BIOGRAPHICAL DICTIONARY
OF
LATIN AMERICAN
AND
CARIBBEAN
POLITICAL LEADERS

EDITED BY

ROBERT J. ALEXANDER

Greenwood Press
NEW YORK • WESTPORT, CONNECTICUT • LONDON

Library of Congress Cataloging-in-Publication Data

Biographical dictionary of Latin American and Caribbean
  political leaders.

  Bibliography: p.
  Includes index.
  1. Politicians—Latin America—Biography—Dictionaries.
  2. Politicians—West Indies—Biography—Dictionaries.
  3. Statesmen—Latin America—Biography—Dictionaries.
  4. Statesmen—West Indies—Biography—Dictionaries.
  5. Latin America—Biography—Dictionaries. 6. West
Indies—Biography—Dictionaries. I. Alexander,
Robert Jackson, 1918–
F144.2.B48   1988   972.9′009′92 [B]   87–17805
ISBN 0–313–24353–0 (lib. bdg. : alk. paper)

British Library Cataloguing in Publication Data is available.

Copyright © 1988 by Robert J. Alexander

All rights reserved. No portion of this book may be
reproduced, by any process or technique, without the
express written consent of the publisher.

Library of Congress Catalog Card Number: 87–17805
ISBN: 0–313–24353–0

First published in 1988

Greenwood Press, Inc.
88 Post Road West, Westport, Connecticut 06881

Printed in the United States of America

The paper used in this book complies with the
Permanent Paper Standard issued by the National
Information Standards Organization (Z39.48-1984).

10 9 8 7 6 5 4 3 2 1

To Maureen Alexander

CONTENTS

Preface   ix

Biographical Dictionary   1

APPENDIX A: Chronology   467

APPENDIX B: Biographies by Country   473

Index   481

Contributors   507

PREFACE

To some degree, the present volume is a complement to *Political Parties of the Americas*, which I edited and Greenwood published in 1982. First, the two volumes cover the same parts of the Western Hemisphere, with the major difference that the present one does not include Canada. Second, the considerable majority of contributors to the present volume were participants in the previous work. As in the earlier book, each contributor has written entries for one or more countries.

In the process of editing this volume, my most serious problem was dealing with the plethora of intellectual data which my contributors presented to me. In some cases, I was forced to severely cut many of the entries, and after much soul-searching even drop some of the contributors' favorite subjects. It is my hope that my "ruthlessness" has not cost me too many friends among my contributors.

What we have ended up with, hopefully, are over 450 biographical sketches of the most important political figures in the nineteenth and twentieth centuries in Latin America and the Caribbean. Although the personalities of both periods are treated adequately, it is probably true that more contemporary figures are represented in this work.

The various entries emphasize the political significance of the biographies. In addition, detailed information is presented on his/her political career, as well as family background, education, and nonpolitical activities where relevant.

Inevitably, readers will not be universally happy with the coverage of this volume, for there is no universally acceptable criterion as to which personalities must be included. The editor takes full responsibility for final selection.

The entries in this volume are alphabetized, but for easy reference, an appendix has been added which lists entries by country or territory. Another appendix presents a chronology of the major events in the area from 1804 to the present. Finally, the index gives ready access to the people included in the volume.

As editor of this work, I owe many debts and obligations. Of course, I owe my greatest debt to my contributors, whose knowledge and hard work are principally responsible for this volume. Next, I want to thank Mary Sive, Cynthia Harris, and Mildred Vasan of Greenwood Press, who were constantly available to answer questions and resolve problems, and have seen the book through from conception to publication. I also owe much to Laurie McGuiness, of the Rutgers University Bureau of Economic Research, who did a large part of the final typing, and to Andra Velsor who gave her some help in this effort.

Finally, I have to thank my wife, Joan P. Alexander, for bearing with me while I worked on this volume, and for her painstaking and valuable work in preparing the index.

BIOGRAPHICAL DICTIONARY OF LATIN AMERICAN AND CARIBBEAN POLITICAL LEADERS

A

ADAMS, SIR GRANTLEY HERBERT (1898–1971), dominated the politics
of Barbados between 1937 and 1961. A Barbadian coloured (of mixed African
and European descent), Adams went to Oxford University to study classics and
law and qualified as a barrister at Gray's Inn. In 1925 he returned to Barbados
where he became a journalist, a practicing lawyer, and a politician. At first
embracing the traditionally conservative position of the coloured middle class,
he began a political assault against the progressives, particularly Charles Duncan
O'Neale* and Clennel Wilsden Wickham.* He eventually won a seat in the
House of Assembly in 1934 and, under the influence of a few white progressives,
quickly came to identify with the radical forces for change. He saw labor disturbances and riots to be rooted in labor exploitation. When he visited London
that year, he was influenced by the increasingly radical West Indian political
groups there and by the Fabian Society.

Returning to Barbados, Adams became the central figure in the formation of
the Barbados Progressive League which undertook the struggle against the old
regime of white oligarchs that totally and absolutely dominated the political
affairs of the colony. He lost the support of his coloured middle-class constituency
but quickly fashioned the League into a political party, renaming it the Barbados
Labor Party (BLP). He built up a wide mass following, using his gift of oratory
and his powerful charismatic appeal. In 1941 he helped form the Barbados
Workers Union (BWU) and became its president.

The first major political change was lowering the qualifications for voting in
1944, which allowed the BLP to assume control of the government in 1946 with
Adams as chief minister. After the introduction of universal adult suffrage in
1951, the constitution was further amended to provide limited internal self-
government. Adams became the first premier in the British West Indies. In 1958
the constitution was further changed to one of a cabinet system and full self-
government.

With Adams at the helm, winning successive electoral victories in 1946, 1948,
1951, and 1956, the BLP introduced progressive tax legislation, provided sig-

nificant credit to small landholders, modernized the country's health facilities, significantly increased old-age pensions, legislated a minimum wage, introduced a 44-hour week, and introduced a host of labor legislation including the right to strike and picket, workers' compensation, and protection from industrial accidents. The result was a notable increase in the standard of living in the Barbadian working class and protection from exploitation characteristic of the plantation economy.

As president of the Barbados Workers Union (BWU), by 1944 Adams won the union's right of collective bargaining. He was concerned about the overlap of labor and government, however, and in 1949 he formalized the separation between his governing party and the union despite retaining the union presidency until 1954 when he became premier.

Adams was elected president of the Caribbean Labour Congress in 1947 and began a strong commitment to Caribbean integration. When the West Indian Federation was established in 1958, he was installed as the first federal prime minister, relinquishing his post as premier of Barbados. However, after four frustrating years, the federation finally collapsed and was formally dissolved on May 31, 1962.

Adams' growing emphasis on international and federal issues, and what some saw as a shift away from progressive politics began to take a serious toll on both the BLP and the BWU. In 1954 the BWU, under President Frank Leslie Walcott,* formally broke all ties with Adams. The following year a few younger members of the BLP under leadership of Errol Walton Barrow* seceded to form the Democratic Labor Party (DLP). In the elections of 1961, one year before the breakup of the federation, the BLP lost to the DLP and Adams returned to find his party in near shambles. He worked until his resignation from the BLP leadership in 1970 to rebuild the party and mold it into a powerful and effective opposition.

BIBLIOGRAPHY

Ayerst, M. *The British West Indies: The Search for Self-Government*. London: George Allen and Unwin, 1960.
Hoyos, F. A. *Builders of Barbados*. London: Macmillan Co., 1972.
———. *Grantley Adams and the Social Revolution*. London: Macmillan Co., 1974.
Lewis, G. K. *The Growth of the Modern West Indies*. New York: Monthly Review Press, 1968.
Tree, R. A. *A History of Barbados*. 2d ed. London: Granada, 1977.
                                                      PERCY C. HINTZEN AND W. MARVIN WILL

ADAMS, JOHN MICHAEL G.M. (TOM) (1931–1985), led the Barbados Labor Party (BLP) back to power after 15 years in opposition. Following in the footsteps of his famous father, Sir Grantley Herbert Adams,* he won the Barbados Island Scholarship in 1950 and went to Oxford University to study political philosophy and economics. He subsequently became a practicing barrister. In

1957 he joined the British Broadcasting Company (BBC) where he remained until 1962. He was also politically active in the British Labor Party. In 1957 Tom Adams also represented his father's Barbados Labour Party at a conference in London.

Adams returned home in January 1963, was soon admitted to the local bar, and immediately launched his political career. His main task was to assist in the reorganization of the BLP which, just two years earlier, had suffered its first electoral defeat. In 1966 he was elected to the Barbadian Parliament for the first time, and with his father and other elected BLP representatives he made the party a formidable opposition.

When Sir Grantley Adams resigned in 1970, Tom Adams continued active in the party under its new chairman, Harold Bernard St. John.* In 1971 the party suffered its most severe setback at the polls winning only 6 seats against the 18 constituencies of the ruling Democratic Labour Party (DLP). Among the defeated BLP candidates was party leader St. John. The party then elected Tom Adams as leader of the parliamentary opposition. On January 21, 1973, he was also elected chairman of the party.

Under Adams' leadership, the BLP won a dramatic electoral victory in 1976, and he became prime minister. He was firmly committed to a moderate economic policy and to a pro-Western, particularly pro-U.S., foreign policy. He assumed the portfolio of minister of finance and, in 1977, was chosen to be the spokesperson for the Commonwealth at the annual meeting of the International Monetary Fund and the World Bank.

The advent of a revolution in neighboring Grenada in 1979 was a major concern for Barbados. Tom Adams was the principal politician in the Caribbean to criticize the coup and the failure of its leaders to schedule elections. Yet it was also Adams who would tell President Ronald Reagan at the March 1983 mini-summit in Barbados that he perceived no significant security threat from the Maurice Rupert Bishop* regime and who rejected the Reagan administration's initial intrusions into Grenadian internal affairs. After the murder of Maurice Bishop and other Grenadians by the Coard-Austin segment in November 1983, however, Adams gave full support to the U.S.-led intervention into Grenada and supplied Barbadian troops as well as the use of the Sir Grantley Adams Airport.

Tom Adams' administration modernized the island's archaic legal code and carried out the modernization of the Barbadian physical infrastructure. In 1984 the economy registered a modest 3 percent economic growth, boosting Barbados to third position in all of Latin American in per capita gross domestic product.

Tom Adams died unexpectedly on March 11, 1985.

BIBLIOGRAPHY

Bajan, June 1983.
Caribbean Contact 7 (November 1980) and 12 (April 1985).
Caribbean Digest 1, No. 1 (1977).

Latin America and Caribbean Contemporary Record. Vols. 2 and 3. New York: Holmes
        and Meier, 1984 and 1985.
Personal interviews.
The Nation, January 18, 1983.

                                        PERCY C. HINTZEN AND W. MARVIN WILL

AGÜERO ROCHA, FERNANDO (1918–   ), was one of a group of Traditional
Conservative Party (PCT) leaders who reorganized the Nicaraguan Conservatives
into a more modern party committed to political and social reform in the early
1960s. At Agüero's insistence, the PCT refused to participate in the February
1963 elections. He at first insisted that the party also boycott the February 1967
presidential elections unless they were supervised by the Organization of American States (OAS). However, in the early Fall of 1966, Agüero organized the
National Union of Opposition, a coalition of the PCT, the Independent Liberal
Party, and the Social Christian Party behind his own presidential candidacy.
Agüero went to Washington, in a vain attempt to get State Department help in
petitioning the Human Rights Commission of the OAS to investigate PCT charges
of violations of the electoral code.

On January 22, 1967, Agüero and Pedro Joaquín Chamorro* held a major
political rally in Managua, and a crowd estimated at between 40,000 and 60,000
began calling for the National Guard to overthrow the Somozas. More than 40
demonstrators, 1 Guard officer, and 2 enlisted men were killed, and at least 100
persons wounded. Agüero was put under house arrest until after the election.

Anastasio Somoza Debayle ("Tachito")* won the election. The PCT, however, was given one-third of the seats in the Senate and Chamber of Deputies.

According to the 1950 Constitution, the president was not eligible to succeed
himself. Tachito Somoza, seeking to wiggle out of this prohibition, offered
Fernando Agüero a deal: the PCT would share power in almost every branch of
government, and Congress would dissolve itself and convene a constituent assembly; Tachito would resign and transfer power to a triumvirate—two designated by his party and one by the Conservatives; and the OAS would be invited
to supervise the first elections under the new constitution.

Agüero accepted. Congress dissolved itself, Somoza stepped down, and a
triumvirate was formed, with Agüero representing the PCT. However, following
the December 23, 1972, earthquake which destroyed about three-quarters of
Managua, Tachito Somoza took over effective control as head of both the Guard
and a new National Emergency Committee. Agüero resigned in protest.

When four Conservative factions united in March 1979, Fernando Agüero
was elected one of six members of the executive committee of the new Democratic Conservative Party of Nicaragua. He continued to hold that post after
the overthrow of the Somoza regime by the Sandinista National Liberation Front,
but he soon faded from an active role in Nicaraguan politics.

BIBLIOGRAPHY

English, Burt H. *Nicaragua Election Factbook,* February 5, 1967. Washington, D.C.:
    Institute for the Comparative Study of Political Systems, December 1966.
Millett, Richard. *Guardians of the Dynasty, A History of the U.S.-Created Guardia
    Nacional and the Somoza Family.* Maryknoll, N.Y.: Orbis Books, 1977.
Pearson, Neale J. "Nicaragua," in Robert J. Alexander (ed.). *Political Parties of the
    Americas.* Volume 2. Alexander. Westport, Conn.: Greenwood Press, 1982.
Walker, Thomas W. *Nicaragua, The Land of Sandino.* Boulder, Colo.: Westview Press,
    1980.

                                                            NEALE J. PEARSON

AGUIRRE CERDA, PEDRO (1878–1941), was president of Chile, 1938–
1941. Of humble origins, he attended the Instituto Pedagógico and qualified as
a teacher and lawyer. A Radical Party member, he was first elected deputy in
1915 and senator in 1921. He was minister of education in 1918 and established
compulsory primary education.

Aguirre Cerda was President Arturo Alessandri Palma's* first interior minister.
Under the Carlos Ibáñez del Campo* dictatorship, he studied abroad and managed
a rural estate, and belonged to the Radical faction opposed to the dictatorship.

During the 1930s, Aguirre Cerda opposed Radical participation in the Popular
Front, but in 1938 he was the Front's successful presidential candidate. As
president, he was responsible for establishing the Chilean Development Corporation, stimulating general unionization of urban workers, and considerably
expanding public education.

Aguirre Cerda died in office of natural causes.

BIBLIOGRAPHY

Cortes, Lia, and Jordi Fuentes: *Diccionario Político de Chile.* Santiago: Editorial Orbe,
    1967.
Galdames, Luis. *Historia de Chile.* Santiago: Editorial Zig Zag, 1945.
Olivarría Bravo, Arturo. *Chile Entre dos Alessandri.* Vol. 1 Santiago: Editorial Nasci-
    mento, 1962.
Stevenson, John Reese. *The Chilean Popular Front.* Philadelphia: University of Penn-
    sylvania Press, 1962.

                                                        ROBERT J. ALEXANDER

ALBIZU CAMPOS, PEDRO (1891–1965), the principal leader of the Puerto
Rican Nationalist Party, went to local schools and received a law degree from
Harvard University in 1917. He then entered the U.S. Army and became a
lieutenant. In the army he was subjected to racial segregation, which perhaps
created his lifelong violent enmity for the United States.

Returning to civil life, Albizu Campos became an advocate of Puerto Rican
independence and spent several years in South America preaching that idea. In
1930 he was elected president of the Puerto Rican Nationalist Party, which had
been formed two decades earlier. The party participated in the 1932 election, in

which Albizu Campos was candidate for insular senator-at-large. However, the party received less than 10 percent of the total vote needed to make it a "legal" party.

Thereafter, under Albizu's leadership, the Nationalists turned to personal terrorism. Their greatest "success" was the assassination of insular police chief, Colonel E. Francis Riggs, in February 1936. As a result, Albizu Campos and seven supporters were sentenced to federal prison, part of which sentence he spent in a hospital in New York City. He was finally released in December 1947.

The Nationalists' attempts to murder President Harry Truman and Puerto Rican Governor Luiz Muñoz Marín* in 1950 resulted in Albizu Campos again being given a jail sentence, this time in Puerto Rico. He was pardoned by Governor Muñoz Marín in 1953. However, when the Nationalists made an armed attack on the U.S. Congress in March 1954, Albiza was jailed once again. He was once more pardoned by Governor Muñoz Marín in November 1964.

BIBLIOGRAPHY

Alibizu Campos, Pedro. *La Conciencia Nacional Puertorriqueña*. Mexico: Siglo Vein-
    tiuno Editores, 1972.
Corretjer, Juan Antonio. *Albizu Campos*. Montevideo: Siglo Ilustrado, 1970.
Hanson, Earl Parker. *Puerto Rico, Land of Wonders*. New York: Alfred A. Knopf, 1960.
Intercontinental Press. New York, September 21, 1979, p. 900.
New York Times, April 22, 1965.

                                                               RICHARD E. SHARPLESS

ALEM, LEANDRO NICEBRO (1842–1896), was a major reformist political leader in Argentina in the late 1800s. His organizational activities led to the formation of the Unión Civica Radical (UCR) in 1891. Since then the UCR has provided the main thrust of middle-class opposition to the Argentine oligarchy and to the military.

Alem was born in Buenos Aires. He fought in the Paraguayan War and afterward was elected to the national congress. He galvanized those who were unhappy with the dishonesty of the national political process, who wanted more representation in national politics, and who opposed the oligarchy's domination of the national scene.

In 1877 Alem and his friend Aristóbulo del Valle attempted to organize a political party (the Republican Party) but failed. However, Alem played a central role in the unrest of 1889 and in the 1890 revolt that led to the resignation of President Juárez Celman. Alem was then elected a national senator, becoming a major critic of the Carlos Pellegrini government.

The Radical Civic Union, created under Alem's leadership in 1891, became the primary vehicle for the reformers who opposed the corrupt political practices of the dominant oligarchy. The UCR's main focus was a drive for electoral honesty. The movement represented primarily the urban middle class, but it also attracted other opponents of the government. The Radicals, with Alem playing an important part, attempted a number of unsuccessful provincial revolts against the national government in the early 1890s.

Almost from its inception, the party was weakened by dissent and factionalism. In 1896 Alem committed suicide, claiming that division and opposition within the Radicals was the cause. He was succeeded as Radical leader by his nephew Hipólito Yrigoyen.*

BIBLIOGRAPHY

Ferns, Henry S. *Argentina*. New York: Praeger, 1969.
Gálvez, Manuel. *Vida de Hipolito Yrigoyen: El hombre del misterio*. Buenos Aires: 1939.
Luna, Félix. *Yrigoyen, el templario de la libertad*. Buenos Aires: 1954.
Rock, David. *Politics in Argentina, 1890–1930: The Rise and Fall of Radicalism*. New York: Cambridge Latin American Studies, 1975.
Snow, Peter G. *Argentine Radicalism: The History and Doctrine of the Radical Civic Union*. Iowa City: University of Iowa Press, 1965.

JOHN T. DEINER

ALEMÁN VALDÉS, MIGUEL (1900–1983), was the first Mexican president since the continuing social revolution was initiated in 1917 to work openly for the growth of the private sector. He also began the era of civilian government. From the beginning of the Revolution in 1910, most Mexican leaders and every president from 1920 on, with the exception of two interim presidents under the tutelage of General Plutarco Elías Calles,* had been army generals. Beginning with Alemán, every president has been an attorney by training except for Adolfo Ruíz Cortines (1952–1958), who was an economist.

In addition to starting Mexico on the path of industrialization under civilian governments, Alemán was the father of Mexico's tourist industry. He sponsored the building of Acapulco into a glamorous resort for the international jet set, by a consortium of investors that included the Mexican government, foreign hotel chains, and a holding company in which he was a partner.

Alemán was also the builder of the campus of the National Autonomous University of Mexico. Not until Alemán brought the university modern laboratories did any Mexican university begin to offer graduate research in the physical sciences at a level recognized by North American and European scholars.

Born in the small town of Sayula in the state of Veracruz on September 29, 1900, Alemán went to school in Orizaba and then to the National Preparatory School in Mexico City. He received his law degree from the National Autonomous University in 1928, writing a thesis on labor law. He began to climb the political ladder in 1928 when he became legal adviser to the minister of agriculture. In 1930 Alemán became a member of the Federal Board of Conciliation and Arbitration, gaining a national reputation as a negotiator in labor management talks.

Alemán's father had been a Revolutionary general and later a deputy in the federal Congress. He carried on his father's tradition of supporting the moderates within the Revolutionary establishment and opposing the leftists. He was a member of the Superior Tribunal of the Federal District during 1930–1935, governor of his native state of Veracruz during 1936–1939, and minister of internal affairs (Gobernación) in the presidential cabinet during 1940–1946. His presidential term ran from December 1946 to December 1952, a period in which the government built hydroelectric dams to bring full-scale irrigated farming to Mexico's arid regions plus surplus electric power to fuel the new growth of industries.

Within the Institutional Revolutionary Party, the followers of former President Lázaro Cárdenas* became the left-wingers, and the followers of Alemán became the right-wingers during Alemán's administration and well into the 1960s, when those personalistic descriptions began to fade from popular usage.

In the 1970s as a former president Alemán continued to influence the moderate and conservative groups within the Institutional Revolutionary Party through an ad hoc organization he formed. In 1947 President Alemán had pushed the expansion of both privately and publicly owned steel companies, and in 1970 his civic front persuaded the party to publicly urge construction of the government's proposed steel complex in the state of Michoacán, which began production in 1976.

Both as president and as former president, Alemán worked to promote the Mexican automobile and electronics industries. He inaugurated Mexico's first television station in 1950 and became its first performer by giving his State of the Union address. In the 1960s he encouraged television and radio parts manufacturers in Monterrey, Guadalajara, and Mexico City.

BIBLIOGRAPHY

Alba, Victor. *The Mexicans—The Making of a Nation*. New York: Praeger, 1967.
Alisky, Marvin. *Who's Who in Mexican Government*. Tempe: Center for Latin American Studies of Arizona State University, 1969.
Briggs, Donald C., and Marvin Alisky. *Historical Dictionary of Mexico*. Metuchen, N.J.: Scarecrow Press, 1981.
Camp, Roderic A. *Mexican Political Biographies*. 1935–1975. Tucson: University of Arizona Press, 1976.
Scott, Robert E. *Mexican Government in Transition*. Urbana: University of Illinois Press, 1964.

MARVIN ALISKY

ALESSANDRI PALMA, ARTURO (1869–1950), was the most important Chilean political leader of the first half of the twentieth century. He received his law degree in 1893. While at the university, he was active in the Liberal Party, and was aligned with the faction opposed to President José Manuel Balmaceda,* and edited an anti-Balmaceda periodical, *La Justicia*. In later years Alessandri was to regret his support of Balmaceda's opponents in the 1891 civil war.

Alessandri was first elected to the Chamber of Deputies in 1897 and continued to serve there until 1915. He also practiced law and dabbled in speculation in the nitrate industry, making and losing several small fortunes. As a deputy, he was particularly adept at manipulating the parliamentary system in an attempt to bring about the overthrow of the incumbent cabinet. He himself served short periods as a minister and in 1918 headed a short-lived cabinet as minister of the interior.

Alessandri first gained national popularity in 1915, when elected senator from the nitrate Province of Tarapacá, defeating the entrenched boss of the province, Arturo del Río. That victory marked him as a potential presidential candidate.

In 1920 Alessandri was the nominee of the Liberal Alliance, which included the Radical Party, a major faction of Liberals, and most of the Democratic Party. The contest was so close that it was submitted to a "Tribunal of Honor" of Congress, which finally conceded victory to Alessandri.

Taking office in December 1920, President Arturo Alessandri soon presented a series of projects to Congress: a labor code, an income tax, separation of church and state, establishment of a central bank, and regular salaries for members of Congress to permit poorer people to aspire to membership in that body. However, most of his proposals were blocked because the Senate was controlled by his opponents until early 1924, and Congress continued to frequently upset cabinets. Even after March 1924, when the Liberal Alliance won control of the Senate, Congress only moved to consider the parliamentary salary proposal. In the face of a fiscal crisis that had caused frequent nonpayment of both military and civil servants salaries, the proposal aroused young officers to make a public protest in the Senate chamber on September 3, 1924.

When army chiefs were unwilling to discipline those officers, President Alessandri met with a delegation of them. Agreement was reached on rapid passage by Congress of a series of laws, including much of the president's program, as well as more rapid promotion for officers, and salary increases for the military. However, when the young military then refused to dissolve their military junta, as they had promised they would, Alessandri resigned and went into exile in Europe.

Another military coup in January 1925 resulted in recall of President Alessandri. From his return in March until his second resignation on October 1, Alessandri brought about a long series of reforms. A new constitution (which he largely authored) substituted the presidential for the parliamentary system and separated church and state; social legislation passed in September 1924 was made effective; and a central bank was established. However, when Carlos Ibáñez del Campo,* minister of war and one of the chiefs of the January 1925 coup insisted on running for president, Alessandri resigned once more.

Although elected senator from Tarapacá again in 1926, Alessandri soon resigned and went into exile in Europe, where he remained until the overthrow of Ibáñez in 1931. Soon after his return, Alessandri was nominated for president by the Democratic Party but was defeated in the 1931 election by Juan Esteban Montero.* After the short-lived Montero regime and the 100-day Socialist Republic, new elections were called at the end of 1932. Arturo Alessandri was victorious.

Alessandri's second administration (1932–1938) reestablished supremacy of the civilian government over the military after eight years of domination by the armed forces. This supremacy was to survive until 1973. The Alessandri regime stimulated rapid recovery from the Great Depression and began the deliberate government policy of stimulating industrialization. Finally, it added a significant piece of social legislation, a preventative medicine law.

For a few years after leaving the presidency, Alessandri was the butt of violent antipathy from the left. However, even in the 1942 elections made necessary by the death of President Pedro Aguirre Cerda,* Alessandri's role was decisive. He led a group of Liberals who repudiated their party's support of ex-dictator Ibáñez and backed Juan Antonio Ríos Morales,* which gave Ríos the margin of victory.

In 1944 Alessandri was again elected to the Senate and a year later became its president. In 1946, following the death of President Ríos, Alessandri was named Liberal Party candidate for president but ceded this place to his son, Fernando Alessandri Rodríguez. When no candidate won a majority, Arturo Alessandri negotiated for the Liberals to throw Liberal support in Congress behind Radical nominee Gabriel González Videla,* in return for three places in his cabinet.

Arturo Alessandri's last exercise of political influence came in April 1947 when, after a disastrous showing of the Liberals in municipal elections, he successfully urged withdrawal of the Liberals from the cabinet. This facilitated President González Videla's reorganization of his cabinet, dropping three Communist ministers who had until then shared posts with the Liberals and Radicals.

BIBLIOGRAPHY

Alessandri Palma, Arturo. *Recuerdos de Gobierno*. 3 vols. Santiago: Editorial Nascimento, 1967.
Alexander, Robert J. *Arturo Alessandri: A Biography*. Ann Arbor, Mich.: University Microfilms International, 1977.
Donoso, Ricardo. *Alessandri: Agitador y Demoledor*. 2 vols. Mexico: Fondo de Cultura Económica, 1953, 1954.
Durand, Luis. *Don Arturo*. Santiago: Editorial Zig Zag, 1952.
Feliú Cruz, Guillermo. *Alessandri: Personaje de la Historia 1868–1950*. Santiago: Editorial Nascimento, 1968.

ROBERT J. ALEXANDER

ALESSANDRI RODRÍGUEZ, JORGE (1896–1986), was president of Chile after a successful career as engineer and industrial manager. Son of Arturo Alessandri Palma,* he graduated in 1919 from the School of Engineering of the University of Chile. When his father went into exile in September 1924, Jorge accompanied him to Europe and returned to Chile when his father did in March 1925. In the following year, he was elected to the Chamber of Deputies. However, when Carlos Ibáñez del Campo* became President in May 1927, he forced Jorge Alessandri into exile where he stayed during most of the Ibáñez period.

During most of the 1930s Jorge Alessandri worked with the government's Mortgage Bank as an engineer. In 1938 he became manager of the country's large paper company, a position he kept for 20 years. He gained a reputation as an efficient manager who was able to maintain friendly relations with the unions of the company's employees. He also achieved a reputation as a financial wizard, a fame only slightly tarnished by service as minister of finance in the government of President Gabriel González Videla* from August 1948 until February 1950.

In 1956 Jorge Alessandri was elected senator from Santiago. Two years later he was the candidate of a coalition of parties of the right for the presidency, winning a narrow victory over Socialist Senator Salvador Allende Gossens.* As president, Alessandri carried out a notable public housing program, in conformity with the Alliance for Progress enacted a modest agrarian reform law, and somewhat modified the tax system. In foreign affairs, Alessandri had Chile join the Latin American Free Trade Area.

After retiring from the presidency in 1964, Jorge Alessandri returned to the paper company as board chairman. In 1970 he again ran as the right's candidate for president, losing by a narrow margin to Salvador Allende. He supported the military overthrow of the Allende government, and for a while he served in an Advisory Council of State established by President Augusto Pinochet Ugarte.*

BIBLIOGRAPHY

Alexander, Robert J. *The Tragedy of Chile*. Westport, Conn.: Greenwood Press, 1978.
Cortes, Lia, and Jordi Fuentes. *Diccionario Político de Chile*. Santiago: Editorial Orbe, 1967.

ROBERT J. ALEXANDER

ALFARO, (JOSÉ) ELOY (1842–1912), was the president of Ecuador who began an extended period of Liberal Party rule. He was the son of a Spanish merchant and an Ecuadorian woman. For some years he engaged in business activities in Panama; he married Ana Paredes Arosemena, a member of a wealthy Panamanian family.

Alfaro spent most of his life in political activities, even when he was also engaged in business. His first "political" action was taken when he was only 22 and kidnapped the governor of Manabí Province. For a quarter of a century thereafter, he engaged in almost uninterrupted revolutionary action, ostensibly on behalf of the Liberals, against successive regimes. He spent much of his modest fortune on these activities.

In 1895 Alfaro was in exile. However, when a split in Conservative ranks led to a revolt and gave the Liberals of Guayaquil a chance to mobilize militarily, they called him back to lead their forces. He marched on Quito, defeated government troops in a war that lasted almost a year, and then eliminated his

Conservative allies and seized complete control of the regime. From then until 1944 the Liberals controlled the Ecuadorean government.

Eloy Alfaro presided over the regime from 1895 to 1901. He then turned the presidency over to Leónidas Plaza,* although at the last moment he tried to prevent Plaza's taking office. In 1905 he organized a successful revolt against Plaza's successor, and he stayed in office until 1911. Then, having allowed the election of another successor, Emilio Estrada, he again sought to prevent a president from taking office. He was forcibly removed and sent into exile. When President Estrada died within four months, Alfaro again sought to return to power, but he had little support. He was arrested in Guayaquil and sent a prisoner to Quito where he and a number of close associates were lynched by a mob.

The regimes of Alfaro and his immediate successors carried out the classical Liberal reforms. They separated church and state, provided for freedom of worship and of the press, and removed religious teaching from all government schools. In addition, they suppressed the church tithe which the Gabriel García Moreno* regime had established, confiscated church property, introduced civil registration of births and deaths, and legalized divorce.

BIBLIOGRAPHY

Linkne, Lilo. *Ecuador: Country of Contrasts*. London: Royal Institute of International Affairs, 1954.
Loor, Wilfrido. *Eloy Alfaro*. 3 vols. Quito: 1947.
Pérez Concha, Jorge. *Eloy Alfaro: Su vida y su obra*. Quito: 1942.

ROBERT J. ALEXANDER

ALFARO, RICARDO JOAQUÍN (1882–1971), was provisional president of Panama from January 1931 to September 1932. He was serving as Panama's ambassador to Washington in 1931 when he was called home to assume the presidency following the overthrow of President Florencio Harmodio Arosemena. Alfaro dealt well with an ugly situation caused by Arosemena's arbitrary and corrupt rule and by the general economic crisis, and he presided over the 1932 presidential campaign with honesty and fairness. It was one of the rare times in Panamanian history that the incumbent president did not try to dictate the outcome.

Alfaro returned to be ambassador to the United States. The Hull-Alfaro Treaty of 1936 removed some of the most offensive stipulations of the 1903 Panama Canal treaty, particularly the U.S. right of unilateral intervention, and gave Panama improved economic terms. His role in the treaty made Alfaro a strong candidate for president in 1940, but he withdrew in reaction to the violent and demagogic tactics of incumbent president Augusto Samuel Boyd and Boyd's choice for successor, Arnulfo Arias Madrid.*

Alfaro returned to public service as foreign minister in 1945 under President Enrique Adolfo Jiménez.* However, when President Jiménez yielded to U.S. demands and signed a treaty extending the use of thirteen wartime military bases for twenty years, Alfaro resigned in protest, precipitating street demonstrations and unanimous rejection of the pact by the National Assembly. The United States evacuated all the defense sites in 1948.

Alfaro capped his career as a member of the International Court of Justice in The Hague.

BIBLIOGRAPHY

Alba C., Manuel María. *Cronología de los Gobernantes de Panama 1510–1967*. Panama: 1967.
Alfaro, Ricardo J. *Biográficos esbozos*. Panama: Instituto Nacional de Cultura, 1974.
Ropp, Steve C. *Panamanian Politics: From Guarded Nation to National Guard*. New York: Praeger, 1982.

CHARLES D. AMERINGER

ALFONSÍN FOULKES, RAÚL RICARDO (1927–), became Argentina's president in December 1983, ending almost eight years of military rule. Leader of the Unión Cívica Radical (UCR), the century-old party that represents democratic reformist views in Argentina, he took office under extremely difficult conditions. His victory was widely hailed by Argentinians anxious for a return of political freedom.

Alfonsín graduated from the military academy at age 18 but decided against a military career. He obtained a law degree and almost immediately entered politics, first at the local and provincial level. In 1963 he was elected to the national Congress, in the same election that brought UCR candidate Arturo Umberto Illia* to the presidency.

Alfonsín emphasized the UCR's traditions of individual liberty, populism, and anti-elitism. His views sometimes brought him into conflict with national UCR leaders, whom he considered overly conservative and out of touch with the people. In 1972 he formed a dissident group within the Radical Party, the Movement for Renovation and Change, to push for social reform policies and modernization of the UCR.

At the 1972 UCR convention, Ricardo Balbín* was the overwhelming choice for the party's presidential nomination in the 1973 elections. Alfonsín's bid for nomination was soundly defeated. Balbín in turn was overwhelmed by Juan Domingo Perón's* stand-in, Héctor José Cámpora,* and the nation then underwent three years of Peronist rule followed by nearly eight years of military rule. Argentina suffered enormous economic and human rights problems during these years. Political party activity was banned completely by the military who used extremely repressive measures to eliminate guerrillas then operating in Argentina.

Alfonsín strengthened his position among Radicals and civilians alike during the years of military rule. In speaking out against governmental economic and human rights policies, he was co-founder and co-president of the Permanent Assembly for Human Rights, the most outspoken Argentine organization to criticize the kidnappings, arrests, tortures, and *desaparecidos*.

After the disastrous Malvinas invasion, the Argentine military made plans to return politics to the civilians. With Balbín's death in 1981, Alfonsín was clearly the leader of the Radical Party. He was named its presidential candidate by a wide margin, on a platform for democracy, morality and social justice, and educational and health reforms. He also was critical of the free market economy and of the harmful effect of the penetration of the multinational corporation into the economy. Alfonsín was elected president by an absolute majority, defeating the Peronists for the first time in a freely contested national election.

During the first year and a half of his presidency, Alfonsín moved slowly. He revoked an amnesty which the military had granted itself, and he instituted an investigation of human rights abuses under military rule. Trials for those considered responsible, even including the preceding military presidents, were begun. Alfonsín also tried to deal with Argentina's economic problems, initially by a price freeze and later through an austerity program begun under the prodding of the International Monetary Fund. Peronist-controlled labor resented some of the sacrifices asked of it and demonstrated against the Alfonsín policies.

Internationally, Alfonsín settled Argentina's longstanding boundary dispute with Chile and began circumspect talks aimed at resolving the Malvinas issue. He also took steps to assert civilian control over the military, such as limiting the number of general officers and reducing the military share of the budget. By June 1986 perhaps his biggest accomplishment was that he had survived, was still in office, and remained committed to democracy.

BIBLIOGRAPHY

New York Times, November 1, 1983.
1984 Current Biography Yearbook. New York: H. H. Wilson Co., 1985.
Snow, Peter G. *Argentine Radicalism: The History and Doctrine of the Radical Civic Union*. Iowa City: University of Iowa Press, 1965.
Sobel, Lester A. (ed). *Argentina and Perón, 1970–75*. New York: Facts on File, 1975.
Wynia, Gary N. "Democracy in Argentina." *Current History*, February 1985.

                                                                  JOHN T. DEINER

ALLENDE GOSSENS, SALVADOR (1908–1973), was the only Socialist Party leader to be president of Chile. His promises of a Chilean Road to Socialism ended with his violent overthrow and death at the hands of the military.

Allende received his medical degree in 1932. In 1937 he was elected, as a Socialist, to the Chamber of Deputies. With the victory of the Popular Front in 1938, President Pedro Aguirre Cerda* appointed Allende minister of health. In 1945 he was elected to the Senate where he remained until he became president of the republic.

In 1943 Salvador Allende headed the Socialist Party faction that opposed entry into the cabinet of President Juan Antonio Ríos Morales,* and rejected merger of the Socialist and Communist parties. When the opposing faction, led by

Marmaduque Grove Vallejo,* was defeated and withdrew, Allende was elected secretary general of the Socialist Party.

When another Socialist Party split occurred in 1948, over collaboration with President Gabriel González Videla* and support for a law outlawing the Communist Party, Allende opposed those policies and helped form the Popular Socialist Party (PSP). However, four years later, when the PSP decided to support the presidential candidacy of ex-dictator Carlos Ibáñez del Campo,* Allende withdrew and rejoined the Socialist Party.

The Communists then offered support if he could obtain the presidential nomination of the Socialist Party. As the Socialist Party's nominee in 1952, he came in a poor fourth. He ran again in 1958 as candidate of the Front of Popular Action (FRAP) composed of the reunited Socialist Party, the Communists, and smaller groups, and was very narrowly defeated by Jorge Alessandri Rodríguez,* nominee of the parties of the right.

The election of 1964 was a contest between the FRAP, with Allende once again as its nominee, and the Christian Democratic Party, led by Eduardo Frei Montalva.* Frei won an absolute majority.

With approach of the 1970 elections, the FRAP was expanded to include the Radical Party and some dissident Christian Democrats, and was rechristened Popular Unity (UP). Salvador Allende was the UP candidate. He received a plurality, but the final decision was up to Congress, where the choice lay between Allende and Jorge Alessandri. The Christian Democrats, who held the deciding votes in Congress, demanded that Allende agree to a Statute of Constitutional Guarantees, reflecting their fear that the UP coalition might destroy the traditional democratic regime. When the statute was passed with Allende's backing, the Christian Democrats voted for him. He took office in November 1970.

UP had pledged nationalization of 81 major industrial and other enterprises, rapid completion of the agrarian reform begun under President Frei, and workers' participation in management of state-owned firms. In practice, the Allende government went considerably beyond that program. Hundreds of enterprises, most of them small or medium sized, were "temporarily" taken over by the state. Much land not subject to the agrarian reform was also seized illegally, and the government pushed for the organization of collective farms.

After the first year, the economic situation became increasingly difficult. Inflation was more severe than the country had ever known before, production fell in both industry and agriculture, and the balance of payments was drastically adverse. The Opposition-controlled Congress sought to limit the government's right to seize private firms. Congressional elections in March 1973 left the Opposition still in control, although with a reduced majority. Widespread middle-class opposition was demonstrated during a month-long strike by independent truckers in October 1972, in protest against a move to nationalize trucking enterprises.

Although the Communist Party acted as a force for moderation, Allende's own Socialist Party collaborated closely with the far left Movement of the Revolutionary Left (MIR) in seizures of farms and urban enterprises. Party secretary Carlos Altamirano boasted two days before the overthrow of Allende, that he and other Socialist leaders had frustrated all of the president's efforts to reach a compromise with the Christian Democrats.

The Allende regime faced international complications. The Nixon administration in the United States was overtly hostile and sought rather ineptly to bring about Allende's overthrow. Although Allende was able to get more foreign aid and promises of aid than any previous Chilean government, much of it was slow in coming, and the cutting off of U.S. aid increased the Allende government's economic problems.

The armed forces remained loyal to the Allende regime until after June 29, 1973, when a revolt of army elements in Santiago was crushed. However, with the subsequent removal of army commander General Carlos Prats, who had led the "constitutionalist" forces in the military, the way was paved for a successful conspiracy, which was led by Prats' successor, General Augusto Pinochet Ugarte.*

Allende's decision on September 9, 1973, to break with Socialist Secretary General Carlos Altamirano and to submit to popular plebiscite the issues between himself and the congressional opposition came too late. Two days later the armed forces revolted. President Allende and some of the members of his government barricaded themselves in the presidential palace, La Moneda, which was heavily bombed and strafed. President Salvador Allende died during the final assault on La Moneda.

BIBLIOGRAPHY

Alexander, Robert J. *The Tragedy of Chile*. Westport, Conn.: Greenwood Press, 1978.
Breve Historia de la Unidad Popular: Documento de El Mercurio. Santiago: 1974.
Cortes, Lia, and Jordi Fuentes. *Diccionario Político de Chile*. Santiago: Editorial Orbe, 1977.
Jobet, Julio César. *El Partico Socialista de Chile*. 2 Vols. Santiago: Editorial Prensa Latina Americana, 1971.
Moss, Robert. *Chile's Marxist Experiment*. London: 1973.

ROBERT J. ALEXANDER

ALVAREZ, GREGORIO (1925–   ), was the only military man to serve as president of Uruguay during the armed forces dictatorship of 1973–1985. He graduated from the Escuela Militar in 1945, was assigned to the calvary, and attended various other courses in his specialty. He became chief of the Republican Guard in 1962 and was head of the Institute for Eradication of Unhealthy Rural Housing in 1968–1969. He was named general in 1971 and became secretary of the National Security Council in 1973. After establishment of the military dictatorship, Alvarez was president of the armed forces' Commission of Political Affairs between 1974 and 1978.

General Alvarez succeeded veteran Blanco Party politician Aparicio Méndez Manfredini* as the head of the military-dominated regime in 1981. Hesitatingly, he led the way in reestablishing an elected civilian government, and he turned over the presidency to successful Colorado Party candidate Julio María Sanguinetti* in March 1985.

BIBLIOGRAPHY

McDonald, Ronald H. "Confrontation and Transition in Uruguay." *Current History* (February 1985).
Who Is Who in Government and Politics in Latin America. New York: Decade Media Books, 1984.

ROBERT J. ALEXANDER

ALVES DE LIMA, LUIS (DUQUE DE CAXIAS) (1803–1880), a highly regarded Brazilian military official, was constantly called on by civilian leaders to suppress rebellions and insurrections in various parts of the country, yet he never attempted to make himself dictator or assume a commanding role in the political life of the nation. He first appeared on the national scene in 1823 when, as a lieutenant in Dom Pedro I's* personal Battalion, he was sent to Bahia and defeated a Portuguese force that refused to acknowledge Brazil's independence. He was raised to the rank of captain at the age of 20.

Transferred to the Brazilian province of Uruguay, Alves de Lima fought in the unsuccessful attempt by Dom Pedro I to block the independence movement and maintain this area as a part of Brazil. He returned to Rio de Janeiro in 1828 and was promoted to the rank of major. He was soon caught up in the problems surrounding the unpopularity of Emperor Dom Pedro I. When the emperor abdicated in 1831, his decision was strongly influenced by his loss of military support, including that of his own battalion. The Regency government (1831–1840) relied heavily on Major Alves de Lima to put down civilian disorders that had broken out all over Brazil following the abdication of the emperor.

Promoted to lieutenant colonel in 1837, Alves de Lima was quickly raised to colonel and posted in 1839 to the northern province of Maranhão where an insurrection had erupted. By 1841 he had broken the rebellion, was given the title of Baron of Caxias, promoted to general, and was elected to serve in the Chamber of Deputies as the delegate from Maranhão.

Shortly afterward, General Alves de Lima was sent to southern Brazil, where a nagging civil war (1835–1845) was raging. He took command in 1842 and brought an honorable settlement to this conflict.

Brazil entered into war with Paraguay (1864–1870). Caxias became involved in partisan politics when he became an adviser to the Conservative Party and found himself in conflict with a new political coalition of moderates and Liberals who had organized the short-lived Progressive Party. He actively supported Conservative politicians. When he was offered the post of commander-in-chief of the Brazilian armed forces, a crisis developed and the Progressive cabinet was forced to resign. Although the Liberals had a majority in Parliament, Emperor Pedro II* selected a Conservative Ministry that placed Caxias in full control of the war against Paraguay. Many Brazilians feel that this was the first step in military intervention in the Brazilian political process.

BIBLIOGRAPHY

Carvalho, Alfonso de. *Caxias*. Rio de Janeiro: Biblioteca do Exercito, 1976.
Smith, Michael. "Caxias." *The McGraw-Hill Encyclopedia of World Biography*. Vol. 2. New York: McGraw-Hill, 1973.

JORDAN YOUNG

AMADOR GUERRERO, MANUEL (1835–1909), was the first president of Panama, 1904–1908. A doctor of medicine, he was born in Cartagena and came to the Isthmus in 1855 to work for the Panama Railroad. He was one of the conspirators who led the Panama Revolution in 1903. He traveled to New York and Washington in late summer 1903 and obtained the backing of railroad officials, the French engineer-lobbyist, Philippe Bunau-Varilla, and the U.S. government. Following the independence movement, Amador became constitutional president in February 1904. His tenure was complicated by the price he had to pay to gain U.S. support for the secessionist movement: to appoint Bunau-Varilla as Panama's minister to the United States, and to sign the Hay-Bunau-Varilla Treaty on the Canal, which set the course of U.S.-Panamanian relations and dominated Panamanian politics for the next 70 years.

BIBLIOGRAPHY

Alba C., Manuel María. *Cronología de los Gobernantes de Panama, 1510–1967*. Panama: 1967.
Alfaro, Ricardo J. *Biográficos esbozos*. Panama: Instituto Nacional de Cultura, 1974.
Castillero R., Ernesto J. *Historia de Panama*. Panama: Editora Panama América, 1959.

CHARLES D. AMERINGER

ARAMBURU, PEDRO EUGENIO (1903–1970), was president of Argentina from 1955 to 1958, and his government attempted to remove Peronist influence from the nation. He was later kidnapped and killed by guerrillas in retaliation for his earlier anti-Peronist actions.

Originally a supporter of Juan Domingo Perón's* government, in 1955 Aramburu turned against Perón and joined General Eduardo Lonardi and Admiral Isaac Rojas in the September coup that overthrew Perón. Three months later Lonardi himself was replaced by a junta government and Aramburu became president of this new junta. It took an extremely strong stance in its actions to purge Peronism for all positions of influence in Argentina. Previous Peronist trade union leaders were barred from leadership positions in trade unions. Peronist political parties were banned, and the use of Perón's name in conjunction with political or labor affairs was prohibited. The government began widespread prosecutions of people who had held important offices under the former Peronist regime. The 1949 Peronist Peronist Constitution was revoked, as were many of the laws that had been enacted under Perón.

In general, the government followed a pro-business, free enterprise policy, and was markedly less economically nationalistic than Perón had been. Expropriated entities, such as the newspaper *La Prensa* were returned to their former owners.

The Aramburu government faced its most serious challenge when a group of non-Perón military officers attempted a coup. This revolt was quickly squashed, and its pro-Perón military leaders were quickly tried and executed.

Aramburu supported a return to civilian politics. The government held elections, and in 1958 Arturo Frondizi,* of the Intransigent Radicals, was elected president. The government had barred use of Perón's name in these elections, and former Peronists were not allowed to run. Consequently, Peronists had no chance to express their preferences, and Frondizi came to power without a clear mandate.

In 1970 ex-President Aramburu was kidnapped by Montonero guerrillas. They charged him with responsibility for persecution of Peronist sympathizers and for the summary execution of Peronist generals in 1956. A mock trial was held, and Aramburu was then killed.

BIBLIOGRAPHY

Hodges, Donald C. *Argentina, 1943–1976: The National Revolution and Resistance.* Albuquerque: University of New Mexico Press, 1976.
Potash, Robert. *The Army and Politics in Argentina, 1945–1962: Perón to Fronidizi.* Stanford, Calif.: Stanford University Press, 1980.
Snow, Peter. *Political Forces in Argentina.* New York: Praeger, 1979.
Sobel, Lester A. (ed). *Argentina and Perón 1970–75.* New York: Facts on File, 1975.
Whitaker, Arthur P. *The United States and the Southern Cone.* Cambridge, Mass.: Harvard University Press, 1975.

JOHN T. DEINER

ARANHA, OSWALDO (1894–1960), a dynamic and innovating force in Brazilian politics, was born in Alegrete, Rio Grande do Sul, the southernmost state of Brazil. Trained as a lawyer in Rio de Janeiro, he returned to his home state to practice law and entered local politics.

Aranha served briefly in the Rio Grande do Sul state legislature and in the federal legislature, after which Governor Getúlio Vargas* invited him to take over the post of secretary of the interior and justice of the state. After the March 1930 presidential elections, Aranha became one of the chief organizers of the successful October 1930 revolution that swept Vargas into power for 15 years.

One of the most trusted of the Vargas advisers, Aranha was first named minister of justice; in this post he smoothed the transition to the new "revolutionary" administration of Getúlio Vargas. Aranha carried no vindictiveness into the new government, and so a majority of bureaucrats and previous political appointees retained their posts. Hence, there was little rancor toward the new government by those defeated by the revolutionary movement of October 1930.

In November 1931 Vargas named Aranha finance minister, a position he retained until July 1934. On February 5, 1934, Aranha signed decree law 23,829 which consolidated and reorganized the nation's foreign debt. He also presided over the program that destroyed 12 million sacks of coffee from the overflowing warehouses because they threatened to swamp the world coffee market and further reduce the prices of Brazil's principal export.

Aranha and Vargas had deep political disagreements over the new constitution of 1934. Aranha resigned from the cabinet, but Vargas named him to the Brazilian Embassy in Washington. On February 2, 1935, Secretary of State Cordell Hull and Ambassador Aranha signed a commercial agreement that resulted in closer economic ties between the two countries. Aranha was exceptionally popular in Washington and established strong personal relationships with President Franklin Roosevelt and various cabinet members.

When Vargas and the military in November 1937 set up the dictatorship of the Estado Novo, Oswaldo Aranha resigned as ambassador to the United States. Vargas refused to accept his resignation and by March 1938 had convinced Aranha to become minister of foreign affairs. Aranha, a dedicated ally of the democracies, held this critical post for six years.

As World War II approached, the United States, seeking an alliance with Brazil, concluded a series of strategic economic agreements with Brazil, including a $12 million loan for the purchase of military equipment by the Brazilian army. When the war began, Aranha insisted that Brazil immediately declare its solidarity with the United States. As a result, more economic aid was promised to Brazil. Much of the cordial relationship between the United States and Brazil was linked to the actions of Oswaldo Aranha. Brazil entered the war in August 1942 and was the only Latin American nation to field an army in Europe, against the Germans and the Italians.

In 1944, as it became apparent that the Allies were winning the war, pressure began to build up in Brazil for a return to democracy. There was a general feeling that Vargas should step down as dictator and that presidential elections should be held. Many saw Oswaldo Aranha as a possible substitute for Vargas. Aranha again came into conflict with Vargas and resigned as foreign minister in September 1944.

In February 1947, while Aranha was on a visit to the United States, the new government of President Eunrico Dutra asked him to represent Brazil at the United Nations as a permanent Brazilian representative. Aranha served as president of the General Assembly and presided over the 1948 special session that created the State of Israel. In 1949 Aranha returned to Brazil and private life.

After Vargas was elected constitutional president of Brazil in 1950, Aranha again became minister of finance, a post he held from June 1953 until the Vargas suicide of August 15, 1954. Aranha again returned to private life as a lawyer.

BIBLIOGRAPHY

Alecanstre, Amilcar Gomes. *Oswaldo Aranha, o mundo afro-asiatico e a paz*. 1961.
O'Donnell, Francisco Talaia. *Oswaldo Aranha*. 1976.

JORDAN YOUNG

ARBENZ GUZMÁN, JACOBO (1913–1971), was overthrown as president of Guatemala by an invasion organized by the Central Intelligence Agency in 1954. The son of a Swiss druggist and a Salvadoran woman, he compiled an impressive academic record at Guatemala's national military academy where he later returned as instructor and director.

In 1944 dictator Jorge Ubico y Castaneda* turned the government over to a military triumvirate which continued his political repression. Arbenz, by then a captain, resigned in protest and joined with Major Francisco Javier Arana and businessman Jorge Toriello to oust the triumvirate. They then supervised the December 1944 elections that resulted in the triumph of Juan José Arévalo Bernejo.*

Under Arévalo, Arbenz and Arana emerged as Guatemala's leading political figures. Arévalo and liberal factions endorsed Arbenz, while the right wing rallied behind Arana. Four months before the election of 1950, Arana was assassinated. With his main rival eliminated, Arbenz received 65 percent of the vote.

The centerpiece of Arbenz' legislative program was the 1952 Agrarian Reform Law. Compensation for expropriated land became a bitter issue. The United Fruit Company demanded market value of its land ($15.8 million), and Arbenz offered the figure which the company itself had declared for tax purposes. Opponents of land reform soon labeled it a Marxist program. There was no question that the Communist Party (reorganized as the Guatemalan Labor Party) had gained considerable influence under Arbenz, and decision makers in Washington were soon describing Guatemala as a Soviet satellite. At an Inter-American Conference in Caracas, Secretary of State John Foster Dulles introduced a strong resolution designed to isolate Arbenz, which did not identify the Guatemalan government as Communist but repudiated Marxist ideology in principle.

Arbenz attempted to organize a militia. The army refused to supply the civilians with weapons. When Arbenz obtained a shipment of Czech small arms for the militia, the United States termed this an intolerable step on the road to Communism.

The Central Intelligence Agency organized, trained, and equipped a small invasion force in Honduras under the command of a former Guatemalan army colonel, Carlos Castillo Armas.* When the group crossed the border into Guatemala in May 1954, the armed forces refused to oppose the invaders and the president resigned.

Arbenz lived in various European countries (including Czechoslovakia and the Soviet Union) after his overthrow. He later moved to Uruguay, Cuba, and, finally, Mexico City, where he died of natural causes.

BIBLIOGRAPHY

Aybar, José. *Dependency and Intervention: The Case of Guatemala in 1954*. Boulder: University of Colorado Press, 1979.
Immerman, Richard H. *The CIA in Guatemala*. Austin: University of Texas Press, 1982.
Seiser, Gregorio. *El Guatemalazo*. Buenos Aires: 1961.
Silvert, K. H. *A Study in Government: Guatemala*. New Orleans: Tulane University Press, 1954.
Torriello Garrido, Guillermo. *La Batalla de Guatemala*. Mexico: Ediciones Cuadernos Americanos, 1955.

JOSÉ M. SÁNCHEZ

ARCE, MANUEL JOSÉ (?–1847), was the first president of Central America. A native of El Salvador, he was involved in conspiracies of advocates of independence as early as 1811, when he was jailed for the first time. He was again imprisoned between 1814 and 1819. When Central America gained its independence in 1821, the Liberals supported him for the presidency of the new republic.

As president, however, Arce sided with the old nobility, arousing the opposition of the Liberals, and he was overthrown by forces led by Francisco Morazán.* He was exiled, first to the United States and later to Mexico.

In 1831 Arce invaded El Salvador and for a short while won control of Guatemala, but he was soon defeated and fled again to Mexico. In 1833 he again invaded and again was unsuccessful. He returned to El Salvador in 1840, ran for president, but was defeated. In 1843 he issued a call for reestablishing the Central American Federation, which had been dissolved some years before, but he found little response. In the following years, he launched his last unsuccessful invasion of El Salvador. Subsequently, he was finally allowed to return peacefully to his native land, where he died.

BIBLIOGRAPHY

Flemion, Philip: "States Rights and Partisan Politics: Manuel José Arce and the Struggle for Central American Union." *Hispanic American Historical Review* 53 (1973): 600–618.
García, Miguel Angel (ed.). *General Don Manuel José Arce: Homenaje en el Primer Centenario de su fallecimiento*. San Salvador: Imprenta Nacional, 1944.

ROBERT J. ALEXANDER

ARÉVALO BERMEJO, JUAN JOSÉ (1904–   ), the first president of Guatemala after the 1944 revolution, was the son of a farmer and a schoolteacher whose academic talents earned him a scholarship to the University of La Plata in Argentina. After receiving his doctorate in 1934, he spent two years with the

Guatemalan Ministry of Education before returning to Argentina as a university professor in Tucumán.

The students, intellectuals, and young professionals who had overthrown the dictatorship of Jorge Ubico y Castaneda* in Guatemala designated Arévalo as their presidential candidate, and he was elected president in December 1944, with a remarkable 86 percent of the vote. Arévalo had stressed the concept of "spiritual socialism," a reform program to liberate Guatemala from the domination of foreign interests and the local oligarchy. During his administration, forced labor was abolished, legislation dealing with educational improvements, social security, and democratization of the armed forces was enacted, and the Labor Code of 1947 allowed industrial and agrarian workers to be unionized. The Guatemalan Communist Party took advantage of Arévalo's liberalism to infiltrate and ultimately gain control of the unions.

Arévalo's reforms antagonized the defenders of the old order: those landed interests that had reaped huge profits through the friendly policies of the Ubico dictatorship. Furthermore, a long and bitter fight between the Guatemalan government and the United Fruit Company began in July 1948, when the company ignored the provisions of the Labor Code.

Thirty-two attempts were made to overthrow the Arévalo administration in its four years of existence. Nevertheless, Arévalo completed his term of office and turned the power over to the elected government of Jacobo Arbenz Guzmán.*

Arévalo's following in later years far exceeded his popularity while in office. His image as a bold reformer and uncorrupted administrator was enhanced in exile. His return to Guatemala in 1963 (as a potential candidate for the presidency) provoked the army to overthrow the government. A prolific writer, Arévalo limited his political activity after that to publishing several books.

BIBLIOGRAPHY

Arévalo, Juan José. *El Candidato Blanco y el Huracán.* Guatemala City: 1984.
Dion, M. B. *Las Ideas Sociales y Políticas de Arévalo.* Mexico: 1958.
Medardo Mejía. *Juan José Arévalo.* Guatemala City: Tipografiá Nacional, 1951.
Monteforte Toledo, Mario. *La Revolución de Guatemala.* Guatemala City: 1975.
Suslow, Leo. *Aspects of Social Reform in Guatemala.* Hamilton, N.Y.: Colgate University Bookstore, 1949.

JOSÉ M. SÁNCHEZ

ARIAS MADRID, ARNULFO (1901–   ), was the president of Panama from October 1, 1940, to October 9, 1941; November 24, 1949, to May 10, 1951; and October 1–12, 1968. He was deposed each time.

Educated in the United States and the recipient of an M.D. from Harvard Medical School, Arias entered politics as a leader of Acción Comunal, which staged the revolution of January 1931 that sought to displace the old oligarchy and U.S. influence at the same time. Arias and his followers were professionals and bureaucrats who displayed a nationalism that was not just anti-Yankee, but was opposed to all foreigners, including the Antillean blacks who had migrated to the Isthmus as railroad and canal workers. During the 1930s Arias expressed pro-Nazi attitudes and avowed admiration for Benito Mussolini.

Becoming president for the first time in 1940, Arias censored the press, intimidated the National Assembly, and railroaded through a new constitution that extended his term indefinitely and gave him near-dictatorial power. Using demagogic and chauvinistic appeals, he "nationalized" the businesses of thousands of alien small shopkeepers, especially Chinese, and disfranchised large numbers of Antillean blacks. However, in October 1941 cabinet minister Ricardo Adolfo de la Guardia, with support of the National Police, took advantage of Arias's unauthorized absence abroad to declare the presidency vacant.

Arias went into exile in Argentina but became a viable political force again in the highly nationalistic atmosphere of postwar Panama. Perhaps having won the disputed 1948 election, Arias, after the death in the following year of President Domingo Díaz Arosemena, was installed in the presidency by National Police Chief José Antonio Remón Cantera,* who had thwarted his election in 1948. Arias instituted a regime of incredible corruption and attempted to establish another dictatorship. Impeached by the National Assembly and Supreme Court, he refused to vacate the presidential palace, and a three-hour gun battle with the National Police resulted in 16 deaths.

Arias won the presidency again in 1968, but when he tried to remove certain National Guard officers, he became victim of a military coup for the third time, this time led by Omar Torrijos Herrera. Thereafter, he continued to lead the opposition to the Torrijos government and its successors.

BIBLIOGRAPHY

Alba, C., Manuel María. *Cronología de los Gobernantes de Panama, 1510–1967*. Panama: 1967.
Castillero R., Ernesto J. *Historia de Panama*. Panama: Editora Panama América, 1959.
Pippin, Larry LaRae. *The Remón Era: An analysis of a Decade of Events in Panama, 1947–1957*. Stanford, Calif.: Stanford University Press, 1964.
Ropp, Steve C. *Panamanian Politics: From Guarded Nation to National Guard*. New York: Praeger, 1982.

CHARLES D. AMERINGER

ARIAS MADRID, HARMODIO (1886–1962), was president of Panama, 1932–1936. He was educated abroad, attending the London School of Economics, and received a degree in law and political science from Cambridge University in 1911. He rose to power through a highly nationalistic and racist-oriented movement, Acción Comunal, which staged the Revolution of 1931. In the subsequent election of 1932, Arias emerged as president.

Arias Madrid capably handled the prevailing economic crisis. The Hull-Alfaro Treaty, which eliminated Panama's status as a U.S. protectorate and gave Panama improved economic terms, was a triumph for his presidency. He also established the National University in 1935.

Following his presidency, Arias became a major shaper of public opinion through his newspapers, *El Panama América*, *La Hora*, and *La Crítica*, and a chain of radio and television stations. He used the media to push chauvinistic nationalism and to promote the political career of his brother, Arnulfo Arias Madrid.*

BIBLIOGRAPHY

Alba C., Manuel María. *Cronología de los Gobernantes de Panama, 1510–1967*. Panama: 1967.
Castillero, Ernesto R. *Historia de Panama*. Panama: Editora Panama América, 1959.
Pippin, Larry LaRae. *The Remón Era: An Analysis of a Decade of Events in Panama, 1947–1957*. Stanford, Calif.: Stanford University Press, 1964.
Ropp, Steve C. *Panamanian Politics: From Guarded Nation to National Guard*. New York: Praeger, 1982.

                                                        CHARLES D. AMERINGER

ARRON, HENCK A.E. (1936–   ), as prime minister led Surinam to independence from the Netherlands in November 1975 and continued to lead the government until February 1980, when he was overthrown by a military coup d'etat led by Sergeant Desi Bouterse.* Before entering politics, he had been a bank worker spending some time at the Bank of Amsterdam in the Netherlands and in a local bank upon returning to Surinam.

Henck Arron entered politics in 1963, when he was elected a Surinam National Party (NPS) member of the Surinam legislature, the Staten. After the defeat of the NPS government headed by Johan Adolf Pengel* in 1969, Arron succeeded Pengel as leader of the NPS in the following year.

Arron led his party's election campaign in 1973 and fought on the issue of attaining independence. After two years of negotiations with the Netherlands government and with those parties (principally representing the East Indian population) which until then had been opposed to independence, Minister President (prime minister) Arron was able to lead the country to independence in November 1975.

The Arron government faced serious economic problems rooted in the world oil crisis and complicated by charges of corruption. However, it was its opposition to unionization of members of the country's armed forces which provoked a coup d'état led by sergeants.

Henck Arron was jailed by the new military rulers from February 1980 until 1981. Upon his release he returned to banking activities, becoming director of the Volkscredietbank in Paramaribo in 1982.

BIBLIOGRAPHY

Alexander, Robert J. "Surinam," in Robert J. Alexander (ed). *Political Parties of the Americas*, Vol. 2, Westport, Conn.: Greenwood Press, 1982.
International Who's Who 1985–86. London: Europa Publications, 1985.

ROBERT J. ALEXANDER

ARROYO DEL RÍO, CARLOS ALBERTO (1893–1969), was the last in a long list of Liberal Party presidents of Ecuador which had begun in 1895. He was brought up and educated in the port city of Guayaquil and by the 1930s was a successful lawyer, closely associated with the powerful commercial and industrial interests of the coastal city.

During the first period that José María Velasco Ibarra* was in power, 1934–1935, Arroyo del Río led the Liberal opposition in Congress, provoking a coup d'état by the president, who established a dictatorship. Within less than a year of taking office, however, Velasco Ibarra was forced to resign.

Arroyo del Río continued to be the principal Liberal leader. In 1939 he led a special constitutional convention in scrapping a constitution that had been adopted the year before in a constituent assembly dominated by Socialist elements. In its place the 1939 body reinstated the 1906 Liberal constitution.

In 1940 Arroyo del Río was elected president of Ecuador with "normal fraud," being credited with 35,000 votes against 22,000 for Velasco Ibarra. In the beginning of his term, he received relatively wide popular backing.

In 1941, however, Peru invaded the southern provinces of Ecuador, along the Pacific Coast. In this crisis, the opposition parties offered to participate in a coalition government of national unity, but Arroyo del Río rejected the offer. The Ecuadorians were quickly defeated, and in January 1942 the Arroyo del Río government, due to the intervention of the Pan American Foreign Ministers' Conference, signed the so-called Protocol of Rio de Janeiro, by which Ecuador ceded to Peru most of its Amazonian provinces, a total of 5,392 square miles.

Although at first the popular reaction was one of stunned acquiescence, massive resistance to President Arroyo del Río soon developed. Although he was received with honors on a state visit to Washington, that did him little good in Ecuador. A Democratic Alliance, which included virtually all the country's political parties, from Conservative, through dissident Liberals, to Socialists and Communists, was formed against Arroyo del Río. After violent demonstrations in Guayaquil, in which policemen were lynched, the army moved in to oust President Arroyo del Río in May 1944.

After his removal from the presidency, Carlos Alberto Arroyo del Río played no further role in Ecuadorian national politics.

BIBLIOGRAPHY

Blanksten, George I. *Ecuador: Constitutions and Caudillos*. Berkeley: University of California Press, 1951.
New York Times, November 1, 1969.

Pareja Díez Canseco, Alfredo. *Breve Historia del Ecuador*. Mexico: Biblioteca Enciclopedia Popular, 1946.
ROBERT J. ALEXANDER

ARTIGAS, JOSÉ GERVASIO (1764–1850), was the most outstanding leader
of the movement resulting in the independence of Uruguay. He was born into
a landowning family and was given the education appropriate to his status.
Thereafter, he spent much time on the family estates and acquired the skills
typical of the cattlemen, the gauchos. He was an officer in the militia and
participated in the Spaniards' successful resistance to the British attempt in 1806–
1807 to seize Montevideo.

Within a few months of the beginning of the revolution against Spain in Buenos
Aires in 1810, Artigas joined the movement. Although he particpated in a force
sent by the Buenos Aires authorities to take Montevideo, he soon became the
major leader of a faction in the "Banda Oriental" (the future Uruguay). The
group sought autonomy for the region, against both Argentine and Portuguese
efforts to extend control over it.

Artigas joined with the federalist forces that were opposed to a centralized
regime under Buenos Aires control. However, the Argentine National Assembly
which met in Buenos Aires in 1813 refused to seat a delegation that Artigas sent
there. A year later, the regime in Buenos Aires outlawed Artigas, but since
Artigas controlled most of the Banda Oriental, the Argentines withdrew in 1815.

Artigas established himself as Protector of the Banda Oriental, but he continued
to seek autonomy, not the independence, of Uruguay within the Argentine Confederation. In pursuance of this objective, he established a Federal League, which
at one point controlled not only the Banda Oriental, but also several Argentine
provinces, extending as far as Córdoba.

In 1816 the Portuguese invaded the Banda Oriental once again and took
Montevideo in January 1817. Artigas continued the struggle but by 1820 had
been totally defeated; he fled to Paraguay, where he spent the rest of his life.
He was not present in his native country in 1828, when it was finally established
as an independent buffer state between Argentina and Brazil.

BIBLIOGRAPHY

Acevedo, Eduardo. *José Artigas: Su obra cívica, alegato histórico*. 3 vols. Montevideo:
    1950.
Lowenthal, Maximiliano. *Artigas, Dramaturgo de los Orientales*. San José, C.R.: La
    Pas, 1947.
Sosa, Josualdo. *Artigas: del vasallaje a la revolución*. Buenos Aires: Editorial Claridad,
    1940.
Street, John. *Artigas and the Emancipation of Uruguay*. Cambridge: Cambridge Uni-
    versity Press, 1959.
ROBERT J. ALEXANDER

ARZE, JOSÉ ANTONIO (1904–1955), was founder of one of the major Bolivian leftist parties of the post-Chaco War generation. Educated in the Colegio
Bolivar and Colegio Sucre in Cochabamba, he was director from 1921 to 1926

of the Higher Institute of Artesans in Cochabamba. From 1927 to 1928 he was professor at the University of Cochabamba and became active in the radical Marxist student movement. He and Ricardo Anaya organized the University Federation of Bolivia in 1928.

Arze taught at the University of San Andrés in La Paz (1931–1932) until the outbreak of the Chaco War, when he went into exile in Chile. For a short while after the War, he was adviser to the minister of labor, but his opposition to the military socialism of the David Toro government caused his exile to Chile again. He taught at the University of Chile and organized the Bolivian Leftist Front in April 1939.

Returning home again in February 1940, he was the only opposition candidate against the establishment's presidential nominee, war hero General Enrique Peñaranda. Although lacking a formal party organization, and a relatively unknown political figure, he won 10,000 votes out of 58,000 cast. His showing marked a major shift in Bolivian politics. On July 25, 1940, together with Ricardo Anaya he founded the Party of the Revolutionary Left (PIR).

The PIR was the first avowed Marxist Party in Bolivia and came to control the nonmining labor movement through the Union Confederation of Bolivian Workers (CSTB). In Congress, PIR proposed radical programs such as nationalization of the mines and petroleum, agrarian reform, a state-directed economy, and complete liberation and integration of the Indian into national life. In foreign affairs, the PIR was pro-Soviet, but it became pro-Allied after the Soviet Union was attacked by Germany.

Between 1941 and 1943, Arze was in the United States, where he taught as a visiting lecturer at Williams College, at the Inter-American Training Center in Washington, and at the Communists' Thomas Jefferson School in New York City. He also worked in the Library of Congress. He returned to Bolivia in January 1944 and sought entry of the PIR into the cabinet of President Gualberto Villarroel López,* but was refused. Later in 1944, he ran against Villarroel for president and was elected national deputy from La Paz. He survived an assassination attempt after emergency medical treatment in the United States.

Arze joined the Democratic Antifascist Front with the oligarchical parties against the Villarroel government. When in the United States, Arze lobbied strenuously for U.S. intervention against the "fascist" regime. The power of PIR over unions, teachers, and university students contributed to the successful coup against Villarroel on June 21, 1946.

In 1947 Arze was elected president of the Chamber of Deputies, and PIR members served in the cabinet of conservative governments from 1946 to 1952. Arze ran again for president in May 1950 but won only 5,170 votes out of 126,000 cast. Arze's last political activity was service on the Educational Reform Commission of the revolutionary government that took power in 1952.

BIBLIOGRAPHY

Baptista Gumucio, Mariano. *Historia Contemporánea de Bolivia, 1930–1978*. 2nd ed. La Paz: Gisbert, 1978.

Céspedes, Augusto. *El Presidente Colgado: Historia Boliviana*. 2d ed. La Paz: Juventud, 1971.
Fellmann Velarde, José. *Historia de Bolivia, La Bolivianidad Semicolonial*. Vol. 3. Cochabamba: Los Amigos del Libro, 1981.
Klein, Herbert S. *Bolivia, The Evolution of a Multi-ethnic Society*. New York: Oxford University Press, 1982.

WALTRAUD QUEISER MORALES

ÁVILA CAMACHO, MANUEL (1897–1955), president of Mexico during World War II, created the social security system in Mexico. Born in the state of Puebla in 1897, the son of a farmer, Ávila Camacho took an accounting degree in Puebla, and in 1914 he joined the revolutionary army with the rank of sublieutenant. Only six years later, he became a colonel in charge of General Lázaro Cárdenas'* staff. He became a general in 1926 and in 1933 assistant minister of defense. In January 1938 he was named minister of defense and was promoted to major general. He was elected as the Revolutionary Party's presidential candidate on July 7, 1940.

As president, Ávila Camacho moved Mexico into an alliance against the Axis, and in 1942 he had the Congress declare war on Germany, Italy, and Japan. Hundreds of Nazi agents were rounded up, and bigots who had been broadcasting against minorities in the United States over powerful Mexican borderland radio stations, in English, were jailed. In 1943 Ávila Camacho created the Mexican Institute of Social Security.

To help the United States harvest its crops while most of its men were in uniform, Ávila Camacho signed the Bracero Treaty with the United States in 1942, under which hundreds of thousands of Mexicans came into the United States to raise food for the war effort. The treaty was renewed in 1948 and phased out at the end of 1964. Ávila Camacho died on October 13, 1955, in Mexico City.

BIBLIOGRAPHY

Alba, Víctor. *The Mexicans*. New York: Praeger, 1967.
Briggs, Donald C., and Marvin Alisky. *Historical Dictionary of Mexico*. Metuchen, N.J.: Scarecrow Press, 1981.
Camp, Roderic A. *Mexican Political Biographies, 1935–1975*. Tucson: University of Arizona Press, 1976.
Johnson, William Weber. *Heroic Mexico*. Garden City, N.Y.: Doubleday, 1969.
Turner, Frederic C. *The Dynamics of Mexican Nationalism*. Chapel Hill: University of North Carolina Press, 1968.

MARVIN ALISKY

B

BÁEZ, BUENAVENTURA (1810–1882), was one of the two major political leaders of the Dominican Republic during its first three decades. A mulatto landowner, Báez alternated in power with his major rival, Pedro Santana,* between 1844 and 1861. He was president during 1849–1853 and 1856–1857. After the end of Spain's reannexation of the country as a colony, Báez became president again in 1865. He negotiated a treaty of annexation with the United States, but the U.S. Senate refused to rectify it. Leaving the presidency in 1866, Báez returned to power between 1868 and 1873, and for a last period between 1876 and 1878. During all of his periods in office, Báez governed as a dictator.

BIBLIOGRAPHY

Enciclopedia Universal Ilustrada Europeo-Americana. Barcelona: José Espasa e Hijos.
Rodman, Selden. *Quisqueya: A History of the Dominican Republic*. Seattle: University of Washington Press, 1964.
Welles, Sumner. *Naboth's Vineyard*. New York: Payson and Clarke Ltd., 1928.

                                                                    ROBERT J. ALEXANDER

BÁEZ, CECILIO (1862–?), was the founder of the Liberal Party of Paraguay. He first gained prestige as a professor of law, history, and sociology in the University of Asunción, and wrote extensive studies of Paraguayan history.

Báez was elected to the Chamber of Deputies for the first time in 1895, where he led the opposition to successive Colorado Party governments and molded that opposition into the Liberal Party. With the advent of the Liberals to power in the early 1900s, Báez was chosen as provisional president in 1906. Subsequently, he served as Paraguayan minister to Spain, France, Italy, and the United Kingdom.

BIBLIOGRAPHY

Enciclopedia Universal Ilustrada Europeo-Americana. Barcelona: José Espasa e Hijos.
                                                        JOHN T. DEINER

BALAGUER, JOAQUÍN (1907–   ), was the last hand-picked president of the dictatorial regime of Rafael Leónidas Trujillo Molina* but emerged from that traumatic period as virtually the only experienced politician with a national reputation. He had not participated in any of the bloodier aspects of the Trujillo regime. He was elected president again four times in the 1960s, 1970s, and 1980s.

Balaguer's early career was that of a scholar and university professor. However, in 1958 Trujillo chose him to be vice president on a ticket headed by the dictator's brother Héctor Trujillo. When Héctor resigned in 1960, Balaguer succeeded to the presidency.

After the murder of Rafael Trujillo in May 1961, Balaguer sought to dismantle the dictatorship, allowing the return of exiles and the establishment of several opposition parties. The Trujillo family's attempt in November 1961 to reassume control was thwarted by the armed forces, with the support of the U.S. administration of John Kennedy. However, Balaguer was ousted by a military coup in January 1962 and went into exile in New York City.

After the 1965 civil war, Balaguer returned and formed the Partido Reformista, serving as its presidential candidate. He was elected in 1966 and reelected in 1970 and 1974. During his administration, he largely brought the military under civilian control and carried out modest economic development and social reform programs.

Running for a fourth term in 1978, Balaguer was defeated by Antonio Guzmán, nominee of the Partido Revolucionario Dominicano. Pressure by U.S. President Jimmy Carter thwarted an attempt by the military to block Balaguer's defeat. Balaguer's attempt to return to the presidency in the 1982 election was unsuccessful. He was finally reelected, for a fourth time, in 1986.

BIBLIOGRAPHY

Crassweiler, Robert D. *Trujillo: Life and Times of a Caribbean Dictator.* New York: Macmillan Co., 1966.
Personal Contacts.
Who Is Who—in Government and Politics in Latin America. New York: Media Books, Inc., 1984.
                                                        ROBERT J. ALEXANDER

BALBÍN, RICARDO (1904–1981), became leader of the Argentine Radical Party (UCR) in the 1940s, based on his outspoken opposition to the regime of Juan Domingo Perón.* He was expelled from Congress by the Peronists and even jailed in 1950. In 1951 Balbín ran against Perón in the national presidential election with Arturo Frondizi* as his running mate as vice president. The UCR was handily defeated by Perón.

In 1956, following the fall of Perón, the UCR split into two parties. Balbín headed the UCRP (Unión Cívica Radical del Pueblo), the Radicals of the People, and Frondizi formed the UCRI (Unión Cívica Radical Intransigente), the Intransigent Radicals. The split was caused by personality conflicts and policy differences. Balbín's faction adamantly opposed both cooperation with the Peronists and the opening up of the Argentine economy to foreign corporations, emphasized traditional individual freedoms, and strongly opposed corruption and dictatorship. Frondizi was more amenable to cooperation with the Peronists, and he and the UCRI, with the help of the Peronist votes, defeated Balbín and the UCRP in the 1958 presidential election. Frondizi was later ousted in a coup in 1962.

In 1963 the UCRP's candidate Arturo Umberto Illia* won the presidential election but was overthrown by a 1966 military coup. Balbín retained control of the party machinery for the following decade, and in 1973 he was twice named the UCR's presidential candidate. In the first election of that year he lost badly to the Peronist candidate Héctor Cámpora,* getting only 21 percent of the vote, while in the second election he was defeated by Perón himself.

During the period of military government after 1976, Balbín remained the dominant figure in the UCR until his death. He called for return to civilian government but was less prominent in denouncing human rights violations than were such younger party leaders as Raúl Ricardo Alfonsín Foulkes,* who succeeded him as UCR leader.

BIBLIOGRAPHY

Alexander, Robert J. *Latin American Political Parties*. New York: Praeger, 1973.
Snow, Peter G. *Argentine Radicalism: The History and Doctrine of the Radical Civic Union*. Iowa City: University of Iowa Press, 1965.
———. *Political Forces in Argentina*. New York: Praeger, 1979.
Wynia, Gary W. *Argentina in the Postwar Era: Politics and Economic Policy Making in a Divided Society*. Albuquerque: University of New Mexico Press, 1978.

JOHN T. DEINER

BALDOMIR, ALFREDO (1884–1948), was the president of Uruguay who brought that country out of the first dictatorship from which it had suffered in the twentieth century. Born in Montevideo, he spent more than three decades in the armed forces and rose to the rank of general by the early 1930s.

Baldomir was a brother-in-law of President Gabriel Terra,* who had been democratically elected in 1930 but had carried out a coup and established a dictatorship in 1933, with the support of part of his own Colorado Party and of the opposition Blanco Party. Baldomir served as Terra's minister of national defense in 1935–1936.

General Baldomir was his brother-in-law's choice to succeed him in 1938 and so was elected president. However, he found it difficult, and finally impossible, to work with the constitutional arrangement he had inherited. Following a pro-Allied policy in World War II, he encountered strong opposition from the Blanco Party, then led by pro-Axis Luis Alberto de Herrera,* which was guaranteed equality in the Senate with the Colorados, according to the arrangements of President Terra with Herrera.

A crisis developed in January 1942, when President Baldomir, attempting to overcome Blanco opposition, dissolved Parliament and removed the Blancos from the cabinet. In the November 1942 elections, he submitted proposals for substituting proportional representation for the equal party representation in choosing members of the Senate which had been established by Terra. This paved the way for the full reestablishment of a democratic regime at the end of the Baldomir administration.

After leaving the presidency, Alfredo Baldomir headed one of the many factions of the Colorado Party. He did not again aspire to be president.

BIBLIOGRAPHY

Fitzgibbon, Russell H. *Uruguay: Portrait of a Democracy*. New Brunswick, N.J.: Rutgers University Press, 1954.
New York Times, Feruary 26, 1948.

ROBERT J. ALEXANDER

BALDORIOTY DE CASTRO, RAMÓN (1822–1889), was the first leader of the Autonomists of Puerto Rico. He received his early education from the canons of the Cathedral of San Juan and completed his studies in Paris, from whence he returned home in 1853. He then taught mathematics, physics, and botany in several local schools. He represented Puerto Rico at the Paris Exposition of 1867. In 1869–1870 he represented Mayaguez in the Spanish Parliament, the Cortes. In that period, he rejected an offer of a high post in the Spanish Ministry of Finance.

In 1872 Baldorioty de Castro returned to Ponce, where he founded a newspaper, *El Derecho*. In 1880 he established another paper, *La Crónica*, as the spokesman for the Autonomists. When the Autonomist Party was officially established in 1887, he was elected its first president, an honor that brought him arrest and imprisonment in Moro Castle. However, he had been released by the time he died in Ponce.

BIBLIOGRAPHY

Cruz Monclova, Lidio. *Baldorioty de Castro: Su Vida, Sus Ideas*. San Juan: Instituto de Cultura Puertorriqueña, 1973.
Rosario, Pilar Barbosa de. *De Baldorioty a Barbosa: Historia del Autonomismo Puertorriqueño 1887–1896*. San Juan, 1974.

Sharpless, Richard E. "Puerto Rico," in Robert J. Alexander (ed.). *Political Parties of the Americas*, Westport, Conn.: Greenwood Press, 1982.

RICHARD E. SHARPLESS

BALMACEDA FERNÁNDEZ, JOSÉ MANUEL (1840–1891), was the last Chilean president of the so-called Liberal Republic. His violent overthrow and suicide resulted in the establishment of the Parliamentary Republic.

Balmaceda, a member of the National Party, got his first political experience in the early 1860s as private secretary of ex-President Manuel Montt Torres.* In 1864 he was elected to the Chamber of Deputies where he served until elected to the presidency. In 1878 President Anibal Pinto Garmendia* sent Balmaceda as minister to Argentina, where he persuaded the Argentine government to remain neutral in the War of the Pacific between Chile on the one hand and Bolivia and Peru on the other. Under President Domingo Santa María Gonzalez* he served as minister of foreign relations, minister of justice, and minister of the interior.

In 1886 Balmaceda was elected president by a coalition of the National Party, the Liberal Party, and a faction of the Radicals. As president, he pushed forward the economic and social development of Chile. A thousand kilometers of new railroad lines were constructed, including the beginning of the Chilean portion of the Transandean Railway. New schools were built on all educational levels, and a Superior Council of Health was established.

The president came into growing conflict with Congress. This was the culmination of a quarter-century process in which Congress had been augmenting its powers at the expense of the chief executive. Balmaceda was an advocate of a strong presidency. In addition, he sought to limit the economic and political influence of British interests in the northern nitrate fields, while there was strong opposition in Congress to any limitation of the British role.

By October 1889 a coalition had been formed against Balmaceda in and out of Congress, consisting of his own National Party, the Radical Party, and two Liberal factions. At the end of 1890 opposition forces in Congress sought to pressure Balmaceda by refusing to pass the budget or the annual authorization required in order to maintain a standing army. So, on January 1, 1891, Balmaceda announced that he would continue operating the government on the same budget as that of 1890. On the same day, a majority in Congress declared the president "deposed."

The rebel congressmen went to Valparaiso where most of the navy, commanded by Captain Jorge Montt Alvarez,* supported them. Proceeding to Iquique, they established a rebel government junta of three persons. The army remained loyal to the president and Civil War ensued, until the end of August when the rebels won the decisive Battle of Placilla. On August 28 Balmaceda received asylum in the Argentine legation, and remained in the legation until September 19, the day his constitutional term ended, and then committed suicide.

BIBLIOGRAPHY

Cortes, Lia, and Jordi Fuentes. *Diccionario Político de Chile*. Santiago: Editorial Orbe, 1967.
Galdames, Luis. *Historia de Chile*. Santiago: Editorial Zig Zag, 1965.
Hervey, Maurice. *Dark Days in Chile*. New York: Macmillan Co. 1892.
Monteon, Michael. *Chile in the Nitrate Era*. Madison: University of Wisconsin Press, 1982.
ROBERT J. ALEXANDER

BANGOU, HENRI (1922–   ), principal Communist leader of Guadeloupe, went to local schools in Pointe-à-Pitre, Guadeloupe, and then to both the Law and Medical Faculties of Paris. During that period, he served as vice-president of the Union of Students of France in 1949–1950.

Bangou practiced medicine as a cardiologist in Pointe-à-Pitre from 1953 to 1959. In 1959 he was elected on the Communist ticket as assistant mayor of Pointe-à-Pitre. In 1965 he was elected mayor, and he was reelected in 1971, 1977, and 1983. He also was elected to the Council General of Guadeloupe in 1967 and reelected in 1973. In 1979 he was officially named leader of the Guadeloupean Communist Party.

BIBLIOGRAPHY

Alexander, Robert J. "Guadeloupe," in Robert J. Alexander (ed.), *Political Parties of the Americas*. Vol. 2. Westport, Conn.: Greenwood Press, 1982.
Who's Who in France. 17th ed. Paris: Editions Jacques Lafitte, 1984.
ROBERT J. ALEXANDER

BANZER SUÁREZ, HUGO (1926–   ), was president of Bolivia from 1971 to 1978. He had graduated from the military academy in 1952, and in 1953 when the army was reorganized by the Nationalist Revolutionary Movement (MNR) after the 1952 revolution, Banzer was reincorporated in the armed forces. Never an MNR supporter, he favored the military coup by Generals Alfredo Ovando Candia* and René Barrientos Ortuño* against the third presidential term of Víctor Paz Estenssoro* in November 1964. From then until August 1966, he served as minister of education, and in the Ovando government (1969–1970) he headed the military college. General Juan José Torres González* dismissed him in January 1971, when a coup attempt by Banzer failed. From exile in Argentina, he continued to plot against the government. On August 22, 1971, after a successful revolt, Colonel Banzer assumed the presidency.

President Banzer's governing style was elitist and authoritarian. Until November 1974 the Banzer government found political backing in the Popular Nationalist Front (FPN), a coalition of traditional adversaries—the MNR and the Falange Socialista Boliviana (FSB). Thereafter, the Banzer government became a personalistic dictatorship. A Military-Peasant Pact was used to control the agrarian sector. The Banzer presidency was characterized by extensive development and economic growth. A new economic elite of medium-sized mining, business, petroleum, and agrobusiness interests became entrenched, and foreign firms were courted by lenient investment laws. Extensive foreign loans were contracted for conspicuous development projects. In foreign policy, Banzer stressed a campaign to regain the lost Pacific coastal ports through bilateral talks with Chile's General Augusto Pinochet Ugarte.*

Despite heavy U.S. economic assistance to Banzer, his development policies contributed to a severe economic crisis and growing national debt. Several military coups were thwarted in 1972, 1973, and 1974; in January 1974 Cochabamba peasant leagues protested high food prices, and a hundred people were killed. A new Compulsory Civil Service Law was used to place government officials in positions of union leadership. All strike activity was banned, mining strikes in Janaury 1975, June 1976 and December 1977 were violently repressed, and army troops were stationed in the mines.

On January 24, 1978, after a successful national hunger strike, a general political amnesty was announced. Banzer supported General Juan Pereda Asbún for the presidency in July elections, which were pronounced fradulent by all the participants. Pereda seized power in a bloodless coup. General Banzer continued to agitate as successive coups swept the country. He ran in the 1979 and 1980 presidential elections, coming out a distant third each time. In 1985 he was runner-up.

BIBLIOGRAPHY

Banzer, Suárez, Hugo. *Libro Blanco de Realizaciones del Gobierno de las Fuerzas Armadas*. La Paz: 1978.
Baptista Gumucio, Mariano. *Historia Contemporanea de Bolivia, 1930–1978*. 2nd ed. La Paz: Gisbert, 1978.
Gallardo Lozada, Jorge. *De Torres a Banzer: Diez Meses de Emergencia en Bolivia*. Buenos Aires: Ediciones Periferia, 1972.
Klein, Herbert S. *Bolivia, the Evolution of a Multi-ethnic Society*. New York: Oxford University Press, 1982.

WALTRAUD QUEISER MORALES

BAPTISTA CASERTA, MARIANO (1832–1907), served as president of Bolivia from 1892 to 1896. Active in politics since studying for his law degree at the Universidad de San Francisco Xavier de Chuquisaca, he struggled against the regime of Manuel Isidoro Belzú* and was exiled to Peru. Returning to Bolivia, he established the newspaper, *El Porvenir*, in 1855 and was elected deputy from Chuquisaca to the national Congress.

During 1873–1876 Baptista was minister of government and foreign relations in the governments of Presidents Adolfo Ballivián and Tomás Frías. A prominent lawyer for the mining companies, Baptista was vice president from September 1884 to May 1888 in the administration of Gregorio Pacheco, Bolivia's second largest silver producer and founder of the Democratic Party. Termed the "ideologue of the Conservative Party," Baptista became president in August 1892, after a typically fraudulent election.

The Baptista government promoted public education, passed a law of obligatory military service, and promoted railroad construction and exploration of Bolivia's northeastern region. Baptista signed several partial peace treaties with Chile, and treaties with Paraguay, Argentina, and Brazil, delimiting Bolivia's boundaries with those countries. He handed over the government to the last Conservative president on August 19, 1896.

BIBLIOGRAPHY

Arguedas, Alcides. *Historia General de Bolivia (El Proceso de la Nacionalidad), 1809–1921)*. Vol. 6. La Paz: Arno Hmos., 1922.
Finot, Enrique. *Nueva Historia de Bolivia (Ensayo de Interpretación Sociológica)*. 2d ed. La Paz: Gisbert, 1954.
Guzmán, Augusto. *Baptista*. La Paz: Juventud, 1957.
Klein, Herbert S. *Parties and Political Change in Bolivia, 1880–1952*. Cambridge: Cambridge University Press, 1969.
O'Connor d'Arlach, Tomás. *Los presidentes de Bolivia desde 1825 hasta 1912*. La Paz: González y Medina, 1912.

WALTRAUD QUEISER MORALES

BARBOSA, JOSÉ CELSO (1857–1921), Puerto Rican Autonomist and later pro-statehood leader, was born into a black family in Bayamón. He went to school there and at the Conciliar Seminary in San Juan. After teaching a year in Bayamón, he sought higher education in the United States, obtaining a medical degree at the University of Michigan in 1880. He then practiced medicine in San Juan.

Barbosa joined the Liberal Reform Party, which advocated autonomy for Puerto Rico. In 1894 he became a director of the party, but shortly before the U.S. invasion of Puerto Rico in July 1898, he withdrew from the party. After U.S. occupation, his followers, the "Puros," decided to support statehood for Puerto Rico and to take the name Republican Party.

When the Foraker Act in 1900 set up an appointed Executive Council, Barbosa became a member of that council, remaining until 1917. Thereafter, he was in the insular Senate, provided for in the Jones Act, which in 1917 recognized the Puerto Rican government and made Puerto Ricans U.S. citizens.

BIBLIOGRAPHY

Pedreira, Antonio Salvador. *Un Hombre del Pueblo: José Celso Barbosa*. San Juan: Imprenta Venezuela, 1937.
Rosario, Pilar Barbosa de. *De Baldorioty a Barbosa: historia del autonomismo puertorriqueño 1887–1898*. San Juan: 1974.

Sterling, Philip. *The Quiet Rebels: Four Puerto Rican Leaders: José Celso Barbosa, Luis Muñoz Rivera, José de Diego, Luis Muñoz Marín.* Garden City, N.Y.: Doubleday, 1968.

RICHARD E. SHARPLESS

BARBOSA, RUY (1849–1923), was a brilliant and emotional orator whose speeches and political campaigns left a deep impact on Brazil. He played significant roles in the empire, the provisional government, and the republic.

Born in 1849 in Bahia, Barbosa entered law school in Recife but transferred to São Paulo, where he received his degree in 1871. Entering politics in his native state, he was elected congressman in 1878 for the Liberal Party. As the empire was disintegrating, Dom Pedro II* in 1889 offered him a post in a Liberal Party cabinet, which he refused. Barbosa had become a convert to Republicanism.

On the fall of the empire in November, Ruy Barbosa became finance minister of the provisional government, and attempted to encourage capital formation by freer emission of bank notes and loosening of credit.

Barbosa also was the most important figure on the committee that drafted a new constitution. He is considered the father of the 1891 constitution and personally responsible for the separation of church and state. This constitution governed Brazil until the 1930 revolution.

When a revolt against the army presidents broke out in 1893, Barbosa was accused of siding with the navy rebels and went into exile. From England he wrote a series of letters commenting on Brazilian affairs which were considered brilliant.

Upon his return to Brazil, he was elected senator from Bahia in 1895. In 1907 he was made Brazilian delegate to the Hague Conference where he put on a dazzling performance demanding equality for all nations on the international arbitration court. He had acquired an international reputation as a statesman and jurist.

In 1910, when the major political party selected a general to run for president, Ruy Barbosa threw his hat in the ring and attempted unsuccessfully to rally the country behind his campaign to keep army officers out of politics. In 1918 he again made a half-hearted bid for the presidency and was defeated.

BIBLIOGRAPHY

Barbosa, Ruy. *Cartas de Inglaterra.* Rio de Janeiro, Typ. Leuginger, 1896.
Bastos, Humberto. *Ruy Barbosa, Ministro de Independencia Económica do Brasil.* Rio de Janeiro, Casa de Rui Barbosa, 1949.
Palha, Américo. *Historia da Vida de Rui Barbosa.*

Turner, Charles W. *Ruy Barbosa: Brazilian Crusader for the Essential Freedoms.* New
    York: Abenzáon-Cokesbury Press, 1945.
Viana Filho, Luiz: *A Vida de Rui Barbosa*, Rio de Janeiro, José Olympio Editora, 1977.
                                                                    JORDAN YOUNG

BARRANTES LINGAN, ALFONSO (1928–   ), a Marxist presidential candidate in Peru in 1985, was born in San Miguel de Cajamarca. After completing
his primary and secondary education, he went to the National University of San
Marcos, where he received his law degree. An Aprista Party activist since 1943,
he led the student protest against Vice President Richard Nixon in May 1958.
Suspended from the Aprista Party, Barrantes traveled to the People's Republic
of China to attend an international student congress later in 1958.

Barrantes joined the Peruvian Communist Party in 1960 but resigned from it
in 1972. Thereafter, he considered himself an independent Marxist, follower of
José Carlos Mariátegui's* ideology. He helped establish Unidad Democrática
Popular in 1977, and when eight political organizations in 1980 formed the
United Left (Izquierda Unida–IU), he became its president. Barrantes was elected
first Marxist mayor of Lima with 33 percent of the votes in 1983 but was defeated
as IU presidential candidate in 1985, when he placed second with 24 percent of
the vote.

BIBLIOGRAPHY

Chang-Rodríguez, Eugenio. *Opciones políticas peruanas.* Lima: Centro de Documen-
    tación Andina, 1985.
Garay Seminario, Martín. *Perfiles humanos.* Lima: 1985.
Goldenberg, Sonia (ed). *Decidamos nuestro futuro.* Lima: Universidad del Pacifico-
    Fundación Friedrich Ebert, 1985.
Rojas Samanéz, Alvaro. *Partidos Políticos en el Peru, desde 1872.* Lima: Ediciones A
    & F, 1985.
                                                    EUGENIO CHANG-RODRÍGUEZ

BARRIENTOS ORTUÑO, RENÉ (1919–1969), was president of Bolivia from
1966 to 1969. He attended school in Cochabamba and then entered the military
academy, from which he was expelled because he supported the Germán Busch*
government. He was subsequently readmitted and graduated in 1943. He also
supported the Gualberto Villarroel López* coup in 1943 and participated in the
organization of the 1944 peasant congress. Barrientos entered the Military College of Aviation and studied briefly in the United States, earning his wings in
April 1945. Because of his involvement in the 1949 civil war against the entrenched elites, he was retired from the army. He risked his life for the Nationalist
Revolutionary Movement (MNR) revolution in April 1952, flying supply missions from Santa Cruz. His loyal support of the MNR led to Barrientos' rapid
rise in the military from captain to general of the air force and head of the party's
military cell.

Barrientos successfully pressured Víctor Paz Estenssoro* to nominate him as a vice presidential running mate for the elections of May 1964. However, Paz's third term ended precipitously with a coup on November 3, 1964, by Barrientos and General Alfredo Ovando Candia.* Barrientos and Ovando assumed temporary executive control. Barrientos resigned from the co-presidency, leaving Ovando in charge in January 1966 to run in the July elections.

As one of Bolivia's more flamboyant presidents, Barrientos cultivated a direct, populist leadership style among the peasant masses, especially in the Cochabamba Valley. Fluent in Quechua, he formed personalist alliances with powerful peasant leaders, which he formalized in the Military-Peasant Pact of 1966, which became the basis of military rule in the 1970s. He formed his own political party, the Popular Christian Movement, and a coalition with minor parties, the Bolivian Revolutionary Front, for the 1966 elections. In 1968 he created a single official party, largely a facade for military rule.

Barrientos favored the rise of a new ruling elite of medium-sized mining entrepreneurs, importers, and agrobusinessmen. A new investment code in 1965 encouraged foreign multinational investment. There were bloody clashes of the military and the miners' unions in 1965 and 1967. Although the economy grew, it became more dependent. The labor movement was broken and domesticated by the government. However, Barrientos' popularity with the peasants helped his government in 1967 to rid Bolivia of the Cuban guerrilla *foco* led by Ernesto (Che) Guevara de la Serna.*

On April 27, 1969, Barrientos' heliocopter mysteriously crashed, ending his life and presidency.

BIBLIOGRAPHY

Díez de Medina, Fernando. *El General del Pueblo*. La Paz: Los Amigos del Libro, 1972.
Mitchell, Christopher. *The Legacy of Populism in Bolivia, From the MNR to Military Rule*. New York: Praeger, 1977.
Ríos Reinaga, David. *Civiles y Militares en la Revolución Boliviana*. La Paz: Difusión, 1967.

WALTRAUD QUEISER MORALES

BARRIOS, GONZALO (1902–   ), one of the principal founders and long-time leaders of Venezuela's Acción Democrática Party, was the party's candidate for president in 1968. He had already graduated from the Central University in Caracas when he left the country in 1928 to escape the oppression of the regime of Juan Vicente Gómez.* He spent most of the next eight years in Spain, where he was closely associated with the exiled novelist Rómulo Gallegos.* He also became a member of the ARDI, the exile revolutionary organization established under the leadership of Rómulo Betancourt.*

Barrios returned home with Gallegos early in 1936, after Gómez' death. He became one of the leaders of the Organización Venezolana (ORVE), and then of the National Democratic Party (PDN), into which ORVE merged. In January

1937 he was elected to the Chamber of Deputies, but two months later was one of the PDN leaders deported by the government of President Eleazar López Contreras.* Upon returning home after a year's exile, he became head of the Disciplinc Committee of the still clandestine PDN. Subsequently, in 1942 he became correspondence secretary of the PDN's legal successor, Acción Democrática (AD).

Gonzalo Barrios was a key figure in the conspiracy between AD and a group of young military men which overthrew the government of President Isaías Medina Angarita* in October 1945. He became a member of the Revolutionary Governing Junta and Governor of the Federal District. In the succeeding elected government of President Rómulo Gallegos, he was Secretary of the Presidency.

With the fall of Gallegos in November 1948, Barrios was jailed and then went into exile for more than nine years. Most of the time, he was the principal leader of the AD group in Mexico.

Upon his return home after the overthrow of the Marcos Pérez Jiménez* dictatorship, Gonzalo Barrios was coopted into the National Executive Committee of Acción Democrática. He was elected to Congress in 1958.

In 1968 Gonzalo Barrios actively sought his party's nomination. The AD split; Barrios' major opponent, Luis Beltrán Prieto Figueroa,* and his followers broke away and formed Electoral Movement of the People. Gonzalo Barrios was the AD nominee, and narrowly lost to Rafael Caldera Rodriguez,* candidate of the Social Christian Copei Party.

Subsequent to the 1968 election, Gonzalo Barrios became president of Acción Democrática, a position he still held in the mid–1980s.

BIBLIOGRAPHY

Alexander, Robert J. *The Venezuelan Democratic Revolution*. New Brunswick, N.J.: Rutgers University Press, 1964.
Betancourt, Rómulo. *Venezuela: Oil and Politics*. Boston: Houghton Mifflin, 1979.
Magallanes, Manuel Vicente. *Los Partidos Políticos en la Evolución Histórica de Venezuela*. Caracas: Monte Avila Editores, 1977.
Martz, John D. *Acción Democrática: Evolution of a Modern Political Party in Venezuela*. Princeton, N.J.: Princeton University Press, 1966.

ROBERT J. ALEXANDER

BARRIOS, JUSTO RUFINO (1835–1885), was the first of the Liberal dictators who replaced Conservative caudillos during the last quarter of the nineteenth century in Guatemala. After receiving a law degree from the University of San Carlos, he made a small fortune experimenting with various crops, particularly coffee, on his plantation.

Barrios entered politics at a time when Conservative governments were operating primarily for the benefit of the elite in the capital, and younger army officers, intellectuals, and provincial leaders expressed their grievances through the Liberal Party. In June 1871 Liberal revolutionaries, under Barrios and General

Miguel García Granados, overthrew the Conservative regime. García Granados, an elderly man, became president. Trying to rule through compromise and tolerance of dissent, he only encouraged the remnants of the Conservative Party to plot against him and force him to step down.

Barrios assumed command in 1873 and immediately discarded the traditional idealism of the Liberals and the moderation of García Granados. Barrios believed that economic development was needed to bring Guatemala to the level of affluence of Europe and the United States, and this, not social and political reforms, became the government's top priority. Barrios' projects included building railroads to both coasts, highways, and colonization of the interior. He encouraged foreign investors to exploit mineral and wood resources while protecting coffee and banana growers.

The economic "take-off" never materialized. Instead of contributing to an industrial revolution the wealthy invested abroad. Public works projects of the national government provided only short-term employment. As the Liberals gained wealth and prestige, they emerged as a new ruling class disregarding the interests of the masses. Barrios shaped Guatemala into a unitary republic with legislative and judicial branches clearly subservient to the executive. Through the 1879 constitution Justo Rufino Barrios came to embody the Guatemalan state more completely than anyone else in history.

Barrios allowed landowners to maintain a system of debt peonage. Landowners made loans to Indians who, paid very low wages, were always in debt; their children inherited the debts.

Barrios reshaped two key institutions: the military and the church. He recruited foreign instructors to teach at the national military school founded by García Granados. The more professional army became a source of support for Barrios rather than a nonpolitical force; by gaining greater social status, the army served as a tool for upward mobility among the lower classes.

Barrios, identifying the church as a consistent supporter of the Conservatives, instituted a number of anticlerical measures. When the church excommunicated him, he exiled all the bishops and archbishops. Barrios also originated a number of educational reforms along Positivist lines imposing a secular curriculum on all educational institutions, with the central government supervising its application.

Barrios carried out an activist foreign policy. He intervened in Costa Rica and Honduras and fought a brief war with El Salvador in 1876. On February 28, 1885, he announced that Central America was once again to be united, under his guidance. The government of Porfirio Díaz* in Mexico, wary of a united Central America, encouraged defiance of Barrios' call. Barrios was killed in an aborted invasion of El Salvador.

BIBLIOGRAPHY

Burgess, Paul. *Justo Rufino Barrios*. New York: 1926.
Días, V. M. *Barrios Ante la Posteridad*. Guatemala: 1955.

Holleran, Mary P. *Church and State in Guatemala*. New York, 1949.
McCreery, D. J. *Development and the State of Reforma Guatemala*. Athens, Ohio: 1983.
Martz, John D. *Justo Rufino Barrios and Central American Union*. Gainesville: University
of Florida Press, 1963.

JOSÉ M. SÁNCHEZ

BARROS LUCO, RAMÓN (1835–1919), had a distinguished political career
of more than 55 years, spanning the whole of Chile's Liberal Republic (1861–
1891) and most of the period of the Parliamentary Republic (1891–1924). He
graduated as a lawyer in December 1858. He was first elected deputy in 1861
and except for one three-year period remained in the Chamber of Deputies until
the Revolution of 1891. President of the Chamber in 1879, 1888, 1889, 1891
and 1892, he also served in several cabinet posts under Presidents Domingo
Santa María González* and José Manuel Balmeceda Fernández.

As president of the Chamber of Deputies, Ramón Barros Luco signed the
"Act of Deposition" of President Balmaceda in January 1891, which launched
the Civil War. He was a member of the three-man government junta established
by the rebels in Iquique.

Barros Luco was elected to the Senate and in 1896 was chosen its president.
He remained a senator (except for a short period as minister to France) until
1906. He also served as a member of the Council of State and on four occasions
as minister of the interior (effectively, prime minister).

In 1910 Ramón Barros Luco, already 76 years old, was chosen president under
very peculiar circumstances. When a deadlock in the popular vote threw the
election into Congress, it rejected both contestants and named Barros Luco
instead.

Throughout Barros Luco's five-year term, congressional maneuvering almost
brought governmental stagnation. As one Chilean writer has observed, "The
parade of cabinets continued without ceasing." Some lasted only a few days,
one lucky one being of seven months' duration. Very few constructive accomplishments could be credited to the administration of President Barros Luco.

BIBLIOGRAPHY

Cortes, Lia, and Jordi Fuentes. *Diccionario Político de Chile*. Santiago: Editorial Orbe,
1967.
Galdames, Luis. *Historia de Chile*. Santiago: Editorial Zig Zag, 1946.

ROBERT J. ALEXANDER

BARROW, ERROL WALTON (1920–1987), was the architect of Barbadian
independence. Educated first at Combermere and Harrison College in Barbados,
he left Barbados in 1939 for service in the Royal Air Force. He made 49 combat
flights during World War II and elected to stay in the Royal Air Force after the
war, serving in the Rhine as personal navigation officer to the commander-in-
chief of the British Army there. In 1947 he was seconded to the Colonial Office
in London and began studies at the London School of Economics where he came

under the influence of Professor Harold Laski. Later, Barrow transferred to Lincoln's Inn, taking his bar finals in 1949.

In 1950 Barrow returned to Barbados where he built a flourishing law practice and joined the Barbados Labour Party (BLP) under the tutelage of Sir Grantley Herbert Adams* who, at a massive public meeting, introduced him as the potential future leader of the party. In 1951 Barrow was elected to the Barbados House of Assembly. He became increasingly critical of the BLP leadership, particularly Grantley Adams, as too conciliatory when dealing with the governor and as too conservative. This growing schism was exacerbated by a degree of organizational chaos within the party and unwillingness of the party elders to consult with the younger leadership headed by Barrow.

In October 1954 Barrow left the BLP to help found the Democratic Labor Party (DLP). He became parliamentary leader of the new party in April 1955. The DLP suffered a tremendous defeat in 1956, with only 4 of its 16 candidates winning seats in the Legislature, and in the March 1958 federal elections in which it failed to capture any seats.

Skillfully exploiting an industrial dispute in the sugar industry in the early part of 1958, Barrow was able to break the influence of the BLP over sugar workers and to create for himself an image of defender of the cause of the Barbadian working class. That same year, he was elected in a by-election to a seat in the House of Assembly by an overwhelming margin. He was also elected vice president of the Barbados Transport and General Workers' Union. Almost immediately, Barrow organized a ''Shadow Cabinet'' in the House and was elected chairman of the DLP. In December 1961 the DLP won a convincing victory, getting 14 seats in the House as opposed to 5 seats for the BLP.

The DLP, with Barrow at the helm, ran the government of Barbados for the next 15 years. In August 1965 Barrow's government prepared a White Paper arguing for independence, and a Conference in London agreed that independence would be granted immediately following elections on November 3, 1966. Barrow and his DLP won and formed the first post-independence government of the island.

Barrow's government oversaw a significant expansion in welfare legislation, tourism, and education. The state greatly expanded expenditures on a construction program that made significant inroads into unemployment and supported a growing domestic construction industry. Barrow dispelled fears of the business community, wary of his socialist preelection rhetoric, by pursuing a moderate economic program and attracting foreign investors. He took Barbados into the Organization of American States and helped launch the Caribbean Free Trade Area. In 1971 his party won a landslide victory in the general elections.

In 1976, suffering from the effects of worldwide recession which had particular impact on sugar-producing countries, Barrow and the DLP lost power to a resuscitated BLP headed by John Michael G.M. (Tom) Adams.* Barrow continued to serve the DLP despite long periods of absence from the island, and once again became prime minister when his party won the 1986 election. Barrow died unexpectedly in August 1987.

BIBLIOGRAPHY

Hoyos, F. A. *Barbados: A History*. London: Macmillan Co., 1978.
————. *Builders of Barbados*. London: Macmillan Co., 1973.
Lewis, G. K. *The Growth of the Modern West Indies*. New York: Monthly Review Press, 1968.
Richards, C. *Caribbean Power*. London: Dobson, 1963.
Tree, R. *A History of Barbados*. 2d ed. London: Granada, 1977.

PERCY C. HINTZEN AND W. MARVIN WILL

BATISTA Y ZALDÍVAR, FULGENCIO (1901–1973), was the dominant political and military leader in Cuba from 1933 until 1959. He was born in Oriente Province of humble mulatto parents and received little formal education. As a young boy he had jobs as a cane cutter, railroad brakeman, carpenter's apprentice, and tailor's apprentice. In 1921 he joined the army as a private. By 1928 he was promoted to sergeant-stenographer, a position that allowed him to become widely known among the enlisted men.

In September 1933 Batista engineered an uprising of noncommissioned officers, which deposed the U.S.-backed President Carlos Manuel de Céspedes and led to establishment of the revolutionary government of Ramón Grau San Martín.* By then a colonel, Batista overthrew Grau in January 1934, with approval of the U.S. government. He then installed as president the traditional politician Carlos Mendieta Montefur,* whose task was to secure U.S. recognition and to bring a measure of stability to the island. These goals were achieved, and national presidential elections were held in early 1936.

The next president, Miguel Mariano Gómez,* son of the republic's second president, served less than a year. When he vetoed a bill favored by Batista for a system of rural schools to be operated by the military, Batista had him impeached.

The third Batista puppet president was Federico Laredo Brú,* during whose term Batista implemented much of the highly publicized Three-Year Plan. Legislation provided workers with pensions, workmen's compensation, and minimum wages. Unionization of workers was encouraged through formation of the Confederación de Trabajadores de Cuba. Significant gains were realized in health, sanitation, and public education, and security of tenure was given to tenant farmers.

In 1938 Batista called for a constituent assembly to write a new constitution. A truce between the warring political factions allowed Batista's most formidable political enemy, Ramón Grau, to return to Cuba. In 1940 Fulgencio Batista ran for president, defeating Grau.

For the next four years Batista presided over a stable and peaceful Cuba, made prosperous as chief sugar supplier to the United States and its allies in World

War II. In 1943–1944 Batista had two prominent Communist Party members, Juan Marinello* and Carlos Rafael Rodríguez,* in his cabinet. In 1944 Batista's hand-picked successor, Carlos Saladrígas, lost the election to Ramón Grau. For the next six years Fulgencio Batista lived in self-imposed exile in Florida, but he was elected, in absentia, to the Cuban Senate.

Batista returned to power in Cuba on March 10, 1952, when he led a military coup against the regime of Carlos Prío Socarrás.* He immediately suspended the constitution, closed down Congress, and outlawed all political parties. In November 1954 he held elections, hoping to legitimize his rule. His only real opponent was former President Ramón Grau, who withdrew when he realized the outcome was rigged.

When a small pleasure boat landed in Oriente Province in December 1956 with 82 revolutionaries led by Fidel Castro,* few of Batista's supporters paid much attention. However, throughout the next two years Castro led a classic guerrilla struggle against Batista's army, forcing the dictator to become increasingly more ruthless in his treatment of all dissenters. On the last day of 1958 Fulgencio Batista, the man who had dominated Cuban political life like no one before him, went into exile.

BIBLIOGRAPHY

Batista, Fulgencio. *Cuba Betrayed*. New York: 1962.
Bonachea, Ramón L., and Marta San Martín. *The Cuban Insurrection, 1952–1959*. New Brunswick, N.J.: Transaction Books, 1974.
Farber, Samuel. *Revolution and Reaction in Cuba, 1933–1960*. Middletown, Conn.: Wesleyan University Press, 1976.
Phillips, Ruby Hart. *Cuba: Island of Paradox*. New York: MacDowell, Obolensky, 1959.
Thomas, Hugh. *Cuba: The Pursuit of Freedom*. New York: Harper and Row, 1971.

STEPHEN J. WRIGHT

BATLLE BERRES, LUIS (1897–1964), was president of Uruguay from 1947 to 1951. A nephew of José Batlle y Ordóñez,* Batlle Berres graduated from the Law Faculty of the University of Montevideo. As a youth, he joined the editorial staff of his uncle's newspaper, *El Día*. Between 1923 and 1933 he was a member of the Chamber of Deputies. In the latter year, he accused President Gabriel Terra* of dictatorial ambitions, as a result of which he was expelled from the Chamber, jailed, and finally exiled until 1936. He then returned to the Chamber of Deputies and became president of the Chamber in 1942, serving until 1946. In 1946 he was elected vice president and succeeded President Tomás Berreta when Berreta died in 1947.

In spite of President Batlle Berres' opposition, his uncle's program for a "collegiate" presidency of nine members was adopted at the end of the Batlle Berres presidential term. He continued to struggle for reestablishment of a unitary presidency, which occurred only after his death. During his last years, he was leader of the largest of the many factions of the Colorado Party, as well as being editor of his own newspaper, *Acción*.

BIBLIOGRAPHY

Enciclopedia Universal Ilustrada Europeo Americana, Supplement 1963–1964. Madrid and Barcelona: Espasa Calpe SA, 1984.
New York Times, July 16, 1964.

ROBERT J. ALEXANDER

BATLLE Y ORDÓÑEZ, JOSÉ (1856–1929), was twice president of Uruguay and set the pattern of the economy, society, and polity of Uruguay during most of the twentieth century. He was the son of President Lorenzo Batlle, left the University of Montevideo before receiving a degree, but pursued further studies in France. In 1886 he founded the daily newspaper *El Día* in Montevideo, as the principal organ of the Colorado Party, and thereafter rose in the party's ranks, being elected senator in 1898. In that period, Uruguay continued to be dominated by the pattern of military/party dictatorships which had been characteristic of most of the nineteenth century.

José Batlle was first elected president of Uruguay in 1903 and almost immediately had to face an insurrection of the opposition Blanco Party, led by Aparicio Saravia,* which he succeeded in suppressing. He sent to Congress bills for labor legislation which were not passed until his second term. However, his proposals for legalizing divorce and for establishing secondary schools in every provincial city were passed.

After leaving the presidency the first time, José Batlle spent considerable time in Europe, studying economic, social, and political reforms in those countries. He was particularly impressed with the plural presidency in Switzerland.

Elected again as president in 1911, José Batlle was responsible in his second term for many reforms. He strongly supported the labor movement but did not try to exert government control over it. His proposals resulted in establishing a social security system and in government development of the economic infrastructure. Among the state firms established on his initiative were a government insurance company which 20 years later was writing three-fourths of the country's policies; a government monopoly of electricity and telephone services; and a government firm dominating the petroleum and alcohol industries. He also established government control over the port works of the city of Montevideo, which were considerably expanded.

After leaving the presidency for a second time, Batlle intensified his campaign for the proposal which he had suggested during his second term—to establish a nine-man presidency, two-thirds of whom would represent the majority party and one-third the second largest party. He saw this kind of presidency as both a means of curbing the dictatorial inclinations of the country's presidents, and the tendency of the opposition to resort to coups instead of the electoral process (since in any case they would be represented in the executive power). This proposal was strongly opposed by the opposition Blancos and by a minority of the Colorado Party, which became split between Batllistas and anti-Batllistas.

When Batlle threatened to run for president for a third time, however, his opponents agreed, in the constituent assembly of 1918, to adopt a modified form of the collegiate presidency: a president and a National Council of Administration of nine members, which would have some of the powers which the president had formerly had. In 1926 Batlle served as head of the National Council of Administration.

Few Latin American leaders have had as large an impact on their own countries as did Batlle. However, for a generation after his death, his heirs largely rode on the reforms that had characterized his period, without introducing significant modifications to deal with new problems. For a short while in the 1930s, and then between 1973 and 1985, the result was a subversion of the political democracy that Batlle had established.

BIBLIOGRAPHY

Alisky, Marvin. *Uruguay: A Contemporary Survey*. New York: 1969.
Arena, Domingo. *Batlle y los Problemas Sociales en el Uruguay*. Montevideo: Claudio García y Cia., n.d.
Batlle, Jorge (ed). *Batlle: Su Vida, Su Obra*. Montevideo: 1956.
Fitzgibbon, Russell H. *Uruguay, Portrait of a Democracy*. New Brunswick, N.J.: Rutgers University Press, 1954.
Zavala Muñíz, Justino. *Batlle: Heroe Civil*. Mexico: Fondo de Cultura Económica, 1945.
                                                                        ROBERT J. ALEXANDER

BEDOYA REYES, LUIS (1919–   ), twice Peruvian presidential candidate, was born in Callão. He received his primary and secondary education in his native city and in Lima, respectively. His doctorate in letters and his professional title of attorney at law (1942) were awarded by the National University of San Marcos. Before he practiced law, he taught at several high schools and at the military school Leoncio Prado. After graduating from San Marcos, he taught history at the Catholic University of Lima. In 1944 he helped to found *Jornada*, a political newspaper that supported the successful presidential candidacy of José Luís Bustamante y Rivera.* Four years later he became President Bustamante's press secretary, just before he was ousted from power.

In 1956, after helping to establish the Christian Democratic Party of Peru, Bedoya served as its first secretary general and supported the Acción Popular presidential candidacy of Fernando Belaúnde Terry.* As his party again supported the presidential candidacy of Belaúnde in 1963, Bedoya served as minister of justice from 1963 to 1964 and was assisted by President Belaúnde to get elected mayor of Lima in 1964 for a three-year term. From 1967 he resigned from the Christian Democratic Party and founded the Christian Popular Party, under whose banner he was reelected mayor of Lima. In 1978 he was elected to the Constituent Assembly with the second highest number of preferential votes, after Víctor Raúl Haya de la Torre,* candidate of the Peruvian Aprista Party (PAP).

Bedoya was his party's presidential candidate in the general elections of 1980, coming in third behind Belaúnde of Acción Popular and Armando Villanueva* of the Aprista Party. In the 1985 election, Bedoya's party joined forces with Andrés Townsend Ezcurra's* Movimiento de Bases Hayistas to form Convergencia Democrática, with Bedoya as its presidential candidate. Again he placed third, after Alan García Pérez* of the PAP and Alfonso Barrantes Lingan* of Izquierda Unida.

BIBLIOGRAPHY

Garay Seminario, Martín. *Perfiles humanos*. Lima: 1985.
Goldenberg, Sonia (ed.). *Decidamos nuestro futuro*. Lima: Universidad del Pacífico-Fundación Friedrich Ebert, 1985.
Rojas Samanéz, Alvaro. *Partidos políticos en el Peru desde 1872*. Lima: Ediciones F & A, 1985.

                                                        EUGENIO CHANG-RODRÍGUEZ

BELAÚNDE TERRY, FERNANDO (1912–   ), twice president of Peru, was born in Lima. He studied mechanical engineering in Paris, after which he transferred to the University of Miami and then to the University of Texas at Austin, where he received a B.S. in architecture in 1935. He then returned to Lima to practice his profession. Belaúnde founded *El Arqitecto Peruano*, a professional journal, in 1937 and began to teach at the Faculty of Engineering of the Catholic University in 1943. A few years later he established the Institute of Urbanism, which was to become part of the National School of Engineering.

When the National Democratic Front (FDN) was established in 1944, Belaúnde was appointed its secretary, and in the following year he was elected to the Chamber of Deputies. When a military coup overthrew the government of the FDN in 1948, he resumed his professional activities. He served as dean of the Faculty of Engineering at the National Engineering University from 1955 to 1960.

The Front of Democratic Youth nominated him as its candidate for the presidency in the national elections of 1956. He lost the election to Manuel Prado* but placed second, and he then helped to transform the National Front of Democratic Youth into Acción Popular (AP), a centrist political party. He was AP presidential candidate in 1962, coming in behind Víctor Raúl Haya de la Torre,* candidate of the Peruvian Aprista Party (PAP). But some generals then overthrew the constitutional government and installed a military junta that called new elections in 1963. This time Belaúnde was proclaimed the winner with 39 percent of the votes. Leftist military officers ousted Belaúnde from power in 1968 and named General Juan Velasco Alvarado* as president of a Revolutionary Government of the Armed Forces. Belaúnde lived in exile in the United States from 1969 until May 1977, when he returned to Lima.

In 1980 Belaúnde was reelected president for a five-year term with 45 percent of the votes. His new administration was marked by severe economic problems and a far left guerrilla insurrection. In the general election of 1985, Acción Popular obtained less than 6 percent of the votes.

BIBLIOGRAPHY

Alisky, Marvin. *Historical Dictionary of Peru*. Metuchen, N.J.: Scarecrow Press, 1979.
Belaúnde Terry, Fernando. *La conquista del Peru por los peruanos*. Lima: Ediciones Tawantinsuyo.
Chang-Rodríguez, Eugenio. *Opciones políticas peruanas*. Lima: Centro de Documentación Andina, 1985.
Pike, Frederick B. *The Modern History of Peru*. New York: Praeger, 1967.
Tauro, Alberto. *Diccionario enciclopédico del Peru*. Lima: Editorial Mejía Baca, 1966.

EUGENIO CHANG-RODRÍGUEZ

BELZÚ, MANUEL ISIDORO (1808–1865), one of Bolivia's most controversial caudillos, was seen as a "socialist demagogue" by the aristocracy and as a popular idol by the lower classes. A *cholo* (person of mixed parentage) of humble origins, he had a limited primary education. He joined the army at 13 and spent most of his life in the barracks. He fought in the independence Battle of Zepita in 1823 and became adjutant to Peruvian General Augustín Gamarra.* When the Peruvians invaded Bolivia, he defected to the Bolivian Army.

Belzú became president in December 1848, at the end of a brief civil war. He remained in office until constitutionally replaced by his son-in-law, General Jorge Córdova, in August 1855. Despite over 30 military uprisings against him and a nearly successful assassination attempt in 1850, his was the first peaceful constitutional transfer of power since the presidency of Antonio Jose de Suore Alcala.*

Belzú promulgated Bolivia's fifth constitution in 1851, which limited the presidential term to five years. He revised the penal, civil, military, and mining codes, and conducted a major national census in 1854. The government enacted protective tariffs and promoted national and state enterprises that were vigorously opposed by the rising merchant and mining elites who favored free trade. Belzú was popular among the *cholos* whose cause he championed. With their support, he established a powerful civilian populist movement. His regime attacked the unequal class structure and properties of the rich.

After having served as ambassador to various European courts, Belzú returned to Bolivia. In 1865 he briefly seized the presidency but was deposed and assassinated by President Mariano Melgarejo* and his supporters in the presidential palace on March 27, 1865.

BIBLIOGRAPHY

Crespo Roda, Alfonso. "Historia de un Caudillo." *Kollasuyo*, No. 25 (1941).
Díaz Arguedas, Julio. *Los generales de Bolivia*. La Paz: Imprenta Intendencia General de Guerra, 1929.

Fellman Velarde, José. *Historia de Bolivia*. Vol. 2, 2d ed. La Paz: Los Amigos del
    Libro, 1981.
Guzmán, Augusto. *Historia de Bolivia*. La Paz: Los Amigos del Libro, 1973.
O'Connor d'Arlach, Tomás. *Los presidentes de Bolivia desde 1825 hasta 1912*. La Paz:
    González y Medina, 1912.

WALTRAUD QUEISER MORALES

BENAVIDES, ÓSCAR R. (1876–1945), twice president of Peru, was born in
Lima. He graduated from the Chorrillos Military Academy as second lieutenant
in artillery. Rising steadily in the army hierarchy, he spent some time in Europe
to receive further training and to convalesce from a tropical malady acquired in
the jungle in 1911, during an armed conflict with Colombia. In collaboration
with a powerful banking family, Benavides deposed Constitutional President
Guillermo Billinghurst* in 1914 and proclaimed himself president of the republic.
The following year José Pardo y Barreda,* the presidential candidate of the
oligarchic Partido Civil, was proclaimed winner of the elections and succeeded
him. Benavides' arbitrary actions moved Manuel González Prada* (1844–1918)
to write the book *Bajo el oprobio*.

Subsequent to the assassination in 1933 of President Luís M. Sánchez Cerro,*
who had plunged the country into a bloody civil war after outlawing the Peruvian
Aprista Party (PAP), the manipulated Constituent Assembly promoted Benavides
to division general and elected him provisional president to serve until 1936.
When tabulations of the votes in the 1936 election showed the overwhelming
lead of Luís Antonio Eguiguren, the presidential candidate supported by the
outlawed PAP, Benavides canceled the results and had the Constituent Assembly
extend his mandate for three more years and disband itself. Benavides assisted
Manuel Prado* in 1939 to win a six-year presidential term. In return, the new
millionaire ruler, scion of the family that had helped Benavides overthrow Billinghurst, honored him with the rank of marshal and appointed him ambassador
to Spain (1940–1943) and Argentina (1943–1944). Benavides returned to Peru
in 1944 to help form the National Democratic Front that elected José Luís
Bustamente y Rivero* president of the republic in 1945, thanks mainly to the
support of the Apristas. Marshal Benavides died soon after Bustamante was
proclaimed president-elect.

BIBLIOGRAPHY

Alisky, Marvin. *Historical Dictionary of Peru*. Metuchen, N.J.: Scarecrow Press, 1979.
Eguiguren, Luis Antonio. *El usurpador*. Lima: Ahora, 1939.
González Prada, Manuel. *Bajo el oprobio*. Paris: Tipograffa de L. Bellenand et Fils,
    1933.
Pike, Frederick B. *The Modern History of Peru*. New York: Praeger, 1967.
Tauro, Alberto. *Diccionario enciclopédico del Peru*. Lima: Editorial Majía Baca, 1966.

EUGENIO CHANG-RODRÍGUEZ

BERNARDES, ARTUR (1875–1955), was president of Brazil from 1922 to
1926. He was born in Vicosa, a small town in Minas Gerais, and his father
Antonio da Silva Bernardes was a Portuguese immigrant who held various judicial

posts under Dom Pedro II.* Maria Aniceta Pinto Bernardes, his mother, came from an old and distinguished Minas Gerais family.

Receiving a law degree in 1900 from the São Paulo Law School, Bernardes entered politics in 1904, when he was elected to the municipal council of Teixeiras. In 1906 he was elected president of the Municipal Council of Vicosa, and in 1907 he won a seat in the Minas Gerais state legislature. His brilliant speeches attracted much attention, and in 1910 he became secretary of finances of the state. In 1918 he was elected governor.

Elected president of Brazil with the support of the state of São Paulo, Bernardes was inaugurated in November 1922. Brazil was being governed at the time under a state of siege as a result of unrest caused by young military rebels, the *tenentes*, who in 1924 seized the city of São Paulo. As a result, the state of siege was extended and lasted through Bernardes' entire mandate.

In the presidential election of 1926, Bernardes supported the Paulista candidate Washington Luis* and the Minas Gerais-São Paulo alliance was maintained. Although the Bernardes administration was marked by many positive accomplishments, he was an unpopular president who had to use state of siege powers to remain in office.

Bernardes was largely inactive politically during the 15-year rule of Getúlio Vargas* (1930–1945). After Vargas' fall, Bernardes sought to revive the pre–1930 Republican Party on a national basis, but it never gained much support outside of Minas Gerais, where it remained an important secondary party.

BIBLIOGRAPHY

Almeida Magalhães, Brune de. *Arthur Bernardes, Estadista da República*. 1973.
Amora, Paulo. *Bernardes, O Estadista de Minas na República*. São Paulo: Editora Nacional, 1954.

JORDAN YOUNG

BETANCOURT, RÓMULO (1908–1981), was the most important political leader of Venezuela in the twentieth century. He established the first mass political party, was president twice, and led the process of establishing a stable political democracy in Venezuela for the first time in its history.

Betancourt began his political career in 1928 when, as a second-year law student at the Central University in Caracas, he was one of the three principal leaders of a vehement Student Week protest against the dictatorship of Juan Vicente Gómez.* Betancourt was jailed for a short while and soon after began his first exile. He went to Curaçao, the Dominican Republic, and Baranquilla, Colombia. In Colombia he led other student exiles in establishing the ARDI, a left-wing and vaguely Marxist political movement.

Early in 1932 Betancourt moved to Costa Rica. There he was one of the founders of the Costa Rican Communist Party and edited its paper. That experience convinced him of the need for a national revolutionary party, not one controlled, as the Communists were, from some foreign country.

Upon the death of Juan Vicente Gómez in December 1935, Betancourt returned to Venezuela and helped establish a radical party, Organización Venezolana (ORVE), and became its Secretary General within a few months. When ORVE merged in late 1936 with several other groups to form the National Democratic Party (PDN), Betancourt became the PDN's secretary of organization.

Early in 1937 Gómez' successor, President Eleazar López Contreras,* outlawed the PDN and ordered most of its leaders deported. Betancourt was one of the few able to evade the police, and for three years he dedicated himself to gathering together a group of young intellectuals and trade unionists who were to be the core of the PDN and its successor, Acción Democrática (AD).

In 1940 Betancourt was caught by the police and exiled for a year to Chile. There, he worked closely with leaders of the Socialist Party, particularly Salvador Allende Gossens.*

Upon returning home early in 1941, Betancourt proposed that the PDN name a "symbolic" candidate in the election campaign then underway. He did so even though it had no chance of success because the new president would be chosen by López Contreras' largely hand-picked Congress. The well-known novelist Rómulo Gallegos* was the PDN's nominee, and the party began to be transformed from an underground skeleton organization into an open mass party.

The new president, General Isaías Medina Angarita* legalized the PDN, as Acción Democrática. Betancourt was its secretary general and spent the 1941–1945 period building the party organization throughout the whole country. During this period, too, AD won control of a majority of the labor movement from the Communists.

As the 1945 election approached, AD sought an agreement with President Medina on a candidate whom they could both support, who would be pledged to introducing universal adult suffrage and direct election of the president and all legislators. A mutually acceptable candidate got sick, whereupon Medina refused further negotiations. Betancourt and other AD leaders then accepted overtures by a group of young military men to seek to overthrow Medina. That resulted in the Revolution of October 18, 1945.

The next day Betancourt became president of the Revolutionary Junta and virtually provisional president of Venezuela. Four other civilians—three of them AD members—and two military officers were also in the junta. Betancourt continued to head the government until early 1948, when his elected successor, Rómulo Gallegos, took over. During that period, universal suffrage was introduced, new mass parties were established, and a modern constitution was adopted.

Major economic and social changes occurred. Among the changes were the following: 50 percent of all oil company profits were to stay in Venezuela; an Economic Development Corporation was established; primary school attendance was doubled; an agrarian reform program was begun; and very strong government support was given to the labor and particularly the peasant movement.

On November 24, 1948, however, the armed forces overthrew President Rómulo Gallegos and began a military dictatorship of more than nine years' duration. Betancourt succeeded in getting out of the country. Living in the United
States, Cuba, Costa Rica, and Puerto Rico, at different times, he spent the period
from November 1948 until January 1958 leading the underground and exiled
Acción Democrática.

Finally, in the face of massive civilian resistance to the regime on January
23, 1958, army and navy leaders sent Marcos Pérez Jiménez* into exile. Betancourt then returned home and in the December elections defeated two opponents and soon after became constitutional president. In the face of extreme
difficulties—four major military coup attempts, guerrilla war by the extreme
left, two splits in AD, and very difficult economic circumstances, among others—
he became the first person in Venezuelan history to come into the presidency
by genuine popular elections and to turn over the office to a popularly elected
successor.

The second Betancourt period largely carried forward what had been started
in the first. Among the major programs were strong encouragement to import
substitution industrialization, vast expansion of the educational system, large-
scale agrarian reform, and strong support for organized labor and collective
bargaining.

This time Betancourt was convinced that merely having a majority of votes
was not sufficient to assure a successful democratic administration. So although
at various times he massively mobilized workers and peasants and others to
support the regime when it was threatened by insurrection, he also sought successfully either to win over or to neutralize those elements that might overthrow
the regime—the military, powerful economic groups, and the church.

In March 1964 Betancourt turned over power to President Raúl Leoni.* He
did not want to create difficulties for President Leoni or the democratic system,
and so he went to Europe, where he stayed about eight years. Upon his return
in 1972, he announced that, although constitutionally eligible, he would not run
again for the presidency. He threw strong support behind AD candidate Carlos
Andrés Pérez.*

Rómulo Betancourt remained the Grand Old Man of Acción Democrática and
a bulwark for the democracy he had been so influential in establishing. Although
his relations with President Pérez became rather tense, Betancourt remained
honorary president of his party until his death.

Betancourt died quite unexpectedly of a massive stroke while on a vacation
in New York City.

BIBLIOGRAPHY

Alexander, Robert J. *Rómulo Betancourt and the Transformation of Venezuela.* New
    Brunswick, N.J.: Transactions Press, 1982.
———. *The Venezuelan Democratic Revolution.* New Brunswick, N.J.: Rutgers Uni-
    versity Press, 1964.

Betancourt, Rómulo. *Venezuela: Oil and Politics*. Boston: Houghton Mifflin, 1979.
Caballero, Manuel. *Rómulo Betancourt*. Caracas: Ediciones Centauro, 1977.
Martz, John. *Acción Democrática: Evolution of a Modern Political Party in Venezuela*. Princeton, N.J.: Princeton University Press, 1966.

ROBERT J. ALEXANDER

BETANCUR CUARTAS, BELISARIO (1923–), was president of Colombia from 1982 to 1986, the first Conservative to be elected after the end of the bipartisan National Front. His early career was in journalism, and he was director of the newspaper *El Siglo* and editor of the weekly newsmagazine *Semana* and other periodicals. He was elected to the Chamber of Deputies in 1962 and to the Senate in 1970. In 1963 he became minister of labor in the government of President Guillermo Leon Valencia, and in that capacity he gained considerable sympathy in the organized labor movement. In 1974 he served as Colombian ambassador to Spain.

Betancur was the Conservative Party candidate for president in 1978 but was defeated by Liberal Julio César Turbay. Four years later, however, he won a strong victory.

Betancur dedicated much of his attention as president to ending the guerrilla conflicts that had been plaguing the country for several decades. Although he reached agreements with most of the guerrilla groups and proclaimed amnesty for their members, the president's efforts collapsed in 1985, during which there were several major clashes between government forces and guerrilla groups, particularly the so-called M–19 faction.

BIBLIOGRAPHY

Current Biography Yearbook, 1985. New York: H. W. Wilson Co., 1985.
Wall Street Journal, December 24, 1984.
Who's Who in the World, 1984–1985. Chicago: Marquis, 1984.

RICHARD E. SHARPLESS

BILBAO BARQUÍN, FRANCISCO (1823–1865), was Chile's leading Utopian Socialist. He studied at the Instituto Nacional de Chile. When only 21 years of age, he published *Sociabilidad Chilena*, which advocated wide democratic reforms and was particularly critical of the church. He was tried and convicted of blasphemy and given a 1200 pesos fine. Bilbao then moved to Valparaiso, where for a short while he edited the newspaper *La Gaceta del Comercio*.

In 1845 Bilbao went to Europe, where he had personal contact with Utopian Socialists and advanced democrats of various kinds. Upon return home, he advocated establishment of a working-class party and organized the Sociedad de la Igualdad to carry on education and propaganda among the workers. He was severely persecuted, and an attempt was made on his life, supposedly with police instigation. The society was suppressed after an unsuccessful military coup against President Manuel Bulnes Prieto*, and Bilbao fled into exile in April 1851.

Bilbao spent the rest of his life in Peru, Europe, and finally Argentina. He maintained contacts with supporters in Chile. Some were among the founders of the Radical Party, and his idea of a working-class party was finally achieved in 1887, with the founding of the Democratic Party.

BIBLIOGRAPHY

Cortes, Lia, and Jordi Fuentes. *Diccionario Político de Chile*. Santiago: Editorial Orbe, 1967.
Enciclopedia Universal Ilustrada Europeo-Americana. Barcelona: José Espasa e Hijos.
                                                                 ROBERT J. ALEXANDER

BILLINGHURST, GUILLERMO (1851–1914), president of Peru (1912– 1914), was born in Arica before that city was surrendered to Chile after the War of the Pacific (1879–1883). During this war, because of close collaboration with Nicolás de Pierola,* Billinghurst was appointed chief of the Army General Staff, although only a colonel of the reserves. His wealth financed Pierola's successful uprising against the government of General Andrés A. Cáceres.* During the Pierola administration (1895–1899), Billinghurst served as vice president, senator, president of the Senate, and minister to Chile.

When his friendship with Pierola declined, Billinghurst competed for leadership of the Democratic Party, founded by Pierola in 1884. During the period he served as mayor of Lima (1909–1910), Billinghurst supported important municipal actions in favor of the working class. On September 24, 1912, he was elected president, but his pro-labor legislation led to his ousting by Colonel Óscar R. Benavides* and the oligarchy in February 1914. Shortly after, he died in exile in Iquique, Chile.

BIBLIOGRAPHY

Alisky, Marvin. *Historical Dictionary of Peru*. Metuchen, N.J.: Scarecrow Press, 1979.
Basadre, Jorge. *Peruanos del siglo XX*. Lima: Ediciones Rikchay Peru, 1981.
Martín, José Carlos. *El gobierno de don Guillermo E. Billinghurst, 1913–1914*. Lima: Companía de Impresiones y Publicidad, 1963.
Tauro, Alberto. *Diccionario enciclopédico del Peru*. Lima: Editorial Mejía Baca, 1966.
                                                          EUGENIO CHANG-RODRÍGUEZ

BIRD, VERE CORNWALL (1909–   ), became the first prime minister of Antigua and Barbuda when that colony received independence from Great Britain in November 1981. Born in poverty, he completed primary school in the colony. He joined the Salvation Army while a teenager and had the opportunity to travel to other West Indian territories. He soon left the organizaton over what he saw as its policies of racial segregation, returning to Antigua where he became a clerk.

Bird joined the Antigua Workingman's Association, and when the Antigua Trade and Labour Union (ATLU) was formed on January 16, 1939, Bird was elected to its Executive Council. In 1943 he won the presidency of the union by an overwhelming majority.

In 1945, backed by the union, Bird was elected to the Legislative Council in a by-election. He again won a seat in general elections the next year and proceeded to attack the merchant plantocracy and their political representative who, through appointed positions, comprised a majority on the Council. Between 1944 and 1951, under Vere Bird's leadership, workers in several key sectors gained the right to bargain and considerably improved wages and conditions of work.

A changed constitution providing the vote to all literate adults was enacted in 1950. Bird decided to establish a political committee within the ATLU to fight the 1951 elections. He called this the Antigua Labor Party (ALP), even though it remained part of the ATLU. The ALP won all eight elective seats in the 1951 elections; Bird was then appointed to the Executive Council, the island's main policy-making body. A further change of constitution in 1956 introduced a ministerial system. Again, the ALP won all eight seats, and Bird became minister for trade and production.

On January 1, 1960, Bird was named chief minister and minister of planning. In 1961 elections for a Legislative Council that was expanded to 10 members, the ALP again won all the seats. In 1966 Bird led a delegation to London to press for Associated Statehood for Antigua. This was granted in February 1967, when he became the colony's first premier leading a government with full internal self-rule. Britain retained responsibility only for foreign affairs and defense.

Some members of the union, led by its general secretary, George Herbert Walter,* began to express dissatisfaction that most top union officials were also members of government. Demands that Vere Bird relinquish either his premiership or his presidency of the union led to a split in union ranks. The dissident group, under Walter's leadership, formed the Antigua Workers Union. Out of this emerged a party, the Progressive Labour Movement (PLM), headed by Walter. As a result Vere Bird was forced to give the ALP a separate organizational structure, even though it remained closely identified with the ATLU. Bird resigned as president of the union to become leader of the newly reorganized party. In the 1971 election, the ALP lost badly, with Bird losing his seat in the Legislative Council.

Between 1951 and 1970 Vere Bird had been responsible for considerable change in the lot of the Antiguan population. He instituted a Peasant Development Scheme, fought to maintain the sugar industry, and instituted a self-help housing scheme. Bird led a successful effort to diversify the Antiguan economy by attracting light industries owned by foreign investors and by developing a flourishing tourist industry. Bird also worked assiduously to form a West Indian Federation. When the federation finally collapsed in 1962, he helped organize the Caribbean Common Market among the countries in Anglophone Caribbean.

Elections in 1976 gave Bird and his ALP a victory over the PLM. Again, he focused his efforts on expanding tourism and foreign-led industrial development. After another electoral victory in 1980, Bird began negotiating with Britain for the colony's full independence, which was granted by Britain on November 1, 1981. Vere C. Bird became the first prime minister of the newly independent nation of Antigua and Barbuda.

BIBLIOGRAPHY

Alexander, Robert J. (ed.). *Political Parties of the Americas*. Vol. 1. Westport, Conn.: Greenwood Press, 1983.
Carmody, C. M. "First Among Equals; Antiguan Patterns of Local-Level Leadership." Ph.D. diss., New York University, 1978.
Richards, Colin. *Caribbean Power*. London: Dobson Books, 1973.
Richards, Novell H. *The Struggle and the Conquest: Twenty-Five Years of Social Democracy in Antigua*. St. Johns: Workers Voice Printery, 1964.
Sanders, Ron. "V.C. Bird—Father of the Nation." In *Official Independence Magazine: Antigua and Barbuda*. St. Johns: Government of Antigua and Barbuda, 1981.
                                                  PERCY C. HINTZEN AND W. MARVIN WILL

BISHOP, MAURICE RUPERT (1944–1983), was prime minister and minister of information, defense, and interior of Grenada after his revolutionary New Jewel Movement seized power in an armed rebellion on March 13, 1979. He received his secondary education in Grenada and his university training in Great Britain, where he successfully qualified as a barrister. While in London, he was active in the Campaign Against Racial Discrimination, aimed at securing civil and political rights for Great Britain's migrant population.

Bishop returned to Grenada in 1970, when the Black Power movement was gaining momentum. In May 1970 Bishop helped found a discussion group called FORUM, made up predominantly of young radical intellectuals and professionals. This evolved into the Movement for the Advancement of Community Effort (MACE), which emphasized political education among the urban pooor. Bishop became spokesperson for the country's poor, organizing protests against the government of Eric Matthew Gairy.*

Bishop decided to merge MACE with the Committee of Concerned Citizens, which was composed primarily of younger members of the country's entrepreneurial population, to form the Movement for Assemblies of the People (MAP). Then in March 1973 Bishop decided to merge MAP with a movement called the Joint Endeavour for the Welfare, Education and Liberation of the People (JEWEL), which had organized a farming cooperative and experienced some success in political mobilization of the country's agricultural workers—Gairy's base of support. The new party was named the New Jewel Movement (NJM) and began an immediate campaign of strikes and sending petitions to London to oppose Gairy's efforts to achieve independence without holding an election.

Despite what appeared to be mass opposition, Britain agreed to grant independence to Grenada under the Gairy regime. To protest, Bishop and the NJM organized a massive demonstration of 10,000 persons in November 1973. Two weeks later, leading members of the NJM, including Maurice Bishop, were taken into custody and severely beaten. All the party's leaders were jailed on February

7, 1974, when the country received its independence. Several party members, including Bishop's father, Rupert Bishop, were killed.

In the face of continued political persecution, Bishop and the NJM joined a Peoples Alliance with the Grenada National Party, headed by Herbert Augustus Blaize,* and the United Peoples Party, which represented interests of the Grenadian business class, in order to contest elections in 1976. The Alliance won 6 of 15 seats in the Grenadian house. Bishop was named official Leader of the Opposition.

The NJM began to embrace a much more leftist ideological position after the 1976 election, and this led to fractures in the Alliance as well as to resignations among the party leadership. In the face of the Gairy government's efforts to destroy the NJM, the party developed a clandestine insurrectionist wing called the People's Army. In March 1979, when Gairy left the country, the People's Army, led by Bishop, seized power.

Popular outpouring of support for the People's Revolutionary Government (PRG), Bishop's new regime, was tremendous. Bishop and the NJM immediately rejected the Westminster form of political party government as inappropriate and made efforts to replace it with a system based on more direct participation by the people.

Bishop implemented a program described as "anti-imperialist, non-aligned, pro-socialist." This translated into strong support for nonalignment, and a particularly close relationship with Cuba and friendly ties with the Soviet Union and Eastern Europe, all of which began to provide the country with economic and military assistance. Despite its socialist rhetoric, the Bishop regime maintained a moderate domestic economic policy which kept intact a large private sector and maintained trade ties with the West.

The intensification of relationships between the PRG and the Communist bloc brought economic and political retaliation by the U.S. government, especially under President Ronald Reagan. This contributed to internal conflict within the Bishop government, which escalated in the latter half of 1983, leading to a split between Bishop and his supporters, and those led by Finance Minister Barnard Coard. Bishop's refusal to share party and government leadership with Coard led to his arrest, an act that brought massive outpourings of public support for Bishop. After he and a female companion were set free by a crowd of demonstrators, a military contingent killed Maurice Bishop, along with a number of his government ministers and nearly 100 demonstrators.

These events provided a rationale for a U.S. military invasion of Grenada that was supported by several Anglophone Caribbean states.

BIBLIOGRAPHY

Bishop, Maurice. *Forward Ever: Three Years of the Grenadian Revolution*. Sydney: Pathfinder Press, 1982.

Braveboy-Wagner, Jacqueline Ann. "Grenada," in Jack W. Hopkins (ed.). *Latin America and Caribbean Contemporary Record*. Vol. 1. New York: Holmes and Meier, 1983.

Brizan, George. *Grenada: Island of Conflict*. London: Croom Helm, 1984.
Thorndike, Anthony. *Grenada*. Boulder, Colo.: Lynne Reiner Press, 1985.
                                    PERCY C. HINTZEN AND W. MARVIN WILL

BLAIZE, HERBERT AUGUSTUS (1918–   ), was the first chief minister of Grenada in 1960, its first premier in 1967, and became prime minister in December 1984. Born into relatively modest circumstances on the Island of Carriacou, he gained a matriculation certificate from secondary school. He left Grenada in 1944 to seek work in Aruba. By 1949 he had become an elected representative of the more than 7,000 oilfield workers there.

In 1952 Blaize returned to Grenada's sister island of Carriacou. He entered politics as an independent from the Carriacou constituency in 1954 and was defeated. In 1956 he joined the Grenada National Party (GNP), which represented interests of the predominantly urban-based coloured class.

Almost from its election to power in 1951, Eric Matthew Gairy's* party, the Grenada United Labour Party (GULP), had been plagued by charges of corruption, financial mismanagement, and unparliamentary conduct, and the party had lost considerable popular support. As a result, Blaize became one of the two GNP candidates to win seats to the Legislative Council in elections in 1956. A coalition government was formed between the GNP and two independent members, with Blaize becoming a member of the Executive Council, leader of the new government, and minister of trade and production. A more responsible system of government was enacted in 1960, and Blaize became the colony's first chief minister. However, GULP defeated Blaize's GNP in elections in March 1961. Blaize retained his Carriacou seat and became official Leader of the Opposition.

Findings of financial impropriety led to suspension of the Grenadian constitution in June 1962 and ouster of the Gairy government. In elections in September, the GNP captured six of ten seats in the Legislative Council and Blaize once more became chief minister. The West Indies Federation had collapsed during 1962, and Blaize based his and the GNP's electoral platform on plans to enter into a political union with neighboring Trinidad and Tobago.

The GNP government under Blaize enacted significant reforms in agriculture, education, health, and communications. It initiated a fertilizer subsidy scheme for farmers, established an agricultural bank, and expanded the water supply. It increased the number of primary schools and extended teacher training.

The colony was granted Associated Statehood in March 1967, and Blaize became the country's first premier, responsible for running all affairs of state except defense and external affairs. Blaize's efforts at unity with Trinidad and Tobago were proving futile, and his party was defeated later that year by a resuscitated GULP. Blaize was again Leader of the Opposition. He waged an unsuccessful fight against Eric Gairy's efforts to move the colony to independence, which was granted in 1974, accompanied by an escalation of corruption and a significant increase in political repression. The opposition formed the

People's Alliance to fight elections in 1976, comprised of the GNP, a radical New Jewel Movement under the leadership of Maurice Rupert Bishop;* and the United People's party, representing business interests. The Alliance won 6 of the 15 seats in the House. Maurice Bishop became Leader of the Opposition, and Blaize continued to serve as a member of Parliament.

After a revolutionary coup by the New Jewel Movement ushered in a radical People's Revolutionary Government (PRG), under the leadership of Bishop (1979–1983), Blaize suspended public rallies for his GNP but kept the party intact by holding private meetings. His party reemerged publicly after the collapse of the People's Revolutionary Government following the assassination of Maurice Bishop, an American-led invasion of the island, and the installation of an interim government. Following a merger of the GNP and two moderate parties to form the New National Party (NNP), Blaize led that party to victory in elections in December 1984. Blaize became prime minister of Grenada and embarked on a decidedly moderate and pro-American policy in an attempt to bring the country out of political and economic chaos.

BIBLIOGRAPHY

Braveboy-Wagner, Jacqueline A. "Grenada," in Jack W. Hopkins (ed.). *Latin America and Caribbean Contemporary Record*. Vol. 1. New York: Holmes and Meier, 1983.

Brizan, George. *Grenada: Island of Conflict: From Americans to Peoples Revolution 1498–1979*. London: Zed Books, 1984.

The Grenada Independence Secretariat. *A Short History of Grenada*. St. George's: Government of Grenada, 1974.

McDonald, Frank. *Grenada: Eric Matthew Gairy and the Politics of Extravagance*. New York: Institute of Current World Affairs, 1969.

Payne, Anthony, Paul Sutton, and Anthony Thorndike. *Grenada: Revolution and Invasion*. London: Croom Helm, 1984.

PERCY C. HINTZEN AND W. MARVIN WILL

BLANCO GALDÓS, HUGO (1934–   ), the major leader of Peruvian Trotskyism, was born in Cuzco. He studied at the Colegio Nacional de Ciencias of his hometown, and then his family sent him to Buenos Aires to study agronomy in 1954. There he joined the Trotskyist Partido Obrero Revolucionario (Revolutionary Labor Party).

After his return to Lima, Blanco helped organize Trotskyist cadres and joined the San Marcos University protest against Vice President Richard Nixon in 1958. Blanco soon moved to Cuzco, where he was jailed for supporting workers' and peasants' strikes and clashes with the police, but was released when he declared a hunger strike. He helped found the Federation of Peasants of the Department of Cuzco and the Front of the Revolutionary Left. Subsequently, with the aid of fellow Trotskyists from abroad and funds obtained from bank robberies in Lima, he launched an armed rebellion in the Valley of La Concepción, north of Cuzco. In May 1963 he was captured and tried by a military tribunal. International pressure from parliamentarians, labor leaders, and intellectuals prevented his being condemned to death, but he received a 25-year sentence. President Juan Velasco Alvarado* set him free in 1970, but in September 1971 he was deported to Mexico. He finally settled in Sweden where he was granted asylum.

Hugo Blanco was elected to the Constituent Assembly of 1978 with the highest number of preferential votes obtained by any radical leftist candidate. In 1980 he was elected to the Chamber of Deputies with considerably fewer votes. After serving five years as senator, and when he was prevented from joining the United Left coalition, Blanco decided not to run for public office in the general election of 1985.

BIBLIOGRAPHY

Blanco, Hugo. *Land or Death: The Peasant Struggle in Peru.* New York: Pathfinder Press, 1972.
Chang-Rodríguez, Eugenio. *Opciones políticas peruanas.* Lima: Centro de Documentación Andina, 1985.
Villanueva, Victor. *Hugo Blanco y la revolución campesina.* Lima: Editorial Mejía Baca, 1967.

EUGENIO CHANG-RODRÍGUEZ

BOGLE, PAUL (1822–1865), was leader of the Morant Bay Rebellion in Jamaica in 1865. Probably born a free man, he became a lay preacher in the Native Baptist Church and a peasant proprietor. He was listed as one of only 104 voters in the parish of St. Thomas. In the 1850s he became associated with George William Gordon,* a wealthy coloured planter who was a member of the Legislative Assembly.

During the 1860s economic conditions in the country were deteriorating. As the peasant population's grievances grew, Bogle was selected to present their problems to the governor, who refused to receive him. Bogle began to organize small armed groups which met secretly in the hills. On October 7, 1865, they marched into Morant Bay and disrupted a court case against a black peasant. Policemen attempting to make arrests were beaten back, and Bogle and his followers fled. Three days later police attempting to arrest those involved were overpowered by peasants in the village of Stony Gut where Bogle lived. On October 11, Bogle and 400 followers, armed with sticks and a few guns, marched on the Morant Bay courthouse which was protected by members of the colony's militia. After a verbal confrontation between the *Custos* (chief parish official) and the demonstrators and some throwing of stones, the militia was ordered to open fire. The demonstrators moved in, killing some militiamen and forcing the rest into the courthouse which was set ablaze. Over 28 persons were killed, including the *Custos*, and 30 were wounded. Martial law was declared, resulting in the execution of nearly 500 persons, the flogging of over 500, and the destruction of more than 1,000 homes. Bogle was finally captured on October 22 and was summarily executed two days later.

Bogle was named a national hero of Jamaica in 1965.

BIBLIOGRAPHY

Black, C. V. *The Story of Jamaica*. London: Collins, 1965.

Jacobs, H. P. *Sixty Years of Change 1806–1866*. Kinston: Institute for Social and Economic Research, 1973.

Roberts, W. A. *Jamaica: The Portrait of an Island*. New York: Coward-McCann, 1955.

Underhill, Edward D. *The Tragedy of Morant Bay*. Freeport, N.Y.: Books for Libraries, 1971.

Wynter, Sylvia. *Jamaica's National Heroes*. Kingston: National Trust Commission, 1971.

PERCY C. HINTZEN AND W. MARVIN WILL

BOLÍVAR, SIMÓN (1783–1830), was the principal Liberator not only of Venezuela, but also of Colombia, Ecuador, Peru, and Bolivia. Scion of an aristocratic Caracas family, he got a good education for his time, including tutoring by Simón Rodríguez, a student of the Enlightenment. In 1797 he went to Europe, where he stayed until 1802, returning home with his bride, a young Venezuelan whom he had met in Madrid. When she died shortly afterward, Bolívar returned to Europe.

Back in Venezuela in 1807, he devoted himself to business interests until the first Venezuelan Junta was established in Caracas in April 1810. He put himself at the Junta's disposal as an officer in the local militia, but the Junta sent him to Europe to seek the support of the British government.

Upon his return to Venezuela, Bolívar worked for a formal declaration of independence, which was signed on July 5, 1811. He was then sent to suppress a counterrevolutionary uprising in Valencia which he achieved. However, in July 1812 royalist forces compelled him to surrender the fortress of Puerto Cabello. Shortly afterward he joined other Venezuelan military men in preventing the departure abroad of Venezuelan President Francisco de Miranda,* in accordance with a surrender agreement Miranda had signed, thus virtually assuring Miranda's arrest by the Spanish.

Bolívar fled to New Granada, whence he organized an invasion of Venezuela, seizing Caracas on August 6, 1813. He was virtual military dictator of the Second Venezuelan Republic. However, in June 1814 he was decisively defeated by royalist troops and again fled to New Granada and thence to Jamaica. There he issued his Jamaica Letter, pledging himself to continue the struggle in Venezuela.

Going to Haiti, Bolívar won the support of President Alexandre Pétion,* and with Pétion's help landed on Venezuelan soil in May 1816. Bolívar captured the city of Angostura in July 1817 and made it his capital. In October 1817 he issued a decree promising land and cattle to veterans of the independence struggle. The Congress of Angostura in February 1819 established the legal basis of independent Venezuela.

Bolívar led his forces to New Granada in May 1819, winning the Battle of Boyacá on August 7, which largely freed Colombia from Spanish control. Returning to Angostura, he convinced the Congress to ratify the union of Venezuela, New Granada (Colombia), and Quito (Ecuador) as the Republic of Gran Colombia. Finally, he led his troops to victory at the Battle of Carabobo in June 1821, the definitive defeat of Spanish forces in Venezuela.

Bolívar went from Carabobo to the Colombian city of Cucutá, where the Gran Colombia Congress was sitting. Having adopted a constitution, that body then elected Simón Bolívar as first president of Gran Colombia, and Francisco de Paula Santander,* a Colombian, as vice president.

Leaving Santander in charge of organizing the new government, Bolívar headed with his troops for Ecuador. In July 1822 he met with the Argentine liberator José de San Martín* in Guayaquil. After that meeting, San Martín withdrew from further liberation struggles, and Bolívar moved to complete the freeing of Peru from Spanish rule. When an army mutiny in Callao resulted in Spanish seizure of that port and of Lima, Bolívar established the Peruvian government in Trujillo. The Peruvian Congress granted him dictatorial powers. He defeated the Spaniards at Junín and then went to Lima, which the independence force had recaptured. While he was there, his lieutenant Antonio José de Sucre Alcola* won the Decisive Battle of Ayacucho, which marked the end of Spanish rule in Peru.

From Lima, Bolívar issued an invitation to all Spanish-American states to a congress to be held in Panama. That gathering did not take place until June 1826, and whatever hopes Bolívar had for a federation of Spanish-American states were not fulfilled by it.

With Sucre's conquest of Upper Peru early in 1825, Bolívar went there. At the request of the leaders of the new nation of Bolivia, Bolívar drew up a constitution, which provided for a lifetime president who would choose his own successor. This constitution was of very short duration.

In April 1826 Bolívar's former lieutenant, José Antonio Páez,* led a separatist movement in Venezuela. Although that was halted when Bolívar went to Caracas, and Bolívar pardoned Páez, Bolívar's political problems continued to mount.

A convention met at Ocaña to revise the Gran Colombia constitution but proved abortive. Thereupon, Bolívar established a military dictatorship, severely restricting civil liberties and canceling many of the anticlerical reforms previously enacted. There was a short war with Peru in 1828–1829, and at the end of 1829, Páez led another movement for separation of Venezuela from Gran Colombia which was successful.

A new constitutional convention in Bogotá early in 1830 failed to settle differences among the constituent parts of Gran Colombia. Shortly afterwards, Ecuador also withdrew from it. Bolívar had already resigned the presidency and was on the way into exile when he died at the Colombian port of Santa Marta.

BIBLIOGRAPHY

Belaúnde, Víctor Andrés. *Bolívar and the Political Thought of the Spanish American Revolution*. Baltimore: Johns Hopkins University Press, 1938.
Bolívar, Simón. *Selected Writings*. New York: Banco de Venezuela, 1951.

Bushnell, David (ed.). *The Liberator Simón Bolívar: Man and Image*. New York: Alfred
    A. Knopf, 1970.
Ludwig, Emil. *Bolívar*. New York: Alliance Book Corporation, 1942.
Madariaga, Salvador de. *Bolívar*. New York: Pelligrini and Cudahy, 1952.

ROBERT J. ALEXANDER

BONIFÁCIO DE ANDRADA E SILVA, JOSÉ (1763–1838), a member of
an important family from the city of Santos in the State of São Paulo, dominated
much of Brazilian politics during the early days of independence. Educated at
Coimbra University in Portugal, Bonifácio in addition to his political activities
became a world famous scientist, specializing in minerology.

Bonifácio's greatest contribution was in coordinating and mobilizing support
for the independence movement. His influence was pivotal in Dom Pedro I's*
decision to remain in Brazil rather than return to Portugal as demanded by the
Portuguese Parliament in 1822. When Pedro I broke with Portugal, José Bonifácio was given the unofficial title of "Patriarch of Brazilian Independence."

During the reign of Dom Pedro I (1822–1831), Bonifácio, although appointed
a cabinet minister, clashed with the young emperor. Bonifácio wanted more
Brazilian participation and elimination of the Portuguese faction that surrounded
the young emperor. When Dom Pedro brought his mistress into the Imperial
Court and named her the Marquesa de Santos, Bonifácio returned to Santos and
cut his relations with the emperor. He left the country and returned in December
1829 when Pedro, in an attempt to bolster his falling popularity, appointed an
all-Brazilian cabinet at Bonifácio's suggestion.

The two men were reconciled, and when the emperor abdicated in 1831 he
summoned Bonifácio and turned over his five-year-old son Pedro II* to his care,
requesting that he tutor and prepare the young man for his duties as emperor of
Brazil. Bonifácio carried out this assignment, although many members of the
Regency felt he was too conservative politically.

BIBLIOGRAPHY

Barretto, Vincente. *Ideologia e política no Pensamento de José Bonifácio*. 1977.
Buzaid, Alfred. *José Bonifácio*. 1972.

JORDAN YOUNG

BONILLA, MANUEL (?–1913), was twice president of Honduras. When Policarpo Bonilla* (no relation to Manuel) became president in 1895, it was under-
stood that his minister of war, General Terencio Sierra, would be the Liberal
Party candidate in 1899 and Manuel Bonilla, the vice president, in 1903. However, Policarpo and Manuel Bonilla quarreled, and Manuel Bonilla withdrew
from the vice presidency. He subsequently became President Sierra's minister
of war. However, Sierra announced his support for Juan Angel Arias in the 1903
elections. Bonilla then resigned and founded a new coalition, the Nationalists,
composed of his following among the Liberals and practically all remaining

Conservatives. Bonilla received 28,850 votes, Arias 25,118, and a third nominee 4,857.

When President Sierra blocked Congress' attempt to select a president from between the top two candidates, Bonilla and a group of supporters left the capital for Amapala, where the mayor administered the presidential oath to Manuel Bonilla. After several battles, Sierra fled to El Salvador, and Bonilla was declared president-elect by Congress on May 5, 1903.

When Bonilla balanced his cabinet with Liberals and Conservatives, however, he irritated members of both parties. He suspended the constitution and declared martial law in the first week of 1904. A constitutional convention in 1905 lengthened the presidential term from four to six years and installed him as president for the period 1907–1912.

In December 1906 Nicaraguan troops sent by President José Santos Zelaya* invaded Honduras, supporting insurgents under ex-Presidents Policarpo Bonilla and Sierra. Manuel Bonilla finally fled to Guatemala and thence to British Honduras.

Bonilla returned to the presidency with the help of Samuel Zemurray, president of the Cuyamel Fruit Company, who provided financing and arms for an invasion force. A peace conference finally named Francisco Bertrand provisional president, until the elections of October 1911, when Manuel Bonilla was elected by 82,000 out of 86,000 ballots cast. Bonilla was inaugurated on February 1, 1912, with Bertrand as vice president.

Zemurray's assistance to Bonilla was rewarded with the concession of 10,000 hectares by the Honduran government, making him the only serious competition to the United Fruit Company.

Manuel Bonilla fell ill and died on March 21, 1913, after transferring power the night before to Vice President Bertrand.

BIBLIOGRAPHY

Durón y Gamero, Rómulo E. *Bosquejo Historico de Honduras, 1502 a 1921*. San Pedro Sula: Tipografía del Comercio, 1927.
Meyer, Harvey K. *Historical Dictionary of Honduras*. Metuchen, N.J.: Scarecrow Press, 1976.
Morris, James A. "Honduras," in Robert J. Alexander (ed.). *Political Parties of the Americas*. Westport, Conn.: Greenwood Press, 1982.
Raudales, Luis Amilcar. *Baturrillo Histórico*. Tegucigalpa: Tipografía Nacional, 1958.
Stokes, William S. *Honduras, An Area Study in Government*. Madison: University of Wisconsin Press, 1959.

NEALE J. PEARSON

BONILLA, POLICARPO (1856–1926), was the second of three Honduran Liberal Party presidents who implemented the principles of separation of church and state, representative government, and economic development through foreign investment. He had recognized the Liberals' lack of party organization, and the

1891 Liberal convention under his leadership established a hierarchical administration on a national, departmental, and municipal level.

Conservative Nationalist candidate Ponciano Leíva won the 1891 election through fraud by the incumbent government. Bonilla then went against one of his party's main principles—achievement of power through the ballot alone—and called for a revolution. As a result, he was exiled in May 1892. Soon after, Liberal revolutionaries, helped by President José Santos Zelaya* of Nicaragua, marched into Tegucigalpa, and Congress declared Policarpo Bonilla president on December 15, 1894.

Under Bonilla's administration, the Honduran north coast became a banana-producing area. In 1899 the Vaccaro family, which had been shipping bananas from Central America to New Orleans, received a large concession to develop land in the Aguan River Valley.

Bonilla was a strong supporter of Central American unification. Although he and Presidents Santos Zelaya of Nicaragua and Rafael Antonio Gutiérrez of El Salvador agreed in June 1895 to establish a *República Mayor de Centro America*, and a congress of the new republic met several times, a revolution in El Salvador in November 1898 ended the unity effort.

General Terencio Sierra, the Liberal presidential candidate in 1898, was elected. When he tried to stay in office in 1903, Manuel Bonilla* (no relation to Policarpo) revolted and in May 1903 was formally sworn in. Policarpo Bonilla then organized a plot involving dissatisfied Liberals who had expected Manuel Bonilla to reward them with governmental positions, with help from Nicaraguan President Zelaya. Policarpo Bonilla's conspiracy was cut short when Manuel Bonilla installed himself as dictator. Policarpo Bonilla's estates were confiscated, and he spent nearly two years in prison before he was pardoned.

Upon his release, Bonilla immediately began plotting a new revolt. When Manuel Bonilla's regime was toppled by a coalition of disaffected Hondurans and Nicaraguan forces of Zelaya, Policarpo Bonilla was pacified by the government's offer of restoration of his land and 200,000 pesos.

Policarpo Bonilla continued to be active in politics and made his last unsuccessful bid for the presidency in 1923.

BIBLIOGRAPHY

Deutsch, Hermann B. *The Incredible Yanqui, the Career of Lee Christmas*. London and New York: Longmans, Green and Co., 1931.
Durón y Gamero, Romúlo E. *Boseuejo Histórica de Honduras, 1502 a 1921*. San Pedro Sula: Tipografía del Comercio, 1927.
Mayer, Harvey K. *Historical Dictionary of Honduras*. Metuchen, N.J.: Scarecrow Press, 1970.
Stokes, William S. *Honduras, An Area Study in Government*. Madison: University of Wisconsin Press, 1950.

NEALE J. PEARSON

BORDABERRY, JUAN MARÍA (1928–   ), was the president of Uruguay who established the country's second dictatorship of the twentieth century. A rancher from the interior, Bordaberry began his political career as a member of the Blanco Party. He was a Blanco senator between 1963 and 1965. In 1964 he became leader of the Federal League for Rural Action, the major grass-roots organization supporting the Blanco regime of 1958–1966, upon the death of its founder, Benito Nardone.

After Vice President Jorge Pacheco Areco, a Colorado party leader, succeeded to the presidency upon the death of President Oscar Gestido in 1967, Bordaberry became Pacheco's minister of agriculture and livestock.

In the November 1971 election, the ballot included a constitutional amendment permitting reelection of the incumbent president, as well as candidates for president and vice president. President Pacheco Areco ran for the presidency, with Bordaberry as his vice presidential candidate. Although Pacheco and Bordaberry won, the constitutional amendment was not adopted, as a result of which Bordaberry become president.

President Bordaberry gave wide powers to the military to suppress the left-wing guerrilla group, the Tupamaros. By the end of 1972 the military had effectively suppressed the Tupamaros. However, in June 1973 the president acceded to the demands of the armed forces to dissolve Congress, when it refused to remove parliamentary immunity from Senator Enrique Erro, whom the military accused of having connections with the Tupamaros.

From then until June 1976, President Bordaberry presided over a thinly disguised military dictatorship. However, disagreements betwen the president and leaders of the armed forces led the military leaders to depose Bordaberry and impose old Blanco Party leaders Aparicio Mendez Montrelini* as his successor.

BIBLIOGRAPHY

Facts on File. New York: Facts on File.
Keesings Contemporary Archives. London: Keesings Publications Ltd.

ROBERT J. ALEXANDER

BOSCH, JUAN (1909–   ), emerged as the major leader of the opposition to the Dominican Republic dictatorship of Rafael Leónidas Trujillo Molina.* An essayist and short-story writer, he was exiled by Trujillo in 1935. During his years in Cuba, Costa Rica, and Venezuela, Bosch organized the Partido Revolucionario Dominicano (PRD) as the major opposition party. After the murder of Trujillo in May 1961, leaders of the PRD returned home to organize the party on Domincan soil. In November, Bosch himself went back and, quickly, through a series of radio and television appearances, gained wide popular support.

Juan Bosch was overwhelmingly elected president at the end of 1962. He presided over the first democratic government in more than three decades, but largely as the result of his political ineptitude he was overthrown by the military after only seven months.

Bosch remained leader of the PRD, but his endorsement of the idea of a "dictatorship with popular support" alienated many backers. When he sought to oust Secretary General José Francisco Peña Gómez,* he was defeated, and he withdrew to form the Partido Liberación Dominicana. His unsuccessful candidacy for president on the PLD ticket in several subsequent elections showed that his party represented only a small minority.

BIBLIOGRAPHY

Baciu, Stefan. *Juan Bosch: del exilio e la presidencia.* Buenos Aires: Bases, 1963.
Bosch, Juan. *Pentagonism: A Substitute for Imperialism.* New York: Grove Press, 1968.
———. *The Unfinished Experiment: Democracy in the Dominican Republic.* New York: Praeger, 1972.
Martin, John Bartlow. *Overtaken by Events.* Garden City, N.Y.: Doubleday and Co., 1966.

ROBERT J. ALEXANDER

BOUTERSE, DESI (?–   ), led the military coup of February 25, 1980, which overthrew the elected government of Surinam. A sergeant, he had sought to unionize the enlisted men, following the model of the armed forces of The Netherlands, founding and leading the Nationale Militaire Rand (NMR). It was when the government of Minister President Henck A.E. Arron* banned the NMR that the sergeants, led by Bouterse, revolted.

After ruling through a National Military Council of sergeants and lieutenants, and then through several civilian puppet presidents, the military finally made Bouterse chief of state in 1982. By that time, he was a lieutenant colonel.

BIBLIOGRAPHY

Alexander, Robert J. "Surinam," in Robert J. Alexander (ed.). *Political Parties of the Americas.* Vol. 2. Westport, Conn.: Greenwood Press, 1982.
Who's Who in the World 1984–86. Chicago: Marquis, 1984.

ROBERT J. ALEXANDER

BOYER, JEAN PIERRE (1776–1850), who served as Haiti's President for Life for 25 years after assuming power in 1818, was born a free mulatto. He was sent to France, where he attended military school. At 16, he joined the French Army and served as an officer in several European campaigns.

Upon returning to Haiti, Boyer supported mulatto General André Rigaud's effort to set up a regime in the south dominated by the mulattoes. Rigaud was defeated by Toussaint L'Ouverture in 1800, and Boyer fled to France.

In 1802 Boyer returned to Haiti with the French force sent by Napoleon Bonaparte to regain dominion over the colony. The French Army became increasingly decimated by illness after its reconquest of Haiti. Armed rebels began to inflict heavy casualties on the French, who retaliated with a campaign of terror. Boyer, along with many other black and mulatto officers, joined the insurrection which ended in defeat of the French. He served under Jean Jacques Dessalines,* who took control in December 1803 and declared himself emperor in 1804.

After Dessalines, a black, was assassinated in an insurrection led mainly by mulatto generals, the country was partitioned into a northern kingdom under the black Henri Christophe* and a southern republic under Alexandre Pétion,* to whom Boyer was secretary and confidante. Boyer was elevated to major general and military commander of Port-au-Prince, the capital.

Upon Pétion's death, Boyer used the army to convince a reluctant Senate to declare him President for Life. He wiped out an insurrection that had been plaguing the Pétion regime for 13 years, and then, using the opportunity of the death of Henri Christophe, he reunited the country. In February 1822, taking advantage of internal conflict in the Dominican Republic, Boyer invaded that colony and succeeded in securing its reunification with Haiti. The island remained united during the rest of Boyer's regime.

While inheriting a nearly bankrupt republic, Boyer's treasury was replenished by nearly 11 million pounds from Henry Christophe's coffers. But instead of taking advantage of the industry and organization of the North and the commitment to hard work instilled in its population by Henry Christophe, Boyer followed the more liberal laissez-faire policy of Pétion, relying more on persuasion than force and allowing cultivators free rein.

This approach proved disastrous. The economic crisis deepened as a result of an agreement with France in 1825, which halved the duties, both import and export on goods in French vessels, and granted 15 million francs compensation to former colonists. With the government depending almost entirely on import and export taxes and already approaching bankruptcy, these terms, made in exchange for French diplomatic recognition, made matters even worse.

In 1825 Boyer attempted to return to the economic program developed under Toussaint, Dessalines, and Christophe, by which workers were considered attached to the land and were obliged by law to work that land. The attempt failed. It relied on the presence of large plantations, but they had been broken up and the land parceled out to small freeholders. In the large plantations that survived there was a shift to sharecropping.

Economic decline was accompanied by political turmoil. In the former kingdom of the North, there was black discontent with a mulatto regime. At the same time, mulatto middle-class and intellectual opposition grew. A revolt against Boyer began in January 1843. After making a half-hearted attempt to defend his regime, Boyer left the country for Jamaica and went to Paris where he died.

BIBLIOGRAPHY

Davis, H. P. *Black Democracy: The Story of Haiti*. Toronto: Longmans Green and Co., 1929.
Heinl, R. D., and N. G. Heinl. *Written in Blood*. Boston: Houghton Mifflin, 1978.
Leyburn, James G. *The Haitian People*. New Haven, Conn.: Yale University Press, 1941.
Logan, R. W. *Haiti and the Dominican Republic*. London: Oxford University Press, 1968.

PERCY C. HINTZEN

BRADSHAW, ROBERT LLEWELLYN (1916–1978), dominated the politics of St. Kitts-Nevis-Anguilla for nearly four decades. After attending primary school in St. Kitts, he went to work in a sugar factory. He entered politics through the trade union movement. The St. Kitts Workers League, formed in 1932 by black field and factory workers in the sugar industry, acted as an incipient political organization *and* trade union, and gained significant concessions for the colony's workers. Bradshaw served as its vice president from 1932 to 1940.

In 1940 Bradshaw was a leader of a seven-week walkout from the sugar factory as a result of which he lost his job there. The same year, the government rescinded the law against unions, and the St. Kitts-Nevis Trades and Labour Union was formed. Bradshaw was elected to its Executive Committee. The union and party were two arms of the same movement.

In 1943 Bradshaw was one of the primary organizers of a week-long strike of sugar estate workers. In 1944 he was elected president of the union and vice president of the Workers' League which in 1945 became the St. Kitts-Nevis-Anguilla Labour Party under Bradshaw's presidency.

Bradshaw led the Labour Party in the 1946 elections in which a number of Labour Party candidates, including Bradshaw, were elected to the Legislative Council. The system of Crown Colony government provided little power and influence for the elected Council members from the Labour Party, however, Bradshaw continued his agitation, leading a 13-week strike in the sugar industry in 1948 and in 1950 a massive demonstration in support of Labour's call for more representative government.

In 1945 Bradshaw represented his union at the inaugural meeting of the Caribbean Labour Congress, of which he was elected assistant secretary. In 1949 he was one of the West Indian representatives at the inaugural conference of the International Confederation of Free Trade Unions in London, and became the first West Indian to serve as a member of its Executive Board.

In 1952, after universal adult suffrage was granted, Bradshaw led the Labour Party to another victory and was appointed minister of trade and production in 1956, when St. Kitts-Nevis-Anguilla were combined into one federated colony. Bradshaw's efforts were becoming increasingly focused on the West Indies Federation, however, and he served as second vice president of the West Indies Federal Labour Party between 1956 and 1957. When the federation was inaugurated in 1958, he became minister of finance in the Grantley Herbert Adams* federal government, a post he held until the collapse of the federation in 1962. He returned home to be reelected to a seat on the local Legislative Council.

The Labour Party won the general election of 1966. Bradshaw was sworn in as chief minister of the three-island colony after resuming the position of party leader, which had been handled by his ally Caleb Azariah Paul Southwell* during his absence. On February 27, 1967, the colony was granted Associated Statehood, with Bradshaw as premier of a cabinet fully responsible for internal affairs and with Great Britain retaining responsibility for only defense and external relations.

The political union of the three-island colony was always unstable, and Bradshaw may have exacerbated this situation, since his primary support and strength came from the sugar workers of St. Kitts. The other two islands were characterized by a predominance of small independent agricultural producers, in contrast to the proletarian character of the labor force on St. Kitts.

Two months after Associated statehood had been achieved, there was an uprising in Anguilla. Britain rushed troops to this tiny island and resumed control over its government. The final resolution of the issue came only when Anguilla reverted to British colonial status and independence came to St. Kitts and Nevis.

Bradshaw's tendency to focus almost exclusively on St. Kitts also plagued his relations with Nevis. The Labour Party had very little support there and faced continuous threats of Nevisian secession. After winning the 1975 election on the platform of immediate independence, Bradshaw encountered formidable opposition from the elected politicians of Nevis, who had won their constituencies with support for secession from the union. Independence did not come to St. Kitts-Nevis until 1983, five years after Bradshaw's death.

BIBLIOGRAPHY

Alexander, Robert J. "Saint Kitts-Nevis," in Robert J. Alexander (ed.). *Political-Parties of the Americas*. Vol. 2. Westport, Conn.: Greenwood Press, 1983.

Hopkins, Jack W. "British Colonies and Associated States," in Jack W. Hopkins (ed.). *Latin America and Caribbean Contemporary Record*. Vol. 1. New York: Holmes and Meier, 1983.

Jones-Hendrickson, Simon B. "St. Kitts-Nevis," in Jack W. Hopkins (ed.). *Latin America and Caribbean Contemporary Record*. Vol. 2. New York: Homes and Meier, 1984.

―――. "Strategies for Progress in the Post-Independence Caribbean: A Bradshawian Synthesis." Presidential address at IX Annual Meeting of Caribbean Studies Association, Basseterr, St. Kitts, 30 May–2 June 1984.

Rickards, Colin. *Caribbean Power*. London: Dobson, 1963.

PERCY C. HINTZEN AND W. MARVIN WILL

BRAMBLE, PERCIVAL AUSTIN (1931–   ), served as the second chief minister of Montserrat. He received his primary and secondary education in Montserrat, after which he worked as a lab technician in Curaçao between 1952 and 1961. He returned to Montserrat and became a hardware dealer and building contractor between 1961 and 1965. He joined his father's Labour Party and was elected to the Legislative Council in 1966, served as minister of communication and works between 1966 and 1969, and as minister of fiscal security for one year.

Becoming increasingly critical of his father, William Henry Bramble,* who was chief minister and leader of the Labour Party, the younger Bramble joined with a wealthy businessman, John Alfred Osborne,* to form the Progressive Democratic Party (PDP). He was particularly concerned with the policy of alienating the country's agricultural lands to serve the interests of foreign residents interested in building vacation and retirement homes. In the 1970 elections, the PDP gained an overwhelming victory, winning every seat. Percival Bramble became chief minister and served until 1978, following another impressive victory in 1973.

Bramble implemented programs whereby free drugs and medical care were provided to the aged, school feeding was introduced, and infants were provided with milk. He was successful in protecting Montserrat from the inflation that was sweeping the rest of the Caribbean following the oil crisis of 1973. He initiated a program of industrialization based on attracting small foreign-owned industries, including electronic assembly plants, and he introduced a state-owned cotton spinning and weaving project. Despite these successes, Bramble's party failed to win a single constituency in the 1978 elections. He won a seat in the 1983 elections, however, and assumed the position of Leader of the Opposition in the Legislative Council.

BIBLIOGRAPHY

Alexander, Robert J. "Montserrat," in Robert J. Alexander (ed.). *Political Parties of the Americas*. Vol. 2. Westport, Conn.: Greenwood Press, 1983.
Fergus, H.A. "Electoral Behavior in Montserrat." *Caribbean Quarterly*, 27 (March 1981).
———. "Personalities in Montserratian Politics: Comments on 1983 General Elections." *Bulletin of Eastern Caribbean Affairs* 10 (May/June 1984).
———. *William Henry Bramble: His Life and Times*. Montserrat: University Centre, University of the West Indies, 1983.

                              PERCY C. HINTZEN AND W. MARVIN WILL

BRAMBLE, WILLIAM HENRY (1902–   ), the first chief minister of Montserrat, received his primary education in Montserrat and then secured employment on a plantation. Later he became a dealer in sea island cotton and subsequently worked as a skilled carpenter and an undertaker. His interest in politics and labor union activities was aroused during the latter half of the 1930s when economic suffering throughout the West Indies caused widespread labor disturbances and rioting.

Although legislation enacted in 1939 legalized trade union activity, a system of sharecropping under virtual absolutism of the estate owners prevented any form of political and labor organization among agricultural workers. Only in 1946 did a local politician, Robert Griffith, decide to organize the Montserrat Trades and Labour Union (MTLU).Bramble became active in the MTLU.

In 1951 universal adult suffrage was introduced, and in elections in 1952 Bramble won a seat on the Legislative Council. There he began an intensive struggle against the rich and powerful merchants and planters who dominated Montserrat. He founded the Labour Party, more of an informal organization for the purposes of electoral mobilization than a formally organized political party. Bramble became the chairman of the Social Services and Public Works Committee, as a result of his post on the Council, and made an attempt to improve the housing conditions of the masses and to champion the lot of the homeless and landless.

Bramble also became a dominant figure in the Trades and Labour Union, and was elected its president in 1954. His unceasing efforts to ensure that the poor had access to land for rent led to the end of the system.

In March 1958 Bramble won the Montserrat seat on the federal legislature of the Leeward Islands. Later that year his Labour Party won four of five elective seats in the Montserrat Legislature. After this victory, he concentrated on politics and allowed the union to fall into abeyance. By 1959 it was all but dormant.

In 1960 a new constitution created a ministerial system and an expanded Legislative Council where elected members had an overwhelming majority. Bramble became chief minister, the first for the colony, as well as minister of trade and production, after the 1961 elections, in which the Labour Party won five of seven elective seats on the council. As chief minister, he switched his political strategy from agitation against the dominant economic powers in the island to accommodation with them. He began active promotion of the tourist industry and agricultural development. He also undertook to develop agri-based small-scale industry and to attract foreign capital. Most importantly, he made available large tracts of land for real estate development, catering to foreigners who were encouraged to build vacation and retirement homes. This produced an increase in the tourist trade and a spurt in construction activity.

In 1966 Bramble won another election despite severe criticism of his development program and his seeming authoritarian approach to party and government. By 1970, however, his oldest son, Percival Austin Bramble,* a former minister in his government, was his chief rival, and William Bramble and his Labour Party were swept out of power, failing to win a single constituency. Following his defeat, the elder Bramble quietly faded out of political and union activity.

BIBLIOGRAPHY

Alexander, Robert J. "Montserrat," in Robert J. Alexander (ed.). *Political Parties of the Americas*. Vol. 2. Westport, Conn.: Greenwood Press, 1983.

Fergus, H. A. *History of Alliuagana: A Short History of Montserrat*. Montserrat: University of the West Indies, Department of Extramural Studied, 1975.

————. *William Henry Bramble: His Life and Times*. Montserrat: University Centre, University of the West Indies, 1983.

PERCY C. HINTZEN AND W. MARVIN WILL

BRIZOLA, LEONEL (1922–   ), a contentious and controversial Brazilian politician, was born in Rio Grande do Sul. He attended a variety of schools, finally graduating from the Engineering School of the University of Rio Grande do Sul in 1949.

Brizola joined the Brazilian Labor Party (PTB) in 1945 and was elected to the state assembly in 1947. In March 1950 he married Neusa Goulart, the sister of Jõao Belchior Marques Goulart.*

In October 1954 Brizola won a seat in the federal Congress to represent the PTB. Elected mayor of the city of Porto Alegre in 1955, he developed neighborhood school programs and improved public transportation.

Brizola won an easy victory in the 1958 gubernatorial election. As governor, his most controversial action was expropriation of the Rio Grandense Light and Power Company, a subsidiary of American and Foreign Power. He followed this move with the 1962 takeover of the state's telephone company, owned by International Telephone and Telegraph Company.

The resignation of President Jânio Quadros* in August 1961 brought Governor Brizola into national prominence. When military authorities attempted to block the accession of Vice President Goulart, Governor Brizola organized a radio network that gave unconditional support to Goulart. When Third Army Commander General Machado Lopes sided with the governor, a civil war appeared imminent, as Brizola disributed weapons to a citizens militia. The situation was defused when the constitution was changed to a parliamentary form of government and Goulart was sworn in as president.

In 1962 Brizola ran for a congressional seat from the state of Guanabara on the PTB ticket. He was overwhelmingly elected. The radicalization of Brazilian politics accelerated when Brizola organized clandestine "Groups of 11," which he hoped would get support from the National Sergeants Command and the Sailors Enlisted Men's Organization. However, when the March 31, 1964, revolution occurred, the Groups of 11 never materialized, and Brizola, along with Goulart, fled into exile.

Brizola remained in Uruguay until 1977, when he went to the United States and then to Portugal. Various European Socialist parties took a great interest in him, and when political amnesty was decreed in Brazil in August 1979, he returned to Brazil. He quickly organized the PDT (Democratic Labor Party) and was elected governor of the state of Rio de Janeiro in November 1982.

BIBLIOGRAPHY

Debert, Luisa Grin. *Ideologia e populismo*. 1979.
Nuniz Bandeira, Luis Alberto. *Brizola e o trabalhismo*. 1979.

JORDAN YOUNG

BULNES PRIETO, MANUEL (1799–1866), was the last general to be president of Chile for more than 75 years. In 1811, when only 12 years old, Bulnes enrolled as a cadet in the Royal Veteran Battalion of Infantry of Concepción. However, he was deported to an island in the Pacific Ocean for political reasons in 1816, returning to the mainland only after the Battle of Chacabuco in February 1817, which definitely assured the independence of Chile. Subsequently, Bulnes took part in many of the later battles of the independence war. By 1831 he was a brigadier general, and by 1833 a major general. He led the Chilean troops in the 1838–1839 war with the Peru-Bolivian Confederation.

In 1841 Bulnes was elected president with the support of the so-called *pelucones* (wigged ones), the more conservative current in Chilean politics at that time. In 1846 he was reelected without opposition. Early in his administration he signed a law of amnesty for all political exiles, and another restoring to their posts in the civil and military administration those dismissed for being on the losing side of the 1828–1830 civil war.

The Bulnes administration substantially augmented Chilean territory. It took control of the Straits of Magellen and founded the city of Punta Arenas. It also carried on an extensive public works program, including signing a contract to build a railroad from Santiago to Valparaíso. It established the University of Chile and several other important educational institutions.

The election at the end of Bulnes' second term of Manuel Montt Torres* as his successor, provoked strong opposition and a short civil war. After duly turning over the presidency to his elected successor, General Bulnes took the field once again, successfully commanding the government troops. This was the last serious attempt to overthrow the Chilean government by force until the Civil War of 1891.

In 1852 ex-President Bulnes was elected to the Senate, and he remained a senator until his death.

BIBLIOGRAPHY

Cortes, Lia, and Jordi Fuentes. *Diccionario Político de Chile*. Santiago: Editorial Orbe, 1967.
Enciclopedia Universal Ilustrada Europeo-Americana. Barcelona: Jose Espasa e Hijos.
Galdames, Luis. *Historia de Chile*. Santiago: Editorial Zig Zag, 1943.

ROBERT J. ALEXANDER

BURNHAM, LINDEN FORBES SAMPSON (1923–1985), became Premier of Guyana in 1964 and led the country to independence in 1966. He traveled to England in 1945 on a Guyana scholarship, received his LL.B. degree in 1947, and was called to the bar in 1948. While in Great Britain he served as president of the West Indian Students Union, a leading member of the League of Coloured Peoples comprising students from the West Indies, Africa and Asia, and became a socialist.

Burnham returned to British Guiana in 1949, throwing himself into law practice and politics, and trade union activities. In 1952 he was elected president of the British Guiana Labor Union (BGLU), one of the country's most powerful unions, a post he held until his death. He also became involved in the Political Affairs Committee (PAC), headed by a Marxist dentist, Cheddi Jagan.* By 1950 Jagan and Burnham turned the PAC into the Peoples Progressive Party—the first non-ethnic political party in the country. Burnham became the party's first chairman, and Jagan became party leader.

From its inception, the PPP's stated aim was to win a free and independent British Guiana and the achieve the socialist reorganization of the society. In 1953, in elections under a new constitution that provided for universal adult suffrage for the first time, the PPP won 18 of the 24 seats. Forbes Burnham became minister of education.

Burnham's Fabian Socialism conflicted sharply with the Marxism-Leninism of a faction of the PPP led by Cheddi Jagan and his wife Janet Jagan.* The radicals had clearly gained the upper hand, not only in the party, but also in the new government. In response the Conservative British government of Winston Churchill suspended the new constitution 133 days after it was initiated. Burnham and Jagan immediately went to Great Britain to protest the decision, and then to India to drum up support there. Restrictions were placed on the movement and political activities of the leaders of the PPP. When he returned home, Burnham chose to abide by these restrictions, going against most of the leadership of the party, and was thus spared the prison sentence that was the lot of most of the party's top leaders.

Ideological differences and the different power bases of Jagan and Burnham soon precipitated a split in the PPP. The Burnham faction's base was the urban black working-class population. When elections were held in 1957, after a partial restoration of the 1953 constitution, the Burnhamites managed to capture only 25.5 percent of the popular vote, winning 3 of 14 seats, to the Jaganites' 9 seats and 47.5 percent of the vote. In 1958 Burnham joined forces with a party representing the black urban middle class to form the Peoples National Congress (PNC). The new party again lost to Jagan's PPP in 1961 elections but got 41 percent of the votes and 11 seats. The PPP, with 42.6 percent of the vote, won 20 seats.

As leader of the opposition and head of one of the country's major trade unions, with support from the bulk of the electorate in the capital city, Burnham resisted any effort to grant the colony independence before substantial electoral reform. In a two-year period of political conflict that took on both racial and ideological characteristics, Burnham's predominantly black urban-based supporters became pitted against Jagan's predominantly East Indian rural supporters. Civil strife forced Jagan to accept a political formula, worked out largely by Burnham, which almost guaranteed political victory to Burnham. Elections were held in 1964 with the clear understanding by Britain that independence would be granted during the tenure of the next government. Burnham's Peoples National Congress and the conservative United Force, winning 40.8 percent and 12.5 percent of the votes, respectively, formed a coalition government under the new system of proportional representation. Burnham became prime minister. When Britain granted independence to British Guiana in 1966, Forbes Burnham continued as prime minister.

By encouraging members of the opposition to cross party lines, Burnham managed to gain full control of the government in 1967. After winning an outright victory for his party in 1968, he began to take the country on an increasingly socialist path. In 1970 he led the establishment of the Cooperative Republic of Guyana. Thereafter, all major foreign-owned sectors of the economy were nationalized, and the state came to own over 80 percent of the country's economic assets. Education became totally free, and social security and welfare were considerably expanded. The country became a leading member of the nonaligned movement, establishing strong relations with Cuba, Eastern Europe, China, and Third World socialist countries.

Under Burnham's increasingly authoritarian leadership the government embarked on revision of the constitution in the late 1970s. Under the new constitution, in 1980 Burnham became executive president, a position he retained until his death.

Burnham died unexpectedly in a local hospital from a complication of maladies.

BIBLIOGRAPHY

Burnham, L.F.S. *A Destiny to Mould.* Compiled by C. A. Nascimento and R. A. Burrowes. London: Longman Caribbean, 1970.
Despres, L. A. *Cultural Pluralism and Nationalist Politics in British Guiana.* Chicago: Rand McNally, 1967.
Jagan, C. *The West on Trial.* Berlin GDR: Seven Seas, 1980.
Manley, R. R. *Guyana Emergent.* Cambridge, Mass.: Schenkman, 1979, rev. 1984.
Spinnger, T. J. *A Political and Social History of Guyana, 1945–1983*, Boulder, Colo.: Westview Press, 1984.

PERCY C. HINTZEN AND W. MARVIN WILL

BUSCH, GERMÁN (1904–1939), a reformist military president of Bolivia, became one of the symbolic heroes of left-wing nationalism after the National Revolution of 1952. He was the son of a German doctor and a Bolivian woman, and graduated from the Colegio Militar. During the Chaco War (1932–1935), Busch was one of the few genuine Bolivian military heroes to emerge from the conflict. By the end of the war, he was a colonel.

Colonel Busch as a leader of a group of young officers who seized power from the conservative civilian government in June 1936, a few months after the end of the Chaco War. Although the new president, Colonel David Toro, proclaimed his regime to be "socialist," nationalized the Standard Oil Company's concessions, and for the first time established a Ministry of Labor, some of its original military and civilian supporters became disillusioned in the Toro government.

In July 1937 President Toro was ousted in a coup led by Germán Busch, who was proclaimed president. The Busch government called elections for a national convention, which adopted a constitution modeled on the Mexican Constitution of 1917, and including extensive social and labor legislation. It also issued the Busch Labor Code, the first such Bolivian legislation, and for the first time encouraged the organization of unions among the tin miners.

Busch had associated with him a number of leftist civilians. One was Gustavo Navarro, better known by his pseudonym Tristán Marof, whose followers were particularly active in organizing the miners. Another was a young lawyer and economist, Víctor Paz Estenssoro,* who drew up what was probably the most important decree of the Busch regime. This required the Big Three tin mining companies to sell to the Bolivian Central Bank all foreign exchange they earned and to buy from the bank whatever foreign currency they needed to conduct their business or repatriate profits. The mining firms strongly objected to this decree, the first serious limitation on their freedom of operation in Bolivia.

About two and a half months after the issuance of this decree, President Busch died. The official explanation was that he had commited suicide, although many associated with his regime insisted that he had been killed. In any case, his death ended the short period of post-Chaco War military reformism. After the victory of the Nationalist Revolutionary Movement (MNR), headed by his one-time minister Paz Estenssoro, Busch was pictured as a precursor of the Bolivian National Revolution.

BIBLIOGRAPHY

Cespedes, Augusto. *El Dictador Suicida, 40 Anos de Historia de Bolivia*. 3d ed. La Paz: Juventud, 1979.
Gumucio, Mariano Baptista. *Historia Contemporanea de Bolivia, 1930–1978*. 2nd ed. La Paz: Gisbert, 1978.

WALTRAUD QUEISER MORALES

BUSTAMANTE, SIR WILLIAM ALEXANDER (1884–1977), became the first prime minister of independent Jamaica. The son of an Irish planter and a mixed blood Jamaican mother, Bustamante was born William Alexander Clarke. After attending elementary school and doing some private studies, he worked as a store clerk and in a sugar factory. He left Jamaica in 1905 and lived in several countries during the next 30 years. When he returned to Jamaica in 1934 he had a sizable fortune and set up a flourishing real estate and money-lending business.

By 1936 Bustamante was taking part in protest marches against the colonial government and intervening in strikes. In 1937 "Busta" became treasurer of the Jamaica Workers' and Tradesmen's Union (JWTU) which he had helped organize.

During 1937–1938 there was an escalation of labor and political unrest not only in Jamaica but throughout the West Indies. Bustamante became deeply involved in this turmoil. On May 23, 1938, he was arrested, charged with sedition, and held without bail. Intense labor and political pressure brought his release a week later. Regarded as a martyr as a result of this experience, Bustamante gained even more status as a charismatic hero.

Soon afterward he formed the Bustamante Industrial Trade Union (BITU), and he served as its president until his death. With his cousin, Norman Washington Manley,* he joined in forming the Peoples National Party (PNP) in September 1938. For a time, the BITU was the union arm of the PNP. In February 1939 he attempted to organize a general strike which failed.

In 1940, after threatening to call a general strike, Bustamante was arrested and detained for 17 months for "impeding the war effort." Upon release in

February 1942, he attacked the leaders of the PNP, accusing them of a betrayal of trust. In 1943 Bustamante founded the Jamaica Labour Party (JLP) to contest the impending elections, the first under universal adult suffrage.

Bustamante's charismatic oratory and wit, together with the decision of portions of the Jamaican middle class to support the JLP out of fear of the socialist ideology of Manley's Peoples National Party, brought victory to Bustamante and his party who captured 22 of the 32 seats in the House of Representatives. The PNP won in only four constituencies. Bustamante became minister of communication and works and leader of the elected members of the Executive Council under a new constitution. Bustamante's party was victorious again in 1949, winning 18 of the 32 seats in the House, although the PNP won a majority of the popular votes. Bustamante was then appointed chief minister and presided over a largely elected Executive Council.

In office, Bustamante considerably modified his positions. A confrontation with strikers of the PNP-controlled Trade Union Congress in 1946 that resulted in the death of one of the strikers generated a scandal. Moreover, Bustamante was avowedly antisocialist and a firm believer in the British Crown. He resisted the PNP campaign for increased self-government and accepted a new constitution only at the urging of the governor. Only after a narrow victory in 1949 did he begin to implement modest social welfare programs for workers. Finally, in 1955, the JLP lost to the PNP, getting only 14 seats to the PNP's 18. Bustamante became Leader of the Opposition and was knighted by the queen.

Despite reservations, Bustamante had been one of the West Indian leaders who in 1947 had agreed to form a regional federation as the basis for eventual independence. After his 1955 electoral defeat, he served as the leader of a federal coalition of parties. When federal elections were held in 1958, Bustamante's JLP won 12 of the 17 Jamaican seats in the federal Parliament, but parties allied with his JLP lost to parties in the rival Federal Labor Party elsewhere.

Bustamante became highly critical of the federation. After losing another election to the PNP in 1959, he forced the Manley government to call a referendum on the issue on September 19, 1961. Bustamante won a resounding victory as voters supported secession. This was the death knell of the federation, which came to a formal end on May 31, 1962.

Bustamante then joined with Manley to petition for Jamaica's full independence. He served on the committee to draw up the independence constitution, joined the delegation that went to Britain to negotiate, and was one of the signatories to the agreement for independence. The leaders of the JLP and PNP agreed on an election prior to independence. Bustamante's JLP was swept to power, winning 26 seats to 19 for the PNP. The country became independent on August 6, 1962, and Bustamante became its first prime minister. In 1964 the 80-year-old Bustamante became ill and never returned to full-time involvement in government. He finally retired as prime minister in 1967.

82 BUSTAMANTE Y RIVERO, JOSÉ LUÍS

BIBLIOGRAPHY

Bustamante, Alexander. *The Best of Bustamante: Selected Quotations 1935–1974*. Researched and compiled by Jackie Ranston. Red Hills, Jamaica: Twin Guinep, 1977.
Eaton, George F. *Alexander Bustamante and Modern Jamaica*. Kingston: Kingston Publishers, 1975.
Hamilton, B. St. John. *Bustamante: Anthology of a Hero*. Kingston: Publications and Productions, 1977.
Hill, Frank. *Bustamante and His Letters*. Kingston: Kingston Publishers, 1976.

PERCY C. HINTZEN AND W. MARVIN WILL

BUSTAMANTE Y RIVERO, JOSÉ LUÍS (1894–   ), a president of Peru, was born and educated in Arequipa. There he received his basic education at a Jesuit school, and his professional title of lawyer and doctorate in politics and public administration from the University of San Agustín (1929). After a stint at high school teaching, he was a professor of philosophy, social geography, history of the Americas, and law at the University of San Agustín from 1922 to 1928. He drafted the revolutionary declaration of Commander Luís M. Sánchez Cerro,* leader of the military coup in Arequipa (1930) that overthrew President Augusto B. Leguía,* and served as minister of justice of the new de facto government. General Óscar R. Benavides,* who assumed power after Sánchez Cerro's assassination in 1933, and President Manuel Prado,* Benavides' successor, appointed him to important diplomatic posts.

Because the Peruvian Aprista Party (PAP) was banned from having its own candidate in the 1945 general elections, the National Democratic Front (FND) which the PAP helped to found, elected Bustamante president of the Republic with 66.97 percent of the votes. However, the precarious FND coalition weakened progressively, leading to boycott of legislative sessions by pro-Bustamante and anti-Aprista senators. During the navy revolt in Callao on October 3, 1948, Bustamante outlawed the PAP. Twenty-four days later, General Manuel A. Odría,* his minister of war, overthrew and exiled him.

Bustamante returned to Peru in 1955. Four years later he was elected member of the Peruvian Academy of the Spanish Language, and in 1960 he was elected dean of the Colegio de Abogados de Lima (Lima's Association of Lawyers). In this same year, the United Nations appointed Bustamante member of the International Court of Justice at The Hague. After his tenure in this international body, he retired to reside in Lima.

BIBLIOGRAPHY

Alisky, Marvin. *Historical Dictionary of Peru*. Metuchen, N.J.: Scarecrow Press, 1979.
Bustamante y Rivero, José Luis. *Treinta años de lucha por la democrácia en el Peru*. Buenos Aires: B.U. Chiesino, 1949.

Seminario, Martín Gary. *Perfiles humanos*. Lima: 1985.
Tauro, Alberto. *Diccionario enciclopédico del Peru* (Lima: Editorial Mejía Baca, 1966.
EUGENIO CHANG-RODRÍGUEZ

BUTLER, TUBAL URIAH (1897–1977), had major responsibility for the emergence of a radical working-class movement in Trinidad and Tobago that spread to the rest of the Anglophone Caribbean, and paved the way for eventual independence of most of the territories. He was born in the neighboring territory of Grenada. The son of a blacksmith, he left school at age 13. He joined the West Indian Regiment and went overseas during World War I. He returned to Grenada in 1919 but left in 1922 for Trinidad, where he secured a job in the oil industry.

At the time of his arrival, the Trinidad Workingmen's Association (TWA), under the leadership of Arthur Andrew Cipriani,* was the most important working-class organization in the country. Butler became a member of the TWA. However, in 1934 he mounted a major challenge to Cipriani, when Cipriani refused to sanction a strike by oilfield workers.

Butler's fiery oratory was honed in the Moravian Church, which he served as a pastor. Convinced of his God-appointed mission to free the West Indian masses from colonial bondage, Butler founded his first political party, the British Empire Workers and Citizens Home Rule Party, in 1936, believing that Cipriani had become a spent political force. Between 1935 and 1937 Butler rallied the black workers to his cause. He saw the socioeconomic woes of the Depression as a direct consequence of colonial exploitation. Initially convinced of the necessity to exhaust all channels of negotiation, Butler pleaded with the colonial administration to enact political, economic, and industrial reforms on behalf of the working class. When his pleas failed, he called for a general strike, which, although planned to be peaceful, was met by force and became a violent confrontation that left 14 people dead, 49 injured, and enormous loss of property. The strike served as a catalyst for similar riots thorughout the Anglophone West Indies.

As a result of these events, a West Indian Royal Commission was convened, under the chairmanship of Lord Moyne, to investigate conditions throughout the Anglophone Caribbean. The report, submitted in 1939 but not released until after World War II, made recommendations for labor and political reform, including more representative government and universal adult suffrage.

The Oilfield Workers Trade Union (OWTU), which was initiated by Butler, emerged out of the rioting. Butler's participation in the union was hampered by his arrest for his role in the riots of 1937. He remained in custody until May 6, 1939. Upon his release, as general organizer of the OWTU, he mobilized the workers against the oil companies and attempted to forge a political union between the predominantly black oilfield workers and the predominantly East Indian sugar workers. His expulsion from the OWTU in 1939 was a tremendous blow to organized labor since it led to a 90 percent drop in the union's membership.

Butler was incarcerated for almost the whole of World War II as a "danger to the war effort." On his release in 1945, he formed the Butler Party and a new union, the British Empire Workers, Peasants, and Ratepayers Union to represent the oilfield workers.

The 1946 elections were the first under universal adult suffrage. The Butler Party, which had forged an alliance with East Indian political leaders, won three of the nine constituencies, tying with another mass-based party. This victory was a genuine multiracial effort in an election fraught with racial animosity between the black and East Indian populations. In 1950 the Butler Party won in 6 of 18 constituencies and achieved a voting bloc of eight members after two independents joined its ranks in Parliament. Although winning the largest number of seats, the absence of a clear majority left it up to the governor, who refused to nominate anyone to the cabinet from the Butler group.

After 1950 racial politics led to splintering of Butler's party as the East Indian members deserted him for a new Peoples Democratic Party. By the next general election in 1956, the Butler Party crumbled under the onslaught of Dr. Eric Williams* and his Peoples National Movement. Butler lost his own constituency, and the party was able to capture a mere 2 seats of the 24 contested.

BIBLIOGRAPHY

Brereton, Bridget. *A History of Modern Trinidad 1783–1962*. Port of Spain: Heinemann, 1981.
Malik, Y. K. *East Indians in Trinidad*. London: Oxford University Press, 1971.
Oilfield Workers Trade Union, July 1937-July 1977. San Fernando, Trinidad: OWTU, 1977.
Oxaal, Ivar. *Black Intellectuals Come to Power*. Cambridge, Mass.: Schenkman, 1968.
Ryan, Selwyn D. *Race and Nationalism in Trinidad and Tobago*. Toronto: University of Toronto Press, 1972.

PERCY C. HINTZEN AND W. MARVIN WILL

C

CABALLERO, BERNARDINO (1839–1912), was a leader of Paraguayan cavalry during the War of the Triple Alliance (1865–1870) and founder of the Paraguayan Colorado Party. In 1876 the Brazilian occupying army left Paraguay, and soon afterward President Juan Bautista Gill was overthrown in a coup led by General Caballero, who dominated Paraguayan politics for the next quarter century, either as president (1880–1886) or through control of the military. His economic policies saw large expanses of Paraguayan land pass to foreigners, and government factories, mines, and railroads were sold to get funds.

Caballero's opponents soon formed the Liberal Party, and Caballero established the National Republican Association, popularly known as the Colorado Party because of its red banner. These remained the focal points of Paraguayan politics for the next century.

During the 1890s the Colorado Party was subjected to factionalism and corruption. Caballero tried to consolidate the party with a purge in 1902, but a Liberal invasion succeeded in overthrowing the government in 1904, ending Bernardino Caballero's domination of Paraguay.

BIBLIOGRAPHY

Kolinski, Charles J. *Historical Dictionary of Paraguay*. Metuchen, N.J.: Scarecrow Press, 1973.
Lewis, Paul H. *Paraguay Under Stroessner*. Chapel Hill: University of North Carolina Press, 1980.
Pendle, George. *Paraguay: A Riverside Nation*. London: Royal Institute of International Affairs, 1956.
Raine, Philip. *Paraguay*. New Brunswick, N.J.: Scarecrow Press, 1956.

JOHN T. DEINER

CÁCERES, ANDRÉS A. (1833–1923), twice president of Peru (1886–1890 and 1894–1895), was born in Ayacucho. After completing high school in his hometown, he served in General Ramón Castilla's* rebellious army with the rank of second lieutenant. When Castilla became president, Cáceres was sent to

Europe for medical treatment of wounds received during the civil wars. Afterward he rose rapidly in the army, participating in a conflict with Ecuador, the Battle of Callao (1866) against a Spanish armada, and armed rebellions. The War of the Pacific against Chile started in 1879 when Colonel Cáceres was governor of Cuzco. He fought bravely in several battles until he was wounded again in the defense of Lima. He was saved by Jesuits who sneaked him out of the capital. Cáceres nursed his wounds and organized the resistance in the Andes as supreme political and military commander of central Peru. His heroic deeds in the guerrilla war against Chilean occupying forces gained him the name of ''The Wizard of the Andes.''

Bitterly opposed to the Treaty of Ancón (1883) imposed by victorious Chile and signed by Peruvian President Miguel Iglesias, Cáceres attempted vainly to seize control of the government in 1884. A year later his army succeeded in occupying Lima and forcing General Iglesias to hold elections which Cáceres won. He served as president of the republic from 1886 to 1890. Cáceres had officers in active duty collaborate with civilians and officers of the reserve to found the militarist Constitutionalist Party in 1886. After leaving office, he was appointed minister in Great Britain and France (1891–1892). He won the manipulated elections of 1894, but his presidency was short. In 1895 a general uprising led by Nicolás de Pierola* overthrew him. He lived as a private citizen in Buenos Aires and Paris before becoming minister to Italy (1905–1911) and to Germany (1911–1914). He was promoted to the rank of marshal in 1919.

BIBLIOGRAPHY

Alisky, Marvin. *Historical Dictionary of Peru*. Metuchen, N.J.: Scarecrow Press, 1979.
Basadre, Jorge. *Peruanos del siglo XIX*. Lima: Ediciones Rikchay, 1981.
Pike, Frederick B. *The Modern History of Peru*. New York: Praeger, 1967.
Tauro, Alberto. *Diccionario enciclopédico del Peru*. Lima: Editorial Mejía Baca, 1966.

EUGENIO CHANG-RODRÍGUEZ

CALDERA RODRÍGUEZ, RAFAEL (1916–   ), was the principal founder of the Social Christian Copei party of Venezuela and the first member of that party to be elected president of the republic.

As a youngster, Caldera was active in the youth organization of Catholic Action. Between 1932 and 1934 he was secretary general of the Council of Venezuelan Catholic Youth. After the death of dictator Juan Vicente Gómez,* he was active in the revived Venezuelan Students Federation. However, when it demanded the closing of all religious orders in Venezuela, Caldera organized the National Union of Students (UNE). He also became a member of the League of National Defense, set up in September 1936 to fight an alleged ''Communist'' threat. Both UNE and the league supported the government of President Eleazar López Contreras.*

Caldera, with other UNE leaders, established Electoral Action in 1938 as a political party in the Caracas area. In the next election, Caldera won a seat in the Chamber of Deputies. In 1942 Electoral Action spread beyond Caracas and became National Action. However, in 1945 it dissolved in a dispute over whether to support General López Contreras' aspirations to return to the presidency— which Caldera opposed.

With the overthrow of President Isaías Medina Angarita,* Rafael Caldera accepted Rómulo Betancourt's* offer of the post of attorney general in the new Acción Democrática (AD)-dominated government. In January 1946 the Committee of Independent Electoral Political Organization (COPEI) was established by the leaders and ex-leaders of the UNE, and Caldera associated himself with it. When violent clashes developed in several parts of the country between members of COPEI and AD, Caldera resigned from the government in April 1946, and immediately became head of Copei. He was elected one of the party's 19 deputies in the constitutional assembly in October 1946. In December 1947 Caldera was Copei's nominee for president, getting 22.4 percent of the vote.

Although Copei was strident in its opposition to the Acción Democrática government, neither Caldera nor his party had anything to do with the overthrow of President Rómulo Gallegos* in November 1948. However, when Colonel Carlos Delgado Chalbaud,* head of the new military junta, promised to move to an elected government as quickly as possible, Caldera and his party agreed to allow some Copei members to accept posts in the regime. After the murder of Delgado Chalbaud in 1950, Caldera and Copei broke off all relations with the government.

Colonel Marcos Pérez Jiménez* seized power on December 2, 1952, and ordered a "recount" of votes of the election held a few days earlier. Caldera led his party in forbidding any members to accept a seat in the resulting constitutional assembly. During the Pérez Jiménez regime, Caldera was very closely watched by the secret police and was arrested on several occasions.

When Pérez Jiménez' "constitutional" term neared its end, the three opposition parties, Acción Democrática, Republican Democratic Union (URD), and Copei, agreed to nominate Rafael Caldera as coalition candidate. However, on August 21, 1957, he was once more arrested and held until December 24. On January 19, 1958, he was finally allowed to leave the country for New York City. There, he met with Rómulo Betancourt and Jóvito Villalba,* and they pledged their parties to work together to restore democratic government following the overthrow of Pérez Jiménez on January 23.

When it proved impossible to reach agreement on a joint candidate of the three parties, Copei once again nominated Caldera for president. That time, he came in third. He also ran for the Chamber of Deputies and won a seat. Between 1959 and 1961, he served as president of the Chamber. During the whole of the administration of Rómulo Betancourt (1959–1964), Caldera worked closely with the president, and the Acción Democrática-Copei alliance was one of the keys to the success of the Betancourt administration.

Caldera ran once more for the presidency in December 1963. He came in second, behind Raúl Leoni* of Acción Democrática. However, five years later, in the face of a major split in AD, Rafael Caldera was finally successful and became president.

During his tenure (1969–1974), President Caldera lacked a majority in Congress and so was forced to negotiate compromises with the opposition, particularly with Acción Democrática. He largely continued the programs of agrarian reform, economic development, and expansion of education which had been carried on by the two AD governments of Betancourt and Leoni. One notable innovation was a law limiting the ability of the foreign oil companies to decapitalize the oil industry in the few years still pending before their scheduled nationalization.

President Caldera sought reconciliation with those parties that had engaged in guerrilla warfare during the previous decade. He allowed the Communists, whose party had been legalized under another name by the Leoni administration (after withdrawing from guerrilla activity), to reassume the name Communist Party of Venezuela. He also brought about the relegalization of the Movement of the Revolutionary Left (MIR) when it finally decided to abandon guerrilla activity.

After leaving the presidency, Caldera, as a senator for life, sometimes participated in discussions in the Senate, as in the debate over the nationalization of the oil industry in 1975. However, he spent most of his time in his professional activities and as a professor at the Central University. He frequently traveled abroad.

Copei won the presidential election of 1978. However, the winner, Luis Herrera Campins* had not been Caldera's personal choice, and relations between the two became increasingly distant. In 1983 Rafael Caldera once again ran as the Copei candidate for president. This time he was defeated by Acción Democrática's Jaime Lusinchi.*

BIBLIOGRAPHY

Alexander, Robert J. *The Venezuelan Democratic Revolution*. New Brunswick, N.J.: Rutgers University Press, 1964.
Betancourt, Rómulo. *Venezuela: Oil and Politics*. Boston: Houghton Mifflin, 1979.
Herman, Donald L. *Christian Democracy in Venezuela*. Chapel Hill: University of North Carolina Press, 1980.
Rivera Oviedo, J. E. *Los Social Cristianos en Venezuela*. Caracas: Ediciones Centauro, 1977.
Segal, Alicia Freilich de. *La Venedemocracia*. Caracas: Monte Avila Editores, 1978.
                                                                    ROBERT J. ALEXANDER

CALDERÓN GUARDIA, RAFAEL ANGEL (1900–1970), was president of Costa Rica during 1940–1944. The son of a prominent physician, he studied medicine at the University of Louvain in Belgium, where he experienced the influence of the advanced Social Catholic teachings of Cardinal Mercier. Upon his return to Costa Rica, he established a successful practice in pediatrics and earned a reputation for charitable works. Following an undistinguished term in the National Legislature, he was elevated to the presidency by the outgoing caudillo, León Cortés Castro,* who hoped he would be a puppet ruler.

To Cortés' chagrin, Calderón Guardia, with the support of progressive Archbishop Víctor Sanabria Martínez,* undertook basic reforms, including a labor code and social security system, and a revamping and expansion of education. He alienated the political right, but was unable to obtain the support of moderates and liberals because of his strong-arm and even fraudulent practices in imposing Teodoro Picado Michalski as his successor in 1944. His alliance with Communist Party chieftain Manuel Mora Valverde,* in 1942, despite the continued support of the archbishop, tended to reinforce Calderón's image as an extremist.

In 1948 Calderón again ran for president, and his attempt to annul the apparent victory of Otilio Ulate Blanco* led to the civil war of 1948 and the coming to power of José Figueres Ferrer.* Calderón fled to Nicaragua where, with the support of Anastasio Somoza García,* he led two unsuccessful attempts to invade Costa Rica, in 1948 and 1955. Calderón eventually returned to Costa Rica and undertook another unsuccessful campaign for the presidency in 1962.

BIBLIOGRAPHY

Aguilar Bulgarelli, Oscar R. *Costa Rica y sus hechos políticos de 1948*. San José: Editorial Costa Rica, 1969.
Ameringer, Charles D. *Don Pepe: A Political Biography of José Figueres of Costa Rica*. Albuquerque: University of New Mexico Press, 1979.
Bell, John Patrick. *Crisis in Costa Rica: The 1948 Revolution*. Austin: University of Texas Press, 1971.
Cañas, Alberto. *Los 8 Años*. San José: Editorial Liberación Nacional, 1955.
Mavis, Richard, and Karen Biesanz. *Los Costarricenses*. San José: Editorial Universidad Estatal a Distancia, 1979.

CHARLES D. AMERINGER

CALLES, PLUTARCO ELÍAS (1877–1945), was the Mexican president who dominated the nation longer than any other Revolutionary leader. Elected only to one four-year term, he later ran the government unofficially during the tenure of three interim presidents.

Born in 1877 in Guaymas, in the state of Sonora, Calles was a schoolteacher who became a Revolutionary general. After serving as governor of Sonora in 1917, he joined the cabinet of President Alvaro Obregón* as minister of internal affairs during 1920–1924.

Under the 1917 Constitution, the presidential term was four years with no reelection. Calles served his term during 1924–1928 and then yielded to the pressures of his benefactor and had the Constitution amended to allow a second term. Obregón won in 1928 but was assassinated before he could be inaugurated. The Constitution made no provision for a vice president but instead directed Congress to choose an interim head until a special election could be called. Congress quickly restored the prohibition against a second presidential term and lengthened the term to six years. During 1928–1934 three interim presidents served, and each was guided by Calles.

During the Calles decade, anticlericalism reduced church participation in politics to almost zero. Calles started the Bank of Agricultural Credit and the Bank of Mexico. He died in California in 1945.

BIBLIOGRAPHY

Briggs, Donald C., and Marvin Alisky. *Historical Dictionary of Mexico*. Metuchen, N.J.: Scarecrow Press, 1981.
Clark, Marjorie. *Organized Labor in Mexico*. Chapel Hill: University of North Carolina Press, 1934.
Djed Borquez. *Calles*. Mexico City: Editorial Mexico Nacional, 1923.
Dulles, John W. F. *Yesterday in Mexico: A Chronicle of the Revolution*. Austin: University of Texas Press, 1961.
León, Luis L. "El Presidente Calles." *Historia Mexicana* 10, No. 2 (October-December 1960).

MARVIN ALISKY

CAMACHO, ELIODORO (1831–1899), founder of the Bolivian Liberal Party, was educated at the Colegio San Calixto in La Paz. He joined the army, led a revolt against President Hilarión Daza, and was named brigadier general by the new president, Narciso Campero. Camacho represented the war party opposing territorial concessions to Chilean claims to Bolivia's coastal provinces. When the War of the Pacific broke out, he became a hero of the campaign.

After the war, Camacho founded the Liberal Party in 1884, which attracted many disillusioned war veterans. He ran unsuccessfully for president in 1884 and 1888. Feeling defrauded by these rigged elections, in October 1888 the Liberals revolted under his leadership. They failed, and Camacho was forced to flee to Peru. He masterminded two other unsuccessful revolts in May 1890 and August 1892. The Liberals were finally successful in the 1898 federal revolution led by General José Manuel Pando.* As a loyal Liberal, Camacho was promoted to division general by the new Pando government.

BIBLIOGRAPHY

Arguedas, Alcides. *Historia General de Bolivia (El Proceso de la Nacionalidad), 1809–1921*. Vol. 6. La Paz: Arno Hnos., 1922.
Díaz Arguedas, Julio. *Los generales de Bolivia*. La Paz: Imprenta Intendencia General de Guerra, 1929.
Fellman Velarde José. *Historia de Bolivia*. 2d ed. Vol. 2. La Paz: Los Amigos del Libro, 1981.
Finot, Enrique. *Nueva Historia de Bolivia (Ensayo de Interpretación Sociológica*. 2d ed. La Paz: Gisbert, 1954.

Partido Liberal. *La Política Liberal, formulada por el Jefe del Partido, Eliodoro Camacho*. Nueva Edición. La Paz: Imprenta Andina, 1916.

WALTRAUD QUEISER MORALES

CÁMPORA, HÉCTOR JOSÉ (1909–1980), a long-time Peronist militant, served briefly as president of Argentina before stepping down so that Juan Domingo Perón* himself could be reelected to that office. Born in Buenos Aires Province, the son of Italian immigrants, Cámpora was a leader in student politics. In 1944, while practicing dentistry, he was elected to a municipal office in Buenos Aires Province, as a Peronist supporter. He was elected as a Peronist to the national Chamber of Deputies in 1946 and was its president from 1948 to 1953.

When Perón was ousted in the 1955 coup, Cámpora was imprisoned by the Pedro Eugenio Aramburu* government. He escaped and fled the country, returning to Argentina in 1960. In 1965, with Arturo Umberto Illia's* People's Radical Party government in power, Cámpora again won election to municipal office.

Thereafter, Cámpora served as Perón's liaison to various factions and personalities within the Peronist movement inside Argentina. The movement was divided into political and trade union branches, with each branch further fragmented by contending leaders. Cámpora's work on Perón's behalf was extremely delicate and difficult, compounded by the rise of guerrilla groups, some of which proclaimed themselves Peronists.

Cámpora was chosen as presidential candidate in 1973 of the pro-Peronist coalition Frejuli, although his candidacy was opposed by some labor bureaucrats. He was declared elected.

Some of the policies Cámpora inaugurated as president were more radical and nationalistic than those favored by Perón. Within less than two months of taking office on May 25, Cámpora and his vice president resigned to allow new elections. Perón was elected to the presidency, with his wife, Isabelita* as vice president.

Although Cámpora remained loyal to Perón, Perón was upset with Cámpora's relationship with the more radical part of the Peronist movement. Following his resignation, Cámpora was appointed ambassador to Mexico and served as a spokesman for the more leftist factions of Peronism, particularly after Perón's death in 1974. He returned to Argentina in 1976 and escaped the coup by taking asylum in the Mexican Embassy until 1979, when he was released. He died in Mexico.

BIBLIOGRAPHY

Hodges, Donald C. *Argentina, 1943–1976: The National Revolution and Resistance*. Albuquerque: University of New Mexico Press, 1976.
Snow, Peter G. *Political Forces in Argentina*. New York: Praeger, 1979.
Sobel, Lester A. (ed.). *Argentina and Peron—1970–75*. New York: Facts on File, 1975.

Whitaker, Arthur P. *The United States and the Southern Cone*. Cambridge, Mass.: Harvard University Press, 1976.
Wynia, Gary W. *Argentina in the Postwar Era: Politics and Economic Policy Making in a Divided Society*. Albuquerque: University of New Mexico Press, 1978.
                                                                        JOHN T. DEINER

CAPILDEO, RUDRANATH (1920–1970), was leader of the major opposition party in Trinidad and Tobago between 1960 and 1969. Primarily a scholar and lawyer, he entered politics very late in life, being coopted as a counterforce to Dr. Eric Williams.* He won an island scholarship to London University in 1938, returned to Trinidad in 1945 with a master's degree in mathematics, and taught at Queens Royal College, Trinidad's leading high school. Capildeo returned to London University in 1946 to work on his Ph.D., which he obtained in 1950. After studying for the bar, he returned to Trinidad to practice law and be principal of the Trinidad Polytechnic.

Capildeo's academic achievements and personal prominence appeared excellent credentials for a political career, since Eric Williams' success in leading his Peoples National Movement (PNM) to electoral victory appeared to be based on precisely the same qualities. In 1958 the Democratic Labor Party (DLP) was formed out of a loose amalgam of groups associated preeminently with the Trinidadian business community and the East Indian population. Its de facto leader was an uneducated Hindu, Bhadase Sagan Maraj,* who was extremely popular among the East Indian lower classes but an embarrassment to middle-class opponents of the PNM. Capildeo, identified as "Trinidad's most educated man," seemed a perfect choice for leader of the DLP. He reluctantly accepted the position, although extremely conscious of his political inexperience.

Despite failing health and tremendous political naïveté, Capildeo managed to hold the DLP together and maintain its credibility as an opposition to the PNM. Although suffering a bad defeat in the elections of 1961, the DLP began to concentrate on issues of constitutional safeguards, which were important in view of the racially charged political atmosphere. The DLP had come to be identified with the East Indian community and the PNM with the Trinidadian population that was of African origin.

At the Independence Conference in London, the DLP delegation emphasized its concern about these issues. Although DLP proposals were rejected, Capildeo and Eric Williams agreed to a compromise which, in the eyes of some, averted a racial crisis and assured constitutional safeguards in post-independence Trinidad and Tobago.

By the time of the Independence Conference, Capildeo's health was deteriorating. In addition, his political goodwill within the DLP was almost exhausted by his frequent absences from Trinidad. An attempt to foist the ideology of democratic socialism on the party led to considerable defection, particularly among conservative white businessmen who had been its staunch supporters. Nonetheless, Capildeo continued to lead the DLP while holding an academic post in London, returning only for electioneering, until he was removed from party leadership in 1969.

BIBLIOGRAPHY

Brereton, Bridget. *A History of Modern Trinidad 1783–1962*. Port of Spain: Heinemann, 1981.
Ince, Basil. "Politics Before the Peoples' National Movement: A Study of Parties and Elections in British Trinidad." PhD. diss., New York University, 1966.
Malik, Y. K. *East Indians in Trinidad*. London: Oxford University Press, 1971.
Oxaal, Ivar. *Black Intellectuals Come to Power*. Cambridge, Mass.: Schenkman, 1968.
Ryan, Selwyn. *Race and Nationalism in Trinidad and Tobago*. Toronto: University of Toronto Press, 1972.

                                            PERCY C. HINTZEN AND W. MARVIN WILL

CARAZO ODIO, RODRIGO (1926–   ), was president of Costa Rica from 1978 to 1982. As protegé of José Figueres Ferrer,* he served during Figueres' 1953–1958 presidency as director of the new National Institute of Housing and Urban Development. Subsequently, he spent much of the 1960s as a businessman in Venezuela and as Figueres' personal contact with Democratic Action Party leaders in Caracas. He returned to Costa Rica in 1966 to seek the National Liberation Party (PLN) nomination in 1970, but he encountered Figueres' own determination to return to the presidency. His spirited but unsuccessful challenge resulted in his being virtually driven from the party.

In 1974 Carazo was defeated by the PLN nominee, Daniel Oduber Quiros,* but in 1978, capitalizing on charges of corruption and inefficiency in the Oduber presidency, he led the Unity coalition to victory. As president, however, he failed to develop a coherent economic program and to deal with bureaucratic waste and corruption. Carazo's popularity plunged, and in 1982 Luis Alberto Monge,* the PLN candidate whom Carazo had beaten in 1978, was the victor.

BIBLIOGRAPHY

Ameringer, Charles D. *Democracy in Costa Rica*. New York: Praeger, 1982.
———. *Don Pepe: A Political Biography of José Figueres of Costa Rica*. Albuquerque: University of New Mexico Press, 1979.

                                                    CHARLES D. AMERINGER

CÁRDENAS, LÁZARO (1895–1970), became the prototype reforming president of Mexico of the Revolutionary era. He expropriated the oil companies in 1938 and the railroads in 1937, created the Mexican Federation of Labor and the National Campesino Federation in 1936, and distributed more land to landless peasants than any previous chief executive.

Cárdenas was born in Jiquilpán in the state of Michoacán. After primary school, he worked in a printing plant, then the local jail as a custodian, and later as a clerk.

In July 1913 Cárdenas joined the revolutionary army in Apatzingán, as a lieutenant, and in September was promoted to captain, the youngest company commander in the entire rebel brigade. He fought against rival insurgent factions commanded by Emiliano Zapata* and Pancho Villa.*

Cárdenas became governor of his native state of Michoacán for the first time in June 1920. As a brigadier general, he helped put down the rebellion led by Adolfo de la Huerta in 1923. Then he became commander of the forces in Michoacán and Oaxaca and was promoted to the rank of major general on April 1, 1928. Former President Plutarco Elías Calles* chose Cárdenas as field commander of the army to quash the rebellion of 1929, the last serious military challenge to the Revolutionary establishment.

Cárdenas was again elected governor of Michoacán on September 15, 1928. His army command assignment in 1929 to put down an insurrection came after the state legislature voted him a leave of absence.

As governor, Cárdenas distributed unused lands to peasant farmers. He displayed anticlericalism by limiting the number of priests within the state and by warning priests not to appear outside their churches in clerical garb.

Cárdenas took a second leave of absence as governor to lead an army division against the Cristeros, a right-wing group of pro-clericals. After brief service as minister of internal affairs, he was minister of defense from January 1 to May 15, 1933.

On December 6, 1933, Cárdenas was nominated as the Revolutionary Party's presidential candidate. In a nationwide campaign, visiting hundreds of cities and towns, he had the most elaborate campaign activity seen in Mexico up to that time.

Once inaugurated on December 1, 1934, Cárdenas supported every labor union on strike or threatening to strike, regardless of what company or industry was involved. He angered his benefactor, former President Calles, by supporting the telephone workers' strike, knowing that Calles was a major stockholder in the telephone company. Only 39 years old when he took office, Mexico's youngest president in this century, he put in ten-hour workdays and would rush to troublespots in provincial areas.

Cárdenas stressed the need to carry out provisions of Article 27 of the Constitution on land reform. He distributed unused land and expropriated large estates to villages as communal farms (*ejidos*).

In 1936 the president convened the founding session of the National Campesino Federation (CNC) as the bargaining entity for rural workers and as the political voice for peasant farmers. Also in 1936 Cárdenas personally helped found the Mexican Federation of Labor (the Confederación de Trabajadores de México, CTM).

In 1938 Cárdenas urged employees of the foreign-owned oil companies to strike for higher wages. Oil company managers would not agree to the terms demanded, and on March 18, 1938, Cárdenas expropriated the petroleum industry. He then created Petroleos Mexicanos, or Pemex, which became the prototype for similar public corporations to run national petroleum industries in developing nations. Although Pemex managed all drilling, exploration, and refining of petroleum, retail service stations throughout Mexico were leased by the government corporation to Mexican private citizens or companies.

Cárdenas also expropriated the railroad lines owned by Southern Pacific, Missouri Pacific, and Missouri-Kansas-Texas corporations. Payment for these came in a relatively friendly series of negotiations, but payment to the expropriated foreign oil companies proved to be difficult and Mexico did not finally begin to make payments to the foreign companies until 1941. The last quarterly payment was made in 1951.

Cárdenas also changed the dominant political party, established in 1929 by President Calles as the National Revolutionary Party, as the Party of the Mexican Revolution on a broader basis. The four sectors of the revised party represented peasant-farmers (*campesinos*), labor unions, the army, and a "popular" category for bureaucrats and all others not easily classified in the first three groups.

In his later years, Cárdenas remained active, first as director of the Río Balsas Commission, controlling the flood waters of a river in his beloved state of Michoacán. He got three different administrations to complete hydroelectric dam projects along the Balsas, insuring Michoacán irrigated farming as well as electric energy for new industries.

In 1969 President Gustavo Díaz Ordaz* asked the old general to become head of the Las Truchas Steel Complex Commission in order to plan for a gigantic government steel and iron complex in Michoacán. The former president saw his last big pet project begin before he died on October 19, 1970.

BIBLIOGRAPHY

Ashby, Joe C. *Organized Labor and the Mexican Revolution Under Cárdenas*. Chapel Hill: University of North Carolina Press, 1963.
Brandenburg, Frank R. *The Making of Modern Mexico*. Englewood Cliffs, N.J.: Prentice-Hall, 1964.
Correa, Eduardo J. *El Balance de Cardenismo*. Mexico City: Editorial Acción, 1941.
Munoz, Hilda. *Lázaro Cárdenas*. Mexico City: Fondo de Cultura Económica, 1976.
Townsend, William C. *Lázaro Cárdenas*. Ann Arbor, Mich.: George Wahr Publishing Co., 1952.

MARVIN ALISKY

CARÍAS ANDINO, TIBURCIO (1876–1960), established a period of Honduran National Party ascendance in 1932 which, except for one interlude under Ramón Villeda Morales* (1957–1963), continued until the inauguration of Roberto Suazo Córdova in 1982.

Carías began as a supporter of Manuel Bonilla* who created a coalition of dissatisfied Liberals and Conservatives to seize power when Terencio Sierra refused to support him as his successor in the presidency in 1903. Carías held several posts under President Bonilla.

After two decades of factional disputes among the Liberals and their opponents during which he spent several periods of exile, Carías emerged as leader of the Conservative Nationalists, the former Bonillista group, and won a plurality in the 1923 elections. Congress adjourned without choosing a successor to President Rafael López Gutiérrez who, influenced by American Ambassador Franklin Morales, proclaimed himself dictator. After 40 days of fighting in which the U.S. government withdrew recognition of López Gutiérrez and United Fruit Company donated an airplane to the Nationalist leader, Carías was victorious. But the State Department informed Carías that he could not be president under any circumstance. General Vicente Tosta was installed as provisional president while elections were scheduled within 30 days.

Although General Carías rose in revolt and gained control of Tegucigalpa and the rest of the countryside, in the face of U.S. opposition, Carías withdrew, supporting Dr. Miguel Paz Barahona, who had been his running mate in the 1923 elections. Dr. Vicente Mejía Colindres defeated Carías in the 1928 elections. Carías, then president of Congress, rejected pleas to revolt and called for support of the new government, which increased his popularity. The United Fruit Company increased support for Carías to protect its interests since Samuel Zemurray and his Cuyamel Fruit Company were backing Liberal candidates. Finally, Carías won by a 20,000-vote margin over Angel Zúñiga Hueste of the Liberal Party in the 1932 elections.

Carías quashed three uprisings by Liberals in 1932, 1935, and 1936, respectively. The Nationalist-dominated Congress extended his term of office in March 1936 and again in December 1939 to December 31, 1948.

Carías' government carried out extensive highway construction. In 1942 his Ministry of Public Health and Social Assistance began an attack on malaria, intestinal, and diarrhetic diseases with help from the Pan American Sanitary Bureau and other international organizations. In 1945 his government began to attack illiteracy, which was then estimated at 70 percent of the population over age ten.

Although Carías contributed political stability to a country torn frequently by civil war since the 1880s, it was achieved at the cost of civil liberties, elimination of national and municipal elections, and restrictions of political activity and freedom of the press. Only the official National Party paper, *La Época*, was allowed to survive.

In 1948 Carías turned over the presidency to a hand-picked successor, Juan Manuel Gálvez Durón.* He subsequently sought to return to office on several occasions, but his efforts proved unsuccessful.

BIBLIOGRAPHY

Beals, Carleton. *Banana Gold*. Philadelphia and London: J. B. Lippincott, 1932.
Durón, Rómulo E. *Bosquejo Histórico de Honduras, 1502 a 1921*. San Pedro Sula: Tipografía del Comercio, 1927.

Morris, James A. *Honduras, Caudillo Politics and Military Rulers.* Boulder, Colo.: Westview Press, 1984.
Pearson, Neale J. "Delivery of Services in Rural Areas of Honduras: Institutions and Problems." *Rural Public Services: International Comparisons.* Boulder, Colo.: Westview Press, 1984.
Stokes, William S. *Honduras, An Area Study in Government.* Madison: University of Wisconsin Press, 1950.

NEALE J. PEARSON

CARO, MIGUEL ANTONIO (1843–1909), acting president and president of Colombia (1892–1898), was the principal author of the country's longstanding constitution of 1886. He was born in Bogotá, the son of José Eusebio Caro, Colombia's famed romantic poet, and was strongly influenced by the staunch conservatism of his father. His education in the rigorous Jesuit tradition undoubtedly contributed to the making of his rigid character and political views.

While in his early twenties, Caro became a firm upholder in the Conservative press of the traditional values of hierarchy, order, and authority. He directed the newspaper *El Tradicionalista* in the early and mid–1870s, and advocated the establishment of a strong, centralized state governed by conservative Catholic political principles.

Caro put his ideas into practice when Congress commissioned him to draft a new constitution. This Constitution of 1886 established a unitarian republic, a strong executive with wide-ranging powers, and recognized Roman Catholicism as the religion of the nation, while also giving the church an important role in the social order.

Caro was elected vice president in 1892, at the beginning of what would be the final administration of Rafael Núñez Muledo.* Since Núñez chose not to rule directly, Caro exercised executive power in Núñez' absence. The situation encouraged Núñez' political opponents within the Conservative Party. When the Liberals, excluded from political power, increased their vocal opposition to the government, Caro reacted with repressive measures, closing several Liberal newspapers and imprisoning and exiling opposition leaders. Early in 1895 the Liberals rebelled. Although this uprising was crushed and the Conservative division temporarily overcome, Caro maintained the armed forces at a high level owing to what he called "the danger to which society is exposed." His continuing political intransigence and the strain on the national budget contributed to the unstable political atmosphere that culminated in the War of the Thousand Days (1899–1902).

In addition to the Constitution of 1886, Caro's most notable contribution to the national culture was in the field of letters. In 1870 he was one of the founding members of the Colombian Academy. Later, his contributions to the study of the Spanish language were rewarded with election to the Royal Spanish Academy.

BIBLIOGRAPHY

Fals Borda, Orlando. *Subversion and Social Change in Colombia.* New York: Columbia University Press, 1969.

Henao, Jesús María, and Gerlado Arrubia. *History of Colombia*. Chapel Hill: University of North Carolina Press, 1938.
López de Mesa, Luis. *Escrutinio sociológico de la historia colombiana*. Bogotá: 1956.
Torres García, Guillermo. *Miguel Antonio Caro: su personalidad política*. Madrid: Ediciones Guadarrama, 1956.

RICHARD E. SHARPLESS

CARRANZA, VENUSTIANO (1859–1920), the legalizer of the Mexican Revolution, was the only revolutionary leader with experience in lawmaking, public administration, and diplomacy, as contrasted with the self-made generals who rose to power after 1910. Only Francisco I. Madero* among the makers of the revolution had a similar upper class background and higher education. Yet Madero lacked the experience in administration which allowed Carranza to solidify his authority in contrast to Madero's wobbly temporary hold on the presidency.

Carranza was born in the state of Coahuila into a wealthy landowning family. After managing a cattle ranch, he served in the federal Senate in Mexico City and then returned to the city of Saltillo as governor of his native state of Coahuila. In 1911 he denounced Porfirio Díaz* and became an ally of Madero. When General Victoriano Huerta* murdered President Madero in 1913, Carranza immediately announced that he and his followers would never acknowledge Huerta as the new president, and he called for a national uprising.

With the overthrow of Huerta, in 1914 Carranza took the title of First Chief of the Constitutionalist Army, rejecting the alternate title of provisional president. He tried to negotiate with Generals Pancho Villa* and Emiliano Zapata* in order to forge unity among revolutionary forces. The effort failed, and the Constitutionalists had to fight the forces of both rival generals.

By 1916 Carranza had been accepted as provisional president throughout most of Mexico. He ordered an election of a constitutional convention, which convened in December in Queretaro and promulgated the current federal constitution in February 1917.

The 1917 Constitution broke radically from Mexico's past. Carranza, a moderate, had expected change but not to the extent that resulted. Article 27 on land reform separated surface ownership from subsoil riches and proclaimed that minerals belonged to the Mexican nation. Article 123, lengthy and filled with the rights of organized workers, was the *Magna Carta* of Mexican labor unions, guaranteeing the right to strike, overtime pay, an 8-hour day, and maternity leave for women who were unionized.

In May 1920, when a new insurrection erupted, troops from the state of Sonora loyal to General Alvaro Obregón* captured Mexico City. Carranza fled to Puebla and was murdered there.

BIBLIOGRAPHY

Benson, Nettie Lee. "The Preconstitutional Regime of Venustiano Carranza, 1913–1917." M.A. thesis, University of Texas, 1936.

Cumberland, Charles C. *The Mexican Revolution—The Constitutionalist Years.* Austin: University of Texas Press, 1972.

Quirk, Robert E. *The Mexican Revolution, 1914–1915.* Bloomington: University of Indiana Press, 1960.

Richmond, Douglas W. *Venustiano Carranza's Nationalist Struggle, 1893–1920.* Lincoln: University of Nebraska Press, 1983.

                                                              MARVIN ALISKY

CARRERA, RAFAEL (1814–1865), controlled the government of Guatemala for 26 years (1839–1865) and established the prototype of the caudillos who ruled Guatemala for the next 100 years. Born of Indian parents in a Guatemala City slum, Carrera had no formal education and never attained functional literacy. After a series of menial jobs, he enlisted in the Guatemalan Army in 1828.

Nine years later, Carrera emerged as leader of a peasant revolt in the northern provinces. His style of personal leadership and courage in combat won him the loyalty of the peasants, mobilized for the first time. However, when the peasant army stormed into Guatemala City in 1838, Carrera was content to allow Liberal politicians to form a new government which promised to respond to the demands of the Indian population.

Conservative leaders—rural property holders and church officials, in particular—soon convinced Carrera that the Liberals had lied to him in order to retain power. Carrera reactivated his forces and again attacked the capital. The Liberals called for assistance from the head of the Central American Federation, Francisco Morazán,* who, with a force of 1,000 Salvadoran soldiers, anticipated easy victory but was totally defeated in March 1840.

Following the victory, Carrera (who had endorsed their ideals of traditional elitism and a strong, politically involved Catholic Church but had also led Indian peasants in a campaign against the Guatemalan rural aristocracy) gradually allowed the old Conservative elite to resume its privileges. His government effected some reforms that benefited the masses, but Carrera himself accumulated vast wealth and power, and the Indians dejectedly retreated to their villages.

Liberals were ruthlessly suppressed, and Carrera exacted strict obedience and adulation, creating a "cult of personality." There was little ideological content to his tactics; he would occasionally threaten to bring back the Liberals if the Conservatives did not provide absolute support. The Liberals did in fact unseat Carrera briefly in 1848, but he returned to power after a few months.

A new constitution in 1851 returned Guatemala to a system of oligarchical control by the educated *latifundistas*, merchants, and the church. Congress elected Carrera President for Life in 1854.

Carrera's one lasting legacy was the intense state nationalism pervasive in Central America. The Central American Federation was associated with Morazán and the Liberals, so Carrera supported successful rebellions in El Salvador, Nicaragua, and Honduras against the Central American Federation, with Conservative forces prevailing in each country.

BIBLIOGRAPHY

Karnes, T. L. *Failure of Union: Central America 1824–1975*. Tempe: Arizona State University Press, 1975.
Marroquín Rojas, Clemente. *Francisco Morazán y Rafael Carrera*. Guatemala City: 1965.
Rodríguez, Mario. *Central America*. Englewood Cliffs, N.J.: Prentice-Hall, 1965.
Tobar Cruz, Pedro. *Los Montañeses*, 2 vols. Guatemala City: 1971.
Woodward, Ralph Lee, Jr. *Central America: A Nation Divided*. New York: 1985.

JOSÉ M. SÁNCHEZ

CARRERA VERDUGO, JOSÉ MIGUEL (1785–1821), was one of the two principal Chilean military leaders of the struggle for independence. As a youth, he was sent by his father to Spain, where he came to know the young Argentine captain in the Spanish Army, José de San Martín.* In September 1808 Carrera himself joined the Spanish Army and fought against the Napoleonic armies. He returned to Chile on July 25, 1811.

On September 4 of that year Carrera led a military coup against the government junta then controlling Chile, forcing reorganization of Congress and establishment of another government junta. However, on November 15, after a further coup, he himself became a member of a new government junta together with Bernardo O'Higgins* and Gaspar Marín and Congress was dissolved. When O'Higgins and Marín resigned shortly afterward, Carrera was left in complete charge of the government.

During Carrera's government, Chile established diplomatic relations with the United States, a national flag and coat-of-arms were adopted, and the Constitution of 1812 was ratified by Congress. Several new primary schools as well as the first secondary school, the Instituto Nacional, and the first public library were established, as was a government daily newspaper, *La Aurora de Chile*.

In March 1813 Carrera was named general-in-chief to face an invasion of Spanish troops. With his defeat at the siege of Chillán in August 1813, the government junta then in charge ordered his replacement by Bernardo O'Higgins. Carrera resisted, provoking a deep enmity between the two men.

Carrera returned to Santiago, carried through a coup d'état, and again took power. O'Higgins thereupon marched on the capital from the South. When news was received of the arrival of a new Spanish expedition from Peru, O'Higgins recognized the government of Carrera and turned over the post of commander-in-chief of the army to him.

On October 1 and 2, 1814, Chilean forces suffered a disastrous defeat at the Battle of Rancagua. Spanish power was restored in the country for almost two and a half years, and all independence leaders had to flee, most of them going to Mendoza, Argentina.

José Miguel Carrera and his two brothers were coolly received by the governor of Mendoza, José de San Martín, in contrast to the warm welcome of O'Higgins. Ordered to leave the Mendoza region, the Carreras went to Buenos Aires. In November 1815 José Miguel Carrera left for the United States, where he acquired two small warships. He returned to Buenos Aires in February 1817 and again quarreled bitterly with San Martín, who had just returned from his own and O'Higgins' decisive victory over the Spaniards in the Battle of Chacabuco which assured Chile's independence.

Carrera then moved to Montevideo. There he published a newspaper and carried on vehement polemics against San Martín and Bernardo O'Higgins. He finally organized an invasion of Argentina and was captured near the city of San Juan. Taken to Mendoza, he was tried and condemned to death on September 3, 1821, the sentence being executed on the following day.

BIBLIOGRAPHY

Cortes, Lia, and Jordi Fuentes. *Diccionario Político de Chile*. Santiago: Editorial Orbe, 1967.
Enciclopedia Universal Ilustrada Europeo-Americana. Barcelona: José Espasa e Hijos.
Galdames, Luis. *Historia de Chile*. Santiago: Editorial Zig Zag, 1945.
                                                          ROBERT J. ALEXANDER

CARRILLO COLINA, BRAULIO (1800–1845), was the first president of Costa Rica. He had been governor of the Costa Rican province in 1835–1837, but during his second term, 1838–1842, he led Costa Rica's secession from the Central American Federation. He encountered stiff opposition, ranging from the traditional elites who regarded independence as a threat to their privileged position, to the peasants who preferred colonial rule because it was remote and unintrusive. Although described as liberal and progressive, Carrillo used frankly dictatorial methods. He established San José as the capital, and leaders of Cartago, Heredia, and Alajuela, who had been used to sharing power, had to be put down by force.

Carrillo did away with the *diezmo* (a 10 percent tax on income and goods to support the church). However, when he declared himself President for Life in 1841, he alienated even the Liberals who had supported his policies. He was overthrown in 1842 by a coalition under the leadership of the former president of the Central American Federation, Francisco Morazán.* Carrillo fled to El Salvador, where he was subsequently murdered.

BIBLIOGRAPHY

Barahona Jiménez, Luis. *El pensamiento político en Costa Rica*. San José: Editorial Fernández-Arce, 1971.
Monge, Carlos. *Historia de Costa Rica*. San José: Editorial Fondo de Cultura de Costa Rica, 1948.
                                                          CHARLES D. AMERINGER

CASTELO BRANCO, HUMBERTO (1897–1967), was the first military president to govern Brazil after the 1964 revolution. He was born in Fortaleza, Ceará, in the northeast, son of an army officer, and entered a military academy in Porto Alegre in 1912. In 1918 he was accepted at the military school at Realengo, attaining the position of second lieutenant in 1921. He returned as an instructor in 1927 after having fought the Luis Carlos Prestes* Column in Mato Grosso and Bahia. When the 1930 revolution broke out, he remained loyal to the government but suffered no punishment.

Promoted to captain in 1932, he was assistant director of the Realengo Military School and liaison to the French military mission. In 1940, as a major, he became assistant to the minister of war, Eurico Dutra.

When Brazil declared war on Germany in August 1942, preparations began for the Brazilian Expeditionary Force to go overseas, and many officers were sent to the United States for specialized training. Castelo Branco attended the Command and General Staff School at Fort Leavenworth. In 1943 he became lieutenant colonel and was sent to Italy in July 1944, where he was made a colonel in 1945. He became brigadier general in 1952. As the pressure against President Getúlio Vargas* mounted in 1954, Castelo Branco signed the Generals' Manifesto of August 23 requesting Vargas to resign. After Vargas committed suicide, Castelo Branco served on the general staff of the army.

In the early 1960s Castelo Branco became leading spokesman for the military protesting against the political unrest caused by President João Belchior Marques Goulart's* populist appeals. On March 31, 1964, a skillfully coordinated and popular military movement headed by General Castelo Branco and General Costa e Silva overthrew Goulart. On April 11, 1964, Congress elected Castelo Branco president. He took over on April 15 and ushered in an unprecedented 20 years of military control of Brazil's presidency.

In his first few months Castelo Branco was concerned primarily with stabilizing the economy. He created the powerful office of Minister of Economic Planning to which he appointed Roberto Campos.

The *linhea dura* (hard line) within the military maintained pressure on President Castelo Branco to remove the political rights of many leading politicians. Bowing to this pressure, Castelo Branco stripped three former presidents, Jânio Quadros,* João Goulart*, and Juscelino Kubitschek de Oliveira,* as well as 70 other politicians, of their political rights. Congress, upon the urging of the military, extended Castelo's term for a year to March 15, 1967.

State elections in October 1965 repudiated military control, and *linhea dura* officers urged Castelo Branco to save the revolution by issuing Institutional Act No. 2 of October 27. This law wiped out all existing political parties, proscribed more politicians, and altered the Supreme Court.

Early in 1966 another decree law issued by Castelo Branco called for indirect election of the president. In October 1966, with no opposition candidate, General Artur da Costa e Silva was ''elected'' by the Brazilian Congress and assumed the presidency on March 15, 1967.

After leaving office, Castelo Branco withdrew from public life. He died tragically in an airplane crash in Fortaleza, Ceará.

BIBLIOGRAPHY

Dulles, John W. F. *Castelo Branco: The Making of a Brazilian President*. College Station: Texas A & M Press, 1978.
————. *President Castelo Branco: Brazilian Reformer*. College Station: Texas A & M Press, 1980.
Ianni, Octavio. *Crisis in Brazil*. New York: Columbia University Press, 1970.
New York Times, July 19, 1967.
Viana Filho, Luis. *O Governo Castelo Branco*. 1975.

JORDAN YOUNG

CASTILLA, RAMÓN (1797–1867), president of Peru (1845–1851 and 1854–1862), was born in Tarapacá. He first joined the Spanish Army in Chile and fought against the patriot forces in Chacabuco (1817) and Cerro de Pasco (1820). After being captured by the victorious forces of José de San Martín,* he joined them. After independence, he participated in the civil wars, constantly changing allegiance. He joined two Chilean expeditionary forces that dissolved the Peru-Bolivian Confederation (1838–1839), in recognition of which he was promoted to division general.

Several important events took place during Castilla's tenure as president: a Latin American Congress met in Lima in 1847, and Indian tribute and black slavery were abolished. After leaving office, he was elected senator and president of the Senate. For conspiring against the government, he was deported. While exiled in Chile, he joined a military rebellion to overthrow Peruvian President Mariano Ignacio Prado, but he died on route to Lima.

BIBLIOGRAPHY

Alisky, Marvin. *Historical Dictionary of Peru*. Metuchen, N.J.: Scarecrow Press, 1979.
Pike, Frederick B. *The Modern History of Peru*. New York: Praeger, 1967.
Tauro, Alberto. *Diccionario enciclopédico del Peru*. Lima: Editorial Mejía Baca, 1966.

EUGENIO CHANG-RODRÍGUEZ

CASTILLO, LUCIANO (1896–1980), co-founder of a Socialist Party of Peru (1930), was born in Piura. He studied law at the University of Trujillo until he was expelled for political activities. He transferred to the National University of San Marcos, where he became president of the National Federation of Students. He graduated with a bachelor of laws degree in 1927. As a member of the Executive Committee of the Peruvian Socialist Party founded by José Carlos Mariátegui* in 1928, Castillo opposed its conversion into the Communist Party. When the conversion occurred in 1930, after Mariátegui's death, he resigned and founded his own Socialist Party, which elected him to the Constituent Assemblies of 1931 and 1978, to the Chamber of Deputies in 1945, and to the Senate in 1956 and 1963.

Castillo was his party's candidate for president in 1956, 1962, 1963, and 1980. While exiled in Mexico, he taught at the National University of Mexico, and upon his return to Lima taught political economy at San Marcos. He died shortly after losing the national elections of 1980.

BIBLIOGRAPHY

Chang-Rodríguez, Eugenio. *Opciones políticas peruanas*. Lima: Centro de Documentación Andina, 1985.
Martínez de la Torre, Ricardo. *Apuntes para una interpretación marxista de historia social del Peru*. Lima: Empresa Editorial Peruana, 1947–1949.
Tauro, Alberto. *Diccionario enciclopédico del Peru*. Lima: Editorial Mejía Baca, 1966.

EUGENIO CHANG-RODRÍGUEZ

CASTILLO ARMAS, CARLOS (1914–1957), became leader of Guatemala through an invasion organized and funded by the Central Intelligence Agency (CIA) in 1954. A man of humble origins, he was a colonel in the Guatemalan Army in 1950 when the assassination of Colonel Javier Arana apparently convinced him of then-President Juan José Arévalo Bermejo's* Communism. Arana was the leading opponent of Arévalo's hand-picked successor, Jacobo Arbenz Guzman,* and the murder was widely believed to have been instigated by leftist elements. Castillo Armas attempted an unsuccessful coup before the 1950 elections, spent some time in prison, and then left Guatemala.

In Honduras, Castillo Armas was approached by the Central Intelligence Agency, then organizing an exile army to invade Guatemala and overthrow the Arbenz government. In May 1954 Castillo Armas led a ragtag, but fairly well-equipped, force of some 500 men into Guatemala. Thanks to air raids by American pilots and to the reluctance of the Guatemalan armed forces to support Arbenz, the government collapsed.

Castillo Armas dismantled Arbenz' reforms. Land that had been expropriated and distributed to Indian peasants was returned to its former owners. The United States, anxious to prove the wisdom of its intervention, poured money into Guatemala—$80 million in the three years of Castillo Armas' rule. Few of these funds reached the country's poor. Castillo Armas disbanded all political parties. He attempted to legitimize his rule through oral plebiscite, without a secret, written ballot. With no one opposing him, Castillo Armas was "elected" president and welcomed to the United States as such.

Numerous scandals and several attempted coups characterized the Castillo Armas years. The "Liberator," as he had designated himself, had to declare a state of siege and intensify repressive measures. Unemployment was rife despite the government's persistent anti-unionism. The members of the oligarchy and foreign investors were content to recoup their losses rather than stimulate the economy.

In 1957 a member of Castillo Armas' palace guard shot him at close range and then committed suicide.

BIBLIOGRAPHY

Cardoza y Aragón, Luis. *La Revolución Guatemalteca*. Mexico City: Ediciones Cuadernos Americanos, 1955.

Immerman, Richard H. *The CIA in Guatemala*. Austin: University of Texas Press, 1982.
Melville, Thomas, and Marjorie Melville. *Guatemala: The Politics of Land Ownership*. New York: 1971.
Schlesinger, Stephen, and Stephen Kinzer. *Bitter Fruit: The Untold Story of the American Coup in Guatemala*. Garden City, N.Y.: Doubleday, 1982.
Woodward, Ralph Lee. *Central America: A Nation Divided*. New York: 1985.
JOSÉ M. SÁNCHEZ

CASTRO, CIPRIANO (1858–1924), was the next to the last of the caudillos who dominated Venezuelan public life for a century and a quarter after independence. He began his political career in the mid–1880s as a conservative supporter of the movement headed by José Manuel Hernández* which led to the founding of the Liberal Nationalist Party. He became a member of the Chamber of Deputies in 1890.

In the mid–1890s Castro was driven into exile in Colombia. There he formed a close alliance with another politico-military leader from the state of Táchira, Juan Vicente Gómez.* Finally, on May 23, 1899, forces led by Castro and Gómez invaded Táchira from Colombia to start the "Restoring Liberal Revolution." By October 1899 Cipriano Castro was president of Venezuela.

Many who had at first supported Castro soon turned against him. José Manuel Hernández, after serving only six days in his cabinet, left Caracas, revolted, and was quickly defeated. The business community of Caracas was outraged when Castro jailed most of the city's leading bankers when they refused to give his government a forced loan. General Manuel Antonio Matos organized a revolt of all those opposed to Castro. He was one of the bankers whom Castro had jailed and was a brother-in-law of Antonio Guzmán Blanco.* His so-called Liberating Revolution broke out in April 1902 with the support of virtually all of the old-style caudillos from the llanos and the coastal regions who had dominated national politics since before the Federal Wars of 1859–1863. It took the Castro forces, led by Juan Vicente Gómez, more than a year to completely liquidate the uprising. This was the last really serious effort of the old caudillos to overthrow the Venezuelan government. Establishment of a professional army ended that type of revolutionary movement in Venezuela.

Cipriano Castro had several serious conflicts with foreign powers. Very early, the Venezuelans lost a border conflict with Colombia, and in 1902 there was a blockade of Venezuelan ports by British, German, and Italian ships over debts allegedly owed to those three powers. When U.S. intervention brought an end to the blockade and submission of the issue to the Hague Court, Venezuela came out very badly in the court's decision. By 1908 diplomatic relations with the United States, France, and The Netherlands had been virtually suspended.

Castro's regime was not only very tyrannical, but also profligate. The president and most of those around him—with the notable exception of his vice president, Juan Vicente Gómez—lived "not wisely but too well." By 1908 Castro had severe health problems and finally decided to go to Europe for medical treatment.

Castro had no reservations about leaving the government in the hands of Vice President Gómez, trusting him implicitly. However, about a month after Castro left the country, Gómez seized full power, was proclaimed provisional president, and ordered Castro not to return.

Castro spent the last 16 years of his life in exile, most of the time in the United States and in the West Indies. His various efforts to organize filibustering expeditions to return to power were without success.

BIBLIOGRAPHY

Picón Salas, Mariano. *Los días de Cipriano Castro*. Caracas: Organización Continental de los Festivales del Libro, 1958.
Rourke, Thomas (Daniel Joseph Clinton). *Gómez: Tyrant of the Andes*. New York: William Morrow, 1936.
Salazar Martínez, Francisco. *Tiempo de Compadres: de Cipriano Castro a Juan Vicente Gómez*. Caracas: Libreria Pinango, 1972.
Sullivan, William. "The Rise of Despotism in Venezuela: Cipriano Castro 1899–1908." Ph.D. diss., University of New Mexico, 1974.
Velásquez, Ramón J. *La Caída del Liberalismo Amarillo*. Caracas: Ediciones Roraima, 1973.

ROBERT J. ALEXANDER

CASTRO RUZ, FIDEL (1927–   ), became the unrivaled leader of Cuba after the triumph of the revolution over the forces of Fulgencio Batista y Zaldívar* on January 1, 1959. He was born the eldest illegitimate child of Angel Castro y Argiz, a Spanish immigrant, and Lina Ruz González, a native Cuban. When he was very young, he was sent to his godparents in Santiago, where he attended a Jesuit school. At age 16, he went to the fashionable Colegio Belén, a Jesuit preparatory school in Havana.

Castro enrolled at the University of Havana to study law in 1945. At the university, he was involved in radical student protests against the administrations of Ramón Grau San Martín* and Carlos Prío Socarrás.* He became involved with the political gangsterism of the era and joined the terrorist organization Unión Insurreccional Revolucionaria. He graduated in 1950.

From 1950 until early 1952 Castro practiced law and became active in the Ortodoxo Party of Eduardo Rene Chibás.* Prior to the coup of March 10, 1952, he was an Ortodoxo candidate for Congress.

When Fulgencio Batista overthrew the regime of Carlos Prío, Castro embarked on a new career. On July 26, 1953, he led an unsuccessful assault on the Moncada barracks in Santiago. The attack failed and the rebels were arrested, convicted of treason, and jailed. At his trial, Castro presented a blueprint for revolution, his "History Will Absolve Me" speech, which called for restoration of the Constitution of 1940, elections, free press, free speech, and an independent judiciary.

On May 15, 1955, Fidel Castro was released from prison; he left Cuba in July for Mexico, where he and his compatriots trained for a guerrilla war against

Batista. On December 2, 1956, Castro and 81 fellow revolutionaries landed in Oriente Province aboard a dilapidated yacht named "Granma." A two-year struggle against the armed forces of the U.S.-backed government of Batista followed. Fidel, along with his chief lieutenants, Ernesto (Che) Guevara de la Serna,* his brother Raúl,* and Camillo Cienfuegos, led the struggle which eventually defeated one of the most firmly entrenched dictatorships in the Caribbean.

When Fidel Castro came to power on January 1, 1959, he at first named a provisional government consisting almost entirely of moderate, middle-class, liberal politicians, led by President Manuel Urrutia. However, after some months of hesitation, Fidel threw his support to those of his followers who favored taking the revolution in a Marxist-Leninist direction. In February 1960 Soviet Deputy Premier Anastas Mikoyan visited Havana to formally open the first Soviet trade mission in Cuba. In May of the same year, diplomatic relations were established between Cuba and the Soviet Union.

In 1960 relations between Havana and Washington deteriorated rapidly. In March President Eisenhower approved a plan for training Cuban exiles for an invasion of the island; in July he suspended Cuba's sugar quota. Castro responded by nationalizing American-owned sugar mills in Cuba, and by the end of the year he had expropriated all remaining U.S. investments on the island. Early in 1961 the United States broke diplomatic relations with the Castro government. On April 17, 1961, the ill-fated Bay of Pigs invasion took place. Its defeat greatly strengthened Castro's popularity and the intensity of his revolution.

In December 1961 Castro proclaimed that he was a Marxist-Leninist. Sometime later, he approved Nikita Khrushchev's plan to base Soviet nuclear missiles on Cuban soil, causing a U.S.-Soviet confrontation in October 1962 which brought the world to the brink of nuclear holocaust.

Meanwhile, Che Guevara, in charge of economic policy, was attempting a Soviet-style program of high-pressure industrialization and breaking dependence on sugar production and export, which ended in disaster. By 1963 the decision was made to seek a more gradual transformation of the Cuban economy and to return to reliance on sugar.

In the political arena, the year 1965 witnessed two major events: the formation of a new communist party, the Partido Comunista Cubano (PCC), and the departure of Che Guevara from Cuba to pursue his ideas of revolution elsewhere.

After Guevara left, Castro continued his support of armed revolutionary movements throughout the world. In the 1960s Cuba backed antigovernment guerrillas fighting in several Latin American countries. Subsequently, Cuban troops were dispatched to fight alongside Marxist forces in Angola and Ethiopia. More recently, Cuba has supported leftist guerrillas in El Salvador and the Sandinista regime in Nicaragua.

The Cuban economy has faltered under Castro's leadership. Failure to reach the sugar production goal of 10 million tons in 1970 illustrated not only an overestimation of Cuban productive potential, but also the continued reliance on sugar as the primary export commodity. The U.S. trade embargo continued to place limitations on the Cuban economy; there were widespread shortages of consumer goods, and rationing remained commonplace. The Cuban economy remained as dependent on the USSR as it ever had been on the United States.

Until 1970 the structure of the Castro regime remained very "informal," with Castro making all important decisions and many minor ones. However, after the failure of the 1970 sugar campaign, Castro's Cuba became "institutionalized" as a more or less orthodox Communist regime. The Communist Party held its first congress in 1975, and subsequently a new constitution patterned after the Brezhnev constitution of the USSR was adopted. Under it, Fidel Castro remained president of the Council of State and Council of Ministers, member of the Politburo and first secretary of the Communist Party, and commander-in-chief of the armed forces.

BIBLIOGRAPHY

Bonachea, Rolando, and Nelson P. Valdés (eds.). *Cuba in Revolution*. Garden City, N.Y.: Anchor Books, 1972.
Boorstein, Edward. *The Economic Transformation of Cuba*. New York: Monthly Review Press, 1968.
Domínguez, Jorge I. *Cuba: Order and Revolution*. Cambridge, Mass.: Harvard University Press, 1978.
Mesa-Lago, Carmelo (ed.). *Revolutionary Change in Cuba*. Pittsburgh: University of Pittsburgh Press, 1971.
Thomas, Hugh. *Cuba: The Pursuit of Freedom*. New York: Harper and Row, 1971.
                                                              STEPHEN J. WRIGHT

CASTRO RUZ, RAÚL (1930–), is the younger brother of Fidel Castro,* and his principal lieutenant. He was a member of the Communist Youth, a branch of the Partido Socialista Popular, during his student days at the University of Havana. He left the party to join his brother in the struggle against Fulgencio Batista y Zaldivar* in the early 1950s.

Raúl Castro fought alongside his brother in the Moncada barracks attack in July 1953, was imprisoned with Fidel following its failure, helped plan the invasion of Cuba in Mexico, participated in the "Granma" landing, and was one of the key leaders of the guerrilla struggle.

Following the triumph of the revolution, Raúl married Vilma Espín, one of the founding members of the 26th of July Movement and later president of the Cuban Confederation of Women and a member of the Central Committee of the Communist Party. In October 1959 the Revolutionary Armed Forces were organized under Raúl's leadership. With the "institutionalization" of the Castro regime in the 1970s, Raúl became first vice president of the Council of State and Council of Ministers, as well as a member of the Politburo and second secretary of the Communist Party. He continued as minister of the armed forces.

Raúl Castro's strong organizational skills won him the confidence of key Soviet officials who saw him as the leader best able to continue the process of centralizing and institutionalizing the apparatus of the revolutionary government. Raúl is also credited with bridging the gap between old guard Fidelistas, of which he is one, and a new generation of military-civilian technicians and administrators. He and his associates built a powerful, professionalized, and modern armed forces establishment and more recently have taken control of the Ministry of Interior. Seen by Moscow as both politically reliable and administratively competent, Raúl continues to be the ideal second-in-command to his flamboyant, charismatic, and unpredictable brother.

BIBLIOGRAPHY

Bonachea, Ramón L., and Marta San Martín. *The Cuban Insurrection 1952–1959*. New Brunswick, N.J.: Transaction Books, 1974.
Domínguez, Jorge I. *Cuba: Order and Revolution*. Cambridge, Mass.: Harvard University Press, 1978.
Franqui, Carlos. *The Twelve*. New York: Lyle Stuart, 1968.
Matthews, Herbert L. *Fidel Castro*. New York: Simon and Schuster, 1969.
Thomas, Hugh. *Cuba: The Pursuit of Freedom*. New York: Harper and Row, 1971.
                                                        STEPHEN J. WRIGHT

CATAYÉE, JUSTIN (?–1960), was the principal political figure in French Guiana following World War II. A deputy in the French National Assembly, he led a split of a majority of the Guianese Socialists away from the French Socialist Party (SFIO), to form the Guyanese Socialist Party (PSG) in 1956. He was killed in an airplane accident in 1960.

BIBLIOGRAPHY

Alexander, Robert J. "French Guiana," in Robert J. Alexander (ed.). *Political Parties of the Americas*. Vol. 1. Westport, Conn.: Greenwood Press, 1982.
                                                        ROBERT J. ALEXANDER

CATO, R(OBERT) MILTON (1915–   ), was St. Vincent's first prime minister (1979–1984) and chief minister/premier prior to independence (1967–1972 and 1974–1979). Following grammar school in St. Vincent, he went abroad for undergraduate and legal studies, which were interrupted for military duty with the Canadian Army during World War II. Cato began his legal training in the United Kingdom in 1948, and when he returned to St. Vincent he established a private legal practice.

Entering politics, Cato was first elected chairman of the St. Vincent Town Board (1952–1953) and later a member of that board (1955–1959). He also served on several public advisory and administrative bodies. He was a principal founder of the St. Vincent Labour Party (SLP) in 1954 and remained its leader for more than three decades. Although labeled a "labor" party, the SLP was, in fact, relatively conservative and enjoyed greater support from business interests than from organized labor. By 1957 Cato and the SLP had secured three of nine seats on the appointed Executive Council of colonial St. Vincent. It was not until 1967, however, that the SLP finally won a majority in the colonial Parliament. Cato became the state's first premier when St. Vincent gained Associated State status in 1969.

Cato lost the premiership between 1972 and 1974 but served as head of a coalition government between 1974 and 1979. In the 1979 general election held immediately after independence, Labour, under Cato's leadership, won 11 of 13 seats. Cato and the SLP were handed an electoral defeat by James Mitchell and his New Democratic Party (NDP) in 1984, however, as a weakening economy and Cato's declining health negatively affected Labour.

During his pre-independence administrations, Milton Cato was able to extend the economic infrastructure in St. Vincent, especially electricity and feeder roads. As a result of massive hurricane and volcanic damage which destroyed a high percentage of the banana trees in the late 1970s and 1980, and a drop in demand for arrowroot, the second ranking commercial crop, Cato's post-independence efforts were forced to focus increasingly on attempts to boost tax revenues. This factor, resulting from overall economic conditions, was apparently a major reason for the SLP defeat in 1984.

In foreign affairs, the Cato government signed the Treaty of the Organization of Eastern Caribbean States (OECS) in 1981. In 1983 the Cato government also made St. Vincent a party to the Eastern Caribbean Regional Security and Defense Pact, a regional attempt to share a military force. This force was first used in the Grenada invasion led by the United States in 1983.

BIBLIOGRAPHY

International Who's Who 1985–86. London: Europa Publications, 1985.
Personalities Caribbean. Kingston, Jamaica: Personalities Ltd., 1983.
Who's Who 1985. New York: St. Martin's Press, 1985.
                                                                    PERCY C. HINTZEN AND W. MARVIN WILL

CEREZO, VINICIO (1943–   ), became president of Guatemala in early 1986, the first civilian president in almost 20 years. He received a bachelor's degree in social sciences from the College of Don Bosco and a master's degree in public administration for development. He studied political science at Loyola University in New Orleans and in 1968 he became a lawyer.

Cerezo began his political career as a student leader of the Social Christian Movement. He joined the Christian Democratic Party in 1968 and held a number of positions in the party. In 1985 he was the party's successful candidate for president.

As president, Cerezo had to tread a careful path between the military, which had largely dominated the country for 30 years, and civilian political leaders seeking justice against those who had dominated the military dictatorship for several decades. He also faced difficulties in carrying out the program of social reform on which he had been elected, while at the same time dealing with an exceedingly difficult short-run economic situation and with deep-seated resistance to reform by conservative civilian and military elements.

BIBLIOGRAPHY

Kinzer, Stephen. "Walking the Tightrope in Guatemala." *New York Times Magazine*, November 9, 1986.
New York Times, December 10, 1985.

JOSÉ M. SÁNCHEZ

CÉSAIRE, AIMÉ (1913–), the major political leader of Martinique after World War II, was educated at the Lycée de Fort-de-France in Martinique, and at the Lycée Louis le Grand, Ecole Normale Superieure and Faculté des Lettres Superieure in Paris. He returned to be a faculty member of the Lycée de Fort-de-France from 1940 to 1945.

Césaire was a Communist member of the two French constitutional assemblies of 1945 and 1946. Subsequently, he was Communist deputy from Martinique between 1946 and 1956. Breaking with the Communists over the Hungarian invasion of November 1956, he continued to be a deputy but as an independent. Subsequent to 1974, he was aligned with the Socialist Party group in the French National Assembly.

After 1956 Césaire was president of the Parti Progressiste Martiniquais, a party he founded which advocated "autonomy" for the island. He was mayor of Fort-de-France from 1945 to 1983, and, although reelected in 1983, his election was invalidated by the Tribunal Administratif. Thereafter, he was president of the Regional Council of Martinique.

Césaire was the leading intellectual of the French Antilles. A well-known poet, he was also author of several historical studies and a leading figure in the Francophone "Negritude" movement.

BIBLIOGRAPHY

Alexander, Robert J. "Martinique," in Robert J. Alexander (ed.). *Political Parties of the Americas*. Vol. 2. Westport, Conn.: Greenwood Press, 1982.
Who's Who in France. 17th ed. Paris: Editions Jacques Lafitte, 1984.

ROBERT J. ALEXANDER

CÉSPEDES, CARLOS MANUEL DE (1819–1874), was president of the Cuban "Republic in Arms" from 1869 to 1873. During his youth, he traveled widely in the United States and Europe. While in Spain in the 1840s, he took an active part in revolutionary activity. Upon return to Cuba, he established himself as a prosperous plantation owner. A persistent critic of Spanish policy in Cuba, he led members of the wealthy Creole elite in Oriente in transforming local Masonic lodges into conspiratorial centers.

On October 10, 1868, in the small town of Yara in Oriente Province, Carlos Manuel de Céspedes led a small group of patriots in proclaiming the independence of Cuba and calling for creation of a republic and abolition of slavery. This dramatic "call to arms" was the beginning of the Ten Years' War (1868–1878).

As self-proclaimed president of the fledgling republic, Céspedes was a cautious, conservative, and often dictatorial leader. Nowhere was this more evident than on the slavery issue. In a proclamation in December 1868, Céspedes decreed a cautious policy of abolition which linked it to the final success of the revolution.

Meanwhile, the rebel movement grew rapidly, from the original 147 men that Céspedes had started with in October 1868 to over 12,000 by the end of the first month of the rebellion. Before the end of 1868 most of Oriente Province was under control of the revolutionary forces.

Céspedes finally called a constitutional convention, which met on April 10, 1869, in Guaimaro, where they adopted a constitution establishing a republican form of government, abolishing slavery, and annexing the new republic to the United States. The delegates also elected Carlos Manuel de Céspedes president of the republic.

By late 1869 Céspedes was still the nominal leader of the rebels, although the civilians had lost much of their power to the military commanders. In October Céspedes decreed destruction of sugar plantations to weaken Spanish control of the economy. In November he finally agreed with the more radical rebel leaders that slaves should be encouraged to rise up against their masters. This decision came too late for Céspedes to maintain himself as the unchallenged leader of the republic. He had lost the support of the conservatives on the slavery issue and of the more radical elements when he removed the popular Maximo Gómez* from his military command. Céspedes had isolated himself within the revolutionary movement.

In 1873 a rump meeting of the House of Representatives and major members of the military removed Céspedes from the presidency. In March 1874 he was ambushed and killed by Spanish forces at San Lorenzo in Oriente Province.

BIBLIOGRAPHY

Foner, Philip. *A History of Cuba and Its Relations with the United States*. New York: International Publishers, 1963.
Portell Vilá, Herminio. *Céspedes, el Padre de la Patria Cubana*. Habana, 1931.
Thomas, Hugh. *Cuba: The Pursuit of Freedom*. New York: Harper and Row, 1971.

STEPHEN J. WRIGHT

CHAMBERS, GEORGE MICHAEL (1930–   ), became the second prime minister of Trinidad and Tobago in 1981 and the second leader of the Peoples National Movement (PNM). Largely self-educated, he took a correspondence course in general education from Wolsey Hall, Oxford. He worked with a firm of solicitors and in the legal department of one of the country's oil companies before entering Peoples National Movement politics. He won the largest majority of any of the candidates contesting the general elections of 1966. After 1966 he held many cabinet portfolios. He also represented Trinidad and Tobago at several conferences of the Caribbean Community and the European Economic Community, and at International financial institutions. In the elections of 1971 and 1976 he was returned unopposed.

Chambers proved one of the most popular leaders in the PNM. He worked closely with the prime minister and emerged the natural choice to lead the party and government when Prime Minister Eric Williams* died suddenly in 1981. By this time, weaknesses were beginning to appear in the booming economy of the country. The price of oil had fallen and production was dropping; industrialization projects in which the state was the major investor were losing money; the government was overinvested in many construction and infrastructural projects; and there were numerous corruption scandals. However, Chambers managed to restore confidence in government and led the party to a resounding victory the year he took power.

Chambers took stringent measures to maintain economic stability. He was also able to stem the tide of corruption that plagued the government in the late 1970s. Moreover, he continued the relatively independent foreign policy of his predecessor. He was one of the few Caribbean leaders who did not support or participate in the U.S. intervention in Grenada in 1983.

Chambers' party was defeated by an opposition coalition in elections in early 1987, and he became Leader of the Opposition.

BIBLIOGRAPHY

Hintzen, Percy C. "The Costs of Regime Survival: Racial Mobilization, Elite Domination and Control of the State in Guyana and Trinidad." Unpublished manuscript, University of California at Berkeley, 1985.

Ryan, Selwyn. "Administrative Capability and Choice of Development Strategy: The Case of Trinidad and Tobago." Paper presented at Caribbean Studies Association Annual Meeting, St. Kitts, May 1983.

PERCY C. HINTZEN AND W. MARVIN WILL

CHAMORRO, FRUTOS (1806–1855), although born in Guatemala, was one of the earliest political leaders of Nicaragua. At the end of his university studies in 1823, he opposed a military *pronunciamiento* which was then underway and menacing the constitutional assembly of the Republic of Central America then in progress. In 1836 he was a member of the legislature of Nicaragua, and in 1838 he was a member of the Nicaraguan constitutional assembly, and helped to establish the University of Granada. In 1843, when a confederation of Honduras, Nicaragua, and El Salvador was founded, Chamorro was a member of its Executive Power and avoided a war with Guatemala. In 1845 he was governor of Nicaragua and in 1846 minister of finance. He returned to the second post in 1851 but was forced to resign when he suggested a cut in the military budget. In 1853 he was head of the Executive Power in Nicaragua; when faced with a revolt, he was besieged in Granada for 221 days. The Conservatives were finally ousted from power with the help of the U.S. soldier of fortune William Walker.*

BIBLIOGRAPHY

Diccionario Enciclopedico Hispano Americana. Vol. 5. Barcelona: Montaner y Simon
    Editores, 1890.
Enciclopedia Universal Ilustrada Europeo Americana. Barcelona: José Espasa e Hijos.

                                                                    NEALE J. PEARSON

CHAMORRO CARDENAL, PEDRO JOAQUÍN (1924–1978), was the long-
time editor of the anti-Somoza Nicaraguan newspaper *La Prensa* whose assassination on January 10, 1978 led to a final rupture of most business and professional support for Anastasio ''Tachito'' Somoza Debayle.* Member of a
distinguished Conservative family, Chamorro early went to work for *La Prensa*,
which had been founded by his father Pedro Joaquín Chamorro Zelaya in 1926.
In 1952 he succeeded his father as the paper's editor.

One of the loudest and most consistent critics of the Somoza family, Chamorro
took part in an armed effort to overthrow the government of Luis Somoza
Debayle* in 1959 and was the principal organizer of the campaign of Conservative candidate Fernando Agüero Rocha* against Tachito Somoza in 1967.

Although a lifelong Conservative Party member, Chamorro had distanced
himself from Agüero Rocha in 1963 because of Agüero's personalism and decision that the Conservatives should not participate in the 1963 election. However, he agreed to become coordinator of the National Union of Opposition—a
coalition of Agüero's Traditional Conservative Party, the Independent Liberal
Party and the Social Christian Party—which backed Agüero's 1967 candidacy.

Chamorro's newspaper carried articles on corruption and violations of human
rights by the Somoza regime. There is some evidence that his assassination
occurred because of *La Prensa* articles about an anti-Castro Cuban exile whose
business firm—located in a building owned by Tachito—collected 38,000 pints
of human blood and plasma a month for sale in Miami. Chamorro's murder
provoked a reaction that led a year and a half later to the fall of the Somozas.

BIBLIOGRAPHY

English, Burt H. *Nicaraguan Election Factbook*, February 5, 1967. Washington, D.C.:
    Institute for the Comparative Study of Political Systems, December 1966.
Millett, Richard. *Guardians of the Dynasty, A History of the U.S. Created Guardia
    Nacional and the Somoza Family*. Maryknoll, N.Y.: Orbis Books, 1977.
Pearson, Neale J. ''Nicaragua,'' in Robert J. Alexander (ed.). *Political Parties of the
    Americas*. Vol. 2. Westport, Conn.: Greenwood Press, 1982.
Walker, Thomas W. *Nicaragua, the Land of Sandino*. Boulder, Colo.: Westview Press,
    1980.
Woodward, R. L., Jr. ''Dr. Pedro Joaquín Chamorro (1924–1958), The Conservative
    Party and the Struggle for Democratic Government in Nicaragua.'' *SECOLAS* 10
    (March 1979).

                                                                    NEALE J. PEARSON

CHAMORRO VARGAS, EMILIANO (1871–1966), was the grand old caudillo and perpetual revolutionary of the Nicaraguan Conservative Party. Member
of a prominent family, he was only 22 when he led the first of several revolts

against Liberal President José Santos Zelaya* in 1893. Sixteen years later, Chamorro and Adolfo Díaz, a young secretary of an American-owned mining company, played a major role in organizing a successful uprising against Zelaya late in 1909, under nominal leadership of the Liberal governor of the Mosquito Coast, General Juan J. Estrada.

Subsequently, Estrada—now president—and Conservative leaders Chamorro, Díaz, and Luis Mena agreed on a Constituent Assembly to select Estrada as president for a two-year term and Adolfo Díaz as vice president. In a fight over U.S. participation in control of customs receipts to pay off a loan to the Estrada government, Chamorro was exiled by Estrada, whose government fell shortly thereafter.

Díaz became president (1911–1916) and appointed Chamorro minister to the United States. He signed the controversial Bryan-Chamorro Treaty in 1914, granting the United States exclusive rights to construct a canal across Nicaragua, leasing Great Corn and Little Corn Islands to the United States for 99 years, and giving the United States the right to set up a naval base on the Gulf of Fonseca—all for $3 million.

Chamorro was president from 1917 to 1920. His administration concluded another agreement with the United States establishing a High Commission— with an American commissioner—to control Nicaraguan revenues in order to pay off foreign creditors.

In 1920 Chamorro imposed the election of his uncle, Diego Manuel Chamorro, as president. The new president died unexpectedly in 1923 and was succeeded by Vice President Bartolomé Martínez, an anti-Chamorro Conservative, who created a coalition with Liberal Party elements. Conservative Carlos Solorzano was nominated for president and Liberal Juan Bautista Sacasa as vice president, and easily won the October 1924 elections. Chamorro revolted, and was formally accepted as president by the Nicaraguan Congress on March 13, 1926. However, on October 24, 1926, after various intrigues, Díaz became president again, and Chamorro went into diplomatic exile as minister to several European countries.

As the result of various other conspiracies and of negotiations in 1926–1927 involving Henry L. Stimson, a treaty was signed providing for organization of a nonpartisan National Guard and presidential elections in 1928. Chamorro tried unsuccessfully to prevent the treaty's ratification.

Honest elections under the auspices of the U.S. Marines resulted in Liberal José María Moncada's inauguration for the 1929–1932 term. In addition, an agreement provided for American training of what was hoped would be an honest and nonpartisan National Guard. However, the treaty's objectives were never achieved. A Liberal, General Anastasio Somoza García,* was ultimately able to take over the Guard and use it to establish a dynasty that would dominate Nicaragua from 1936 to 1979.

On numerous occasions, Emiliano Chamorro sought to restore Conservatives to dominance. Finally despairing of success, he signed a so-called Pact of the Generals in 1950 with Anastasio Somoza, which softened Conservative opposition to Somoza's regime in return for a fixed percentage of positions in Congress and the bureaucracy.

BIBLIOGRAPHY

English, Burt H. *Nicaraguan Election Factbook, February 5, 1967*. Washington, D.C.: Institute for the Study of Political Systems, December 1966.
Kantor, Harry. *Patterns of Politics and Political Systems in Latin America*. Chicago: Rand McNally, 1969.
Millett, Richard. *Guardians of the Dynasty, A History of the U.S. Created Guardia Nacional and the Somoza Family*. Maryknoll, N.Y.: Orbis Books, 1977.
Pearson, Neale J. "Nicaragua," in Robert J. Alexander (ed.). *Political Parties of the Americas*, Vol. 2. Westport, Conn.: Greenwood Press, 1982.
Walker, Thomas W. *Nicaragua, the Land of Sandino*. Boulder, Colo.: Westview Press, 1980.

NEALE J. PEARSON

CHARLES, GEORGE FREDERIC (1916–   ), became the first chief minister of St. Lucia in January 1960. Receiving his primary and secondary education in St. Lucia, he worked for a short time with his businessman uncle and then left for the Dutch colony of Curaçao to work in the oil industry. Upon his return to St. Lucia, he became a commission agent.

Charles' political career developed through the labor movement. In 1948 he joined the St. Lucia Workers Union (SWU) and was elected its general secretary the following year. This union, born out of labor struggles in the late 1930s, became the most powerful political force on the island and the basis for formation of the country's first political party, the Saint Lucia Labour Party (SLP), on the eve of the 1951 elections. These elections followed constitutional advances that established universal adult suffrage and provided for a Legislative Council in which a majority of members were elected. The new SLP won six of eight elected seats in the Legislative Council in 1951. Charles, who was then elected to the council, was reelected in September 1954 and became minister of social services when a quasi-cabinet system was introduced two years later.

Charles assumed the presidency of the Saint Lucia Workers Union in 1954. In 1957 he was also elected leader of the SLP and led the party to its second electoral victory as it won seven of eight elected seats in the Legislative Council. Charles became one of the leading advocates for a West Indian Federation, aligning his party with the ultimately victorious West Indies Federal Labour party. His father, James Luc Charles, became Minister without Portfolio in the Grantley Herbert Adams* government when the federation was established in 1958.

In January 1960 a cabinet form of government was established, along with a 13-member Legislative Council, including 10 elected members, and Charles became St. Lucia's first chief minister. In elections the following year, he led the party to yet another victory, winning nine of the ten elected council seats. However, his leadership was under internal attack from a group of younger party officials. They opposed the reelection of Charles as party leader and chief minister. They defected after the 1961 elections to form a new political party, the National Labour Movement (NLM), leaving the SLP with only a bare majority (six of ten elected seats) in the Legislative Council. Charles continued to lead the government until 1964, when further internal conflict produced the defection of two additional elected party members. Elections were forced, and the SLP was defeated.

Charles continued as party leader of the SLP until 1967 and as Leader of the Opposition until 1969. He left the presidency of the St. Lucia Workers Union in 1968.

BIBLIOGRAPHY

Alexander, Robert J. "Saint Lucia," in Robert J. Alexander (ed.). *Political Parties of the Americas*. Vol. 2. Westport, Conn.: Greenwood Press, 1983.
Brana-Shute, Rosemary and Gary Brana-Shute. "St. Lucia." *Latin America and Caribbean Contemporary Record*, Vols. 1–4. New York: Holmes and Meier, 1982, 1983, 1984, 1985.
Rickards, Colin. *Caribbean Power*. London: Dobson Books, 1963.
St. Lucia at Independence. Castries, St. Lucia, February 22, 1979.

PERCY C. HINTZEN AND W. MARVIN WILL

CHARLES, MARY EUGENIA (1919–   ), became the first female prime minister in the Caribbean, after her party was elected to power in Dominica in July 1980. Born into a successful, well-to-do family, she received her primary education and a portion of her secondary education in Dominica, completing her higher studies at a Roman Catholic convent in Grenada. She then attended the University of Toronto where she graduated with a B.A. in 1946. She qualified as a barrister in 1947.

Charles became actively involved in politics in October 1968, when the government of Edward Oliver LeBlanc* passed the Seditious and Undesirable Publication Act. She was in the forefront of organized protest against this legislation. The Dominica Freedom Party (DFP), which she founded and over which she presided, grew out of this protest. Although Charles was defeated in the 1970 general elections in which her party won two seats, she served in the House of Assembly as a nominated member. She was finally elected in 1975. This time, her Freedom Party captured three seats in the House. She became Leader of the Opposition and a leading opponent of the government of Patrick Roland John* who had assuumed the premiership in 1974.

In June 1977 Charles participated in a Committee for National Salvation (CNS), a loose amalgam of opposition groups formed against what was popularly perceived as antiworker and antidemocratic legislation by the John government. She also opposed the granting of independence to the colony under the terms proposed by the John government. Despite these objections, Dominica became independent in November 1978. The political crisis intensified, reaching a peak in May 1979, when opposition to a bill to outlaw strikes and limit freedom of the press led to massive CNS-supported demonstrations.

At one CNS-backed rally, the Dominican Army opened fire, killing three persons and wounding others. This led to a general strike headed by five of the country's most powerful unions. The crisis provoked an exodus of seven of the ruling Dominica Labour Party (DLP) elected representatives in the House, to form a new party that became active in efforts to oust the John government. This was quickly followed by resignation of the president of the country, an appointee of the prime minister. Events forced a dissolution of Parliament and the ouster of the prime minister. An interim coalition government was established on June 21, 1979, by the CNS. However, Charles decided not to involve her party in the coalition government but to remain the official opposition.

In the July 1980 elections, Charles led her DFP to a landslide victory, winning 17 of 21 seats in the House, and Eugenia Charles became prime minister. Under her leadership, the Dominica government was one of the most conservative in the region, firmly committed to private enterprise and to attracting foreign investment, unswervingly pro-West, and particularly pro-United States in foreign policy.

In 1983 Charles assumed the chairmanship of the new Organization of Eastern Caribbean States (OECS). In that capacity, she turned to the United States for help following the collapse of the Maurice Rupert Bishop* government in Grenada and the murder of its top leadership. She was at the side of President Reagan on October 25, 1983, when he announced the decision to invade Grenada. The Charles government was also a major supporter of the Reagan-backed Eastern Caribbean Regional Defense Force, and of Reagan's Caribbean Basin Initiative (CBI), for economic development of the area. However, Charles joined other Eastern Caribbean leaders in stating disappointment over the lack of investment and the relatively low amount of aid provided by the CBI—$10 million for the entire Eastern Caribbean. The candid Charles has stated that she could spend such an amount ten times over in her own economically depressed island.

BIBLIOGRAPHY

Alexander, Robert J. "Dominica," in Robert J. Alexander (ed.). *Political Parties of the Americas*. Vol. 2. Westport, Conn.: Greenwood Press, 1983.
Branda-Shute, Gary, and Rosemary Branda-Shute. "Dominica," in Jack W. Hopkins (ed.). *Latin America and Caribbean Contemporary Record*. Vols. 1, 2, and 3. New York: Holmes and Meier, 1983, 1984, 1985.
Bulletin of Eastern Caribbean Affairs 5, no. 2 (May/June 1979).
Personal Interviews.
Smith, Linden. "The Political Situation in Dominica." *Bulletin of Eastern Caribbean Affairs* 5, no. 3 (July/August 1979).

                                                   PERCY C. HINTZEN AND W. MARVIN WILL

CHÁVES, FEDERICO (1882–?), was the president of Paraguay from 1949 to 1954. He had been a long-time Colorado politician, leader of the "democratic" wing of the party, and rival of Juan Natalicio González* for its control. He had a distinguished career as lawyer and judge.

Cháves formed an alliance with Felipe Molas López after the 1948 coup which brought Molas López to power. In reality, Cháves and his faction of the Colorados held power even though Molas López was titular president. Cháves was president of Congress, president of the Colorado Party, controlled the Ministry of Defense and the police, and had military support. He purged the followers of the deposed violence-prone Juan Natalicio González.

Federico Cháves assumed power in 1949, running as sole candidate in the July 1950 elections, while Liberal Party leaders were under house arrest.

During Cháves' presidency, the Paraguayan economy came under strong inflationary pressure, and Cháves was plagued by constant maneuvering of rival Colorados. Nevertheless, he was reelected in 1952. Although he was leader of the "democratic" faction of the Colorados, in the presidency he showed little support for the democratic process.

Finally, in May 1954 Cháves attempted a showdown against those, including General Alfredo Stroessner,* whom he felt were planning a coup. The police remained loyal, but in extremely fierce fighting the army defeated them, and on May 5, 1954, President Cháves was overthrown.

BIBLIOGRAPHY

Kolinsky, Charles J. *Historical Dictionary of Paraguay*. Metuchen, N.J.: Scarecrow Press, 1973.
Lewis, Paul H. *Paraguay Under Stroessner*. Chapel Hill: University of North Carolina Press, 1980.
Lott, Leo B. *Venezuela and Paraguay: Political Modernity and Tradition in Conflict*. New York: Holt, Rinehart and Winston, 1972.
Pendle, George. *Paraguay: A Riverside Nation*. London: Royal Institute of International Affairs, 1956.
Weil, Thomas, et al. *Area Handbook for Paraguay*. Washington, D.C.: Department of Defense, 1972.

JOHN T. DEINER

CHIARI, RODOLFO E. (1870–1937), was president of Panama during 1924–1928. Born in Panama of Italian immigrant parents, he was educated in Panama, amassed a fortune as a sugar planter, and established the Chiari family as a political power. He wrested control of the Liberal Party from Belisario Porras* and represented oligarchical control over Panamanian politics.

Despite Chiari's strong political base his presidency was stormy. A rent strike in Colón and Panama City in 1926 became violent and obliged him to request the intervention of U.S. troops from the Canal Zone. In the same year, 21 National Police members died suppressing an uprising by the Cuna Indians of San Blas.

Chiari's failure to secure approval of the 1926 Panama Canal Treaty, revising the 1903 agreement with the United States, was his most serious setback. The pact aroused powerful nationalistic sentiment and led to creation of a semi-secret organization, Acción Comunal, led by the Arias Madrid* brothers. Chiari managed to dictate the choice of Florencio Harmodio Arosemena as his successor, but the Revolution of 1931 ended the period of Chiari's dominance of Panamanian politics.

BIBLIOGRAPHY

Alba C., Manuel María. *Cronología de los Governantes de Panama, 1510–1967*. Panama: 1967.
Castillero, R., Ernesto J. *Historia de Panama*. Panama: Editora Panama América, 1959.
Ropp, Steve C. *Panamanian Politics: From Guarded Nation to National Guard*. New York: Praeger, 1982.

CHARLES D. AMERINGER

CHIARI REMÓN, ROBERTO FRANCISCO (1905–   ), was president of Panama twice: once for four days in November 1949, and then for a full term, 1960–1964. Chiari's first brief time in office occurred when Colonel José Antonio Remón,* chief of the National Police, was consolidating power. Remón ousted Chiari when he refused to follow orders. The assassination of Remón in 1955 reversed Chiari's fortunes.

Chiari was the son of former president and long-time boss of the Liberal Party, Rodolfo E. Chiari,* and received his education in Panama. The Liberal Party had declined with the rise of Remón and of the Panameñista movement of Arnulfo Arias Madrid.* However, in an unprecedented achievement for an opposition candidate, Roberto Chiari won the 1960 election. Although Chiari represented a throwback to the old oligarchy, he felt it was necessary to promote economic and social change in order to avoid violent revolution.

Chiari visited the United States in 1962 and pledged support to the Alliance for Progress. However, after an effort to raise the Panamanian flag at Balboa Heights High School in the Canal Zone in January 1964 resulted in the deaths of 20 persons and the injury of hundreds, Chiari broke relations with the United States, charging the United States with aggression, before the Organization of American States and the United Nations. In time, Presidents Chiari and Lyndon Johnson issued a joint statement outlining a series of proposed treaties for resolving the Canal issue.

BIBLIOGRAPHY

Alba C., Manuel María. *Cronología de los Gobernantes de Panama, 1510–1967*. Panama: 1967.
Pippin, Larry LaRae. *The Remón Era: An Analysis of a Decade of Events in Panama, 1947–1957*. Stanford, Calif.: Stanford University Press, 1964.
Ropp, Steve C. *Panamanian Politics: From Guarded Nation to National Guard*. New York: Praeger, 1982.

CHARLES D. AMERINGER

CHIBÁS, EDUARDO RENÉ (1907–1951), was one of the most colorful and controversial politicians in the first 50 years of the Cuban Republic. Eddy, as he was affectionately known to his followers, was the son of a wealthy engineer and politician. He studied law and politics at the University of Havana but was expelled in 1927 for making a fiery speech against President Gerardo Machado y Morales.* He then studied law and English at Georgetown University in Washington, D.C. Returning to the island, Chibás once again took up the struggle against Machado. He was imprisoned for 18 months, spending part of the time in a jail on the Isle of Pines where he met his future political ally and adversary, Ramón Grau San Martín.*

In September 1933 Chibás nominated Grau for president of the revolutionary junta. In the period from Grau's downfall in January 1934 until his reelection to the presidency in 1944, Chibás belonged to the Auténtico Party and was one of Dr. Grau's strongest supporters. In 1939 he was elected to the constituent assembly, and the next year ran successfully for a seat in the House of Representatives. He gained a Senate seat in 1944.

Disillusioned with the corruption and broken promises of Grau's first two years, Chibás broke with the Auténticos in 1946. The next year he founded a new political party, El Partido del Pueblo Cubano. Known as the Ortodoxo party, its slogan was "Honesty versus Money."

Chibás and his Ortodoxo movement proved that they were a force to reckon with in the 1948 presidential election. In his campaign, Chibás advocated distribution of land to landless farmers, creation of a central bank, and expansion of social security. He voiced the hopes of thousands of Cubans who were disillusioned with the failure and corruption of the Auténticos, and his campaign was, in reality, based on the single issue of moral reform and a complete housecleaning in government. Despite the absence of any real party structure, organization, or money, Chibás polled 325,000 votes to Carlos Prío Socarrás'* 900,000 and Ricardo Núñez Portuondo's 600,000. The Communist candidate, Juan Marinello,* finished a distant fourth with 142,000 votes in what was to be the last free election that Cuba experienced.

Chibás' radio show on station CQM every Sunday night was a national event for over seven years. On August 5, 1951, Eddy Chibás shot himself following one of his broadcasts. He had been depressed by his inability to provide proof in support of his accusations against one of Prío's cabinet ministers. His last broadcast was an emotional appeal to continue the fight for honest government.

BIBLIOGRAPHY

Conte Agüero, Luis. *Eduardo Chibás: El Adalid de Cuba.* Mexico City: Editorial JUS, 1955.
Farber, Samuel. *Revolution and Social Structure in Cuba, 1933–1959.* Middletown, Conn.: Wesleyan University Press, 1976.
Ruíz, Ramón Eduardo. *Cuba: The Making of a Revolution.* New York: W. W. Norton, 1968.
Suchlicki, Jaime. *University Students and Revolution in Cuba 1920–1968.* Coral Gables, Fla.: University of Miami Press, 1969.

STEPHEN J. WRIGHT

CHRISTOPHE, HENRI (1767–1820), who was proclaimed king of Haiti in 1811, was born a slave in the British island of Grenada. When 12 years old, he ran away, persuading the skipper of a vessel to take him aboard. While in port at Cap Français in St. Domingue, he was sold to a French officer of Admiral d'Estaing's fleet, as a mess boy. When the fleet returned to St. Domingue, Christophe was sold to a black freedman who owned a hotel at the Cap. He was able to earn enough money to purchase his emancipation, married the daughter of his ex-master, and remained at the hotel.

Christophe apparently stayed clear of the violent turmoil that plagued the colony after 1789, until 1794, when he joined Toussaint L'Ouverture's* forces as a sergeant, at the age of 27.

In 1796, already with the rank of major, Christophe distinguished himself in a campaign against mulatto commanders and became a colonel. In 1801, when civil war erupted between the mulattoes who held the South and the blacks under Toussaint, Christophe again distinguished himself and was named brigadier by Toussaint.

After Toussaint secured absolute domination over the island with defeat of the Spanish in Santo Domingo, Christophe was given divisional jurisdiction in a system of military administration which divided the island into districts run by senior military personnel.

With a French attempt in 1802 to restore dominion over Haiti, Toussaint and his generals, Jean-Jacques Dessalines* and Christophe, were beaten back. After running low on food and supplies, Christophe suspended hostilities and was given a command in the French Army, with 1,500 of his regular troops. This was soon followed by the surrender and imprisonment of Toussaint.

As the French forces became weakened with illness, Leclerc was increasingly forced to depend on the black and mulatto generals, particularly in the face of a revolt as word spread of impending restoration of slavery. As French atrocities against blacks and mulattoes increased, Christophe joined the rebels. With the black and mulatto generals united under Dessalines, the French forces were defeated.

Under Dessalines, Haiti was declared independent on January 1, 1804. The country was divided into four districts with Christophe becoming the general in command of the North. When Dessalines invaded Santo Domingo in 1804, Christophe led the invasion force in the North, quickly overcoming French and Spanish troops. Dessalines was killed in 1806 during an attempt to quell an uprising of generals in the South.

Christophe was declared provisional leader, but a constitutional assembly, controlled by mulatto generals, drafted a republican constitution that provided President Christophe with very little power. In response, Christophe led his black forces from the North toward the capital, Port-au-Prince. After some initial success, Christophe was forced to retreat back to the North.

There, he set up a separate state. The country remained divided for 13 years, and in 1811 Christophe declared himself King. His organization of the North rested on a combination of military despotism, with certain benevolent qualities, and a nobility that he created and cultivated.

Christophe adapted the system he had developed under Toussaint: estates, now in government hands, were given on five-year leases to loyal supporters and the wealthy; labor was organized along militaristic lines with a heavy emphasis on hard work and discipline. The workers got a quarter of the income of the plantations and were also provided small plots of land to provide for their personal needs.

Under this system, the society became highly polarized between the workers and the small clique of mostly black aristocrats. There was an insignificant middle class of urban artisans, ex-soldiers, and midsized cultivators. Christophe imported English teachers to staff the few schools that he opened, but this served the class interests of the new aristocracy, the only ones able to avail themselves of the opportunity to educate their children.

The system was economically successful, allowing Christophe to raise revenue equaling that of the immediate prerevolutionary period when St. Domingue was France's richest colony. However, the system was rooted in firm class divisions and rested on a labor force with little civil and political rights.

The laissez-faire system of the South enticed many from the North. When, in 1811, some people fled to the South, Christophe revived hostilities with Alexandre Pétion's* republic. He lost the encounter and proceeded to kill and torture captured prisoners. He also punished his officers, blaming them for the loss. Hostilities with the South intensified Christophe's dislike and distrust of the mulatto population. He began to persecute them.

In 1820, suffering from paralysis and with members of his army defecting, Henri Christophe decided to take his own life.

BIBLIOGRAPHY

Beard, John R. *The Life of Toussaint L'Ouverture*. Westport, Conn.: Negro University Press, 1970.
Cole, Herbert. *Christophe: King of Haiti*. London: Eyre and Spottiswoode, 1967.
James, C. L. R. *The Black Jacobins*. London: Allison and Busby, 1980.
Moran, Charles. *Black Triumvirate*. New York: Exposition, 1957.
Syme, Ronald. *Toussaint: The Black Liberator*. New York: William Morrow, 1971.

PERCY C. HINTZEN

CIPRIANI, ARTHUR ANDREW (1875–1945), contributed most to building a national consciousness in Trinidad and Tobago. From a white landowning Trinidadian family of Corsican ancestry, he emerged the unlikely leader of the predominantly black and East Indian masses during the 1920s and 1930s. At the outbreak of World War I in 1914 he enlisted in the British Army and was placed in charge of the West Indian Regiment. With a regiment that was predominantly black, he found himself embroiled in constant conflict with the War Office over its humiliating treatment of the soldiers under his command. He became a hero and an idol among the members of the regiment for his defense of their interests.

Upon returning to Trinidad, Cipriani soon became president of the Soldiers and Sailors Union and later of the Trinidad Workingmen's Association (TWA), which, under his leadership, would become the most important working-class organization in the country. This era was dominated by strikes and demonstrations in the face of a postwar economic decline. Between 1919 and 1934 Cipriani forged the TWA into the leading left-wing movement in the entire Caribbean. By 1930 it boasted 42 affiliated sections in Trinidad and 13 in Tobago and a total membership, by 1935, of 130,000. Cipriani's slogan "Agitate, Educate, Confederate" became the rallying cry of the masses for the whole generation that he was the effective political leader in the colony.

Cipriani was a Fabian Socialist strongly committed to the tradition of the British Labour Party. His union and political activities catapulted him into successive electoral victories as an independent member of the Trinidadian Legislative Council, where he served continuously between 1925 and 1945. He also served an unbroken spell in the Port of Spain City Council between 1926 and 1941 and was mayor of Port of Spain for eight terms.

In the Trinidad Legislative Council and the City Council, Cipriani carried on a constant struggle for labor and social legislation. However, given the relative weakness of labor laws eventually passed in 1932, and in view of his growing belief that political agitation and reform had to take precedence over labor agitation, he refused to register the TWA and its two affiliate unions in 1932. Instead, he chose to concentrate on political activities and changed the name of the TWA to the Trinidad Labour Party (TLP) in 1934.

This was a time of increasing labor discontent in the face of growing economic woes that came with the worldwide Depression. Always a constitutionalist and opposed to the use of violence, Cipriani opposed direct action as a strategy. Moreover, the TLP remained a loosely organized body. His inability to share leadership compounded his problems. In 1936 he was deserted by his major lieutenants, Tubal Uriah Butler* and Andrian Rienzi. Butler, with his willingness to employ direct action to confront the colonial system, quickly replaced Cipriani as the champion of the people. Although Cipriani retained political office until 1945, he was relatively ignored during the last decade of his life.

BIBLIOGRAPHY

Brereton, Bridget. *A History of Modern Trinidad 1783–1962*. Port of Spain: Heinemann, 1981.
James, C. L. R. *The Life of Captain Cipriani*. Nelson, Lancs.: Coulton and Co., 1932.
Lewis, Gordon K. *The Growth of the Modern West Indies*. New York: Monthly Review Press, 1968.
Oxaal, Ivar. *Black Intellectuals Come to Power*. Cambridge, Mass.: Schenkman, 1968.
Ryan, Selwyn: *Race and Nationalism in Trinidad and Tobago*. Toronto: University of Toronto Press, 1972.

PERCY C. HINTZEN AND W. MARVIN WILL

COMPTON, JOHN GEORGE MELVIN (1926–   ), led St. Lucia as head of the government from 1964 until independence in 1979. Born in the neighboring island of St. Vincent, he attended secondary school in St. Lucia, and worked in the Curaçao oil refineries between 1946 and 1948. In 1948 he left for Great Britain to study law and economics. He received a BSc. from the London School of Economics and an LLB. in 1951.

Returning to St. Lucia, Compton ran as an independent candidate for the Legislative Council in 1954. In 1956 he joined the St. Lucia Labour Party (CLP), which had won elections in 1951 and 1954. Compton won a seat in the St. Lucian Legislative Council on the SLP ticket in 1957 and was minister of trade and industry between 1958 and 1961. With the introduction of cabinet government in 1960, George Frederic Charles,* leader of the SLP, was made chief minister.

Compton, leader of a new generation of SLP officials, younger and more educated than the old guard, began to challenge Charles' leadership. After the party won the 1961 general election, Compton broke ranks with the SLP to form and head the National Labour Movement (NLM), taking two other SLP officials with him. Despite the defection of three of its elected officials, the SLP managed to control six of ten elective seats in the legislature.

Further defections in 1964 forced the government to call elections. Compton then merged his NLM with the Peoples Progressive Party, long the official opposition to the SLP, to form the United Workers Party (UWP), under his leadership. When the UWP won an electoral victory in its very first year, getting six of ten seats in the Legislative Council, Compton became chief minister. Following an abortive effort at eastern Caribbean federation in the aftermath of the 1958–1962 West Indies Federation, Compton negotiated the Associated State status for St. Lucia in 1967, which gave the elected government control of every aspect of administration except foreign affairs, defense, and internal security. Compton became premier, and the Legislative Council became the House of Assembly, with 17 of its 18 members elected.

During his 15 years as head of government, John Compton orchestrated an extensive program of infrastructural development, particularly in the road network and the electrical and water and sewer systems. His government made enormous strides in education and stimulated development of tourism, the banana industry, and industrialization based on attracting foreign investors.

Negotiations with Britain resulted in granting St. Lucia independence in February 1979, when Compton became the country's first prime minister. In elections called in June 1979, however, Compton and the UWP lost 12 of 17 seats in the House of Assembly to a resuscitated SLP, which was now under a new leadership. Compton was Leader of the Opposition until 1982, when his party was again victorious and he resumed the post of prime minister.

BIBLIOGRAPHY

Alexander, Robert J. "St. Lucia," in Robert J. Alexander (ed.). *Political Parties of the Americas*. Vol. 2. Westport, Conn.: Greenwood Press, 1983.
Brana-Shute, Rosemary, and Gary Brana-Shute. "St. Lucia," in Jack W. Hopkins (ed.). *Latin America and Caribbean Contemporary Record*. Vols. 1–4. New York: Holmes and Meier, 1982, 1983, 1984, 1985.

Caribbean Studies, 1979–1985.
Smith, Lindel. "St. Lucia Elections, 2nd July 1979." *Bulletin of Eastern Caribbean Affairs* 3 (July/August 1979).

                                                         PERCY C. HINTZEN AND W. MARVIN WILL

CONCHA ORTIZ, LUIS MALAQUÍAS (1859–1921), was founder of Chile's first Socialist Party. He began his political career as a member of the Radical Party, after graduating from law school in 1880. In 1887 Concha led a group of labor leaders and young intellectuals who split from the Radical Party to establish the Democratic Party. He was that group's first national secretary, and between 1896 and 1909, and again from 1915 until his death, he was president of that party.

Concha supported President José Manuel Balmaceda Fernandez* in the Civil War of 1891, and as a consequence was jailed several times for short periods in the years that followed. However, in 1900 he was elected to the Chamber of Deputies, where he remained until 1918, when he was elected senator. He served as a cabinet member for short periods between 1917 and 1920. He published several books and pamphlets elaborating on the Democratic Party's programs.

BIBLIOGRAPHY

Alexander, Robert J. "Chile," in Robert J. Alexander (ed.). *Political Parties of the Americas*. Westport, Conn.: Greenwood Press, 1982.
Cortes, Lia, and Jordi Fuentes. *Diccionario Político de Chile*. Santiago: Editorial Orbe, 1967.

                                                                     ROBERT J. ALEXANDER

CONSTANT BOTELHO DE MAGALHÃES, BENJAMIN (1836–1891), is one of the founding fathers of the Brazilian Republic, his impact being based on the influence which the Positivist philosophy he taught at the military school in Rio de Janeiro had on young army officers.

Benjamin Constant came from an impoverished middle-class family from the city of Niteroi in the state of Rio de Janeiro. He was able to enter the military school attached to the Imperial Court of Dom Pedro II,* graduating with highest honors in mathematics. He received an appointment as professor in the Dom Pedro II College and later served as a captain in the Paraguayan War.

Upon his return to Rio de Janeiro, Constant was promoted to the rank of colonel and resumed his teaching career. He became a dedicated republican and staunch abolitionist. In 1887 he was one of the founders of the politically powerful Military Club of Rio de Janeiro. Constant was attracted to the Positivist philosophy of Auguste Comte which attempted to offer scientific solutions to many of the social and political problems of the period.

Constant was a gifted teacher and had an extraordinary impact on many young cadets who passed through the school. These young men were not the wealthy sons of plantation owners but rather represented an ambitious rising middle class not in tune with the monarchy of Dom Pedro II. Many were deeply impressed with Constant's support of republican ideas, and he became their idol. He was considered important enough to be at the side of Marshal Manuel Deodoro da Fonseca* and Floriano Peixoto* when the republic was proclaimed.

During the provisional government many of these young army officers, and even senior officials, turned to Colonel Benjamin Constant for advice. He was appointed minister of war in the first Republican cabinet. The provisional government also elevated him to general for his services to the republic. He was offered a senatorial seat from the state of Pará but refused.

BIBLIOGRAPHY

Barros Lins, Ivan Monteiro de. *Tres Abolicionistas Esquecidas*. 1938.
Mendes, Raymundo Teizeira. *Benjamin Constant*.

JORDAN YOUNG

CORTÉS CASTRO, LEÓN (1882–1946), was president of Costa Rica from 1936 to 1940. His election was a reaction against over 30 years of liberal government, which had nurtured individual freedoms and extended public education, but neglected developing social and economic problems. Costa Rica's coffee barons, who sensed their declining power, wanted a strongman to restore their power and selected Cortés.

As president, Cortés took a hard line toward the incipient labor movement and suppressed the new Communist Party, denying Communist leader Manuel Mora Valverde* the seat in Congress that he had won. Cortés even manifested some pro-Nazi sympathies. Ineligible to run again in 1940, he sponsored the candidacy of Rafael Angel Calderón Guardia,* mistakenly believing he would be an easily managed puppet.

Cortés tried a political comeback in 1944 but faced Teodoro Picado Michalski, the hand-picked candidate of the new strongman, Calderón. Cortés' authoritarian past came back to haunt him and undermined his credibility.

BIBLIOGRAPHY

Ameringer, Charles D. *Don Pepe: A Political Biography of José Figueres of Costa Rica*. Albuquerque: University of New Mexico Press, 1979.
Bell, John Patrick. *Crisis in Costa Rica: The 1948 Revolution*. Austin: University of Texas Press, 1971.
Mavis, Richard, and Karen Biesanz. *Los Costarricenses*. San José: Editorial Universidad Estatal a Distancia, 1979.

CHARLES D. AMERINGER

CRESPO, JOAQUÍN (1845–1898), was the most important Venezuelan political figure between the end of the Antonio Guzmán Blanco* period in 1888 and the assumption of power by the caudillo forces from the Andean state of Táchira in 1899. He rose to a certain prominence during the Federal Wars (1859–1863), becoming a general in the Federal armies led by Juan Cristósomo Falcón.* Subsequently, he became a loyal lieutenant of Antonio Guzmán Blanco.*

In 1884 Gusmán Blanco rewarded Crespo by having him chosen president for the two-year term 1884–1886. After Crespo's period, Guzmán Blanco was elected for his own last two years as chief executive. In 1886 Crespo sought to return to the presidency, but Guzmán Blanco chose Juan Pablo Rojas Paúl, who in turn chose as his successor Raimundo Andueza Palacio.

When President Andueza Palacio sought to illegally extend his term of office in 1892 Joaquín Crespo organized and led the so-called Legalist Revolution, which deposed Andueza and brought Crespo back to the presidency. Crespo called a constitutional convention which more or less restored the Federalist constitution of 1864, which had been abrogated by Guzmán Blanco. Crespo was then elected constitutional president for the 1894–1898 term.

The Crespo regime faced serious economic difficulties. As a result, it negotiated loans in Europe on very onerous terms for Venezuela.

In the 1897 election Crespo's choice for a successor, General Ignacio Andrade, was confronted by General José Manuel Hernández,* "El Mocho," an exceedingly popular figure. Although Hernández may well have won the election, Andrade was officially declared the victor. As a consequence, Hernández revolted soon after Andrade had taken office. General Crespo led the government forces against Hernández and was killed in battle.

BIBLIOGRAPHY

Enciclopedia Universal Ilustrada Europeo-Americana. Barcelona: José Espasa e Hijos.
Magallanes, Manuel Vicente: *Los Partidos Políticos en la Evolución Histórica de Venezuela*. Caracas: Monte Avila Editores, 1977.
Velásquez, Ramón J. *La Caída del Liberalismo Amarillo.* Caracas: Ediciones Roraima, 1977.

ROBERT J. ALEXANDER

CRITCHLOW, HUBERT NATHANIEL (1884–1958), founder of the modern trade union movement in Guyana, was undoubtedly one of the most important political actors in that country's twentieth-century history. He was son of a wharf foreman, left primary school at the age of 14, one year before graduation, and worked at odd jobs before becoming a dockworker. At the time he had some national celebrity as one of the colony's top sportsmen. In 1906 he was falsely charged with assault during a strike of dockworkers, but was subsequently acquitted. From then on, he took a leadership role in labor organization.

Critchlow was one of two leaders to meet with the country's Chamber of Commerce during January 1917 in the midst of a wave of strikes for increased wages and better working conditions. By January 1918 he became the undisputed leader of waterfront workers. In January 1919 he formed the British Guiana Labor Union (BGLU), which reached a total membership of 7,000 to 9,000 in its first year. It became affiliated with the International Federation of Trade Unions and the Socialist International.

Critchlow was the person most responsible for development of the Caribbean labor movement. He helped organize the Guianese and West Indian Federation of Trade Unions and Labour Parties which eventually evolved into the Caribbean Labour Congress (CLC) in 1945.

In 1930 Critchlow began to call on workers to struggle to overthrow capitalism and to mobilize for socialist reconstruction. He visited the Soviet Union in 1932 and, on his return, for some time praised the social and political order that he had observed in the Soviet Union and advocated adoption of some of that country's programs in the West Indies.

The trade union movement was officially recognized in 1940 and was provided with political representation in 1943 when Critchlow and fellow unionist Ayube Edun were nominated to the Legislative Council as trade union representatives. In 1941 Critchlow became the first secretary of the newly formed Trades Union Council, an umbrella organization of trade unions. He was finally ousted from control of the BGLU by more radical elements in the early 1950s.

BIBLIOGRAPHY

Chase, A. *A History of Trade Unionism in Guyana: 1900–1961*. Georgetown: New Guyana Company, 1964.
Daly, Vere T. *A Short History of the Guyanese People*. Georgetown: Daly, 1966.
Hintzen, P. C. "Problems of National Integration in Guyana: A Study of Four Urban Areas." M.A. Thesis, Clark University, 1975.
Trinidad and Tobago Government Broadcasting Unit. *Caribbean Emancipators*. Port of Spain: GBU, 1976.

PERCY C. HINTZEN AND W. MARVIN WILL

CROES, GILBERT FRANÇOIS (BATICO) (1938–   ), emerged in the early 1970s as the principal political leader of Aruba and advocate of its separation from the Netherlands Antilles. He was educated in Hilversum, in The Netherlands, after which he returned home to teach school. He founded the Movimiento Electoral del Pueblo (MEP) in 1970, as a party seeking greater autonomy for Aruba. Subsequently, he served in both the island legislature of Aruba and the Staten (Parliament) of Netherlands Antilles.

During 1983–1984 there were extended negotiations among the governments of Aruba, Netherlands Antilles, and The Netherlands. Agreement was finally reached that on January 1, 1986, Aruba would become separate from the Netherlands Antilles, although maintaining a common currency, at least for the time being. Croes did not emerge as the first minister president of the newly autonomous Aruban regime, because in November 1985 his party was defeated in general elections by a rival coalition. In fact, Croes was badly wounded in an automobile accident the day before the transfer of power to the Aruban regime and could not participate in it.

BIBLIOGRAPHY

Alexander, Robert J. "Netherlands Antilles," in Robert J. Alexander (ed.). *Political Parties of the Americas*. Vol. 2. Westport, Conn.: Greenwood Press, 1982.

El Pais (Madrid), January 6, 1986.
Personalities Caribbean, Seventh Edition 1982–83. Binghamton, N.Y.: Vail Ballou Press,
    n.d.

ROBERT J. ALEXANDER

D

DE LA MADRID, MIGUEL (1934–   ), president of Mexico during 1982–1988, had to preside over an austerity program to rescue Mexico from the brink of bankruptcy. Born in Colima, de la Madrid took his law degree at the National Autonomous University of Mexico and a master's degree in public administration from Harvard, the first Mexican president to hold a graduate degree from a U.S. university. He served as assistant finance director for Pemex, the government's oil corporation, public credit director for the Finance Ministry, and then minister of planning and the budget in the José López Portillo* cabinet.

As soon as de la Madrid was inaugurated as president on December 1, 1982, he announced his austerity policies and an anticorruption campaign that exposed the wholesale graft of the Echeverría and López Portillo administrations. The opposition was predictable. The Mexican Federation of Labor, the federal bureaucrats, and the leaders of the Institutional Revolutionary Party all complained.

De la Madrid retreated to a modest degree in the second half of 1984 and in 1985, reintroducing several subsidies to "protect the purchasing power of workers." In 1985 the government's Basic Commodities Corporation and its National Supply System obtained larger roles in supplying low-cost goods to retail stores run by labor unions, bureaucratic unions, and farm groups.

Despite such problems, de la Madrid, with the help of emergency loans and credits from the United States, managed to rescue his nation from sliding into bankruptcy.

BIBLIOGRAPHY

Briggs, Donald C., and Marvin Alisk. *Historical Dictionary of Mexico*. Metuchen, N.J.: Scarecrow Press, 1981.
Camp, Roderic A. *Mexican Political Biographies, 1935–1975*. Tucson: University of Arizona Press, 1976.
Grayson, George W. "Oil and Politics in Mexico." *Current History* 82, No. 488 (December 1983).

Ross, Stanley R. "Divergent Approaches to the Presidential Succession." *The Mexican Forum* 3, No. 1 (January 1983).
Street, James H. "Mexico's Development Dilemma." *Current History* 82, No. 488 (December 1983).

MARVIN ALISKY

DELGADO CHALBAUD, CARLOS (1909–1950), was a member of the Venezuelan Revolutionary Government Junta which first brought the Acción Democrática (AD) party to power in 1945; and president of the military junta that overthrew the AD regime three years later. His mysterious murder paved the way for the advent to power of dictator Marcos Pérez Jiménez.*

Delgado Chalbaud was the son of an old caudillo, Román Delgado Chalbaud, who in 1919 failed in an attempt to overthrow Juan Vicente Gómez* and spent the next seven years in one of Gómez' dungeons. Carlos went with his mother to France and was educated in French schools, including engineering training in a military school. He accompanied his father, who had been released in 1926, in the ill-fated attempt to invade Venezuela with a revolutionary force in 1929. Román Delgado Chalbaud was killed in this invasion; Carlos returned to France.

Carlos Delgado Chalbaud went back to Venezuela after the death of Juan Vicente Gómez in December 1935 and was given a commission as captain of engineers in the Venezuelan Army by President Eleazar López Contreras.* He had risen to major by 1945.

When junior officers formed the Military Patriotic Union, to conspire against President Isaís Medina Angarita* in 1945, Delgado Chalbaud joined only a few weeks before the coup of October 18, 1945. However, he became one of the two military men in the Revolutionary Government Junta set up after the coup, serving also as minister of war. He continued as minister of war under elected President Rómulo Gallegos* after February 1948. In that capacity, he allowed Major Marcos Pérez Jiménez* to return home from a decorous exile, and subsequently he did nothing to thwart Pérez Jiménez' plotting against the Gallegos government.

With the downfall of Gallegos on November 24, 1948, Colonel Delgado Chalbaud insisted on being head of the new military junta. He remained in that post until he was kidnapped in broad daylight in Caracas and then murdered. Full details of the plot behind his murder have never been revealed, although the assassin was himself killed by the police.

BIBLIOGRAPHY

Alexander, Robert J. *Rómulo Betancourt and the Transformation of Venezuela.* New Brunswick, N.J.: Transactions Press, 1981.
Betancourt, Rómulo. *Venezuela: Oil and Politics.* Boston: Houghton Mifflin, 1979.
Kolb, Glen L. *Democracy and Dictatorship in Venezuela 1945–1958.* New London: Connecticut College, 1974.

Martz, John D. *Acción Democrática: Evolution of a Modern Political Party in Venezuela.* Chapel Hill: University of North Carolina Press, 1966.

ROBERT J. ALEXANDER

DE LUGO, RON (1930–   ), a leader of the U.S. Virgin Islands Democratic Party, was educated in the Virgin Islands and Puerto Rico. He was a member of the Territorial Senate from 1956 to 1966, and was administrator of St. Croix in 1961. He was the Virgin Islands' nonvoting member of the U.S. House of Representatives from 1969 to 1973 and from 1983 to 1987. He was a delegate to the National Democratic Convention in 1956, 1960, 1964, and 1968 and a member of the Democratic National Committee after 1959. He was a member of the Virgin Islands Constitutional Convention in 1971–1972.

BIBLIOGRAPHY

Sharpless, Richard E. "Virgin Islands of the United States," in Robert J. Alexander (ed.), *Political Parties of the Americas.* Vol. 2. Westport, Conn.: Greenwood Press, 1982.
Who's Who in America, 1984–1985. 43rd ed. Chicago: Marquis Who's Who, 1984.

RICHARD E. SHARPLESS

DEODORO DA FONSECA, MARSHAL MANUEL (1827–1892), was the leader of the military faction that overthrew the imperial rule of Dom Pedro II* in 1889, and the first president of Republican Brazil in 1891, but he proved to be an inept political leader.

Born in the northeastern state of Alagoas, he served all his adult life in the army. He took part in the Paraguayan War (1864–1870). As early as 1879 the army began to disagree with government policies aimed at reducing the size of the armed forces. By taking their case to the nation's newspapers, the officials broke the law but were not punished for their actions.

In 1883 sharper disagreements began to develop between the army and the civilian ministers of war of Dom Pedro II. The army, overwhelmingly abolitionist, resented being assigned to return runaway slaves and felt that Dom Pedro did not recognize their contribution to the nation since the war with Paraguay ended in 1870.

By 1883 General Deodoro da Fonseca had emerged as the most popular officer in the Brazilian military after the death of Luis Alves de Lima, the Duque de Caxias, and younger army officers looked to him for leadership in their opposition to the emperor. The founding of the Military Club in 1887 with General Deodoro as its first president accelerated the role of the military in the Brazilian political arena. A series of incidents that pitted the civilian army ministers against General Deodoro took place.

When rumors began to circulate that the emperor was planning to cut the size of the army, arrest General Deodoro, and transfer all military garrisons out of the capital, Republican Party politicians convinced the general that he must proclaim Brazil a republic to save the army and his comrades in arms. It was a reluctant General Deodoro da Fonseca, backed only by the garrisons of Rio de Janeiro, who under pressure from Republican Party politicians and Benjamin Constant Botelho de Magalhães* and Aristides Lobo, proclaimed Brazil a republic on November 15, 1889.

A provisional government was set up while a republican constitution was prepared by a constituent assembly and delivered to the nation on February 24, 1891. During the provisional government period, General Deodoro da Fonseca proved to be an incompetent politician unable to deal with the civilian political leaders. Nevertheless, the constituent assembly after writing the new constitution elected him to serve as Brazil's first president.

In November 1891 a civil war threatened to break out against Deodoro. To remain in power he quickly dissolved Congress and assumed dictatorial powers. When it became apparent that he had little support from either civilians or the armed forces, he resigned on November 23, 1891. Vice President General Floriano Peixoto* took office and served out the remainder of his term.

BIBLIOGRAPHY

Magalhaes, R. Jr. *Deodoro-a Espada contra o Imperio*. São Paulo: Editora Nacional, 1957.

JORDAN YOUNG

DESSALINES, JEAN-JACQUES (1758–1806), declared Haiti independent on January 1, 1804, after defeating French forces sent to restore colonial rule on the island. From an early age as fieldhand slave, Dessalines displayed a rebellious character. In 1792, with the colony wracked by internecine conflict—among the whites between royalists and supporters of the French Revolution, and between the whites and mulattoes demanding equal political rights—Dessalines joined a slave uprising led by a Jamaican, Boukman. Soon, the rebellious slaves controlled the North, pushing the French to the coastal towns.

Dessalines was noticed by Toussaint L'Ouverture.* There began what was to prove an extremely loyal attachment of Dessalines to L'Ouverture during a period when the changing of allegiances was commonplace. Dessalines played a crucial role in Toussaint's victories over the British, Spanish, and mulatto forces which resulted in eventual unification of the island.

Dessalines was most instrumental in defeating the mulatto general, André Rigaud, who had established an autonomous regime in the South. For this, he was made governor of the South and promoted to general. He reportedly slaughtered between 5,000 and 10,000 mulatto supporters of Rigaud. After Toussaint captured Santo Domingo, Dessalines was posted to the West and South with responsibility for defense, internal security, and restoration of the economy based on cane, coffee, cotton, and indigo production.

In 1802 Napoleon Bonaparte dispatched a military force under his brother-in-law, General Leclerc, to restore French dominion over the colony. Toussaint and his generals, Dessalines and Henri Christophe,* were defeated, and Toussaint surrendered his forces and was taken to France where he died a year later. In the wake of the defeat, Dessalines joined the French forces, along with Henri Christophe.

Meanwhile the United States, in an effort to prevent restoration of French control of St. Domingue, allowed American merchants to send arms and supplies to the ex-slaves. A declaration of war against France by Great Britain prevented Bonaparte from resupplying his troops, among whom illness was taking an extremely large toll. Dessalines and mulatto commander Alexandre Pétion* decided on a united front against the French, launching the War of Independence. After initial successes, the combined forces, now joined by Henri Christophe, declared Dessalines the commander-in-chief. He captured Port-au-Prince on October 3, 1803, after which the French forces were quickly defeated.

Dessalines assumed the title of governor general. He rounded up and slaughtered all but a few of the whites who remained on the island, thus losing most of the country's skilled manpower and isolating Haiti internationally.

Dessalines proclaimed himself emperor on October 8, 1804. In 1805 he invaded Santo Domingo, defeating French and Spanish troops and imposing a cruel regime which many consider the root of the cycle of hatred and hostility that has characterized the two nations of Hispaniola. Alienated from both blacks and mulattoes, isolated and shunned internationally, Dessalines was finally assassinated after an insurrection.

BIBLIOGRAPHY

Beard, John R. *The Life of Toussaint L'Ouverture*. Westport, Conn.: Negro University Press, 1970.
Heinl, R. D., and N. G. Heinl. *Written in Blood*. Boston: Houghton Mifflin, 1978.
James, C.L.R. *The Black Jacobins*. London: Allison and Busby, 1980.
Moran, Charles. *Black Triumvirate*. New York: Exposition, 1957.
Syme, Ronald. *Toussaint: The Black Liberator*. New York: William Morrow, 1971.

PERCY C. HINTZEN

DÍAZ, PORFIRIO (1830–1915), was Mexico's long-time dictator-president whose 35-year rule (1876–1911) provoked the revolt that began the Mexican Revolution. His distinctive first name becames a noun to describe his era, the *porfiriato*.

Díaz was born into a poor *mestizo* family in Oaxaca City. His father died when he was a teenager, and he had to work to support his mother. He studied first at a seminary and then at the Institute of Oaxaca.

A revolution erupted in 1855, and Díaz volunteered as a cavalry lieutenant. His political orientation to the Liberal Party had begun during his days as an Institute student. Within five years he had risen to the rank of brigadier general. In the war against the French Army of occupation and the monarchy of Emperor Maximilian, Díaz became a hero leading Mexican troops in Puebla in 1862 and 1863.

Designated commander of the Army of the East in 1864, Díaz drove the French out of Oaxaca City, only to have the enemy retake the city and capture him. He overpowered his guards, established his own guerrilla camp in the mountains, and soon was leading groups of irregulars in attacks on the French garrisons in Oaxaca and Guerrero. His campaign in southern Mexico culminated in June 1867 with his capture of Mexico City.

Díaz then retired from the Army and took up ranching and farming. However, he kept planning to run for the presidency, counting on his popularity in the Liberal Party. He lost out to President Benito Juárez.*

In 1875, Díaz again ran for president on a platform whose slogan was "Effective Suffrage, No Reelection," a slogan that thirty-five years later would be turned against him. Defeated for the presidency a second time, Díaz and his followers revolted in 1876, ousted Sebastián Lerdo de Tejada* as president, and installed Díaz in his place. A perfunctory election then gave Díaz a regular four-year term, 1876–1880.

Technically out of office for four years while a puppet president held the title during 1880–1884, Díaz actually continued to rule Mexico. Thereafter, every four years he went through the motions of having himself reelected.

During this 35-year period, Díaz transformed Mexico into a stable nation but at the expense of individual liberties. Díaz built roads, linked most major Mexican cities with railroads, revitalized the mining industry, began the oil industry, and promoted Latin America's first steel mill. Much of the economic growth and activity was funded by foreign investors, which engendered antiforeign nationalism among Díaz's opponents.

Internal law and order were maintained by Díaz's elite constabulary, the *Guardias Rurales* or Rural Police. However, to the majority of Mexicans laboring in the fields at subsistence wages, the federal officers seemed highly repressive.

Díaz did not abrogate the Constitution of 1857 but simply ignored much of it. The charter's anticlerical provisions were particularly ignored.

By 1905 a definite anti-Indian racism had crept into government policies and decisions. White and *mestizo* Mexicans could attain services and privileges that Indians could not. A group of presidential advisers, known as the *científicos* (or scientific thinkers), more and more made policy for the president. They stressed the need for technology for urban centers but displayed little concern for the problems of the countryside at a time when a majority of Mexicans were rural.

Díaz' last decade in office witnessed growing opposition from labor unions, peasant leaders, and anticlerical politicians. Despite his pro-management views, Díaz allowed unions for railroad workers and mine workers to grow because the owners were foreigners and demands for pay raises did not directly hurt his own circle of Mexican advisers and friends.

In 1908 Díaz granted an interview to a journalist from the United States, James Creelman, published in the widely read *Pearson's Magazine*, whoe subscribers included many U.S. officials. In it, Díaz, then almost 78 years old, stated that he had achieved his major goals for Mexico and would not run again for president in the forthcoming 1910 election. He even welcomed the formation of opposition parties.

A few months later, he retracted these statements, but it was too late. Washington had taken him seriously, and so had Mexico's leading intellectuals, including Francisco I. Madero.* Using the reneged promises of 1908 as the launching pad for his own presidential campaign, Madero served as the rallying symbol for various groups bitterly opposed to Díaz. When civil war erupted in 1910, Díaz reportedly was surprised by its intensity.

When Ciudad Juárez fell to the insurgents on May 11, 1911, Díaz resigned and fled to France. He spent the remaining four years of his life in Paris, living at the level of an ex-monarch, surrounded by servants. He died unmourned by a majority of Mexicans.

BIBLIOGRAPHY

Arnaiz y Freg, Arturo. *Juárez, Su Obra y Su Tiempo*, Mexico: Universidad Nacional Autónoma de Mexico Obras del Maestro Sierra, 1956.
Bulnes, Francisco. *La Verdad Sobre la Intervención y El Imperio*. Mexico: Librería Bouret, 1904.
Cumberland, Charles. *Mexican Revolution—Genesis Under Madero*. Austin: University of Texas Press, 1952.
Prewett, Virginia. *Reportage on Mexico*. New York: E. P. Dutton, 1941.
Tannenbaum, Frank. *Peace by Revolution*. New York: Columbia University Press, 1933.

MARVIN ALISKY

DÍAZ ORDAZ, GUSTAVO (1911–1979), will be remembered as the president who successfully defeated the most serious challenge to the power of the Revolutionary establishment since the Mexican Revolution began its nonmilitary phase in 1920. He was also the chief executive who presided when Mexico hosted the Olympics, the only Latin American nation ever to have done so.

Prior to the Olympics of 1968 Díaz Ordaz endured two and a half months of orchestrated violence by the far left. The National Student Strike Committee claimed that daily riots were intended to force the Ministry of Education to simplify entrance requirements for the universities and prep schools. Actually, their aim was to force the government to cancel the Olympic Games scheduled for October.

On October 2, 1968, the so-called Student Strike Forces, in which middle-aged riflemen and snipers intermixed with genuine students, killed a few police, and in return 200 of them were killed. That Battle of the Plaza of the Three Cultures ended in capitulation by the rioters, with 2,000 of them sent to jail. The next week President Díaz Ordaz opened the Olympics.

Born into a middle-class family in the town of San Andrés in the state of Puebla, Díaz Ordaz took his law degree from the University of Puebla, in contrast to a majority of the Mexican presidents after 1946 who obtained their law degrees at the National Autonomous University of Mexico. A professor of law at the University of Puebla, he became president of the university in 1940.

In 1941 Díaz Ordaz launched his political career as municipal chairman of the dominant Institutional Revolutionary Party (PRI) for the city of Puebla. Elected a deputy to the federal Congress for the 1943–1946 term, he then served as a senator during 1946–1952. Briefly between his deputy and senatorial terms in 1946, he was secretary of state (lieutenant governor) of the state of Puebla and solidified his contacts within the Ministry of Internal Affairs in Mexico City.

In 1953 Díaz Ordaz became director of legal affairs for the Gobernación Ministry. In 1956 he became that ministry's executive administrator, and in 1958 he was named minister of internal affairs by President Adolfo López Mateos.*

In addition to hosting the Olympics and defeating a leftist attempt to destabilize the government, the Díaz Ordaz administration launched an investment thrust in Central America. By 1970 the government's development bank, Nacional Financiera, had led a consortium of public and private entities in investment larger than that of corporate and governmental Mexico in any previous administration.

After his term as president, Díaz Ordaz became Mexico's ambassador to Spain, but in August 1977 he resigned in disagreement with President José López Portillo's* policies toward the Spanish government. He returned to private law practice in Mexico City, where he died.

BIBLIOGRAPHY

Briggs, Donald C., and Marvin Alisky. *Historical Dictionary of Mexico*. Metuchen, N.J.: Scarecrow Press, 1981.
Camp, Roderic A. *Mexican Political Biographies, 1935–1975*. Tucson: University of Arizona Press, 1976.
Cosio Villegas, Daniel. *La Sucesion Presidencial*. Mexico City: Editorial Joaquin Mortiz, 1974.
Padgett, L. Vincent. *The Mexican Political System*. Boston: Houghton Mifflin, 1976.

MARVIN ALISKY

DUARTE, JOSÉ NAPOLEÓN (1925–   ), was a founder of the Christian Democratic Party of El Salvador and twice president of that republic. He obtained his higher education at the University of Notre Dame in South Bend, Indiana, where he graduated in 1945. Upon his return to El Salvador, he practiced civil engineering until 1964.

One of the founders of the Christian Democratic Party in 1960, Duarte was the party's first general secretary. He was its victorious candidate for mayor of San Salvador, the nation's capital, in 1964, and he was twice reelected.

In 1972 Duarte was the principal opposition candidate for president, with Guillermo Ungo of the National Revolutionary Movement (MNR) as his vice presidential running mate. Although it is generally agreed that Duarte and Ungo won, the military regime then in power counted the ballots differently. Duarte was jailed, beaten, and exiled to Venezuela, where he remained until 1979.

After overthrow of the government of General Carlos Humberto Romero in 1979, Duarte returned to El Salvador. In 1980–1982 he was president of the ruling government junta and sought both to carry out promised reforms and to confront the left-wing guerrilla insurrection, the titular head of which was his one-time running mate, Guillermo Ungo. He was elected constitutional president in 1984.

Although Duarte was elected on a platform of fulfillment of agrarian reform and other changes decreed after the overthrow of Romero, he met strong opposition from the economic-social oligarchy and elements of the military. In addition, his efforts to enter into negotiations with the guerrilla rebels were blocked by elements in his own regime, in the guerrilla forces, and the U.S. government.

BIBLIOGRAPHY

International Who's Who 1985–86. London: Europa Publications, 1985.
McDonald, Ronald H. "El Salvador," in Robert J. Alexander (ed.). *Political Parties of the Americas*. Vol. I. Westport, Conn.: Greenwood Press, 1982.
New York Times, May 8, 1984.
Webre, Stephen. *José Napoleón Duarte and the Christian Democratic Party in San Salvadoran Politics, 1960–1972*. Baton Rouge: Louisiana State University Press, 1979.

ROBERT J. ALEXANDER

DUARTE, JUAN PABLO (1813–1876), was the principal leader of the struggle for independence of the Dominican Republic. Educated in Haiti during the period when Haiti occupied his native land, Duarte returned to Santo Domingo to organize in 1838 a secret society, La Trinitaria, dedicated to achieving Dominican independence. He was exiled by the Haitians in 1842. With the overthrow of Haitian President Jean Pierre Boyer* in 1844, Duarte was able to lead La Trinitaria in a successful effort to free the Dominican Republic from Haitian control.

Juan Pablo Duarte was quickly driven from control of the new Dominican government by General Pedro Santana* and was once again driven into exile, this time to Germany and Venezuela. He did not return home until 1864, at a time when General Santana had agreed to the country's once again becoming a Spanish colony. Although Duarte helped lead the struggle against Spanish domination, he was again exiled by the provisional government of the republic reestablished in 1865. He lived in Venezuela the rest of his life.

BIBLIOGRAPHY

Enciclopedia Universal Ilustrade Europeo Americana. Barcelona: José Espasa e Hijos.
Rodman, Selden. *Quisqueya: A History of the Dominican Republic*. Seattle: 1964.

Welles, Sumner. *Naboth's Vineyard: The Dominican Republic 1844–1924*. 2 vols. New York: 1928.

ROBERT J. ALEXANDER

DUEÑAS, FRANCISCO (?–1875?), was three times chief executive of El Salvador. Little is known of his early career, but in 1851 he was first elected president. During his first term, he reorganized national finances, established the University, and built the country's first customs house. In 1856, as vice president of El Salvador, he was one of the leaders of the struggle against the North American filibusterer William Walker,* who had seized control of Nicaragua.

Dueñas' third period in office was as president of El Salvador between 1863 an 1871. His administration stimulated economic development, established the Military College, built the National Palace, extended the nation's water supply system, and established the first telegraph lines. However, he was overthrown by a coup, put on trial, and though exonerated, driven into exile. He died abroad sometime after 1875.

BIBLIOGRAPHY

Enciclopedia Universal Ilustrada Europeo-Americana. Barcelona: José Espasa e Hijos.

ROBERT J. ALEXANDER

DUVALIER, FRANÇOIS (1907–1971), became president of Haiti in 1957 and established the country's only hereditary regime, which lasted until his son Jean-Claude was overthrown in 1986. He was born in Haiti's capital, Port-au-Prince, the son of a schoolteacher. He was educated in local schools, including the Lycée Pétion, where Dumarsais Estimé* was one of his teachers, and the School of Medicine of the national university, where he graduated in 1934.

Duvalier worked in government service for the next ten years. He was associated with the American Sanitary Mission, directing programs of preventive medicine. In 1944 he went to the University of Michigan on a fellowship to study public health, failed his course, and later attended a short course in tropical public health in Puerto Rico. He was involved in the Sanitary Mission's malaria eradication and anti-yaws campaign.

During the 1930s Duvalier joined a group of black intellectuals, the Griots, who had begun to study and sanctify Haiti's African heritage. The group's work marked the beginning of a new campaign against the mulatto elite and an emerging ideology of black power, Haitian style. It was on this ideology that Duvalier later based his political leadership. His pro-black sentiments led to his advocacy of voodoo.

In 1946 Duvalier joined the Worker-Peasant Movement (MOP), a political party formed by a young mathematics teacher, Daniel Fignolé, of which Duvalier became secretary general. Through the party, he built a political constituency in Port-au-Prince.

Mulatto President Élie Lescot* was deposed by a military coup in 1946. Upon assumption of power by President Dumarsais Estimé, Lescot's black successor, Duvalier was appointed director general of public health and later secretary of labor and public health.

When the black commander of the Presidential Guard, Paul Eugène Magloire,* succeeded Estimé in December 1950, after a coup, he was opposed by Duvalier. Duvalier went into hiding until August 1956.

On September 7, 1956, Duvalier became a candidate to succeed Magloire, who was forced to leave the country in November 1956. During the next few months, there were five provisional governments.

Duvalier fought the campaign as representative of the Griots, proclaimed himself heir to Dumarsais Estimé, and had the firm support of the military leaders. The campaign became a two-man race between Duvalier and a wealthy mulatto businessman, Louis Dejoie. With the army in full command, when the results were announced Duvalier won, and his supporters received 23 of the 37 seats in the Chamber of Deputies and all those in the Senate.

Duvalier began to organize a system of coercion, control, and patronage. He began a reign of terror which by some estimates, resulted in killing between 30,000 and 60,000 opponents during his 14-year rule. He removed all powerful officers from the military, and in 1959 he created a militia, the *tonton macoutes*, over which he had absolute personal control. They conducted a campaign of terror and repression against the population. In 1963 he also created the National Security Volunteers, recruited from among the black underclass and absolutely loyal to him.

The encouragement of voodoo served as a means of both recruiting rural support and spreading fear. Similarly, the *tonton macoutes* and the National Security Volunteers both recruited support and instilled fear. Many leaders of these two organizations were local leaders in rural constituencies.

Duvalier moved to undermine the influence of the church by expelling foreign clergy and by securing the appointment of personally acceptable Haitians to the hierarchy of the Roman Catholic and Anglican churches. Like the military, the organized church soon became an accomplice of his regime.

Duvalier institutionalized corruption which transferred enormous wealth to him, his family, and his associates. Power became increasingly personalized. Parliament was dissolved in 1961, two years before its term was up, and a unicameral legislature was decreed in the elections for which only candidates personally chosen by the president* participated. Duvalier's name was placed at the head of every ballot. All of Duvalier's candidates were declared elected, and he announced himself to be elected to another six-year term of office, by virtue of the presence of his name on the ballot. In 1963 he had himself declared President for Life, and in a plebiscite to confirm his status, it was reported that there were 2.8 million votes in favor and 3,234 against. Persons voting ''no'' were promptly arrested for defacing the ballot.

Although in the beginning Duvalier secured a considerable amount of American economic and military assistance, after 1961 this aid was finally ended by the Kennedy administration. Although Duvalier at first managed to attract considerable private foreign investment, this too ended, and there was rapid deterioration of the economy, with growth of absolute poverty and degenerating conditions.

Duvalier was able to retain power until his death in April 1971. Upon foreseeing his imminent death, he announced on January 22 that Jean-Claude Duvalier, his 19-year old son, was his chosen successor, and in a plebiscite this was "confirmed" by a vote of 2,391,916 to 0.

BIBLIOGRAPHY

Diederich, B., and Al Burt. *Papa Doc: The Truth About Haiti Today*. New York: McGraw-
      Hill, 1969.
Duvalier, François. *Memoires D'un Leader du Tiers Monde*. Port-au-Prince: Hachette,
      1969.
Gingras, Jean-Pierre. *Duvalier, Caribbean Cyclone*. New York: Exposition Press, 1967.
Heinl, R. D., and N. G. Heinl. *Writtin in Blood*. Boston: Houghton Mifflin, 1971.
                                                                     PERCY C. HINTZEN

DUVALIER, JEAN-CLAUDE (1951–   ), became President for Life of Haiti after the death of his father, dictator François Duvalier* on April 21, 1971. He was born in Port-au-Prince a few years before his father took office. He attended primary and secondary schools in the capital, and spent one year at the law school. On January 22, 1971, his ailing father made the announcement that Jean-Claude was to be his successor, a decision confirmed in a "plebiscite" held one month later, with a vote of 2,391,916 to 0 in favor. When François Duvalier died, Jean-Claude, then only 19 years old, became the nominal head of state. For a while, real power rested with his mother, Simone Ovide Duvalier, and, to a less extent, his sister, Marie-Denise.

Gradually, Jean-Claude put his personal stamp on the regime. He began to recruit members of the elite whom he had met in school into positions of power. He also began to emphasize development and to invite qualified Haitians to return home. Gradually, criticism of the regime began to appear in the local media, and in 1979 some political parties emerged. These developments were aided somewhat by President Jimmy Carter's emphasis on human rights and by an increasing dependence on U.S. investments and U.S. foreign aid to bail out the economy.

Support for the regime of François Duvalier, rooted in the black middle class, became eroded, and formerly powerful Duvalierists became alienated. Outwardly, the ideology of black domination was maintained, as was Jean-Claude's support for voodoo, but in reality the regime became firmly entrenched in the mulatto elite.

Jean-Claude moved to reinvigorate the educational system by inviting foreign specialists. Agricultural development was attempted with the help of projects from the United States, Israel, France, and Canada. Most importantly, he used the extremely low wages of urban workers to attract over 200 assembly-type industries employing over 40,000 people and producing for export to the industrial countries.

The test of the regime's sincerity about restoring political liberty came in legislative elections in 1979. But the regime used bribery, terror, and force to ensure victory in all but one constituency. The election of President Reagan, with his emphasis on supporting friendly regimes rather than on human rights, contributed to a political crackdown in November 1980, with the arrest of nearly 200 persons, the expulsion of many, and the use of the country's courts, under absolute control of the president, to convict members of the opposition.

Duvalier became even more closely aligned with the mulatto elite when, in 1980, he married Michele Bennett, daughter of a nouveau riche mulatto family. At the same time, economic problems began to escalate. The high price of imported oil, increasing foreign indebtedness, and high interest rates began to depress Haiti's already impoverished economy.

Duvalier was becoming even more isolated from the black middle-class support base of his father. At the end of 1985 high school students began a series of strikes, and his machinery of control began to falter in areas outside the capital. Massive demonstrations against his regime and a shutdown by the business sector convinced the government of the United States to encourage him to leave the country. In February 1986 he left the presidency, and was transported on an American military plane into exile in France.

BIBLIOGRAPHY

Diederich, B., and Al Burt. *Papa Doc: The Truth About Haiti Today*. New York: McGraw-Hill, 1969.
Nicholls, David. *Haiti in Caribbean Context*. London: Macmillan Co., 1985.
Rotberg, Robert I. *Haiti: The Politics of Squalor*. Boston: Houghton Mifflin, 1971.
Weinstein, Brian, and Aaron Segal. *Haiti: Political Failures, Cultural Successes*. New York: Praeger, 1984.

PERCY C. HINTZEN

E

ECHANDI JIMÉNEZ, MARIO (1915–), was president of Costa Rica from 1958 to 1962. A wealthy lawyer-businessman, he represented conservative and traditional elements in Costa Rican politics. In the election of 1948, he supported Otilio Ulate Blanco.* Following the civil war of 1948, which was fought to uphold Ulate's election, Echandi served as Costa Rican ambassador to the United States and as foreign minister.

During the subsequent presidential term of José Figueres Ferrer* (1953–1958), Echandi serving in the national legislature, became a hero of anti-Figueres elements. In January 1955 armed forces under the exiled Rafael Angel Calderón Guardia* unsuccessfully invaded Costa Rica from Nicaragua, with the aid of that nation's dictator, Anastasio Somoza García.* Figueres became convinced that Ulate and Echandi were involved in the conspiracy. When Figueres used his majority in the Legislative Assembly to lift congressional immunity of Echandi in order to bring him to trial on charges of treason, the courts refused to try Echandi, and he returned to Congress in triumph. Figueres had inadvertently given the opposition a presidential candidate.

Echandi won the 1958 election. Although he had been a major critic of recent changes in Costa Rican society, he did not undo economic and social reforms, concentrating on strengthening the private sector, attracting foreign investment, and promoting public works. Echandi faced perilous international coditions marked by the fall of long-time Caribbean dictators and the rise of Fidel Castro* in Cuba. He steered a neutral course during this period, and Costa Rica benefited from the Alliance for Progress.

Echandi ran for president again in 1970, at the head of a coalition of opposition parties, but got only 41.2 percent of the vote against Figueres. In 1982 he was again a candidate, but this time he headed a splinter right-wing group and won only 3.3 percent of the vote.

BIBLIOGRAPHY

Ameringer, Charles D. *Democracy in Costa Rica*. New York: Praeger, 1982.
————. *Don Pepe: A Political Biography of Jose Figueres of Costa Rica*. Albuquerque: University of New Mexico Press, 1979.
Mavis, Richard, and Karen Biesanz. *Los Costarricenses*. San José: Editorial Universidad Estatal a Distancia, 1979.

                                                            CHARLES D. AMERINGER

ERRÁZURIZ ECHAÚREN, FEDERICO (1850–1901), son of a former president of Chile, Federico Errázuriz Zañartu,* was the second chief executive during the so-called Parliamentary Republic established after the Civil War of 1891. He received his law degree from the University of Chile in 1873. Three yeras later he entered the Chamber of Deputies, where he remained until his election as senator.

Under President Domingo Santa María González,* Errázuriz was one of the leaders of the congressional opposition. Subsequently, although minister of war and navy in the cabinet of President José Manuel Balmaceda Fernández* for a short time, he sided with Congress against the president in the civil war of 1891.

In 1894 Errázuriz was elected to the Senate. In that same year President Jorge Montt Alvarez named him* minister of justice and public instruction.

In 1896 Errázuriz was elected president as the nominee of the Coalition, made up of some factions of the Liberals, the Conservative Party, and the National Party. His margin of victory was so narrow, however, that the issue had to be decided by Congress.

The administration of President Errázuriz Echaúren was most notable for a boundary dispute with Argentina which almost resulted in war. However, the Chilean president and his Argentine counterpart, Julio Argentina Roca,* finally decided to submit the issue to arbitration. Domestically, expansion of the education system and installation of a modern water supply system in Santiago and Valparaiso were the most significant occurrences.

In 1900 Errázuriz' health seriously declined. On May 1, 1901, he retired as chief executive, turning over power to Vice President Anibal Zañartu, and died before the inauguration of his elected successor.

BIBLIOGRAPHY

Cortes, Lia, and Jordi Fuentes. *Diccionario Político de Chile*. Santiago: Editorial Orbe, 1967.
Galdames, Luis. *Historia de Chile*. Santiago: Editorial Zig Zag, 1945.
Torribio Medina, José. *Los Errázuriz: Notas Bibliográficas y Documentos para la Historia de Esta Familia en Chile*. Santiago: Editorial Universitaria, 1964.

                                                            ROBERT J. ALEXANDER

ERRÁZURIZ ZAÑARTU, FEDERICO (1825–1877), was the first Liberal to be president of Chile. He received his law degree in 1846, after which he began his political career as a member of the municipal government of Santiago. In

1849 he was elected to the Chamber of Deputies. He strongly opposed election of Manuel Montt Torres* in 1851 and participated in the abortive uprising that sought to prevent Montt's taking office. He was then exiled for some time to Peru but upon his return was again elected to the Chamber of Deputies.

During the administration of President José Joaquín Pérez* (1861–1871), Errázuriz Zañartu held several cabinet portfolios. He served as minister of war and marine during the war against Spain, in which Chile was allied with Peru and Bolivia. In 1867 he was elected to the Senate.

In 1871 Federico Errázuriz Zañartu was elected president, as the outgoing government's candidate and with support of the Liberal and Conservative parties. During his administration, Liberals, Radicals, and National Party members in Parliament proposed a variety of measures to limit the power of the church: extension of government control of education; ending the right of clergymen to be tried in ecclesiastical instead of civil courts; civil control of cemeteries; civil marriage; and separation of church and state. Although compromises were reached on some of these issues, the controversy ended the Liberal-Conservative alliance that had dominated Chilean politics for a decade.

Several steps were taken to limit the power of the president. One increased the power of the "Continuing Committee" of Congress that met regularly when the Senate and Chamber were not in session.

The Errázuriz Zañartu government encouraged economic development. Construction of new railroads was undertaken, and foreign capital was encouraged to invest in expansion of mining. In addition, a major effort was undertaken, under the direction of Benjamin Vicuña MacKenna,* whom Errázuriz appointed mayor of Santiago, to modernize and beautify the capital city.

Ex-President Errázuriz Zañartu died only about nine months after turning over his office to his elected successor late in 1876.

BIBLIOGRAPHY

Cortes, Lia, and Jordi Fuentes. *Diccionario Político de Chile*. Santiago: Editorial Orbe, 1967.
Enciclopedia Universal Ilustrada Europeo Americana. Barcelona: José Espasa Hijos.
Galdames, Luis. *Historia de Chile*. Santiago: Editorial Zig Zag, 1945.
Torribio Medina, José. *Los Errázuriz: Notas Bibliográficas y Documentos para la Historia de Esta Familia en Chile*. Santiago: Editorial Universitaria, 1964.

ROBERT J. ALEXANDER

ESQUIVEL, MANUEL (1940–), became Belize's second prime minister in December 1984. After attending primary and secondary schools in Belize City, Esquivel attended Loyola University in New Orleans, where he earned a bachelor's degree in physics; Bristol University in England, acquiring certification in physics education; and postgraduate work at New York University. Esquivel then accepted a teaching post at the Jesuit-associated St. John's College in Belize City. He held that post until 1984.

Esquivel helped to form the United Democratic Party (UDP) in 1973 out of a merger of three of the country's opposition parties. His first elective post came in 1974, when his party won control of the Belize City Council. He was again successful in municipal elections in 1977 and 1980. In the interim, he contested and lost a seat in the country's House of Representatives in 1979, an election the ruling party was expected to lose to the UDP, but in which the UDP was able to capture only 5 of 18 seats. Esquivel was appointed to the Belizean Senate, however.

Dissatisfaction with UDP leadership as a result of the party's electoral loss led to a shakeup in the party with Esquivel being chosen party leader in January 1983. He had previously been chairman of the party.

Under Esquivel's leadership the UDP grew in strength, particularly in Belize City, the country's largest city and port, where a majority of the country's population resides. The country had been granted independence from Great Britain on September 21, 1981. However, unemployment in the port city was estimated to be more than 40 percent, which worked to the advantage of Esquivel and his UDP in the country's first post-independence elections. Esquivel emphasized an economic development program based on attracting foreign multinationals as a way out of the country's economic plight, which he blamed on mismanagement by the country's then ruling party. He presented a more pro-Western position in the country's foreign relations, harshly criticizing the government of Prime Minister George Price* for its relations with the socialist states of Cuba and Nicaragua. Esquivel led the UDP to a stunning landslide victory in 1984.

BIBLIOGRAPHY

Alexander, Robert J. "Belize," in Robert J. Alexander (ed.). *Political Parties of the Americas*. Vol. 1. Westport, Conn.: Greenwood Press, 1982.
"The Comet of Belize: Manuel Esquivel." *The New York Times*, December 16, 1984.
Personal Communication.
Young, Alma. "Belize," in Jack W. Hopkins (ed.). *Latin America and Caribbean Contemporary Record*. Vols. 3 and 4. New York: Holmes and Meier, 1984, 1985.
————, and Jacqueline Braveboy-Wagner. "Territorial Disputes in the Caribbean Basin," in Marvin Will and Richard Millett (eds.). *Crescents of Conflict*. New York: Praeger Publishers, 1985.

PERCY C. HINTZEN AND W. MARVIN WILL

ESTIGARRIBIA, JOSÉ FÉLIX (1888–1940), president of Paraguay from 1937 to 1940, was the only Paraguayan besides Francisco Solano López* to attain the title of marshal, as successful commander of the country's army in the Chaco War against Bolivia between 1932 and 1935. After graduating from the military academy and pursuing a more or less routine career in the armed forces, he only became a major figure in national affairs during and after the war.

Following the Chaco conflict, Paraguay experienced a year of turmoil. The Liberals, under President Eusebio Ayala, were overthrown in February 1936 in a coup that brought Colonel Rafael Franco,* a popular military hero, to the presidency. However, Franco's anti-Liberal revolutionary government was deeply divided among various factions, and in August 1937 a successful coup brought the Liberals back to power.

Marshal Estigarribia was made head of the new government. He favored the reformist-minded New Liberal faction of the party, but his attempts at social reform were blocked by Congress, controlled by the traditional Liberals. So Estigarribia dissolved Congress, declared himself dictator, and brought in a new constitution (1940), which provided for increased state power and an exceptionally strong president. Estigarribia seemed to be instituting a kind of corporativist structure in Paraguay, with representation of group interests rather than individuals. However, he was killed in an airplane crash less than a month after the new constitution went into effect.

BIBLIOGRAPHY

Kolinski, Charles J. *Historical Dictionary of Paraguay*. Metuchen, N.J.: Scarecrow Press, 1973.
Lewis, Paul H. *Paraguay Under Stroessner*. Chapel Hill: University of North Carolina Press, 1980.
Lott, Leo B. *Venezuela and Paraguay: Political Modernity and Tradition in Conflict*. New York: Holt, Rinehart and Winston, 1972.
Warren, Harris G. *Paraguay: An Informal History*. Norman: University of Oklahoma Press, 1949.
Weil, Thomas, et al. *Area Handbook For Paraguay*. Washington, D.C.: Department of Defense, 1972.

JOHN T. DEINER

ESTIMÉ, DUMARSAIS (1900–1953), became president of Haiti in 1946, marking the return of the black political elite to power. Born in a small village, he was orphaned at a young age and reared by an uncle, a magistrate and member of the national Senate. After primary and secondary education in Port-au-Prince, he became a mathematics teacher at his alma mater, Lyceé Pétion, where he taught François Duvalier,* the future dictator.

Estimé was active in politics at an early age and lost his teaching job for opposing President Louis Borno during the U.S. occupation. When Borno was replaced by President Stenio Vincent* in 1930, Estimé became a member of the Chamber of Deputies and president of it for a time. During his tenure as minister of education, he organized the system of higher education to be based on merit and improved significantly the salaries of the country's teachers. Estimé also served in other portfolios in President Vincent's cabinet.

Vincent was replaced by mulatto President Élie Lescot,* who was deposed in January 1946 by a military coup. With the backing of the only black member of the three-man Executive Military Committee, Major Paul Eugène Magloire,* and with support of the black intellectual community, Estimé was elected president by the National Assembly.

Estimé embarked on a program of reform which he labeled "socialist" but was more nationalist and populist in character. He restored the ban on foreign ownership of land and broke the monopoly of Standard Fruit in production of bananas, nationalizing their holdings and dividing them into seven sections that were parceled out to his supporters. Retaliation from the former owners resulted in almost total destruction of the industry.

Estimé restored independence to the judiciary and the legislature, allowed freedom of the press, and encouraged formation of political parties and trade unions which were legalized and which freely criticized the government. He also undertook educational reform, expanding the school system. He increased the salaries of state employees, partly as a means of providing upward mobility through the civil service to the blacks.

President Estimé was blessed with a booming economy when he came to office, which helps explain the success of his social reform policies. He continued to receive U.S. economic assistance, while making efforts to end American financial control established during occupation.

Some of Estimé's policies alienated both left and right. His efforts to create and encourage a black elite came to be resented and became a burden on the country's fiscal resources. Despite successful efforts to encourage tourism, much of the inordinate sums spent on development of tourist facilities was unaccounted for. He imposed, for the first time, an income tax that particularly hit the elite. Moreover, he at least passively encouraged the practice of voodoo and attempted to curb and Haitianize the Catholic Church.

In 1950 Estimé decided to have himself reelected. He declared martial law and attempted to intimidate his opponents by mob violence. In May 1950 he was finally removed from office by the same junta that had paved the way for his assumption of power. He left Haiti and died in New York three years later. He was granted a state funeral by President Paul Magloire, and when François Duvalier came to power was named a national hero. Both his widow and son served in the Duvalier regime.

BIBLIOGRAPHY

Diederich, B., and Al Burt. *Papa Doc: The Truth About Haiti Today*. New York: McGraw-Hill, 1969.
Gingras, Jean-Pierre. *Duvalier, Caribbean Cyclone*. New York: Exposition Press, 1967.
Heinl, R. D. and N. G. Heinl. *Written in Blood*. Boston: Houghton Mifflin, 1978.
Logan, R. W. *Haiti and the Dominican Republic*. London: Oxford University Press, 1968.
Nicholls, David. *Haiti in Caribbean Context*. London: Macmillan Co., 1985.

                                                                        PERCY C. HINTZEN

ESTRADA CABRERA, MANUEL (1857–1923), was a Liberal dictator who held power for 22 years in Guatemala, longer than anyone else in its history. After his "election" to the presidency in 1898, he amended the Constitution to eliminate the single-term presidential limitation. He was then reelected four times in electoral exercises that were flimsy façades for his personal autocracy.

As Justo Rufino Barrios* had done earlier, Estrada attempted to promote prosperity through extensive public works. Roads, bridges, and ports were built. A new elite of coffee producers and outside companies emerged under Barrios and Estrada Cabrera, and displaced the old landed oligarchy.

Estrada Cabrera created a large, permanent bureaucracy through which the government penetrated rural areas that had never been integrated into the political system. At the same time, personalities replaced ideas as political activity was limited to jockeying for power by the military or to internecine struggles among various Liberal factions.

Estrada continued the anticlericalism inaugurated by Barrios, confiscating church lands and banning a number of religious activities. Some services previously provided by the church were assumed by the governmental bureaucracy.

When labor unions began to organize, strikes and labor demonstrations were harshly suppressed by the armed forces. Most industrial establishments were small shops that successfully resisted unionization.

Estrada Cabrera made exceedingly generous concessions to outside planters, merchants, and financiers. German coffee growers and North American and British transportation and commercial interests became extremely influential. In 1904 Estrada granted the United Fruit Company a 99-year concession to own and operate the country's principal rail line, and it soon controlled all the railroads in Guatemala. He also granted United Fruit large portions of prime banana land, enabling the company to become the dominating entity in the economy.

When El Salvador assisted Guatemalan rebels in 1906, Estrada Cabrera declared war. The United States and Mexico negotiated an armistice and then sponsored a treaty signed by all Central American states in which they agreed to stop intervening in each other's affairs.

By 1920 discontent had reached nearly every sector of Guatemalan society. With the murder of an antigovernment legislator in the halls of Congress, national outrage was such that Estrada Cabrera tried to appease the opposition by allowing return of all political exiles. However, Congress declared him insane and forced his resignation. He died in exile.

BIBLIOGRAPHY

Karnes, T. L. *Failure of Union: Central America, 1824–1975*. Tempe: Arizona State University Press, 1975.
Rodríguez, Mario. *Central America*. Englewood Cliffs, N.J.: Prentice-Hall, 1965.
Vidaurre, Adrián. *Los Ultimos Treinta Años de ela Vida Política de Guatemala*. Havana: 1921.
Woodward, Ralph L., Jr. *Central America: A Nation Divided*. New York: 1985.
                                                          JOSÉ M. SÁNCHEZ

ESTRADA PALMA, TOMÁS (1835–1907), was the first president of the Cuban Republic, serving from 1902 to 1906. In 1876, during the Ten Years' War (1868–1878), he was declared president of the rebel "Republic in Arms," a position he held only briefly before being captured by the Spaniards. Following release from prison, Estrada was named by the revolutionary forces to carry on diplomatic negotiations abroad, primarily with the United States. Throughout the 1880s, he operated a Quaker school for boys in upstate New York and became a naturalized U.S. citizen. In 1895 he was chief for a year of the Cuban junta in New York, succeeding José Martí,* who had departed for Cuba to lead the revolution.

On May 29, 1902, Tomás Estrade Palma became Cuba's first president. Elected without opposition, with support of most of the leading politicians and military leaders, he unfortunately was the wrong man for the position. He was not a true representative of Cuban nationalism, preferred a politically dependent Cuba, and prior to assuming office had anticipated annexation of Cuba by the United States. Once in power, he made it clear that he supported the Platt Amendment.

Coming to power without any meaningful political party or platform, Estrada carried on programs initiated by Leonard Wood during the first U.S. occupation. Over 300 kilometers of new roads, improved sanitation, expanded public works, and continued growth of educational programs were his accomplishments. The treasury reserve grew from $539,000 in 1902 to $7,099,000 in 1906. However, he was unsuccessful in getting Congress to approve legislation necessary for establishment of political order. The Constitution of 1901 called for the promulgation of 43 organic laws. 15 had been adopted during the first U.S. occupation, and under Estrada Palma only 4 were passed. With a reputation for financial integrity, Estrada Palma was perhaps the only Cuban president prior to 1959 who failed to enrich himself in office.

The most lasting legacy of the republic's first president was legitimization and institutionalization of U.S. intervention in Cuban domestic affairs. In 1905 Estrada Palma agreed to run for reelection with support of the Moderate (Conservative) Party, and the Liberal Party boycotted the election. In August 1906, with the Liberals in rebellion, Estrada Palma virtually begged the United States to invoke the Platt Amendment and intervene. When President Theodore Roosevelt hesitated, Estrada Palma resigned, thereby creating a political vacuum that forced the United States to intervene.

BIBLIOGRAPHY

Dominguez, Jorge I. *Cuba: Order and Revolution.* Cambridge, Mass.: Harvard University Press, 1978.
Fagg, John Edwin. *Cuba, Haiti and the Dominican Republic.* Englewood Cliffs, N.J.: Prentice-Hall, 1965.
Fitzgibbon, Russel H. *Cuba and the United States, 1900–1935.* New York: Russell and Russell, 1935.

STEPHEN J. WRIGHT

EVANS, MELVIN (1917–), the first elected governor of the United States Virgin Islands, received his primary and secondary education in the Virgin Islands. He then studied at Howard University in Washington, D.C., where he received a bachelor of science degree in 1940 and a medical degree in 1944. He subsequently received a master of public health degree at the University of California at Berkeley in 1967.

Evans was the physician in charge of the Frederikstad Municipal Hospital in St. Croix from 1945 to 1948, and chief municipal physician of the Virgin Islands government in St. Croix during 1951–1956 and 1957–1959. Between 1959 and 1967, he was Virgin Islands commissioner of health.

Evans led the reorganization of the Progressive Republican Party in the Virgin Islands and was its successful candidate for governor, serving from 1969 to 1975. In 1979–1980 he was the Virgin Islands' nonvoting member of the U.S. Congress. In 1981 he was named ambassador to Trinidad and Tobago by the Reagan administration.

BIBLIOGRAPHY

Sharpless, Richard E. "Virgin Islands of the United States," in Robert J. Alexander (ed.). *Political Parties of the Americas*. Vol. 2. Westport, Conn.: Greenwood Press, 1982.
Who's Who in America, 43rd ed., 1984–1985. Chicago: Marquis Who's Who, 1984.

RICHARD E. SHARPLESS

F

FALCÓN, JUAN CRISTÓSOMO (1820–1870), leader of the Liberal or Federal forces in Venezuela in the Federal Wars of 1859–1863, served for nearly four years as president of the republic. He first came into prominence in his home state of Coro (now Falcón) during the administrations of the Monagas brothers, José Tadeo* and José Gregorio* (1847–1858), as military and political leader of the Liberals there. When José Tadeo Monagas was overthrown by a coalition of Conservatives and disillusioned Liberals under Julián Castro in March 1858, Falcón at first supported Castro. However, when Castro turned against the Liberals, Falcón fled to the Antilles.

In July 1859 Falcón returned to Venezuela with an invading Liberal force. Proclaimed head of the Liberal cause (now rechristened Federalist), with Ezequiel Zamora as its military chief, Falcón assumed the military chieftancy as well after Zamora was killed in battle in January 1860. A series of defeats forced Falcón to flee to Colombia and then the Antilles in April 1860. It was more than a year before he was able to return with a new invading force.

This time, the Federal cause was successful. By October 1861 Conservative leader General José Antonio Páez* consented to peace negotiations, but agreement proved impossible. Devastating conflict continued through 1862. Finally, in April 1863 Falcón and Páez signed the Treaty of Coche which recognized Federalist victory in the war.

Falcón became provisional president. He called a constitutional convention, which completed its work by March 18, 1865, when he was sworn in as constitutional president. His principal task was to begin reconstruction from the devastation of the Federalist War. His agent in Europe, Antonio Guzmán Blanco,* negotiated extensive loans that were invested in public works. However, criticism of Guzmán Blanco grew rapidly, and this finally turned into opposition to Falcón. In 1867 he was overthrown by the so-called Blue Revolution led by José Tadeo Monagas,* and went into exile.

BIBLIOGRAPHY

Diccionario Biográfico de Venezuela. Madrid: Cardenas-Sáenz de la Calzada y Cia.,
    1953.
Enciclopedia Universal Ilustrada Europeo-Americana. Barcelona: José Espasa e Hijos.
Magallanes, Manuel Vicente. *Los Partidos Políticos en la Evolución Histórica de Ven-
    ezuela.* Caracas: Monte Avila Editores, 1977.

ROBERT J. ALEXANDER

FEIJÓ, PADRE DIOGO ANTÔNIO (1784–1843), was a cleric who served
as head of the Brazilian government (1834–1837) and managed to keep Brazil
a single unified country during the difficult period of the regency following Dom
Pedro I's* abdication in 1831. He was one of several regents and served as
minister of justice in 1831. Fearing insubordination of the army, he created a
national guard to suppress regional disorders. He was elected sole regent of
Brazil in October 1834.

Feijó succeeded in putting down regional revolts that had broken out in various
parts of the nation. However, he stirred up considerable controversy with the
Catholic Church by favoring abolition of clerical celibacy and encouraging the
Brazilian church to act more independently of Rome. In 1835 a bill to separate
the Brazilian church from Rome was narrowly defeated in the Chamber of
Deputies. On September 19, 1837, Feijó resigned when the Chamber of Deputies
refused his request for more troops to put down a rebellion in the province of
Rio Grande do Sul.

BIBLIOGRAPHY

Davis, Harold. *Latin American Leaders.* New York: Cooper Square Publishers, 1949 and
    1968.
Ellis, Alfredo. *Feijó Su Epoca.* 1940.
Haring, C. H. *Empire in Brazil: A New World Experiment with Monarchy.* Cambridge,
    Mass.: Harvard University Press, 1958.
Real, Miguel (ed.). *Diogo Antonio Feijó.* 1967.
Sousa, Octavio Tarquinio de. *Diogo Antonio Feijó (1784–1843).* Rio de Janeiro: José
    Olympio, 1942.

JORDAN YOUNG

FERNÁNDEZ OREAMUNO, PRÓSPERO (1834–1885), was president of
Costa Rica from 1882 to 1885. He came to power following the 12-year dictatorship of Tomás Guardia Gatiérrez* and ushered in a decade of change that
set Costa Rica's course for the next 50 years. The Guardia dictatorship, a period
of material progress, had ended the domination of the landed elites and provided
the opportunity for the emerging commercial and professional classes of San
José to seize political power. Fernández, a general, chose to represent these new
groups when he assumed the presidency upon the dictator's death.

Fernández began a series of liberal reforms. He expelled the Jesuits and activist
Bishop Bernardo Augusto Thiel.* He proclaimed civil marriage and divorce,

secularization of cemeteries, the right to work on holy days, and restrictions on religious processions. Many of the young men, such as Ricardo Jiménez Oreamuno* and Cleto González Viquez,* who took part in drafting these reforms, governed Costa Rica through the first third of the twentieth century.

BIBLIOGRAPHY

Ameringer, Charles D. *Democracy in Costa Rica*. New York: Praeger, 1982.
Gamboa G., Francisco. *Costa Rica: ensayo histórico*. San José: Ediciones Revolució, 1971.
Monge, Carlos. *Historia de Costa Rica*. San José: Editorial Fondo de Cultura de Costa Rica, 1948.

CHARLES D. AMERINGER

FERRÉ AGUAYO, LUIS ANTONIO (1904–), governor of Puerto Rico from 1969 to 1973, was educated in Ponce, the Morristown School (Morristown, N.J.), and then received two degrees from the Massachusetts Institute of Technology in the 1920s. He thereupon entered his family's business and by the 1950s was the island's most important industrialist.

Ferré was an active member of the Statehood Republican Party. He ran unsuccessfully for mayor of Ponce in 1940, and was in the 1951 constitution convention and in the insular House of Representatives from 1952 to 1956. He was the party's unsuccessful nominee for governor in 1956, 1960, and 1964.

When, in 1967, his party voted to abstain from a plebiscite on the island's status, Ferré opposed this position and led a dissident movement that formed the New Progressive Party (NPP). He was the successful NPP candidate for governor in 1968, but his administration faced serious economic problems and several damaging scandals. He lost his 1972 bid for reelection. In 1976 he was elected to the insular Senate.

BIBLIOGRAPHY

Personalities Caribbean. 7th ed. Kingston, Jamaica: Personalities Ltd., 1983.

RICHARD E. SHARPLESS

FIGUERES FERRER, JOSÉ (1906–), dominated Costa Rican political affairs for three decades after 1948. The son of a physician, he was born in San Ramón, shortly after his parents emigrated from Spain. In 1924 he went to the United States to study engineering at Massachusetts Institute of Technology but dropped out. He returned to Costa Rica in 1928 and acquired a rundown farm, where he created an agricultural-industrial enterprise, manufacturing coffee bags and rugs from cabuya fiber. He shared the proceeds with the peasants and workers in the form of housing, schools, recreational facilities, and clinics.

Figueres burst on the national scene in 1942, when he made a radio speech criticizing President Rafael Angel Calderón Guardia* for his failure to prevent mob violence in the aftermath of a German submarine attack on Puerto Limón. After two years' exile in Mexico, Figueres returned home as a hero of those opposed to Calderón, whose regime had grown repressive. When President Teodoro Picado attempted to annul the victory of opposition candidate Otilio Ulate Blanco* in the presidential election of 1948, Figueres rallied his supporters to overthrow Picado in a six-week civil war in March-April 1948. Although Figeures eventually installed Ulate in the presidency, he first presided over the Founding Junta of the Second Republic for 18 months.

The Founding Junta undertook a major transformation of the economy, while maintaining Calderón's social programs and restoring Costa Rica's democracy. It nationalized banking, insurance, energy, communications, and transportation, and instituted the concept of national planning. These progams and others were incorporated in the Constitution of 1949. Figueres also abolished the Costa Rican Army.

Figueres organized the National Liberation Party (PLN) and won the presidency in 1953. The PLN became the dominant party in Costa Rica. Much of the creative phase of Figueres' career had occurred during the Founding Junta, and he spent his presidencies implementing and fine-tuning his program. He was especially active in the fight to achieve better international prices for basic commodities, courting the United States in this endeavor. He argued that Latin Americans did not want handouts, only just prices for their products. He linked economic justice to the struggle for democracy.

Figueres strongly opposed the Caribbean dictators by giving shelter to refugees and supporting exile movements. The dictators, in turn, attempted to overthrow Figueres several times. Without an army, Figueres called on the Inter American System for defense.

During the 1960s Figueres remained very much the international statesman. He became the symbol not merely of the antidictatorial forces but also a model for the democratic alternative to Fidel Castro. He promoted collaboration among Latin American parties of the Democratic left.

In Costa Rica, Liberacionista leader Francisco José Orlich Bolmarcich* won the 1962 presidential election, but in 1966 the PLN standard-bearer, Daniel Oduber Quiros,* lost. This defeat convinced Figueres that he had to run in 1970.

Figueres became president again in 1970. This last presidency was very controversial, as Figueres, in his quest for better prices for coffee, opened trade talks and established diplomatic relations with the Soviet Union, which conservative groups protested vigorously. He caused a major scandal when he allowed "fugitive financier" Robert Vesco to settle in Costa Rica.

President Figueres undertook a "war on poverty," setting up the Combined Institute of Social Assistance to aid the chronically poor. Moreover, for the first time since its founding, the PLN succeeded itself in the presidency at the end of his term, with the victory of Daniel Oduber in 1974.

BIBLIOGRAPHY

Ameringer, Charles D. *Don Pepe: A Political Biography of José Figueres of Costa Rica.* Albuquerque: University of New Mexico Press, 1979.

Araya Pochet, Carlos. *Historia de los partidos políticos: Liberación Nacional*. San José: Editorial Costa Rica, 1968.
Baeza Flores, Alberto. *La Lucha Sin Fin*. B. Costa-Amic, (ed.) Mexico: 1969.
Barahona Jiménez, Luis. *El pensamiento político en Costa Rica*. San José: Editorial Fernández-Arce, 1971.
Castro Esquivel, Arturo. *José Figueres Ferrer: El hombre y su obra*. San José: Imprenta Tormo, 1955.

CHARLES D. AMERINGER

FIGUEROA LARRAÍN, EMILIANO (1866–1931), was president of Chile for two short periods. He received his law degree at the University of Chile in 1889 and for some time thereafter served in the municipal government of Santiago. In 1900 he was elected to the Chamber of Deputies, keeping that post until he became vice president (acting president) in 1910. He also served short periods as minister of justice and minister of the interior.

When President Pedro Montt Montt* fell ill and abandoned the presidency, he was at first succeeded by Elías Fernández Albano. However, upon the death of Vice President Fernández, Emiliano Figueroa Larraín succeeded to that position, as minister of the interior. He served as vice president from September 6 through December 23, 1910. He presided over ceremonies celebrating the centenary of Chilean independence.

In 1911 Figueroa Larraín was named Chilean minister to Spain, and then in 1914 minister to Argentina, in which post he remained until 1920.

At the time of the second resignation of President Arturo Alessandri Palma* on October 1, 1925, all existing parties organized a convention to select a nominee to oppose the candidacy of Colonel Carlos Ibáñez del Campo.* The convention chose Figueroa Larraín, a member of the Liberal Democratic Party.

Although ex-President Alessandri warned Figueroa against naming Ibáñez minister of war, Figueroa submitted to military pressure and did put Ibáñez in that post. As a consequence, Ibáñez was in a position to make it almost impossible for President Figueroa Larraín to govern. Finally, in February 1927 he named Ibáñez minister of the interior, and two months later presented his resignation, leaving Ibáñez as vice president.

BIBLIOGRAPHY

Alexander, Robert J. *Arturo Alessandri: A Biography*. Ann Arbor, Mich.: University Microfilms International, 1977.
Cortes, Lia, and Jordi Fuentes. *Diccionario Político de Chile*. Santiago: Editorial Orbe, 1967.

ROBERT J. ALEXANDER

FLORES, JUAN JOSÉ (1801–1864), was the first president of Ecuador. Born in Puerto Cabello, Venezuela, the son of a Spanish merchant and a local woman, whose family name he took, he had little formal education. At 14, he joined the forces of Spain in the independence war, but two years later joined the rebels after becoming their captive. He was a cavalry officer under Simón Bolívar* in the Battle of Carabobo in June 1821, which was decisive in obtaining Venezuelan independence.

By 1824 Flores was governor of Pasto Province in southern Colombia, in Simón Bolívar's Republic of Gran Colombia. Shortly thereafter, he was named governor of Quito (in present-day Ecuador), and by 1830 he was deputed to control all of Ecuador. He had been named a general in 1829.

When the Republic of Gran Colombia broke up in 1830, General Flores, who had both civil and military authority in Ecuador, called together a constituent assembly of the Ecuadorian provinces, which declared independence in May 1830. It chose Flores as provisional president, and he was elected constitutional president a few months later.

Flores organized a viable state in Ecuador, with the backing of the rural and commercial ruling class, and the Venezuelan soldiers who were still the main contingents of the Ecuadorian armed forces. In 1834 he suppressed a revolt of Liberals, based in the port city of Guayaquíl, led by Vicente Rocafuerte.* As the result of an agreement between the two men, Rocafuerte became president of Ecuador in January 1835.

After Rocafuerte had been president for four years, Flores returned to power in 1839. Four years later, he had himself reelected. However, this provoked a revolt, and in 1845 Flores agreed to go into exile for two years in return for certain concessions.

Subsequently, Flores tried unsuccessfully on several occasions to invade Ecuador and return to power. It was not until 1859 that, once Gabriel García Moreno* had seized control of the Quito region, Flores was able to capture the Guayaquil coastal area in support of García Moreno. Two years later, he presided over a constitutional congress that legalized the García Moreno regime. Later, he led troops on several occasions in defense of the García Moreno government; he died during one of these expeditions.

BIBLIOGRAPHY

Blanksten, George. *Ecuador: Constitutions and Caudillos*. Berkeley: University of California Press, 1951.
Enciclopedia Universal Ilustrada Europeo Americana, Barcelona: José Espasa e Hijos.
Laso, Elias. "Biografía del General Juan José Flores." *Boletín de la Academia Nacional de Historia* (1924).
Linke, Lilo. *Ecuador: Country of Contrasts*. London: Royal Institute of International Affairs, 1955.
Rolando, Carlos A. *Biografía del General Juan José Flores*. Guayaquil: 1930.

                                                          ROBERT J. ALEXANDER

FLORES, VENANCIO (1808–1868), was twice president of Uruguay. Although his landowning family hoped he would enter the church, instead he joined Uruguayan military forces which in 1825 were fighting against Brazilian domination. By 1830 he was a captain. After a short period as a civilian, he returned in 1832 to military action in support of President Fructuoso Rivera,* who was then faced with an insurrection led by Juan Antonio Lavalleja.*

In 1836 Flores escaped from prison, where he had been held by President Manuel Oribe* of the Blanco Party. He joined Fructuoso Rivera's revolt against Oribe and became commander in San José Department when Rivera's forces triumphed. He supported Rivera's war against Argentine tyrant Juan Manuel de Rosas,* and for a short while was commander of Rivera's Colorado Party forces in Montevideo.

In 1851 Flores joined the Argentine Army of Justo José de Urquiza,* which raised the nine-year long siege of Montevideo by forces supported by Rosas. In the following year, he served as minister of war and navy. After the overthrow of President Juan Francisco Giró, he became a member of a ruling three-man Junta, shortly afterward being elected constitutional president to fill out Giró's unexpired term. Although supported by a 4,000-man Brazilian Army, Flores was forced to resign in September 1853.

Joining forces with his old antagonist Manuel Oribe to put Gabriel Antonio Pereira in the presidency, Flores soon quarreled with Pereira and went to Argentina, where he spent several years as a rancher and a lieutenant of Bartolomé Mitre.* He returned to Uruguay in April 1863 in order to lead a revolt against the Blanco Party government then in power. By early 1865 he had triumphed, with the support of Brazilian troops, and became president again.

Flores' victory served as *causus belli* for the War of the Triple Alliance, when Paraguayan dictator Francisco Solano López* came to the support of the Uruguayan Blancos and was faced with the forces of Argentina, Uruguay, and Brazil. Flores commanded the Uruguayan troops in that conflict until December 1866, when he returned to Montevideo. In the face of growing discontent, he allowed the calling of elections and then resigned in February 1868. Shortly afterward, he was assassinated.

BIBLIOGRAPHY

Enciclopedia Universal Ilustrada Europeo Americana. Barcelona: José Espasa e Hijos.
Lepro, Alfredo. *Años de Forja: Venancio Flores*. Montevideo: 1962.
María, Isidoro de. *Rasgos biográficos de hombres notables de la República Oriental del Uruguay*. 4 vols. Montevideo: 1939.

ROBERT J. ALEXANDER

FONSECA AMADOR, CARLOS (1930?–1976), was the principal founder of the Sandinista Front of National Liberation (FSLN) in Nicaragua. After Fidel Castro* came to power in January 1959, a small group of Cubans and Nicaraguans—including Fonseca Amador—had landed on the Caribbean coast but were decimated by the Nicaraguan National Guard.

Fonseca, together with a group of other dissidents from the Socialist Party of Nicaragua, the country's orthodox Communist Party, created the Sandinista Liberation Front in 1962, to wage guerrilla war on the Somoza regime in the same region that Augusto Cæsar Sandino* had fought the U.S. Marines in 1927–1928. In late 1964 Fonseca Amador was arrested. Then, in the aftermath of university student sit-in strikes, as well as efforts to discipline Guard officers engaged in unauthorized violence and torture, President René Schick Gutiérrez intervened and saved Fonesca from almost certain death. After being sentenced to prison by a civilian court, he was allowed to go into exile.

In late 1966 a group of FSLN fighters, fresh from training in Cuba, surfaced in Pancasán, Matagalpa. Fonseca Amador's activities for the next four years remain obscure. However, some FSLN elements sought to establish an urban guerrilla force, an effort that was smashed by the Guard by July 1969.

The focus of the Frente activities then shifted briefly to Costa Rica. In September 1969 Fonseca Amador was arrested there on a charge of bank robbery. Numerous efforts to secure his release failed until in October 1970 a FSLN team hijacked a Costa Rican airliner with four U.S. citizens aboard. The plane and passengers were released only after Fonseca Amador and three fellow FSLN members were freed and flown to Cuba.

After Fonseca's flight to Cuba, the FSLN began to build a network of student organizations, neighborhood committees, rural organizations, women's groups, and sectors within the Roman Catholic Church. However, in the wave of repression that followed the December 27, 1974, seizure by FSLN of many prominent guests at a farewell party for U.S. Ambassador Turner Sheldon, and the resulting release of 14 prisoners and payment of a $1 million ransom, Carlos Fonseca Amador was killed in the northern mountains.

After the FSLN came to power in July 1979, Fonseca Amador's picture—along with Sandino's—came to adorn the National Palace, billboards, wall murals, and textbooks.

BIBLIOGRAPHY

Crawley, Eduardo. *Dictators Never Die, a Portrait of Nicaragua and the Somoza Dynasty*. London: C. Hurst and Co., 1979.
Marcus, Bruce (ed.). *Sandinistas Speak, by Tomás Borge, Carlos Fonseca, Daniel Ortega, Humberto Ortega and Jaime Wheelock*. New York: Pathfinder Press, 1982.
Millett, Richard. *Guardians of the Dynasty, A History of the U.S. Created Guardia Nacional and the Somoza Family*. Maryknoll, N.Y.: Orbis Books, 1977.
Pearson, Neale J. "Nicaragua," in Robert J. Alexander (ed.). *Political Parties of the Americas*. Vol. 2. Westport, Conn.: Greenwood Press, 1982.
Walker, Thomas W. (ed.). *Nicaragua in Revolution*. New York: Praeger Special Studies, 1982.

NEALE J. PEARSON

FRANCIA, DR. JOSÉ GASPAR RODRÍGUEZ DE (1766–1840), the first great Paraguayan political leader, was born in Córdoba, Argentina. He received an education in both theology and the law. He finally settled in Asunción, where he practiced law in the last years of the colonial period.

With the outbreak of the independence movement in Paraguay in 1811, Dr. Francia was a member of the country's five-man ruling junta. However, the country's leaders had little financial and economic experience, the wealthy families were divided in their loyalties, and the Argentines had a strong desire to annex Paraguay. By 1813 Dr. Francia had emerged as the new nation's dominant political figure. He was one of the very few Paraguayans with a university education, and in 1814 Congress voted him dictator for life.

Francia ruled Paraguay as a kind of socialist state. He created a strong army in which all males between 17 and 60 were required to serve. Property of the upper classes was confiscated, and the land was worked by peasants or the army, under state direction. Paraguay's borders were sealed, and the state undertook to supply all the citizen's needs. No foreign trade or travel was allowed without Francia's permission, and even internal travel was closely regulated.

Political opposition was not tolerated. Dr. Francia turned against the wealthy families and soon destroyed Paraguay's small upper class. Executions and prison camps were used against suspected political plotters, and those who could escape Francia fled into exile. This merciless attack on political enemies began a Paraguayan tradition still followed in the twentieth century.

When Francia ("El Supremo") died in 1840, he left a Paraguay without a privileged upper class and untouched by changes occurring in the outside world. The peasants were loyal to the government, grateful for the land they had been given. Francia had united the country from above, primarily by destroying political opposition. He spared Paraguay the anarchy endemic in many Latin American countries of the time, but his complete intolerance for political opposition and his opposition to foreign contacts were controversial precedents for later Paraguayan leaders.

BIBLIOGRAPHY

Kolinski, Charles J. *Historical Dictionary of Paraguay*. Metuchen, N.J.: Scarecrow Press, 1973.
Lewis, Paul H. *Paraguay Under Stroessner*. Chapel Hill: University of North Carolina Press, 1980.
Pendle, George. *Paraguay: A Riverside Nation*. London: Royal Institute of International Affairs, 1956.
Warren, Harris G. *Paraguay: An Informal History*. Norman: University of Oklahoma Press, 1949.
Weil, Thomas, et al. *Area Handbook for Paraguay*. Washington, D.C.: Department of Defense, 1972.

JOHN T. DEINER

FRANCO, RAFAEL (1897–1973), was president of Paraguay from February 1936 to August 1937, a major hero in the Chaco War, and founder of the Febrerista Party. He first came to national attention in 1928 when he led an attack on a Bolivian fort in the Chaco. When the Chaco War broke out in 1932, Franco, removed from the army for his 1928 action, was reinstated as a colonel. He gained a reputation as a capable commander and as a leader who treated his soldiers well.

At the conclusion of the war, Franco became involved in plans to overthrow the Liberal Party government then in power. He was sent into exile, but on February 17, 1936, President Eusebio Ayala was overthrown, and Colonel Franco returned home as head of the new government, which represented a very wide range of outlooks.

Despite internal differences, the Franco government inaugurated serious reforms during its brief stay in office: land reform which expropriated some large *latifundios* and distributed the land to peasants on easy terms; and new labor laws giving workers the right to unionize and strike and providing social benefits. Despite its achievements, the government was overthrown in a coup in August 1937. Once again Franco went into exile.

Rafael Franco continued to command the loyalty of substantial numbers of workers, students, and others. In October 1945 they formally organized the Concentración Revolucionaria Febrerista. Theye were invited to take part in the coalition government formed by President Higinio Morinigo* in 1946, and after bitter debate, the party's leaders agreed. As a consequence, Franco returned to Asunción in August 1946.

Colonel Franco urged a policy of moderation, and the Febreristas began preparing for promised elections. However, the Guión Rojo, a group of shock troops under Juan Natalicio González,* leader of the radical wing of the Colorado Party, attacked Febreristas student and labor supporters.

In January 1947 the Febrerista party demanded that the coalition government be replaced by an all-military cabinet to handle the growing violence and unrest. Morinigo replied by dissolving the cabinet, declaring a state of siege, exiling leading Febreristas, including Colonel Franco, and precipitating the 1947 civil war.

Colonel Franco returned to Paraguay to take charge of rebel troops. In the siege of Asunción, August 3-August 19, Franco's troops were defeated, and he and his followers again fled abroad.

Following the civil war, most of Franco's political activities took place in exile. An effort to return to Paraguay in 1956 was foiled by the government. In the early 1960s Franco brought about the expulsion of groups of party members inspired by Fidel Castro* and alleged Communist supporters.

In 1964 Alfredo Stroessner* granted the Franco faction legal recognition, and Franco once again returned from exile. Once home he greatly reduced his political activity and tried to avoid factionalism. The weakness of his party was demonstrated by its extremely poor showing in the 1967 election. The party was still divided between a radical youth group and a much more moderate leadership headed by Franco. The death of Franco removed the only unifying symbol left to the Febreristas.

BIBLIOGRAPHY

Kolinski, Charles J. *Historical Dictionary of Paraguay*. Metuchen, N.J.: Scarecrow Press, 1973.

FREI MONTALVA, EDUARDO 165

Lewis, Paul H. *Paraguay Under Stroessner*. Chapel Hill: University of North Carolina Press, 1980.
———. *The Politics of Exile: Paraguay's Febrerista Party*. Chapel Hill: University of North Carolina Press, 1968.
Lott, Leo B. *Venezuela and Paraguay: Political Modernity and Tradition in Conflict*. New York: Holt, Rinehart and Winston, 1972.
Weil, Thomas, et al. *Area Handbook for Paraguay*. Washington, D.C.: Department of Defense, 1972.

JOHN T. DEINER

FREI MONTALVA, EDUARDO (1911–1982), was the only Christian Democrat to be president of Chile. His years of university study largely coincided with those of the Carlos Ibáñez del Campo* dictatorship. Frei and his colleagues at the Catholic University were active in the National Association of Catholic Students (ANEC) and in "study circles" under the aegis of ANEC. He got his law degree in 1933.

Soon after graduation, Frei, as president of ANEC, attended an International Congress of Catholic University students in Rome, and he served as secretary general. Subsequently, he traveled to France and Belgium, where he made contact with a number of people of Christian Democrat orientation, and attended the classes of Jacques Maritain.

Frei and his friends entered the Conservative Party after the overthrow of Ibáñez. They organized the National Movement of Conservative Youth. In April 1935 Frei moved to Iquique, to edit the most important daily newspaper of the city, *El Tarapacá*. In 1937 he ran for Congress, losing by only 60 votes in an area where candidates of the left were usually the victors.

The advanced social ideas of Eduardo Frei and other leaders of the Conservative youth, which in 1936 took the name Falange Nacional, aroused the growing opposition of the Conservative Party leadership. After the presidential elections of 1938, the party sought to "reorganize" the Falange Nacional, to which the Falange responded by establishing a separate political party.

In 1941 Eduardo Frei was elected president of the Falange Nacional. He led it in supporting the candidacy of Radical Party leader Juan Antonio Ríos Morales,* after the death of President Pedro Aguirre Cerda. In May 1945 Frei was named minister of public works by President Ríos. However, he resigned in January 1946, after a bloody clash between police and trade unionists in Plaza Bulnes in Santiago.

In 1949 Frei first won electoral office, as senator, after having on four occasions unsuccessfully sought election to the Chamber of Deputies. He remained in the Senate until his election to the presidency.

The Falange Nacional nominated Frei as prospective candidate of a left-center coalition in the 1952 elections. However, when he was rejected, the Falange supported Pedro Enrique Alfonso of the Radical Party.

In 1958 the Falange Nacional merged with two other small groups to establish the Christian Democratic Party. Eduardo Frei was its nominee in that year's presidential election. He came in third, getting slightly more than 20 percent of the vote. In the next congressional election, the Christian Democratic Party became the country's most voted party.

Eduardo Frei was nominated for president again by the Christian Democrats in 1964. His only serious competitor was Salvador Allende Gossens,* the Socialist leader. This time Frei won, receiving over 56 percent of the popular votes.

The Frei administration carried out extensive social and economic reforms: an agrarian reform, under which Frei began the process of redistributing the country's large landholdings; a law legalizing unionization of agricultural workers, which brought major increases in levels of living and independence and self-respect to the country's peasants; and a law for "Chileanization" of the mining industry, reorganizing the copper, nitrate, and coal mining firms as Chilean corporations in which the government held a majority of the stock. The Frei administration also substantially altered the tax system, making it considerably more progressive, and pushed development of several new export-oriented and manufacturing industries.

President Frei took two foreign policy initiatives of considerable importance: leadership in formation of the Andean Bloc for economic unity of the Andean countries; and an effort to develop an organization of copper exporting countries comparable to the Organization of Petroleum Exporting Countries (OPEC) among the oil exporters.

In spite of considerable progress in a number of its programs, inflation which had developed during the two previous administrations continued under Frei. This, together with resentment at increased taxation, the presence of ex-President Jorge Alessandri Rodríguez* as a candidate, and the attempt of the Christian Democrat nominee Radomiro Tomic to assume a far left position, brought defeat of the Christian Democrats in the 1970 election. Salvador Allende, the Socialist leader and nominee of the left-wing coalition, Popular Unity, won a narrow plurality. His election was confirmed later in Congress, with support of the Christian Democrats.

Eduardo Frei was once again elected to the Senate in March 1973 and became its president. He did not support the military coup of September 11, 1973, which overthrew the government of Allende, although he recognized it as virtually inevitable. Early in 1974 he strongly denounced the military dictatorship of General Augusto Pinochet Ugarte.* For the rest of his life Frei was the most prominent leader of the opposition to the dictatorship.

BIBLIOGRAPHY

Alexander, Robert J. *The Tragedy of Chile*. Westport, Conn.: Greenwood Press, 1978.
Cortes, Lia, and Jordi Fuentes. *Diccionario Político de Chile*. Santiago: Editorial Orbe, 1967.

Grayson, George. *El Partido Demíocrata Cristiano Chileno*. Santiago de Chile: Editorial Francisco de Aguirre, 1968.

                                                    ROBERT J. ALEXANDER

FREIRE SERRANO, RAMÓN (1787–1851), three times Supreme Director of Chile, was the most important political figure during the chaotic period (1823–1829) of rule by the *pipiolos* (novices), predecessors of the Liberal Party. He began his military career as a cadet in 1811, participated in several early battles of the war for independence, and after defeat of the Chilean Army at Rancagua on October 1, 1814, he fled to Buenos Aires. Two years later, he returned with José de San Martín's* Army of the Andes, and captured Talca.

In March 1823 Freire opposed the dictatorship of Bernardo O'Higgins.* With the resignation of O'Higgins, Freire was chosen a Supreme Director of the Nation, which he remained until July 9, 1826. During much of that time, he deputed the powers of the office to others, while fighting to drive the Spaniards out of their southern strongholds, which he finally did in early 1826.

In July 1824 Freire carried out a coup d'etat, dissolving the existing Congress and calling new elections. Throughout his tenure, Freire faced strong opposition from the *pelucones* (wigged ones), the forerunners of the Conservatives, as well as from supporters of Bernardo O'Higgins.

Although he retired amid considerable popular acclaim in July 1826, Freire returned to power in January 1827, after successfully organizing military forces against a coup that had deposed his successor. Although Congress elected Freire for a two and a half year term, he resigned after only three months, following a quarrel with Congress.

With the outbreak of the civil war of 1829–1830, Ramón Freire became head of a three-man government Junta set up in Santiago when the president, Joaquín Vicuña, fled to Valparaiso. However, that body never gained effective control over the country. Freire led the *pipiolo* military forces but was decisively defeated at the Battle of Lircay in April 1830.

After victory of the *pelucones*, Freire was sentenced to death. However, he succeeded in getting away and finally went into exile in Tahiti.

BIBLIOGRAPHY

Cortes, Lia, and Jordi Fuentes. *Diccionario Político de Chile*. Santiago: Editorial Orbe, 1967.
Enciclopedia Universal Ilustrada Europeo Americana. Barcelona: José Espasa e Hijos.
Galdames, Luis. *Historia de Chile*. Santiago: Editorial Zig Zag, 1945.

                                                    ROBERT J. ALEXANDER

FRONDIZI, ARTURO (1908–), was one of the major Argentine political figures of the Peronist and post-Perón* periods. Born in Corrientes Province, he, like a number of politicians of his generation, was the son of Italian immigrants. By the time he graduated from the University of Buenos Aires Law

School in 1930, he was already active in Radical Party (UCR) politics. He served as a member of Congress from 1946 to 1951 when he became famous for his speeches attacking the undemocratic nature of the Peronist regime.

By 1950 Frondizi and Ricardo Balbín* were the two most prominent Radicals, and Frondizi was Balbín's vice presidential running mate in the 1951 election against Perón. They were soundly defeated, partly because of Perón's popularity and partly because of governmental control over the election process. Frondizi continued his outspoken criticism of the Perón regime.

Following Perón's overthrow, the UCR split into two parties: the UCRI (Unión Cívica Radical Intransigente), headed by Frondizi, and the UCRP (Unión Cívica del Pueblo) headed by Balbín. Frondizi's party was the more leftist of the two, advocating an industrially developed, but democratic, Argentina. His programs were supported by intellectuals, industrialists, and even some Peronists. It called for the reintegration of Peronists into political life, and this prospect was frightening to large portions of the middle class.

Frondizi defeated Balbín in a 1958 election in which the military had prohibited the Peronists from running. At the last moment, Perón endorsed Frondizi and many Peronists cast their ballots for him.

President Frondizi had to face more than 30 military coup attempts against him and to rule a nation polarized by ten years of Peronist rule, followed by three years of anti-Peronist repression. The single largest group, the Peronists, was excluded from legal political activity, and the strongest political force, the military, was deeply divided. Under these conditions, Frondizi had a constant struggle merely to stay in power, but he did institute some major programs during his four years in office.

One of Frondizi's most controversial actions was contracting with foreign oil companies to reinvigorate Argentina's oil industry. As a result, Argentina became self-sufficient in oil, but Frondizi was criticized for dealing with foreigners. His attempts to draw closer to both the United States and Cuba also drew criticism.

Internally, Frondizi's main problem was how to reincorporate the Peronists into national politics. Initially, his policy of a price freeze gained him support from labor, but the austerity program begun in 1959 at the International Monetary Fund's urging served to drive a wedge between Frondizi and the Peronist workers.

Frondizi finally convinced the military that the Peronists should be allowed to participate in elections by assuring them that Peronist candidates had no chance of winning. However, when the Peronists won half of the contested congressional seats and control of the key province of Buenos Aires in the 1962 elections, military leaders, always suspicious of Frondizi's linkages with the Peronists and of his alleged sympathies for Che Guevara* and Cuba, ousted him in a coup, put him in prison on Martín García Island, and later kept him under house arrest until he was freed by the Arturo Umberto Illia* government which came to power in 1963.

When he returned to political activity, Frondizi formed a new party, the Movimiento de Integración y Desarrollo (MID). In 1973 it joined the Peronist Frejuli coalition.

Frondizi continued as a controversial and often pungent critic of Argentine politics in his later years. MID never beame a major party, however.

BIBLIOGRAPHY

Ferns, Henry S. *Argentina*. New York: Praeger, 1969.
Hodges, Donald C. *Argentina, 1943–1976: The National Revolution and Resistance*. Albuquerque: University of New Mexico Press, 1976.
Johnson, Kenneth F. *Argentina's Mosaic of Discord*. Washington, D.C.: Institute for the Comparative Study of Political Systems, 1969.
Snow, Peter G. *Political Forces in Argentina*. New York: Praeger, 1979.

JOHN T. DEINER

G

GAIRY, ERIC MATTHEW (1922–   ), largely dominated the politics of Grenada for three decades until his overthrow in 1979. He received his primary education in Grenada but in his late teens went to Trinidad to work on a U.S. military base, and then migrated to the Dutch colony of Aruba to work in an oil refinery.

While in Aruba, Gairy became a trade union organizer, the traditional route for incipient political activists. He met Theophilus Albert Marryshow,* the Grenadian political and labor activist, a meeting that led to his decision to return to Grenada in December 1949.

In Grenada, Gairy found a society politically and economically dominated by a small group of predominantly white elites. In his hometown of Grenville, Gairy took up the cause of the peasants, in their dealings with authorities and landowners. He also formed the Grenada Manual and Mental Workers Union in July 1950. After successfully mobilizing for better wages and conditions of work on behalf of sugar workers, Gairy began efforts to secure his union as the bargaining agent in other sectors of the economy. He called a general strike in February 1951. British troops were called in, and Gairy was held in custody for 11 days on the Island of Carriacou. This action precipitated serious rioting, looting, and burning, which forced the governor to bargain with Gairy. When his demands were met, Gairy successfully ended the protests.

In early 1951 Gairy formed the colony's first political party, the Grenada United Labour Party (GULP). As with his union, Gairy assumed the position of president-general. Under a new constitution providing for universal adult suffrage and an elected majority of eight members on the Legislative Council, Gairy led his party to victory in six of eight constituencies in 1951. After serving less than a year, however, Gairy was suspended from the Legislative Council in 1952 for abusive behavior. In 1954 he lost his seat on the Executive Council, only to be reinstated six months later when GULP captured seven of the eight elective seats. In 1955 Gairy was again suspended from the Legislative Council for disruptive behavior; nonetheless, in March 1956 he became minister of trade and production.

Gairy's party lost the general elections in September 1957, winning only two of eight seats, although GULP received 51.9 percent of the popular vote. A coalition of opposition parties under the leadership of Herbert Augustus Blaize* assumed power until 1961. When a new constitution ushered in a ministerial system, it was Blaize and not Gairy who became the country's first chief minister.

During the 1957 electoral campaign, Gairy had been disenfranchised and proscribed from holding elective office for violating the electoral law. Although not an officeholder after the March 1961 elections when his party won eight of ten elective seats, he assumed the role of "adviser to the government," which was nominally run by a friend and nominee. When his franchise was restored in June of the same year, Gairy won a seat in a by-election, and became chief minister and minister of finance on August 17, 1961.

The Gairy government, and Gairy personally, demonstrated increasing evidence of financial impropriety. A Commission of Inquiry produced evidence of misuse and waste of public funds by Gairy and his government, and of a campaign to force members of the civil service to commit or condone financial improprieties. The Grenadian Constitution was suspended, and when elections were called in September 1962, GULP won 45.9 percent of the vote but was victorious in only four constituencies. The Grenada National Party (GNP) captured the remaining six seats, and Herbert Blaize once more was chief minister.

In March 1967 Grenada was granted Associated Statehood, thereby giving the legislature and cabinet full control of all government affairs except defense and external affairs. In elections a few months after Associated Statehood was acquired, Gairy led GULP in winning seven of ten constituencies. Gairy became premier, a post he held until February 1974, when Grenada became fully independent and he became the country's first prime minister.

In the period between 1967 and 1979, the Gairy government carried on state-directed violence and intimidation against political opponents by the "Mongoose Gang," and patronage and corruption were rife. The period also witnessed severe economic decline and strong allegations of electoral fraud.

After Gairy's ouster in March 1979 by an armed takeover by the New Jewel Movement, Gairy took up residence in the United States. He returned to Grenada after the violent collapse of the Peoples Revolutionary Government in late 1983 and subsequent military intervention by the United States.

Gairy resuscitated his party to contest elections held in December 1984, but GULP won only 1 of 15 seats and approximately one-third of the popular vote. The victorious GULP candidate soon resigned, leaving Gairy's group without representation in Parliament.

BIBLIOGRAPHY

The Grenada Independence Secretariat. *A Short History of Grenada*. St. George's Grenada: Government of Grenada, 1974.

McDonald, Frank. *Grenada: Eric Matthew Gairy and the Politic of Extravagance.* New York: Institute of Current World Affairs, 1969.
Richardson, Bonham C. "Grenada," in Robert J. Alexander (ed.). *Political Parties of the Americas.* Vol. 1. Westport, Conn.: Greenwood Press, 1982.
Singham, A. W. *The Hero and the Crown in a Colonial Polity.* New Haven, Conn.: Yale University Press, 1968.
Thorndike, Anthony. *Grenada.* Boulder, Colo.: Lynne Reiner Press, 1985.

PERCY C. HINTZEN AND W. MARVIN WILL

GAITÁN, JORGE ELIÉCER (1898–1948), was one of the most influential Colombian political leaders of the twentieth century. He was born in Bogotá into a lower middle-class family. His father was a bookseller and his mother a schoolteacher and early advocate of women's rights. Educated by his mother and in private schools, he later earned a law degree at the National University, and another at the University of Rome, where he also studied the techniques of Benito Mussolini, the Italian fascist leader.

Gaitán first won national prominence during congressional debates over the Abadía Méndez administration's handling of strikes in the "banana zone" in 1928–1929. After investigating an army massacre of workers, he made a series of sensational speeches that exposed complicity of high government officials with the foreign-owned banana company. His revelations made him a nationalist hero, and he quickly became a leading Liberal Party figure and member of the party's directorate. In Congress, he proposed legislation, including agrarian reform, protection of workers' rights, and social welfare measures.

Frustration over failure to bring about passage of progressive legislation resulted in his organizing the Unión Nacional Izquierdista Revolucionaria (UNIR). Based on a union of unorganized urban workers, rural laborers, and small landowners, UNIR was short-lived (1934–1935). When the Liberal administration of Alfonso López Pumarejo* initiated reforms in the mid–1930s, Gaitán abandoned UNIR and again assumed a leadership role in the Liberal Party. He served briefly as mayor of Bogotá and as minister of education and minister of labor. He also was elected to the Senate.

During the early 1940s, years of political turmoil and economic dislocation, Gaitán remained somewhat apart from struggles that were factionalizing the Liberal and Conservative parties. In 1944, however, as the second López administration dissolved in chaos, Gaitán launched a campaign for the presidency and organized a populist movement which cut across class and party lines, appealing to urban and rural working classes and emerging middle sectors. His program called for sweeping social and economic changes in the interests of the country's poor. It was a movement, radical in the context of the times, that threatened the entire structure dominated by what Gaitán called the ruling "oligarchy."

Gaitán utilized modern techniques of political mobilization, including radio and the airplane. He built a grass-roots movement, particularly in the cities and towns, that involved many people in politics for the first time. His flamboyant oratory and charismatic personality complemented his program.

When the Liberal Party made Gabriel Turbay its official presidential candidate, Gaitán refused to retire from the race. This Liberal split resulted in election of the Conservative, Mariano Ospina Pérez,* in 1946. Gaitán then set out to capture leadership of the Liberal Party, which was in complete disarray. He did so in 1947 and began to reorient the party in a more progressive direction. Accelerating violence in the countryside between the majority Liberals and the minority but ruling Conservatives, however, increasingly occupied his attention. The violence was exacerbated by Conservative efforts to consolidate power and throttle growing demands for social and economic changes. Gaitán himself became a victim. An assassin fatally shot him on a Bogotá street on April 9, 1948.

BIBLIOGRAPHY

Gaitán, Jorge Eliécer. *Las ideas socialistas en Colombia*. Bogotá. 1963.
————. *Los mejores discursos de Jorge Eliécer Gaitán, 1919–1948*. Bogotá: 1958.
Osorio Lizarazo, J. A. *Gaitán: Vida, muerte y permanente presencia*. Buenos Aires: Ediciones López Negri, 1952.
Sharpless, Richard E. *Gaitán of Colombia: A Political Biography*. Pittsburgh: University of Pittsburgh Press, 1978.
Valencia, Luis Emiro (ed.). *Gaitán: Antología de su pensamiento social y económico*. Bogotá: 1968.

RICHARD E. SHARPLESS

GALLEGOS, RÓMULO (1884–1969), was the most famous Venezuelan literary figure of his time, one of the founders of Acción Democrática (AD), and president of the republic for a short time in 1948.

Gallegos entered the Central University in Caracas with the intention of being a lawyer, but soon abandoned the law. In 1909 he helped establish a literary review, *La Alborada*, and in 1913 he published his first book, *Los Aventureros*. His first novel, *Reinaldo Solar*, appeared in 1920, and his most famous novel, *Doña Bárbara*, in 1929.

In 1912 Gallegos became director of the Colegio Federal in the provincial city of Barcelona. Then he transferred to Caracas, where he was assistant director of the Liceo do Caracas between 1912 and 1918. However, his most important role as a teacher came between 1922 and 1930, when he was director of the Liceo Andrés Bello, as well as teaching philosophy there. In this capacity he taught many of those young men who were to be the principal civilian political leaders of Venezuela for almost a generation.

In 1931 Gallegos was elected to the Senate. However, rather than serve under the regime of dictator Juan Vicente Gómez,* Gallegos went into voluntary exile in Spain. He returned home early in 1936, a few weeks after Gómez' death. He served a few months in 1936 as minister of education of President Eleazar López Contreras,* but also became active in Organización Venezolana, the core of what was to become Acción Democrática. In 1937 he was elected to the Chamber of Deputies, where he was one of the principal spokesmen for the opposition to the López Contreras government.

As the end of López Contreras' administration approached, Rómulo Betancourt* and other leaders of the still semiclandestine National Democratic Party (PDN) launched the "symbolic" candidacy of Rómulo Gallegos for the presidency, even though it was clear that, through his control of Congress, the president was going to impose the election of Colonel Isaías Medina Angarita.*

Gallegos' candidacy permitted the PDN to campaign openly on his behalf. Soon after Medina's inauguration, Gallegos summoned a conference to convert the underground PDN into the open Acción Democrática. When AD was finally legalized in September 1941, Gallegos became its president.

Although Gallegos took no part in the negotiations leading to the overthrow of President Medina by young military men and Acción Democrática in October 1945, he did not oppose the move. When it came time for AD to choose a candidate for president in the 1947 election, the logical nominee was Rómulo Gallegos. Gallegos was overwhelmingly elected and took office in February 1948.

During the short period of Gallegos' presidency several important measures were passed, most notably a general agrarian reform law. However, the same young military officers who had facilitated AD's ascension to power in 1945 had become increasingly unhappy with their civilian allies. Although plotting by Colonel Marcos Pérez Jiménez* and others was virtually in the open, President Gallegos was unwilling or unable to do anything to curb it. As a consequence, he was overthrown on November 24, 1948.

Soon after his ouster, Gallegos went into exile. He spent the next nine years principally in Cuba and Mexico, and published several more novels. He returned to Venezuela only after overthrow of the Pérez Jiménez dictatorship early in 1958. Thereafter, he had the role of senior statesman and respected figurehead of Acción Democrática.

BIBLIOGRAPHY

Acción Democrática y la Cultura. Caracas: Ediciones Centauro, 1971.
Betancourt, Rómulo. *Venezuela: Oil and Politics*. Boston: Houghton Mifflin, 1979.
Cuarenta Años de Acción Democrática: Cuatro Presidentes. Vol. I. Cracas: Ediciones de la Presidencia de la Republica, 1981.
Cuatro Figuras Blancas. Caracas: Foción Serrano Producciones, 1975.
Kolb, Glen L. *Democracy and Dictatorship in Venezuela 1945–1958*. New London: Connecticut College, 1977.

ROBERT J. ALEXANDER

GALTIERI, LEOPOLDO FORTUNATO (1926–   ), who took over the presidency of Argentina on December 22, 1981, led Argentina into a disastrous war with Great Britain over the Malvinas (Falkland) Islands and was forced to resign in June 1982, following Argentina's humiliating defeat. A career army officer, he was born into a working-class family in suburban Buenos Aires and entered the military academy in 1943. He received regular promotions and commands in the army, ultimately being named army commander-in-chief in 1980. He was considered a moderate within the armed forces.

By early 1981 Argentina faced serious economic problems and was having border problems with Chile. Galtieri visited the United States, warmly welcomed by the Reagan administration, which approved of his strong anti-Communist statements. He became an increasingly vocal critic of President Roberto Viola's ineptitude. Finally, Viola was forced to resign, and Galtieri took over as president.

The country was in a deep recession, inflation was soaring out of control, and the country's monetary reserves were disappearing. Public opposition, dormant for years, was becoming more visible, and at the end of March there were large antigovernment demonstrations in Buenos Aires and other cities. Two days later, Argentina invaded the Malvinas, bringing a tremendous outpouring of support from Argentines who have always regarded these islands as belonging to them. However, the Argentines were defeated and humiliated by the British forces, with serious losses of life on both sides.

The Argentine public, so supportive in April, massed angrily in front of the presidential palace when news of Argentina's surrender came on June 15. Galtieri was removed on June 17, 1982, and by the end of 1983 a civilian government had been elected, ending seven years of military rule.

The Raúl Ricardo Alfonsín Foulkes* government elected in 1983 initiated trials of Galtieri and the other junta leaders, trying to make them accountable for their actions while in power. Galtieri was sentenced to a long prison term.

BIBLIOGRAPHY

Current Biography, 1982.
International Who's Who, 1982–83.
Newsweek 99:41, May 3, 1982.
Time 119:26, April 19, 1982.
Washington Post, June 13, 1982.

                                                              JOHN T. DEINER

GÁLVEZ, MARIANO (1794–1862), was an early president of Guatemala. Although of humble origin, he received a legal education and, with the outbreak of the independence movement, urged union with Mexico. After separation of Central America from Mexico, he held offices in both the Central American and Guatemalan governments. In 1831 he became president of Guatemala. As such, he sought to limit the influence of the Catholic Church, seizing much of its property, establishing religious toleration, and establishing free public education. He sought to stimulate economic development through extensive foreign colonization.

Gálvez' policies generated extensive opposition from vested interests. They supported the revolt of Rafael Carrera,* which ousted Gálvez in 1838. He fled to Mexico, where he lived until his death.

BIBLIOGRAPHY

Diccionario Enciclopédico Hispano Americano. Vol. 9. Barcelona: Montaner y Simón
    Editores, 1892.
Enciclopedia Universal Ilustrade Europeo Americano. Barcelona: José Espasa e Hijas.
                                                                JOSÉ M. SÁNCHEZ

GÁLVEZ DURÓN, JUAN MANUEL (1887–1972), was the chosen successor
of Tiburcio Carías Andino,* when the National Party strongman decided to leave
after 16 years in the presidency of Honduras. He had been a long-time lawyer
of the United Fruit Company, a judge, a deputy to the 1924 constituent assembly,
minister of government and private secretary to President Paz Barahona (1925–
1928), and minister of defense under Carías. Gálvez surprised people when he
ruled in a constitutional manner from January 1949 to November 1954. He
traveled widely through Honduras by jeep and light airplane and enhanced his
image as a "simple democratic citizen."

Important institutional changes under Gálvez included introduction of the
income tax, creation of the Central Bank and a National Development Bank,
and passage of the banking law and commercial code. The Francisco Morazán
Military School was established during his tenure. A non-Communist labor
movement developed as a politically potent force after a 69-day banana workers
strike in May-July 1954, when Gálvez insisted on the signing of a collective
labor contract.

In 1954 both Tiburcio Carías and his former vice president, Abraham Williams
Caldernó, sought the presidency. The reorganized Liberal Party nominated Ramón Villeda Morales.* Although Villeda Morales and the Liberals won a plurality, there was no clear winner. Gálvez left the country suddenly on November
16 for medical treatment at Gorgas Hospital in Panama, turning the presidency
over to Vice President Julio Lozano Días.

Only the Liberal deputies showed up at Congress for selection of a president
from the top two candidates. Lozano, basing his authority on a clause in the
1936 Constitution which covered this impasse, assumed dictatorial powers on
December 5. Gálvez returned to Tegucigalpa two days later, but did not contest
his fellow Nationalist's assumption of dictatorial power. Later, Lozano appointed
Gálvez president of the Supreme Court.

Subsequently, Gálvez continued to live his usual modest life, enjoying general
respect and recognition.

BIBLIOGRAPHY

Ideario de Una Democracia, Declaraciones del Dr. Juan Manuel Gálvez. Tegucigalpa:
    Talleres Tipo-Litograficos "Ariston," 1951.
Kantor, Harry. *Patterns of Politics and Political Systems in Latin America*. Chicago:
    Rand McNally, 1964.
Morris, James A. *Caudillo Politics and Military Rulers*. Boulder, Colo.: Westview Press,
    1984.

New York Times, November 19, 1957, and August 27, 1972.
Parker, Franklin D. *The Central American Republics*. London and New York: Oxford University Press, 1964.

NEALE J. PEARSON

GAMARRA, AGUSTÍN (1785–1841), president of Peru (1829–1833 and 1839–1841), was born in Cuzco. He enrolled in the Spanish Army in 1810 and fought against patriot forces until 1820, when he joined José de San Martin's* army. Under the command of Simón Bolívar's* generals, Gamarra fought bravely in the battles of Junín and Ayacucho (1824). After serving as governor of Cuzco and participating in conflicts against Bolivia and Ecuador, he deposed President José de la Mar in 1829 and ruled Peru for four years. He continued to be active in politics and in the civil wars, constantly changing allies.

Gamarra and other Peruvian generals assisted Chile's expeditionary forces that battled against President Andrés de Santa Cruz* and dissolved the Peruvian-Bolivian Confederation in 1838. The following year, he had the electoral college elect him president, but he did not finish his second term, being killed on November 8, 1841, while leading troops to force Bolivia to join a new confederation with Peru, this time under his leadership. His domineering wife, Francisca, became known as La Mariscala (the lady Marshall), and was credited with making important decisions for him.

BIBLIOGRAPHY

Alisky, Marvin. *Historical Dictionary of Peru*. Metuchen, N.J.: Scarecrow Press, 1979.
Basadre, Jorge. *Peruanos del siglo XX*. Lima: Ediciones Rikchay, 1981.
Pike, Frederick A. *The Modern History of Peru*. New York: Praeger, 1967.
Tauro, Alberto. *Diccionario enciclopédico del Peru*. Lima: Editorial Mejía Baca, 1966.

EUGENIO CHANG-RODRÍGUEZ

GARCÍA IÑIGUÉZ, CALIXTO (1839–1898), was one of the most prominent military commanders in the Cuban revolutionary armies from 1870 to 1898. During both the Ten Years' War and the final struggle that began in 1895, Calixto García served as General Maximo Gómez's* second-in-command. In mid–1872 García took over from Gómez command of the revolutionary forces in Oriente Province. In the fall of 1874, García was captured by the Spaniards, and he remained in prison until cessation of hostilities in 1878. General García then traveled to New York, where he organized the Comité Revolucionario Cubano to foster continuation of the revolutionary struggle against Spain.

Enlisting the support of Antonio Maceo y Grajales,* García tried to organize another insurrection. Both had refused to recognize the peace agreement. In August 1879 García met with Maceo in Jamaica, and from that meeting came the Kingston Proclamation which stated that the promised reforms had not been adopted by the Spanish in Cuba. This "call to arms" for what would come to be known as La Guerra Chiquita was doomed when García removed Maceo from his command of forces in Oriente Province only days after outbreak of hostilities, believing that Maceo's color was a detriment to the success of the uprising. It was not until May 1880 that García made his ill-prepared invasion of the island. He surrendered to the Spanish in August 1880 and was sent to prison in Spain.

In spite of García's dismal failure in the "little war," he attained a measure of brilliance in the final struggle against Spain during 1895–1898. Once again, he found himself as Gómez' second-in-command. His most memorable contribution was as intermediary between the U.S. government and the Cuban revolutionary forces symbolized in the famous "message to García."

BIBLIOGRAPHY

Miranda, Luis Rodolfo. *Calixto Garciá Iñiguéz: Estratega.* La Habana: Academia de la Historia de Cuba, 1951.
Pérez, Louis A., Jr. *Cuba Between Empires 1878–1902.* Pittsburgh: University of Pittsburgh Press, 1983.
Portell Vilá, Herminio. *Historia de Cuba en sus Relaciones con Los Estados Unidos y España.* Habana: Jesús Montero, 1939.
Thomas, Hugh. *Cuba: The Pursuit of Freedom.* New York: Harper and Row, 1971.
                                                                      STEPHEN J. WRIGHT

GARCÍA MORENO, GABRIEL (1821–1875), twice president of Ecuador, sought to reestablish the union of church and state which had existed during Spanish colonial rule. Born in Guayaquil of a Spanish father and an Ecuadorian mother, he went to Quito to study for the priesthood when he was 15. However, he gave up his priestly aspirations and got a law degree.

García Moreno became involved in politics in his twenties. He married into a powerful Quito family, thus establishing bases in both of the country's major centers of power. His first participation in politics was as a supporter of Vicente Rocafuerte,* founder of Ecuador's Liberal tradition.

During the early 1850s he twice visited Europe. In 1857 he was elected mayor of Quito, rector of the University of Quito, and a national senator. During the next three years, he engaged in revolutionary activities, which finally brought him to power in September 1860. His rule was confirmed by a convention in the following year.

García Moreno strongly allied himself with the Catholic Church. His regime decreed that only Roman Catholicism could be practiced in the country and that only its adherents could be Ecuadorian citizens. He brought back the Jesuits who had been expelled by an earlier administration. In 1873 García Moreno's administration had the country officially dedicated to the Sacred Heart of Jesus.

When his four-year term expired in 1865, García Moreno allowed the election of a successor. However, he again seized power in 1869, remaining in office for six years. His second administration was marked by considerable expansion of education, as well as by construction of the country's first railway and the building of a highway from Quito to the Pacific Coast.

When his constitutional term expired the second time in 1875, García Moreno had himself reelected once again. However, before he could be inaugurated for the third time, he was assassinated.

BIBLIOGRAPHY

Enciclopedia Universal Ilustrada Europeo Americana. Barcelona: José Espasa e Hijos.
Link, Lilo. *Ecuador: Country of Contrasts*. London: Royal Institute of International Affairs, 1954.
Pattee, Richard. *Gabriel García Moreno y el Ecuador de su Tiempo*. Quito: 1941.
                                                                    ROBERT J. ALEXANDER

GARCÍA PÉREZ, ALAN (1949–   ), president of Peru (1985–   ), was born in Lima in a family that had been active in the Peruvian Aprista Party (PAP) since its inception in 1930. He studied in public schools of Barranco and then at Lima's Catholic University, San Marcos, and the Universidad Complutense of Madrid. His law degree was awarded by San Marcos in 1972, and his doctorate in jurisprudence by the Complutense. In France he did postgraduate work at the University of Paris under the direction of François Bourricaud, a sociologist who specialized in Peruvian affairs.

After five years in Europe (1973–1977), García returned to Peru. He was elected member of the Constituent Assembly in 1978 and deputy in 1980. In 1982 he was elected secretary general of PAP. He was elected president of the republic on April 14, 1985, with 48 percent of the votes. In his writings and speeches, Alan García proposed a decentralized government, the promotion of agriculture and industry, and concerted Latin American action to obtain better conditions for the payment of the country's huge international debt. He made significant contributions to the modernization of the Plan de Gobierno Aprista prepared by a team of experts of PAP's Council of National Planning. He favored keeping Peru as a non-aligned member of the Third World, and he supported international disarmament and noninterference in the domestic affairs of the developing countries especially of El Salvador and Nicaragua.

BIBLIOGRAPHY

Chang-Rodríguez, Eugenio. *Opciones políticas peruanas*. Lima: Centro de Documentación Andina, 1985.
Garay Seminario, Martín. *Perfiles humanos*. Lima: 1985.
Goldenberg, Sonia (ed.). *Decidamos nuestro futuro*. Lima: Universidad del Pacífico-Fundación Friedrich Ebert, 1985.
Rojas Samane, Alvaro. *Partidos Políticos en el Peru desde 1872 a nuestros días*. Lima: Ediciones F & A, 1985.
                                                            EUGENIO CHANG-RODRÍGUEZ

GARVEY, MARCUS MOSIAH (1887–1940), was one of the greatest of all West Indian mass leaders. Born into rural poverty near St. Ann's Bay, Jamaica, he was forced to discontinue his schooling at age 14. He moved to Kingston and began work in the Jamaican government printery. Later he became publisher of his own newspaper, *Our View*, and an important tabloid *The Watchman*. In 1909–1914 Garvey traveled to Panama and Costa Rica, making contact with large numbers of expatriate black West Indians and Jamaicans, and then to London, where he spent 1912–1914 and became acquainted with early Pan Africanists.

Upon return to Jamaica in July 1914, Garvey organized the United Negro Improvement Association (UNIA) to unite all black people and establish "our" country and government. Part of his effort centered on developing black leadership in black colleges, using Tuskegee Institute in Alabama, directed by his friend Booker T. Washington, as a model. When Washington died in 1916, just prior to Garvey's departure from Jamaica to meet with him, the trip evolved into a 38-state lecture tour and Marcus Garvey did not return to Jamaica until 1927.

While in the United States, Harlem became the center of Garvey's movement. By 1919, 30 UNIA branches with 2 million members had been established throughout the United States. Total membership exceeded 5 million by 1927. This rapid increase owed much to a weekly publication Garvey initiated in 1919, *The Negro World*.

At the UNIA convention held in 1920, with 25,000 delegates from the Caribbean, Central America, and the United States, Garvey proclaimed return to Africa as the ultimate goal. The convention drafted a Declaration of Rights of the Negro Peoples of the World demanding self-determination for blacks, political and legal equality, and liberation of Africa.

Garvey's detractors ranged from racists to black leaders such as W. E. B. Du Bois, to the U.S. government. Du Bois found an opportunity to attack him when the Black Star Line which Garvey had initiated in 1919 failed in 1922, largely as the result of incompetent management, and Garvey was indicted for fraudulent use of the mails, although these charges still remain dubious. Garvey was imprisoned for nearly three years between 1924 and 1927. Upon his release, he was deported to Jamaica.

Back home, Garvey began publishing the *Black Man* and later the *New Jamaican*. In 1929 he also founded the People's Political Party (PPP). Franchise restrictions hampered the PPP, which won no parliamentary seats and only his election to the Kingston Corporation. Garvey was even sentenced to a three months' imprisonment for a campaign speech attacking fairness of the electoral system. Disillusioned with Jamaica, Garvey departed for London in 1935, where he died, penniless.

In 1964 the government of Jamaica brought his remains back to Jamaica for interment, and proclaimed him a National Hero of Jamaica. In addition, the government of Jamaica placed Garvey's bust in the Pan American Union building in Washington, D.C., as a representation of their nation's most important hero.

BIBLIOGRAPHY

Black, C. V. *The Story of Jamaica*. London: Collins, 1965.
Roberts, W. A. *Jamaica: The Portrait of an Island*. New York: Coward-McCann, 1955.
                                             PERCY C. HINTZEN AND W. MARVIN HILL

GÉFFRARD, FABRE NICHOLAS (1806–1878), president of Haiti from 1859 to 1867, was born in the south of Haiti, the son of a mulatto father and a black mother. Coming from an elite family, he managed to acquire an education before joining the army.

Géffrard served as a general in the campaigns of President Faustin Soulouque* to reestablish Haitian dominion over the Dominican Republic. When the Haitian empire was established by Soulouque, Géffrard was given the title Duke of Tabara. He became the emperor's most trusted adviser. As bankruptcy, corruption, graft, and military, political, and administrative incompetence intensified, the idea of Géffrard as a possible successor to Soulouque began to grow. The emperor ordered Géffrard's arrest, but Géffrard led a successful insurrection and was made president by acclamation of January 20, 1859.

Géffrard's administration, while somewhat more partial to the mulatto elite, incorporated many powerful blacks from the Soulouque government. The army, the bastion of black elitism, survived intact.

Géffrard inherited a pattern of state decision making that subverted the rule of law and the constitution. He reintroduced, with minor modifications, the relatively progressive constitution of Jean Baptiste Riche, who had preceded Soulouque. Although the government had less dictatorial power, Géffrard was President for Life.

Géffrard halved the army from 30,000 to 15,000 men. He was moderately successful in improving roads and the coastal steamboat service, but he failed in his attempts to introduce electric telegraphy and to improve irrigation and the capital city's water supply. He improved the educational system, starting a number of primary and high schools, reestablishing a medical school, and founding a law school, a school of navigation, and a school of art. However, education still retained its elite character.

Géffrard acted vigorously to curb the influence of voodoo which had gained tremendously under Soulouque. He signed a concordat with the Vatican in 1860 which restored the power of the Catholic Church.

President Géffrard paid considerable attention to international affairs. He reached a detente with the Dominican Republic, but when, two years later, that country returned to being a Spanish colony, Géffrard provided crucial assistance to insurgents there. Spain sent a squadron to Haiti's capital city and obtained a commitment from Géffrard not to support the rebels, to grant Spain an apology, and to pay a $200,000 indemnity. Five months later, however, Géffrard managed to get diplomatic recognition of Haiti by the United States for the first time.

Problems that plagued previous regimes persisted: use of state funds for personal enrichment, and the fiscal deficit which quadrupled between 1859 and

1865. In 1865 and 1866 devastating crop failures particularly affected the country's export of cotton.

Géffrard was faced with 15 attempted coups during his eight years in power. Because of constant rebellion, he dissolved the elected legislature in 1863, replacing it with one guaranteed to rubber stamp his edicts. In 1865 an insurrection led by a powerful black general, Sylvain Salnave, was put down with British help. In 1867, with Salnave again rebelling and with a mutiny in the ranks of his palace guard, Géffrard left for Jamaica, where he died 11 years later.

BIBLIOGRAPHY

Davis, H. P. *Black Democracy. The Story of Haiti*. Toronto: Longmans, Green and Co., 1929.
Heinl, R. D., and N. G. Heinl. *Written in Blood*. Boston: Houghton Mifflin, 1978.
Leyburn, James G. *The Haitian People*. New Haven, Conn.: Yale University Press, 1941.
Logan, R. W. *Haiti and the Dominican Republic*. London: Oxford University Press, 1968.
Nicholls, David. *Haiti in the Caribbean Context*. London: Macmillan Co., 1985.

PERCY C. HINTZEN

GHIOLDI, AMÉRICO (1899–   ), was a major Socialist spokesman in Argentina from 1930 to 1980. Born in Buenos Aires and graduated from the normal school in 1920, he became an editor of the Socialist periodicals *La Vanguardia* and *Acción Socialista*. In 1931 and 1936 he was elected to the Chamber of Deputies, where he became a leader of the Socialist delegation.

Ghioldi was a bitter critic of Juan Domingo Perón* and was eventually forced into exile. He and other Socialists strongly attacked the undemocratic nature of the Peronist labor movement and condemned the violent and repressive measures used to force the ouster of anti-Peronist labor leaders.

Ghioldi returned to Argentina after Perón's ouster in 1955 and again served as *La Vanguardia*'s editor. However, the Socialists soon split into several factions and ceased to be a significant force in political or labor affairs. Always a violent anti-Peronist, Ghioldi served for a while as ambassador to Portugal in the government of General Jorge Videla in the late 1970s.

BIBLIOGRAPHY

Alexander, Robert J. *Latin American Political Parties*. New York: Praeger, 1973.
Baily, Samuel L. *Labor, Nationalism and Politics in Argentina*. New Brunswick, N.J.: Rutgers University Press, 1967.
Rock, David. *Politics in Argentina, 1890–1930: The Rise and Fall of Radicalism*. New York: Latin American Studies, 1975.

Smith, Peter H. *Argentina and the Failure of Democracy, 1904–1955*. Madison: University of Wisconsin Press, 1974.

JOHN T. DEINER

GOMES, ALBERT (1911–1978), was Trinidad's most important political leader in the decade after World War II. Returning to Trinidad after spending 1928–1930 in New York as a student, he began to publish a magazine, *The Beacon*, which became the center of radical activity. It took up the cudgel for the lower classes, attacking the privileged on a number of issues.

In 1937 Gomes decided to enter politics at the behest of a close acquaintance, Quintin O'Connor, an erstwhile follower of Arthur Andrew Cipriani,* and leader of the Federated Workers Trade Union. Gomes and O'Connor mounted a campaign that brought Gomes' election to the Port of Spain Municipal Council. In 1941 Gomes became the principal spokesperson for the left in favor of universal adult suffrage, which he was largely responsible for winning in a new constitution in 1946.

In elections in 1946 Gomes won a seat in the Legislative Council. The next year he was nominated to the Executive Council. Gomes then became decidedly more cautious. He argued for gradual political change to avoid "dislocation, recantation, and remorse" in making a "fetish of democracy." This seeming ideological about-face cost him his seat in the capital city's municipal council which he had held since 1938, serving three times as deputy mayor.

Gomes was again elected to the Legislative Council in 1950, under a new constitution which he had helped prepare, providing a ministerial form of government. He became minister of industry, labor and commerce. For the next five years, he dominated the politics of the colony. Gomes, de facto head of the five ministers, began attracting foreign investors to the colony, keeping tax rates and social overhead expenditure low. He also successfully fought to retain imperial protection and preferential prices for the country's agricultural staples. Finally, he set the stage for a program of industrial diversification. He mediated between employees and employers and kept strikes and work stoppages to a minimum, by forcing unions and employers to make concessions before industrial disputes went out of control.

By 1955 Gomes, as one of the leaders of the Party of Political Progress Group, dominated by the country's conservative white businessmen, contested elections which were to usher in responsible government for the colony. They suffered a severe defeat by the newly formed Peoples National Movement headed by Dr. Eric Williams.* After participating in opposition politics, Gomes retired to Great Britain.

BIBLIOGRAPHY

Brereton, Bridget. *A History of Modern Trinidad 1783–1962*. Port of Spain: Heinemann, 1981.

Gomes, Albert. *Through a Haze of Colour*. Port of Spain: Key Caribbean Publications, 1974.

Malik, Y. K. *East Indians in Trinidad*. London: Oxford University Press, 1971.

Oxaal, Ivar. *Black Intellectuals Come to Power*. Cambridge, Mass.: Schenkman, 1968.

Ryan, Selwyn. Race and Nationalism in Trinidad and Tobago. Toronto: University of Toronto Press, 1972.

PERCY C. HINTZEN AND W. MARVIN WILL

GÓMEZ, JOSÉ MIGUEL (1858–1921), was president of Cuba from 1909 to 1913. A major general during the Wars of Independence, where he had compiled a distinguished record, he was appointed governor of his native province of Las Villas during the first U.S. occupation (1899–1902) and was elected to the same post under the republic. Unlike his predecessor in the presidency, Tomás Estrada Palma,* Gómez was seen by his supporters as a genuine charismatic leader.

Gómez' presidency occurred during years of relative prosperity; sugar harvests expanded, industrialization was initiated, and electrification began. He built a small army and started a navy and coast guard. Some progress was realized in education; several agricultural schools were opened. He made attempts to improve the lot of Cuba's working classes by constructing low-cost housing, advocating development of a university for workers, and seeking passage of a law requiring that rural workers be paid in cash rather than chits redeemable at company stores. Gómez also sought to establish diplomatic relations with nearly every nation in the world.

The Gómez years were also years of rampant graft. To many, he came to be known as El Tiburón (The Shark) because of his unabashed personal involvement with many forms of graft. During his presidency, legislature, judiciary, and bureaucracy all succumbed to graft schemes. By restoring the national lottery, Gómez expanded the opportunities for dishonesty to many thousands of additional citizens, particularly those in his own Liberal Party.

Gómez faced several demands on his government by the Taft administration, which was concerned with maintaining stability on the island. When the United States landed marines in 1912 to quell an uprising of blacks, Gómez strongly protested the violation of Cuban sovereignty.

President Gómez decided to seek reelection despite a 1908 pledge to support Alfredo Zayas y Alfonso* in the 1913 presidential election. In an effort to secure the nomination for himself, Gómez even had one of Zayas' major supporters in the army assassinated. When that failed, Gómez worked to have his fellow Liberal defeated, resulting in the election of Conservative Party candidate Mario García Menocal.*

BIBLIOGRAPHY

Fagg, John Edwin. *Cuba, Haiti and the Dominican Republic*. Englewood Cliffs, N.J.: Prentice-Hall, 1965.

Millet, Allan Reed. *The Politics of Intervention: The Military Occupation of Cuba, 1906–1909*. Columbus: Ohio State University Press, 1968.

Ruíz, Ramón Eduardo. *Cuba: The Making of a Revolution*. New York: W. W. Norton, 1968.

Strode, Hudson. *The Pageant of Cuba*. New York: Harrison Smith and Robert Haas, 1934.

Thomas, Hugh. *Cuba: The Pursuit of Freedom*. New York: Harper and Row, 1971.

STEPHEN J. WRIGHT

GÓMEZ, JUAN VICENTE (1857–1935), was the last of the great Venezuelan caudillos. Unwittingly, he brought about changes that made his breed of politician extinct in Venezuela.

Although he reputedly learned to read only when he was already grown, Gómez was able in his youth to amass a small fortune as a cattle driver and ranch owner. Losing that fortune in 1892 by backing a revolt that failed, he living during the next few years in Colombia, where he again gained considerable wealth through cattle raising (and, allegedly, rustling).

Gómez associated himself politically with Cipriano Castro,* who like Gómez was a native of Táchira and a temporary exile in Colombia. When Castro returned to Táchira in 1899 with a small armed force, Gómez was his chief lieutenant. During the next few months which brought success to the Castro forces, Gómez was their principal field commander.

President Castro made Juan Vicente Gómez first governor of the Federal District, then governor of Táchira, and in 1903 first vice president. In 1902 Gómez as commander of the army put down several attempts by rival caudillos to topple the regime. When President Castro went to Europe in 1908 for medical treatment, Vice President Gómez saw him off on the boat. Soon afterward he sent orders that Castro not return home, had himself proclaimed provisional president, and in 1910 was elected constitutional president for the first time.

In the beginning, Gómez had the support of many people disgusted with the libertine Cipriano Castro, including many intellectuals, who objected to the oppressiveness of the Castro regime. He also had support of foreign investors alienated by Castro's xenophobia. By 1914, however, many backers were alienated, having realized that Gómez had established a very oppressive personal dictatorship.

During the next 21 years, Gómez stayed in power despite numerous attempts by rival caudillos—including Cipriano Castro—to organize internal revolts or invasions against him. He also successfully faced down a protest movement by students in 1914 and an even more massive one in 1928.

Two basic changes brought about during the Gómez period spelled the end of the old-style caudillo. One was his building up of a professional army. By the mid–1930s the lower and middle ranks of officers consisted of military school graduates. So, although the generals continued to be people who owed their posts to their personal loyalty to Gómez, those below them were professional soldiers.

The second major change under Gómez was growth of the oil industry. Even before World War I, Gómez began giving concessions to foreign oil companies to search for petroleum. By the early 1920s they had found it in abundance, in and around Lake Maracaibo—and later in the eastern part of the country. They were allowed to exploit it under a law that the foreign oil companies' officials themselves had largely written. At the same time, Gómez and those closest to him used the opening up of the oil industry to get very large financial returns for themselves.

Gómez used the country's vastly increased revenues to pay off the national debt, to build roads, and to construct public works. Those revenues resulted in growth not only of a substantial wage-earning working class in and around the oil industry, but also of other workers and middle-class elements in the major cities.

Gómez considered Venezuela one huge personal hacienda. He acquired landed property, forcibly or otherwise, all over the country, and not infrequently he used the armed forces to cultivate or improve those properties. Virtually all of the country's revenues and wealth were at his disposal.

Although Gómez was in power from 1908 until his death in bed in December 1935, he was not president during all of that period. He was president from 1908 to 1914; although formally president from 1915 to 1922, he allowed his vice president to carry out most executive functions. He was again president in fact as well as in name from 1922 to 1929, and again from 1931 until his death. Gómez always held the reins of power, particularly control over the armed forces.

Juan Vicente Gómez never married, but he was reputed to have had as many as 100 children.

BIBLIOGRAPHY

Fuenmayor, Juan Bautista. *Historia de la Venezuela Política Contemporánea 1899–1969*. Vol. 2. Caracas: 1976.
Magallanes, Manuel Vicente. *Los Partidos Políticos en la Evolución Histórica de Venezuela*. Caracas: Monte Avila Editores, 1973.
Rourke, Thomas (Daniel Joseph Clinton). *Gómez: Tyrant of the Andes*. New York: William Morrow, 1936.
Vallenilla Lanz, Laureano. *Césarismo Democrático*. Caracas: Tipografía Garrido, 1961.
Velázquez, Ramón J. *La Caída del Liberalismo Amarillo*. Caracas: Ediciones Roraima, 1977.

ROBERT J. ALEXANDER

GÓMEZ, LAUREANO (1889–1965), was the often strident but effective reviver of Colombia's Conservative Party after its fall from power in 1930. He served as president of Colombia (1950–1953) until overthrown in a coup led by General Gustavo Rojas Pinilla.*

Gómez was born and educated in Bogotá. Gifted with a talent for polemical expression, he became a spokesman, as editor of *La Unidad* (1909–1916), for a group of young Conservative nationalists disenchanted with Colombia's weakness revealed by the loss of Panama. Through the years of Conservative rule until 1930, he served in various provincial and national positions, including representative, senator, and minister to Argentina.

The victory of the Liberal Party in the presidential election of 1930, together with Conservative disarray, convinced Gómez that his party needed a new direction. While minister to Germany in 1931, he became interested in rightist ideologies which were then growing in influence. Upon his return, he became the leader of the Conservative Party.

Growing Liberal electoral majorities and the conviction that Colombia was moving toward socialism caused Gómez to intensify his attacks on Liberalism. By the late 1930s he cast himself in the role of savior of a country experiencing political and moral decay. He championed Spanish falangism, openly sympathized with European fascism, and even advocated extralegal action to reassert Conservative hegemony.

From the pages of his daily *El Siglo*, as well as in Congress, Gómez steadily attacked and undermined the chaotic second administration of Liberal Alfonso López Pumarejo* (1943–1945). As party chief, Gómez whipped the Conservatives into line behind the candidacy of Mariano Ospina Pérez,* who won the presidency in 1946. Gómez himself was elected president in 1950 in an election from which the Liberal abstained.

The years of Gómez' presidency were marred by savage violence in the countryside and political polarization. His attempts at constitutional reform split the Conservative Party. For health reasons, Gómez turned over the presidency to Roberto Urdaneta Arbeláez in 1951, and when he attempted to resume office in 1953, he was stopped by a military coup.

Gómez worked against dictator Rojas Pinilla from his exile in Spain. Finally, he convinced the Conservatives to join the Liberals in forming the National Front, which was designed to restore constitutional rule after 1958, to bring about an end to violence, and to achieve political peace between the parties.

BIBLIOGRAPHY

Dix, Robert H. *Colombia: The Political Dimensions of Change*. New Haven, Conn.: Yale University Press, 1967.
Fluharty, Vernon Lee. *Dance of the Millions*. Pittsburgh: University of Pittsburgh Press, 1957.
New York Times, July 15, 1965.

RICHARD E. SHARPLESS

GÓMEZ, MÁXIMO (1836–1905), was the predominant military leader in both Cuban Wars of Independence (1868–1878 and 1895–1898). A Dominican by birth, Gómez came from a prosperous family and had the benefit of a good education. He fled his native island after losing all his property in the Civil War of 1866, and he settled in Bayamó, Cuba, as a farmer. Shortly after the Grito de Yara (the first proclamation of independence) in 1868, Goméz joined the forces of Carlos Manuel de Céspedes* as a sergeant and led a contingent of Dominican exiles in skirmishes with Spanish forces in Oriente Province during the early phases of the Ten Years' War (1868–1878). The experience he had gained fighting the Spanish in Santo Domingo was invaluable to the incipient revolutionary forces in Cuba.

Gómez rose to the rank of commander of rebel forces in Oriente, and his genius as a military strategist and leader was clear. He was the principal leader of a group that included Calixto García Iñiguéz* and Antonio Maceo y Grajales* and that developed and refined the art of guerrilla warfare. Many of Gómez' ideas on the topic would be carefully studied by a later generation of Cuban revolutionaries led by Fidel Castro* and Ernesto ''Che'' Guevara.*

Throughout the Ten Years' War, Gómez repeatedly advocated military invasion of the western provinces of Cuba, which represented the greatest wealth to Spain. He waged a campaign of devastation in the Province of Las Villas in 1875. When the civilian leadership of the revolution continued to thwart his demands to wage a concentrated campaign in the west, Gómez became disillusioned and urged that a peace treaty be arranged with Spain. Following the Pact of Zanjón which ended the Ten Years' War, Gómez went into exile in Honduras.

During the next 15 years, Maximo Gómez laid plans for a future revolution against Spain with José Martí* and Antonio Maceo. In January 1893 Gómez was appointed chief of the Cuban Revolutionary Party, created by Martí in New York in 1881. In March 1895 Gómez and Martí issued the Manifiesto de Monti Cristi, a declaration of war against Spain. Two weeks later, Gómez and Martí landed on Cuban soil.

Following the death of Martí, Gómez was declared *general en jefe* by the Republic in Arms. As both the major military and political leader of the rebellion, Gómez launched a campaign to capture control of western Cuba, the goal that had eluded him in the Ten Years' War. To achieve the military and economic defeat of Spain, Gómez again ordered that sugarcane fields and *centrales* be destroyed and workers terrorized. Although his policy of carrying fire and sword indiscriminately into the western part of the island may have set the stage for Spain's final defeat, that same policy devastated the island's economic base and crippled the young republic soon to be born.

A special constitutional provision was passed making Gómez eligible for the presidency of the republic. However, he refused to run for office, believing that the first president should be a native-born Cuban.

BIBLIOGRAPHY

Flint, Grover. *Marching With Gómez*. New York, Lamson, Wolfee and Co., 1898.
Foner, Philip. *A History of Cuba and Its Relations with the United States*. New York: International Publishers, 1963.
Guerra y Sánchez, Ramiro, et al. *Historia de la Nación Cubana*. Habana: Ed. Hist. de la Nación Cubana, 1952.

Pérez, Louis A., Jr. *Cuba Between Empires 1878–1902*. Pittsburgh: University of Pittsburgh Press, 1983.

Roig de Leuchsenring, Emilio. *La guerra libertadora Cubana de los treinta años 1868–1898*. Habana: Historiador de la ciudad de La Habana, 1952.

STEPHEN J. WRIGHT

GÓMEZ, MIGUEL MARIANO (1890–1951), was Cuba's sixth constitutionally elected president and son of José Miguel Gómez,* the second president. He was a conservative politician of Cuba's traditional governing elite; he served 12 years in the House of Representatives and was mayor of Havana for a while during the administration of Gerardo Machado y Morales.* However, he attacked the repressive nature of the Machado regime. With the backing of Fulgencio Batista y Zaldivar* and the Liberal Party, Gómez easily won the presidential election of January 1936, defeating former President Mariano García Menocal.*

Inaugurated in May, Gómez immediately blundered when he selected his cabinet without consulting army chief Batista. Relations deteriorated further when Gómez opposed a bill Batista had had introduced to establish a 9 cent tax on every bag of sugar produced, for construction of army-operated schools. Obsessed with the importance of reasserting civilian authority, Gómez felt that army control over rural education would erode the constitution and civilian power. Three days after Gómez vetoed the rural schools bill, he was impeached by the Senate, becoming the first Cuban president removed from office by Congress.

BIBLIOGRAPHY

Gellman, Irwin. *Roosevelt and Batista*. Albuquerque: University of New Mexico Press, 1973.

Thomas, Hugh. *Cuba: The Pursuit of Freedom*. New York: Harper and Row, 1971.

STEPHEN J. WRIGHT

GONZÁLEZ, JUAN NATALICIO (1897–1966), was a scholar, historian, and literary figure, and a president of Paraguay. Born in the interior, and with little formal schooling, he became a frequent contributor of polemical essays to the Colorado Party paper, *Patria*. He was a charismatic leader, and by age 40 had participated in protests, been exiled, become editor of the party paper, and been elected president of the party. During the Rafael Franco* government (1936–1937), he was exiled to Argentina, where he lived during World War II, writing prolifically and moving in nationalistic leftist political and intellectual circles.

Gónzalez' political model called for the national government to intervene in society to provide economic and social gains for the peasants and lower classes. He was particularly opposed to foreign economic influence in Paraguay, and urged expropriation and redistribution of foreign wealth.

When González returned to Paraguay at the close of World War II, his chief rivals in the Colorado Party were Federico Cháves,* leader of the "democratic" faction, and Felipe Molas López. González used tactics of violence and intimidation to achieve control of the party, through the Guión Rojo, a well-disciplined and completely loyal group of strong-arm followers.

González and the Guión Rojo gained tremendous power during the 1947 civil war. They they took over the job of policing Asunción and were given virtually unlimited power to root out rebel sympathizers in the capital. Following the war, the country was clearly in Colorado hands, but the party remained divided between González' Guionista faction and Cháves' "democratic" faction. The 1947 convention to nominate a presidential candidate was a González-Cháves showdown. After much violence and intimidation of the "democratic" faction by the Guionistas, the meeting unanimously chose J. Natalicio González. Running unopposed, he won and took office in August 1948.

Following González' election, but before he took power, another Colorado leader, Felipe Molas López, led a coup that removed President Higinio Morínigo,* allegedly to prevent a coup by Morínigo against President-Elect González. Molas López was then able to severely limit González' control over appointments. González' attempt to purge Molas López' followers resulted in his overthrow in a January 1949 coup.

Natalicio González went into exile in Mexico. Later he was named ambassador to that country by President Alfredo Stroessner.*

BIBLIOGRAPHY

Kolinski, Charles J. *Historical Dictionary of Paraguay*. Metuchen, N.J.: Scarecrow Press, 1973.
Lewis, Paul H. *Paraguay Under Stroessner*. Chapel Hill: University of North Carolina Press, 1980.
Lott, Leo B. *Venezuela and Paraguay: Political Modernity and Tradition in Conflict*. New York: Holt, Rinehart and Winston, 1972.
Raine, Philip. *Paraguay*. New Brunswick, N.J.: Scarecrow Press, 1956.
Weil, Thomas, et al. *Area Handbook for Paraguay*. Washington, D.C.: Department of Defense, 1972.

JOHN T. DEINER

GONZÁLEZ FLORES, ALFREDO (1877–1962), was president of Costa Rica from 1914 to 1917. He was appointed by Congress in 1914, when elections failed to produce a winner with a majority. He had to deal with the economic dislocations caused by World War I. Cut off from traditional European markets, Costa Rican coffee sales plummeted and government revenues declined. González Flores attempted to meet the crisis by cutting government costs, raising taxes, and extending credit to small farmers. He levied taxes on coffee exports, imposed exchange controls, proposed an income tax, and lowered salaries of government employees, including teachers.

These measures made him highly unpopular. In a coup, Defense Minister Colonel Federico Tinoco Granadas* overthrew him in January 1917. González Flores fled to the United States, where he enlisted the support of President

Woodrow Wilson, who refused to recognize Tinoco, which contributed to Tinoco's eventual resignation.

BIBLIOGRAPHY

Ameringer, Charles D. *Democracy in Costa Rica*. New York: Praeger, 1982.
Creedman, Theodore S. *Historical Dictionary of Costa Rica*. Metuchen, N.J.: Scarecrow Press, 1977.
Mavis, Richard, and Karen Biesanz. *Los Costarricenses*. San José: Editorial Universidad Estatal a Distancia, 1979.

CHARLES D. AMERINGER

GONZÁLEZ PRADA, MANUEL (1844–1918), organizer and leader of one of the first Peruvian parties, Unión Nacional, was born in Lima into an aristocratic and conservative family. He received his education in schools in Valparaiso, Chile, and San Marcos University. He abandoned San Marcos to administer a family farm in Canete, south of Lima, where he engaged in scientific research and writing poetry, essays, and plays. In the war with Chile (1879–1883), he was an officer in the reserves.

In 1885 he became president of the Círculo Literario, a club of liberal writers. Under its auspices he wrote radical articles and speeches to criticize social and economic conditions, defend the Indians, and attack the aristocracy, the army, and the church, the three pillars of oligarchic Peru. When the Círculo Literario became the Unión Nacional in 1891, González Parada drafted its Declaration of Principles and then departed for Europe.

During the seven years he spent in Europe, González Prada attended lectures by famous professors of the Collège de France, and went to theaters, museums, and libraries. His first book was published in 1894. When it was distributed in Peru, copies wre burned publicly to protest its liberal ideas. He returned to Peru in 1898 to resume leadership of Unión Nacional and continue publishing articles critical of socioeconomic conditions. As the government and the conservative forces closed down newspapers where his writing appeared, González Prada radicalized his political thinking and defended more and more openly anarchist philosophy and anticlericalism. During the political maneuvering prior to the 1904 elections, González Prada was proposed as presidential candidate of the Unión Nacional and the Liberal Party, but he declined. In 1912 he was finally persuaded to accept the directorship of the National Library, which he held until he resigned in protest for the overthrow of Guillermo Billinghurst,* the constitutional president. In 1915 a new constitutional president reappointed González Prada director of the National Library, which he remained until his death.

González Prada belongs to the history of political ideas for espousing Positivist ideas, for promoting anarchist ideology, and for preparing the basis of Peru's modern political parties. The Apristas acknowledge him as one of their precursors, and the Indianist ideological and artistic movement recognize him as one of its founders.

BIBLIOGRAPHY

Chang-Rodríguez, Eugenio. *La literature política de González Prada, Mariátaegui y Haya de la Torre*. Mexico: Studium, 1957.
Cutler, John Henry. "Manuel González Prada, Precursor of Modern Peru." Ph.D. diss. Harvard University, Cambridge, Mass., 1936.
Palmer, Judith Walker. "The Influence of Manuel González Prada on Modern Peruvian Essayists." Ph.D. diss., University of Florida, Gainesville Fla., 1972.
Podesta, Bruno. *El pensamiento político de González Prada*. Lima: Instituto Nacional de Cultura, 1975.
Sánchez, Luis Alberto. *Don Manuel*. 4th ed. Lima: Populibros Peruanos, n.d.

EUGENIO CHANG-RODRÍGUEZ

GONZÁLEZ VIDELA, GABRIEL (1898–1980), was the last of three Radical Party presidents of Chile between 1938 and 1952. He received his law degree in 1922. He entered national politics eight years later when he first became a member of the Chamber of Deputies. Although this was the famous "thermal Congress" hand-picked by dictator Carlos Ibáñez del Campo,* González Videla belonged to the Radical Party faction less well disposed to the Ibáñez regime than was the party's president Juan Antonio Ríos Morales.* As a consequence, after the overthrow of Ibáñez, Gabriel González Videla was elected president of the Radical Party.

In the presidential election of 1932, González Videla threw his influence in the Radical Party behind endorsement of ex-President Arturo Alessandri Palma.* As a member of the Chamber of Deputies, González Videla tried to find grounds for the Radicals' collaboration in the Alessandri government. However, he did not oppose the Radical's joining the Popular Front in 1936.

With victory of the Popular Front in 1938, President Pedro Aguirre Cerda* named González Videla Chilean ambassador in Paris and then in Rio de Janeiro. He returned home in 1945 to be elected to the Senate. By then, he was identified with the group in the Radical Party which favored working closely with the Communist Party.

When the death of President Ríos in mid–1946 made a new presidential election necessary, González Videla was the Radical Party nominee. He also had the backing of the Communist Party and the small Falange Nacional.

Although González Videla received a plurality, the final decision was thrown into Congress. After extensive negotiations with ex-President Alessandri, the Liberals agreed to support González Videla, assuring his election. In return, he agreed to take three Liberals into his cabinet, along with members of his own party and the Communists.

Between November 1936 and April 1947 González Videla governed with this tripartite cabinet. The Communists were particularly militant, seeking to use their government influence to crush their opponents in the labor movement. The president became convinced that the Communists thought they could use him and their presence in his government to gain power in Chile, as they were then doing in Eastern Europe.

González Videla took advantage of Liberal Party withdrawal from his government in April 1947 to completely reorganize the cabinet, leaving out the Communists. There then began a bitter struggle between the president and the Communists, culminating in González Videla's pushing through Congress in mid–1948 a statute outlawing the Communist Party.

González Videla continued strong support for economic development which had characterized his two predecessors. He sponsored establishment of the Technical University of the State and pushed the successful search for petroleum in the far South. Another important step of his administration was granting the vote to women in parliamentary and presidential elections.

After leaving the presidency in 1952, González Videla returned principally to business activity. He did not exercise any significant leadership in the Radical Party, even behind the scenes. He supported overthrow of the Salvadore Allende Gossens* government by the military under General Augusto Pinochet Ugarte.* When he died, he was vice-chairman of an advisory Council of State which Pinochet established.

BIBLIOGRAPHY

Alexander, Robert J. *The Tragedy of Chile*. Westport, Conn.: Greenwood Press, 1978.
Bowers, Claude G. *Chile Through Embassy Windows*. New York: Simon and Schuster, 1958.
Cortes, Lia, and Jordi Fuentes. *Diccionario Político de Chile*. Santiago: Editorial Orbe, 1967.
Enciclopedia Universal Ilustrada Europeo Americana. Barcelona: Jose Espasa e Hijos.
                                                              ROBERT J. ALEXANDER

GONZÁLEZ VÍQUEZ, CLETO (1858–1937), was one of two great Liberal presidents of twentieth-century Costa Rica. "Don Cleto," along with Ricardo Jiménez Oreamuno,* dominated Costa Rican politics between 1906 and 1936. He was president twice, 1906–1910 and 1928–1932.

Don Cleto embraced the liberal reforms of the late nineteenth-century, particularly in education and separation of church and state, making them the guiding principles of his administrations. He worked hard to uphold law and extend the suffrage and political rights to all citizens. He believed strongly in individual freedom and the unobtrusiveness of government.

González Viquez and Ricardo Jiménez failed to organize a permanent political party or to develop potential successors. They largely ignored economic and social problems. They achieved clean government and electoral democracy, but did not interfere with the economic power of the coffee barons.

BIBLIOGRAPHY

Ameringer, Charles D. *Democracy in Costa Rica*. New York: Praeger, 1982.
Barahona Jiménez, Luis. *El pensamiento político en Costa Rica*. San José: Editorial Fernández Arce, 1971.

Creedman, Theodore. *Historical Dictionary of Costa Rica*. Metuchen, N.J.: Scarecrow Press, 1977.
Gamboa G., Francisco. *Costa Rica: ensayo histórico*. San José: Ediciones Revolución, 1971.
Mavis, Richard, and Karen Biesanz. *Los Costarricenses*. San José: Editorial Universidad Estatal a Distancia, 1979.

CHARLES D. AMERINGER

GORDON, GEORGE WILLIAM (1820–1865), was born into slavery in Jamaica, the illegitimate son of a wealthy white planter and a black slave woman. Gordon taught himself to read and write and mastered the rudiments of accounting. In 1836, two years before the formal end of slavery, he set himself up as a produce dealer in Kingston. He later became a planter in the parish of St. Thomas. By 1842 he had accumulated enough wealth to provide European educations for his twin sisters and an older sister, and to save his white father from bankruptcy. Gordon became a magistrate in St. Thomas Parish and, after 1850, a member of the Jamaican House of Assembly.

Instead of affiliating with the white rural or "Country" political party, he joined the so-called Town party of fellow "men of color," who for the most part were merchants, government officials, and lawyers, with ideas ranging from progressive to radical. The Town party's early role was one of close support for critics of the callous, conservative policies of Governor Eyre, in the face of a deep economic crisis. Gordon, who together with a peasant leader, Paul Bogle,* led the struggle for the rights of impoverished blacks, predicted rebellion if more enlightened policies were not adopted.

Gordon's words proved to be prophetic. In October 1865 the Morant Bay uprising, led by Paul Bogle, occurred, with the loss of dozens of lives. Martial law was declared. Although Gordon was in Kingston at the time of the uprising and was not directly linked to the disturbance, he was arrested, taken to Morant Bay, and court-martialed for conspiracy. Finally, he was hanged.

In 1969 the government of independent Jamaica recognized George William Gordon by naming him a Jamaican National Hero.

BIBLIOGRAPHY

Black, C. V. *The Story of Jamaica*. London: Collins, 1965.
Gordon, G. W.: A Biography. Jamaica Now, October 1960.
Roberts, W. A. *Jamaica: The Portrait of an Island*. New York: Coward-McCann, 1955.
———. *Six Great Jamaicans: Biographical Sketches*. 2d ed. Kingston: Pioneer Press, 1957.
Underhill, Edward D. *The Tragedy of Morant Bay*. Freeport, N.Y.: Books for Libraries, 1971.

PERCY C. HINTZEN AND W. MARVIN HILL

GOULART, JOÃO BELCHIOR MARQUES (1919–1976), unexpectedly became president of Brazil in 1961 when the popular and charismatic Jânio Quadros* resigned and served until 1964. Born in 1919 in São Borja, Jango, as he was popularly called, grew up on a ranch close to that of Getúlio Vargas*. Although he received a law degree from the Faculty of Juridical and Socal Science of Porto Alegre, he never exercised his profession, becoming a rancher instead. When Vargas returned to Rio Grande do Sul after being overthrown in 1945, a strong personal friendship developed between young João Goulart and the former dictator. At Vargas' urging, Goulart began to organize the PTB (Labor Party) in Rio Grande do Sul.

Goulart became a political protegé of Vargas and chief coordinator of the Vargas campaign for president in Rio Grande do Sul. At the same time he ran for a congressional seat on the PTB ticket. With the Vargas victory in 1950, Goulart also won but did not assume his seat in Congress. He was appointed secretary of justice and the interior in the Rio Grande do Sul state government. He made the PTB the most powerful party in the state. He was also named president of the PTB in 1952.

In May 1952 Vargas ordered Goulart to reassume his seat in Congress. In June 1953 he was named minister of labor, an appointment that created tension in the army and middle class who feared that Goulart was a follower of Juan Domingo Perón* and would try to create a workers' republic in Brazil. Vargas, under heavy military pressure, removed Goulart as minister of labor, and Jango returned to Congress.

Shortly after the August 1954 suicide of Vargas, Goulart attempted to win a Senate seat from the state of Rio Grande do Sul but was defeated. In 1955, however, he was elected Juscelino Kubitschek de Oliveira's* vice president.

Presidential elections in 1960 resulted in the victory of Quadros who was of the opposition party, UDN, but Brazilian law permitted voters to select the vice president from another slate. Goulart of the PTB party was elected vice president under Quadros.

When Quadros unexpectedly resigned on August 25, 1961, army and civilian politicians who had opposed Goulart refused to accept him as president of Brazil. General José Machado Lopes of the Third Army, stationed in Porto Alegre, and the governor of Rio Grande do Sul, Leonel Brizola* (Goulart's brother-in-law), opposed any attempt to block Goulart's right to assume the presidency. Politicians devised a plan that made Brazil a parliamentary democracy, which in theory stripped power from the president and transferred it to a prime minister approved by Congress. Tancredo Neves* of Minas Gerais was the first prime minister.

President Goulart took office on September 6. The new parliamentary system did not function well, and in a referendum on January 24, 1963, full power was returned to the president.

During the next 14 months the battle lines were drawn between labor unions, peasants, students, and underprivileged supporting the president and the middle class, businessmen, large landowners, the U.S. government, and the army opposing him.

Goulart did not seem to have any clear-cut program, and he became increasingly isolated, eventually losing the support of the governors of the powerful states of São Paulo, Minas Gerais, and Rio Grande do Sul. In the last days of his administration, in a desperate attempt to maintain himself in power, President Goulart organized giant political rallies where decree laws expropriating foreign oil refineries and land reform were issued. Goulart's final move came in March 1964, when the president gave an impassioned speech supporting the demands of the army sergeants against the government.

When revolution broke out on March 31, the public did little to support Goulart. He spent the rest of his life in exile and died of a heart attack on December 6, 1976, in Argentina.

BIBLIOGRAPHY

Deodato, Alberto. *Nos Tempos do João Goulart.* Belo Horizonte: Editora Itatiala Ltd., 1965.
Jurema, Abelardo. *Sexta-Feira*, 13. Rio de Janeiro, J. Alvaro 1964.
Muniz Bandeira. *O Governo João Goulart, 1961–1964.* 1977.
Pedreira, Fernado. *Marco 31.* Rio de Janeiro, J. Alvaro 1964.
Toledo, Caio Navarro de. *O Governo Goulart, e o Golpe de 1964.* 1982.

JORDAN YOUNG

GRAU SAN MARTÍN, RAMÓN (1887–1969), served as president of Cuba from September 10, 1933, until January 14, 1934, and again from October 1944 until October 1948. The son of a wealthy merchant, he received his secondary education from private tutors before going to the University of Havana where he earned his medical degree in 1908. Grau undertook further medical studies in Europe and then returned to Cuba to establish one of the largest and most lucrative medical practices on the island. In 1921 Dr. Grau became professor of physiology at the University of Havana, where he later served as dean of the medical school.

During the late 1920s Grau gained a popular following among students for his courageous stands against the dictator Gerardo Machado y Morales.* He spent most of 1929 in prison as a result of his antigovernment activities. When, on September 4, 1933, Cuba's student revolutionaries toppled the regime of Carlos Manuel de Céspedes with the aid of an unknown army sergeant, Fulgencio Batista y Zaldíva,* they invited Grau to become president.

For four months Grau instituted a number of economic and social programs to improve the lot of the lower classes and weaken the hold of U.S. companies on the island. His nationalization of labor law required all business enterprises in Cuba to employ native Cubans for at least 50 percent of their total payroll. Other laws provided for women's suffrage, granting women the right to hold public office, construction of rural housing, reduction of rents, a minimum wage and establishment of the 8-hour work day, totally free education for poor students, establishment of a Ministry of Labor, and assumption of control of U.S.-owned electric and telephone companies.

Failing to receive diplomatic recognition from the United States, Grau's government fell on January 15, 1934. He went into exile until 1939 when he returned to assume the presidency of the Constituent Assembly. During his exile, Grau was instrumental in forming a new political party, called the Partido Revolucionario Cubano (Auténtico). In July 1940 Grau ran unsuccessfully for the presidency against Batista. Four years later, however, he was victorious against Batista's hand-picked successor, Carlos Saladrigas.

Ramón Grau's second presidency was a disappointment to many who expected that he would continue the nationalistic, reformist policies of his first administration. Grau and his Auténtico Party made several ineffective attempts to reduce the control of U.S. companies over vital aspects of the Cuban economy, but dropped most of their more nationalistic demands. During his second term there was an almost religious concern for protection of basic freedom and civil liberties, despite the fact that gangsterism and urban terrorism increased. The major exception was in the area of organized labor, where the Communists were purged from control of the powerful Labor Confederation with the help of Grau's Minister of Labor Carlos Prío Socarrás.* Grau also tilted his policies in labor's direction, with hundreds of decrees that gave labor almost everything it demanded—so much so that wages increased in excess of 150 percent during his administration. Some felt that this had the effect of discouraging necessary investment and thereby undercut the possibility of diversifying the economy.

Ramón Grau failed to implement the progressive, democratic-reformist regime he had promised. With a few notable exceptions, those close to President Grau were lacking in both idealism and honesty. Subsequently, Grau himself was indicted for corruption but was never brought to trial. All this discredited social democratic ideals in Cuba and helped prevent the evolutionary development of the country toward a more progressive state.

After Batista seized power again in 1952, Grau sought to organize a "legal" opposition, without much success. He stayed in Cuba under the Fidel Castro* regime until his death.

BIBLIOGRAPHY

Aguilar, Luis. *Cuba 1933: Prologue to Revolution*. Ithaca, N.Y.: Cornell University Press, 1972.
Farber, Samuel. *Revolution and Reaction in Cuba, 1933–1960*. Middletown, Conn.: Wesleyan University Press, 1976.
Gellman, Irwin F. *Roosevelt and Batista*. Albuquerque: University of New Mexico Press, 1973.
Thomas, Hugh. *Cuba: The Pursuit of Freedom*. New York: Harper and Row, 1971.
Wright, Stephen J. "Cuba, Sugar and the United States: Diplomatic and Economic Relations During the Administration of Ramon Grau San Martin, 1944–1948." Ph.D. diss., Pennsylvania State University, 1983.

STEPHEN J. WRIGHT

GROVE VALLEJO, MARMADUQUE (1879–1954), had a distinguished military career, led two coups d'ètat, became the founder of the Socialist Party of Chile, and for a few years was the country's most popular political figure. He graduated from the military school as an artillery lieutenant. The slow promotion of officers in the early decades of the twentieth century resulted in his only having reached the rank of major by 1924.

Grove participated in the Military Junta of junior officers whose demands ultimately forced the resignation of President Arturo Alessandri Palma* in September 1924. Four months later, in January 1925, he was co-leader with Carlos Ibáñez del Campo* of another junior officers' coup that resulted in Alessandri's being summoned back to the presidency. He became colonel by 1926 and founded the Chilean Air Force. In that year, he was named Chilean military attaché in London, but two years later he was dismissed by President Ibáñez because of a meeting with exiled ex-President Alessandri. In 1930 Grove participated in an unsuccessful coup against Ibáñez and was exiled to Easter Island, but made a spectacular escape and went back to Europe.

With the overthrow of Ibáñez in August 1931, Marmaduque Grove returned home, to command the Chilean Air Force. He led the coup of June 4, 1932, which proclaimed the Socialist Republic of Chile. Although Grove led the Socialist Republic for less than two weeks, he rallied wide support among trade unionists and left-wing intellectuals.

In elections for president in November 1932, Grove was candidate of the Socialist Alliance, a group of small parties that had supported his regime in June. He got almost one-third of the votes but lost to ex-President Alessandri.

In April 1933 the Socialist Alliance became the Socialist Party. Grove was soon after elected to the Senate and was proclaimed Life President of the new party. In 1938 it supported him as candidate of the Popular Front, but the Radicals and Communists imposed the nomination of a Radical, Pedro Aguirre Cerda,* who was ultimately elected. However, in this period Grove undoubtedly had more popularity among rank-and-file Chileans than any other political leader, more because of personal charisma than because of exposition of clear political ideas.

In 1943 Grove split with the majority of the Socialist leaders when he advocated entering the cabinet of President Juan Antonio Ríos Morales* and supported ultimately merging the Socialist and Communist parties. He split away to organize the Authentic Socialist Party. When that party finally decided to merge with the Communists, Grove returned to the Socialist Party. He remained a senator until 1949.

BIBLIOGRAPHY

Alexander, Robert J. "Chile," in Robert J. Alexander (ed.). *Political Parties of the Americas*. Vol. 1. Westport, Conn.: Greenwood Press, 1972.
Charlín, Carlos. *Del Avion Rojo a la República Socialista*. Santiago: Editorial Nacional Quimantú, 1972.

Jobet, Julio César. *El Partido Socialista de Chile*. Santiago: Editora Prensa Latino Americana, 1971.

ROBERT J. ALEXANDER

GUARDIA, ERNESTO DE LA (1904–   ), was the first post-World War II president of Panama to serve out his full term, 1956–1960. He was educated in the United States, receiving a business administration degree from Dartmouth. Despite his conservative leaning and the disintegration of the late President José Antonio Remón's* National Patriotic Coalition, de la Guardia continued economic and social programs begun by the martyred president. He extended government planning, undertook low-cost housing, established a minimum wage, and sponsored significant improvements in education. He created the Electoral Tribunal to assure free and fair elections.

In spite of de la Guardia's commendable record, he was generally unpopular because of the turbulence of the times. In April 1959 an invasion from Cuba was thwarted when the invading force surrendered. More seriously, on November 3, Panama's Independence Day, Panamanian students "peacefully invaded" the Canal Zone to place Panamanian flags, leading to rioting in Panama City, with numerous injuries and major property damage. Although President Dwight Eisenhower ordered display of the Panamanian flag in the Zone, President de la Guardia was offended when he was not invited to raise the first flag.

De la Guardia was the first Panamanian president to deliver the sash of office to a winner from the opposition.

BIBLIOGRAPHY

Alba C., Manuel María. *Cronología de los Gobernantes de Panama, 1510–1967*. Panama, 1967.
American University Foreign Area Studies. *Panama: A Country Study*. Washington, D.C.: March 1980.

CHARLES D. AMERINGER

GUARDIA, RICARDO ADOLFO DE LA (1899–1970), seized the presidency of Panama on October 9, 1941, and kept it until June 15, 1945. He was educated in Panama and his early career was in journalism. As minister of government and justice, de la Guardia deposed President Arnulfo Arias Madrid* when Arias travelled to Cuba without congressional authorization. He had the backing of most Panamanian political parties, the National Police, the Supreme Court, and the U.S. government.

De la Guardia declared war on the Axis powers and cooperated fully with the United States in defense of the Canal. He negotiated an agreement with the United States for constructing military bases in the republic outside the Zone. This cooperation proved controversial after the war but contributed to Panama's wartime economic well-being, with full employment and increased government revenues. De la Guardia handled these funds in a relatively honest fashion and undertook a program of public works. He restored the liberties Arias had suppressed and annulled the Constitution of 1941 that the dictator had imposed.

BIBLIOGRAPHY

Alba C., Manuel María. *Cronología de los Gobernantes de Panama, 1510–1967*. Panama: 1967.
Alfaro, Ricardo J. *Biográficos esbozos*. Panama: Instituto Nacional de Cultura, 1974.
Castillero R., Ernesto J. *Historia de Panama*. Panama: Editora Panama América, 1959.

CHARLES D. AMERINGER

GUARDIA GUTIÉRREZ, TOMÁS (1831–1882), one of the few authoritarian figures and military heroes in Costa Rican history, achieved distinction for defense against the filibusterer William Walker* in 1856 and quickly gained political influence. Costa Rica had been dominated by a conservative, landowning oligarchy, whose feuds tended increasingly to involve the military in politics. Growing impatient over his role as a mercenary of the ruling class, Guardia seized power in April 1870 and was either president or backstage manipulator for the next 12 years.

Guardia's rule was a transition period from the "patriarchal" republic to the "liberal" republic. He shared the Positivist philosophy of many of his Latin American contemporaries and launched an ambitious program of public works, although his effort to have a railroad built from San José to Puerto Limón failed, and the project was only completed several decades later. Guardia's policies provided the opportunity for a new class of coffee planters, businessmen, and professionals to assume power after his death.

BIBLIOGRAPHY

Creedman, Theodore S. *Historical Dictionary of Costa Rica*. Metuchen, N.J.: Scarecrow Press, 1977.
Mavis, Richard, and Karen Biesanz. *Los Costarricenses*. San José: Editorial Universidad Estatal a Distancia, 1979.
Monge, Carlos. *Historia de Costa Rica*. San José: Editorial Fondo de Cultura de Costa Rica, 1948.

CHARLES D. AMERINGER

GUEVARA ARZE, WALTER (1912–), Bolivian politician, lawyer, and president, attended secondary school in Cochabamba, Oruro, and La Paz, and received his law degree in the Universidad de San Andrés in 1936. A deputy to the constitutional convention of 1938, he was active in political parties that predated the founding of the Movimiento Nacionalista Revolucionario (MNR). He was director of the Mining Bank in 1939. With the fall of the reformist military government of Germán Busch,* he became professor of sociology in San Andrés University in 1940; and chief lawyer for the Railway Workers Social Fund. He served in the MNR-Gualberto Villarroel López* rule as secretary general of the governing junta in 1944.

With the triumph of the National Revolution in April 1952, Walter Guevara Arze was named minister of foreign relations and culture (and later minister of government) in the Victor Paz Estenssoro* administration. He was successful in securing U.S. recognition of the regime a few months after the MNR came to power. He allied himself with the Hernán Siles Zuazo* wing of the MNR, which represented the "right" wing of the party. In the preelection convention of 1956, Guevara attacked the party's labor left under Juan Lechín Oquendo* and was censured. With Siles as president, Guevara Arze was again minister of foreign relations and minister of government.

It was assumed that Guevara Arze would be the MNR's presidential candidate in 1960. But at the party congress, when he openly opposed the personalistic leadership of Paz Estenssoro, who planned to run himself, Guevara was expelled and formed the Movimiento Nacionalista Revolucionario Auténtico (MNRA). He was the MNRA's presidential candidate, and the party won 14 legislative seats. Guevara lost his congressional seat and left for self-imposed exile to Chile, charging the MNR government had manipulated the election. During preparations for the 1962 congressional elections, he formed the Partido Revolucionario Auténtico (PRA).

When Paz was elected to a third term, Guevara Arze—with other MNR dissidents like Lechín and Siles—supported the military coup of Vice President René Barrientos Ortuño.* In one of Barrientos' cabinets, Guevara Arze served as minister of foreign relations.

In June 1978 Guevara Arze ran for the vice presidency with Paz Estenssoro. The elections were soon nullified by a military coup. In 1979 he was elected to the Senate and became its head. He finally became president when the vote was indecisive among the top presidential contenders—Paz Estenssoro, Siles, and Hugo Banzer Suarez*—and Guevara, next in line as president of the Senate, was chosen interim president by Congress. He assumed office on August 6, 1979, but was overthrown by a military coup on November 1. In 1980 he ran as the presidential candidate of PRA, but the military coup of García Meza, the "cocaine general" (allied with cocaine smugglers) suspended civilian rule.

A founder of Bolivia's major revolutionary party, the MNR, Guevara Arze was an important theoretician and strategist. In his youth a member of the Marxist group of José Aguirre Gainsborg, founder of the Revolutionary Workers Party, and in the early 1940s associated with leftist currents of the MNR, by the late 1940s Guevara believed that a Marxist proletarian revolution was impossible for Bolivia. His concept of a broad, multiclass revolutionary alliance, proved the winning strategy for the MNR.

BIBLIOGRAPHY

Alexander, Robert J. *Bolivia, Past, Present and Future of Its Politics*. New York: Praeger, 1982.
Céspedes, Augusto. *El Dictador Suicida: (40 años de historia de Bolivia)*. 2d ed. La Paz: Juventud, 1968.

Fellman Velarde, José. *Víctor Paz Estenssoro: el hombre y la revolución*. La Paz: A Tejerina, 1954.

Malloy, James M., and Richard S. Thorn (eds.). *Beyond the Revolution, Bolivia Since 1952*. Pittsburgh: University of Pittsburgh Press, 1971.

Mitchell, Christopher. *The Legacy of Populism in Bolivia, From the MNR to Military Rule*. New York: Praeger, 1977.

WALTRAUD QUEISER MORALES

GUEVARA DE LA SERNA, ERNESTO (CHE) (1928–1967), was one of the most controversial revolutionary figures of the mid-twentieth-century. Although closely linked with the Cuban Revolution and Fidel Castro,* his most significant contributions were his writings on guerrilla warfare. Che Guevara viewed armed guerrilla struggle as the only viable means to destroy the forces of imperialism in Third World nations, and Marxism-Leninism as the means by which societies could be made more just and humane.

Ernesto Guevara was born in Rosario, Argentina, and grew up in Córdoba Province, coming of age during the Peronist era of the late 1940s. Young Che was influenced most by his mother, who had distinctly radical tendencies.

After graduating from medical school in 1953, Che traveled to Bolivia, then experiencing a revolution under the leadership of the Movimiento Nacionalista Revolucionario. He wandered throughout much of the rest of Latin America, ending up in Guatemala. There he sympathized with the Marxist-Leninist tendencies of the revolution then in process. When, in 1954, the United States sponsored a coup that deposed Jacobo Arbenz Guzmán's* leftist government, Guevara fled to Mexico. From his Guatemalan experiences, he concluded that it was necessary to utilize the armed struggle to defeat the forces of imperialism. In Mexico City Che met Fidel Castro and his compatriots who were preparing for their armed invasion of Cuba, and studied theories of revolution, including the major works of Marx and Lenin, and the guerrilla strategy used in the Spanish Civil War, China, and Vietnam.

Ernesto Guevara traveled to Cuba on the "Granma" with Fidel Castro and 80 other revolutionaries. For two years he was one of the key leaders in the guerrilla struggle against the forces of Fulgencio Batista y Zaldívar.* From his experiences waging the guerrilla struggle, he developed ideas and theories embodied in *Guerrilla Warfare*.

Guevara played a major role in the first five years of Fidel Castro's regime. More than any other individual, he was responsible for moving Castro in the direction of Marxism-Leninism. He served as minister of industry and president of the National Bank. His efforts to promote high-pressure industrialization to break the hold of sugar on the economy were disastrous. He was the main protagonist of the use of only "moral incentives," which he expounded in his work entitled *Man and Socialism in Cuba*.

Apparently quarreling with Castro, Guevara left Cuba in 1965. In 1967 he lost his life attempting to apply his ideas on guerrilla warfare in Bolivia.

BIBLIOGRAPHY

Bonachea, Ramón L., and Marta San Martín. *The Cuban Insurrection 1952–1959*. New
    Brunswick, N.J.: Transaction Books, 1974.
Bonachea, Rolando E., and Nelson P. Valdés. *Che: Selected Works of Ernesto Guevara*.
    Cambridge, Mass.: MIT Press, 1969.
Guevara, Ernesto. *Reminiscences of the Cuban Revolutionary War*. New York: Grove
    Press, 1968.
James, Daniel. *Che Guevara*. New York: Stern and Day, 1969.
Sinclair, Andrew. *Che Guevara*. New York: Viking Press, 1971.

STEPHEN J. WRIGHT

GUZMÁN, ANTONIO LEOCADIO (1801–1884), was the principal founder
of the Liberal Party of Venezuela. By the late 1830s he was one of the leading
figures in a group that opposed the political dominance of José Antonio Páez,*
and that had its sociological base particularly among the country's agricultural
landlords and the urban artisans. In 1840 this group established the Liberal
Society of Caracas, which shortly afterward became the Liberal Party, and
established a weekly newspaper, *El Venezolano*, of which Guzmán became
editor. Largely through that journal he became, after 1845, undisputed leader
of the party.

In 1846 Guzmán was Liberal candidate for president against the victorious
General José Tadeo Mongas,* backed by Páez. When a feeble attempt at military
insurrection was made in Guzmán's name, but probably without his support, he
was arrested and sentenced to death. However, President Monagas commuted
his sentence to permanent exile.

Although backed by Páez, Monagas soon formed an alliance with the Liberals,
as a consequence of which Guzmán was soon allowed to return and was shortly
afterward chosen vice president. He again ran for president in the election of
1850, this time against the president's brother, José Gregorio Monagas*, who
was victorious. However, the Monagas brothers soon quarreled, and Guzmán,
who continued to be vice president, became the closest adviser of President José
Gregorio Monagas while seeking to reunify the Liberal Party.

In April 1852 Guzmán went to Peru, on a private mission, returning only in
December, after his vice presidential term had expired. Soon afterward, President
José Gregorio Monagas named him minister to Peru, Bolivia, Chile, and
Argentina.

Ex-president José Tadeo Monagas was reelected in 1855 but was overthrown
by a military coup led by General Julián Castro and backed by the Conservatives
and dissident Liberals in March 1858. Soon, the five-year-long civil war (1859–
1863), the Federal War, began between the Conservatives of General Páez, and
the Liberals, renamed the Federal Party.

The government of Julián Castro exiled Guzmán in June 1858. In St. Thomas,
in the Danish Virgin Islands, he joined several other Liberal exiles to establish
the Patriotic Junta of Venezuela. This became the nucleus of the Federal Party,

which gave political leadership to the struggle against José Antonio Páez and the Conservatives.

By the end of the Federal War, however, Guzmán had been superseded as the principal figure in the Liberal ranks by his son, Antonio Guzmán Blanco.* Although Antonio Leocadio Guzmán was elected to Congress after the victory of the Federales in the war, it was his son who became vice president.

For some years, the situation remained turbulent. In August 1869 a physical attack on Guzmán Blanco's home resulted in his seeking diplomatic asylum in the U.S. Legation and Antonio Leocadio Guzmán seeking refuge in the Brazilian legation. When the legations were attacked, the Guzmáns fled to La Guaira and from there were able to get to Curaçao. In the following year, they returned with an armed force, were able to overthrow the incumbent government, and Antonio Leocadio Guzmán's son became president.

BIBLIOGRAPHY

Diccionario Biográfico de Venezuela. Madrid: Cardenas-Sáenz de la Callzada y Cia., 1953.
Enciclopedia Universal Ilustrade Europeo Americana. Barcelona: José Espasa e Hijos.
Magallanes, Manuel Vicente. *Los Partido Políticos en la Evolución Histórica de Venezuela*. Caracas: Monte Avila Editores, 1977.

ROBERT J. ALEXANDER

GUZMÁN BLANCO, ANTONIO (1829–1899), was the single most important Venezuelan political leader in the last half of the nineteenth century. As son of Antonio Leocadio Guzmán, founder of Venezuelan Liberalism, he was immersed in politics from his childhood, but rose to prominence only during the Federal War (1859–1863) during which he acquired the title of general and was a principal adviser of Liberal leader Juan Cristósomo Falcón.* With Liberal victory, he became Falcón's vice president (1863–1868). He remained in Europe during much of this period and negotiated a large loan from Great Britain, from which, his opponents claimed, he profited very much personally.

In June 1868 Falcón was overthrown and exiled by a coalition of Conservatives and dissident Liberals. Soon afterward, Guzmán Blanco returned home to mobilize the Liberal forces. However, he was forced to go into exile in Curaçao, whence he returned in February 1870. By June he was president, remaining in office for seven years.

During this first term, Guzmán Blanco virtually liquidated the Conservatives. Some who revolted were executed; the party as such was not allowed to function; and a number of Conservatives were coopted into Guzmán Blanco's administration.

Guzmán Blanco largely turned public finances over to a group of private businessmen. They lent money to the government for its current expenses and in return were allowed to collect 85 percent of the government's principal tax source, customs duties. Although severely criticized, this arrangement did assure the government of regular continuing revenues.

Guzmán Blanco carried out an extensive public works program, building roads, railroads, telegraph lines, and aqueducts and modernizing the principal ports. He strongly encouraged foreign investment, and foreign capital participated in many government projects.

During much of his term, Guzmán Blanco carried out a traditional Liberal anticlerical program. Seminaries, monasteries, and convents were suppressed; all religious instruction was transferred to the Central University; and civil marriage and civil registration of vital statistics, were decreed. At one point, the archbishop of Caracas was exiled. However, after the archbishop resigned in 1876, Guzmán Blanco and the Papal Nuncio negotiated an agreement in which the church finally accepted Guzmán Blanco's reforms as well as official separation of church and state.

Guzmán Blanco encouraged a "cult of personality" around himself and sought to associate his name with those of earlier national heroes. He established the National Pantheon, as the burial place for great leaders of the past, and had numerous statues of many of them set up throughout the country, on the base of which, of course, the name of Antonio Guzmán Blanco appeared prominently. He also encouraged the use of encomiums for himself, the most widely used of which was Illustrious American.

In 1877 Guzmán Blanco sponsored the election of General Francisco Linares Alcántara as president for a two-year term. He himself went to Europe. However, when a revolt drove the president from Caracas, Guzmán Blanco returned home, quickly led the Liberal forces to victory, and became provisional president in February 1879. In the following year he was elected constitutional president for a two-year term. He was reelected for another two years in 1882.

In 1884 Guzmán Blanco again allowed the election of a hand-picked successor, General Joaquín Crespo,* for a two-year term. However, when Crespo showed signs of wanting to acquire power as well as the presidency, Guzmán Blanco once more returned home from Europe, to run for his last period in the presidency, 1886 to 1888. He then returned to Europe, leaving another chosen successor, General Juan Pablo Rójas Paúl, in the presidency. This time he did not return to Venezuela.

BIBLIOGRAPHY

Gilmore, Robert. *Caudillismo and Militarism in Venezuela*. Athens: Ohio University Press, 1984.

Magallanes, Manuel Vicente. *Los Partidos Políticos en la Evolución Histórica de Venezuela*. Caracas: Monte Avila Editores, 1977.

Nava, Julian. "The Illustrious American: The Development of Nationalism in Venezuela Under Antonio Guzmán Blanco." *Hispanic American Historical Review* No. 45, 1965.

Velásquez, Ramón J. *La Caída del Liberalismo Amarillo*. Carcas: Ediciones Roraima, 1977.

Wise, George S. *Caudillo: A Portrait of Antonio Guzmán Blanco*. New York: Columbia University Press, 1951.

ROBERT J. ALEXANDER

GUZMÁN REYNOSO, ABIMAEL (1934–   ), founder and maximum leader of the Peruvian guerrilla movement, Communist Party–Shining Path, was born in Molleno. He studied in a Callao grade school and in a highly disciplined Catholic high school in Arequipa. He obtained his doctorate at the National University of San Agustín and joined the philosophy faculty of the National University of San Cristobal de Humanga in Ayacucho in 1962. There he held important administrative positions, taught philosophy courses, and indoctrinated his students with his own Marxist political ideas. A Communist, he was already an important Maoist leader when the Partido Communista Peruano-Bandera Roja was formed in 1964. He acted openly in this party until 1974, when he went underground with the name of Comrade Gonzalo. In 1980 his party, the Partido Comunista–Sendero Luminoso, began its guerrilla campaign in the Ayacucho area. After 1984, his partisans, through announcements on San Marcos University walls and Shining Path clandestine literature, referred to Guzmán as "President Gonzalo."

BIBLIOGRAPHY

Chang-Rodríguez. *Opciones políticas peruanas*. Lima: Centro de Documentación Andina, 1985.

Mercado, Roger. *El Partido Comunista del Peru: Sendero Luminoso*. Lima: Ediciones de Cultura Popular, 1982.

Rójas Samanéz, Alvaro. *Partidos politícos en el Peru desde 1872 hasta nuestros dias*. Lima: Ediciones F. & A., 1985.

EUGENIO CHANG-RODRÍGUEZ

H

HAYA DE LA TORRE, VÍCTOR RAÚL (1895–1979), founder of the APRA (American People's Revolutionary Alliance), was born in Trujillo, Peru. He attended the National Universities of Trujillo and San Marcos, as well as the London School of Economics and Ruskin College, Oxford. During his student days, he assisted Lima's workers in obtaining the 8-hour day, founded the People's Universities, fought for university reforms, and led the protest against President Augusto B. Leguía's* attempt to dedicate Peru to the Sacred Heart. After becoming president of the Federation of University Students in 1923, he was jailed and deported.

During the years of his first exile (1923–1931), Haya helped to found the José Martí* People's University in Havana, worked for José Vasconcelos,* Mexican minister of education, founded APRA in Mexico City, visited the USSR, attended the 1927 International Congress of Anti-Imperialists, lectured in the United States, Mexico, and Central America, and widely published his views.

The Peruvian Aprista Party (PAP), founded in September 1930 after the overthrow of President Leguía, elected Haya its presidential candidate in the elections of 1931. After electoral irregularities, his rival, Luís M Sánchez Cerro,* leader of the military revolt that overthrew Leguía, was proclaimed winner. During the reign of terror against the Apristas by the new oligarchical ruler, Haya was placed in solitary confinement. He was freed after Sánchez Cerro was assassinated in 1933. Following a few months' truce while General Óscar R. Benavides* consolidated himself in power, Haya went into hiding to lead his party's underground struggle. In 1945, when the Apristas were barred from having their own presidential candidate, he helped form a National Democratic Front which elected José Luís Bustamante y Rivero.* Three years later, the PAP was again outlawed, and Haya complied with his party's directive to seek asylum in the Colombian Embassy in Lima. For five years the Manuel A. Odría* government refused to give him safe conduct, and Haya's residence in the embassy became a *cause celèbre* in international law.

Under international pressure, Haya was permitted to leave Peru in 1954 and spent the following three years abroad. In 1962 he was again his party's presidential candidate. Although he received the highest number of votes, the National Electoral Board declared his candidacy a few thousand votes short of the 33 percent requirement. A subsequent military coup installed a new military junta that organized a new election. This time victory went to Fernando Belaúnde Terry,* although the Apristas had obtained more than 34 percent of the votes. In 1978 Haya was elected member of the Constituent Assembly with the highest number of preferential votes. Thus, he presided over the Assembly and signed the 1979 Constitution just before he died.

Haya's international fame does not rest entirely on his attempt to bring democracy to his country and lead the millions of Indians to the mainstream of Peruvian life. He was the leader and philosopher of APRA, from which many other democratic leftist parties in Latin America borrowed widely in their ideology and basic program. The PAP was the first modern organized political party in Peru. Haya's platform of fundamental reforms advocating the social democratic transformation of Peru and promotion of a United States of Indoamerica was attacked as extremist and utopian by conservatives and as centrist and reformist by radical Marxists. After his death, the governments of Peru and Venezuela decreed a day of national mourning. Two million people, about 30 percent of the voting population of the country, attended his funeral procession.

BIBLIOGRAPHY

Alexander, Robert J. (ed.). *Aprismo: The Ideas and Doctrines of Víctor Raúl Haya de la Torre*. Kent, Ohio: Kent State University Press, 1973.
Astíz, Carlos S. *Pressure Groups and Power Elites in Peruvian Politics*. Ithaca, N.Y.: Cornell University Press, 1969.
Chang-Rodríguez, Eugenio. *La literatura política de González Prada, Mariátegui, y Haya de la Torre*. Mexico: Studium, 1957.
Cossio del Pomar, Felipe. *Víctor Raúl: Biografía de V.R. Haya de la Torre*. 2 Vols. Mexico: Editorial Cultura, 1961–1969.
Sánchez, Luis Alberto. *Haya de la Torre y el Apra*. 2d ed. Lima: Editorial Universo, 1980.

EUGENIO CHANG-RODRÍGUEZ

HÉDER, LÉOPOLD (1918–   ), was both deputy and senator from French Guiana in the French National Assembly. In his early career he was a hospital official. In 1958 he was elected alternate to Socialist deputy Justin Catayée,* and he succeeded as full deputy when Catayée died in an accident in 1960. He was reelected in 1962 but was defeated by a Gaullist in 1967. In 1971 he was named to the French Senate and served until 1978. Between 1970 and 1973 he also was president of the General Council of French Guiana.

BIBLIOGRAPHY

Alexander, Robert J. "French Guiana," In Robert J. Alexander (ed.), *Political Parties of the Americas*. Vol. 1. Westport, Conn.: Greenwood Press, 1982.
Dictionnaire de la Politique Française. Paris: La Librarie Française, 1967.

ROBERT J. ALEXANDER

HERNÁNDEZ, JOSÉ MANUEL (1853–1919), although a Venezuelan caudillo of the typical nineteenth-century mold, conducted one of the few really popular presidential campaigns of the century in 1897. When only 17 years of age, he participated in a revolt in 1870 against the government of Antonio Guzmán Blanco.* Hernández was severely wounded, being left with a shriveled hand, which accounted in later years for his nickname El Mocho Hernández (Crippled Hernández).

In 1892 Hernández participated in the "Legalist Revolution" which restored General Joaquín Crespo* to power. Elected to Congress in the following year, he soon became a major leader of the opposition to Crespo. He organized the Liberal Nationalist Party.

At the end of Crespo's term in 1897, Hernández was the principal opposition candidate for president. In a way then unknown in Venezuela, he organized local groups of the Liberal Nationalist Party in virtually every part of the country, and he conducted a wide-ranging popular campaign, evincing enthusiastic support among many common people. His platform called for extension of the suffrage, proportional representation and a secret ballot, improvements in education, honesty of public officials, and independence of the courts.

When the government "counted him out," El Mocho Hernández attempted to overthrow the regime. In a battle against him, ex-President Joaquín Crespo was killed, but subsequently Hernández' forces were decisively defeated. Although Hernández at first supported the "Liberal Restoring Revolution" led by Cipriano Castro* in 1899 and was offered a cabinet post by Castro, he almost immediately turned against it. When he rose in revolt, he was quickly defeated and jailed. However, in 1903–1904 there was a short reconciliation between Castro and Hernández, Hernández serving for a few months as minister to Washington. However, Hernández was soon in exile.

When in 1908 Juan Vicente Gómez* seized power, Hernández was allowed to return. Though greeted with great popular enthusiasm in Caracas, he played no further significant role in national politics.

BIBLIOGRAPHY

Diccionario Biográfica de Venezuela. Madrid: Cardenas-Sáenz de la Calzada y Cia., 1953.
Magallanes, Manuel Vicente. *Los Partidos Políticos en la Evolución Histórica de Venezuela*. Caracas: Monte Avila Editores, 1977.

Velásquez, Ramón J. *La Caída del Liberalismo Amarillo*. Caracas: Ediciones Roraima, 1977.

ROBERT J. ALEXANDER

HERNÁNDEZ COLÓN, RAFAEL (1936–   ), twice governor of Puerto Rico and president of the Popular Democratic Party, was educated in local schools in Ponce, in Valley Forge Military Academy in Pennsylvania, and at Johns Hopkins University. He finally received a law degree from the University of Puerto Rico.

After privately practicing law in 1959–1960, Hernández served as commissioner of public service (1960–62). Between 1961 and 1966 he was professor of law in the Catholic University of Puerto Rico in Ponce.

Hernández Colón entered politics as secretary of justice, in which capacity he was responsible for writing the Political Code, Mortgage Code, and Plebiscite Act of 1967. In 1968 he was elected senator-at-large, and between 1969 and 1972 he was president of the Popular Democratic-controlled Senate. In 1969 he was chosen president of the party.

Hernández Colón served as governor of Puerto Rico from 1973 to 1977 but, unable to deal adequately with the island's growing economic problems, was defeated for reelection. He remained head of the Popular Democratic Party and was its victorious candidate for governor in 1984.

BIBLIOGRAPHY

New York Times, January 2, 1972.
Personalities Caribbean. 7th ed. Kingston, Jamaica: Personalities Ltd., 1983.

RICHARD E. SHARPLESS

HERNÁNDEZ MARTÍNEZ, MAXIMILIANO (1883–1966), was dictator of El Salvador between 1931 and 1944. He studied at the Escuela Politécnica Militar, and thereafter experienced a more or less normal military career, reaching the post of commander-in-chief of the army by 1931. He became president in December, upon the resignation of elected President Arturo Araújo. In 1935 he was elected to a term in his own right. Subsequently, constituent assemblies extended his term until (in theory) 1949.

General Hernández Martínez presided over a particularly brutal dictatorship. In 1932 he suppressed a peasant uprising, led by Communists, but with wide support among the rural population, in which as many as 45,000 people were reported to have perished. A second attempted uprising in February 1944, in protest against General Hernández' further extension of his term of office, was suppressed with equal brutality.

Less than a month later, on March 8, 1944, Hernández Martínez was forced out of office by a general strike and lockout of protest against his regime. He fled to Honduras. Although he sought to return home during the 1956 presidential election campaign, a hostile reception resulted in his again seeking refuge in

Honduras. He was murdered there by his chauffeur, apparently as a result of a personal quarrel.

BIBLIOGRAPHY

Enciclopedia Universal Ilustrada Europeo Americana. 1936–39 Supplement and 1965–66 Supplement. Madrid: Espasa Calpe.

ROBERT J. ALEXANDER

HERRERA, LUIS ALBERTO DE (1875–1959), was leader of the the Uruguayan Blanco Party from 1920 until his death. Born in Montevideo, as a young man he participated in the Blanco Party revolts of 1897 and 1904. In 1905 he was first elected to the national legislature. In 1920 he was chosen as the Blanco Party president.

Between 1925 and 1927 Herrera served as president of the National Council of Administration, established in the Constitution of 1918 to share the executive power with the president of the republic. After President Gabriel Terra* carried out a coup in 1933 which ended the Constitution of 1918, Luis Alberto de Herrera worked out with Terra an arrangement, incorporated in the Constitution of 1934, that provided equal representation of the president's Colorado Party, Herrera's Blanco Party in the Senate, and the Blancos in the cabinet.

After Terra's successor, Alfredo Baldomir,* ended the 1934 Constitution, Luis Alberto de Herrera was leader of the opposition. He ran for president on various occasions and in several cases received more votes than any Colorado Party nominee, but under the Uruguayan system which summed up the various candidates of the two parties who ran to determine which party won, Herrera never had more votes than all of the Colorado nominees. Thus, he was never elected president.

During most of the rest of his life, Herrera continued to be the most important opposition leader. In the election of 1958, the Blancos won for the first time in almost 100 years, but only six weeks later Herrera died.

BIBLIOGRAPHY

Alisky, Marvin. *Uruguay: A Contemporary Survey.* New York: 1969.
Fitzgibbon, Russell H. *Uruguay: Portrait of a Democracy.* New Brunswick, N.J.: Rutgers University Press, 1954.
New York Times, April 10, 1959.

ROBERT J. ALEXANDER

HERRERA CAMPINS, LUIS (1925–   ), was the second president of Venezuela belonging to the Social Christian Party. He was the head of the National Union of Students (UNE), the Catholic students' group, at the time of the October 18, 1945, coup d'ètat which brought the Acción Democrática Party to power for the first time, and he expressed his strong support for the new revolutionary government. Subsequently, with the establishment of the Christian Social Copei

Party under the leadership of Rafael Caldera Rodríguez,* Herrera Campins became the head of its youth group.

After the overthrow of the Acción Democrática government in 1948, Luis Herrera Campins went abroad. He became the principal spokesman for exiled members of Copei. He received his law degree at Santiago de Compostella University in Spain in 1954 and represented Copei at the First World Conference of Christian Democratic Parties in 1956.

With the overthrow of Marcos Pérez Jiménez* dictatorship in January 1958, Herrera Campins returned to Venezuela. He served in the Chamber of Deputies from 1959 to 1964, and was a senator until his election as president. He was president of the Copei Party in 1961, president of the parliamentary bloc of his party from 1963 to 1970, and between 1969 and 1977 was secretary general of the Latin American Congress of Christian Democratic Organizations.

Herrera Campins won a bitter contest for the Copei nomination for president in 1978. He was victorious in the election. He came to power when world oil prices were beginning to drop, and his regime was faced with a severe economic crisis, marked by substantial inflation, growing unemployment, and a rapidly mounting foreign debt. Congress was controlled by the Opposition, and there was substantial dissidence within the Copei Party. As a consequence, President Herrera Campins appeared to be a weak and relatively ineffective leader. When ex-President Rafael Caldera ran again, he was substantially defeated by Acción Democrática candidate Jaime Lusinchi.*

BIBLIOGRAPHY

Blank, David Eugene. *Venezuela: Politics in a Petroleum Republic*. New York: Praeger, 1984.
Herman, Donald L. *Christian Democracy in Venezuela*. Chapel Hill: University of North Carolina Press, 1980.
International Who's Who in 1985–86. London: Europa Publications, 1985.
New York Times, December 6, 1978.
Riera Oviedo, J. E. *Los Social Cristianos en Venezuela*. Caracas: Eidiciones Centauro, 1977.

                                                                    ROBERT J. ALEXANDER

HEUREAUX, ULÍSES (1845–1899), was dictator of the Dominican Republic from 1882 until 1899, during which the country experienced considerable economic development but also suffered one of the most tyrannical regimes in its history. A black, perhaps of Haitian origin, he presided over an exceedingly cruel and barbarous regime.

The government of Heureaux was dominated by the army and the civil bureaucracy, and the dictator considerably enriched himself from his control of the state. However, the sugar industry expanded, and the republic's social infrastructure was substantially increased. He borrowed very large sums abroad to finance his government, a debt that was a weight on succeeding regimes and contributed to ultimate U.S. intervention in the republic.

Heureaux was assassinated in 1899.

BIBLIOGRAPHY

Bailey, Helen Miller, and Abraham P. Nasatir. *Latin America: The Development of Its Civilization*. Englewood Cliffs, N.J.: Prentice-Hall, 1960.

Herring, Hubert. *A History of Latin America from the Beginnings to the Present*. New York: Alfred Knopf, 1964.

Rodman Selden. *Quisqueya: A History of the Dominican Republic*. Seattle: University of Washington Press, 1964.

Welles, Sumner. *Naboth's Vineyard*. New York: Payson and Clarke, Ltd., 1928.

ROBERT J. ALEXANDER

HIDALGO Y COSTILLA, MIGUEL (1753–1811), was the father of Mexico's independence. The War of Independence began as a struggle to create a Mexican monarchy independent of the Spanish crown, so that Mexican-born Spaniards (creoles) would have equal rights with Iberian-born Spaniards but would remain the ruling class. Hidalgo himself began by championing autonomy for a monarchical Mexico in order to insure more social justice. Later, he added to his goals citizenship for Indians.

Born on a plantation in the state of Guanajato, Hidalgo studied for the priesthood at the College of San Nicolás in the state of Michoacán. Later he became dean of the college, after achieving fame as a teacher of literacy to the Indians. The viceroy considered Hidalgo too nonconformist and ordered him to resign his deanship to serve as a parish priest in his native state of Guanajuanto, in the town of Dolores.

There Hidalgo met a young landowner, Ignacio Allende, also born in Guanajuato, who resented the preference given to leaders born in Spain. Both agreed that if Mexico could attain political autonomy, such inequities would vanish.

On September 15, 1810, in the evening, ringing the church bells, Hidalgo gave the *grito* (''Cry'') for independence. The viceregal government had been warned by a priest who betrayed his religious vows by relaying information about the *grito* which he had heard as a part of Hidalgo's confession. Before dawn on September 16, Hidalgo was warned that Spanish troops were en route to arrest him. He armed his Indian followers with machetes and a few muskets and suddenly found himself a military leader. Using a banner of the Virgin of Guadalupe as his battle flag, Hidalgo joined forces with Allende and capture the Guanajuato town of San Miguel.

Hidalgo gathered Indians and *mestizos* into the rebel army. He issued proclamations in favor of an elected Congress, to make laws for Mexico under the nominal authority of King Ferdinand of Spain. But the viceregal generals ignored that chance to retain at least token control over Mexico. Meantime, a village priest who had studied under Hidalgo at the College of San Nicolas, José Morelos, joined the rebellion and recruited troops in Acapulco.

In March 1811 Spanish forces captured Hidalgo. The Inquisition declared him and Morelos defrocked and excommunicated. Despite Hidalgo's numerous public prayers for liberty and independence, his church persecutors accused him of not believing in God because he rejected papal guidance. A companion edict warned that all priests who supported the revolution would suffer excommunication.

No longer recognized by viceregal generals as a priest, Hidalgo was turned over to civil authorities for punishment. Stripped to a loincloth, Hidalgo was publicly flogged, as an example to any priest who might defy royal authority. Then, on July 30, 1811, Hidalgo was shot in Chihuahua by a firing squad, less than one year after he had led the opening battle in Mexico's War of Independence.

As a military leader, Hidalgo must be regarded as a failure. As a leader of Mexican people, symbolizing a bond between creoles and Indians and as a rallying voice for Mexican nationhood, Hidalgo became the father of his country.

BIBLIOGRAPHY

Bancroft, Hubert H. *History of Mexico*. Vol. 1. San Francisco: Bankcroft Library reprint, 1940.
Cuevas, Mariano. *Historia de la Iglesia en Mexico*. El Paso: 1821.
Meecham, J. Lloyd. *Church and State in Latin America*. Chapel Hill: University of North Carolina Press, 1966.
Parkes, Henry B. *A History of Mexico*. Boston: Houghton Mifflin, 1970.
Sierra, Justo. *The Political Evolution of the Mexican People*. Austin: University of Texas Press, 1969.

MARVIN ALISKY

HOSTOS Y BONILLA, EUGENIO MARÍA DE (1839–1903), was an early advocate of Puerto Rican self-government. He had his secondary and university training in Spain, but was disappointed by the refusal of the First Spanish Republic to grant Puerto Rican autonomy. He went to New York in 1869, associating with Cuban revolutionaries there. Then, after a long tour of South America, Hostos settled in the Dominican Republic, where he was a major force in reorganizing the educational system. Between 1889 and 1898 he was a teacher in both secondary schools and the University of Chile.

Throughout his exile from Puerto Rico, Hostos continued to advocate autonomy for the island, and at one point advocated a confederation of Cuba, Puerto Rico, and the Dominican Republic. In April 1898 he went to New York, but by the time of his arrival, the United States had occupied Puerto Rico. Hostos urged the quick establishment of a civilian government there, but when the United States was unresponsive, he returned to the Dominican Republic, where he stayed until his death.

BIBLIOGRAPHY

Enciclopedia Universal Ilustrada Europeo-Americana. Barcelona: José Espasa e Hijos.
Hostos, Eugenio Carlos de. *Eugenio María de Hostos, a Promoter of Pan Americanism.*
Madrid: Imp. J. Bravo, 1954.

RICHARD E. SHARPLESS

HUERTA, VICTORIANO (1854–1916), a Mexican general who briefly usurped the presidency, is remembered as the man who murdered the apostle of the Revolution, Francisco I. Madero.* He was born in a village in the state of Jalisco to Indian parents. A brilliant student at the Colegio Militar, he denied his pure Indian heritage and claimed to be a *mestizo.* Displaying hatred for his Indian origin, Huerta as an army officer in 1880 slaughtered dozens of Mayas in the uprising in Yucatán. As a general, in 1911 Huerto indiscriminately ordered attacks against civilians and rebels alike in an attempt to defeat the forces of Emiliano Zapata.* In 1912 President Madero appointed Huerta chief of staff. On February 22, 1913, Huerta had Madero imprisoned and then shot in the back, "while trying to escape." Huerta proclaimed himself president of Mexico.

Defeated by the constitutionalist forces, Huerta resigned on July 15, 1914, and fled to the United States. He attempted to return to Mexico but was arrested on June 27, 1915, for illegally running guns across the border. He died as a prisoner at Fort Bliss.

BIBLIOGRAPHY

Brieb, Kenneth J. *The United States and Huerta.* Lincoln: University of Nebraska Press, 1969.
Johnson, William Weber. *Heroic Mexico.* Garden City, N.Y.: Doubleday, 1968.
Meyer, Michael C. *Huerta: A Political Portrait.* Lincoln: University of Nebraska Press, 1972.
Womack, John. *Zapata and the Mexico Revolution.* New York: Alfred A. Knopf, 1968.

MARVIN ALISKY

I

IBÁÑEZ DEL CAMPO, CARLOS (1877–1960), presided for four years over one of the two dictatorships which Chile has suffered in the twentieth century. He entered the military school in 1896. Among his assignments as a career officer were those of commanding the Carabineros School, directing the Cavalry School, and heading a mission that gave the first formal training to the officers of the army of El Salvador. However, because of the slow rate of military promotions during the first decades of the twentieth century, he was only a major by 1924.

Ibáñez was a member of the Military Junta of junior officers in September 1924 which led to the fall of President Arturo Alessandri Palma.* In January 1925 he was co-leader with Marmaduque Grove Vallejo* of the second young officers' coup, which resulted in President Alessandri being summoned back to office.

Alessandri confirmed Ibáñez in the post of minister of war, which he had had since the January coup. However, when Ibáñez made it clear that he intended to run for president, Alessandri resigned the presidency in protest. That temporarily forced Colonel Ibáñez to postpone his presidential ambitions. The new president elected in October 1925, Emiliano Figueroa Larrain,* reappointed Ibáñez minister of war.

Because of President Figueroa's inability to control the actions of his war minister, he first named Ibáñez as minister of interior in February 1927, and then two months later he resigned, turning over to Ibáñez the post of vice president (acting president). Ibáñez presided over elections in which his only rival was Elías Lafertte Gaviño,* the Communist leader then being held prisoner on Easter Island. Ibáñez became president of Chile on July 21, 1927.

During Ibáñez' presidency, most political parties continued to function legally, although many leading party personalities were driven into exile. When congressional elections were scheduled in early 1930, President Ibáñez called party leaders together at the hot springs at Chillán, where he was on summer vacation, and told them how many candidates each party would have and who they should be. So only one candidate was named for each post, and according to laws then in effect, elections were unnecessary. This legislature was known as the "thermal congress" owing to its place of origin.

During his 1927–1931 administration Ibáñez put into effect social and labor legislation passed in September 1924, bringing into existence a legally recognized labor movement, and establishing collective bargaining and a social security system. During his first two years, Ibáñez borrowed heavily abroad to finance extensive public works. He established the national militarized police, the Carabineros. He also signed a final peace treaty with Peru, formally ending the War of the Pacific and providing that the city of Tacna, occupied by Chile for 50 years, should be returned to Peru.

The Great Depression destroyed the stability of the Ibáñez dictatorship. The drop in Chile's national income was the most severe of any nation for which the League of Nations kept statistics. Growing unemployment and social unrest culminated in July 1931 in clashes at the University of Chile, a general student strike, and finally a general strike and lockout by workers and employers throughout the country. Ibáñez resigned on July 26 and went into exile.

Ibáñez stayed abroad for about five years. Then, in the election of 1938, he was presidential nominee of the Popular Liberating Alliance Coalition, consisting of his own followers and the Chilean Nazi Party. After an attempted uprising against the government of President Arturo Alessandri by the Nazis on September 5 was suppressed with considerable bloodshed, Ibáñez withdrew his candidacy and supported Pedro Aguirre Cerda,* nominee of the Popular Front, who was victorious.

Ibáñez again ran for president in 1942, following the death of Aguirre Cerda, this time with the backing of the Conservative Party and most of the Liberal Party. However, ex-President Alessandri was able to organize a sufficiently large defection of Liberals in support of Ibáñez' opponent, Juan Antonio Ríos Morales,* to bring about the general's defeat. In 1949 Ibáñez was elected to the Senate.

At the end of the term of President Gabriel González Videla,* there was a certain revulsion against the traditional political parties. Many turned to General Ibáñez, who was seen as a somewhat benign elderly man and whose earlier tyranny had been forgotten by many. He was reelected president in 1952.

During his second administration, President Ibáñez governed democratically. He had to face very severe inflation, and he adopted a drastic stabilization program. He sponsored a law to reorganize the copper mining industry and enacted a new labor law specifically for that industry. The law passed in the Gonzalez Videla administration to outlaw the Communist Party was repealed over Ibáñez' veto, and a new electoral law virtually established universal adult franchise.

President Ibáñez' second term ended in November 1958. When he died a year and a half later, he was running for the Senate.

BIBLIOGRAPHY

Boizard, Ricardo. *Cuatro Retratos en Profundidad: Ibanez, Lafertte, Leighton, Walker.* Santiago: Imprenta El Imparcial, n.d.
Contreras Guzman, Victor. *Bitacore de la Dictadura, Administración Ibanez 1927–1931.* Santiago: Imprenta Cultura, 1942.
Correa Prieto, Luis. *El Presidente Ibáñez, La Política y los Políticos, Apuntes para la Historia.* Santiago: Editorial Orbe, 1962.
Cortes, Lia, and Jordi Fuentes. *Diccionario Político de Chile.* Santiago: Editorial Orbe, 1967.

                                                        ROBERT J. ALEXANDER

IGLESIAS CASTRO, RAFAEL (1861–1924), was president of Costa Rica for two terms, 1894–1898 and 1898–1902. He was the dominant political figure during the last decade of the nineteenth century, having forced recognition of the election of his father-in-law, José Joaquín Rodríguez in 1890, when President Bernardo Alfaro Soto* tried to impose his own candidate. During Rodríguez' term, Iglesias was "the power behind the throne."

Iglesias governed in the wake of the liberal reform administrations of the 1880s, and his authoritarian style caused the young Liberals much discomfort. He was impatient with opposition and frequently violated individual rights, and he amended the constitution to permit his reelection. He sponsored significant construction projects, such as the National Theater and Pacific Railroad. He managed to frustrate the Liberals for an additional term with election of a compromise candidate Ascensión Esquivel in 1902.

BIBLIOGRAPHY

Creedman, Theodore S. *Historical Dictionary of Costa Rica.* Metuchen, N.J.: Scarecrow Press, 1977.
Mavis, Richard, and Karen Biesanz. *Los Costarricenses.* San José: Editorial Universidad Estatal a Distancia, 1979.
Monge, Carlos. *Historia de Costa Rica.* San José: Editorial Fondo de Cultura de Costa Rica, 1948.

                                                        CHARLES D. AMERINGER

IGLESIAS PANTÍN, SANTIAGO (1872–1939), Puerto Rico's foremost labor leader, organized the island's first important working-class party, the Socialist Party, which became a major political force during the 1920s and 1930s. He was born in Coruña, Spain, to working-class parents. At the age of 15, he settled in Havana, Cuba, where he became involved in union activities, serving as secretary of the city's Workers Circle from 1889 to 1896. At the outbreak of Cuba's second War for Independence in 1895, Iglesias and other labor leaders came under suspicion of Spanish authorities, and he fled to Puerto Rico.

Discovering that no labor movement existed in Puerto Rico, Iglesias began the task of building one. On May Day, 1897, he launched a small newspaper,

Ensayo Obrero, advocating working-class organization. This won Iglesias the attention of Spanish officials, and he was jailed.

Iglesias was still incarcerated when the American occupation of Puerto Rico occurred in July 1898. An attempt by the Spaniards to have him deported to Spain came to the attention of the American military governor, General John Brooke, who released him and made him a personal aide. Under the Americans' protection, he resumed his pro-labor activities and lobbied successfully for reduction of the workday to 8 hours.

Iglesias soon traveled to the United States, where he established a long and influential relationship with Samuel Gompers, president of the American Federation of Labor (AFL). Iglesias' ties to Gompers paid off after his return to Puerto Rico in 1900. The Americans' attitudes about labor had changed. Iglesias was charged with conspiracy and was given a long prison term; Gompers' intervention with President Theodore Roosevelt resulted in his release.

Next, Iglesias edited a series of labor newspapers. His Free Federation of Puerto Rican Workers was affiliated with the AFL, whose Puerto Rican representative he became. In 1925 he was named secretary of the AFL-sponsored Pan American Federation of Labor, a post he held until his death. In 1908 he first sought political office as the Free Federation's candidate for Resident Commissioner in Washington.

Iglesias was convinced that statehood was the only means of insuring protection for workers against capitalist interests seeking to destroy the labor movement. This was the position of the Socialist Party, which he organized in 1915.

Under Iglesias' direction, the Socialists grew rapidly. They elected him to the new insular Senate in 1917 (where he served until 1933) and sent several representatives to the lower house. In 1928, in alliance with the conservative but pro-statehood Republicans, they gained almost half the seats in the legislature. But as the junior partner in the alliance, the Socialists' popularity began to recede. Their failure to formulate a convincing program during the Great Depression added to their troubles. Undoubtedly, an additional reason for the Socialists' decline was Iglesias' absence in Washington as Resident Commissioner from 1933 until his death. By 1938 many Socialist leaders and rank-and-file members bolted to the new Popular Democratic Party of Luis Muñoz Marín.*

BIBLIOGRAPHY

Anderson, Robert W. *Party Politics in Puerto Rico*. Stanford, Calif.: Stanford University Press, 1965.
Carreras, Juan. *Santiago Iglesias Pantín*. San Juan, n.d.
Iglesias Pantín, Santiago. *Luchas Emancipadoras*. San Jaun: 1929.
Lewis, Gordon K. *Puerto Rico: Freedom and Power in the Caribbean*. New York: Monthly Review Press, 1963.
Lopez, Adelberto, and James Petras (eds.). *Puerto Rico and the Puerto Ricans*. New York: John Wiley, 1974.

RICHARD E. SHARPLESS

ILLIA, ARTURO UMBERTO (1900–   ), was president of Argentina from 1963 to 1966. Born in Buenos Aires Province and graduated from the medical school of the University of Buenos Aires, he began to practice medicine in a small town in the province of Córdoba. In 1948 he was elected to the national Congress where he served for four years. When the Radical Party split after 1955, Illia sided with Ricardo Balbín* and the People's Radicals (UCRP), which reflected his own moderate and traditional Radical views.

In 1963 Illia was nominated as the UCRP's presidential candidate. Although garnering only about 25 percent of the popular vote, he managed to get the support of enough minor parties in the electoral college to be elected president. However, he came to power without a working legislative majority.

Illia's problems were exacerbated in 1965 and 1966 when Peronists were allowed to take part in local and congressional elections. Their important victories caused unease among the military and other anti-Peronist sectors. Students also posed problems for the Illia government, taking to the streets to protest government educational policy. The regime was further rocked by rumors of corruption. Compounding all these problems was Argentina's difficult economic situation. One of Illia's most visible moves, cancellation of oil contracts, was understandable from a political point of view but caused Argentina again to become an oil importer.

By early 1966 Argentine political journals were openly speculating on when, not if, Illia would be overthrown. When the expected coup came in June, it was welcomed by large numbers of Argentines from various political perspectives. They did not realize that Illia's overthrow was the beginning of a new political era of increased violence and repression.

BIBLIOGRAPHY

Cantón, Dario. *Elecciones y partidos políticos en la Argentina: historia, interpretación y balance, 1910–1966.* Buenos Aires: 1973.
Johnson, Kenneth F. *Argentina's Mosaic of Discord.* Washington, D.C.: Institute for the Comparative Study of Political Systems, 1969.
Potash, Robert. *The Army and Politics in Argentina, 1945–1962: Perón to Frondizi.* Stanford, Calif.: Stanford University Press, 1980.
Snow, Peter G. *Argentine Radicalism: The History and Doctrine of the Radical Civic Union.* Iowa City: University of Iowa Press, 1965.
Wynia, Gary W. *Argentina in the Postwar Era: Politics and Economic Policy Making in a Divided Society.* Albuquerque: University of New Mexico Press, 1978.

JOHN T. DEINER

ISAACS, KENDALL GEORGE LAMON (1925–   ), the leader of the opposition political party in the Bahamas, the Free National Movement (FNM), is of mixed racial stock. He graduated from Government High School in Nassau and then volunteered for World War II service in the Bahamas Battalion, where he reached the rank of lieutenant. In 1946 he enrolled in Queens College,

Cambridge University, receiving a bachelor's degree in 1949, a law degree in 1950, and a master's degree in 1953.

Isaacs spent two years in private law practice before becoming a circuit magistrate in 1952, solicitor general, 1955–1963, and attorney general in 1963–1965. He accepted appointment to the Bahamian Senate in 1965, where he was vice president from 1968 to 1971. He was elected to the House of Assembly in 1982 and led the Free National Movement to nearly 45 percent of the popular vote.

The FNM was formed in 1970 by eight MPs led by Cecil Wallace, former Progressive Liberal Party (PLP) chairman and a cabinet member in the Premier Lynden Oscar Pindling* cabinet. In 1976 the FNM suffered a major schism when a majority of its elected members formed the Bahamian Democratic Party (BDP), but by the 1982 election this separation had been healed and almost all opposition parties except the Marxist-oriented Vanguard Party were represented in the restuctured FNM, led by Isaacs.

BIBLIOGRAPHY

Alexander, Robert J. "The Bahamas," in Robert J. Alexander (ed.) *Political Parties of the Americas*. Vol. 1. Westport, Conn.: Greenwood Press, 1982.
Collingwood, Dean. "The Bahamas," in Jack W. Hopkins (ed.). *Latin American and Caribbean Contemporary Record*. Vols. 1–3. New York: Holmes and Meier, 1983, 1984, 1985.
Personal Interviews.
Personalities Caribbean. Kingston, Jamaica: Personalities Ltd., 1975.
Symmonett, Chris. "Pindling Accused of Lack of Prudence." *Caribbean Contact* 12 (January 1985).

PERCY C. HINTZEN AND W. MARVIN WILL

ITURBIDE, AGUSTÍN DE (1783–1824), an army officer, made himself emperor of newly independent Mexico as Augustín I. Born in Valladolid in Michoacán in 1783, he studied at the Valladolid Seminary, and at age 14 he entered the colonial militia as a second lieutenant because of his father's aristocratic status. When Miguel Hidalgo y Costilla* began the revolution for independence in 1810, Iturbide became an officer with the Spanish troops. By 1820 he was a colonel.

In Spain in 1820, constitutional government was revived. This prompted monarchist Iturbide to favor independence for Mexico to keep out liberalism. He negotiated independence with the last Spanish Viceroy Juan O'Donojú, on September 27, 1821. On May 20, 1822, he proclaimed himself emperor of Mexico. The army ousted him on March 23, 1824, and executed him on July 19 for attempting to overthrow the new republic.

BIBLIOGRAPHY

Flores Caballero, Romeo. *Counterrevolution*. Lincoln: University of Nebraska Press, 1974.

Hale, Charles A. *Mexican Liberalism in the Age of Mora, 1821–1853*. New Haven, Conn.: Yale University Press, 1968.

Robertson, William Spence. *Rise of the Spanish American Republics as Told in the Lives of Their Liberators*. New York: D. Appleton and Co., 1918.

Zorrilla, Juan Fidel. *Los Ultimos Días de Iturbide*. Mexico: Librería de M. Porrua, 1969.

MARVIN ALISKY

J

JAGAN, CHEDDI (1918–   ), has been one of the most important twentieth-century political figures in Guyana. His parents were East Indian laborers on the sugar estates, who managed to enroll him in the country's top secondary school. Jagan subsequently attended Howard University in Washington, D.C., and Northwestern University in Chicago, where he graduated in 1942 with a degree in dental surgery. He married Janet Rosenberg* in 1943, and that year returned home where he almost immediately became involved in political activity in the capital city of Georgetown. In 1945 he was elected treasurer of the Man Power Citizen's Association, the trade union representing the predominantly East Indian labor force in the sugar industry. Rejecting that union's moderate approach, Jagan resigned in 1946 and formed the Guyana Industrial Workers Union which quickly became the largest sugar workers' organization. Jagan also formed the Political Affairs Committee (PAC) with a program of nationalism and socialism. In 1947 the PAC elected him to the Legislative Assembly. As the only radical member of that body, he was catapulted into national prominence by the outrage over the shooting of 21 workers of his union during a strike in 1948.

In 1950 Jagan and Linden Forbes Samson Burnham* formed the Peoples Progressive Party (PPP), the first multiracial nationalist party in the country. In 1953, in the first elections under universal adult suffrage, the PPP won a majority of seats and Jagan became Leader of Government, under a constitution providing a modified form of self-rule. The Jagan government lasted a mere 133 days. Britain, claiming a "Communist threat," suspended the constitution and reverted to a nonelective form of government. Jagan was sentenced to six months in prison in 1954 for disobeying conditions of a state of emergency imposed by the government.

Soon after release from prison, Jagan became embroiled in a conflict with Forbes Burnham, co-leader of the PPP. Jagan's Marxist-Leninist ideology, his emphasis on confrontation, and his predominantly East Indian support generated considerable opposition within the party. In 1955 the PPP split into Jaganite and Burnhamite wings. Jagan's faction won a majority in elections in 1957 under a revised constitution, and he became chief minister. In 1961 this title was changed to premier, and he was accorded increased powers.

Operating under considerable political restrictions between 1957 and 1964, Jagan nonetheless managed an impressive array of accomplishments. Development planning was introduced, extensive surveys of the country's resources were made for the first time, and electricity-generating capacity was upgraded and expanded with state takeover of the Canadian-owned electric companies. Agricultural production, particularly rice and vegetables, was considerably expanded. As minister of labor, health and housing, his wife carried out extensive programs in those fields. There was great educational expansion at the primary and secondary level, with the state assuming full control of all primary schools, and a University of Guyana was established.

Jagan's Marxism-Leninism and his increasingly close relationship with Fidel Castro's* Cuba and the Soviet bloc caused increasing concern among Western governments, particularly Britain and the United States, which were determined that Jagan would not head a post-independence government. During a series of violent political confrontations and racial rioting between 1962 and 1964, Jagan, unable to maintain order, agreed to allow Britain to dictate the terms under which the country would get independence. A new constitution, by changing the electoral process, virtually guaranteed his defeat. His party lost the elections in 1964 and never regained power.

Out of power, Jagan remained the Leader of the Opposition. In 1971, in exchange for support for a constitutional amendment that made possible nationalization of the country's major bauxite company, Jagan secured some degree of consultation with the government over major issues. Then in 1975 Jagan, feeling that the ruling party had been pushed into a progressive direction, offered "critical support" to the regime. Subsequently, his party entered into a loose alliance with other radical opponents of the regime.

BIBLIOGRAPHY

Depres, L. A. *Cultural Pluralism and Nationalist Politics in British Guiana*. Chicago: Rand McNally, 1967.
Jagan, C. *The West on Trial*. Berlin, GDR: Seven Seas Books, 1980.
Manley, Robert H. *Guyana Emergent*. Cambridge, Mass.: Schenkman, 1979.
Smith, R. T. *British Guiana*. London: Oxford University Press, 1962.
Spinner, Thomas J. *A Political and Social History of Guyana, 1945–1983*. Boulder, Colo.: Westview Press, 1984.

PERCY C. HINTZEN AND W. MARVIN WILL

JAGAN, JANET (née ROSENBERG) (1920–   ), married Cheddi Jagan* in Chicago in 1943, and then returned with him to Guyana, working as a dental hygienist while they put together the country's first nationalist movement. As a committed Marxist-Leninist, she played a major role in her husband's development and became a major force in Guyanese politics.

Janet Jagan helped organize the Political Affairs Committee (PAC) and published a bulletin that propagandized the group's commitment to radical nationalism. Her political intellect, skills, and commitment to the cause of nationalism made her popular in the capital city, where she narrowly lost as an independent candidate to national elections in 1947. She was also active in the trade union movement, being field secretary for a union of clerical workers, and was instrumental in forming the Guiana Industrial Workers Union (GIWU), organized by her husband to represent the country's sugar workers.

When the People's Progressive Party (PPP) was formed in 1950, Janet Jagan became its first general secretary, editor of the party newspaper *Thunder*, and general secretary of the party's women's wing. That year, she became the first woman elected to the Town Council of the capital city.

With the working classes mobilized behind it, the PPP won a sweeping victory in national elections in 1953, the first under universal adult suffrage. Janet Jagan, one of the successful candidates, became one of the first three women elected to the Legislative Assembly. She was made deputy speaker, another first for the country's women.

The election of the PPP was reversed after 133 days, when Britain suspended the constitution, landed Royal Marines, and reverted to crown colony government. Under emergency restrictions on the PPP leadership, Janet Jagan was prohibited from leaving the capital and from engaging in political activity. She spent five months in prison for violating these restrictions.

In 1955 the PPP split into two factions, and Janet Jagan retained her position as general secretary and editor of *Thunder* in the Jaganite faction. In the 1957 elections, that faction won 9 of the 14 seats in the new Legislative Council. Janet Jagan was appointed minister of labor, health, and housing, the first time that a cabinet post was held by a woman. She became instrumental in developing the governments' ties with Eastern Europe and with post–1959 Cuba. Her ministry was credited with eradicating malaria in the interior and filaria in the entire country, developing a successful vaccination campaign against polio and typhoid, and providing potable water in the rural areas. She built numerous health centers and cottage hospitals, and established maternity and child welfare clinics in rural areas. Janet Jagan's ministry was responsible for elimination of the barracks-type housing characteristic of sugar estate workers and for an extended Rent Restriction Ordinance. She established wage councils and advisory committees, got legislation passed that resulted in improved wages and conditions for all categories of workers, and introduced numerous welfare and social security benefits.

In 1961 the PPP was returned to power. Janet Jagan was made minister of home affairs. The years between 1961 and 1964 were years of civil strife. Fueled by racial animosity, opposition to the government took on such violent proportions that Janet Jagan was unable to maintain order. Feeling that she had no control over the police, she resigned in protest on June 1, 1964. Later that year, the PPP lost power to a coalition of the two major opposition parties. Janet Jagan continued as a leading member of the opposition, editor of the party's publication, and general secretary of the PPP.

BIBLIOGRAPHY

Chase, A. *A History of Trade Unionism in Guyana, 1900–1961*. Georgetown: New Guyana, 1964.
Despres, L. A. *Cultural Pluralism and Nationalist Politics in British Guiana*. Chicago: Rand McNally, 1967.
Jagan, C. *The West on Trial*. Berlin, GDR: Seven Seas, 1980.
People's Progressive Party. *21 Years, 1950–1971*. Georgetown: New Guyana, 1971.
Spinner, T. J. *A Political and Social History of Guyana, 1945–1983*. Boulder Colo.: Westview Press, 1984.

                                                    PERCY C. HINTZEN AND W. MARVIN WILL

JALTON, FRÉDERIC (1924–   ), principal leader of the Socialist Party of Guadeloupe from the 1960s on, was a medical doctor, practicing his profession after 1952. As a Socialist, he was elected mayor of Abymes, and councillor general for the Canton of Abymes. He was elected to the French National Assembly in 1973 but refused to sit with Socialist Party delegation until the Socialist leader François Mitterand agreed that the Guadeloupean Socialists did not have to follow the French party's policy of collaborating with the Communists. He was reelected in 1978 and 1981.

BIBLIOGRAPHY

Alexander, Robert J. "Guadeloupe," in Robert J. Alexander (ed.). *Political Parties of the Americas*. Vol. 2. Westport, Conn.: Greenwood Press, 1982.
Who's Who in France. 17th ed. Paris: Editions Jacques Lafitte, 1984.

                                                                ROBERT J. ALEXANDER

JAMES, CYRIL LIONEL ROBINSON (1901–   ), Trinidadian political activist, author, and Marxist ideologist, was born into a coloured middle-class family. He won a scholarship to Queens Royal College, the country's most prestigious secondary school, where he subsequently became a teacher. He became an ardent admirer of Arthur Andrew Cipriani,* whose biography he wrote.

James went to Great Britain in 1932 as a political liberal. By 1934 he was a leader of the Trotskyists working within the Independent Labour Party (ILP), while supporting himself as a cricket correspondent for several newspapers.

While in the ILP, James wrote several books, contributed to the party's press, and was its principal spokesman on the issue of the Italian-Abyssinian War. James also edited *International African Opinion*, the journal of the International African Service Bureau, where he was associated with George Padmore, Jomo Kenyatta, and Kwame Nkrumah.

In 1938 James went to the United States on a lecture tour but remained for 15 years. Active in the Socialist Workers Party, he was for a while the U.S. Trotskyists' principal spokesman on race problems. In 1940 he was a leader of a dissident group that formed the Workers Party, but by the early 1950s he headed a small group of his own, which was no longer Trotskyist but independent Marxist.

In 1953 James was deported from the United States to England. In 1958, after the Peoples National Movement (PNM), headed by his former student, Dr. Eric Williams,* was elected to power in Trinidad, James returned there. He became secretary of the Federal Labour Party, the governing party of the new West Indian Federation, joined the PNM, and was editor of its newspaper, *The Nation.* As leader of the party's left wing, he attempted with some initial success to push the PNM in a progressive direction.

Under considerable pressure from Britain and the country's business elite, the PNM leadership soon began to reduce James' influence. It rejected an international policy of nonalignment in favor of a pro-Western position. As a result, James resigned his position in the party. In 1962, just a few days before the country received its independence under a PNM government, James returned to Britain. He next visited Trinidad as a cricket correspondent in 1965, when the government placed him under house arrest, but public outcry soon brought his release. He remained in the country, founding a newspaper, *We the People*, and forming the Workers and Peasants Party. However, James soon returned to Britain and subsequently continued his writing; he also taught at Northwestern University in Illinois and at Federal City College in Washington, D.C.

BIBLIOGRAPHY

James, C.L.R. *Beyond a Boundary.* London: Hutchinson, 1963.
———. *The Future in the Present.* London: Allison and Bushy, 1977.
LaGuerre, J. G. *The Social and Political Thought of the Colonial Intelligentsia.* Mona, Jamaica: ISER, 1982.
Lopez, Consuelo. "C.L.R. James: The Rhetoric of a Defiant Warrior." Ph.D. diss., University of Indiana, 1983.
Oxaal, Ivar. *Black Intellectuals Come to Power.* Cambridge, Mass.: Schenkman, 1968.

                                        PERCY C. HINTZEN AND W. MARVIN WILL

JIMÉNEZ, ENRIQUE ADOLFO (1888–1970), was president of Panama from June 15, 1945, to September 30, 1948. His presidency was distinguished for its productiveness and rectitude. He sponsored major public works, including the first phase of University City, the International Airport at Tocumén, and numerous schools, hospitals, and institutions. He created the Free Port of Colón and the Ministry of Social Welfare, Labor and Public Health.

Jiménez was a member of the Liberal Party. Coming from a family of modest means, he received a high school education in Panama and went to work in the offices of the Pacific Mail Steamship Company. However, in 1908, having participated in the campaign of the successful presidential candidate, José Domingo de Obaldia, he was appointed to the Panamanian consulate in New York, where he spent four years improving his education. From that point on, Jiménez filled numerous government positions, including treasury minister in 1931 and ambassador to the United States during World War II.

President Jiménez faced his most serious problem in 1947 when the United States sought to extend for 20 years the agreement covering military bases it had built outside the Zone during World War II. The president, against advice of Foreign Minister Ricardo Joaquín Alfaro,* accepted this agreement. Alfaro resigned, protesting crowds filled the plazas, and the National Assembly unanimously rejected the pact.

BIBLIOGRAPHY

Alba C., Manuel María. *Cronología de los Gobernantes de Panama, 1510–1967*. Panama: 1967.
Alfaro, Ricardo J. *Biográficos esbozos*. Panama: Instituto Nacional de Cultura, 1974.
                                                              CHARLES D. AMERINGER

JIMÉNEZ OREAMUNO, RICARDO (1859–1945), was president of Costa Rica for three terms: 1910–1914, 1924–1928, and 1932–1936. He and Cleto González Víquez* dominated Costa Rica between 1908 and 1936. Jiménez strove to render efficient and honest government and to maintain absolute separation of church and state. Although he extended the suffrage, he made no other changes. His concept of government was to limit it to upholding the law and providing public services and education.

Development of commercial agriculture, increasing dependence on export of bananas and coffee, and growth of population brought new social and economic problems to which Jiménez' policies seemed unresponsive. However, he did not oppose the new labor movement. His strengthening of electoral democracy and popular representation made it possible subsequently for activist politicians to achieve power. He and González Víquez failed to develop a party structure to carry on their work.

BIBLIOGRAPHY

Ameringer, Charles D. *Democracy in Costa Rica*. New York: Praeger, 1982.
Barahona Jiménez, Luis. *El pensamiento político en Costa Rica*. San José: Editorial Fernández-Arce, 1971.
Creedman, Theodore S. *Historical Dictionary of Costa Rica*. Metuchen, N.J.: Scarecrow Press, 1977.
Mavis, Richard, and Karen Biesanz. *Los Costarricenses*. San José: Editorial Universidad Estatal a Distancia, 1979.
                                                              CHARLES D. AMERINGER

JOHN, PATRICK ROLAND (1937–   ), became the first prime minister of independent Dominica in November 1978. He received his primary and secondary education in Dominica and became a secondary school teacher. He left teaching in 1960 for a job as a shipping clerk. He helped form the Seamen and Waterfront Workers Union and served as its first general secretary. John also became a member of the Dominica Labour Party (DLP) and was its general secretary between 1966 and 1972. He was elected to the City Council of Dominica's capital and was mayor between 1965 and 1968.

In 1970 the DLP split. John threw his lot with the existing party leader, Edward Oliver LeBlanc,* who led the government after 1961 and now headed the LeBlanc Labour Party. John won a House seat in 1970 and held several cabinet posts under Premier LeBlanc. The rift in the party was soon healed, and the two factions realigned as the Dominican Labour Party.

This was a period of political and economic crisis. With unemployment and underemployment growing, a radical political organization patterned after the Rastafarian group of Jamaica emerged among the black lower classes. In the midst of these problems, Premier LeBlanc resigned, and Patrick John became leader of the party and premier. He embarked on a campaign against political dissent and legislated extremely unpopular measures against the Rastafarians and the opposition in general.

John and the DLP won the election of 1975. He then began negotiations with Britain which resulted in the granting of independence to Dominica in November 1978. John became the country's first prime minister.

The passage of even more repressive legislation led to the formation in June 1977 of a Committee for National Salvation (CNS), which included most of the political opposition. The anti-Patrick John campaign reached its peak in 1979 with mounting public demonstrations and an increasing cycle of state retaliation and military force, with resultant casualties. Particularly at issue was a bill introduced in the House of Assembly to outlaw strikes and limit press freedom. A general strike was called by five of the most powerful trade unions. In the midst of the turmoil, seven members of John's party in the House resigned, followed by the resignation of the president, and John was forced to call new elections.

On June 21, 1979, before elections could be scheduled, John was ousted by the House and replaced by an interim government headed by members of the DLP who had defected. John retained his position as leader of the DLP and contested the elections in 1980 as part of a coalition with the Dominica Liberation Alliance, which lost in all constituencies it contested.

After leaving office, Patrick John was jailed several times. In March and April 1981 plans for a coup were revealed, and John was jailed for his alleged conspiracy with Texas millionaire Michael Eugene Perdue and several other foreigners. Released from jail in May 1982, he was reincarcerated in December when the West Indies Court of Appeals returned an adverse ruling.

BIBLIOGRAPHY

Branda-Shute, Rosemary, and Gary Branda-Shute. "Dominica," in Jack W. Hopkins (ed.). *Latin America and Caribbean Contemporary Record*. Vols. 1, 2, and 3. New York: Holmes & Meier, 1983, 1984, 1985.
Bulletin of Eastern Caribbean Affairs 5, No. 2 (May/June 1979).

Dies Dominica (pamphlet). Public Relations Division, Premier's Office. Roseau, Dominica: 1972.
Smith, Linden. "Dominica: The Post-Hurricane David Period." *Bulletin of Eastern Caribbean Affairs* 5, No. 4 (September/October 1979).
————. "The Political Situation in Dominica." *Bulletin of Eastern Caribbean Affairs* 5, no. 3 (July/August 1979).

PERCY C. HINTZEN AND W. MARVIN WILL

JONCKHEER, EFRAÍN (1910–?), was the first important political leader to emerge in Curaçao, Netherlands Antilles. One of the organizers of the Curaçao Democratic Party in the early 1940s, he emerged as the first minister president (prime minister) of Netherlands Antilles, when an autonomous elected regime was established in 1954. With continuing victories of the Curaçao Democratic Party and its allies in the other islands, he continued to hold that position. He led the government for the following decade.

BIBLIOGRAPHY

Díaz, Augustín Miguel. "Informe Sobre el Partido Democrático de Curazao." Curaçao: 1978. Mimeo.
Personal contacts of the writer.

ROBERT J. ALEXANDER

JORDAN, EDWARD (1800–1869), was one of a very small number of black and brown Jamaicans who held elective office during and immediately following slavery. The son of a mulatto freedman from Barbados, he was jailed for a short while in 1831 on charges of fomenting slave rebellion. However, he was elected to the Jamaican House of Assembly in 1835, three years before the formal end of slavery. He also served on the Kingston Common Council and, ultimately, became mayor of Kingston, serving for 12 years beginning in 1854. Jordan and a fellow mulatto, Robert Osborn, attempted to provide leadership for previously unrepresented brown and black Jamaicans, and together published a newspaper, *The Watchman*. Some critics accused Jordan of compromising too much with the white colonial establishment.

BIBLIOGRAPHY

Augier, F. R., et al. *The Making of the West Indies*. London: Longmans, 1960.
Black, W. A. *The Story of Jamaica*. London: Collins, 1965.
Murray, R. N. *Nelson's West Indian History*. London: Nelson, 1971.
Roberts, W. A. *Jamaica: The Portrait of an Island*. New York: Coward-McCann, 1955.
————. *Six Great Jamaicans: Biographical Sketches*. 2d ed. Kingston: Pioneer Press, 1957.

PERCY C. HINTZEN AND W. MARVIN WILL

JUÁREZ, BENITO (1806–1872), Mexico's most beloved president, led his nation intermittently during 1858–1872. A Zapotec Indian, he was born in an Indian village in the mountains of the state of Oaxaca. He was unable to speak

Spanish until the age of 12. He came to the city of Oaxaca, the state capital, to be a household servant. His wealthy employer soon sent young Benito as a full-time student to a nearby primary school. He rapidly became fluent in Spanish and a prodigious reader.

Passing the bar examination, Juárez began to practice law in Oaxaca City and in Mexico City. In 1846 Oaxaca elected Juárez governor. He inherited a bankrupt state government, but by the end of his term, the state treasury had a surplus for the first time since Mexican Independence from Spain in 1821. In 1853 the centralists of General Antonio López de Santa Anna* returned to power in Mexico City, forcing Juárez and other federalists into exile in the United States. In New Orleans, Juárez supported himself by rolling cigarettes at a tobacco factory.

In November 1855 Juan Alvarez became president of Mexico and chose a cabinet of fellow Liberals, including Juárez as minister of justice. Juárez by decree abolished separate courts which had guaranteed priests and military leaders that they could be tried only in their own courts by their friends and peers. Two years later he wrote a similar curbing of clerical and military special privileges into the new constitution. Juárez also included in the 1857 charter the nationalization of church cemeteries.

Juárez became president in 1857 and largely defeated the Conservatives in an ensuing civil war. However, in 1861 French Emperor Napoleon III landed an army in support of the Conservatives. After winning the Battle of Puebla on May 5, 1862, the Mexican patriotic forces under General Ignacio Zaragoza began to retreat before the better armed French Army. By March 1864 the Juarez government controlled only northernmost Mexico.

In April 1864 the Austrian Archduke Maximilian was told by his French advisers that he had been "elected" emperor of Mexico, and formally accepted the crown. In the far north, Juárez asserted that the coronation was illegitimate and that Mexicans would continue the struggle until the presidency was restored in Mexico City.

Juárez declared his carriage the seat of government, flush against the border with the United States, just south of El Paso, Texas. Later, a city would arise on the spot to honor him, Ciudad Juárez.

In the spring of 1865, the United States' Civil War was drawing to a close, and President Abraham Lincoln sent President Juárez arms and other vital supplies. In 1866 General Ulysses S Grant began opening recruiting stations for volunteers to go to Mexico to fight in the army of Juárez. The Mexican president wrote Grant that "you too are a great Mexican patriot." By late 1866 French troops were on the run.

Maximilian indicated he would abdicate and retire as a private citizen, but President Juárez ordered a court martial. The verdict was death by firing squad. Maximilian was executed.

Juárez was reelected to the presidency in 1867. He had to devote his considerable administrative skill to patching the wounds which the French had inflicated on the political system. He was also eager to rebuild the Mexican economy. He ordered resumption of construction of the railroad linking Veracruz with Mexico City, begun in 1850 but abandoned during the monarchy. It was opened to traffic in 1873, after Juárez' death.

The cause closest to Juárez' heart was education. He had the old Jesuit College of San Ildefonso converted into the National Preparatory School in order to train lay teachers. Owners of haciendas were ordered by presidential decree to build primary schools on their premises. The theory of Positivism imported from Europe inspired the new education officials, and its emphasis on the study of sciences was Juárez's big thrust against clerical scholasticism.

The next presidential election, in 1871, found Juárez a candidate for his fourth term, but he did not gain a clear popular majority of the votes over the two other major candidates. Congress, sitting as an Electoral College, finally chose Juárez. He died of a heart attack a year later.

BIBLIOGRAPHY

Hanna, Alfred J., and Kathryn A. Hanna. *Napoleon III and Mexico*. Chapel Hill: University of North Carolina Press, 1971.
Juárez, Benito. *Apuntes para Mis Hijos*. Mexico City: Cuadernos Americanos, 1960.
Parkes, Henry B. *A History of Mexico*. Boston: Houghton Mifflin, 1970.
Sterne, Emma G. *Benito Juárez, Builder of a Nation*. New York: Alfred A. Knopf, 1967.
                                                                    MARVIN ALISKY

JUSTO, AGUSTÍN PEDRO (1878–1943), was a career military officer who served as president of Argentina from 1932 to 1938. He was born in Entre Ríos Province and graduated from the military academy in 1892. He later taught at and was director of that academy. In 1922 Justo served as minister of war for a Radical government, and in 1930 he was named commander-in-chief for the Uriburu government that overthrew Hipolito Yrigoyen.* He was then elected president by a coalition of conservative groups known as the Concordancia.

Justo's most pressing problem was to revive the Argentine economy which had been badly hurt by the world Depression. To this end, his government signed the Roca-Runciman Pact, in order to preserve Argentina's traditional trading relationship with Great Britain. The agreement provided an outlet for Argentine meat products, but was denounced by industrialists, Socialists, and nationalists who charged the government had sold out to foreign interests.

The Justo government was politically very conservative and engaged in widespread fraud to ensure that government candidates won elections. In 1932 the Radical Party boycotted elections to protest electoral dishonesty. Justo's government constantly supported oligarchical interests against the newly emerging forces: urban workers, the middle class, and industrialists.

In 1938 Justo ceded power to the governmental candidate Roberto Ortíz in an extremely dishonest election. When Ortíz' health failed, he was succeeded in office by his vice president, Ramón Castillo, who was the final representative

JUSTO, JUAN BAUTISTA

of the Concordancia to hold power. He was overthrown in the 1943 coup that led to Domingo Juan Perón.*

BIBLIOGRAPHY

Alexander, Robert J. *The Perón Era*. New York: Columbia University Press, 1951.
Bucich, Escobar, Ismael. *Historia de los Presidentes Argentinos*. Buenos Aires: Roldán, 1934.
Levene, Gustavo Gabriel. *Historia de los presidentes argentinos*. 2 vols. Buenos Aires: 1973.
Smith, Peter H. *Argentina and the Failure of Democracy, 1904–1955*. Madison: University of Wisconsin Press, 1974.
Whitaker, Arthur P. *The United States and Argentina*. Cambridge, Mass.: Harvard University Press, 1954.

JOHN T. DEINER

JUSTO, JUAN BAUTISTA (1865–1928), the founder of Argentina's Socialist Party, was born in Buenos Aires and received a medical degree from the University of Buenos Aires in 1888. He later studied in Europe and introduced many innovations to Argentine medicine. He also became active in Radical politics but left that party once Hipólito Yrigoyen* became its leader.

Justo joined Alfredo Lorenzo Palacios* and others in 1895 to found the Socialist Party, which would represent the cause of the workers. Under Justo's leadership, the Socialists called for reform through the electoral process, rather than violent revolution. In 1894 Justo established and was first editor of *La Vanguardia*, the Socialist newspaper. He also wrote several books related to socialist themes and translated Marx's *Das Kapital* into Spanish.

In 1912 Justo was elected to the Chamber of Deputies from Buenos Aires, and in 1924 to the Senate. Throughout his legislative career, Justo fought for worker benefits and for honesty in government and the electoral process.

BIBLIOGRAPHY

Cantón, Darío. *Elecciones y partidos políticos en la Argentina: historia, interpretación y balance*. Buenos Aries: 1973.
Cuneo, Dardo. *Juan B. Justo y las luchas sociales en la Argentina*. Buenos Aires: 1956.
Levene, Ricardo. *A History of Argentina*. Chapel Hill: University of North Carolina Press, 1937 (reprint 1963).
Rock, David. *Politics in Argentina, 1890–1930: The Rise and Fall of Radicalism*. New York: Cambridge Latin American Studies, 1975.
Smith, Peter H. *Argentina and the Failure of Democracy, 1904–1955*. Madison: University of Wisconsin Press, 1974.

JOHN T. DEINER

K

KING, CYRIL EMMANUEL (1921–   ), governor of the U.S. Virgin Islands from 1975 to 1979, was born in St. Croix. After going to local schools, he attended American University in Washington, D.C., where he received a bachelor of science degree in public administration. He served in the U.S. Army from 1944 to 1946.

Between 1949 and 1961 King was an aide to Senator Hubert Humphrey (D.–Minn.). He returned home to become government secretary and sometimes acting governor between 1961 and 1969. In 1968 he organized a Democratic Party liberal dissident group, the Independent Citizens Movement (ICM). It elected him to the insular Senate, where he served from 1972 to 1974. In 1974 he was the ICM's successful candidate for governor.

BIBLIOGRAPHY

Sharpless, Richard E. "Virgin Islands of the United States," in Robert J. Alexander (ed.). *Political Parties of the Americas*. Vol. 2. Westport, Conn.: Greenwood Press, 1982.
Who's Who in America 1978–79. 40th ed. Chicago: Marquis Who's Who, 1978.

RICHARD E. SHARPLESS

KROON, CIRO DE (?–?), was the second leader of the Curaçao Democratic Party. He succeeded Efrain Jonckheer* as leader of the party and minister-president of Netherlands Antilles in the mid–1960s. However, his government resigned and called new elections in the summer of 1969 as a result of strikes that degenerated into very serious rioting throughout Curaçao. The Democratic Party was defeated in these elections, and some time later Ciro de Kroon gave up his party leadership.

BIBLIOGRAPHY

Alexander, Robert J. "Netherlands Antilles," in Robert J. Alexander (ed.). *Political Parties of the Americas*. Vol. 2. Westport, Conn.: Greenwood Press, 1982.
Personal contacts of the writer.

ROBERT J. ALEXANDER

KUBITSCHEK DE OLIVEIRA, JUSCELINO (1902–1976), a flamboyant, popular, and dynamic president of Brazil, was born in Diamantina, a small historical mining town in Minas Gerais. In 1922 he entered medical school, graduating in 1927. His first job was in the surgery clinic of the Santa Casa de Misericordia in Belo Horizonte, and he then went to study in Europe.

Returning to Brazil shortly after the October 1930 revolution, he entered politics in 1933 and served as federal congressman from 1935 to 1937. When President Getúlio Vargas* closed Congress in 1937 and instituted the Estado Novo dictatorship, Kubitschek returned to the practice of medicine.

In 1940 Kubitschek was appointed mayor of Belo Horizonte and dramatically modernized the Minas Gerais state capital with sweeping boulevards and a complex that contained an ultramodern Catholic Chuch designed by Oscar Niemeyer with paintings and frescoes by Candido Portinari.

One of the organizers of the Partido Social Democratico (PSD) political party when the Vargas dictatorship ended in 1945, Kubitschek was elected to the federal Chamber of Deputies. In 1950 he won the governorship of the state of Minas Gerais. As governor from 1951 to 1955 his major objective was to transform the state from an agricultural producer to a sophisticated and highly industrialized section of the country. Kubitschek was an extremely popular governor.

In the wake of Vargas' suicide in 1954, Kubitschek was put forward as the natural candidate of the pro-Vargas forces for the 1950 presidential elections. His running mate was João Belchior Marques Goulart.*

Elections were held on October 3, 1955, amidst a great deal of tension, for it appeared that some elements of the military allied with Carlos Lacerda* would block the elections or annul the election results if Kubitschek won. When the final count favored Kubitschek, the major military leaders pledged their loyalty, assuring the inauguration of Kubitschek and Goulart on January 31, 1956.

Kubitschek set up a target program that focused on development of energy, an expanded road-building program, and expansion of heavy industry. It was crowned with the construction of a new twenty-first-century capital Brasilia, in the center of the country. President Kubitschek formally transferred the seat of government to Brasilia.

Kubitschek opened Brazil to foreign industrialists who poured capital and equipment into the country. As a result, he provoked criticism that Brazilian industry was being "denationalized"since multinationals established many of the nation's new basic industries.

All of these development plans were costly and were financed in part by inflationary loans by government banks. When in 1959 the International Monetary Fund demanded curtailment of development as the price for new loans, President Kubitschek broke off negotiations which raised his standing with the nationalists. For the years 1957 to 1960 the gross national product (GNP) growth rate for Brazil was 7.8 percent, and the country built the infrastructure needed for the intensification of development during the 1970s.

On November 25, 1958, Brazil recognized the USSR. Nonetheless, President Dwight Eisenhower paid a special visit to Brazil in February 1960. Kubitschek suggested to him a new hemisphere-wide approach to the problems of Latin America called Operation Pan America, but the U.S. government largely ignored it.

Kubitschek turned power over to his elected successor, Jânio Quadros* in January 1961. A few months later a Senate vacancy occurred in the state of Goyaz, and Kubitschek won that seat, in a special election on June 4, 1961. When Quadros resigned in August 1961, Kubitschek opposed the amendment that established a parliamentary system. As conditions deteriorated under Goulart, Kubitschek was constantly urged to take a stand against Goulart but he refused.

After the military revolt of March 31, 1964, toppled Goulart, Kubitschek was deprived of his political rights and went into voluntary exile in June. He returned to Brazil in October 1965, but was harassed by the military and went into exile again in November 1965.

In October 1966 Carlos Lacerda,* by then an active opponent of the military government, attempted to organize a new political party, the Frente Ampla, led by Kubitschek, Goulart, and himself. However, the government ordered the Frente Ampla to disband. From that date on, Kubitschek abandoned politics and dedicated himself to business activities. When he died in an automobile accident, he was still the most popular politician in Brazil.

BIBLIOGRAPHY

Benevides, María Victoria de Mesquita. *O Governo Kubitschek: Desenvolvimento Económico e Estabilidade Política*. Rio de Janeiro: Paz e Terra, 1976.
Corbisier, Roland. *JK e a luta pela Presidencia*. 1976.
Kubitschek, Juscelino. *Meu Caminho para Brasilia*. 1978.
————. *Uma Campanha democrática*. 1959.
Maranhão, Ricardo. *O Governador Juscelino Kubitschek*. 1981.

JORDAN YOUNG

L

LACERDA, CARLOS (1914–1977), a brilliant and tempestuous Brazilian politician and newspaperman, was the son of Mauricio Paiva de Lacerda and Olga Werneck de Lacerda. His father was a newspaperman, national congressman, and leading left-wing politician.

As a law student at the University of Rio de Janeiro, Carlos Lacerda was one of the organizers of the Communist Youth Federation. He was jailed briefly in 1937 but was quickly released, and began his newspaper career. He broke with the Communist Party in 1939.

In February 1945, by publishing an interview with an opposition political leader, Lacerda first gained national prominence. When President Getúlio Vargas* did not punish Lacerda, freedom of the press was reestablished.

The Vargas dictatorship fell in October 1945. In 1947 Lacerda was elected a National Democratic Union (UDN) member of the Rio de Janeiro City Council. He founded his own newspaper, *Tribuna da Imprensa*, as the major critic of those who supported former dictator Vargas. When Vargas was democratically elected president in 1950, Lacerda continued his most violent opponent. He organized the Lantern Club in order to expose the corruption of the Vargas government.

On August 5, 1954, an attempt to murder Lacerda failed, but an air force officer who was with him was killed. This event provoked a major crisis that ended only when President Vargas committed suicide on August 24. The general public felt that Lacerda had been the catalyst in these events, but his effort to get the 1955 election postponed for fear that a pro-Vargas politician would be elected failed.

Juscelino Kubitschek de Oliveira* and João Belchior Marques Goulart,* former labor minister under Vargas, were elected president and vice president respectively, in October 1955. When Lacerda and Acting President Carlos Luz attempted to carry out a coup against President-elect Kubitschek, they were thwarted by Minister of War Henrique Lott. Lacerda went into temporary exile for a year in the United States.

Throughout the Kubitschek administration, Lacerda became one of the important leaders of the UDN. With the 1960 presidential election approaching, he successfully supported Quadros, even though Quadros was not a member of the UDN, as the only possible candidate to defeat the Vargas forces. Quadros won, and Lacerda won the governorship of the city of Rio de Janeiro, which had been established as the state of Guanabara.

Lacerda played a significant role in the August 1961 resignation of President Quadros. He sought unsuccessfully to dissuade Quadros from giving a decoration to Ernesto (Che) Guevara,* Fidel Castro's* economic minister. Lacerda charged Quadros with cutting traditional ties with the United States and preparing a coup d'ètat. President Quadros resigned on August 15, 1961.

The administration of João Goulart, the vice president who assumed office after Quadros (September 1961–March 1964), was a period of intense political warfare between Governor Carlos Lacerda and President Goulart. Plans for the March 1964 coup against Goulart deeply involved Lacerda. However, after the coup, when the army blocked any attempt by Lacerda to capitalize on it, he was soon in conflict with the military government. His attacks on President Humberto Castelo Branco* soon equaled those he had leveled against Vargas and Goulart.

In 1966 Lacerda attempted to create a new political party, the Frente Ampla, an alliance with former Presidents Kubitschek and Goulart. The military reaction was predictable. Lacerda was stripped of his political rights for ten years and he was imprisoned briefly.

Lacerda then left politics and returned to journalism. He also founded a publishing house. He died unexpectedly, after a brief illness.

BIBLIOGRAPHY

Lacerda, Carlos. *Depoimento*. Rio de Janeiro: 1978.
———. *O Poder das Ideas*. Rio de Janeiro: Distribuidora Record, 1963.

                                                                                     JORDAN YOUNG

LACHMON, JAGGERNATH (?–   ), was for several decades the most important political leader of the East Indian community in Surinam. The leader of the Progressive Reformed Party (VHP), founded in the late 1940s, he participated in governments led by the Surinam National Party (NPS) during the early 1950s. In the last half of the decade, he led the major opposition in Parliament. Between 1963 and 1973 Lachmon continued his alliance with the NPS in the government of Minister-President Johan Adolf Pengel* and in the opposition.

Lachmon broke with the NPS over the issue of independence, which the East Indians at first opposed. After reelection of the NPS in 1973, he negotiated for two years with Minister-President Henck A.E. Arron* for acceptable constitutional terms for independence. On Independence Day, November 21, 1975, Lachmon had a public reconciliation with Arron. However, Lachmon was officially Leader of the Opposition until the overthrow of the civilian government by a military coup in February 1980.

BIBLIOGRAPHY

Alexander, Robert J. "Surinam," in Robert J. Alexander (ed.). *Political Parties of the Americas*. Vol. 2. Westport, Conn.: Greenwood Press, 1982.
                                                                    ROBERT J. ALEXANDER

LAFERTTE GAVIÑO, ELÍAS (1886–1981), was titular leader of the Communist Party of Chile for more than half a century. He went to work at 11 years of age in the nitrate fields, became active in mutual benefit societies and other workers groups, and after the violent clash of nitrate strikers with soldiers in Iquique in 1907 became a convinced revolutionary.

In 1911 Lafertte first met Luis Emilio Recabarren Serrano.* He soon became one of Recabarren's principal lieutenants, working with him on periodicals in Iquique and Valparaiso, as well as in founding the Socialist Labor Party (PSO), and in the Labor Federation of Chile (FOCh), which after 1917 was led by Recabarren. He supported changing the PSO to the Communist Party in 1922.

In 1923 Lafertte was elected to the Executive Committee of the FOCh, and after Recabarren's death at the end of 1924, he became its principal leader. In 1927 he was the Communist Party's candidate for president, the only nominee to run against Colonel Carlos Ibáñez del Campos,* although he was then a prisoner on an island in the Pacific Ocean.

During the Ibáñez regime, Lafertte spent a great deal of time in jail or in exile. After Ibáñez' overthrow, Lafertte worked to revive the FOCh. In 1932 he went to Montevideo for a Latin American Communist Trade Union Conference and to the Soviet Union for the first time.

Elías Lafertte was the Communist Party's candidate for president in both the 1931 and 1932 elections. He received only a few thousand votes in either of them.

During the regime of President Arturo Alessandri Palma,* which came to power in December 1932, Lafertte was again arrested and exiled. However, in congressional elections in 1937, he was elected to the Senate. He remained a member of that body most of the years until his death. From the late 1930s, he was also president of the Communist Party, although he had very little to do with determining the party's policies.

BIBLIOGRAPHY

Alexander, Robert J. *Communism in Latin America*. New Brunswick, N.J.: Rutgers University Press, 1957.
Boizard, Ricardo. *Cuatro Retratos en Profundidad: Ibáñez, Lafertte, Walker, Leighton*. Santiago: Imprenta del Imparcial, 1950.

Cortes, Lia, and Jordi Fuentes. *Diccionario Político de Chile*. Santiago: Editorial Orbe, 1967.

ROBERT J. ALEXANDER

LANUSSE, ALEJANDRO AGUSTÍN (1918–   ), a career military man, was president of Argentina for two years in the early 1970s. He presided over elections that led to the return of civilian government and the second presidency of Juan Domingo Perón.*

Lanusse was born in Buenos Aires and attended military schools. His military career showed progress until 1951, when he was involved in an unsuccessful revolt against Juan Perón. Lanusse was jailed, but was released and restored to his rank after the 1955 coup that ousted Perón. He served as commander of the presidential guard from 1955 to 1957, and was promoted to colonel and made assistant director of the war college. In 1962 he was promoted to brigadier general and in 1966 was active in the coup that overthrew President Arturo Umberto Illia,* bringing General Juan Carlos Onganía* to power. Onganía made Lanusse commander-in-chief of the army in 1968.

In 1969 the Onganía government was startled by the violence that broke out in Cordoba: three days of rioting, students and workers united against the police, with regular army troops called in to restore order. Widespread dissatisfaction with the military regime was all too evident.

In 1970 Lanusse formed a junta with the commanders-in-chief of the navy and air force, and replaced Onganía with General Roberto Levingston as president. But when Levingston made the crucial mistake of trying to remove Lanusse as commander-in-chief, the military rebelled, removed Levingston, and installed Lanusse as president on March 26, 1971.

Faced with political violence and economic malaise, Lanusse sought to get the military out of politics. He allowed renewal of political party activity, including the Peronists, although prohibiting Perón himself from running for office. When the presidential election was held in March 1973, a Peronist coalition headed by Héctor José Cámpora* captured the presidency. Within two months, Cámpora resigned, and in elections later that year, Perón became president.

BIBLIOGRAPHY

Hodges, Donald C. *Argentina, 1943–1976: The National Revolution and Resistance*. Albuquerque: University of New Mexico Press, 1976.
Page, Joseph A. *Perón: A Biography*. New York: Random House, 1983.
Snow, Peter G. *Political Forces in Argentina*. New York: Praeger, 1979.
Sobel, Lester A. (ed.). *Argentina and Perón, 1970–1975*. New York: Facts on File, 1975.

JOHN T. DEINER

LAREDO BRÚ, FEDERICO (1875–1946), was president of Cuba from December 1936 until October 1940. Born in Santa Clara Province, he fought in the War of Independence, becoming a colonel. A traditional conservative politician, he was in the cabinet of Carlos Manuel de Céspedes in 1933, and president of the Council of State under President Carlos Mendieta y Montefar,* and ran successfully for vice president with Miguel Mariano Gómez.* When President Gómez was impeached in December 1936, Laredo Brú became president.

Unlike Gómez, who refused to acknowledge the paramount position of General Fulgencio Batista y Zaldívar,* Laredo Brú accepted his position vis-à-vis Batista and attempted to provide stable civilian leadership. His cabinet consisted of Batista's friends, who assured that the military chief got what he desired from the civilian authorities. However, he must be credited with restraining Batista's natural authoritarian tendencies.

Under Laredo Brú, an impressive body of social legislation was adopted, as called for in Batista's Three-Year Plan. This included labor laws and strengthening the rights of tenant farmers. In addition, a constituent assembly met to write the highly progressive Constitution of 1940.

BIBLIOGRAPHY

Gellman, Irwin F. *Roosevelt and Batista*. Albuquerque: University of New Mexico Press, 1973.
Thomas, Hugh. *Cuba: The Pursuit of Freedom*. New York: Harper and Row, 1971.
                                                                STEPHEN J. WRIGHT

LAVALLEJA, JUAN ANTONIO (1784–1853), was a major figure in Uruguay's struggle for independence. His parents were wealthy Spanish ranchers, but he joined revolutionary forces in 1811, after the outbreak of the struggle against Spain. He was a supporter of José Gervásio Artigas* in conflicts with both the Argentines and the Portuguese-Brazilians. In 1825, he led a group of Uruguayans, "the immortal thirty-three," who invaded Brazilian-held Uruguay, seeking to obtain its independence. In the resulting war between Argentina and Brazil in 1825–1828, he was the principal leader of Uruguayan forces, and in 1827–1828 he established his own dictatorship.

Lavalleja was provisional president of Uruguay in 1830 but did not succeed in being elected the first constitutional president. In 1832 and 1835 he led revolts against President Fructuoso Rivera,* and in 1836 he supported President Manuel Oribe* when Rivera revolted against him.

When Oribe was defeated, Lavalleja took part in an Argentine invasion and was blamed for its defeat. Although long a leader of the Blanco Party, he was a member of a triumvirate that took power with Brazilian support in 1853, after the ouster of the Blanco government of President Juan Francisco Giró. Lavalleja died while in that post.

BIBLIOGRAPHY

Castellanos, Alfredo Rául. *Juan Antonio Lavalleja, libertador del pueblo oriental: Ensayo biográfico*. Montevideo: 1955.

Salberain Herrera, Eduardo de. *Lavalleja: La redención patria*. Montevideo: 1957.
Vázquez, Juan Antonio. *Lavalleja y la campaña de 1825*. Montevideo: 1927.

ROBERT J. ALEXANDER

LEBLANC, EDWARD OLIVER (1923–   ), was the first premier of Dominica.
After attending primary school in Dominica, he embarked on a period of self-
education, obtaining the London Matriculation Certificate in 1948. Between 1941
and 1953 LeBlanc was an agricultural instructor, and in 1944 he completed a
course at the Imperial College of Tropical Agriculture in Trinidad. In 1953 he
joined the Dominica Banana Association.

LeBlanc entered politics by securing election to the Vieille Case Village Board.
He joined the Dominica Labour Party (DLP) and won a seat in the Legislative
Council in August 1957. LeBlanc resigned from the Dominica Legislature to
become one of the two Dominica members of the Parliament of the West Indies
Federation in 1958.

After two years in the federal Parliament, LeBlanc returned to Dominica in
1960 to assume leadership of the party. He led the DLP to its first victory in
January 1961, winning 7 of 11 elective seats in the Legislative Council. He
became chief minister and minister of finance. Surviving internal party turmoil,
which resulted in ouster of the party's founder and former leader, Phyllis Alfrey,
in 1961, LeBlanc increasingly concentrated on constitutional reform. With the
breakup of the West Indies Federation in 1962, he sought formation of a federation of the Little Eight Windward and Leeward Islands plus Barbados. When
this plan proved impossible, LeBlanc led the Dominica delegations to a conference in London which paved the way for Dominica's Associated State status on
March 1, 1967. The Dominica government took full responsibility for internal
affairs of the colony, and Britain controlled only defense and foreign affairs.
LeBlanc became the first premier. The DLP captured 10 of 11 elective seats in
the Legislative Council in 1966.

As premier, LeBlanc brought about the inclusion of Dominica in the Caribbean
Free Trade Area (CARIFTA) in 1968. As a result of internal turmoil, in 1970
the DLP split into two factions: the LeBlanc Labour Party and the Dominica
Labour Party. LeBlanc's faction swept the elections of 1970, winning 8 of 11
elective seats. After the elections, the two factions reunited as the DLP.

Poverty and underdevelopment were particularly depressing in Dominica. In
the late 1960s, a Rastafarian movement patterned after the movement then flourishing in Jamaica emerged in the colony, reflecting a growing rebelliousness by
the black underclass.

Edward LeBlanc tendered his resignation from the Dominica premiership, the
House of Assembly, and the DLP leadership on July 26, 1974.

BIBLIOGRAPHY

Alexander, Robert J. "Dominica," in Robert J. Alexander (ed.), *Political Parties of the
Americas*. Vol. 2. Westport, Conn.: Greenwood Press, 1983.

Bulletin of Eastern Caribbean Affairs 5, No. 2 (May/June 1979).
Dies Dominica (Pamphlet). Public Relations Division, Premier's Office, Roseau, Dominica: 1972.
Smith, Linden. "Dominica: The Post-Hurricane David Period." *Bulletin of Eastern Caribbean Affairs* 5, No. 5 (September/October 1979).
———. "The Political Situation in Dominica." *Bulletin of Eastern Caribbean Affairs* 5, No. 3 (July/August 1979).

PERCY C. HINTZEN AND W. MARVIN WILL

LECHÍN OQUENDO, JUAN (1920–   ), was Bolivia's major labor leader for more than 40 years after 1944. Born of middle-class parents of Lebanese extraction, he was a veteran of the Chaco War (1932–1935). Thereafter, he worked as a clerk in the Patiño Company's mines; he was also the star of the company's soccer team.

When the Movimiento Nacionalista Revolucionario (MNRO)–military government of Gualberto Villarroel López* seized power in December 1943, Lechín was made subprefect of Catavi. He gained the respect of the miners by refusing to be a "company man" as had his predecesors. In 1944 he was elected executive secretary of the Miners Federation (FSTMB), which quickly became the country's most powerful union. Despite the opposition of the other labor groups to the MNR–military government, Lechín and the FSTMB gave critical support to the regime until its fall in 1946.

Lechín, despite misgivings, agreed to the radical labor platform, the Thesis of Pulacayo, which had been drafted by Guillermo Lora,* a law student and Trotskyite leader, and adopted at the FSTMB Congress in 1946. In 1947 Lechín, along with several other national labor representatives, was elected to Congress on the ticket of the Miners' Bloc.

Between 1946 and 1952 Lechín experienced repeated exile and repression. After the April 1952 triumph of the National Revolution, which he and Hernán Siles Zuazo* largely led, Lechín and the FSTMB created the Bolivian Labor Central (COB), of which Lechín became executive secretary. He also served as minister of mines in the new government of President Víctor Paz Estenssoro.* Between 1956 and 1960 he was president of the Senate and acting vice president of the republic. Lechín expected to run for the presidency in 1960, but deferred his candidacy to 1964 in order to permit Paz Estenssoro to run again. He served as vice president during the second Paz administration. However, when his presidential ambitions were again thwarted in 1964, he broke with the MNR and founded his own party, the Revolutionary Party of the National Left.

Although Lechín supported the coup against Paz in November 1964, the Miners Federation soon fell out with President René Barrientos Ortuño,* and Lechín was forced into exile in May 1965. He regained influence in the reformist governments of Generals Alfredo Ovando Candia* (1969–1970) and Juan José Torres González* (1970–1971). Lechín served as president of the radical Peoples' Assembly until Torres' overthrow in August 1971.

Lechín was in exile in Chile during most of the succeeding Hugo Banzer Suarez* government, and again after the military coup of 1980. With the election of Siles Zuazo in Ocrober 1982, Lechín continued to play a central role as chief spokesman of the labor movement. He led several general strikes against the Siles government's austerity program. With the reelection of President Víctor Paz Estenssoro in 1985, Lechín's role as principal leader for organized labor continued.

BIBLIOGRAPHY

Barrios Villa, Erasmo. *History Sindical de Bolivia*. Oruro: Imprenta Universitaria, 1966.
Delgado G., Trifonio. *100 Años de Lucha Obrera en Bolivia*. La Paz: Editorial Isla, 1984.
Lechín Oquendo, Juan. *Discurso Inaugural del Secretario Ejecutivo de la COB al Tercer Congreso Nacional de Trabajadores*. La Paz: Talleres Graficos Bolivianos, 1962.
————. *Lechín y la Revolución Nacional*. La Paz: Caja Nacional de Seguro Social, n.d.
Lora, Guillermo. *Historia del Movimiento Obrero Boliviano*. La Paz: Editorial Amigos del Libro, 1967.
                        WALTRAUD QUEISER MORALES AND GUILLERMO DELGADO

LÉGITIMUS, HÉGÉPAPPE (18 ?–19 ?), was the first important black political leader of Guadeloupe in the twentieth century. At about the turn of the century, he founded the island's first party, the Socialist Party, which a few years later became the Guadeloupe Federation of the French Socialist Party. He was deputy in the French Chamber of Deputies from 1903 to 1906, and Mayor of Pointe-a-Pitre for many years.

BIBLIOGRAPHY

Alexander, Robert J. "Guadeloupe," In Robert J. Alexander (ed.), *Political Parties of the Americas*. Vol. 2. Westport, Conn.: Greenwood Press, 1982.
                                              ROBERT J. ALEXANDER

LEGUÍA, AUGUSTO B. (1863–1932), twice president of Peru, was born in Lambayeque. He completed his early education in an English school in Valparaíso, Chile. Although short and very thin, he first applied his great energy to business. He was successively general manager of the Peruvian and Ecuadorean branches of the New York Life Insurance Company; exporter of hides to the United States and Chile; Peru's manager of the British Sugar Company Limited founded in London in 1896; president of the Board of Directors of the Compañía de Seguros Sudamérica which he founded in Lima in 1900; and president of the National Bank of Peru.

Leguía served twice as minister of finance (1903–1904 and 1904–1907); the second time he was also prime minister. His prestige in the Partido Civil led to his election to the presidency in 1908 to a four-year term. When he broke with the oligarchic Partido Civil, he was exiled by President José Pardo in 1913. After six years of business activities in Great Britain and the United States,

Leguía returned to Peru to run for the presidency as an independent. In 1919 he won the election, but he staged a preventive coup to begin his second term in office. He remained in power for 11 years, thanks to his manipulated reelections in 1924 and 1929. He promulgated the Constitution of 1920, but interpreted constitutional law so as to govern in an autocratic manner. He made a token gesture toward decentralized power by creating three regional legislatures to deal with nonvital provincial matters. He maintained good relations with the Catholic church, and in 1923 had the country officially dedicated to the Sacred Heart, a move that caused widespread protest, particularly among students and workers.

During his dictatorship, Leguía attempted to check the power of the old artistocratic oligarchy while encouraging the rise of a new financial and commercial oligarchy. He multiplied the national debt tenfold by obtaining loans in the United States. After the economic Depression of 1929 dried up investments, his administration began to weaken until an army revolt in Arequippa forced Leguía to resign. He died in a Lima jail.

BIBLIOGRAPHY

Alisky, Marvin. *Historical Dictionary of Peru*. Metuchen, N.J.: Scarecrow Press, 1979.
Capunay, Manuel A. *Leguía*. Lima: 1957.
Hooper López, René. *Leguía, ensayo biográfico*. Lima: Ediciones Peruanas, 1964.
Pike, Frederick B. *The Modern History of Peru*. New York: Praeger, 1967.
Tauro, Alberto. *Diccionario enciclopédico del Perú*. Lima: Editorial Mejía Baca, 1966.
                                                    EUGENIO CHANG-RODRÍGUEZ

LEÓN DE VIVERO, FERNANDO (1906–   ), three times president of the Chamber of Deputies of Peru, was born in Ica. He studied law at the National University of San Marcos, where he was a student leader and became active in the Aprista movement. When the Peruvian Aprista Party was outlawed in 1931, León de Vivero became an important revolutionary leader with a high price on his head, hunted mercilessly by the secret police. When the political situation improved, he was elected to the Chamber of Deputies in 1945. He was the first member of his party to preside over that body.

When the constitutional government was overthrown by General Manuel Odría* in October 1948, León de Vivero resumed his revolutionary work, until he was forced to seek asylum in the Cuban Embassy in Lima. He lived in exile in Mexico and later in New York until 1962. In 1963 he was again elected deputy and was president of the Chamber of Deputies for a year. For a short period of time he served as Peruvian ambassador in Chile.

León de Vivero was elected member of the Constituent Assembly in 1978 and deputy for a five-year term in 1980. He served as secretary general of the Peruvian Aprista Party from 1980 to 1982. In the general elections of April 14, 1985, he was chosen a senator.

BIBLIOGRAPHY

Cárdenas, Eduardo. *20,000 biografías breves*. Hanover, Pa.: Libro de America, 1963.
Léon de Vivero, Fernando. *Avances del imperialismo fascista en el Peru*. Mexico: Manuel
     Arevalo, 1938.
————. *El tirano quedó atrás*. Mexico: Editorial Cultura, 1951.
                                                   EUGENIO CHANG-RODRÍGUEZ

LEONI, RAÚL (1906–1972), was one of the founders of Acción Democrática and third member of that party to serve as president of Venezuela. He was a third-year law student at the Central University of Venezuela and president of the Students Federation in February 1928, at the time of the vigorous Student Week protest against the dictatorship of Juan Vicente Gómez.* He was jailed and exiled to Baranquilla, Colombia, where he and some colleagues conducted a small business. One of the collaborators of Rómulo Betancourt* in organizing the Revolutionary Group of the Left (ARDI), a radical but non-Communist political organization, in 1931, he remained in Colombia until the death of Gómez in December 1935.

Leoni became a leader of the Organización Venezolana (ORVE), the core of a new national revolutionary party, and of the National Democratic Party (PDN), into which the ORVE merged late in 1936. He was elected to the Chamber of Deputies in January 1937, but his victory was not recognized by the government. He was one of the PDN leaders deported in March 1937 by President Eleazar López Contreras.*

After more than a year of exile during which he finally got a law degree from the National University of Bogotá, Colombia, Leoni returned home. Upon the deportation of Betancourt in late 1939, he became the ranking figure in the PDN leadership. With legalization and conversion the PDN into Acción Democrática (AD) early in the administration of President Isaías Medina Angarita* in September 1941, Leoni was a major collaborator of Secretary General Rómulo Betancourt in spreading the party organization throughout the country.

When AD sought agreement with President Medina on a joint candidate for his successor in 1945, Leoni and Betancourt went to Washington to convince Ambassador Diogenes Escalante to be that candidate. They succeeded, but Escalante soon became sick and had to withdraw.

When AD was then approached by junior officers concerning possible cooperation in a coup against President Medina, Leoni and Betancourt were the AD leaders who negotiated with them. After the coup, Raúl Leoni became a member of the Revolutionary Government Junta formed on October 19, 1945. He was also minister of labor and supported the rapid spread of unionization; participated in negotiations for the first nationwide collective bargaining agreement in the oil industry in 1946; and formed a strong alliance with the AD leaders in organized labor.

With the overthrow of President Rómulo Gallegos* by the military in November 1948, Leoni went into exile. He spent most of the ensuing nine years working for the International Labor Organization of the United Nations, while at the same time playing a leading role in the AD exile organization.

After the overthrow of the dictatorship of General Marcos Pérez Jiménez* in January 1958, Leoni returned home. He again became a member of AD's National Executive Committee, in December 1958 was elected senator, and soon afterward president of AD.

In the 1963 election process to choose a successor to President Rómulo Betancourt, Raúl Leoni won the nomination, even though he was not the choice of Betancourt for AD candidate. He won owing to the backing of the Trade Union Bureau of the party. He won a plurality in a widely divided vote and in February 1964 was inaugurated as president. Leoni refused to continue the coalition with the Christian Social Copei Party which had existed during the Betancourt administration; during his term he had several different combinations in his cabinet.

President Leoni largely continued the policies of his predecessor: he pushed industrialization, continued the agrarian reform, and further expanded the educational system. However, his administration made at least two innovations. First, he took tentative conciliatory steps toward far-left elements that had launched a guerrilla war during the Betancourt period, and when the Communist Party withdrew from guerrilla activity, Leoni relegalized the party for the 1968 elections under the name Unión para Avanzar. Second, in 1966 he also introduced a law to levy an excess profits tax on the oil companies which the petroleum firms strongly resisted. A compromise was reached by which the companies paid a substantial additional amount to the Venezuelan government.

After the Social Christian Copei Party's victory in the 1968 election, Raúl Leoni made Venezuelan history as the first president to peaceably turn over power to an opposition party.

During his last years, President Leoni returned to the practice of law. He also remained active in the leadership of the AD. However, with his health deteriorating, he went abroad for treatment; he died in New York City.

BIBLIOGRAPHY

Alexander, Robert J. *The Venezuelan Democratic Revolution*. New Brunswick, N.J: Rutgers University Press, 1964.
Betancourt, Rómulo. *Venezuela: Oil and Politics*. Boston: Houghton Mifflin, 1979.
Cuarenta Años de Acción Democrática: Cuatro Presidentes. Vol. 2. Caracas:Ediciones de la Presidencia de la Republica, 1981.
Cuatro Figuras Blancas. Caracas: Foción Serrano Producciones, 1975.
Martz, John. *Acción Democrática: Evolution of a Modern Political Party in Venezuela*. Princeton, N.J.: Princeton University Press, 1966.

ROBERT J. ALEXANDER

LERDO DE TEJADA, SEBASTIÁN (1827–1889), president of Mexico after Benito Juárez,* could not prevent a power vacuum developing after Juárez' death. Born in Jaapa in the state of Veracruz, Lerdo got a law degree and served as president of San Ildefonso College during 1852–1853. He became minister of foreign relations in 1857, a deputy in Congress during 1861–1863, and chief justice of the Supreme Court in 1867. When President Juárez died in office in 1872, Lerdo succeeded to the presidency under the 1857 Constitution. General Porfirio Díaz* ousted him from the presidency in 1876. Lerdo lived in exile in New York until his death.

BIBLIOGRAPHY

Bulnes, Francisco. *El Verdadero Juárez*. Mexico City: Libreria Bouret, 1904.
Callcott, Wilfird H. *Liberalism in Mexico, 1857–1929*. Palo Alto, Calif.: Stanford University Press, 1931.
Knapp, Frank A. *The Life of Sebastián Lerdo de Tejada*. Austin: University of Texas Press, 1951.
Scholes, Walter V. *Mexican Politics During the Juárez Regime, 1855–1872*. Columbia: University of Missouri Press, 1957.
Sinkin, Richard N. *The Mexican Reform, 1855–1876, A Study in Liberal Nation Building*. Austin: Institute of Latin American Studies of the University of Texas, 1979.

MARVIN ALISKY

LESCOT, ÉLIE (1883–1974), was president of Haiti between 1941 and 1946. A member of the mulatto elite, he went to primary and secondary school in Cape Haitien, and then joined his uncle's import-export business. He became an interpreter for the customs service in 1905 and six years later was a member of the Chamber of Deputies. Subsequently, he was director of the major secondary school in Port-au-Prince, justice of the peace, consul in Cuba, judge of a civil tribunal, held various cabinet posts, and was ambassador to the United States.

Lescot developed strong ties with Rafael Leónidas Trujillo,* dictator of the Dominican Republic, who provided him with funds to bribe members of the Haitian Assembly to elect him president in 1941. After failure of an unconstitutional attempt by President Sténio Vincent* to remain in office, Vincent, under pressure from Washington, stepped down and on May 15, 1941, was succeeded by Lescot.

Lescot's regime was tyrannical and corrupt. He established military tribunals with jurisdiction over all offenses and persons, thus circumventing the judiciary. There were numerous arbitrary arrests of political opponents, critical journalists, and the clergy. Corruption and nepotism were rampant. Ostensible social security and economic development schemes became mechanisms for enriching Lescot, his family, and a small clique of elites. He took exclusive personal control over the budget and, in 1944, using the excuse of the war, appropriated all foreign assets in the country. He also created six regional delegates with absolute power in their local jurisdictions, who answered directly to him through his minister of interior.

Lescot established strong ties with the United States. U.S. and Haitian entry into World War II proved highly opportune. Declaring "extraordinary powers," he virtually suspended the constitution and negotiated with Washington for increased economic aid and military assistance. The United States agreed to buy all of Haiti's cotton and sisal. Haiti was provided artillery, military aircraft, and a detachment of the U.S. Coast Guard.

Using the excuse of the war, Lescot suspended national elections to the assembly in 1944, giving himself the power to appoint its members, and extended his presidential term from five years to seven. As soon as the war ended, however, Lescot came under attack from a local newspaper, *La Ruche*. His move in January 1946 to ban the paper and detain its editors sparked massive demonstrations by students and civil servants. On January 11, three high-ranking officers, including the commander of the Presidential Guard, Major Paul Eugene Magloire,* deposed the president. He left Haiti for Miami, flying later to Montreal. He eventually returned to Haiti, where he died.

BIBLIOGRAPHY

Diederich, B., and Al Burt. *Papa Doc: The Truth About Haiti Today*. New York: McGraw-Hill, 1969.
Logan, R. W. *Haiti and the Dominican Republic*. London: Oxford University Press, 1968.
Nicholls, David. *Haiti in Caribbean Context*. London: Macmillan Co., 1985.
Rothberg, Robert I. *Haiti: The Politics of Squalor*. Boston: Houghton Mifflin, 1971.
Weinstein, Brian, and Aaron Segal. *Haiti: Political Failures, Cultural Successes*. New York: Praeger, 1984.

PERCY C. HINTZEN

LIBERIA-PETERS, MARIA (1942–   ), became the first woman to be minister-president (prime minister) of Netherlands Antilles in 1984. She had a university education in The Netherlands, and became a kindergarten teacher and school administrator after her return home in 1962. She was elected a National People's Party member of the Curaçao insular legislature in 1976, and in the 1984 election she was her party's most popular candidate for the Netherlands Antilles Parliament, the Staten. Party leaders thereupon picked her to preside over a new coalition government. Her administration was faced with particularly severe economic problems when the Shell Company threatened to shut down its oil refinery, which for half a century had been Curaçao's major economic activity.

BIBLIOGRAPHY

New York Times, August 19, 1985.

ROBERT J. ALEXANDER

LLERAS CAMARGO, ALBERTO (1906–   ), was twice president of Colombia during periods of crisis when conciliation rather than partisan politics were required. Born in Bogotá and educated at the prestigious Colegio del Rosario and the Externado de Derecho he became a journalist for the leading Liberal daily *El Tiempo*. He was a member of the Directorate of the Liberal party during the administration of Enrique Olaya Herrera* in the early 1930s. When Liberal reformer Alfonso López Pumarejo* assumed the presidency in 1934, Lleras, secretary to the presidency and later minister of government, took a leading role in designing legislation and in organizing the Confederación de Trabajadores Colombianos (CTC), the leading trade union confederation. López made him the chief spokesman and propagandist for the "Revolution on the March." He founded the newspaper *El Liberal* in 1939.

Lleras was again named minister of government during López' second term. The administration came under increasing attack from Conservatives and dissident Liberals, and faced growing social unrest due to deteriorating economic conditions. Lleras became interim president in 1945, following López' resignation, and made possible orderly transfer of power to Mariano Ospina Pérez,* the Conservative victor in the 1946 election.

Lleras represented Colombia abroad and served as secretary general of the Organization of American States in Washington from 1948 to 1954. When the military toppled the dictatorship of General Gustavo Rojas Pinilla* in 1957, he served as Liberal negotiator with exiled Conservative leader Laureano Gómez* in discussions that led to creation of the bipartisan National Front. As the only candidate acceptable to the majority leadership in both parties, Lleras was elected president in 1958 of the first National Front government.

The Lleras administration started a program of civil action in reducing the level of violence. Agrarian reform legislation was passed, and the Colombian Institute of Agrarian Reform was established. The National Planning Office was revitalized, and a ten-year economic and social development plan was drawn up in accordance with the Alliance for Progress. Politically, Lleras adhered to the bipartisanship of the National Front, encouraged democratic processes, and allowed the former dictator Rojas to return home. In 1959 he ended a ten-year state of siege in most of Colombia.

After leaving the presidency in 1962, Lleras continued as a respected elder statesman and sometime adviser to the National Front governments. He resided for years in the United States, where he directed the continental magazine *Visión*.

BIBLIOGRAPHY

Dix, Robert H. *Colombia: The Political Dimensions of Change.* New Haven, Conn.: Yale University Press, 1967.
Hellman, Ronald, Albert Berry, and Mauricio Solaun. *Politics of Compromise.* New Brunswick, N.J.: Transaction Books, 1980.
Lleras Camargo, Alberto. *Sus mejores páginas.* Bogotá: 1960.
República de Colombia. *Un Año de gobierno, 1945–1946.* Bogotá: 1946.

RICHARD E. SHARPLESS

LLERAS RESTREPO, CARLOS (1908–   ), was president of Colombia (1966–1970) during the period of the bipartisan National Front. He was born and educated in Bogotá. As a Liberal student leader, he took an active role in politics in the late 1920s. A continuing interest in agrarian questions was aroused by his involvement in disputes over land problems while an official of the Cundinamarca departmental government in the early 1930s. A protegé of the Liberal reform president, Alfonso López Pumarejo* (1934–1938), Lleras was a representative, senator, and minister of finance under both López and Eduardo Santos (1938–1942). On six different occasions, he served as a member, or president, of the Liberal Party's National Directorate.

In 1948 Lleras assumed leadership of the Liberal opposition to the Conservative government of Mariano Ospina Pérez* following the assassination of Jorge Eliécer Gaitán.* In 1952 he was forced into exile during the presidency of Laureano Gómez.*

Lleras served on the boards of directors of several banks, and on the board of the Federación Nacional de Cafeteros de Colombia, which controlled the country's major export, coffee. In 1961 he pushed through congress agrarian reform legislation.

As president, Lleras brought to the government a strong technocratic emphasis. He strengthened the state planning apparatus, created autonomous institutes to develop various social programs, reformed the tax system, and imposed regulations on foreign direct private investment. He sponsored development of peasant organizations to support the agrarian reform. During his administration, Colombia achieved notable economic growth rates.

Lleras was named director of the Liberal Party in 1972. But his bid for another presidental nomination in 1974 was defeated by Alfonso López Michelson,* who subsequently was elected president.

BIBLIOGRAPHY

Dix, Robert H. *Colombia: The Political Dimensions of Change*. New Haven, Conn.: Yale University Press, 1967.

Hellman, Ronald, Albert Berry, and Mauricio Solaun. *Politics of Compromise*. New Brunswick, N.J.: Transaction Books, 1980.

Hirschman, Albert O. *Journeys Toward Progress*. New York: Twentieth Century Fund, 1963.

Lleras Restrepo, Carlos. *De la república a la dictadura*. Bogotá: 1955.

                                                    RICHARD E. SHARPLESS

LOMBARDO TOLEDANO, VICENTE (1894–1968), was Mexico's most powerful Marxist labor leader, founder of the Popular Socialist Party, and the only serious Marxist presidential candidate. He was born in Tezuitlan in the state of Puebla. He received his law degree from the National Autonomous University of Mexico in 1919 and a Ph.D. from the same institution in 1933. Off and on he taught part time as a law professor at his alma mater. He founded and became director of the Workers University of Mexico (a vocational institution at the skilled-trade technology level) in 1936.

In 1923 Lombardo Toledano was named secretary of educational affairs of the Mexican Regional Confederation of Labor (CROM—Confederación Regional Obrera Mexicana). He argued within the CROM with the more politically moderate labor leaders, and on September 19, 1932, resigned from the CROM, declaring himself to be a radical Marxist not in sympathy with CROM's traditional approaches.

In 1933, with some dissident CROM unions, he organized the General Confederation of Mexican Workers and Peasants (CGOCM—Confederación General de Obreros y Campesinos Mexicanos). In 1936 the president of Mexico, Lázaro Cárdenas,* chose Lombardo to be the founding secretary general of the Confederation of Workers of Mexico (CTM—Confederación de Trabajadores de Mexico), absorbing some CROM, some CGOCM, and other union groups. When Lombardo aligned himself with the Communists' oppostion to the Allies in World War II in the 1939–1941 period, the CTM ousted him as its head.

Lombardo's first political post was as a deputy in the federal Congress during 1926–1928, representing the Mexican Labor Party (PLM), the political arm of the CROM. He later affiliated with the government party, the Institutional Revolutionary Party (PRI), but in 1948 decided to found the Popular Party as a socialist party to compete with the PRI. He avoided including the word "socialist" in the party's original title in hopes of luring some non-Marxist activists from the PRI to his party. Later, he did add the word, being secretary general of the Popular Socialist Party (PPS).

In 1952 Lombardo ran as the PPS candidate for president, receiving 75,000 votes, whereas the winner from the PRI, Adolfo Ruíz Cortines, received 2.7 million votes. Yet, Lombardo's campaign helped establish the PPS as a major force in two states, Oaxaca and Nayarít.

Lombardo's CGOCM unions, revived in the 1950s as the Unión General de Obreros y Campesinos Mexicanos (UGOCM), survived after his death but remained small. In his last years, Lombardo influenced millions of Mexicans through his regular political column in the leftist magazine *Siempre*.

BIBLIOGRAPHY

Brandenburg, Frank R. *The Making of Modern Mexico*. Englewood Cliffs, N.J.: Prentice-Hall, 1964.

Camp, Roderic. *Mexican Political Biographies, 1935–1975*. Tucson: University of Arizona Press, 1976.

Johnson, William Weber. *Heroic Mexico*. Garden City, N.Y.: Doubleday, 1968.

Millon, Robert P. *Mexican Marxist: Vicente Lombardo Toledano*. Chapel Hill: University of North Carolina Press, 1966.

Scott, Robert E. *Mexican Government in Transition*. Urbana: University of Illinois Press, 1964.

                                                                                   MARVIN ALISKY

LÓPEZ, CARLOS ANTONIO (1792–1862), was the second of three powerful dictators who ruled Paraguay during its first 60 years of independence. A wealthy *estanciero*, López succeeded in gaining control of the country after six months of turbulence following the death of his predecessor, Dr. José Gaspar Rodríguez Francia.* From 1842 until his death, he was the undisputed master of his country.

Under López, the government increased its ownership of the land to include almost the entire country. He reversed Francia's policy of closing Paraguay off from the world, opened the country's borders, and the nation experienced a period of economic and cultural stimulation. There was even modest immigration. López favored economic development; one of the continent's first railways was built under his government's auspices.

López became embroiled in the turbulent politics of neighboring Argentina. From 1845 until 1852 he sided with those elements who were fighting to oust tyrannical Juan Manuel de Rosas.*

Because of the number of innovations and changes introduced under Carlos Antonio López, and the disasters suffered under his successor, the 1844–1862 period is sometimes referred to as Paraguay's Golden Age.

Although very much a political tyrant, López maintained the façade of a constitutional regime, with a functioning but subservient Congress. But he never allowed the legislature to limit his control of national affairs.

Upon his death, López was succeeded by the third of Paraguay's powerful nineteenth-century dictators, his son Francisco Solano López,* whom he had named as commander-in-chief of the army as early as 1845.

BIBLIOGRAPHY

Graham, R. Cunninghame. *Portrait of a Dictator: Francisco Solano López*. London: Heinemann, 1933.

Kolinski, Charles J. *Historical Dictionary of Paraguay*. Metuchen, N.J.: Scarecrow Press, 1973.

———. *Independence or Death! The Story of the Paraguayan War*. Gainesville: University of Florida Press, 1965.

Lewis, Paul H. *Paraguay Under Stroessner*. Chapel Hill: University of North Carolina Press, 1980.

Weil, Thomas et al. *Area Handbook for Paraguay*. Washington, D.C.: Department of Defense, 1972.

JOHN T. DEINER

LÓPEZ, FRANCISCO SOLANO (1826–1870), was the last of three powerful dictators who ruled Paraguay during the first 60 years of its independence. He led the country into a disastrous war with Argentina and Brazil (1865–1870) which cost Paraguay more than 150,000 square kilometers of territory, and led to the death of over half of the 550,000 Paraguayans alive at the beginning of the conflict. Of those 250,000 Paraguayans left alive at the conclusion of the war, only 14,000 were adult males.

The first son of Paraguay's second president, Carlos Antonio López,* Francisco Solano López was largely educated by his father, who made him a brigadier general at the age of 19. He participated in a short war against the Juan Manuel de Rosas* regime in Argentina in 1845.

Between 1853 and 1856 Francisco Solano López was in Europe, heading an effort to seek immigrants, investments, and armaments. His mission was successful, and in addition to many contracts, he brought back an Irish mistress, Elisa Alicia Lynch. He had a new diplomatic assignment from his father in 1859, seeking to mediate a conflict between the Province of Buenos Aires and the Argentine Confederation.

When Carlos Antonio López died in 1862, Franciso Solano López became his father's successor. The first years of his rule were marked by economic prosperity. However, the devastating War of the Triple Alliance (Argentina, Brazil, and a puppet government of Uruguay) against Paraguay began when Francisco Solano López declared war on Brazil because of Brazil's invasion of Uruguay in 1865. Argentina denied the Paraguayan Army permission to cross Argentine territory to fight against Brazil, and when the Paraguayans did so anyway, they ended up in battle against both the Argentines and Brazilians.

Although the Paraguayans did well in the early years of the war, they were ultimately overwhelmed. Asunción was burned, and López was forced into the jungle with his troops. He was finally killed in the Battle of Cerro Cora in 1870, after which the war ended.

BIBLIOGRAPHY

Graham, R. Cunninghame. *Portrait of a Dictator: Francisco Solano López*. London: Heinemann, 1933.
Kolinski, Charles J. *Historical Dictionary of Paraguay*. Metuchen, N.J.: Scarecrow Press, 1973.
————. *Independence or Death! The Story of the Paraguayan War*. Gainesville: University of Florida Press, 1965.
Lewis, Paul E. *Paraguay Under Stroessner*. Chapel Hill: University of North Carolina Press, 1980.
Weil, Thomas, et al. *Area Handbook for Paraguay*. Washington, D.C.: Department of Defense, 1972.

JOHN T. DEINER

LÓPEZ ARELLANO, OSWALDO (1921–   ), was the dominant military officer in Honduras after 1957 and was twice president. He had joined the army in 1939, and was one of the senior colonels when the armed forces ousted Julio Lozano Díaz on October 21, 1956. When Major Robert Gálvez Barnes withdrew from the three-member military junta on November 16, 1957, López, then minister of defense, took his vacant seat on the Junta. He continued to serve as minister of defense in the administration of President Ramón Villeda Morales,* inaugurated in December 1957.

On October 3, 1963, military forces loyal to López ousted Villeda in the face of the electoral victory of Liberal candidate Modesto Rodas Alvarado, who had talked about ending the military's budgetary autonomy and ability to nominate candidates for chief of staff. López served as head of a military government that supervised February 1965 elections for a constituent assembly which elected him as constitutional president.

Promoted to general, López appointed Ricardo Zúñiga Augustinius as secretary of the presidency and subsequently minister of government. A short-lived war with El Salvador in 1969 demonstrated the military incompetence and corruption of many senior officers and the weak loyalty of many upper-class and middle-class groups to the regime, in contrast to the strong loyalty of organized peasant and trade union groups.

As the 1971 elections for president and Congress approached, the National Party named colorless Ramón Ernesto Cruz. With Zúñiga masterminding the Cruz campaign, the Nationalists won, but Cruz was overthrown by the military, still under the command of López, on December 4, 1972. In an effort to mobilize public support for López' regime, 29 senior army officers, informally charged with incompetence and corruption were "retired," and land distribution was speeded up under the December 1974 agrarian reform decree.

President López was finally forced out of office for the last time by his military colleagues on April 22, 1975, in the face of charges he had accepted a $1.25 million bribe from United Brands (formerly United Fruit) to evade the export taxes.

BIBLIOGRAPHY

Meza, Víctor. *Historia del Movimiento Obrero Hondureño*. Tegucigalpa: Editorial Guaymuras, 1980.
Morris, James A. *Honduras, Caudillo Politics and Military Rulers*. Boulder, Colorado: Westview Press, 1984.
New York Times, November 19, 1957.
Pearson, Neale J. "Peasant Pressure Groups and Agrarian Reform in Honduras, 1962–1977," in William P. Avery, Richard E. Lonsdale and Ivan Volgyes (eds). *Rural Change and Public Policy, Eastern Europe, Latin America and Australia*. New York: Pergamon Press, 1980.

NEALE J. PEARSON

LÓPEZ CONTRERAS, ELEAZAR (1883–1973), was the successor of long-term Venezuelan dictator Juan Vicente Gómez.* He became a professional soldier in the army of Cipriano Castro,* the first caudillo from the mountain state of Táchira, whence López Contreras also came. Juan Vicente Gómez gave him his first major military post, director of war, in charge of purchases for the armed forces. By 1928 he was commander of the Caracas garrison. He suppressed an attempted coup by junior officers supported by student leaders who had organized the Student Week protest against the Gómez regime.

López Contreras' loyalty to Gómez led to his appointment as minister of war and marine in 1931. He still held that post when Gómez died, and he immediately assumed the presidency. Congress confirmed him as provisional president and subsequently elected him as constitutional president for the 1936–1941 period.

As president, López Contreras relaxed the Gómez dictatorship. He deported most members of Gómez' numerous family and confiscated their very large landed estates. For about a year, he allowed the organization of political parties, most of them opposition groups, as well as the establishment of a labor movement, permitted considerable freedom of the press, and brought enactment of a new labor law and a new petroleum law. However, after crushing an oil strike, he deported about three score leaders of the new parties in February 1937. Except in Caracas, he conducted rigged elections.

At the end of his term, President López Contreras chose Colonel Isaías Medina Angarita,* his minister of war, as his successor, whose election was assured by López Contreras' control over Congress, which then chose the chief executive.

As Medina's term neared an end, López Contreras aspired to return to the presidency. He organized a party, Agrupación Cívica Bolivariana, which nominated him. Rumors were rife that López Contreras might try to overthrow Medina by a coup, since he had little chance of election by the Congress dominated by Medina. When a coup did occur, it came from young officers in alliance with Acción Democrática, which ended all possibility of López Contreras returning to power.

After the October 1945 coup, General López Contreras was deported. He stayed abroad until the end of the Acción Democrática regime in 1948. He played no further part in national politics.

BIBLIOGRAPHY

Alexander, Robert J. *Rómulo Betancourt and the Transformation of Venezuela*. New Brunswick, N.J.: Transaction Press, 1982.
Betancourt, Rómulo. *En 18 de Octubre de 1945: Génesis y Realizaciones de Una Revolución Democrática*. Caracas: Editorial Sei Barral, 1979.
————. *Venezuela: Oil and Politics*. Boston: Houghton Mifflin, 1979.
Fuenmayor, Juan Bautista. *Historia de la Venezuela Política Contemporanea 1899–1969*. Tomo II and Tomo III, Vol. 1. Caracas: 1976.

ROBERT J. ALEXANDER

LÓPEZ MATEOS, ADOLFO (1910–1970), was the Mexican president who nationalized the electric power industry and created the profit-sharing law for private sector workers. He described himself as "a leftist within the limits of the Constitution." He was born in the town of Atizapán in the state of Mexico. His father, a dentist, died when Adolfo was very young, and his mother was left to support five children on a small income. Young Adolfo completed his primary studies at the Colegio Francés in Mexico City on a full scholarship, and his secondary studies in Toluca. He received his law degree from the National Autonomous University of Mexico in 1934. As a student, he supported philosopher and educator José Vasconcelos'* unsuccessful campaign for the government party's presidential nomination in 1929 against the hand-picked candidate of former president Plutarco Elías Calles.*

López Mateos launched his political career in 1934 as an adviser to the National Workers Bank of Development, while employed as an attorney for the Ministry of Finance. As minister of labor during 1952–1958, he developed his public image as a friend of organized labor.

As president of Mexico during 1958–1964, López Mateos ended the costly railroad strikes of 1959 by having Demetrio Vallejo, secretary general of the Railroad Workers Union and a leader of the Communist Party, jailed on charges of sedition. In 1969, when he expropriated all foreign and domestic privately owned electric power companies, he restored his popularity among union workers. Then in 1962 he had Congress amend Article 123 of the constitution, and enact enabling legislation for the profit-sharing law, according to which a tripartite government-management-labor committee was formed in every private corporation of Mexico to determine what percentage of profits would be shared among full-time employees.

In foreign policy, López Mateos stressed verbiage and policies that seemed to make Mexico City independent of Washington, such as endorsing the early period of the Fidel Castro* government in Cuba. In 1962, when the Organization of American States condemned Castro's intervention in the domestic politics of Venezuela, Mexico alone supported Cuba. When other Latin American governments began recalling their ambassadors to Havana, López Mateos continued to praise Castro.

Thanks to understanding from Washington, López Mateos was able to take credit for transfer of the Chamizal territory in southernmost El Paso to Mexican sovereignty. The Rio Grand over the years had shifted; the United States readily admitted that fact and expedited the transfer.

BIBLIOGRAPHY

Camp, Roderic A. *Mexican Political Biographies, 1935–1975.* Tucson: University of Arizona Press, 1976.
———. *Mexican's Leaders, Their Education and Recruitment.* Tucson: University of Arizona Press, 1980.
Meyer, Michael C., and William L. Sherman. *The Course of Mexican History.* New York: Oxford University Press, 1983.
Purcell, Susan Kaufman. *The Mexican Profit-Sharing Decision.* Berkeley: University of California Press, 1975.
Vernon, Raymond. *The Dilemma of Mexico's Development.* Cambridge, Mass.: Harvard University Press, 1963.

MARVIN ALISKY

LÓPEZ MICHELSON, ALFONSO (1913–   ), was president of Colombia in 1974–1978. The son of President Alfonso López Pumarejo,* he was educated in Europe and at the Georgetown School of Foreign Service in Washington, D.C. He received his law degree at the University of Chile.

After pursuing private law practice, López Michelson became active in his father's political movement in the 1930s. Subsequently, he continued active in the leadership of the Liberal Party. In 1958 he established the Movimiento Revolucionario Liberal (MRL) to oppose the National Front arrangement between Liberals and Conservatives for alternating power between the two parties. He was elected senator by the MRL.

López Michelson made his peace with the leadership of the Liberal Party and the National Front. As a consequence, he was named governor of César Province in 1967–1968 and became a leading figure in the Liberal Party.

Alfonso López Michelson served as president of Colombia between 1974 and 1978, the first president to be elected after expiration of the National Front agreement. His administration was particularly plagued with the expansion of the international drug trade, especially involving the shipment of cocaine from Colombia to the United States.

Alfonso López Michelson ran for president again in 1982 but was defeated by Conservative nominee Belisario Betancur Cuartas.*

BIBLIOGRAPHY

Who's Who in Government and Politics in Latin America. New York: Decade Media
    Books, 1984.

                                                            RICHARD E. SHARPLESS

LÓPEZ PORTILLO, JOSÉ (1920–   ), was president of Mexico during 1976–1982. Born in Mexico City, he graduated from a public primary school and in 1937 from the National Preparatory School. He received a law degree from the University of Santiago, Chile, in 1945, and a second one from the National Autonomous University of Mexico in 1946, where he immediately became a part-time professor of law until 1958. He was one of the founders of the Ph.D. program in public administration at the university in 1950.

López Portillo launched his career in government as administrative assistant to the executive administrator of the Ministry of National Properties in 1959. He became assistant minister of the presidency during 1968–1970, then assistant director of government properties during 1970–1972, and finally director general of the Federal Electric Commission during 1972–1973. President Luis Echeverría appointed him minister of finance and public credit in 1973. The two had been close friends since the sixth grade in primary school.

López Portillo's administration developed a National Development Plan that divided Mexico into 11 zones, in an attempt to decentralize industry. Under the plan, tax credits were given to investors who opened plants away from the three largest metro areas of the republic. During his administration Mexico became the world's fourth largest exporter of petroleum.

Just before leaving office, López Portillo expropriated all private banks in Mexico and drastically devalued the peso. Post-auditing of the petroleum operations by President Miguel de la Madrid's* attorney general in early 1983 brought charges of vast embezzlement of government income by López Portillo's close associate, Jorge Díaz Serrano, his director general of Pemex, the government oil firm. López Portillo himself entered the presidency as a professional man moderately well off; his conspicuous wealth after leaving office could not be explained in terms of his presidential salary and his known assets in 1976.

After leaving the presidency, López Portillo traveled abroad, living in luxury in Europe and avoiding news interviews completely.

BIBLIOGRAPHY

Camp, Roderic A. *Mexican Political Biographies, 1935–1975.* Tucson: University of Arizona Press, 1976.
———, and Miguel A. Basanez. ''The Nationalization of Banks and Mexican Public Opinion.'' *The Mexican Forum* 4, No. 2 (April 1984).
Godoy, Emma. *Margarita López Portillo y los Días en la Voz.* Mexico City: Editorial Costa Amic, 1977.
Mejía Prieto, Jorge. *Llamenme Pepe-Trazos biográficos de José López Portillo.* Mexico City: Editores Asociados, 1976.
Ross, Stanley R. ''LEA and Don Pepe, 1976 and 1982.'' *The Mexican Forum* 3, No. 1 (January 1983).

MARVIN ALISKY

LÓPEZ PUMAREJO, ALFONSO (1886–1959), as president of Colombia (1934–1938), initiated the country's first modern social and economic reform legislation in the twentieth century. Born in Honda, Tolima, into a prominent regional family with interests in the coffee trade, he was educated in Bogotá and England, and then worked in the family firm, representing it in New York. Eventually, he founded a commercial bank. Although he had early been involved in politics, he did not achieve national importance until the Liberal Party convention in 1929. The long-ruling Conservative Party was divided, and López issued a call to Liberals to take power with new ideas and programs. The old-line Liberals prevailed at the convention, but the party did succeed in electing Enrique Olaya Herrera* president in 1930, in coalition with dissident Conservatives.

López served under Olaya as ambassador to the United Kingdom. However, he became the center of a group of young, progressive-minded Liberals. Named the party's presidential candidate for 1934, he was elected when the Conservative Party, led by Laureano Gómez,* abstained from the election.

Under the slogan ''Revolution on the March,'' López pushed through Congress measures that were startlingly radical for the time: universal male suffrage, limitations on the secular role of the Roman Catholic Church; and constitutional changes that gave the state an activist role in economic affairs, a graduated income tax, laws that protected the rights of workers to organize, and definition of property as having a ''social function.'' An agrarian reform law was also passed. Primary education was nationalized and made obligatory, the National University was reorganized, and substantially increased expenditures were made for education at all levels.

Although limited in both scope and effectiveness, the "Revolution on the March" made López the most popular president in modern Colombian history. However, Olaya's followers, including big businessmen, saw the reforms, especially those concerning labor and state economic policy, as potentially dangerous to their interests. The Conservatives railed against what they called anticlericalism and the general direction of the López administration. Faced with mounting opposition in Congress and from the traditional political leadership, he slowed his program considerably in 1937.

The following administration of Liberal Eduardo Santos (1938–1942) was called "the pause." No significantly new social programs were begun, and the Liberals were divided. López won a second term in 1942. During that time, social and economic conditions were worsening, the frustration of the working and middle classes was rising, and political polarization occurred as the Liberals split and the Conservatives under the rightist Laureano Gómez mounted vitriolic opposition. Serious labor troubles marred his administration, and scandals, including some within his own family, demoralized it. López was briefly arrested by a rebellious army unit in 1944. Although the coup failed, it further discredited him. López finally resigned and turned the presidency over to Alberto Lleras Camargo* in 1945.

Although López represented Colombia in the United Nations between 1946 and 1948, he played no prominent role in national politics until the 1950s. Then, as Colombia was engulfed by widespread rural violence and military dictatorship, he originated the idea of a National Front government of Liberals and Conservatives which was eventually adopted.

BIBLIOGRAPHY

Dix, Robert H. *Colombia: The Political Dimensions of Change*. New Haven, Conn.: Yale University Press, 1967.
Lattore Cabal, Hugo. *Mi novela; Apuntes autobiográficos de Alfonso López*. Bogotá: 1961.
Zuleta Angel, Eduardo. *El presidente López*. Bogotá, 1966.

RICHARD E. SHARPLESS

LORA ESCOBAR, GUILLERMO (1924–   ), Bolivia's most famous Trotskyist leader, was the son of a miner father and a Quechua woman. His grammar and high school were completed in the mining camp of Uncia. He refused to finish his law studies at San Andrés University, becoming active in the Revolutionary Workers Party (POR), and the labor movement. He wrote the Thesis of Pulacayo, the Trotskyist-oriented statement of principles adopted at the Fourth Miners' Congress in November 1946. Lora was a member of the Bloque Minero Parlamentario, a group of working-class deputies elected to Congress in 1947.

The POR under Lora's direction worked closely with the Nationalist Revolutionary Movement (MNR) in the labor movement between 1946 and 1952, when both parties were illegal. For a few months after the April 1952 National

Revolution, the POR dominated the newly established labor confederation, the Central Obrero Bolatino (COB), but in October was ousted by the MNR. Subsequently, the POR was hit by political and theoretical schisms. Many POR labor leaders joined the MNR, and the POR suffered from conflicts within the Fourth International. It finally split in 1956. Lora remained head of the POR faction that centered around the newspaper *Masas*.

Lora continued to maintain some influence in the Miners Federation. In 1971 he was a leader of the short-lived Popular Assembly during the administration of President Juan José Torres,* and he ran as a presidential candidate for his party in the 1985 elections.

In a number of books, and in *Masas* Lora has been a prolific chronicler of political and labor history of Bolivia.

BIBLIOGRAPHY

Alexander, Robert J. *Trotskyism in Latin America.* Stanford, Calif.: Hoover Institution Press, 1973.
Lora, Guillermo. *Contributión a la Historia Política de Bolivia.* 2 vols. La Paz: Isla, 1978.
————. *Formación de la Clase Obrera Boliviana.* La Paz: Ediciones Masas, 1980.
————. *History of the Bolivian Labor Movement.* London: Cambridge University Press, 1977.

GUILLERMO DELGADO

LOUISY, ALLAN (?–), became prime minister of St. Lucia four months after the country attained its independence in 1979. He received his primary and secondary education in St. Lucia, and was called to the bar in 1945, and entering private practice for one year. During the following 28 years he served as crown attorney or magistrate in St. Lucia, Antigua, Montserrat, Dominica, and Jamaica, ending up as a Puisne Judge in the West Indies Associated States Supreme Court in Antigua.

Louisy returned to St. Lucia as the St. Lucia Labor Party (SLP) was at a low ebb. After winning elections in 1951, 1954, 1957, and 1961, the party lost power to the United Workers Party led by John Compton* in 1964. A group of young radical activists, headed by George Odlum, had joined the party in 1973 and managed to radicalize it. To further strengthen the appeal of the party and to bolster its legitimacy, Louisy was invited to join and he emerged as the compromise choice for party leader in 1974. He became Leader of the Opposition, after winning a seat to the House of Assembly.

Louisy became embroiled in conflict with the more radical members of the party under Deputy Leader Odlum. Nonethless, he was able to lead the SLP to victory in June 1979, a few months after the country became independent, and became the country's second prime minister. The victory was due, in large part, to Odlum's appeal. Trade union leaders played a much more active role, with four holding ministerial posts. The SLP government pushed economic reform based on expansion and development of domestic agriculture and stressed close economic ties with the rest of the English-speaking Caribbean. With Odlum as minister of external affairs, foreign policy measures included association with the "nonaligned" nations, a pact with the Maurice Rupert Bishop* regime in Granada and the Serephan government of Dominica, and overtures to Cuba.

In 1981 Louisy was forced to resign as prime minister and SLP leader after a parliamentary defeat of his budget. The party managed to hold onto power until 1982 when it was defeated in an election following loss of a vote of confidence in Parliament.

BIBLIOGRAPHY

Alexander, Robert J. "Saint Lucia," in Robert J. Alexander (ed.) in *Political Parties of the Americas*. Vol. 2. Westport, Conn.: Greenwood Press, 1983.
Saint Lucia At Independence. Castries, St. Lucia, February 22, 1979.
Smith, Lindel. "St. Lucia Elections, 2nd July 1979." *Bulletin of Eastern Caribbean Affairs* 5, No. 3 (July/August 1979).

PERCY C. HINTZEN AND W. MARVIN WILL

L'OUVERTURE, TOUSSAINT (1743?–1803), led the only successful slave revolution in modern history, that of Haiti. The French Revolution precipitated revolts by both blacks and mulattoes and conflicts among the whites in St. Domingue, France's most prosperous colony. When the insurrections began, Toussaint remained faithful to his master, Monsieur Bayou, who had provided him with the opportunity to gain some education. He worked as a coachman and apparently also as a veterinarian.

After helping his master flee to the United States, Toussaint joined the slave insurgents under Jean-François, who had declared himself a royalist, fighting against the Republican forces. Toussaint rose quickly to the post of commander. He defeated French forces sent to capture him on November 17, 1792.

Toussaint held the post of military secretary to one of the two acknowledged leaders of the insurrectionist slaves, Biassou. He soon commanded a force of 4,000 blacks, training them with the help of French deserters in drill, weaponry, and discipline. With the acknowledged rank of colonel, he became elevated to a status of near equality with his erstwhile leaders, Jean-François and Biassou.

February 14, 1794, the French Republic abolished slavery, and accepted black and mulatto deputies from St. Domingue in the National Assembly. This apparently made a profound impression on Toussaint.

Under siege from Spanish forces and from the British, who had also invaded the island, the French governor Laveau began to engage in secret communications with Toussaint. Undoubtedly disappointed by restoration of slavery in the colony by both the Spanish and British, and promised promotion to general in the French Army. Toussaint made a *volte-face* and soon recaptured portions of the colony which were in Spanish hands.

Meanwhile, the British invaded Port-au-Prince. They were supported by white royalists bent on reestablishing slavery. Two mulatto generals, André Rigaud and Villatte, held the south of the island and one of its major ports, Cap Haitien, while Toussaint was firmly in control of the center. With support of the black population fearing reenslavement by the Spanish and British, he soon moved against the mulatto general Villatte, who had imprisoned the French governor, marched to the governor's rescue, and was given the title of lieutenant governor of the colony.

In May 1796 the French sent commissioners to try to reestablish their authority. Under Sonthonax, they expelled many mulatto leaders, including Villatte. Following consolidation of Sonthonax's power, he and Toussaint were the two most powerful men in the colony, although the mulatto General Rigaud ran a virtually autonomous state in the South.

Toussaint, bearing the title of general-in-chief of the St. Domingue Army, and with alliances with former planters, emigrés, and royalists, marched on the Cap and forced Sonthonax to return to France. His replacement, Hédouville, had instructions to regain control over both Toussaint and Rigaud and to support both against the English, who still held Port-au-Prince and the western part of the island.

The English were routed in the West, and Toussaint encircled Port-au-Prince. The British general quickly agreed to evacuate peacefully if Toussaint would agree to a truce. Joining Rigaud, Toussaint was quickly able to rout the remaining British forces.

An insurrection broke out against Hédouville after rumors circulated that he intended to restore slavery, and he was forced to flee. Toussaint then defeated Rigaud and his mulattoes, and in February 1801 they marched into Spanish Santo Domingo and won control of all Hispaniola. Even though Haiti was, de facto, a sovereign nation, Toussaint refused to declare it independent from France.

Toussaint developed international alliances, particularly with the United States, and with President John Adams' assistance negotiated a treaty with Britain. Adams' help with supplies and ships was crucial in his defeat of Rigaud.

Toussaint organized a military administrative system and prepared a constitution that named him Governor General for Life. He took over land left by former French and mulatto owners, and instituted a system by which agricultural workers were guaranteed modest wages, medical care, and housing, but were not free to move about. Abandoned plantations were leased to army officers and senior government officials.

Toussaint's victory was short-lived. Napoleon Bonaparte soon launched an invasion of the colony, led by his brother-in-law, General Charles Leclerc. Assisted by Rigaud and other mulatto leaders, Leclerc landed 22,000 veteran troops on the island, gaining spectacular victories. Toussaint surrendered on May 5, 1802, after most of his lieutenants had joined the French. He was transported to France and imprisoned until his death.

BIBLIOGRAPHY

Beard, John R. *The Life of Toussaint L'Ouverture*. Westport, Conn.: Negro University
    Press, 1970.
James, C.L.R. *The Black Jacobins*. London: Allison and Busby, 1980.
Moran, Charles. *Black Triumvirate*. New York: Exposition, 1957.
Syme, Ronald. *Toussaint: The Black Liberator*. New York: William Morrow, 1971.
Watman, Percy. *The Black Napoleon: The Story of Toussaint L'Ouverture*. New York:
    Harcourt Brace, 1931.

PERCY C. HINTZEN

LUIS, JUAN (1940–   ), an elected governor of the United States Virgin Islands,
was born in Vieques, Puerto Rico, but his family moved to St. Croix when he
was two months old. He was educated in Christiansted public schools and at the
Inter American University in Puerto Rico. After serving in the United States
Army, he taught primary school and held several positions in management of
local businesses. Between 1972 and 1974 he served as insular senator, elected
by the Independent Citizens Movement. He was that party's successful candidate
for lieutenant governor, and in 1978 he was elected governor.

BIBLIOGRAPHY

Sharpless, Richard E. "Virgin Islands of the United States," in Robert J. Alexander
    (ed.). *Political Parties of the Americas*. Vol. 2. Westport, Conn.: Greenwood
    Press, 1982.
Personalities Caribbean. 7th ed. Kingston, Jamaica: Personalities Ltd., 1983.

RICHARD E. SHARPLESS

LUIS, WASHINGTON (1869–1957), was the last Brazilian president of the
"old republic." Born in the state of Rio de Janeiro, the scion of a distinguished
family that had served the empire of Dom Pedro II* in many important posts,
he received a law degree from the São Paulo law faculty in 1891 and won his
first elected post in 1897 as a member of the Batatais Town Council. In 1900
he moved to the state capital and married a wealthy coffee heiress.

   Washington Luis was elected in 1904 to the state assembly as representative
of the Paulista Republican Party (PRP), and two years later he was appointed
state secretary of justice, serving until 1912. In 1912 he was elected again to
the state legislature, but the next year the city council of São Paulo chose him
as mayor. In 1917 he was returned to office in a direct election. He earned a
reputation as a tough law and order administrator by smashing the strikes that
swept the city.

   Elected governor of São Paulo in 1920, two years later Washington Luis threw
the support of his state to the candidacy of the Minas Gerais politician Arthur
Bernardes* for the presidency, with the tacit understanding that the Minas Gerais
politicians would suport a Paulista in 1926. Washington Luis was virtually
unopposed as the presidental candidate in 1926.

As president, Luis was trapped by the economic crash of 1929, which destroyed the São Paulo coffee economy. In his effort to salvage the economic fortunes of São Paulo, he decided to support another Paulista, Governor Julio Prestes, in the presidential election of 1930. He thus broke the unwritten agreement of alternating the presidency between Minas Gerais and São Paulo. The Minas Gerais politicians sought out another candidate, Governor Getúlio Vargas* of Rio Grande do Sul, which resulted in a bitterly contested election.

Putting the entire force of the national administration behind his candidate, Washington Luis managed to gain a victory for Prestes, but created the conditions that led to the October Revolution, which brought Getúlio Vargas to power.

Washington Luis left the country after the revolution and went into exile in Europe and the United States, not returning to Brazil again until 1947.

BIBLIOGRAPHY

Dicionario Histórico-Biográfico Brasileiro 1930–1983. Vol. 3. Editora Forense Universitaria Ltda., 1984.

JORDAN YOUNG

LUSINCHI, JAIME (1924–), was the fifth member of Acción Democrática (AD) to be elected president of Venezuela. He studied medicine at the Central University in Caracas and the University of the East. While still very young, he became a local leader of AD in the state of Anzoátegui, being elected president of the state legislature in 1948. From 1948 to 1952 he served as regional secretary general of Acción Democrática, but then was arrested and exiled by the Military Junta then in power. He spent the next six years in Argentina, Chile, and the United States.

Upon returning to Venezuela after the fall of Pérez Jiménez,* Jaime Lusinchi became a member of the National Executive Committee of AD, and served as the party's international secretary from 1958 to 1961. He was a member of the Chamber of Deputies in 1959–1967 and subsequently was elected to the Senate. 222 President of the Acción Democrática parliamentary group from 1968 to 1978, he was secretary general of the party between 1980 and 1983, until he became AD's candidate for president.

Jaime Lusinchi decisively defeated ex-President Rafal Caldera Rodríguez* of the Social Christian Copei Party in the 1983 election. He took office in February 1984.

BIBLIOGRAPHY

Lusinchi, Jaime. *Frente el Futuro*. Caracas: Comisión Electoral, 1983.
New York Times, December 6, 1983.
Personal Contacts.

ROBERT J. ALEXANDER

M

MACEO Y GRAJALES, ANTONIO (1845–1896), was one of the preeminent military leaders of the Cuban Wars of Independence from 1868 until his death. Maceo was from a free Negro family in Santiago, Cuba, received little formal education, and went to work at the age of 16. In his late teens he began to show interest in politics and joined a group of merchants and political activists in Santiago who were dissatisfied with Spanish rule.

Maceo, possessing the most dash and brilliance of all the military leaders of the Wars of Independence, became a folk hero to Cuba's black population. He proved to be a great guerrilla fighter, displaying audacity and willingness to take all risks in exercising daring military maneuvers. However, always willing to subordinate his enormous power and popularity to the cause of the Republic in Arms, he was loyal to his military superior, Máximo Gómez.*

Maceo quickly worked his way up through the ranks of the revolutionary army. From March 1873 through mid–1875 he won a series of major battles in campaigns in eastern Cuba. He instilled in his men notions of duty, discipline, and honor, and the idea of loyalty to civilian authority and to the larger goals of the revolution. In return, his men displayed respect and love for him. He was promoted to brigadier general in 1872 and just prior to the end of the Ten Years' War, in 1878, was promoted to major general.

Along with Calixto García Iñiguéz*, Maceo rejected the pact ending the Ten Years' War. With the collaboration of García, Maceo launched the so-called Guerra Chiquita (1879–1880), which failed. From 1880 until 1895, Maceo spent time in Haiti, Honduras, Mexico, Panama, and Costa Rica. In 1884 he met the great spiritual and intellectual leader of the revolutionary movement, José Martí.*

Although Maceo was rejected in the assignment of several military commands by both Martí and Gómez, he nevertheless played a crucial role in the fighting during 1895 and 1896. Prior to his death at the hands of the Spanish in December 1896, Maceo had commanded the triumphant Army of Liberation as it crossed Cuba from east to west scoring major victories against the Spanish Army.

BIBLIOGRAPHY

Foner, Philip. *Antonio Maceo*. New York: Monthly Review Press, 1977.
Pando, Magdalen M. *Cuba's Freedom Fighter*. Gainesville, Fla.: Felicity Press, 1980.
Pérez, Louis A., Jr. *Cuba Between Empires 1879–1902*. Pittsburgh: University of Pittsburgh Press, 1983.
Ruíz, Ramón Eduardo. *Cuba: The Making of a Revolution*. Amherst: University of Massachusetts Press, 1968.

STEPHEN J. WRIGHT

MACHADO, GUSTAVO (1898–   ), one of the earliest Communist leaders of Venezuela, for four decades was that country's most outstanding Marxist-Leninist. He was born of an aristocratic family of Caracas. In high school in the upper class Catholic German School, by 1914 he was already a student leader. He suffered his first year in jail when the General Association of Students was suppressed by Juan Vicente Gómez.* In 1919 he took part in an aborted civil-military plot against Gómez and fled to Bonaire.

Machado spent the next 17 years in exile in the United States, France, Cuba, Mexico, and Colombia. In Cuba in 1924 he was one of the founders of the Communist Party of Cuba. In Mexico he was one of the founders of the pro-Communist Venezuelan Revolutionary Party and of the Anti-Imperialist League of the Americas. In 1928 he spent a short while in Nicaragua with the guerrilla band of Augusto César Sandino.* In 1929 Machado joined an expedition that seized control of the Dutch Island of Curaçao for several days, but failed in efforts to launch an invasion of Venezuela.

Upon his return home, Machado sought to unite those who claimed to be followers of the Communist Party but did not succeed. He was one of the 43 people deported in February 1937 by the government of President Eleazar López Contreras.* He again spent several years abroad. Upon his return home, he was involved in the one dissident movement within Communist ranks in which he was ever to participate, but returned to the orthodox party in 1946. He was a member of the 1946 Constituent Assembly and the Chamber of Deputies in 1948. He was Communist candidate for president in 1947.

Machado was editor of the Communists' daily *Tribuna Popular*, which he continued to put out for a year and a half after overthrow of the government of President Rómulo Gallegos* in November 1948. In April 1950 he was again arrested and later was deported to Mexico.

With the fall of the Pérez Jiménez* dictatorship, he returned to Venezuela. Elected to the Chamber of Deputies in 1958, he reportedly opposed his party's recourse to guerrilla war at the end of 1961 but was jailed in September 1963, as a result of the guerrilla campaign, and stayed in jail until 1968.

Gustavo Machado continued to be active in the leadership of the Communist Party after his last release from jail. The party had a national celebration in 1978 on his eightieth birthday.

BIBLIOGRAPHY

Alexander, Robert J. *The Communist Party of Venezuela*. Stanford, Calif.: Hoover Institution Press, 1969.
Fuenmayor, Juan Bautista. *Historia de la Venezuela Política Contemporanea, 1899–1969*. Tomo II and Tomo III, Vol. 1. Caracas: 1976.

ROBERT J. ALEXANDER

MACHADO Y MORALES, GERARDO (1871–1939), was president of Cuba from 1925 to 1933, heading the first dictatorship in the Republic. He had a very poor childhood, working for many years in a butcher shop; prior to the War of Independence in 1895, he and his father were cattle rustlers. He had little opportunity for a formal education. During the years immediately before he entered politics, he managed the Cuban branch of General Electric.

Machado entered politics as mayor of Santa Clara. Later, he joined the cabinet of José Miguel Gómez,* where he gained a reputation for toughness when he suppressed a strike of sewage workers. In 1924 he was nominated for the presidency by the Liberal Party and won handily.

The first two years of Machado's presidency indicated that he might purge the corruption of his predecessors. His first cabinet contained many highly respected men. He proposed a public works bill that called for building a central highway and construction of a national capitol. In 1926 Machado sponsored the Verdeja Act, which was intended to control sugar production and prevent the periodically disastrous drop in sugar prices. He also pressed for construction of much needed technical schools. In late 1926 Gerardo Machado was one of the most popular presidents in the history of Cuba.

In 1927 Machado, riding a wave of national popularity persuaded a compliant legislature to reform the Constitution to permit him to run for reelection in 1928 and, if successful, to serve a six-year term. This produced a wave of protest from students at the University of Havana. As Machado's rule became more strong-handed, the labor unions and the new Communist Party also opposed his regime. However, his prestige soared in 1928 when he hosted the Sixth International Conference of American States and entertained U.S. President Calvin Coolidge. Later in 1928 Machado was reelected, after barring his only serious rival, Carlos Mendieta y Montefur,* from participating in the election.

As Machado began his second term, the economy appeared robust, and he enjoyed the strong support of Washington. However, with the onset of the Depression, sugar prices plummeted from 2.18 cents in 1928 to 1.23 cents per pound in 1930. The economy and the nation were devastated.

In September 1930 protests exploded at the University of Havana, led by the left-leaning Student Directorate. Machado responded by closing the campus and suspending constitutional guarantees. Earlier, he had suspended public meetings by political groups not legally approved by the government. When the army broke up one such "illegal" meeting, eight people were killed. In November 1930 nationwide anti-Machado protests led to the closing of all Cuban schools.

Two months later Machado had the entire membership of the Student Directorate arrested and imprisoned.

In August 1931 two leaders of the more moderate opposition, Carlos Mendieta and Mario García Menocal,* initiated an unsuccessful rebellion against Machado. Also in 1931 Machado created the Porra, a special paramilitary force to dispose of enemies of the government. For its part, the secret political organization, ABC, sought through the use of terror to counter the violence of Machado and his Porra. Throughout 1932 violence became commonplace in the streets of Cuba's cities. Constitutional guarantees were suspended again in mid-June.

The new U.S. president, Franklin Roosevelt, appointed Sumner Welles as U.S. ambassador to Cuba, with the mission of bringing stability to Cuba by mediating between Machado and the factions opposing him. After weeks of negotiations failed to find a solution that would keep Machado in power, the beleaguered dictator fled the country in August 1933.

BIBLIOGRAPHY

Aguilar, Luis E. *Cuba 1933: Prologue to Revolution*. Ithaca, N.Y.: Cornell University Press, 1972.
Domínguez, Jorge I. *Cuba: Order and Revolution*. Cambridge, Mass.: Harvard University Press, 1978.
Gellman, Irwin F. *Roosevelt and Batista*. Albuquerque: University of New Mexico Press, 1973.
Ruíz, Ramón Eduardo. *Cuba: The Making of a Nation*. New York: W. W. Norton, 1968.
Thomas, Hugh. *Cuba: The Pursuit of Freedom*. New York: Harper and Row, 1971.
                                                    STEPHEN J. WRIGHT

MACIVER RODRÍGUEZ, ENRIQUE (1845–1922), was a major figure in the Radical Party of Chile for more than half a century. He got his law degree in 1869. In 1876 he was first elected to the Chamber of Deputies in which he served until 1900. The rest of his life, MacIver was a senator and, on several occasions, a minister. He signed the document "deposing" President José Manuel Balmaceda Fernández* and spent most of the 1891 civil war in exile.

MacIver, a very distinguished lawyer and a large landowner, led the "free enterprise" faction of the Radical Party. The faction was defeated in the party's Third Congress in 1906, which committed the party to an ill-defined "socialism." In spite of that defeat, MacIver remained in the party. As late as 1920 he was one of three contestants for the presidential nomination of the Liberal Alliance, of which the Radical Party was the core, losing out to Arturo Alessandri Palma.*

BIBLIOGRAPHY

Alexander, Robert J. "Chile," in Robert J. Alexander (ed.). *Political Parties of the Americas*. Vol. 1. Westport, Conn.: Greenwood Press, 1982.

Cortes, Lia, and Jordi Fuentes. *Diccionario Político de Chile*. Santiago: Editorial Orbe, 1967.

ROBERT J. ALEXANDER

MADERO, FRANCISCO I. (1873–1913), the father of the Mexican Revolution, was the first president elected after the end of the dictatorship of Porfirio Díaz.* He was born in Parras, Coahuila, into one of the most powerful families in Mexico. From 1887 to 1892 he studied economics in France, and then he spent one year studying agriculture at the University of California in Berkeley. Returning to Mexico, he developed the Laguna Ranching District in Coahuila. In 1908 Madero published *The Presidential Succession in 1910*, a call for new leadership to replace the 35-year rule of Porfirio Díaz. In 1909 Madero established the National Antireelectionist Party, which nominated him as a presidential candidate.

Madero was arrested in Monterrey in June 1910 and in October fled to the United States, where he issued his Plan of San Luís, calling for armed struggle against the government. That fighting began the Revolution on November 20, 1910. Madero returned to Mexico in February 1911. Díaz resigned on May 25 and went into exile. Madero formed the Constitutional Progressive Party, which nominated him for the presidency and José Piño Suárez of Yucatán for the vice-presidency. Madero occupied the presidency from November 6, 1911, until he resigned at the point of a gun on February 19, 1913. His chief reforms had been to sell public lands and to make loans to communal farms (*ejidos*). He also created a Department of Labor. Madero lost the support of General Emiliano Zapata* when he failed to pursue a vigorous land reform program.

Madero made a fatal mistake by appointing General Victoriano Huerta* as his chief of staff. Huerta rewarded him by ordering Madero and Piño Suárez shot in the back "while trying to escape" on February 22, 1913. Madero in death became the apostle of the Revolution, and his slogan, "Effective Suffrage, No Reelection," the battle cry of the Revolution.

BIBLIOGRAPHY

Cabrera, Luis. *Veinte Años Después*. Mexico City: Ediciones Botas, 1937.

Cumberland, Charles C. *Mexican Revolution, Genesis Under Madero*. Austin: University of Texas Press, 1952.

García Granados, Ricardo. *Historia de Mexico Desde 1867 Hasta la Caída de Huerta*. Vol. 2. Mexico City: Editorial Jus, 1956.

Ross, Stanley R. *Francisco I. Madero, Apostle of Mexican Democracy*. New York: Columbia University Press, 1956.

Valadés, José C. *Imaginación y Realidad de Francisco I. Madero*. Mexico City: Editorial Porrua, 1960.

MARVIN ALISKY

MAGLOIRE, PAUL EUGÈNE (1907–   ), was Haiti's thirty-third president. He was born to a black elite family in Cap Haitien, attended primary schools there, and graduated from Lycee Philippe Guerrier. He taught at his alma mater for a year and then enrolled in Haiti's military academy, graduating in 1931. Later, he took a law degree from the national university.

After graduation from military school, Magloire served as aide-de-camp to President Sténio Vincent,* adjutant to several regional military commanders, governor of the national prison, and commandant of the Palace Guard. When, in January 1946, opposition to the oppressive and corrupt regime of President Élie Lescot* mounted, Magloire joined with two mulatto military leaders to depose the president. He was instrumental in securing the election of President Dumarsais Estimé,* the representative of black intellectuals and other black elites. Magloire was named minister of interior, after which he returned to his position as commander of the Palace Guards.

In 1950, when Estimé sought to remain in office in defiance of the existing constitution, Magloire joined a military coup. The Executive Military Committee, of which Magloire was part, then dismissed Parliament and, in a revised constitution, for the first time provided for the president to be elected by universal male franchise. Magloire was overwhelmingly elected president in December 1950, with the backing of the military, the Roman Catholic Church, and the United States.

Magloire failed to pursue policies of reform implemented in the early years of his predecessor. He concentrated on economic development, negotiating an agreement with the United States for assistance in soil conservation, cattle farming, drainage, and irrigation; and formulated a five-year plan which would be financed by foreign aid, concentrating on improvement of transportation and port facilities. His regime saw the opening of bauxite mines by Reynolds Metals, as well as development of a tourist industry and attraction of foreign investment.

In 1954, however, the coffee crop began to fail, and in October a vicious hurricane destroyed crops and property. At the same time, government projects were proving more costly than anticipated, and there was growing evidence of corruption among members of Magloire's family and some charges of politically motivated killings. A dispute arose over the date when the president's term legally ended, with Magloire insisting on May 1957 and members of the growing opposition claiming May 1956.

Magloire was soon faced with intense opposition. A student insurrection spread to strikes by unions. In November 1956 Magloire banned all public meetings and political broadcasts and publications; he finally declared a state of siege and dissolved the legislature. At the time, he decided to leave Haiti for Jamaica, but he ultimately settled in New York.

BIBLIOGRAPHY

Diederich, B., and Al Burt. *Papa Doc: The Truth About Haiti Today*. New York: McGraw-Hill, 1969.
Heinl, R. D., and N. G. Heinl. *Written in Blood*. Boston: Houghton Mifflin, 1978.
Nicholls, David. *Haiti in Caribbean Context*. London: Macmillan Co., 1985.
Rotberg, Robert I. *Haiti: The Politics of Squalor*. Boston: Houghton Mifflin, 1971.

Weinstein, Brian, and Aaron Segal. *Haiti: Political Failures, Cultural Successes*. New
    York: Praeger, 1984.

PERCY C. HINTZEN

MALESPÍN, FRANCISCO (?–1846), was a major leader of the Conservatives
of El Salvador in the 1840s. Little is known about his early life, but by early
1841 he was commander-in-chief of the army of El Salvador and imposed the
provisional presidency of Juan Lindo. He joined with Guatemala, Honduras,
and Nicaragua to overthrow Francisco Morazán,* the president of Central
America.

In 1844 Malespín was elected president of El Salvador by the National As-
sembly. Soon afterward, he unsuccessfully invaded Guatemala and then attacked
Nicaragua, where he finally captured the city of Léon in January 1845. His
brutality in this campaign alienated even his Salvadorean followers, and the
National Assembly deposed him in February 1845. Malespín then took refuge
in Honduras, where he mobilized forces to invade El Salvador but was defeated.
Some time later, when he returned to El Salvador, he was lynched by a mob in
San Fernando.

BIBLIOGRAPHY

Enciclopedia Universal Ilustrada Europeo Americana, Barcelona: José Espasa e Hijos.

ROBERT J. ALEXANDER

MANLEY, MICHAEL NORMAN (1924–   ), served as prime minister of
Jamaica between 1972 and 1980. The son of Norman Washington Manley,* he
followed in his footsteps in high school at Jamaica College, graduating in 1942.
He then went to McGill University in Canada, but enlisted in the Royal Canadian
Air Force and served as a pilot officer. In 1945 he entered the London School
of Economics, graduating with a B.Sc. in economics in 1949, and spent an
additional year doing graduate work. In 1950–1951 he worked as a freelance
journalist for the BBC.

Manley returned to Jamaica in 1951, became associate editor of *Public Opinion*, the semiofficial organ of the People's National Party (PNP), and wrote a
political column for it. In 1952 he was elected to the National Executive Council
of the PNP.

In 1952 Manley joined the staff of the National Workers Union (NWU), formed
under PNP influence. At the time, the largest labor group was the Bustamante
Industrial Trade Union (BITU), aligned with its founder Sir William Alexander
Bustamante* and his Jamaica Labour Party. Manley assumed the post of NWU
Sugar Supervisor in August 1953. In 1954 his efforts were largely responsible
for an NWU victory in representational elections at three major sugar estates.
In two years, the NWU support among sugar workers became equal to that of
the BITU. Manley became Island Supervisor and first vice president of the NWU.

Manley was credited with significant innovations in union negotiations. A bargaining victory over Aluminum Company of Canada in 1953, in which wages became tied to the ability of the mining companies to pay, resulted in a 300-percent wage increase for the workers. In 1962 Manley proved to a Commission of Inquiry that the sugar industry had had $4 million in unreported profits between 1945 and 1950, and sugar workers were awarded $2.5 million. Manley became president of the Caribbean Bauxite, Mineworkers, and Metal Workers Federation in 1964.

Michael Manley served as an appointed PNP member of the Senate between 1962 and 1967. When the number of constituencies was increased in 1967, he decided to contest an electoral seat and narrowly won election to the House of Representatives. When illness forced his father to retire from politics in 1969, Manley was elected PNP president and Leader of the Opposition. His dynamic personality, honesty, and sincerity, together with his political program helped return the PNP to office in 1972, after two terms in opposition, by the biggest victory margin to date by a political party in Jamaica. Upon assuming power, Manley moved more decidedly to the left, reemphasizing that his party embraced the philosophy of democratic socialism. The PNP won an even greater landslide victory in 1976.

Between 1972 and 1980 the Manley government made significant innovations both domestically and in foreign policy, embarking on a kind of Third World "New Deal." He taxed the country's foreign-owned bauxite producers to secure revenue to finance domestic reform and development, and he encouraged the local private sector to become less reliant on ties to the metropole. He handed land titles to small farmers and squatters. In addition, he built feeder roads and supported a program of rural electrification and irrigation; established a literacy program for adults and set up cooperatives for the sugar workers; set a minimum wage law and maternity leave with pay for female workers; established a commitment to nonaligned and other Third World countries; and took special interest in supporting liberation struggles in Southern Africa. He insisted on his country's sovereign right to establish relations with whomever it pleased, and he developed relations with Cuba and China.

Manley's government faced considerable political and economic retaliation, primarily from the United States. Beset by economic problems, partly the result of the worldwide economic crisis, Manley made a number of policy mistakes that resulted in loss of confidence in the economy by domestic investors and efforts at economic destabilization, principally by the United States. Manley was finally forced to accept the International Monetary Fund's stringent terms to keep Jamaica's economy afloat. The consequences were politically disastrous. Facing a campaign of political violence, which resulted in the death of over 750 persons during the latter half of the 1970s, his government began to appear unable to maintain order. His party lost the 1980 elections to the Jamaica Labour Party headed by a pro-U.S. conservative politician, Edward P.G. Seaga.* Manley became Leader of the Opposition.

In December 1983 Manley and the PNP refused to participate in national elections, in protest against violation of an agreement between the ruling party and the PNP about the way general elections would be called. Although Manley remained leader of the PNP, this decision left the party without elected representatives in the Jamaican House of Assembly.

BIBLIOGRAPHY

Arawak, Christopher (pseud). *Jamaica's Michael Manley: Messiah. . . . Meddler. . . . or Marionette?* Miami: Sir Henry Morgan Press, 1980.
Manley, Michael. *Struggle in the Periphery.* London: Third World Media Ltd., 1982.
Personal Interviews.
Stone, Carl. *Perspectives on Jamaica in the Seventies.* Kingston: Jamaica Publishing House, 1981.
Will, W. Marvin. "Jamaica." *Collier's 1984 Yearbook.* New York: Macmillan Co., 1983.

PERCY C. HINTZEN AND W. MARVIN WILL

MANLEY, NORMAN WASHINGTON (1893–1969), was the founder of Jamaica's first national party, the People's National Party (PNP). Of Irish and black descent, he was born in rural Jamaica and grew up in modest circumstances. After graduation in 1913 from Jamaica College, he taught school for nearly two years before leaving Jamaica on a Rhodes Scholarship at Oxford University. His university studies were interrupted by World War I, and he served in an artillery regiment of the British Army. Returning to Oxford, he received a bachelor's degree in 1920 and was called to the bar at Gray's Inn in 1921. Back in Jamaica by 1922, Manley rocketed to prominence as a lawyer and was appointed King's Counsel within only ten years.

The 1930s were a period of growing unrest in the West Indies, including Jamaica. An incident on May 2, 1938, in which rioting strikers were bloodily suppressed by the police, was the beginning of serious labor and political turmoil. Manley was retained by the West Indian Sugar Company to defend its actions against the rioters. Shortly afterward, however, his cousin, William Alexander Bustamante,* the recognized labor leader at the time, was arrested, and Manley represented Bustamante, whose release he secured.

Manley led in forming the People's National Party which, from its inception on September 19, 1938, had a socialist and nationalist ideology. The PNP became the model for nationalist parties throughout the West Indies in the postwar era. For a time, the Bustamante Industrial Trade Union (BITU), headed by Bustamante, served as labor wing of the party.

The two-party system was inaugurated in 1943, with formation of the Jamaica Labour Party (JLP) by Bustamante, who had fallen out with Manley. At the same time, the PNP formed the Trade Union Congress. Largely as a result of the PNP's efforts, universal suffrage was granted for the 1944 elections under a new constitution. The PNP lost the 1944 elections to the JLP, with Manley losing in his own constituency. The PNP also lost the election of 1949, despite winning a majority of the popular vote. Manley, however, was elected and was Opposition Leader between 1949 and 1955. He campaigned for a West Indian Federation as logical extension of Jamaican nationalism, and he became one of the most committed West Indian leaders to this cause.

In 1953 a ministerial system of government was inaugurated, and two years later Manley led his PNP to victory over Bustamante's JLP. He became chief minister and promptly began the task of reforming the economy, agriculture, and education. He secured increased revenue from the bauxite companies operating within Jamaica. There was substantial economic growth, particularly in manufacturing and tourism. He also pressed Britain for full internal self-government which was granted in 1959, at which time he became premier.

Manley contributed significantly to the inauguration of the West Indies Federation in 1958, even though the loosely linked federal party with which his PNP was associated and over which he presided lost badly in Jamaica to Bustamante's Jamaica Labour Party. Despite this defeat, Manley led the PNP to victory in the 1959 national elections.

Almost immediately, however, Bustamante called for Jamaica's secession from the federation. Manley agreed to call a referendum in 1961, and the electorate voted overwhelmingly for secession. The PNP and JLP jointly prepared the independence constitution, and Britain agreed to grant independence after elections were held in 1962. Manley and the PNP lost the elections, relegating him to Leader of the Opposition when the country received its independence in August 1962, under a JLP government headed by Bustamante as prime minister.

In opposition, Manley assumed the role of elder statesman and began to restructure his party to win back the support it had lost over the years. He decided to return to greater emphasis on democratic socialism, although supporting some private enterprises, as well as joint ventures between the private and state sectors. Manley resigned his position as party leader and member of the House of Representatives shortly before his death.

Norman Manley was declared a National Hero of Jamaica in 1969, the year of his death.

BIBLIOGRAPHY

Manley, Norman W. *Manley and the New Jamaica: Selected Speeches and Writings, 1938–68*, edited by Rex Nettleford. London: Longmans Caribbean, 1971.

Munroe, Trevor. *The Politics of Constitutional Decolonization: Jamaica 1944–62*. Mona, Jamaica: Institute for Social and Economic Research, 1972.

Nettleford, Rex. *Manley and the Politics of Jamaica: Toward an Analysis of Political Change in Jamaica, 1938–1968*. Mona, Jamaica: Institute for Social and Economic Research, 1971.

Sherlock, Philip. *Norman Manley: A Biography*. London: Macmillan Co., 1980.

Wynter, Sylvia. *Jamaica's National Heroes*. Kingston: National Trust Commission, 1971.

PERCY C. HINTZEN AND W. MARVIN WILL

MARAJ, BHADASE SAGAN (1919–1971), was the first and most important of the powerful Trinidadian leaders who transformed the East Indian community into a politically powerful bloc. The son of a leader of a Hindu faction in the sugar belt, Maraj was only minimally educated, but he amassed a fortune after World War II through disposal of surplus war goods from American military bases on the island.

Giving liberal financial support to the poor, initiating and financing Hindu schools and temples, organizing Hindu festivals, and lending his support to striking East Indian workers, Maraj acquired a huge following of loyal supporters and admirers. He was first elected to political office in 1950, as an independent. In 1953 he formed the Peoples Democratic Party (PDP) and by 1955 it was the best organized and most powerful political organization in the country. In 1953 Maraj became president general of the Federation of Sugar Workers and Cane Farmers, which represented the sugar workers of the country, the majority of whom were Hindus.

Postponement of general elections from 1955 to 1956 allowed the formation and consolidation of the Peoples National Movement (PNM) under Dr. Eric Williams.* The emergence of this party, the economically and politically conservative policies of Maraj, and his strong Hindu identity resulted in defeat of the PDP in the elections of 1956.

Cognizant of his narrow political base, Maraj agreed to enter into an alliance for the 1958 elections for the West Indies Parliament. This effort, initiated by Sir William Alexander Bustamante* of Jamaica, was a confederation of national parties within the Parliament of the West Indies Federation. Maraj entered the new Trinidadian unit, the Democratic Labour Party (DLP), of the confederal coalition.

Although Maraj did not hold an executive position in the "new" DLP, it was clear that his followers were the most powerful element in the Trinidadian coalition. An extremely strong showing among the rural Hindu population won the DLP six of ten Trinidad seats in the federal Parliament. By early 1958 he and the PDP had almost full control of the DLP, and the party was recognized as the official Opposition in the Trinidadian Parliament. Maraj was unanimously elected parliamentary head of the DLP.

Although Maraj's power to mobilize the Hindu rural masses was legendary, his exclusively Hindu identity was too narrow to mount a successful national campaign, in view of the multiethnic character of the DLP leadership. In addition, his reliance on machine politics and patronage was a political embarrassment to many of his colleagues, while his lack of education and social and intellectual sophistication proved anathema to the middle classes, both East Indian and non-East Indian, who were potential DLP supporters. Severe illness in 1959 made him relatively inactive, with long periods of absence from Parliament. This permitted malcontents in the DLP to organize his ouster. Dr. Rudranath Capildeo* accepted an offer to become leader of the party.

Maraj left the DLP in 1971 to form the Democratic Liberation Party. He decided to contest the elections called in 1971 by a government recovering from a period of intense civil opposition, when almost all the rest of the political opposition called for a boycott of the elections. Maraj's political demise was made evident when his new party garnered support from only 4.22 percent of registered voters.

BIBLIOGRAPHY

Brereton, Bridget. *A History of Modern Trinidad 1783–1962*. Port of Spain: Heinemann, 1981.

Klass, Morton. *East Indians in Trinidad: A Study of Cultural Persistence*. New York: Columbia University Press, 1961.

Malik, Y. K. *East Indians in Trinidad: A Study in Minority Politics*. London: Oxford University Press, 1971.

Ryan, Selwyn. *Race and Nationalism in Trinidad and Tobago*. Toronto: University of Toronto Press, 1972.

PERCY C. HINTZEN AND W. MARVIN WILL

MARIÁTEGUI, JOSÉ CARLOS (1894–1930), Peru's major Marxist theoretician, was born in Moquequa in southern Peru. Shortly after he began his primary school in Huacho, he suffered a blow to his knee which left him with a permanent limp. At 15 he had to abandon his studies in Lima to work as a copy boy in *La Prensa* to help support his family. In time he became its parliamentary chronicler. Dissatisfied with the conservative trends of *La Prensa*, in 1918 he joined the staff of *El Tiempo* and established the journal *Nuestra Epoca*. The following year he founded the daily *La Razón*, in which he openly supported the University Reform and the 1919 general strike. President Augusto B. Leguía* appointed him "Peruvian Agent of News, Propaganda and Publicity" in Italy in late 1919 in order to keep Mariátegui out of Peru for a few years.

During the four years he spent in Europe Mariátegui embraced Marxism, married Anna Chiape in Florence, had a son, and learned French, Italian, and German. Back in Lima in 1923, he lectured at the González Prada* People's University at the invitation of his friend Víctor Raúl Haya de la Torre.* Before Haya was sent into exile, he designated Mariátegui as his successor in the editorship of the journal *Claridad*. Following the deportation of Haya, Mariátegui became the outstanding leftist personality in the country. As González Prada and Haya before him, Mariátegui believed in a united front of workers and intellectuals. In 1926, in a cooperative venture with his brother Julio César, he established the Minerva publishing house and bookstore. There he published *7 ensayos de interpretación de la realidad peruana* (1928), which was of particular significance in influencing both the Marxist and non-Marxist left in Latin America.

Mariátegui had returned from Europe with the thought of founding a leftist publication to stimulate new ideas and promote socialism. He turned out the first issue of *Amauta* in September 1926. In November 1928 he started publication of *Labor*, a newspaper that prepared the ground for founding the General Confederation of Peruvian Workers (CGTP). After polemics with Haya de la Torre, Mariátegui founded the Socialist Party of Peru (PSP). The party was "a blend of Aprismo and Communism," according to Comintern agents attending the first meeting of Latin American Communist Parties held in Buenos Aires in 1929. Mariátegui sent a working paper on his Marxist ideas to the meeting, and at the gathering he received a harsh rebuke for having established a socialist party instead of an outright Communist Party. Frustrated, Mariátegui resigned as secretary general of the PSP just before he died.

Mariátegui is widely recognized as one of the few important Marxist theorists to have appeared in Latin America.

BIBLIOGRAPHY

Carnero Checa, Genaro. *La acción escrita: José Carlos Mariátegui, periodista*. Lima: Biblioteca Amauta, 1980.
Chang-Rodríguez, Eugenio. *Poética e ideología en José Carlos Mariátegui*. Madrid: José Porrua Turanza, 1983.
Garrels, Elizabeth. "The Young Mariátegui and His World, 1894–1919." Ph.D. diss., Harvard University, 1974.
Kromkowski, John A. "The Emergence and Ongoing Presence of J. C. Mariátegui in Peru and the Soviet Union," Ph.D. diss., University of Notre Dame, 1972.
Melis, Antonio (ed.). *José Carlos Mariátegui: Correspondencia*. Lima: Biblioteca Amauta, 1984.

EUGENIO CHANG-RODRÍGUEZ

MARINELLO, JUAN (1898–1977), was one of the top intellectuals of the prerevolutionary Communist movement in Cuba. Son of a wealthy sugar family, he received a law degree from the University of Havana in 1920, studied at the Central University of Madrid, and returned to Havana to take a doctorate in 1929. He held posts as professor of modern languages at the University of Havana, professor of Spanish-American history and literature at the National University of Mexico, and professor of Spanish and Cuban literature at the Escuela Normal para Maestros in Havana. He was editor of a number of literary and political periodicals, and carried out extensive research on the political and social philosophies of José Martí,* whom he concluded was not a disciple of Marx.

Juan Marinello fought alongside the radical students of the 1920s to protest excesses of the Alfredo Zayas y Alfonso* and Gustavo Machado* regimes. He was imprisoned and fled to Spain, France, and Mexico from 1930 to 1933. Back in Cuba, he organized the Unión Revolucionaria as a legal front for the outlawed Communist Party. In 1939 Fulgencio Batista y Zaldívar* allowed the merger of the two groups as the Unión Revolucionaria Comunista, of which Marinello became president.

In 1940 Marinello was a Communist member of the Constituent Assembly, and two years later, he was elected to the House of Representatives. In 1943 and 1944 he was Minister Without Portfolio in the cabinet of President Fulgencio Batista. In 1944 he was elected to the Senate, two years later its vice president, and in 1948 he was his party's candidate for president, coming in a poor fourth.

Juan Marinello was head of the Partido Socialista Popular at the time of the triumph of the Revolution. Although he never played a leading role in the Fidel Castro* regime, he served Castro as ambassador to UNESCO and was president of the World Peace Council.

BIBLIOGRAPHY

Blasier, Cole, and Carmelo Mesa-Lago. *Cuba in the World.* Pittsburgh: University of Pittsburgh Press, 1979.
Karol, K. S. *Guerrillas in Power: The Course of the Cuban Revolution.* New York: Hill and Wang, 1970.
Ruíz, Ramón Eduardo. *Cuba: The Making of a Revolution.* New York: W. W. Norton, 1968.
Thomas, Hugh. *Cuba: The Pursuit of Freedom.* New York: Harper and Row, 1971.
                                                                    STEPHEN J. WRIGHT

MARIÑO, SANTIAGO (1788–1854), was one of Simón Bolívar's* principal lieutenants and one of Venezuela's important political leaders after independence. With the outbreak of the independence movement, he was a leader of the struggle in the Guayana region. After Francisco de Miranda* surrendered, however, Mariño went into exile in Trinidad. In 1813 he headed a group of returning exiles who joined Simón Bolívar in the east, but returned to Trinidad after the defeat of independence forces in the first Battle of Carabobo.

Mariño returned home again in 1816. At the Congress of Guayana, he opposed Bolívar, although subsequently he pledged support to him. Elected to the second Venezuelan Congress in February 1819, Mariño quickly returned to military activity. He was chief of staff at the Battle of Carabobo which assured Venezuelan independence.

Mariño supported José Antonio Páez* in separating Venezuela from the Republic of Gran Colombia in 1830. In the following year, he suppressed the revolt against Páez led by General José Tadeo Monagas.*

In 1834 Mariño was an unsuccessful candidate for president. In 1835 he headed the Reformist Revolution which overthrew President José María Vargas, but he was defeated by troops led by General Páez, who restored Vargas to office.

Mariño then retired to his estates in Aragua. However, in 1848, he led the army that defeated General Páez, who had revolted against his hand-picked successor, General José Tadeo Monagas.* In 1850 Mariño was again an unsuccessful candidate for president.

BIBLIOGRAPHY

Diccionario Biográfico de Venezuela. Madrid: Cárdenas-Saenz de la Calzada y Cia., 1953.
Enciclopedia Universal Ilustrada Europeo-Americana. Barcelona: José Espasa e Hijos.

Magallanes, Manuel Vicente. *Los Partidos Políticos en la Evolución Histórica de Venezuela*. Caracas: Monte Avila Editores, 1977.

ROBERT J. ALEXANDER

MARRYSHOW, THEOPHILUS ALBERT (1887–1958), was the first major political leader of Grenada. He emerged from extremely humble surroundings and was apprenticed to a carpenter, after leaving primary school before reaching seventh standard.

Marryshow's political education and career in journalism began at 17 when he joined the staff of *The Federalist and Grenada*, a newspaper edited by William Donavan, a radical advocate of West Indian nationalism and the rights of black West Indians. Marryshow soon developed an intense commitment to the cause of self-determination for the West Indies and to the idea of a West Indian federation. In 1909 he became editor of *St. George's Chronicle and Grenada Gazette*, which was then the oldest newspaper in the West Indies, and in 1915 he helped to found *The West Indian*, dedicated to popularizing the twin causes of representative government and federation for the West Indies. Marryshow eventually acquired sole ownership of the paper and continued as its editor until 1934.

In 1914 Marryshow founded the Representative Government Association, with its immediate goal being to end the system under which all members of legislative bodies were nominees of the governor. The association fought for representative elected government with the ultimate aim of an independent West Indian federation. Not content with confining the association's activities to Grenada alone, Marryshow actively participated in the formation of similar bodies in other islands of the Anglophone Caribbean. In 1921 he took the fight to Great Britain, paying his own expenses on a one-man mission, and convinced the British government to send a commission to inquire into constitutional reform for the West Indies. As a result of its report, the legislative councils of the Windward and Leeward Islands, including Grenada and Trinadad, were made partially elective in 1925. Marryshow was elected to the Legislative Council and served as an elected member for 33 consecutive years, until his death, including service as a member of the colony's Executive Council, 1942–1954, and deputy president of the Legislative Council, 1951–1955.

Marryshow founded the Grenada Workers' Association and presided over it during the second decade of the century. During the 1920s he also began intense efforts to establish a Caribbean-style labor movement, helping to organize the British Guiana and West Indies Labour Congress, which was later renamed the Caribbean Labour Congress. This body, of which Marryshow was elected president in 1946, became a major instrument in the fight for a federated West Indies and for national self-determination.

Marryshow played an important role when final plans for the federation were formulated in Jamaica in 1957. With the inauguration of the West Indies Federation in February 1958, he was appointed to the federal Parliament as a senator from Grenada and served until his death in October of the same year.

BIBLIOGRAPHY

Emannuel, P. A. *Crown Colony Politics in Grenada, 1917–1951*. Cave Hill, Barbados: Institute of Social and Economic Research, University of the West Indies, 1978.
Government Broadcasting Unit. *Caribbean Emancipators*. Port of Spain, Trinidad: Government of Trinidad and Tobago, 1973.
Richardson, Bonham C. "Grenada," in Robert J. Alexander (ed.). *Political Parties of the Americas*. Vol. 1. Westport, Conn.: Greenwood Press, 1982.
Singham, A. W. *The Hero and the Crowd in a Colonial Polity*. New Haven, Conn.: Yale University Press, 1968.
Thorndike, Anthony. *Grenada*. Boulder, Colo.: Lynne Reiner Press, 1985.

                                                      PERCY C. HINTZEN AND W. MARVIN WILL

MARTÍ, JOSÉ (1853–1895), was the most brilliant spokesman of the radical revolutionary movement which led the struggle for Cuban independence during the 1880s and 1890s. Both of Martí's parents were Spaniards. Neither parent encouraged young José in the direction of education, but fortunately, he came under the mentorship of the respected Havana schoolmaster, Rafael María Mendive. At the age of 16, encouraged by Mendive, who was himself a strong supporter of Cuban independence, Martí wrote a letter critical of Spain which led to his imprisonment and exile to Spain in 1871. There he immersed himself in a heady revolutionary atmosphere while studying law. In 1874 he earned a degree and left for France before departing for the New World. During the late 1870s he lived in Guatemala and Mexico before moving to New York City, where he became the president of the Cuban revolutionary committee.

As a writer for the *New York Sun*, Martí traveled widely and became the chief interpreter of North American culture to a vast readership throughout South and Central America. He was always organizing his fellow Cuban exiles, and in his political writings he developed a series of revolutionary objectives. He advocated a brief war with Spain which would avoid destruction of the island and intervention by the United States, and he also advocated a republic founded on social and racial equality. He believed that without economic freedom there could be no liberty for all, and he foresaw a Cuban democracy based on a smallholding peasantry in a diversified economy.

In 1892 Martí founded the Cuban Revolutionary Party. Three years later, after recruiting three of Cuba's greatest revolutionary generals to his cause—Máximo Gómez,* Antonio Maceo y Morales,* and Calixto García Iñignéz*—Martí landed on Cuban soil to personally lead the final struggle against Spain. He died in battle while fighting Spanish forces in Oriente Province.

BIBLIOGRAPHY

Gray, Richard. *José Martí, Cuban Patriot*. Gainesville: University of Florida Press, 1962.
Kirk, John M. *José Martí: Mentor of the Cuban Nation*. Tampa: University Presses of Florida, 1983.

Lizaso, Felix. *Martí: Martyr of Cuban Independence*. Albuquerque: University of New Mexico Press, 1953.
Onis, Juan de (ed). *The America of José Martí*. New York: Minerva Press, 1954.
Thomas, Hugh. *Cuba: The Pursuit of Freedom*. New York: Harper and Row, 1971.

STEPHEN J. WRIGHT

MÉDICI, EMÍLIO GARRASTAZÚ (1905–), the third general to be president of Brazil (1968–1974) after the 1964 revolution, was born in Baje, Rio Grande do Sul, of a family of modest landowners. He entered military school in 1918 in Porto Alegre and ultimately graduated from the Realango Military School in Rio de Janeiro. He moved up the military hierarchy, attaining the rank of general in 1961.

When General Artur Costa e Silva became president in 1967, he appointed Médici to direct the Serviço Nacional de Inteligencía (SNI), which is equivalent to the American Central Intelligence Agency except that it also functions inside Brazil. Then, with the death of President Costa e Silva in August 1969, the army resolved that General Médici would be his successor. On October 25, 1969, the Brazilian Congress carried out the orders of the army, voting 239 for Médici, with 76 abstentions.

In the first years of his administration, left-wing elements intensified efforts to bring down the military regime, and the government increased repressive measures, using torture and imprisonment. Various army units were very successful and on November 4, 1969, succeeding in killing Carlos Marighela, considered one of the leading terrorists. Leftist terrorists were not the only victims. Over 4,000 were arrested in November 1971 for alleged subversion, including Catholic Church activists.

Economic development plans were in the hands of a civilian economist, João Paulo Reis Velloso. The regime stressed expansion of the infrastructure, modernization of agriculture, and development of manufactured exports. Some people dubbed the results "the Brazilian miracle."

BIBLIOGRAPHY

Dicionario Histórico Biográfico Brasileiro, 1930–1983. Vol. 3.

JORDAN YOUNG

MEDINA ANGARITA, ISAÍAS (1897–1953), was the last president of Venezuela to rise to military leadership during the dictatorship of Juan Vicente Gómez.* He was one of the first graduates, in 1914, of the military school established by Gómez, and his rise in the military ranks was steady if unspectacular. In 1935 he was chief of staff of the army; between 1936 and 1941 minister of war and navy under Gómez' successor, President Eleazar López Contreras;* and in 1940 a brigadier general.

General López Contreras chose Medina as his successor, and Medina took office in early 1941. His administration was much more liberal than that of his predecessor. Among its most important acts were legalization of the hitherto underground National Democratic Party (PDN), led by Rómulo Betancourt,* as Acción Democrática (AD) and of the Communist Party under the name Venezuelan Popular Union. Medina also had his own followers organized into the Venezuelan Democratic Party (PDV). He established the first stages of a social security system and a substantial middle-income housing program in Caracas. He reorganized relations with the petroleum companies, establishing closely similar dates for expiration of their concessions and substantially increasing the amount concessionaires had to pay the government.

Although substantially liberalizing the regime, President Medina refused to allow establishment of universal adult suffrage or direct popular election of his successor. However, he negotiated with AD to select a mutually acceptable candidate who would promise to introduce these two measures. Although agreement was reached on Diógenes Escalante, Venezuelan ambassador to Washington, no additional agreement was possible when Escalante fell ill and had to withdraw. Medina insisted that the PDV name his personal choice, Angel Biaggini. As a consequence, AD accepted the overtures of junior army officers to cooperate in the overthrow of Medina. On October 18, 1945, Medina's government fell.

Ex-President Medina went into exile in the United States, returning home in 1948 only after the Acción Democrática government had been overthrown. He played no further role in politics.

BIBLIOGRAPHY

Betancourt, Rómulo. *El 18 de Octubre de 1945: Génesis y Realizaciones de Una Revolución Democrática*. Caracas: Seix Baral, 1979.
Fuenmayor, Juan B. *1928–1938, Veinte Años de Política*. Madrid: Editorial Mediterraneo, 1969.
Medina Angarita, Isaías. *Cuatro Años de Democracia*. Caracas: Pensamiento Vivo, 1963.
                                                                    ROBERT J. ALEXANDER

MELGAREJO, MARIANO (1820–1871), a Bolivian president, is remembered as the worst of South America's nineteenth-century strongmen. An illegitimate *mestizo*, he joined the army of Andrés de Santa Cruz* in 1835, fought in the campaigns to establish the Bolivian-Peruvian Confederation and, later, in the Battle of Ingavi to repulse the second Peruvian invasion. By 1848 he had achieved the rank of colonel, and in 1862 he became Bolivia's youngest general when he put down a rebellion against President José Maria Achá. Although related to Achá, Melgarejo led a revolt against him in December 1864 and became president. His rule lasted until January 15, 1871, when he himself was deposed by another military strongman, General Agustín Morales.

Melgarejo spent much of his rule defeating rebellions around the country. Rarely sober and easily flattered by honors bestowed on him from abroad, he signed several unfavorable territorial treaties with Brazil, Chile, and Peru, which decreased Bolivia's territory and economic resources. He also granted tax exemption to Chilean mineral exports shipped from Bolivian ports, an issue which in 1879 precipitated the War of the Pacific whereby Bolivia lost the rich coastal provinces.

Melgarejo despised the masses and was equally alienated from the upper classes. His government dismantled populism and economic protectionism in favor of free-trade capitalism and the interests of the new silver mining oligarchy. Hardest hit by these policies were the urban artisans and the Indian communities that had survived after independence, which provoked bloody peasant uprisings. In January 1871 a massive revolt broke out against him, and Melgarejo fled to Peru, where he was killed by colonel José Aurelio Sánchez, the brother of his favorite mistress.

BIBLIOGRAPHY

Díaz, Arguedas, Julio. *Los generales de Bolivia*. La Paz: Imprenta Intendencia General de Guerra, 1929.
Gutiérrez, Alberto. *El melgarejismo, antes y después de Melgarejo*. 2d ed. La Paz: González y Medina, 1918.
O'Connor d'Arlach, Tomás. *El general Melgarejo: hechos y dichos de este hombre celebre*. La Paz: González y Medina, 1913.
————. *Rozas, Francia y Melgarejo*. La Paz: González y Medina, 1914.
Paredes, M. Rigoberto. "El General Mariano Melgarejo y su tiempo, conclusión." *Kollasuyo* 59 (1945).

WALTRAUD QUEISER MORALES

MÉNDEZ MANFREDINI, APARICIO (1904–   ), was the second civilian to preside over the military dictatorship that controlled Uruguay between 1973 and 1985. He was educated at the Universidad de la República in Montevideo, and practiced law between 1920 and 1970. He was a history teacher in two secondary schools, and professor of administrative law at the Universidad de la Republica, 1930–1955. He served as legal advisor and head of the Juridical Office of Montevideo, 1935–1938; and member of the Electoral Court, 1943–1946.

Méndez was a leader of the Blanco Party, serving as member of the Chamber of Deputies and as minister of public health between 1961 and 1964. In 1973 he became a member of the Council of State created by the military regime and its first vice president between 1974 and 1976. The military chose him to succeed President Juan María Bordaberry* whom they deposed in 1976. Méndez served in the presidency until 1981.

BIBLIOGRAPHY

Facts on File 1976. New York: Facts on File, 1976.
International Who's Who 1985–1986. 49th ed. London: Europa Publications Ltd., 1985.

ROBERT J. ALEXANDER

MENDIETA Y MONTEFUR, CARLOS (1873–1960), served as provisional president of Cuba from January 1934 to December 1935. He fought with Antonio Maceo y Grajales* in the war against Spain, served in the national legislature for 22 years, and ran unsuccessfully for vice president on the Liberal Party ticket in 1916. Along with former President Mario García Menocal,* he unsuccessfully attempted to overthrow the Gustavo Machado* dictatorship in 1931, was captured, and imprisoned.

When Fulgencio Batista y Zaldívar* deposed the Ramón Grau San Martín* government in January 1934, he turned to Mendieta, whose reputation for honesty, moderation, and inability to make firm decisions made him the ideal candidate for a president whom Batista could easily manage. Mendieta governed Cuba without any real political or social program other than restoration of domestic peace, which was not finally achieved until late 1935. His government was immediately recognized by the United States, and he enjoyed the good fortune of seeing the Platt Amendment repealed during his stay in office.

BIBLIOGRAPHY

Domínguez, Jorge I. *Cuba: Order and Revolution*. Cambridge, Mass.: Harvard University Press, 1978.
Gellman, Irwin F. *Roosevelt and Batista*. Albuquerque: University of New Mexico Press, 1973.
Thomas, Hugh. *Cuba: The Pursuit of Freedom*. New York: Harper and Row, 1971.

                                                                 STEPHEN J. WRIGHT

MENOCAL, MARIO GARCÍA (1866–1941), was president of Cuba from 1913 until 1921. He spent most of his youth in the United States, receiving an engineering degree from Cornell. Following graduation, he worked for a U.S.-owned company in Nicaragua.

Menocal returned to Cuba when the rebellion against Spain resumed under José Martí* in 1895. He joined the rebel forces as a private and by the war's end was a general. Serving as Calixto García Iñiguez'* chief of staff, he established himself as a war hero. For two years following the war, he served as chief of Havana police.

Menocal resigned this position to enter the sugar business, co-founding the Cuban-American Sugar Company with U.S. Congressman R. B. Hawley. This experience proved helpful during his presidency, when the sugar industry experienced unparalleled expansion.

Menocal won a close election in 1912, when Liberal Party President José Miguel Gómez* refused to support fellow Liberal Alfredo Zayas y Alfonso.* Menocal's Conservative Party also won control of both houses of Congress. The early years of his first term saw relative economic depression resulting from the loss of sugar markets in war-torn Europe. In 1915 he pushed through Congress laws to provide compulsory workers' insurance, a new monetary system, and a mechanism for state mediation of labor disputes.

Menocal was one of the most corrupt politicians Cuba has ever seen. His estimated worth in 1913 was $1 million; when he left office eight years later it had grown to $40 million. Menocal built fewer roads in his eight-year administration than Gómez had in four years, yet they cost three times as much.

Following reelection in 1917, Menocal was party to even more extreme corruption. However, he retained the support of the United States, which was eager to maintain order on the island to insure the flow of sugar to the Allied cause during the Great War.

The most controversial episode of the Menocal years was the election of 1916 and the subsequent Liberal Party revolt in February 1917. Like Gómez before him, Menocal pledged that he would not seek reelection, but he changed his mind and received the Conservative Party nomination. Observers agreed that the election in which Menocal was declared winner was the most fraudulent to date in the short history of the republic. Led by José Miguel Gómez, the Liberal Party revolted in 1917. The United States came to Menocal's aid with rifles and ammunition, and the revolt was put down.

Menocal was a strong supporter of the United States during World War I. Sugar prosperity spiraled during 1919–1920, when prices rose from 8.65 cents to 22.5 cents per pound. The so-called Dance of the Millions symbolized the graft-infested climate of the period.

BIBLIOGRAPHY

Aguilar, Luis. *Cuba 1933: Prologue to Revolution*. Ithaca, N.Y.: Cornell University Press, 1972.
Domínguez, Jorge I. *Cuba: Order and Revolution*. Cambridge, Mass.: Harvard University Press, 1978.
Fagg, John Edwin. *Cuba, Haiti, and the Dominican Republic*. Englewood Cliffs, N.J.: Prentice-Hall, 1965.
Thomas, Hugh. *Cuba: The Pursuit of Freedom*. New York: Harper and Row, 1971.
STEPHEN J. WRIGHT

MERWIN, JOHN DAVID (1921–   ), was governor of the United States Virgin Islands from 1958 to 1961. He served in the U.S. Army in World War II, rising to captain. He studied at the University of Lausanne, the University of Puerto Rico, and Yale, and received a bachelor of laws degree at George Washington University in 1948. He practiced law in St. Croix in the 1950s and 1960s, and was senator at large in the Virgin Islands legislature from 1955 to 1957 and government secretary in 1957. He was the principal leader of the Progressive Republican Party. After leaving the governorship, Merwin returned to business activities.

BIBLIOGRAPHY

Sharpless, Richard E. "Virgin Islands of the United States," in Robert J. Alexander (ed.). *Political Parties of the Americas*. Vol. 2. Westport, Conn.: Greenwood Press, 1982.
Who's Who in America. 43d ed. Chicago: Marquis Who's Who, 1984.
RICHARD E. SHARPLESS

MIRANDA, FRANCISCO DE (1750–1816), the first great advocate of Venezuelan independence and head of the first Venezuelan republic, came from a well-to-do Caracas family, got his education in Caracas, and then went to Spain, where he bought a military commission. He rose to colonel, participating in campaigns in North Africa and the West Indies.

Miranda aroused the enmity of his Spanish military colleagues, perhaps because of his colonial origins. In 1783 he fled to the United States, where he stayed two years, traveling widely and meeting many leaders of the new republic. He then moved to England. In the 1780s he traveled widely on the European continent. In the early 1790s he rose to the rank of general with the French revolutionary armies.

By then, Miranda was committed to the cause of Spanish-American (and specifically Venezuelan) independence. He sought the backing of the British government and also tried to get U.S. government support. In 1805 he went to the United States, whence, in February 1808, he undertook a private expedition to try to free Venezuela. Although he captured the city of Coro, he was soon defeated and returned to Britain.

With the outbreak of revolution in Caracas in 1810, Francisco de Miranda hurried home. His long advocacy of independence and his revolutionary experience made him a natural leader of the independence movement. He strongly urged a declaration of independence and on July 5, 1811, such a document was signed. Shortly afterward, he suppressed a counterrevolutionary movement in Valencia.

The new republic adopted a loose federal form of government, over the objections of both Miranda and Simón Bolívar.* In spite of the incursion of new Spanish forces against the republic, other leaders of the independence movement hesitated to give Miranda the centralized authority he thought necessary. After a very disastrous earthquake in March 1812, however, and substantial advances by Spanish troops, Miranda was finally given dictatorial power to confront the emergency.

The forces led by Miranda were defeated by the Spaniards. On July 25, Miranda signed a document of capitulation which permitted him to leave the country. However, Bolívar and others prevented Miranda's departure, and shortly afterward he was arrested by the Spanish forces, in violation of the agreement they had signed with him. He was shipped off to a Spanish prison, where he died four years later.

BIBLIOGRAPHY

Madariaga, Salvador de. *Bolívar*. New York: Pellegrini and Cudahy, 1952.
Miranda, Francisco de. *South American Emancipation*. London: 1810.
Parra Pérez, Caracciolo. *Historia de la Primera República de Venezuela*. Caracas: Academía Nacional de Historia, 1959.
Robertson, William Spence. *The Life of Miranda*. Chapel Hill: University of North Carolina Press, 1929.
Thorning, Joseph Francis. *Miranda: World Citizen*. Gainesville: University of Florida Press, 1952.

ROBERT J. ALEXANDER

MITCHELL, JAMES FITZ ALLEN (1931–   ), premier of St. Vincent from 1972 to 1974 and prime minister after 1984, was born on the island of Bequia. Following his education in St. Vincent, he enrolled at the Imperial College of

Tropical Agriculture in Trinidad and later attended the University of British Columbia in Vancouver. Prior to entering politics, he spent three years as an agricultural research officer, two years as a school teacher, and one and a half years with the British Ministry of Overseas Development in London. He also put out several works on Caribbean agriculture.

Mitchell won election to the legislature from the Grenadines constituency as a member of the St. Vincent Labour Party (SLP) in 1966, and in 1967 was appointed minister of trade, production, labour, and tourism in the SLP government headed by Robert Milton Cato.* By 1972, however, Mitchell had broken with Labour and had won the Grenadines seat as an independent. In this election, the SLP and opposition Peoples Political Party (PPP) were deadlocked in legislative support, paving the way for Mitchell, the independent, to become the compromise choice for premier. He lost this position in a no confidence vote brought by the SLP and PPP two and a half years later (1974). Mitchell then attempted to build a new party, which put forward 11 candidates in the next election. Only Mitchell emerged victorious, again representing the Grenadines.

Mitchell's concern for the Grenadines was unstinting. His fear of emasculation of these small islands by larger St. Vincent induced him to oppose independence. But independence did come to St. Vincent in 1979. That same year Mitchell founded the New Democratic Party (NDP) and led it to second-rank and "loyal opposition" status. Mitchell himself was defeated, however, in a head-to-head race against Ebenezer Joshua, leader of the PPP. In the 1984 election Mitchell was vindicated and assumed the prime ministership following victory by the NDP.

In the context of St. Vincentian politics, Mitchell can be described as middle-of-the-road to slightly "left of center." In a May 1985 interview he stated his desire to see an active Vincentian private sector, although acknowledging need for strong government regulation, espcially to protect local real estate from purchase by overseas interests. He particularly promoted peasant agriculture. His government opposed the Reagan administration's attempts to increase militarization in the region via the Eastern Caribbean Regional Security and Defense Pact signed in 1983.

BIBLIOGRAPHY

Dictionary of Latin American and Caribbean Biography. London: Melrose Ltd., 1971.
International Who's Who 1985–86. London: Europa Publications, 1985.
Personalities Caribbean. Kingston: Personalities Ltd., 1983.
                                        PERCY C. HINTZEN AND W. MARVIN WILL

MITRE, BARTOLOMÉ (1821–1906), was the first president of the Argentine Republic (1862–1868). Born in Buenos Aires, he spent much of his early life in exile in Uruguay and other South American countries because of activities against Juan Manuel de Rosas.* He joined Justo José de Urquiza's* forces and commanded the artillery in the final battle that ousted Rosas.

Thereafter, Mitre became military commander and governor of Buenos Aires Province. He commanded Buenos Aires forces which defeated the provincial armies in 1861, spent the next year working to form the provinces into a new federal government, and was unanimously elected the first president of the new republic in 1862.

Many projects that shaped the future of Argentina were developed under Mitre. Buenos Aires was made provisional capital. In addition, he struggled to replace caudillo rule with institutionalized government throughout the provinces, encouraged immigration, and worked to establish public education. His government improved the ports, promoted agriculture and trade, and fostered the growth of shipping facilities and construction of railroads. These projects aided Argentina's economic growth and modernization, based on the processing and export of agricultural products. Mitre also served as commander of the united armies against Paraguay in the War of the Triple Alliance.

Following his presidency, Mitre increasingly turned his attention to historical investigations. He wrote the four-volume *Historia de Belgrano y de la independencia argentina* in 1887, probably the most important work on Argentina's struggle for independence. In 1870 Mitre founded *La Nación*, which continued for a century as one of Argentina's most prestigious newspapers.

In 1874 Mitre was defeated for the presidency by Nicolás Avellaneda, charged fraud, and attempted an unsuccessful revolt. However, he was soon pardoned; he served as a diplomat and senator, ending his career as president of the Senate. Mitre was one of the founders of the Unión Cívica in 1890.

BIBLIOGRAPHY

Ferns, Henry S. *Argentina*. New York: Praeger, 1969.
Jeffrey, William H. *Mitre and Argentina*. New York: 1952.
Levene, Gustavo Gabriel. *Historia de los presidentes Argentinos*. 2 vols. Buenos Aires: 1973.
Levene, Ricardo. *Las ideas históricas de Mitre*. Buenos Aires: 1948.
Wright, Ione S., and Lisa M. Nekhom. *Historical Dictionary of Argentina*. Metuchen, N.J.: Scarecrow Press, 1978.

JOHN T. DEINER

MONAGAS, JOSÉ GREGORIO (1795–1858), second of two brothers to be president of Venezuela in the midnineteenth century, helped establish Liberal domination of Venezuelan caudillo politics. He participated in the Wars of Independence in the eastern part of the country. After the separation of Venezuela from Gran Colombia, Monagas joined the opposition to the first Venezuelan president, José Antonio Páez.* He strongly supported establishment of the Liberal Party in 1840. He also backed his brother, President José Tadeo Monagas'* move to form an alliance with the Liberals, even though he had been chosen by Páez, a Conservative.

José Tadeo chose his brother José Gregorio to be his successor as president in 1851, and he served out his term until 1855. The most notable event of José Gregorio Monagas' administration was the abolition of slavery in 1854.

José Gregorio Monagas did not play any major role in national politics after leaving the presidency.

BIBLIOGRAPHY

Diccionario Biográfico de Venezuela. Madrid: Cárdenas-Sáenz de la Calzada y Cia., 1953.
Enciclopedia Universal Ilustrada Europeo-Americana. Barcelona: José Espasa e Hijos.
Magallanes, Manuel Vicente. *Los Particos Políticos en la Evolución Histórica de Venezuela*. Caracas: Monte Avila Editores, 1977.

ROBERT J. ALEXANDER

MONAGAS, JOSÉ TADEO (1784–1868), was the president of Venezuela who ended the rule of the Conservative oligarchy. One of the principal leaders of the struggle for independence from Spain in eastern Venezuela, he supported the separation of Venezuela from the Republic of Gran Colombia, but in 1831 led an unsuccessful revolution against the government of General José Antonio Páez.* For several years he sought to bring about the establishment of a separate country in eastern Venezuela.

In 1835–1836 Monagas led a revolt against the government of President José María Vargas, who had been placed in charge by José Antonio Páez. Although that revolution overthrew Vargas, it was defeated when Páez returned and defeated the revolutionary forces, restoring Vargas to power. Monagas was pardoned by the Vargas regime and Páez.

Monagas did not take part in organizing the Liberal Party, although his brother José Gregorio* did. José Tadeo was thus acceptable in 1847 as a compromise presidential candidate, and was backed by José Antonio Páez.

Monagas as president from 1847 to 1851 aligned himself with the Liberals and against Páez, and defeated an attempt of Páez in 1848 to overthrow him. At the end of his term in 1851 he successfully supported his brother José Gregorio Monagas as his successor.

At the end of José Gregorio's term, José Tadeo returned to the presidency. This time, José Tadeo Monagas was overthrown in March 1858 by a coalition of Conservatives and dissident Liberals, headed by General Julián Castro. Shortly afterward, the Federal War (1859–1863) began.

Although the Liberals triumphed in the Federal War, José Tadeo Monagas led a movement, the "Blue Revolution," against the government of General Juan Cristósomo Falcón,* which had resulted from that triumph. Upon taking Caracas in July 1868, Monagas installed a civilian to head a new regime. He died five months later, without ever having reassumed the presidency.

BIBLIOGRAPHY

Diccionario Biográfico de Venezuela. Madrid: Cárdenas, Sáenz de la Calzada y Cia., 1953.

Enciclopedia Universal Ilustrada Europeo Americana. Barcelona: José Espasa e Hijos.
Magallanes, Manuel Vicente. *Los Partidos Políticos en la Evolución Histórica de Venezuela.* Caracas: Monte Avila Editores, 1977.

                                                                    ROBERT J. ALEXANDER

MONGE ALVAREZ, LUIS ALBERTO (1926–   ), president of Costa Rica, 1982–1986, was a founder of the National Liberation Party (PLN) in 1951. His origins and schooling were more humble than those of many of the other PLN founders. Monge began his career in the "Rerum Novarum" trade union movement under Padre Benjamín Nuñez in the 1940s, which brought him to the side of José Figueres Ferrer* in the 1948 civil war.

During the 1950s Monge was general secretary of the Inter American Regional Organization of Workers (ORIT), with headquarters in Mexico City. In 1959 he, Figueres, and Núñez established the Inter-American Institute of Political Education in San José, for development of democratic left movements, in Latin America, and he was managing editor of the institute's journal, *Combato.*

In 1963, during the administration of Francisco José Orlich Bolmarcich,* Monge served as ambassador to Israel, but personal problems and concern over the conservative drift of the PLN caused him to withdraw from politics momentarily. In 1966 he assumed the position of PLN secretary general.

As secretary general of the PLN, Monge slowly built a political base. He won a seat in the Legislative Assembly in 1970 and served as its president during Figueres' 1970–1974 term. He won the PLN nomination in 1978, lost that election, but won in 1982.

Monge dedicated his presidency to dealing with Costa Rica's economic ills by cutting waste and inefficiency in the bureaucracy and trimming social programs. Some of the balance-of-payments problems were ameliorated as a result of the drop in the price of oil, and Monge received important U.S. economic assistance because of his cooperative attitude toward U.S. policy on Nicaragua.

BIBLIOGRAPHY

Ameringer, Charles D. *Democracy in Costa Rica.* New York: Praeger, 1982.
————. *Don Pepe: A Political Biography of José Figueres of Costa Rica.* Albuquerque: University of New Mexico Press, 1979.

                                                                    CHARLES D. AMERINGER

MONTERO RODRÍGUEZ, JUAN ESTEBAN (1880–1948), was the first member of the Radical Party to become president of Chile. In October 1925 on behalf of the Radicals he signed the agreement of most of the country's parties to support the candidacy of Emiliano Figueroa Larraín,* in an effort to thwart the presidential aspirations of Colonel Carlos Ibáñez del Campo. Then, in July 1931, two weeks before the fall of Ibáñez, he became minister of interior and sought to dismantle many of the authoritarian aspects of that regime, efforts that gained him considerable popularity. With Ibáñez' resignation on July 26, Montero became vice president (acting president), resigning on August 20 to be a candidate in the coming presidential election. He was supported by the Radical Party as well as by the Conservatives and Liberals.

As president, Montero had to face the worst period of the Great Depression. Social and economic discontent, together with violent political controversy over his refusal to dissolve the Congress he had inherited from the Ibáñez dictatorship, culminated in his overthrow on June 4, 1952. He played no further role in politics.

BIBLIOGRAPHY

Alexander, Robert J. "Chile," in Robert J. Alexander (ed.). *Political Parties of the Americas*. Vol. 1. Westport, Conn.: Greenwood Press, 1982.
Charlín, Carlos. *Del Avión Rojo a la República Socialista*. Santiago: Empresa Editora Nacional Quimantú, 1972.
Cortes, Lia, and Jordi Fuentes. *Diccionario Político de Chile*. Santiago: Editorial Orbe, 1967.

ROBERT J. ALEXANDER

MONTES, ISMAEL (1861–1933), was twice president of Bolivia (1904–1909, 1913–1917) and a major figure in the Liberal Party. Born in the city of La Paz, he graduated at 16 from the National College of Ayacucho in La Paz and began to study law. When the War of the Pacific began, he enlisted in the army and in 1884, after having reached the rank of captain, left the army to continue his law studies. In 1886 he began a political career as a national representative from La Paz. With the Liberal Party's "Federal Revolution" of 1898, he became minister of war in the administration of President José Manuel Pando.*

Montes was elected president in 1904. His greatest achievement was expansion of the economy, resulting from the boom in tin exports, and sizable foreign loans, which were later criticized as irresponsible. In 1906 Montes negotiated the Speyer Contract, which estabalished the Bolivia Railway Company with backing from the National City Bank of New York. The 416 miles of track laid by the Speyer Company cost Bolivia $22 million. The government's inability to pay off the debt permitted the British Antofagasta and Bolivia Railway Company to gain control of Bolivia's rail system. The new system linked together major cities and mining centers with the Peruvian network. Like previous governments, that of Montes favored laissez-faire economic policies, and the tin entrepreneurs and landed elites were taxed only minimally.

The Montes government also supported large public works: urban construction, new roads, and telegraph lines. There was major reorganization of the army under a French military mission. Education was reformed by a Belgian Pedagogical Mission; many Bolivian teachers were sent abroad for training. In 1904 Montes concluded the treaty with Chile which ceded to Chile Bolivia's rights to the coastal provinces for 300,000 pounds sterling, allowed construction of the La Paz-Arica rail line by Chile, and provided for the use of Arica as a permanent seaport for Bolivia. Despite opposition, the Montes government viewed normalization of relations with Chile as necessary to continued economic development.

In 1909 Montes engineered the election of his successor, Dr. Eliodoro Villazón. In August 1913 Montes secured his own reelection. His second term continued his earlier development efforts but a severe economic recession in 1913–1914 led to unrest. The opposition protested recent elections as fraudulent, and in 1914 dissident Liberals formed the Republican Party. Limited economic recovery permitted Montes to hold on until the end of his term and to turn over the government to José Gutiérrez Guerra, the last Liberal Party president. In 1917 Montes was appointed minister to France and remained there until 1928. Returning to Bolivia, he supported the Chaco War until his death.

BIBLIOGRAPHY

Díaz Arguedas, Julio. *Los generales de Bolivia*. La Paz: Imprenta Intendencia General de Guerra, 1929.
Fellman Velardo, José. *Historia de Bolivia*. Vol. 3. 2d ed. La Paz: Los Amigos del Libro, 1981.
Fifer, J. Valerie. *Bolivia: Land, Location and Politics Since 1825*. Cambridge: Cambridge University Press, 1972.
Klein, Herbert S. *Parties and Political Change in Bolivia, 1880–1952*. Cambridge: Cambridge University Press, 1969.
O'Connor d'Arlach, Tomás. *Los presidentes de Bolivia desde 1825 hasta 1912*. La Paz: González y Medina, 1912.

WALTRAUD QUEISER MORALES

MONTT ALVAREZ, JORGE (1845–1922), the only military officer to serve as president of Chile between 1851 and 1924, came to power as a result of the only successful effort in that period to overthrow the incumbent government. He entered the naval school in 1858 and received his commission three years later. He saw action in both the 1865–1866 war with Spain and the War of the Pacific of 1879–1883 against Peru and Bolivia. He was named maritime governor of Valparaiso in 1887.

When a majority in Congress rebelled against President José Manuel Balmaceda Fernández* in January 1891, Captain Jorge Montt led the navy in support of the congressional action. He was named head of a rebel Government Junta established in Iquique in April, which took over in Santiago on August 31, after the victory of the rebels. On December 26, 1891, with the support of the Conservative, Liberal, and Radical parties, he took office as constitutional president.

During his five-year term, President Jorge Montt relied principally on the Conservative Party. However, he had eight total reorganizations of his cabinet, reflecting the beginning of the parliamentary regime that had been brought about by victory of the rebels in the 1891 civil war. During Montt's period there was a return to a constitutional regime in which, after at first suffering some persecution, the followers of deposed President Balmaceda were able to participate fully.

After leaving the presidency in 1896, Jorge Montt returned to active navy service. He did not retire until 1913.

BIBLIOGRAPHY

Alexander, Robert J. "Chile," in Robert J. Alexander (ed.). *Political Parties of the Americas*. Vol. 2. Westport, Conn.: Greenwood Press, 1982.
Cortes, Lia, and Jordi Fuentes. *Diccionario Político de Chile*. Santiago: Editorial Orbe, 1967.
Enciclopedia Universal Ilustrada Europeo-Americana. Barcelona: José Espasa e Hijos.
Harvey, Maurice H. *Dark Days in Chile*. New York: Macmillan Co., 1892.
Monteón, Michael. *Chile in the Nitrate Era*. Madison: University of Wisconsin Press, 1982.

ROBERT J. ALEXANDER

MONTT MONTT, PEDRO (1846–1910), was one of the presidents of Chile who suffered most from the ministerial instability that characterized the Parliamentary Republic. Son of President Manuel Montt Torres,* he received his law degree from the University of Chile in 1870. Nine years later he was elected a National Party member of the Chamber of Deputies, where he remained until his election as senator in 1900, a position he held until he became president. For several years he was president of the Chamber of Deputies.

During the presidency of José Manuel Balmaceda Fernández* Montt held several cabinet posts. However, he sided with the congressional rebels in the Civil War of 1891 and visited the United States and several European countries as a representative of the rebel Government Junta. Subsequently, he became president of the National Party and was minister of interior in the cabinet of President Jorge Montt Alvarez.*

Pedro Montt ran for president for the first time in 1901, as candidate of the coalition consisting of his own National Party and the Conservative Party, but was defeated. Five years later, he ran successfully as nominee of the Liberal Alliance, which the National Party had by that time joined.

President Pedro Montt faced strong opposition in Congress, headed by Arturo Alessandri Palma* and Enrique Zañartu, who succeeded in forcing frequent changes in the president's cabinet. Social tensions also ran high, a nitrate workers strike of 1907 culminating in a massacre of strikers and their families in Iquique by police and soldiers. President Montt resigned the presidency in July 1910 for health reasons and went to Europe for medical treatment. He died in August in Bremen, Germany.

BIBLIOGRAPHY

Alexander, Robert J. *Arturo Alessandria: A Biography*. Ann Arbor: University Microfilm International, 1977.
Cortes, Lia, and Jordi Fuentes. *Diccionario Político de Chile*. Santiago: Editorial Orbe, 1967.

Enciclopedia Universal Ilustrada Europeo-Americana. Barcelona: José Espasa e Hijos.
Galdames, Luis. *Historia de Chile*. Santiago: Editorial Zig Zag, 1945.

ROBERT J. ALEXANDER

MONTT TORRES, MANUEL (1809–1880), president of Chile for two consecutive terms, received his law degree in 1831. As vice-rector of the Instituto
Nacional, he took a major role in extending the national education system, being
responsible for establishing more than 100 schools, as well as the University of
Chile. He also organized the Astronomic Observatory, conducted hydrographic
surveys along the coast, and carried out Chile's first population census.

During the administration of President Joaquín Prieto Vial* and Manuel Bulnes
Prieto,* Manuel Montt held several cabinet posts, as well as being for a short
while on the Supreme Court and early in 1851 its Chief Justice. He was a member
of the Chamber of Deputies from 1840 until his election to the presidency.

Manuel Montt was elected president in 1851, as candidate of the political
faction then known as the *pelucones* ("wigged ones"). His election provoked
an armed insurrection that continued in the first months of his presidency, but
was finally suppressed by Montt's predecessor in the presidency, but was finally
suppressed by Montt's predecessor in the presidency, General Manuel Bulnes,
whom Montt put in charge of the military campaign.

Montt was reelected in 1856 and served for a total of ten years. During that
period, he energetically stimulated the country's economic and social development, a railroad from Santiago to Valparaiso was completed and one from
Santiago to Talca was begun. The electric telegraph was introduced, and a prepaid
and relatively cheap postal service was established. There were numerous public
works projects, the educational system was extended further, and a new workers'
savings bank and a mortgage bank were set up.

Bitter political controversies centering on church-state relations marked the
Montt administration. The *pelucones* had generally favored the church, in contrast to the anticlerical Liberal Party. However, an incident in 1856 provoked a
conflict between the church authorities and the Supreme Court. When President
Montt and his principal collaborator, Antonio Varas de la Barra,* supported the
Supreme Court, the *pelucones* broke into two separate parties—the Conservative
Party, favorable to the archbishop, and the National Party, formed by the sup-
porters of Montt and Varas. Efforts to reunite the two groups failed. The Conservatives formed a somewhat unnatural opposition coalition with the anticlerical
Liberal Party.

In 1859 a second military uprising against the Montt government was suppressed with some difficulty. However, that was to be the last serious uprising
against the Chilean government until the Civil War of 1891.

Upon leaving the presidency in September 1861, Manuel Montt was named
to the Council of State and in 1864 he was elected once again to the Chamber
of Deputies. However, President José Joaquín Pérez Mascayano* named Montt
to be minister of Peru in 1864, and he remained in that country for four years.

At the time of his death, Manuel Montt was a senator and still a leading figure in the National Party.

BIBLIOGRAPHY

Cortes, Lia, and Jordi Fuentes. *Diccionario Político de Chile*. Santiago: Editorial Orbe, 1967.
Edwards Vives, Albert. *La Fronda Aristocrática*. Santiago: Editorial del Pacífico, 1945.
Galdames, Luis. *Historia de Chile*. Santiago: Editorial Zig Zag, 1945.

ROBERT J. ALEXANDER

MOORE, LEE LLEWELLYN (1939–   ), became premier of St. Kitts-Nevis on May 18, 1979. He attended primary and secondary school in St. Kitts, won a scholarship in 1957, and went to Kings College of the University of London. He graduated in 1962, but remained at the University to complete an Ll.M. in 1963, after which he became a lecturer in law at the City of Birmingham College of Commerce.

In 1967 Moore returned to St. Kitts to set up private practice, joined the staff of Premier Robert Llewellyn Bradshaw* as public relations officer, and became involved in the St. Kitts-Nevis-Anguilla Labour Party and the St. Kitts and Nevis Trades and Labour Union. He was elected vice president of the labor union. In 1971 Moore first won a seat in the legislature on the Labour ticket. He was immediately appointed attorney general and minister of legal affairs, and later external affairs as well. He served in this position and held the party post of vice president until the death of party leader Robert Bradshaw in May 1978.

Moore mounted an unsuccessful challenge to Caleb Azariah Paul Southwell,* who had succeeded Bradshaw both as party leader and premier. When Southwell died suddenly in May 1979, Moore, as party leader, assumed the premiership.

Moore inherited the problem of strong Nevisian resistance to association with St. Kitts and to independence under such an arrangement. Deciding to seek an immediate mandate for independence and to consolidate the power of the Labour Party, Moore called elections in February 1980. Labour managed to win only four of nine seats, and a coalition between the Peoples Action Movement (PAM), led by Dr. Kennedy Alphonse Simmonds,* and the Nevis Reformation Party (NRP), led by Simeon Daniel, replaced Labour in the government. Lee Moore became Leader of the Opposition, a post he continued to hold after Labour lost the elections of June 1984.

BIBLIOGRAPHY

Caricom Perspectives 18 (March/April 1983).
Hopkins, Jack W. "British Colonies and Associated States," in Jack W. Hopkins (ed.). *Latin America and Caribbean Contemporary Record*. Vol. 1. New York: Holmes and Meier, 1983.
Johnes-Hendrickson, Simon B. "St. Kitts-Nevis," in Jack W. Hopkins (ed.) *Latin America and Caribbean Contemporary Record*. Vol. 2. New York: Holmes and Meier, 1984.

The Nation (Barbados), September 15, 1983, supplement.
Personal Interview.

PERCY C. HINTZEN AND W. MARVIN WILL

MORALES BERMÚDEZ, FRANCISCO (1921–   ), president of Peru (1975–
1980), was born and educated in Lima. He graduated from the Escuela Militar
de Chorrilos and was commissioned in the army corps of engineers in January
1943. He also graduated from the Escuela Superior de Guerra and from the
Center for Higher Military Studies (CAEM) in 1967. Morales Bermúdez served
as minister of finance and economy from March 19 to May 31, 1968, in the
cabinet of President Fernando Belaúnde Terry.* He then became director of
logistics for the Army General Staff. He was promoted to brigadier general in
1968 and to division general in 1972.

Morales Bermúdez joined the Revolutionary Government of the Armed Forces
and served as minister of finance and commerce from February 1, 1969, to
January 1, 1974, the day he was appointed commanding general of the army.
A few months later he became minister of war and head of the cabinet. General
Morales Bermúdez staged a military coup in August 1975, which forced General
Juan Velasco Alvarado* to resign. The two most significant acts of his administration were the 1978 elections for the Constituent Assembly that approved the
1979 Constitution and the 1980 general elections won by Fernando Belaúnde
and Acción Popular.

In 1982 Morales Bermúdez organized the Democratic Front of the National
Union, which proclaimed him its presidential candidate in the general elections
of 1985. He did poorly in that election.

BIBLIOGRAPHY

Alisky, Marvin. *Historical Dictionary of Peru*. Metuchen, N.J.: Scarecrow Press, 1979.
Chang-Rodríguez, Eugenio. *Opciones políticas Peruanas*. Lima: Centro de Documen-
    tación Andina, 1985.
Rójas Samanéz, Alvaro. *Partidos políticos en el Peru*. Lima: Centro de Documentación
    e Información Andina, 1983.
Tauro, Alberto. *Diccionario Enciclopédico del Peru*. Lima: Editorial Mejía Baca, 1966.

EUGENIO CHANG-RODRÍGUEZ

MORA PORRÁS, JUAN RAFAEL (1814–1860), was Costa Rican president
from 1849 to 1860. A prosperous coffee planter, he belonged to one of the oldest
families of the ruling oligarchy. His principal problem was rivalry for power
with other oligarchical families. He used his office to favor economic activities
of relatives and friends, enabling a small group to monopolize credit and trade
and virtually dictating his reelection in 1853. This led to decline in his popularity
and to doubts that he could complete his second term.

Mora rallied the Costa Ricans and much of Central America in a war of
resistance against the filibusterer William Walker.* The conflict transformed
Mora's troubled rule into popular acclaim, but when he tried to extend his rule

for a third term in 1859, his enemies and the generals removed him. When, in 1860, he attempted to return to power at the head of an invading column, government forces under President José Maria Montealegre captured and executed him.

BIBLIOGRAPHY

Gamboa G., Francisco. *Costa Rica: ensayo histórico*. San José: Ediciones Revolución, 1971.
Mavis, Richard, and Karen Biesanz. *Los Costarricenses*. San José: Editorial Universidad Estatal a Distancia, 1979.
Monge, Carlos. *Historia de Costa Rica*. San José: Editorial Fondo de Cultura de Costa Rica, 1948.

CHARLES D. AMERINGER

MORA VALVERDE, MANUEL (1908–   ), was founder of the Costa Rican Communist Party in 1931 and led it for more than 50 years thereafter. During the 1930s as a champion of electoral reform and individual freedoms in opposition to strongman President León Cortés Castro,* the Communist Party gained prestige. It also built a base in the new labor movement.

Mora enjoyed his greatest success during the 1940s, when he supported Presidents Rafael Angel Calderón Guardia* (1940–1944), and Teodoro Picado Michalski (1944–1948), in achieving significant social reforms. Changing the party's name to Popular Vanguard (PVP), Mora formed the Victory Bloc with the ruling National Republican Party. He served in the national Congress as an effective spokesperson for his party.

With defeat of the government in the 1948 civil war, the Communist Party was outlawed, and Mora spent a period in exile. After a brief hiatus, the Communists continued to participate in elections under different labels. After returning to Costa Rica, Mora resumed his leadership of the party and was elected to Congress several times.

In 1983 Manuel Mora was finally removed as secretary general of the PVP, which provoked a split in the party.

BIBLIOGRAPHY

Ameringer, Charles D. *Don Pepe: A Political Biography of José Figueres of Costa Rica*. Albuquerque: University of New Mexico Press, 1979.
Barahona Jiménez, Luis. *El pensamiento político en Costa Rica*. San José: Editorial Fernández-Arce, 1971.
Bell, John Patrick. *Crisis in Costa Rica: The Revolution of 1948*. Austin: University of Texas Press, 1971.
Gamboa G., Francisco. *Costa Rica: ensayo histórico*. San José: Ediciones Revolución, 1971.

CHARLES D. AMERINGER

MORAZÁN, FRANCISCO (1792–1842), was the last leader of the Central American Federation. Born in Honduras, Morazán was the son of a creole family from the French Caribbean. He initially joined the armed forces but spent most of his time in politics, rapidly moving up through the ranks of the Liberal Party, then in opposition.

Although the Conservatives were in power from 1826 to 1829, Morazán led the Liberals to victory and in 1830 began his first term as president of Central America. He sought vicious revenge against Conservative leaders; most of them were jailed, exiled, or deprived of their civil and political rights. Claiming extraordinary powers, he shifted the federation's capital from Guatemala City, the hotbed of Conservative activity, to San Salvador.

In the 1834 presidential election, José Cecilio del Valle,* a moderate, emerged the winner but died before taking office. Congress then reelected Morazán, who pushed for increased taxation, a system of coerced labor for three days a month, and foreign colonization of the more sparsely inhabited reaches of Guatemala.

Morazán's controversial economic reforms alienated small farmers, merchants, and artisans who had initially backed the Liberals. When, in 1837, the Guatemalan Indians were galvanized by the Conservatives and by Rafael Carrera,* a peasant leader, Morazán was initially unconcerned with these developments. When he decided to move against Carrera, the relatively inexperienced Guatemalan won a crushing victory in 1840. Carrera's success inspired the other provinces to install Conservative, anti-Morazán regimes.

Following his humiliating loss to Carrera, Morazán fled to Panama. He made one last attempt to regain power, but was captured and executed by firing squad in San José, Costa Rica.

BIBLIOGRAPHY

Chamberlain, R. S. *Francisco Morazán, Champion of Central American Federation.* Miami: 1950.
Montufar, Lorenzo. *Morazán.* San José: 1970.
Townsend Ezcurra, Andrés. *Las Provincias Unidas de Centro America.* 2d ed. San José: 1973.
Villacorta Calderón, J. A. *Historia de la República de Guatemala.* Guatemala City: 1960.
Woodward, R. L., Jr. "The Rise and Decline of Liberalism in Central America." *Journal of Inter American Studies and World Affairs* 26 (August 1984).

JOSÉ M. SÁNCHEZ

MORÍNIGO, HIGINIO (1897–   ), was president of Paraguay from 1940 to 1948. Born in Paraguarí, he attended the military college, graduating in 1922. He received regular promotions, served in the Chaco War, and was named war minister in the José Félix Estigarribia* government, assuming the presidency when Estigarribia was killed in an airplane accident in 1940.

During World War II, Morínigo and three pro-Axis military men ruled Paraguay as a dictatorship. Paraguay's official neutrality did not hide the pro-fascist nature of the regime. All political activity was suspended, and strict censorship and controls were placed on the population.

At the close of the war, Morínigo decided to allow political party activity to resume, got rid of the three pro-Axis members of the wartime junta, and called for the formation of a coalition government of Febreristas and Colorados. Within a year, however, his experiment in party cooperation proved unworkable. At the beginning of 1947 Morínigo dissolved the coalition government. Party leaders went into exile, and a few weeks later the 1947 Civil War broke out.

Most military officers deserted Morínigo during the civil war, although some, including then Colonel Alfredo Stroessner,* gave him support, as did the Guión Rojo faction of the Colorado Party and a peasant militia. Aided by some military supplies sent by Argentina's President Juan Domingo Perón,* and by tactical mistakes by the rebels, Morínigo was able to defeat the insurgents and drive them into exile.

At the end of the Civil War, Morínigo fell victim of intense factionalism in the Colorado Party and finally was removed from office in a coup staged by Colorado leaders and some military men (including Stroessner). Following the coup, Morínigo retired from politics and went to live in exile in Buenos Aires.

BIBLIOGRAPHY

Kolinski, Charles J. *Historical Dictionary of Paraguay*. Metuchen, N.J.: Scarecrow Press, 1973.
Lewis, Paul H. *Paraguay Under Stroessner*. Chapel Hill: University of North Carolina Press, 1980.
Lott, Leo B. *Venezuela and Paraguay: Modernity and Tradition in Conflict*. New York: Holt, Rinehart and Winston, 1972.
Warren, Harris G. *Paraguay: An Informal History*. Norman: University of Oklahoma Press, 1949.
Weil, Thomas, et al. *Area Handbook for Paraguay*. Washington, D.C.: Department of Defense, 1972.

JOHN T. DEINER

MOSQUERA, TOMÁS CIPRIANO DE (1798–1878), Colombian president and general, was born in Popayan into an old landed family of considerable wealth and prestige. The family's members had a prominent place in national affairs. Mosquera's oldest brother, Joaquín, was vice president of the new republic from 1833 to 1835; another brother, Manuel, became archbishop of Bogotá in 1835. Tomás first won fame on the battlefield.

At the age of 17, Mosquera joined the forces fighting for Colombia's independence. By 1824 he was a lieutenant colonel, commander of his home province of Popayán. His military successes and loyalty to the Liberator Simón Bolívar* resulted in his appointment as intendent of Guayaquil in 1826 and of Cauca in 1828. The following year Mosquera was on a diplomatic mission in Lima, Peru.

Mosquera went abroad during the early 1830s, studying military science in Europe and the United States. On his return to Colombia, from 1834 to 1837 he represented Cauca in the national congress, where he was a strong advocate of economic development and a promoter of international trade.

President José Ignacio Márquez (1837–1841) named him minister of war, and in 1840 he joined General Pedro Alcántara Herran in suppressing the uprising led by José María Obando.* Subsequently, he led a successful campaign against other insurgent groups in central and northern Colombia.

His reputation as a soldier, the support of the military, his social position, and the influence of his brother, the archbishop of Bogotá, combined to bring Mosquera the presidency in 1845. Although he remained staunchly conservative in social views, Mosquera appointed the able Florrentino Gonzáles secretary of the treasury, and together they designed a national economic policy based on free trade which encouraged the country's export sectors. This policy divided the country's ruling classes and initiated a period of intense national strife, which included a Liberal electoral victory in 1849.

Artisan groups opposed to free trade, students from the new National University, influenced by ideas from the revolutionary Europe of 1848, and young liberal members of the upper class were instrumental in electing Liberal General José Hilario López to the presidency in 1848. They strongly backed his anticlerical and abolitionist initiatives. When the populist hero, General José María Obando was elected president in 1853, the country appeared on the verge of an authentic social revolution. However, Obando was overthrown in April 1854 by General José María Melo.

Mosquera, meanwhile, had left the country for the United States in 1850. In the chaos following the overthrow of Obando, urgent appeals were made for his return. He did so in 1854 and succeeded in overthrowing the dictatorship of José María Melo. Mosquera then returned to his home province of Cauca, which he helped reorganize as a state within the Granadine Confederation, represented it as senator, and served as governor after 1858. He was an unsuccessful candidate for president in 1857 representing the National Party, made up of Liberals and a faction of the Conservatives.

Conservative Doctor Mariano Ospina Perez,* elected president in 1857, attempted to impose centralized authority over the near-sovereign states. Mosquera emerged as leader of the states-rights advocates. The upshot was civil war in 1860. Mosquera, joined by his former opponent General Obando, finally succeeded in taking Bogotá and ousting Ospina in 1861. Mosquera assumed the title of Provisional President of the United States of New Granada.

Mosquera immediately moved to strengthen the states' authority. He sharply curtailed the power of executive appointees, and he broke the economic power of the Catholic Church by disentailing all property held by corporations or religious communities, ordered the Jesuits out of the country, suppressed all religious orders, and imprisoned the archbishop of Bogotá for disobeying the government.

A new federalist constitution creating the United States of Colombia was framed in 1863. It took effect while Mosquera was in southern Colombia defeating an invasion by an Ecuadorian Army. Congress elected Mosquera president for a one-year term. He was reelected in 1867 for a fourth term, but by this time he had recognized the weaknesses of extreme federalism. His efforts to restrain it and impose national unity led to his ouster by a group of dissident Liberals supported by a faction of the army.

Mosquera was exiled to Peru in 1867. He remained there three years. The inevitable shifts in political fortunes resulted in his return, however, and until his death he represented Cauca as a senator and a governor.

BIBLIOGRAPHY

Estrada Monsalve, Joaquín. *Mosquera: Su grandeza y su comedia*. Bogotá: 1945.
Fals Borda, Orlando. *Subversion and Social Change in Colombia*. New York: Columbia University Press, 1969.
Helguera, J. Leon, and Robert H. Davis, (eds). *Archivo Epistolar del General Mosquera*. 3 vols. Bogotá: 1966.
Henao, Jesús María, and Gerardo Arrubia. *History of Colombia*. Chapel Hill: University of North Carolina Press, 1938.
Tamayo, Joaquín. *Don Tomás Cipriano de Mosquera*. Bogotá: 1936.

RICHARD E. SHARPLESS

MUÑOZ MARÍN, LUIS (1898–1980), Puerto Rico's first elected governor, was the island's dominant political figure of the twentieth century. He was born several months before American military occupation during the Spanish-American War. His father, Luis Muñoz Rivera,* was a leading political figure before and after the U.S. occupation.

Muñoz Marín spent much of his youth in the United States, attended Georgetown Preparatory School in Washington, and Georgetown University. After his father's death, he lived in New York as a freelance writer and translator, and published several books of poetry.

Muñoz was secretary (1916–1918) to the resident commissioner in Washington, when the Jones Act (1917) granted citizenship to Puerto Ricans. Soon afterward, despite the opposition of his father's old associates, he joined the Socialist Party of Puerto Rico.

Following his return to Puerto Rico, Muñoz became publisher and editor of *La Democracia*, the principal pro-independence newspaper, and an advocate of the rights of the *jíbaros*, rural smallholders and landless peasants. He was elected to the insular Senate in 1932 by the Liberal Party.

Muñoz soon became an ardent supporter of Franklin D. Roosevelt's New Deal; in several trips to Washington, he persuaded administration officials to provide massive recovery aid to Puerto Rico. He also led a successful effort to have an unpopular U.S.-appointed governor removed. These efforts increased his popularity and influence among his electorate, but also brought him into conflict with Antonio Barceló, leader of the Liberals.

Finally expelled from the Liberals, Muñoz, in a radical departure from previous practice, organized the Popular Democratic Party in 1938, not around the question of Puerto Rico's status, but around economic and social issues. Independence or statehood, he argued, could be put aside until the most pressing problems of the people were met.

Muñoz and his followers campaigned strenuously for the 1940 election, urging
agrarian reform, improved wages and working conditions, and public projects
aimed at improving the lot of the people. The Popular Democrats won a close
victory, which began a period of political domination that lasted two and a half
decades.

Muñoz was elected president of the senate and entered into an alliance with
the new governor, Roosevelt-appointee Rexford Tugwell, who was sympathetic
to Muñoz' goals. A Land Authority was established to purchase and redistribute
land, agricultural and industrial development projects were started, a state-owned
electric power authority was established, and numerous public housing projects
were launched. In 1944 the Popular Democrats polled twice as many votes as
all other parties combined.

After the war, Muñoz turned his attention to Puerto Rico's industrialization.
The Industrial Incentives Act of 1947 and creation of the development agency
Fomento opened the island to U.S. capital. Building on government-built infrastructure programs of transportation, communications, education, health facilities, and energy, private investment flooded in and turned Puerto Rico into
a modern, urban, industrialized society. Despite criticism that Puerto Rico was
becoming merely a cheap labor dependency of the U.S. economy and that its
society was losing its Hispanic heritage to mass consumerism, voters continued
to return Muñoz and the Popular Democrats to power in every election.

The status question also was addressed. In 1948 Muñoz became the first elected
governor. He then campaigned for definition of Puerto Rico as a commonwealth
or Free Associated State with the United States. Almost 70 percent of the voters
approved in a 1951 plebiscite; the following year they voted for a new commonwealth constitution that gave Puerto Rico broad self-rule.

Through the 1950s and early 1960s, Muñoz presided over a rapidly changing
Puerto Rico. While hundreds of thousands left the island to seek jobs on the
mainland, those who remained constructed the most materially advanced state
in the Caribbean. Although per capital income never reached levels of the poorest
U.S. state and unemployment remained a nagging problem, the *jíbaros* became
industrial workers, a new middle class grew rapidly, and education, health care,
and housing accelerated.

Muñoz finally retired from the governorship in 1964, handing power over to
his hand-picked protegé, Roberto Sánchez Vilella. Muñoz took a Senate seat.
During the 1970s he retired from active politics; he was in bad health for several
years before his death.

BIBLIOGRAPHY

Aitken, Thomas. *Poet in the Fortress: The Story of Luis Muñoz María*. New York: New
    American Library, 1964.
Anderson, Robert W. *Party Politics in Puerto Rico*. Stanford, Calif.: Stanford University
    Press, 1965.
Lewis, Gordon K. *Puerto Rico: Freedom and Power in the Caribbean*. New York:
    Monthly Review Press, 1963.

Lopez, Adalberto, and James Petras. *Puerto Rico and the Puerto Ricans*. New York: Schenkman Publishing, 1974.

Sharpless, Richard E. "Puerto Rico," in Robert J. Alexander (ed.). *Political Parties of the Americas*. Vol. 2. Westport, Conn.: Greenwood Press, 1982.

                                                             RICHARD E. SHARPLESS

MUÑOZ RIVERA, LUIS (1859–1916), Puerto Rican political leader, first gained prominence during the final years of Spanish rule. Born in Barranquitas into a family of modest means, he reeived an elementary education in his hometown but expanded his learning through self-study.

By the late 1880s sentiment for political autonomy was growing, and Muñoz Rivera became one of its leading advocates. He joined an autonomist group in Ponce in 1887 and launched the newspaper *La Democracia* as its voice in 1890. His editorials soon brought the opposition of the Spanish authorities, but within a short time he was a leader of the new Autonomist Party.

Persecution by Spanish authorities resulted in fracturing the Autonomists. Some members, from exile in New York City, aligned themselves with José Martí's* Cuban Revolutionary Party, which advocated armed struggle for independence. Muñoz Rivera disagreed with that strategy, seeking instead agreement with Spanish Liberals. In 1897, following negotiations in Spain, he signed a charter by which the Liberal Sagasta government granted Puerto Rico substantial internal autonomy. In elections, the Autonomists won an impressive victory, and Muñoz Rivera became the first head of the insular cabinet. However, American occupation of the island, only a few days after the first Parliament met, resulted in dissolution of the administration and eventual disappearance of the Autonomist Party.

Muñoz Rivera accepted American occupation hopefully. He traveled to Washington, where he argued for free trade between the United States and Puerto Rico and a charter of self-government. When the U.S. Congress passed the Foraker Act, which sharply limited Puerto Ricans' political roles, Muñoz Rivera entered the opposition and organized the Federal Party. The Federalists remained a minority in opposition to the pro-statehood Republicans until 1904, when dissident Republicans joined with them to form the Unionist Party. It won the elections of that year on an autonomist platform. Two years later, Muñoz Rivera was elected to a four-year term in the House of Delegates. Following that, his party elected him resident commissioner in Washington.

In the U.S. capital Muñoz Rivera was a fervent advocate of Puerto Rican political rights. Through articles in *La Democracia*, he also kept Puerto Ricans informed of his activities. He was very influential in getting the Jones Act of 1917 passed, which granted Puerto Ricans U.S. citizenship, a Bill of Rights, and a popularly elected two-house legislature. Although he did not live to see the passage of the act, his role in its formulation gained wide-spread acclaim among his people.

BIBLIOGRAPHY

Anderson, Robert. *Party Politics in Puerto Rico*. Stanford, Calif.: Stanford University Press, 1965.
Boletín Histórico de Puerto Rico. San Juan: 1923. Fernández García, Eugenio. *El Libro de Puerto Rico*. San Juan: 1923.
González Ginorio, José. *Luis Muñoz Rivera a la luz de sus obras y de su vida*. San Juan: 1919.
Sharpless, Richard E. ''Puerto Rico,'' in Robert J. Alexander (ed.). *Political Parties of the Americas*. Vol. 2. Westport, Conn.: Greenwood Press, 1982.

RICHARD E. SHARPLESS

N

NABUCO DE ARAUJO, JOAQUIM BARRETO (1849–1910), a distinguished abolitionist, was of primary significance in the elimination of slavery in Brazil. Born in Pernambuco where his father had served as senator under Dom Pedro II,* he studied at the Dom Pedro College and received a law degree from the University of Recife. Entering journalism, he took up the cause of abolition, publishing many articles denouncing slavery.

After serving two years in Washington with the Brazilian Foreign Service, he entered politics, winning a seat in the Chamber of Deputies in 1878. There he launched a violent attack on slavery and became one of its most vocal critics, which brought him into constant conflict with the emperor, who wished to proceed quietly and cautiously on the slavery question, but Joaquim Nabuco's eloquence would not let the matter rest. He also founded and was president of the Brazilian Anti-Slavery Society, and set up a network of abolitionist clubs all over Brazil.

Nabuco served as correspondent for the Brazilian newspaper *Journal of Commerce* in London from 1882 to 1884. Reelected to Parliament in 1884, he played a leading role in getting the abolition bill through the Parliament in spite of clashes with his own Conservative Party.

When the republic was established in 1889, Nabuco was hostile at first and retired temporarily from active politics. However, his talents as an astute negotiator were needed to settle a dispute over the Brazil-British Guiana border. He argued Brazil's case before the Italian King Vittorio Emanuel III. He was next appointed to serve in London but was quickly moved to Washington in 1902 as the first ambassador of republican Brazil. He died in Washington.

BIBLIOGRAPHY

Nabuco, Caroline. *Joaquim Nabuco.* 1950.
Nabuco, Joaquim. *Abolitionism: The Brazilian Anti-Slavery Struggle.* Urbana: University of Illinois Press, 1977.

JORDAN YOUNG

NEVES, TANCREDO (1910–1985), first civilian president elected after 21 years of military rule in Brazil, died in March 1985 before taking office. Born in São João del Rey, Minas Gerais, he belonged to a traditional but not wealthy family of the area. He participated in the political campaign of 1930, supporting the Liberal Alliance and Getúlio Vargas.* Graduating from law school in 1933, he was a founder of the Progressive Party of Minas Gerais. Elected in 1935 to the city council of São João del Rey, he lost his seat when Vargas shut down Brazil's political system in 1937 with establishment of the fascist-modeled Estado Novo.

Neves won election to state assemblyman in January 1947 after the Vargas dictatorship had fallen. In 1950 he was elected a Social Democratic Party (PSD) congressman and became leader of the PSD Minas Gerais delegation. Vargas named him minister of justice in 1953, and he served until Vargas committed suicide in August 1954.

Returning to Congress, Neves became the leading spokesman for Juscelino Kubitschek de Oliveira's* drive for the presidency. In 1955 Neves became director of the Banco de Credito Real de Minas Gerais, and a year later a director of the Bank of Brazil. In 1958 he became secretary of finances of Minas Gerais. In 1960 he suffered his one political defeat, when he ran unsuccessfully for governor of Minas Gerais.

After the August 1961 resignation of President Jânio Quadros,* the Brazilian Army split on whether to permit Vice President João Belchior Marques Goulart* to assume the presidency. Tancredo Neves helped work out a compromise of a parliamentary system, and traveled to Montevideo to convince the vice president to accept it. When Goulart was inaugurated on September 7, 1961, Neves became the first prime minister. As such, he favored a more independent foreign policy, agrarian reform, and entrance of foreign capital to help Brazilian economic development. In June 1962 Neves and the cabinet resigned so that they would not be disqualified from running in the October 1962 election.

Tancredo Neves returned as congressman from Minas Gerais and became majority leader of the Chamber of Deputies. When in March 1964 the military overthrew Goulart, Neves resigned as majority leader but remained as a deputy.

The decree law of 1965 which dissolved all existing parties resulted in Neves joining the newly created opposition Brazilian Democratic Movement (MDB), whereas most of his former PSD colleagues entered the pro-government party. He was elected to three successive terms in Congress. Throughout this period, he maintained opposition to the military government. In 1978 he was elected senator from Minas Gerais and in 1982 was overwhelmingly elected governor.

When the military decided to permit free elections in the 1984 presidential race, Tancredo Neves became the opposition nominee. Massive desertions from the government party gave Neves and the PMDE (Partido Movimiento Democratico Brasileiro) party a victory in the January 1985 electoral college. Before he could take the oath of office on March 15, however, Neves became seriously ill. He died from a series of surgical operations, and Vice President José Sarney became president of Brazil.

BIBLIOGRAPHY

Delgado, Lucilia de Almeida Neves. *Tancredo Neves, A Trajetoria de Um Liberal*. Rio de Janeiro: 1984.

JORDAN YOUNG

NÚÑEZ MOLEDO, RAFAEL (1825–1894), twice president of Colombia, was born in the Atlantic coastal city of Cartagena, where he also was educated. After receiving a law degree, he became active in politics. In 1844 he was president of the local Democratic Society and editor of *La Democracia*, both of which espoused freedoms proclaimed in recent European revolutions. In the early 1850s, he was elected to the Chamber of Representatives. There he became a firm supporter of the radical Liberal General José María Obando* and a staunch anticlerical. He served for a time as secretary of government under Obando. Núñez also held several ministerial posts in different administrations during the period. As secretary of the treasury in 1862, he strongly defended a decree nationalizing church properties.

In 1863 Núñez left Colombia for the United States, and then went to England and France, where he was consul in Liverpool and Le Havre. He contributed articles to Colombian periodicals on developments in Europe and came under influence of the Positivist school of philosophy and sociology. Disenchanted by the extreme federalism and economic stagnation that afflicted his country, he saw in the Positivist slogan "Order and Progress" the formula of stability and material development.

Núñez returned to Colombia in 1874. In alliance with like-minded Liberals—known as Independents—he lost his first bid for the presidency, but in 1879 was elected by a coalition of Independents and Conservatives. By this time, he stressed the necessity for gradual, ordered progress restrained by conservative institutions and values. During his first term, he emphasized economic development. A national bank was established and a protective tariff enacted. Several of the more extreme anticlerical measures of previous Liberal administrations were repealed.

Núñez was again elected president in 1884, primarily because of Conservative endorsement. His election further split the Liberals, many of whom viewed him as an opportunist and betrayer. In 1885 Liberal dissidents rebelled. The uprising was crushed with Conservative support. The event marked Núñez' final embrace of his former political enemies.

Now fully convinced that the federalist constitution of 1863 was unworkable, Núñez called a constitutional convention made up of Conservatives and Independents. Their final document, ratified and signed in 1886, embodied Núñez' ideas: a unitary republic, strengthened executive, role for the Roman Catholic Church, especially in education, and a clear definition of "responsible" individual liberties. The following year a Concordat with the Vatican formally recognized the church's place and gave the church an influential voice in education at all levels.

The delegates who wrote the Constitution of 1886 also elected Núñez to a six-year term, but he served actively only until 1888. At that time he retired to Cartagena, leaving day-to-day running of the government to Presidential Alternate Carlos Holguín. Núñez was again elected in 1891 but, considering his primary work accomplished, allowed Vice President Miguel Antonio Caro to act as executive. Núñez limited himself to making his views known in the capital through correspondence with the acting executive and articles in various newspapers and periodicals.

The Liberals felt themselves excluded as a political force, and the increasingly intolerant and reactionary actions of Núñez' allies resulted in continuing political instability. On several occasions, Núñez threatened to come out of retirement and reassume active running of the government. He was preparing to do so when he died suddenly.

BIBLIOGRAPHY

Castillo, Nicolás del. *El primer Núñez*. Bogotá: 1971.

Henao, Jesús María, and Geraldo Arrubla. *History of Colombia*. Chapel Hill: University of North Carolina Press, 1938.

Lievano Aguirre, Indalecio. *Rafael Núñez*. Bogotá: 1946.

Otero Muñoz, Gustavo. *Un hombre y una epoca: La vida azarosa de Rafael Núñez*. Bogotá: 1951.

Vergara, José Ramón. *Escrutinio histórico: Rafael Núñez*. Bogotá: 1939.

RICHARD E. SHARPLESS

O

OBANDO, JOSÉ MARÍA (1795–1861), Colombian caudillo, general, and president (1853–1854), was born near Caloto in the lower Cauca Valley. He first emerged as a successful guerrilla leader of blacks and Indians during the Wars for Independence, fighting on the side of the royalists in an area of southern Colombia where the conflict took on a decidedly class and racial character.

Late in 1822 Simón Bolívar* arrived in southern Colombia. Obando, sensing that the tide was turning against the royalists, visited Bolívar, who persuaded him to join forces with the army of Gran Colombia. He distinguished himself in subsequent battles and was promoted to colonel.

Obando remained in Popayán. In 1828, following assumption of dictatorial powers by Bolívar, Obando joined with General Francisco de Paula Santander* in the struggle against the dictator. When peace was restored, Obando emerged as the principal caudillo of southern Colombia.

During the confusion surrounding Bolívar's death in 1830, Venezuelan General Rafael Urdaneta* seized power in Bogotá. In the Cauca, Obando and General José Hilario López joined forces, declared the region annexed to Ecuador, and prepared to march on the capital. When Urdaneta's government collapsed, Obando was named vice president by a constitutional convention and provisional head of state in late 1831.

Following the election of Santander as the first president of the Republic of Nueva Granada in 1832, Obando successfully undertook to reannex the Cauca region. Although Santander's supporters made Obando their candidate for president in 1836, civilian opposition to continued rule by military men coalesced around José Ignacio Márquez, who was elected by Congress.

After his defeat, Obando retired to Popayán until 1839, when a popular uprising broke out in neighboring Pasto Province, provoked by an attempt by the central government to close local religious institutions. When President Márquez sent in troops, Obando supported the regional forces against the national government and again gathered a guerrilla army, but when he was finally defeated in July 1841 he fled to Peru.

Only when Liberal General José Hilario López was elected president in 1849, largely with the support of the Democratic Societies made up of artisans and college students, did Obando return home to take up military and diplomatic positions in the administration. With the Democratic Societies behind him, Obando won the presidential election of 1852.

As president, Obando supported the new federalist constitution of 1853, which expanded civil liberties, and included separation of church and state, universal suffrage, and popular election of provincial governors. However, when the alliance of Democratic Societies and students split apart, civil strife broke out and the specter of class war loomed. On April 17, 1854, General José María Melo seized power in the name of the artisans and offered dictatorial powers to Obando. When Obando refused, Melo assumed them himself. A Liberal-Conservative coalition overthrew Melo after a short but brutal civil war.

Obando was removed from the presidency. He retired from political life until 1860, when he again joined a federalist revolt, and was killed in a battle near Bogotá.

BIBLIOGRAPHY

Fals Borda, Orlando. *Subversion and Social Change in Colombia*. New York: Columbia University Press, 1969.
Henao, Jesús María, and Geraldo Arrubia. *History of Colombia*. Chapel Hill: University of North Carolina Press, 1938.
Ortíz, Venancio. *Historia de la revolución del 17 de abril de 1854*. Bogotá: 1855.
Rodríguez Plata, Horacio. *José María Obando, intimo*. Bogotá: 1958.
Samper, José María. *Ensayo sobre las revoluciones políticas y la condición social de la repúblicas colombianas*. Paris: E. Thunot Co., 1861.

RICHARD E. SHARPLESS

OBREGÓN, ALVARO (1880–1928), was the first president of Mexico after the fighting phase (1910–1920) of the Revolution ended and the political reform phase began. Born on a farm in Alamos in the state of Sonora, he managed a cigar factory, and then a flour mill. In 1911 he supported the Revolution by becoming mayor of Huatabampo, Sonora's southern port. In 1912 he formed his own army of 300 Indians, named himself general and supported President Francisco I. Madero.* He helped Venustiano Carranza* occupy Mexico City in 1914. In 1916 he became minister of war. After Carranza was assassinated in May 1920, Obregón became president on November 30, succeeding Acting President Adolfo de la Huerta.

Obregón launched an anticlerical campaign, pushed benefits for organized labor, and began the process of agrarian reform. He pressured his successor, President Plutarco Elías Calles, to get the no-reelection principle taken out of the Constitution, and in 1928 he won a second term. But before he could assume office again he was assassinated by a seminary student seeking to avenge the antichurch policies of Obregón.

BIBLIOGRAPHY

Gil, Feliciano. *Biografía del General Alvaro Obregón*. Hermosillo: Editores del Partido Antireelecionista, 1914.
Grieb, Kenneth J. *The United States and Huerta*. Lincoln: University of Nebraska Press, 1969.
Obregón, Alvaro. *Ocho Mil Kilómetros en Campaña*. Mexico City: Fondo de Cultura Económica, 1959.
Sáenz, Aaron. "Alvaro Obregón." *Historia Mexicana*. 10, No. 2 (October-December 1960).

MARVIN ALISKY

ODRÍA, MANUEL A. (1907–1974), president of Peru (1948–1956), graduated from the Chorrillos Military Academy (1919) and studied at the Escuela Superior de Guerra (1927–1929), of which he later served as director. Odría was promoted to brigadier general by Congress in 1946. The following year he became minister of the interior of President José Luís Bustamante y Rivero,* whom he ousted from power on October 29, 1948. During his autocratic rule, Odría kept the Peruvian Aprista Party outlawed and undertook a public works program, especially during the Korean War (1950–1953), when prices of Peruvian exports rose sharply and foreign investment expanded the national economy. At the end of his dictatorship, Odría traveled to the United States and Europe until 1961, when he returned to Lima to found the Unión Nacional Odriísta (UNO), which nominated him for president in the elections of 1962 and 1963. Although UNO came in third in both elections, the party remained active until the reformist military leaders came to power in 1968. Odría then faded from public view in retirement.

BIBLIOGRAPHY

Alisky, Marvin. *Historical Dictionary of Peru*. Metuchen, N.J.: Scarecrow Press, 1979.
Astíz, Carlos A. *Pressure Groups and Power Elites in Peruvian Politics*. Ithaca, N.Y.: Cornell University Press, 1969.
Chang-Rodríguez, Eugenio. *Opciones políticas peruanas*. Lima: Centro de Documentación Andina, 1985.

EUGENIO CHANG-RODRÍGUEZ

ODUBER QUIRÓS, DANIEL (1921–   ), was president of Costa Rica, 1974–1978. He was one of a group of students at the Liceo de Costa Rica and the Law School who formed the Center for the Study of National Problems in 1940. He later received a master's degree in philosophy from McGill University and studied in France at the Sorbonne.

Oduber helped found the Social Democratic Party in 1945 and participated in the 1948 civil war. Following the triumph of José Figueres Ferrer* in that conflict, he served as secretary general of the Founding Junta of the Second Republic. He was a founder in 1951 of the National Liberation Party (PLN), of which he became secretary general in 1956. He headed the PLN caucus in Congress for the 1958–1962 term and was foreign minister under President Francisco José Orlich Bolmarcich.*

Oduber was the PLN's candidate for president in 1966 but lost. He took the defeat very hard and sued the conservative newspaper, *La Nación*, for libel. His disappointment was compounded when Figueres sought the PLN nomination in 1970. However, he succeeded Figueres as president in 1974, the first time the PLN had won two consecutive terms.

As president, Oduber was not successful in dealing with inflation and other problems caused by the energy crisis of the 1970s. He also resisted public pressure for expulsion of "fugitive financier" Robert Vesco from the country. His party suffered electoral defeat in 1978.

After leaving the presidency, Oduber was active in the Socialist International, as its vice president, and in lecturing in universities in Europe and the United States.

BIBLIOGRAPHY

Ameringer, Charles D. *Democracy in Costa Rica*. New York: Praeger, 1982.
———. *Don Pepe: A Political Biography of José Figueres of Costa Rica*. Albuquerque: University of New Mexico Press, 1979.
Barahona Jiménez, Luis. *El pensamiento político en Costa Rica*. San José: Editorial Fernández-Arce, 1971.
Oduber, Daniel. *Una Campaña*. San José: Editorial, "Eloy Morua Carrillo," 1967.
                                                                    CHARLES D. AMERINGER

O'HIGGINS, BERNARDO (1778–1842), the illegitimate son of one of the last of Spain's captains general of Chile (and a native of Ireland), was the principal liberator of that country. As a youth, he attended schools in Lima, Peru, and in London. He did not return to Chile until 1802. He then took over a family hacienda near the city of Los Angeles and in 1804 was named mayor of Chillán.

When the movement for Chilean independence began on September 18, 1810, O'Higgins raised militia groups for the new regime. Elected to the Constitutional Assembly of 1811, he belonged to its Independence faction. When José Miguel Carrera Verdugo* seized power in November 1811, he named O'Higgins a member of a new Government Junta, but O'Higgins soon resigned and returned to his hacienda.

When a new Spanish expedition arrived from Peru in March 1813, O'Higgins again raised troops. He occupied Los Angeles but was unable to seize Chillán. In October 1813 he was wounded. However, in January 1814 the Government Junta decided to replace Carrera with O'Higgins as field commander of the independence army, thus starting a long feud between the two men.

With defeat of the Chileans in the Battle of Rancagua in October 1814, O'Higgins fled to Argentina. He returned to Chile two years later as a brigadier general in the Army of the Andes of José de San Martín.* On February 12, 1817, he took part in the victorious Battle of Chacabuco.

Four days after Chacabuco, Bernardo O'Higgins was chosen Supreme Director of Chile by a meeting of citizens and with the support of San Martín. In 1820 he also became Captain General of Chile. As a ruler, O'Higgins was arbitrary but was also a strong republican and a reformer. He abolished all titles of nobility and coats of arms, and attempted to suppress the right of primogeniture. He established a national army and organized a military school.

War continued with the Spaniards, in the southern part of the Central Valley. At one point the Spanish forces threatened Santiago. However, on April 5, 1818, the Chileans' victory at the Battle of Maipú assured the country's independence.

O'Higgins was responsible for the enactment of two successive constitutions, one in 1818 and another in 1822. He was frequently accused of acting high-handedly and rigging elections.

Some progress occurred in several fields under O'Higgins. Regular mail service was established between Santiago and Valparaiso, and several new schools, a national orphanage, and a military hospital were established. Some progress was also made in modernizing Santiago, including the opening of its main street, the Alameda. The United States extended diplomatic recogition to O'Higgins' government.

The war with the Spaniards continued until almost the end of O'Higgins' period in office. He appointed an English seaman, Admiral Thomas Cochrane, to organize a Chilean navy, which later helped José de San Martín to liberate Peru. General San Martín named O'Higgins a grand marshal of Peru in 1821.

Finally, opposition to the O'Higgins dictatorship resulted in uprisings in Concepción and La Serena in January 1823. Thereupon on January 28, an "open meeting" was organized in Santiago before which, after at first refusing, O'Higgins finally appeared and at last agreed to resign as Supreme Director. The new government soon deported O'Higgins to Peru. He lived near Lima for the next 19 years and died just when he was preparing to return home.

BIBLIOGRAPHY

Cortes, Lia, and Jordi Fuentes. *Diccionario Político de Chile*. Santiago: Editorial Orbe, 1967.
Enciclopedia Universal Ilustrada Europeo-Americana. Barcelona: José Espasa e Hijos.
Galdames, Luis. *Historia de Chile*. Santiago: Editorial Zig Zag, 1945.

ROBERT J. ALEXANDER

OLAYA HERRERA, ENRIQUE (1881–1937), served as president of Colombia (1930–1934) during a period of transition to Liberal Party rule following almost two decades of Conservative domination. His candidacy was the result of a coalition of Liberals and dissident Conservatives known as the National Concentration.

Olaya was born into a prominent family in Guateque, Boyacá. He served on the Liberal side against the Conservatives in the Civil War of the Thousand Days

(1899–1903), and later joined the opposition to the government of General Rafael Reyes.* He played a leading role in the overthrow of Reyes in 1909.

Olaya was an early advocate of cooperation between the parties. He accepted the fact that the Liberals were a minority, but argued that they should have a role in the government. Despite his own party's opposition, he accepted the post of minister in Washington during the Conservative administration of Pedro Nel Ospina (1922–1926) and served until 1929.

As president, Olaya was faced with severe economic problems resulting from the Great Depression. He moved cautiously. He carefully balanced the political interests of Liberals and Conservatives, while initiating limited social measures. He also established controls over the petroleum industry. Connections with North American financial circles made while he represented Colombia in Washington helped him in dealing with foreign creditors. He was, however, criticized by nationalists for concessions he made to U.S. oil interests.

Local Liberal attempts to assert political domination over Conservatives in Santander and Boyacá resulted in rural violence, which threatened to upset the delicate political balance that Olaya maintained. When a border conflict with Peru erupted, Olaya successfully used the opportunity to call for national peace and unity. Colombians were gratified when the League of Nations settled the dispute in Colombia's favor.

During the reformist Liberal administration of Alfonso López Michelson* (1934–1938), Olaya assumed leadership of the moderate wing of the party. He served López briefly as minister of foreign relations and ambassador to the Vatican.

BIBLIOGRAPHY

Dix, Robert H. *Colombia: The Political Dimensions of Change*. New Haven, Conn.: Yale University Press, 1967.
Fluharty, Vernon Lee. *Dance of the Millions*. Pittsburgh: University of Pittsburgh Press, 1957.
García, Antonio. *Gaitán y el problema de la revolución colombiana*. Bogotá: 1955.
Sharpless, Richard E. *Gaitán of Colombia: A Political Biography*. Pittsburgh: University of Pittsburgh Press, 1978.

RICHARD E. SHARPLESS

O'NEALE, CHARLES DUNCAN (1879–1936), was a major precursor of the mass political movement that emerged in Barbados during the 1930s. He left Barbados for Scotland in 1899 to study medicine at Edinburgh University. After graduating, he worked as a doctor in the English city of Newcastle, also becoming involved in the Independent Labor Party and winning a seat in the Sunderland County Council.

O'Neale returned to Barbados before World War I but soon moved to Trinidad, where he practiced medicine and was involved in local politics. He returned home in 1924 and found the political climate for propagating socialist ideas much

more receptive, largely as the result of the work of Clennell Wilsden Wickham*
and Clement Innis, who published a progressive newspaper, the *Weekly Herald*.
In October 1924 O'Neale and Wickham formed the Democratic League, which
was rooted in the principles of socialism with a program aimed at obtaining
universal adult suffrage, recognition of trade unions, collective bargaining, compulsory education, and welfare and social security measures. O'Neale also
formed the Workingmen's Association, which became the labor appendage to
the league.

In 1924 the league enjoyed its first electoral success when one of its members
was elected to the House of Assembly. O'Neale himself finally won a seat in
the House in 1932. However, in the four years he spent in the House, he was
unable to secure legislation on most of his demands because of the conservative
nature of the Assembly, chosen by an upper- and middle-class electorate. However, O'Neale's importance lay in his success in galvanizing the Barbadian
masses and workers into an effective political organization.

BIBLIOGRAPHY

Bajan Magazine, September 1959.
Hoyos, F. A. *Barbados: A History*. London: Macmillan Co., 1978.
————. *Builders of Barbados*. London: Macmillan Co., 1973.
————. *Our Common Heritage*. Bridgetown, Barbados: Advocate Press, 1953.
Tree, Ronald. *A History of Barbados*. 2d ed. London: Granada, 1977.

                                    PERCY C. HINTZEN AND W. MARVIN WILL

ONGANÍA, JUAN CARLOS (1914–   ), was president of Argentina from 1966
to 1970. Born in provincial Buenos Aires, he attended parochial schools before
entering the military academy. He rose to brigadier general by 1959 but was not
politically prominent until he emerged as head of the Azules faction that defeated
the Colorados in a 1962 military confrontation. The Azules believed that the
military should stay out of politics; the Colorados believed that the military
should rule.

Onganía was a powerful force behind the government's calling elections which
were won by Arturo Umberto Illia* in 1963. In 1965 Onganía retired from active
duty in protests over military promotions. Less than a year later he became
president by the June 1966 coup which overthrew Illia.

Onganía was welcomed by many Argentines dismayed by the country's economic stagnation and political unrest. However, the Onganía government soon
disbanded all political parties and confiscatd their property; political and labor
demonstrations were banned; and Congress, all provincial legislatures, and the
Supreme Court were dissolved. Opposition groups were suppressed, and their
leaders were jailed. The government also intervened in the universities and purged
many outstanding academics. Outstanding Argentine scholars and scientists left
the country.

In the economic area, the government emphasized private enterprise and welcomed foreign investment. Prices were allowed to increase faster than wages. By 1969 there was substantial discontent. In May protests spilled over into violence in the industrial and university city of Córdoba, the center of the most radical wing of the Peronist labor movement, which combined with students to defeat the police in street fighting and take over the city. Onganía finally had to send in the military to restore order.

Following the "Cordobazo," violence increased. Guerrilla activity began, militant Peronist youth groups became active, the radical part of the Catholic Church stepped up its efforts, and there was a violent struggle for control of the Peronist labor movement. In 1970 Onganía was ousted in a bloodless coup headed by army commander-in-chief Alejandro Agustín Lanusse.* Onganía then retired to private life.

BIBLIOGRAPHY

Ferns, Henry S. *Argentina*. New York: Praeger, 1969.
Hodges, Donald C. *Argentina, 1943–1976: The National Revolution and Resistance*. Albuquerque: University of New Mexico Press, 1976.
Johnson, Kenneth F. *Argentina's Mosaic of Discord*. Washington, D.C.: Institute for the Comparative Study of Political Systems, 1969.
Page, Joseph A. *Perón: A Biography*. New York: Random House, 1983.
Snow, Peter G. *Political Forces in Argentina*. New York: Praeger, 1979.

JOHN T. DEINER

ORIBE, MANUEL (1792–1857), was the second president of Uruguay and founder of the Blanco Party. He was born into a leading Montevideo family and joined the independence struggle when it began in 1811. He was first against the federalists who, under José Gervásio Artigas,* opposed the Buenos Aires authorities, but subsequently joined forces with Artigas and became a captain. However, after the Portuguese seized Montevideo in 1817, Oribe went to Buenos Aires, where he was given a captain's commission.

In 1821 Oribe returned to Montevideo to join the Portuguese forces there, but when they withdrew three years later, he returned to Buenos Aires. He was a leading figure in the Thirty-Three, led by Juan Antonio Lavalleja,* who went from Buenos Aires to Montevideo to launch the struggle for Uruguayan independence.

Oribe supported the first Uruguayan president, Fructuoso Rivera,* opposed Lavalleja's attempts to challenge him, and became minister of war and navy. Oribe succeeded Rivera in March 1835 but soon fell out with Rivera, who began a revolt in 1836. Oribe organized his followers during the conflict into the Blanco Party, and insisted that all government employees wear the White (Blanco) insignia.

Oribe was finally forced to resign in 1838 and went to Buenos Aires. There he participated in various campaigns launched by Juan Manuel de Rosas* against his opponents. As a consequence of success in those struggles, he was able to return to Uruguay in 1843 at the head of a force that soon gained control of most of the countryside. However, a nine-year siege of Montevideo, during which he presided over a Blanco government in Restauración, was ultimately unsuccessful. Oribe ostensibly retired to private life in 1851 and subsequently went to Europe. He returned to Uruguay in 1855 and, although continuing to be active in national politics, was unable to return to power. He died two years later, of natural causes.

BIBLIOGRAPHY

Carnelli, Lorenzo. *Oribe y su época*. Montevideo, n.d. *Enciclopedia Universal Ilustrada Europeo-Americana*. Barcelona: José Espasa e Hijos.
Pereda, Setembrino. *Los partidos históricos uruguayos*. Montevideo, 1918.

ROBERT J. ALEXANDER

ORLICH BOLMARCICH, FRANCISCO JOSÉ (1907–1969), was president of Costa Rica from 1962 to 1966. He was a close friend and collaborator of Costa Rica's dominant politician, José Figueres Ferrer.* Orlich, a wealthy coffee-grower, helped finance Figueres' agricultural venture during the 1930s.

Orlich and Figueres organized a liberal faction called Acción Demócrata, which merged with the Center for the Study of National Problems to form the Social Democratic Party in 1945. Orlich commanded the "Northern Front" during the 1948 civil war and was a leading member of the Founding Junta of the Second Republic (1948–1949), as minister of public works. The National Liberation Party (PLN) was founded at Orlich's finca in 1951; two years later he won a seat in the Legislative Assembly and was party leader in Congress. He was Figueres' choice for the PLN nomination in 1958 but lost the election, principally because the PLN was split. Four years later he got a second chance and won.

As president, Orlich was more conservative than many members of his party. He was reluctant to take new initiatives. He faced strong opposition within the PLN from those who felt he had caused it to lose its revolutionary character and from those who charged that he bungled disaster relief during the two-year eruption of the Irazú volcano. However, Orlich's presidency was not as conservative as critics charged; he gave attention to housing for the poor and to the problem of agrarian reform. Nevertheless, when the PLN lost the election of 1966, Orlich received the blame. He died of cancer three years later.

BIBLIOGRAPHY

Ameringer, Charles D. *Don Pepe: A Political Biography of José Figueres of Costa Rica*. Albuquerque: University of New Mexico Press, 1979.
Araya Pochet, Carlos. *Historia de los partidos políticos: Liberación Nacional*. San José: Editorial Costa Rica, 1968.

Creedman, Theodore S. *Historical Dictionary of Costa Rica*. Metuchen, N.J.: Scarecrow Press, 1977.

                                                              CHARLES D. AMERINGER

ORTEGA SAAVEDRA, (JOSÉ) DANIEL (1945–   ), the first among equals of the victorious Sandinista Liberation Front (FSLN) leaders who dominated Nicaraguan policy after civil war toppled the Somoza family dynasty which had dominated the country from 1936 to 1979, was inaugurated president in January 1985. His father was a middle-class merchant, and both Daniel's father and mother had been in trouble with the police for taking part in conspiracies.

In 1959 several invasions from Honduras and Costa Rica failed to remove the regime, then headed by Luis Somoza Debayle.* Frustrated students then formed Nicaraguan Patriotic Youth in 1960; one of its early members was Daniel Ortega who, at 15, was arrested for the first time. After graduating from secondary school, he entered the Jesuit-run Universidad Centro-Americana in Managua to study law, but dropped out after a year and joined the FSLN which had been founded some months earlier. He helped organize student protests and went to Havana to attend a congress convened by Fidel Castro* to support revolutionary movements in the hemisphere.

When Ortega returned to Managua, he helped establish FSLN urban guerrilla cells. Robberies of banks and businesses became a principal source of funds for the Sandinistas. Captured in 1967, Ortega spent the next seven years in jail, until December 30, 1974, when he and 13 other political prisoners were released as part of a FSLN ransom payment.

Ortega and the others were flown to Cuba, where they received several months of military training. But in the wave of repression that followed the release of Ortega and the other prisoners—along with entry of new recruits into the FSLN ranks—a split developed between the original Prolonged Popular War Tendency, which focused on building up forces in the countryside, and another group known as the Proletarian Tendency, which sought to build a revolutionary apparatus among urban workers. There also developed an Insurrectionist or Tercerista group led by Daniel Ortega, which sought to build alliances with progressive business groups and upper class intellectuals. This group gave rise to the Broad Front of Opposition, formed in April 1978 by Rafael Córdova Rivas, a Conservative Party attorney who had defended various FSLN prisoners, and Alfonso Robelo Callejas, an industrialist. However, in December 1978 the three FSLN factions set up a unified command.

In June 1979 the FSLN established a government-in-exile in Costa Rica, headed by a five-member junta made up of Daniel Ortega; Moisés Hassan Morales, a Marxist engineer heading the People's United Movement, an FSLN-created working-class group; Sergio Ramírez Mercado, a lawyer-writer; Alfonso Robello Calleja; and Violeta Barrios de Chamorro, widow of Pedro Joaquín Chamorro,* the murdered *La Prensa* editor. When the Sandinistas marched into Managua July 19, this Junta of National Reconstruction under the chairmanship of Ortega was placed in charge of day-to-day operations of the government, although the nine-member FSLN Directorate was really the ultimate governmental authority.

In the aftermath of unilateral changes in the regime by the FSLN, Violeta Barrios de Chamorro and Alfonso Robelo resigned from the Junta in 1980. After intense negotiations involving Ortega, they were replaced by Rafael Córdova Rivas and Arturo Cruz Porras, former president of the Central Bank. Córdova and Cruz resigned in 1981 over postponement of elections and media censorship—especially that of *La Prensa*.

With every sector of the economy in crisis in 1979 and much of the population in danger of starvation, Ortega sought help from both the West and the East. In September 1979 he went to the Havana Summit Meeting of the Non-aligned Nations, then chaired by Fidel Castro.

Soon after Ronald Reagan took office in 1981, U.S. policy toward Nicaragua shifted abruptly from conciliatory efforts by the Carter administration to hostility. The Reagan administration sought to "destabilize" the Sandinista regime before it could consolidate its power. It subsidized those seeking to mount a guerrilla war against the regime.

Following the U.S. invasion of Grenada in October 1983, Ortega tried to defuse American opposition to the Sandinista regime. Amnesty for exiles was proclaimed, and elections were scheduled for November 4, 1984. Two opposition parties—the Democratic Coordination Council, headed by Arturo Cruz Porras, and the Independent Liberal Party—complaining of press censorship and restrictions on the right of assembly, chose not to compete.

Although Ortega and his vice presidential candidate Sergio Ramírez Mercado were assured of election, Ortega ran as if he had a serious chance of losing. When votes were counted, Ortega had won 63 percent of the 1,170,142 votes cast, and the FSLN had won 61 of the 90 seats contested in the National Assembly.

BIBLIOGRAPHY

Current Biography, October 1984.
Ortega, Daniel. "Nothing Will Hold Back Our Struggle for Liberation," in Pedro Camejo and Fred Murphy, (eds.). *The Nicaraguan Revolution*. New York: Pathfinder Press, 1979.
Pearson, Neale J. "Nicaragua," in Robert J. Alexander (ed.). *Political Parties of the Americas*. Vol. 2. Westport, Conn.: Greenwood Press, 1982.
———. "Nicaragua in Crisis." *Current History*, February 1979.
Walker, Thomas W. (ed.). *Nicaragua in Revolution*. New York: Praeger Special Studies, 1982.

NEALE J. PEARSON

OSBORNE, JOHN ALFRED (1936–   ), became chief minister of Montserrat in 1978 after his party swept all seats in the country's election. He received his elementary and secondary education in Montserrat, after which he left for Great

Britain where he attended Paddington Technical College. Returning to Montserrat in 1960, he established himself as a shipbuilder and shipowner, amassing considerable wealth.

Osborne was first elected to the Legislative Council in 1966 and then won his constituency five successive times, the last in 1983. Opposed to William Henry Bramble* during the latter half of the 1960s, Osborne joined with Bramble's son and heir apparent, Percival Austin Bramble* in 1970, to found the Progressive Democratic Party (PDP), which was swept to power that year. Osborne served for a short time as minister of agriculture in the Percival Bramble government but soon left the party, criticizing Bramble for his socialist policies and autocratic leanings.

With the support of a powerful intellectual and union leader, James Irish, Osborne formed the Peoples Liberation Movement (PLM) in 1976. In 1978 the PLM won all the seats in the Legislative Council, and Osborne became chief minister. This victory was repeated in 1983, when the PLM won all but two seats.

Osborne pursued a policy of ardent support for free enterprise. As a result, he gained strong backing from the powerful local business class and attracted North American investors to the country. His government also sought to revive local agriculture through production of cotton, red peppers, and vegetables. At the same time, Osborne allowed the social and welfare programs of the previous government, which he once regarded as evidence of its socialist leanings, to remain intact.

BIBLIOGRAPHY

Alexander, Robert J. "Montserrat," in Robert J. Alexander (ed.). *Political Parties of the Americas*. Vol. 2. Westport, Conn.: Greenwood Press, 1983.
Fergus, H. A. "Electoral Behavior in Montserrat." *Caribbean Quarterly* 27 (March 1981).
Fergus, H. A. "Personalities in Montserratian Politics: Comments on 1983 General Elections." *Bulletin of Eastern Caribbean Affairs* 10 (May/June 1984).
                                    PERCY C. HINTZEN AND W. MARVIN WILL

OSORIO, OSCAR (1910–1969), was president of El Salvador (1950–1956). He studied at the Escuela Politecnica Militar and had a normal military career until 1945 when, implicated in a conspiracy, he was exiled to Mexico. He returned in 1948, after the overthrow of President Castañeda Castro, to become a member of a new Revolutionary Council.

The young military organized the Revolutionary Party of Democratic Unification (PRUD), and it elected Osorio president in 1950. His presidency established social security, and legalized trade unions and collective bargaining for urban, but not rural, workers. It also established the Salvadoran Institute for Development of Production and began a large hydroelectric project on the Lempa River. He was succeeded by his minister of interior, José María Lémus.

Osorio soon broke with his successor. In 1960 he formed the PRUD (Auténtico), but it did not prosper. Thereafter, he ceased to be a major factor in national politics.

BIBLIOGRAPHY

Directory of Latin American and Caribbean Biography, 1971–72. London: Melrose Press, 1971.
Martz, John D. *Central America: The Crisis and the Challenge.* Chapel Hill: University of North Carolina Press, 1959.
McDonald, Ronald H. "El Salvador," in Robert J. Alexander (ed.). *Political Parties of the Americas.* Vol. 1. Westport, Conn.: Greenwood Press, 1982.
New York Times, March 8, 1969.

ROBERT J. ALEXANDER

OSPINA PÉREZ, MARIANO (1891–1975), was the Conservative president of Colombia during the turbulent years 1946–1950. He was born in Medellín into a politically prominent Antioquía family. His grandfather, Mariano Ospina Rodríguez, was president of Colombia from 1857 to 1861, and an uncle, Pedro Nel Ospina, was president from 1922 to 1926. Educated in private schools in Medellín, Ospina studied business and engineering at universities in Medellín, the United States, and Belgium. Subsequently, he was active for years in managing the family's vast commercial holdings. For a time he directed the Federación Nacional de Cafeteros de Colombia.

Ospina entered politics at an early age. He served in city and departmental offices, and then was elected a senator from Antioquía in 1923. In 1926 he was minister of public works. Ospina earned a reputation for moderation and conciliation. He generally stayed apart from the intense internal strife and tendencies toward extremism that wracked the Conservative Party during the 1930s and early 1940s. Yet, when the rightist party leader, Laureano Gómez,* looked for a candidate to oppose the divided Liberals in the election of 1946, he settled on Ospina, who won because of the Liberal split, although the Liberals retained majorities in Congress.

The Ospina administration passed limited social legislation of benefit to the workers. Ospina, however, appeared to agree with other Conservative—and some Liberal—leaders that it was time to limit change, or even to reverse gains made by the "popular classes" during the years of Liberal reformism.

When the Liberals confirmed their majority in the 1947 congressional elections, and popular Jorge Eliecer Gaitán* won control of the Liberal Party, the Ospina administration appeared paralyzed. This seemed to be confirmed by increasing rural violence between Liberals and Conservatives in which tens of thousands lost their lives, and by the president's apparent inability to control it.

Following the assassination of Gaitán on April 9, 1948 and the uprising known as the *Bogotázo.* Ospina brought Liberals into his administration. But the contradictions of a Conservative president representing a minority of the voters and a Liberal Congress representing a majority, as well as the antagonisms between reactionary Conservatives and reformist Liberals, led Ospina to close Congress and declare a state of siege in 1949. His action paved the way for the election of Gómez in 1950, when the Liberals abstained from voting.

Following the formation of the National Front governments in the late 1950s, Ospina assumed the role of an elder statesman of the Conservative Party. An important, sometimes majority, faction of the party identified as Ospinistas.

BIBLIOGRAPHY

Dix, Robert H. *Colombia: The Political Dimensions of Change*. New Haven, Conn.: Yale University Press, 1967.
Ospina Pérez, Mariano. *Una política conservadora para Colombia*. Bogotá: 1969.
Sharpless, Richard E. *Gaitán of Colombia: A Political Biography*. Pittsburgh: University of Pittsburgh Press, 1978.

RICHARD E. SHARPLESS

OVANDO CANDIA, ALFREDO (1917–   ), president of Bolivia in 1966 and 1969–1970, attended primary and secondary school in Sucre and La Paz and entered the military academy. With the outbreak of the Chaco War, he briefly served at the front. In 1936 he graduated and subsequently received further training in the Higher War College and in Argentina. He was a major by 1948. After the Nationalist Revolutionary Movement (MNR) victory in 1952, he was further promoted, rising to general of division by December 1962. He taught at the Higher War College, served as military attaché to Paraguay and Uruguay, was army chief of staff in 1957, and commander-in-chief of the armed forces by 1962. On December 24, 1964, he was promoted to general of the army.

Ovando was the military power behind the overthrow of the MNR in November 1964. He served as co-president of the military government until 1966, and he ruled alone until René Barrientos Ortuño* took over in August. With the death of Barrientos in April 1969, Ovando permitted Vice President Luis Adolfo Siles Salinas to assume the presidency briefly, but carried out a coup against him on September 26, 1969.

Ovando launched a Peruvian-style "revolution from above." He formed a civilian-military cabinet of the "national left," revoked the Petroleum Code of 1955, and nationalized the Bolivian Gulf Oil Company on October 17, 1969. Labor unions were permitted to organize, and wages were increased. Troops were withdrawn from the mines.

These radical moves proved confusing. Earlier, Ovando had ordered troops into the mines during the general strike of May 1965, had directd the campaign against the Cuban guerrilla *foco* of 1967, and put down the Teoponte guerrilla *foco* in July 1970. Economic nationalism and the influence of radical young civilian reformers in his cabinet encouraged anti-imperialist measures and a foreign policy of "independence neutralism." He sent an ambassador to Moscow in January 1970 and received a $27.5 million loan from the USSR.

The United States recognized the Ovando government, but after the nationalization of Gulf, major oil companies refused to purchase or refine Bolivian crude, and U.S. government aid was reduced by 75 percent. In September 1970, shortly before his ouster, Ovando promised to compensate Gulf with $78 million. Internal turmoil came to a head on October 4, 1970, in a right-wing military coup. It failed, but on October 7, Ovando resigned, and General Juan José Torres González* secured control. Ovando was named ambassador to Spain by Torres and remained there in exile after Torres fell ten months later.

BIBLIOGRAPHY

Gumucio, Mariano Baptista. *Historia Contemporánea de Bolivia, 1930–1978*. 2d ed. La Paz: Gisbert, 1978.

Mitchell, Christopher. *The Legacy of Populism in Bolivia, From the MNR to Military Rule*. New York: Praeger, 1977.

Por Qué? Para Qué?: Documentos del Gobierno Revolucionario de Bolivia. La Paz: Editorial del Estado, 1969.

Ríos Reinaga, David. *Civiles y Militares en la Revolución Boliviana*. La Paz: Difusión, 1967.

                                                    WALTRAUD QUEISER MORALES

P

PÁEZ, JOSÉ ANTONIO (1790–1873), was the first president of Venezuela. He had only the most rudimentary formal education. Before the outbreak of the movement for independence, he was employed as a ranch-hand in the great plains or llanos. Once the independence struggle began in 1810, Páez joined the rebel forces, mobilizing the llanos cattlemen for the cause. When the movement was temporarily defeated in 1814, Páez continued the struggle.

When Simón Bolívar* returned from exile to renew the war for independence in 1816, José Antonio Páez recognized his authority. Páez was one of the major commanders in Bolívar's great victory at Carabobo in 1821, which assured Venezuelan independence. Then, when Bolívar went on to pursue the war else-where, Páez' influence was preponderant in the regime he left in charge in Venezuela.

Páez became increasingly discontented with the Gran Colombia regime, pre-sided over by Bolívar and with its seat in Bogotá, Colombia. In 1826, summoned to Bogotá to explain his conduct, he was not punished. In the next year, he led an abortive revolt, which ended when Bolívar pardoned him.

When a new revolt began in 1829, Páez joined it and soon became its head. In 1831 he became first president of Venezuela and served for one four-year term. He was succeeded by a hand-picked civilian named José María Vargas, but a few months later a revolt led by Santiago Mariño* and José Tadeo Monagas* overthrew Vargas. Thereupon Páez rallied his supporters and restored Vargas to office.

However, Vargas was again forced out in 1836 and was succeeded by another Páez loyalist, Vice President Carlos Soublette.* Páez then returned to the pres-idency for the 1839–1843 term, and was succeeded by Soublette for the 1843–1847 period.

With the exit of President Soublette, domination of Venezuelan politics by Páez and the so-called Conservative oligarchy came to an end. Páez chose as his candidate in 1847 General José Tadeo Monagas, a leader of the 1831 revolt, who had subsequently made his peace with Páez. Once in office, Monagas formed an alliance with the Liberals. As a consequence, Páez led a revolt against Monagas, but was defeated and went into exile.

Returning to Venezuela with a small force of armed followers in 1849, José Antonio Páez was this time not only defeated but also captured. He was exiled in 1850 and spent the next eight years in New York City.

With the overthrow of the Liberal regime in 1858 by General Julián Castro, Páez went back to Venezuela. However, in July 1859 he again went abroad. This time he stayed overseas until 1861 when he was called back by his Conservative followers to lead their military forces in the Federal War that had been underway for two years. Soon afterward he was declared dictator of Venezuela by the Conservative forces.

Meanwhile, the Conservatives were losing the Federal War. Finally, in the middle of 1863 an agreement was signed between José Antonio Páez and the Federalist (Liberal) leader General Juan Cristósomo Falcón,* which put an end to the conflict and recognized Falcón as president. Páez then returned to his exile in New York City, where he died.

BIBLIOGRAPHY

Graham, Robert B. C. *José Antonio Páez*. Philadelphia: Macrae, 1929.
Magallanes, Manuel Vicente. *Los Partidos Políticos en la Evolución Histórica de Venezuela*. Caracas: Monte Avila Editores, 1977.
Páez, José Antonio. *Autobiografiá del General José Antonio Páez*. 2 vols. New York: 1969.

ROBERT J. ALEXANDER

PAIEWONSKY, RALPH (1907–   ), the last appointed governor of the United States Virgin Islands, was the son of Jewish immigrant parents and born in St. Thomas, Virgin Islands. He went to local schools, and later to New York University, where he received a chemistry degree. Between 1940 and 1960 he was Virgin Islands member of the Democratic National Committee. He was also president of the Virgin Islands Legislative Assembly for some years. He largely dominated Virgin Islands politics during the Kennedy-Johnson period, being appointed governor by President John F. Kennedy and remaining until the end of the Johnson administration. Upon retiring from politics, Paiewonsky pursued a business career in the islands.

BIBLIOGRAPHY

Personalities Caribbean. 7th ed. Kingston, Jamaica: Personalities Ltd., 1983.
Sharpless, Richard E. "Virgin Islands of the United States," in Robert J. Alexander (ed.). *Political Parties of the Americas*. Westport, Conn.: Greenwood Press, 1982.

RICHARD E. SHARPLESS

PALACIOS, ALFREDO LORENZO (1879–1963), was one of the group of outstanding Socialist politicians who became active in Argentine politics at the close of the nineteenth century and continued to be active into the 1950s. He received his law degree from the University of Buenos Aires, and later was professor and dean of the University of Buenos Aires law faculty, and professor, dean, and president of the University of La Plata. His academic speciality was labor legislation, but his passion was politics.

Palacios was one of the founders of the Socialist party and in 1904 became the first Socialist deputy in the national Congress. Reelected several times, he was later elected to the national Senate, serving from 1935 to 1943. He was responsible for much pioneering labor legislation.

Palacios was one of Juan Domingo Perón's* most bitter critics. In 1944 he resigned all his academic positions in protest against what Palacios felt was Perón's destruction of the free labor movement in Argentina. Along with many other Socialist labor and political figures, Palacios was forced to go into exile.

Although over 70 years old by the time Perón was overthrown, Palacios was named ambassador to Uruguay in 1955 and participated in the constitutional reform convention of 1957. He was elected senator again in 1958, but resigned in protest against the military's overthrow of the constitutional government of President Arturo Frondizi* in 1962.

BIBLIOGRAPHY

Alexander, Robert J. *Labor Relations in Argentina, Brazil and Chile*. New York: McGraw-Hill, 1962.
Baily, Samuel. *Labor, Nationalism and Politics in Argentina*. New Brunswick, N.J.: Rutgers University Press, 1967.
Whitaker, Arthur P. *The United States and Argentina*. Cambridge, Mass.: Harvard University Press, 1954.
Wright, Ione S., and Lisa Nekhorn. *Historical Dictionary of Argentina*. Metuchen, N.J.: Scarecrow Press, 1978.

JOHN T. DEINER

PANDO, JOSÉ MANUEL (1849–1917), was president of Bolivia (1899–1904) and founder of the Republican Party. Born in Arica, Pando spent most of his youth in La Paz, where he received his bachelor's degree at 16 and completed six years of medical school. In an effort to topple the dictator Mariano Melgarejo,* he abandoned his medical career and joined the army in 1871. Although progressing rapidly through the ranks, he retired while a lieutenant colonel. During the War of the Pacific, he rejoined the army as a captain and emerged from the war a hero.

After the war, Pando became chief of the Liberal Party and led various Liberal revolts against entrenched Conservative governments, causing his exile to Chile and confinement to the Acre wilderness in northeastern Bolivia. While exploring the northeastern jungles, he became aware of the Brazilian encroachments and the need to incorporate the wealthy rubber region into the nation.

In December 1898 Pando led the Liberals in the successful Federal Revolution. A governing junta was established, headed by Colonel Pando. A Liberal-dominated constitutional assembly proclaimed José Manuel Pando as president.

The Pando government was active in developing roads, railroads, and communications. It was more closely tied to the new tin mining elite than to the landlord-silver oligarchy. The government attracted major foreign investments into mining, railroad construction, and the rubber boom. Despite their initial program of federalism, the Liberals instituted a unitary system not unlike that of the Conservatives. Although the Liberals had enlisted Indian support for the revolution with promises of agrarian reform, once in power they continued to despoil Indian community lands and espoused the racist-Positivist philosophies of the day which characterized the Indian as subhuman.

In the Acre region, rubber tappers, instigated by Brazil, revolted four times between 1899 and 1902. In 1901 Pando assigned concessionary rights for rubber exploitation to North American investors for 33 years, expecting in return U.S. political and diplomatic support for Bolivia against Brazilian encroachments, but the North Americans failed to intervene. The Pando government finally negotiated the Treaty of Petropolis with Brazil in 1903, which gave most of Acre to Brazil for a promised payment of $10 million and construction of a railway outlet to the Amazon.

After leaving office, Pando remained much involved in politics. He and other prominent Liberals broke with the Liberal Party and founded the Republican Party in 1914. Three years later Pando was assassinated by a political opponent.

BIBLIOGRAPHY

Diaz, Arguedas, Julio. *Los generales de Bolivia*. La Paz: Imprenta Intendencia General de Guerra, 1929.
Fellman Velarde, José. *Historia de Bolivia*. Vol. 3. 2d ed. La Paz: Los Amigos del Libro, 1981.
Fifer, J. Valerie. *Bolivia: Land, Location and Politics Since 1825*. Cambridge: Cambridge University Press, 1972.
Klein, Herbert S. *Parties and Political Change in Bolivia, 1880–1942*. Cambridge: Cambridge University Press, 1969.
O'Connor d'Arlach, Tomás. *Los presidentes de Bolivia desde 1825 hasta 1912*. La Paz: González y Medina, 1912.

WALTRAUD QUEISER MORALES

PARDO Y BARREDA, JOSÉ (1864–1947), President of Peru (1904–1908 and 1915–1919), was born in Lima. Son of Manuel Pardo y Lavalle,* Peru's first full-term civilian president, he was awarded a B.A. in literature (1883), a doctorate in political science (1885), and the professional title of lawyer in 1886 from San Marcos University, where he taught international law from 1903 to 1904. He was minister of foreign relations from 1903 to 1904, when he was nominated presidential candidate of the Partido Civil founded by his father. After his first administration, Pardo lived in Europe for five years. Upon his return to Lima in 1914, he was elected president of San Marcos University. The following year, he was again his party's successful candidate. His second administration ended with a preventive coup by Augusto B. Leguía,* the winner of the 1919 general elections. Pardo lived in Europe from 1919 to 1940. He died in Lima.

BIBLIOGRAPHY

Basadre, Jorge. *Historia de la República del Peru.* Lima: Editorial Universitaria, 1968.
Martín, José Carlos. *José Pardo y Barreda, el estadista.* Lima: Compañía de Impresiones y Publicidad, 1948.
Pike, Frederick B. *The Modern History of Peru.* New York: Praeger, 1967.

                                        EUGENIO CHANG-RODRÍGUEZ

PARDO Y LAVALLE, MANUEL (1834–1878), president of Peru, was born in Lima, son of the conservative writer Felipe Pardo y Aliago (1806–1868). His early schooling was in Chile; he finished high school in Lima and then studied at the universities of Barcelona and Paris. He returned to Lima in 1853 to launch a business career. Pardo expounded his nationalist and moderate Positivist ideas in the *Revista de Lima.* He was commissioned to negotiate a loan for Peru in Europe in 1864, and upon his return he joined the Huancayo uprising headed by Colonel Mariano Ignacio Prado. When Prado assumed dictatorial power to repel the attack on Callao by a Spanish Armada, Pardo was appointed minister of the treasury in 1865. Three years later he was named director of the Lima Public Beneficence Society and served as mayor of Lima from 1869 to 1870.

In 1871 Pardo founded the Partido Civil purportedly to promote civilian government and modernize the country. One year later he was elected as the first civilian president of the country. He assumed office after a military uprising against him was crushed by the civilian population of Lima. The most important accomplishments of his administration were the establishment of the faculty of public administration at San Marcos University and the founding of the Schools of Engineering, Agriculture, and Arts and Crafts. Ironically, he urged his party to elect General Mariano Ignacio Prado as presidential candidate. General Prado succeeded him in 1876. After spending two years in Chile, Manuel Pardo returned to Lima to become senator of Junin and president of the Senate. A sergeant guarding the Parliament killed him when he was about to enter the building.

BIBLIOGRAPHY

Alisky, Marvin. *Historical Dictionary of Peru.* Metuchen, N.J.: Scarecrow Press, 1979.
Pike, Frederick B. *The Modern History of Peru.* New York: Praeger, 1967.
Tauro, Alberto. *Diccionario enciclopédico del Peru.* Lima: Editorial Mejia Baca, 1968.

                                        EUGENIO CHANG-RODRÍGUEZ

PAZ ESTENSSORO, VÍCTOR (1907–   ), was a founder and leader of the party that made the 1952 revolution, the Nationalist Revolutionary Movement (MNR), and president of Bolivia (1952–1956, 1960–1964, and 1985–   ). He got his early education in Tarija and the Colegio Nacional Bolívar of Oruro. At San Andrés University in La Paz, he received his law degree. In 1927 he worked as an attorney and then served in various government financial agencies. In 1939, as president of the Mining Bank in the Germán Busch* government, he was responsible for a stringent foreign exchange law that required the large tin companies to sell their foreign exchange to the Central Bank at fixed rates.

Paz entered politics in 1938 as representative from Tarija to the National Convention called by President Busch. He was reelected as a national deputy from Tarija in 1940 and became first vice president of the Chamber of Deputies for 1940–1941. In 1941, he served briefly in the cabinet of President Enrique Peñaranda as minister of economy, but resigned in protest when many Busch reforms were revoked. A Chaco War veteran, he led in founding the MNR in January 1941. The MNR and RADEPA, the secret veterans' lodge, made the "revolution" of December 20, 1943. In the new government of Major Gualberto Villarroel López,* Paz became minister of finance. He and other MNR cabinet officers resigned in early 1944 because of U.S. refusal to recognize the revolutionary regime, but he returned to his post several months later and only resigned again shortly before the July 1946 coup against Villarroel. Paz went into a six-year exile (1946–1952) in Argentina, where he worked in the banking system but continued to keep in touch with the MNR underground at home.

Paz, though in exile, ran as the MNR candidate in the presidential elections of 1951. Although Paz and his running mate, Hernán Siles Zuazo,* won a plurality, they lacked the necessary constitutional majority. To prevent an MNR government, the oligarchical forces under President Mamerto Urriolagoitia turned the country over to military rule. However, with the MNR revolutionary victory on April 9, 1952, Paz returned triumphantly and was inaugurated president on April 16. During his first presidential term, the MNR extended the franchise to all Bolivians; a sweeping land reform decree was signed in 1953; the large mining companies were nationalized; and extensive development of the eastern lowlands was begun. After his term ended in 1956, Paz served as ambassador to Britain.

In 1960 the MNR split over the presidential nomination. Paz had returned and won the nomination of his party over Walter Guevara Arze,* who formed the Authentic Revolutionary Party (PRA). His second term imposed stringent economic measures under the Triangular Plan in the mines, which led to great labor unrest. Vigorous economic development programs were instituted with $205 million in U.S. economic assistance.

In 1964, although it had been expected that Vice President Juan Lechín Oquendo* would run for the presidency, Paz sought a third term, irrevocably fragmenting the MNR. General René Barrientos Ortuño* was his vice presidential candidate. Barrientos launched a coup against Paz on November 4, and Paz left for an extended exile in Lima, where he taught economics in a university.

The MNR was part of the conspiracy with the Bolivian Socialist Phalange (FSB) and military that overthrew President Juan José Torres González* in August 1971. With the presidency of Hugo Banzer Suarez,* Paz returned to Bolivia, but he soon broke with the military and was again exiled.

In July 1978 Paz ran in the presidential elections, but the results were annulled and the military took over. He again participated in the July 1979 elections, coming in second. He condemned the military takeover by Colonel Natusch Busch on November 1, 1979, against Interim President Guevara Arze. In the June 1980 election Víctor Paz drew about 21 percent of the vote, but again no one received the majority required to elect a president. Congress was to decide, and Paz had agreed to support Hernán Siles, but on July 17, 1980 a bloody military coup by General Luis García Meza again thwarted civilian rule, and Paz went back into exile. He returned to Bolivia again when Siles Zuazo was sworn in as president in October 1982.

When President Siles called a new election in July 1985, Paz Estenssoro ran once again. Although he came in slightly behind General Banzer in the popular vote, no candidate had a majority, and Congress chose Paz Estenssoro over Banzer. He was inaugurated for the fourth time on August 6, 1985, and immediately sought to come to grips with the country's economic chaos: 50,000 percent inflation, international bankruptcy, and stagnating production.

BIBLIOGRAPHY

Alexander, Robert J. *Prophets of the Revolution*. New York: Macmillan Co., 1962.
Fellman Velarde, José. *Víctor Paz Estenssoro: El Hombre y la Revolución*. La Paz: A. Tejerina, 1954.
Loayza Beltrán, Fernando. *Campos de Concentración en Bolivia: Tres Años Prisionero de Víctor Paz Estenssoro*. La Paz: Burillo, 1956.
Navarro, Gustavo Adolfo (Tristán Marof). *Víctor Paz Estenssoro*. La Paz: Editorial La Paz, 1949.
Reinaga, Fausto. *Víctor Paz Estenssoro*. La Paz: Editorial La Paz, 1949.

WALTRAUD QUEISER MORALES

DOM PEDRO I (ALCÂNTARA DE BRAGANÇA E BOURBON) (1798–1834), commands an imposing place in Brazilian history by his simple act of declaring Brazil an independent nation and successfully severing the more than 300-year relationship with the mother country, Portugal. Although born in Portugal, he came to Brazil at the age of nine when his father King João VI and his mother, Queen Carlota Joaquina, fled to Brazil in 1808 to escape the invading armies of Napoleon Bonaparte. In 1821 King João VI reluctantly returned to Portugal but left his 23-year-old son, Pedro, as regent.

When the Portuguese Parliament ordered Dom Pedro to return to Portugal for further education, he declared, "Tell the people that I will stay." The phrase "I will stay" ("fico") became famous as the first step in Brazil's independence.

Pedro reorganized his cabinet to include politicians reflecting Brazilian nationalist sentiment most notably Brazilian-born José Bonifácio de Andrada e Silvo,* from São Paulo. As pressure mounted from Portugal, and after much discussion with members of his cabinet and enthusiastic street demonstrations, Dom Pedro declared Brazil an independent nation on September 7, 1822, and took the title Pedro I, Emperor of Brazil. In approximately 15 months, with relatively little bloodshed, independence was assured.

Pedro I, governed for the next nine years. He enacted a constitution after disbanding a constituent assembly he had called. His autocratic actions displeased many of his Brazilian supporters, but the constitution of 1824 was considered liberal for the time. In addition to the traditional three branches of government, it contained an innovative "Moderating Power" which made the emperor responsible for preserving the balance among the other branches of government. When the empire ended in 1889, the army unofficially took over this function.

Although his early role as a symbol of the nation's independence movement was invaluable, Brazilians soon tired of Pedro's autocratic personality and heavy dependence on Portuguese monarchists who had remained in Brazil. Financial mismanagement, loss of the southernmost province of Uruguay, flaunting of the constitution, and scandalous affairs with many women brought many calls that he abdicate. Pedro finally decided to do so in 1831 when his own Imperial Guard joined those urging his departure from the country.

One of his last acts as emperor was to name his five-year-old son, Brazilian-born Pedro de Alcântara* as prince regent and heir to the throne. He also ordered that his former Minister of State José Bonifácio be named as tutor to his young son.

Pedro returned to Portugal where he sought to regain control of that country by naming his daughter Maria I queen of Portugal in 1834.

BIBLIOGRAPHY

Correa da Costa, Sergio. *Every Inch a King*. New York: 1953.
Gama, Annibal. *D. Pedro na regença*. Rio de Janeiro: Gráfica Laenment, 1943.
Rangel, Alberto. *Dom Pedro I e a Marquesa de Santos*. São Paulo: Editora Brasilense, 1969.
Sousa, Octavio Tarquinio de. *A Vida de D. Pedro I*. Rio de Janeiro: José Olympio, 1952.
Vianna, Velio: *D. Pedro I e D. Pedro II: Acresas suas biografias*. São Paulo: Editora Nacional, 1966.

JORDAN YOUNG

DOM PEDRO II (DE ALCÂNTARA) (1825–1891), for 49 years emperor of Brazil, created an historical, social, and political superstructure that continued to some extent into the twentieth century. His personality and his ability to pull together divergent groups and to serve as a unifying force contributed to maintaining Brazil as a single nation.

During his long reign, Pedro became one of the greatly admired statesmen of the nineteenth century. His friendships stretched from French philosophers to men of science such as Alexander Graham Bell. He studied and spoke many languages, wrote poetry, experimented in science, and was a liberal in his religious beliefs. He was considered a "philosopher king" by many observers as he governed Brazil with honesty, integrity, and moderation.

He became emperor in 1831 when his father Dom Pedro I* abdicated. Although the constitution stated that he could be crowned only when he was 18 years of age, a political deadlock between Conservative and Liberal leaders finally led them to turn to the emperor when he was 14 years old and he was crowned in 1841. Although in the first few years of his reign he was virtually the puppet of his political advisers, by 1847 he had become truly the head of the Brazilian nation.

The 1824 constitution granted Pedro a great deal of power. By the time he was 18, he had begun to appoint his own ministers as well as the presidents of the provinces. He frequently used the "moderating power" to change cabinets and call new elections. Yet he did not act as an autocratic tyrant, and generally used persuasion and compromise to work out administrative deadlocks.

After 1847 Pedro governed through a prime minister whom he nominated and who enjoyed majority support in the Parliament. In 49 years, Pedro changed prime ministers 36 times, and on 11 occasions he disbanded the lower house and ordered new elections. Throughout most of his reign, however, he managed to maintain a balance between the Conservative and Liberal parties. Personal liberty was respected, and life and property were safe. As free speech was recognized, the emperor was often the target of severe criticism in the press.

The war with Paraguay (1864–1870) made the emperor realize how backward and inefficient Brazil was in communications, transportation, and industry. Immediate steps were taken to improve the situation. Railroad companies were formed and industry encouraged in the state of São Paulo.

One of the biggest problems faced by Dom Pedro II was the persistence of slavery. He freed his own slaves and worked for the gradual emancipation of all slaves. He granted honors and titles to those who freed their slaves. In 1871 he supported and sponsored the Rio Branco Law which mandated that children of slaves would henceforth be born free, although they would serve their mother's masters until the age of 21. In 1885 he backed a bill to free all slaves over the age of 65. When Pedro was traveling in Europe in May 1888, his daughter, Princess Isabel, supported the law which freed all slaves without compensation to their owners.

As Pedro aged and became ill, support for the monarch declined. The possibility that his daughter, Isabel, and her French husband, the Comte d'Eu, would rule was not welcomed by most Brazilians. A combination of factors including loss of Catholic Church support, plantation owners' anger at the abolition of slavery, the rise of a small but clamorous Republican Party, but most important of all, a discontented but well-organized military faction, resulted in the downfall of Dom Pedro II on November 15, 1889. Sixty-four year old Dom Pedro was sent into exile in Paris, where he died.

BIBLIOGRAPHY

Bernstein, Harry. *Dom Pedro II*. New York: Twayne Publishers, 1973.
Lyra, Hector. *Historia de Dom Pedro II, 1825–1891*. 2 vols. São Paulo: Companhia Editora Nacional, 1938–1940.

Williams, Mary Wilhelmine. *Dom Pedro the Magnanimous, Second Emperor of Brazil*. Chapel Hill: University of North Carolina Press, 1937.

JORDAN YOUNG

PEIXOTO, FLORIANO (1839–1895), a professional army officer was a key figure in the overthrow of the empire and was the second president of Brazil.

Born in northeastern Brazil, he came from a very modest family and opted for a military career to escape the crushing poverty of the Northeast. He received university degrees in mathematics and physical sciences, served with distinction in the war with Paraguay and by 1889 had risen to be adjutant general to Marshal Manuel Deodoro da Fonseca.* He backed Deodoro da Fonseca's revolt against the emperor on November 15, 1889, support which was decisive in the proclamation of the Republic. He was appointed minister of war in the provisional republican government.

A constituent assembly elected Deodoro da Fonseca president and Floriano Peixoto vice president of the new republic. When General Deodoro resigned on November 11, 1891. Vice President Peixoto assumed the presidency. He was ruthless in suppression of the opposition, banning and jailing army officers and civilian politicians. He favored rapid economic development and drew his support from the middle-class Positivists who felt that the discipline he had imposed on the nation was necessary for survival of the new republic. He also successfully defeated rebellions against his government in Rio Grande do Sul.

When his presidential term expired, Peixoto permitted presidential elections, and Prudente de Morais, a civilian from São Paulo, was elected.

BIBLIOGRAPHY

Bello, José María. *A History of Modern Brazil, 1889–1964*. Stanford, Calif.: Stanford University Press, 1966.
Carneiro, Glauco. *Historia das Revolucões Brasileiras*. Rio de Janeiro: Edicões O Cruzeiro, 1965.
Peixoto, Sylvio. *No Tempo de Floriano*. 1940.
Simmons, Charles Willis. *Marshal Deodoro and the Fall of Dom Pedro II*. Durham, N.C.: Duke University Press, 1966.

JORDAN YOUNG

PEÑA GÓMEZ, JOSÉ FRANCISCO (19?–   ), succeeded Juan Bosch* as principal leader of the Partido Revolucionario Dominicano (PRD) of the Dominican Republic. At the time of the death of dictator Rafael Leónidas Trujillo Molina* in 1961, Peña Gómez was a student in the University of Santo Domingo, where he ultimately graduated as a lawyer. He was an early recruit to the PRD and was one of a group of young members sent for training in Venezuela and Peru.

After the overthrow of the PRD government of Juan Bosch in September 1963, Peña Gómez was one of those principally responsile for reorganizing the party and for establishing contacts in the armed forces. With the outbreak of the

Constitutionalist Revolution in April 1965, he broadcast a call to all PRD members and supporters to back the insurrection.

In 1966 Peña Gómez was elected secretary general of the PRD. With Juan Bosch living abroad, he was largely in charge of running the party. Although he formally accepted Bosch's rather ill-defined notion of a "dictatorship with popular support," by 1970 there were clearly differences between the two.

Between September 1970 and February 1973, Peña Gómez pursued advanced law studies in Paris, although keeping the title of PRD secretary general. Upon his return, a conflict soon developed between him and Bosch and in August 1973, he resiged as secretary general. However, when Bosch was defeated in an attempt to purge Peña Gómez' supporters, and in November 1973 resigned from the party, Peña Gómez was then reelected secretary general and became generally recognized as the PRD's principal figure.

Peña Gómez cultivated relations with other parties of the democratic left in Latin America and in Europe and among liberals in the United States. In 1976 he led the party into the Socialist International, of which he soon became vice president.

These international contacts were largely responsible for forcing the army to back down when it attempted to block the election in 1978 of PRD candidate Antonio Guzmán as president. In that same election, Peña Gómez was chosen mayor of Santo Domingo. Peña Gómez also led the PRD to its third electoral victory in 1982, when Salvador Jorge Blanco was its presidential nominee.

BIBLIOGRAPHY

Personal contacts.
Who Is Who—Government and Politics in Latin America, New York: Decade Media
  Books.

ROBERT J. ALEXANDER

PENGEL, JOHAN ADOLF (1916–   ), was leader of the Suriname National Party (NPS) and Minister President of the country during most of the 1960's. He studied law and entered the civil service in 1938. He was first elected to the colony's legislature, the Staten, as an NPS member in 1949. He succeeded D. H. Emanuels as the second leader of the NPS and in that capacity became prime minister (Minister President) or a coalition government in 1963.

The Pengel government carried out policies of economic development, stressing expansion of the infrastructure and modest industrialization. However, social unrest, culminating in strikes by teachers and many other groups, brought the fall of the Pengel cabinet in 1969. In subsequent elections the NPS suffered a severe defeat, and in 1970 Pengel gave up leadership of the party to Henck A. E. Arron.*

BIBLIOGRAPHY

Alexander, Robert J. "Surinam," in Robert J. Alexander (ed.)., *Political Parties of the
  Americas*. Vol. 2. Westport, Conn.: Greenwood Press, 1982.

Dictionary of Latin American and Caribbean Biography 1971–2. London: Melrose Press
    Ltd., 1971.

                                                                           ROBERT J. ALEXANDER

PÉREZ, CARLOS ANDRÉS (1922–   ), was president of Venezuela from
1974 to 1979, the fourth member of Acción Democrática (AD) to hold that post.
He graduated from the Central University in Caracas. After the Revolution of
October 18, 1945, he became private secretary of Rómulo Betancourt,* president
of the Revolutionary Junta. In 1947 he was elected to the Chamber of Deputies.
After the fall of the AD government, Pérez spent most of the next nine years in
Costa Rica, where from 1953 to 1958 he was chief editor of the daily newspaper
La República. He was also very active in the exile leadership of AD.

Returning home with the fall of the Marcos Pérez Jiménez* dictatorship early
in 1958, Carlos Andrés Pérez was elected to the Chamber of Deputies, where
he remained until he became president. During the Betancourt administration of
1959–1964, he was first vice minister of the interior and in 1963–1964 minister
of the interior. He was principally in charge of the government's efforts to
suppress the urban guerrilla efforts of the far left parties.

After the split in Acción Democrática in 1967–1968 which resulted in formation of the Electoral Movement of the People by the dissidents. Pérez became
secretary general of AD. He also began to work for his party's nomination for
president. He was assured of the candidacy when Rómulo Betancourt finally
announced that he would not himself run again and endorsed Pérez. He won a
very strong victory in December 1973.

During the Pérez administration the government undertook extensive economic
development. There were major increases in the size of the steel industry, expansion of the hydroelectric system, large-scale irrigation projects, subsidization
of agriculture, and expansion of the petrochemical industry. The Pérez regime
also sponsored laws nationalizing the iron mining and petroleum industries.

Pérez took advantage of the oil prosperity to make Venezuela's weight felt
abroad to an unprecedented degree. He became an important spokesman for the
Third World and developed substantial aid programs for the countries of Central
America and the Caribbean. His style in foreign affairs was flamboyant.

After retiring from the presidency, Carlos Andrés Pérez continued to be very
active politically. He remained a major force within Acción Democrática, and
he also played a significant role in the Socialist International, with which his
party was affiliated. He was particularly involved with the International's intervention in the Central American crisis of the early 1980s.

BIBLIOGRAPHY

Alexander, Robert J. *The Venezuela Democratic Revolution.* New Brunswick, N.J.:
    Rutgers University Press, 1964.
Cuarenta Años de Acción Democrática: Cuatro Presidentes. Vol. 2. Caracas: Ediciones
    de la Presidencia de la República, 1981.

Cuatro Figuras Blancas. Caracas: Foción Serrano Producciones, 1975.
Equipo Proceso Politico. *CAP 5 Años: Un Juicio Critico*. Caracas: Caracas: Editorial
   Ateneo de Caracas, 1978.

ROBERT J. ALEXANDER

PÉREZ JIMÉNEZ, MARCOS (1914–   ), was the last of a series of military dictators of Venezuela from the Andean state of Táchira which had begun with Cipriano Castro* in 1899. He graduated from the military school in 1934, and for a decade his military career was unspectacular. By 1945 he had only reached the rank of major.

In 1944–1945 Pérez Jiménez organized the Unión Patriótica Military (UPM) to plot the overthrow of President Isaías Medina Angarita.* He also led a delegation of the UPM which conferred with Rómulo Betancourt* and Raúl Leoni* about Acción Democrática (AD) participation in that conspiracy. On October 18, 1945, it was the arrest of Marcos Pérez Jiménez, which triggered the UPM to go into action. By the next day the uprising had triumphed.

Pérez Jiménez was not included in the Revolutionary Government Junta established on October 19, 1945, a fact he reportedly deeply resented and held Rómulo Betancourt, president of that Junta, responsible for. However, he was made chief of the General Staff and in 1946 was promoted to lieutenant colonel.

Rómulo Betancourt had doubts about Pérez Jimenez' loyalty to the Acción Democrática regime. Therefore, just before turning the government over to his elected successor, Rómulo Gallegos,* Betancourt dispatched Pérez Jiménez on an extensive "diplomatic" mission to keep him out of the country for a long period. However, Minister of Defense Carlos Delgado Chalbaud* permitted Pérez Jiménez to return home prematurely. There Pérez Jiménez began to plot President Gallegos' overthrow, which took place on November 24, 1948. Army leaders established a military government junta with Pérez Jiménez as a member but presided over by Minister of War Delgado Chalbaud. When, on November 13, 1950, Delgado Chalbaud was murdered, his place was taken by a civilian, with Pérez Jiménez and Colonel Luis Felipe Llovera Páez continuing as the other two members.

In November 1952 the Junta called elections. When it became clear that the opposition Republican Democratic Union (URD) had won, counting of the votes was suspended, and Colonel Marcos Pérez Jiménez announced over the radio that he had assumed the presidency "in the name of the armed forces." He remained president from December 2, 1952, until January 23, 1958, and presided over one of the most repressive dictatorships than existing in Latin America.

Much of the Pérez Jiménez period was marked by vastly increased oil revenues, for various international crises had raised the demand for Venezuelan oil. Moreover, Pérez Jiménez reversed the AD governments' policy of not granting new concessions to foreign firms, and many firms spent large amounts to acquire new concessions. The regime had an extensive public works program, principally construction of roads and of pharaonic projects in Caracas. Corruption was also of monumental proportions.

The downfall of Pérez Jiménez came after he chose to have a "plebiscite" where voters answered yes or no to the proposal that he remain in power, a device that appeared utterly ridiculous to most Venezuelans and eclipsed for the moment fear of the regime. The military finally deposed Pérez Jiménez on January 23, 1968.

Pérez Jiménez was deported and ended up in the United States, but in August 1963 the government of President Rómulo Betancourt extradited the ex-dictator. In a trial lasting five years he was convicted of having stolen a substantial amount of money, was sentenced to the time he had already been in jail, and was allowed to go into exile once more.

In 1968 supporters of Pérez Jiménez organized a political party, which named him candidate for the Senate from Caracas. He was elected but was subsequently disqualified on the ground that he had not been in Venezuela during the election campaign or on election day. Subsequently, a constitutional amendment provided that no ex-officeholder convicted of a felony connected with his tenure in office could be eligible to run for any post again.

Following his release from jail, Pérez Jiménez lived in self-imposed exile in Spain.

BIBLIOGRAPHY

Betancourt, Rómulo. *Venezuela: Oil and Politics*. Boston: Houghton Mifflin, 1979.
Kolb, Glen L. *Democracy and Dictatorship in Venezuela, 1945–1958*. New London: Connecticut College, 1974.
Libro Negro 1952. Caracas: José Agustín Catalá, 1974.
Pérez Jiménez, Marcos. *Diez Años de Desarrollo*. Caracas: 1972.
Proceso a Un Ex-Dictador: Juicio al General (R) Marcos Pérez Jiménez. Caracas: Editora José Agustín Catalá, 1969.

ROBERT J. ALEXANDER

PÉREZ MASCAYANO, JOSÉ JOAQUÍN (1801–1889), was the first president of Chile during the so-called Liberal Republic. As a young man, he had a diplomatic career in the United States, France and Argentina. In 1834 he was first elected alternate member of the Chamber of Deputies. From 1837 to 1852 he was a full member of the Chamber; he became a senator in 1852 and stayed in the Senate until his election as president.

During the administration of President Manuel Bulnes Prieto* (1841–1851), Pérez served as minister of finance, of interior, and of foreign relations. During the following administration of President Manuel Montt Torres,* he was a member of the Council of State. When a split developed among those supporting President Montt, Pérez, as a supporter of the president, became a member of the National Party.

When the 1861 presidential election approached, the pro-government forces first proposed to run Antonio Varas de la Barra,* a chief lieutenant of President Montt. When Varas absolutely refused to run, both government and opposition forces turned to José Joaquín Pérez. He ran without opposition, backed by the National, Liberal, and Conservative parties. His first cabinet contained members of all three parties.

The National Party was not satisfied with its secondary role. Moreover, a group of militant young Liberals was unhappy with the policies of both their party and the Pérez government; they broke away to form the Radical Party, and together with the Nationals, by 1862 they formed the parliamentary opposition to the Pérez regime.

Political controversy was temporarily suspended in 1865–1866 during the short war with Spain during which Spanish warships blockaded most Chilean ports and bombarded Valparaiso.

President Pérez was reelected in 1876 with support of the Liberals and Conservatives. Shortly before the end of Pérez' second term, the constitution was amended to prohibit reelection to any of his successors. Another important political reform was the Freedom of Worship Law of 1865, providing that denominations other than the Catholic Church were free to carry on their ceremonies indoors and to maintain their own educational institutions.

There was considerable economic expansion during the Pérez decade. New railrods were built, telegraph lines were extended, and European immigrants, particularly Germans, as well as native Chileans were settled in lands around Valdivia in the southern part of the Central Valley.

Two years after leaving the presidency, José Joaquín Pérez was elected to the Senate. From 1873 until 1882 he served as its president.

BIBLIOGRAPHY

Cortes, Lia, and Jordi Fuentes. *Diccionario Político de Chile*. Santiago: Editorial Orbe, 1967.
Enciclopedia Universal Ilustrada Europeo-Americana. Barcelona: José Espasa e Hijos.
Galdames, Luis. *Historia de Chile*. Santiago: Editorial Zig Zag, 1945.

ROBERT J. ALEXANDER

PERÓN, EVA MARÍA DUARTE DE (EVITA) (1919–1952), was Juan Domingo Perón's* second wife and one of Argentina's most controversial political figures. Evita was an illegitimate child, born in the provincial Buenos Aires town of Los Toldos. She and her family were ostracized because of this illegitimacy, thereby initiating a dislike for Argentina's class system which she never forgot. Evita left home in her early teens to join a traveling theater group and ended up in Buenos Aires. She prospered as a radio actress and began to meet a number of the important officers who were behind the 1943 coup. While working on disaster relief for victims of the San Juan earthquake in January 1944, Evita met Colonel Juan Perón and soon became his mistress.

In 1944 and 1945 Evita assisted Perón in his efforts to attract worker support. When, in October 1945, Perón was ousted from his government positions and imprisoned by a faction of the military, Evita helped mobilize a demonstration in his support, and on October 17 the massive outpouring of workers into the streets of Buenos Aires resulted in Perón's return from prison. Instead of resuming his governmental posts, he announced his candidacy for president and married Evita.

Perón was elected president in 1946, and Evita became responsible for government relations with labor. Evita's pro-worker sympathies, hard work, and charisma made her extremely effective in gaining and coordinating worker support for Perón. Although she was truly pro-worker, she would not tolerate any who refused to bow to Peronist control.

In addition to her activities with trade unionists, Evita mobilized governmental support from the poor through her Eva Duarte de Perón Welfare Foundation, a gigantic organization which she created to replace the traditional charity organizations run by upper class women. It received governmental funds, as well as private ''donations,'' which were inevitably given by both employers and workers after the signing of collective bargaining agreements. Businesses that did not ''volunteer'' money to the Foundation soon found themselves the object of governmental harassment.

Evita was also active in the area of women's rights. She strongly backed giving women the right to vote, which came about in 1947. She also organized the Feminine Peronist Party. Evita intended to formalize her power by running for vice president in the 1952 election, but the military, many of whose officers detested and distrusted her, caused her to drop her candidacy.

On June 26, 1952, Evita died of cancer. There was a huge outpouring of public grief, with the lines of people waiting in the rain to pass before her coffin stretching for 20 blocks.

In the years following her death, Evita's life assumed the proportions of a myth. The most radical and leftist elements of the Peronist movement looked to Evita as their model, and ultimately those elements could not support the more conservative Perón when he returned in 1973. For Peronistas, Evita symbolized the fight to achieve social, economic, and political justice for Argentina and the workers, but for anti-Peronists she symbolized the worst of Peronist antidemocratic practices and demagogic excesses.

BIBLIOGRAPHY

Ackridge, Sharon A. Hollenback. *Cinderella from the Pampas: María Eva Duarte de Perón, Argentine First Lady, 1919–1952*. Santa Barbara, Calif.: Akridge, 1976.

Barnes, John. *Evita, First Lady: A Biography of Eva Perón*. New York: Grove Press, 1978.

Fraser, Nicholas, and Marysa Navarro. *Eva Perón*. London: André Deutsch, 1980.

Kirkpatrick, Jeane. *Leader and Vanguard in Mass Society: A Study of Peronist Argentina.* Cambridge, Mass.: MIT Press, 1971.

JOHN T. DEINER

PERÓN, JUAN DOMINGO (1895–1974), dominated Argentine politics from 1943 to the time of his death. He brought the urban workers into Argentine politics as a major political actor, and his policies raised fundamental issues about the nature of democracy and development in Argentina.

Juan Domingo Perón was born in the small Buenos Aires provincial town of Lobos, into a lower-middle-class family. He entered the Colegio Militar in 1911 and moved slowly up the army ranks thereafter. He taught at the military academy, gaining a reputation as a scholar and historian, and was a military attaché in Chile and in Mussolini's Italy. Upon returning from Europe, Perón became a leading organizer of the coup that brought the military to power in 1943.

Following that coup, Perón rose quickly to power. Put in charge of labor affairs as secretary of labor, he aided labor's organizational and collective bargaining efforts. He became vice president and minister of war under his friend President Edelmiro Farrell in February 1944.

Not all military men supported Perón, however, and in October 1945, he was forced out of his positions and arrested by a group of officers. Within a week his labor supporters staged a massive march on downtown Buenos Aires, and Perón was brought back from imprisonment on October 17, 1945, his opponents in the military were purged, and he became the most powerful man in Argentina.

During this period, Perón was aided by Eva Duarte, a radio actress who had become his mistress. Following Perón's return on October 17, he and Evita were married, and he resigned his governmental positions to run for the presidency. He won the February 1946 election, one of the most honest in Argentina's history, with a campaign based on the theme of social justice and strong nationalism.

Once in power, Perón formulated a philosophy called Justicialismo, which called for social justice, economic independence, and political sovereignty. His power rested on the military and the trade unionists. Perón had to perform a sort of juggling act between them. Evita was given much responsibility for mobilizing and controlling labor, and Perón dealt more with the military and other political affairs.

The labor movement was purged of leaders with a personal following of their own. Non-Peronists were coopted, forced into exile by government harassment, or saw their followers desert them for the rival unions created by the government. However, the major reason for governmental control of labor was that the majority of workers liked Perón and supported him for positive, not negative, reasons, and leaders and workers alike looked to Perón and Evita as their benefactors.

Perón's strategy with the military was to provide benefits such as higher salaries and improved facilities. Many officers supported his nationalistic foreign policies and his buildup of military forces to keep them competitive with rival Brazil. Officers who opposed Perón were purged.

Argentina emerged from World War II in a good economic position. It had accumulated extensive credits by selling food products to the Allies, some of which were used to purchase foreign-owned railroads, shipping companies, and public utilities, as well as to fund accelerated industrialization. But the government gained control over the infrastructure at a relatively high cost for a somewhat outdated physical plant. Government policy of paying low prices to Argentine producers caused some to leave agriculture. The industrialization program was weakened by governmental corruption and mismanagement.

Perón appointed Peronist university rectors and purged faculties of anti-Peronists. The quality of education declined and became more politicized.

Near the end of Perón's first term, the government increased pressures for conformity. *La Prensa*, the last remaining newspaper to oppose Peron, was shut down and then reopened under General Confederation of Labor (CGT) control. The government dealt harshly with labor opposition in several unions. A declining economic situation, caused partly by bad weather conditions but also by governmental mismanagement, forced Perón to cut back on worker benefits.

In 1952 Perón won reelection for a second term. Evita died of cancer the same year, depriving the president of one of his major sources of support. Economic problems forced Perón to seek a loan from the United States and aid from U.S. oil companies; both acts were resented by Argentine nationalists.

Perón's difficulties were greatly exacerbated by his struggle with the Catholic Church in 1954–1955, which culminated in Perón being excommunicated. His battles with the church were particularly distressing to some rightist Catholics within the military who were active in the September 1955 coup that ousted him.

Although Perón was overthrown, his political influence in Argentina was far from over. By 1962, when they were allowed to vote for their own candidates again, the Peronists elected half of the congressional nominees and gained control of Buenos Aires Province. The military then ousted President Arturo Frondizi* and annulled the Peronist electoral victories.

During Perón's exile, his followers in Argentina were divided, and Perón tried to make sure that no individual could arise to take his place as leader of the movement. Conflicts among Peronist factions in the labor movement grew violent, resulting in many assassinations of labor leaders. With the 1969 "Cordobazo," when large-scale fighting broke out in the city of Córdoba, there was a major upsurge of guerrilla activity and of radical Peronist youth groups.

President Alejandro Agustín Lanusse* (1971–1973) realized that the military had no solutions for the deteriorating economic and political situation, and desired to remove the military from the government before it was damaged as an institution. Reluctantly, he allowed the Peronists to run a candidate for president in elections he called in 1973.

Héctor Cámpora,* a long-time Perón confidant, was elected president. He ruled for only two months and then resigned. In new elections, Perón, who had returned from exile, was elected with over 60 percent of the popular vote.

Perón supported the rightists in the Peronist movement, particularly the leaders of the labor bureaucracy. His policies were successful at first. Guerrilla activity stopped, and inflation was drastically reduced. After about six months, however, the situation began to deteriorate. Leftist guerrillas, both Peronist and non-Peronist, resumed their activities. Inflation again became a problem.

By this time Perón was sick and was unable to work full time at his job. He died on July 1, 1974, and was succeeded in office by Vice President Isabelita Perón.*

BIBLIOGRAPHY

Alexander, Robert J. *Juan Domingo Perón: A History*. Boulder, Colo.: Westview Press, 1976.

Barager, Joseph R. (ed.). *Why Perón Came to Power: The Background to Peronism in Argentina*. New York: Alfred A. Knopf, 1968.

Page, Joseph A. *Perón: A Biography*. New York: Random House, 1983.

Smith, Peter H. *Argentina and the Failure of Democracy, 1904–1955*. Madison: University of Wisconsin Press, 1974.

Sobel, Lester A. (ed.). *Argentina and Perón, 1970–75*. New York: Facts on File, 1975.

                                                            JOHN T. DEINER

PERÓN, MARÍA ESTELA MARTÍNEZ DE (ISABELITA) (1931–   ), third wife of Juan Domingo Perón,* succeeded him as Argentine president on June 29, 1974, and ruled until March 24, 1976. She was the first woman president in Latin America.

Isabelita was born into a poor family in La Rioja Province. She studied music, theater, and dance, and met Perón in Panama while dancing with an Argentine "folklore" company. She became his "secretary," and they married in 1960. When Juan Perón was elected president in 1973, Isabelita was elected his vice president, as a compromise candidate.

Isabelita became president when Perón died in office in 1974. She proved herself unable to rule the country. There was a wave of labor and guerrilla violence, the economy degenerated, with soaring inflation and lack of growth. She constantly shifted cabinet members. Finally, the military ousted her, placed her under house arrest, but eventually permitted her to go into exile in Spain. She remained titular head of the Peronist movement.

BIBLIOGRAPHY

Hodges, Donald C. *Argentina, 1943–1976: The National Revolution and Resistance*. Albuquerque: University of New Mexico Press, 1976.

Page, Joseph A. *Perón: A Biography*. New York: Random House, 1983.

Pavón Pereyra, Enrique. *Isabel, historia de una voluntad*. Buenos Aires: Ediciones Mares del sur, 1983.

Snow, Peter G. *Political Forces in Argentina*. New York: Praeger, 1979.
Sobel, Lester A. (ed.). Argentina and Perón, 1970–75. New York: Facts on File, 1975.

JOHN T. DEINER

PÉTION, ALEXANDRE (1770–1818), who introduced a republican form of government in Haiti, was the son of a wealthy French colonist and a mulatto woman. As a youth, he worked as a blacksmith and silversmith. He enlisted in the colonial militia at the age of 18, and three years later, he joined the cause of the mulattoes against the French colonists, who were refusing to grant political equality to the mulattoes.

Under the black general Toussaint L'Ouverture,* Pétion was instrumental in routing British forces from the island. Later, he joined mulatto General André Rigaud, who held the South, in an attempt to establish mulatto dominance, but after defeat by Toussaint, Pétion fled into exile in 1800.

Pétion returned to St. Domingue with French forces under General Charles Leclerc, sent in 1802 by Napoleon Bonaparte, in an attempt to dislodge Toussaint. Toussaint's forces were routed, and Toussaint's generals joined the French forces.

Soon, however, French atrocities and fear of reestablishing slavery sparked new rebellion. Pétion joined the rebel forces in October 1802. He agreed to a united front with the black general, Jean-Jacques Dessalines,* against the French. The United States allowed arms and supplies to be shipped to them, while war with Great Britain prevented the French from resupplying their forces.

The colony was declared independent on January 1, 1804, under Dessalines, as governor general. The country was divided into four administrative districts, and Pétion was given jurisdiction over the west. Dessalines proclaimed himself emperor in October 1804. Problems between them stemmed partly from racial tensions between blacks and mulattoes (of whom Pétion was the acknowledged leader) and partly from Pétion's unhappiness wiith the atrocities of the regime. The relationship further cooled with Pétion's refusal to marry Dessalines' daughter at the emperor's request.

There was an uprising against Dessalines by mulatto generals in the south, including Pétion. The emperor was ambushed and assassinated on his way to quell the uprising.

The black general, Henri Christophe,* was considered the acknowledged successor to Dessalines. There was strong mulatto resistance to him, however. Pétion, while immediately proclaiming Christophe provisional chief of state, devised a republican constitution that gave real power to the elected Senate, of which the mulattoes had absolute control.

Christophe gathered his army from the north and attempted to capture Port-au-Prince. Pétion's forces managed to repulse Christophe just outside Port-au-Prince. Forced to retreat North, Christophe set up an independent regime. The assembly in Port-au-Prince then elected Pétion in Christophe's places, as president of Haiti. This division remained until 1820, two years after Pétion's death.

Pétion's first allegiance was to the mulatto population. The initial two or three years of his regime were spent reversing the land policy of Toussaint and Dessalines. Lands appropriated by the state were returned to their former owners, the majority of whom were wealthy mulatto aristocrats. Moreover, a law granted payment to the original owners equal to the total value of the crops lost to them under Dessalines.

Pétion subsidized the cultivators, with the state purchasing crops to maintain acceptable price levels. Moreover, he abolished the land tax and moved to fix security of tenure through government registration of ownership and sale of property.

Pétion also organized massive land redistribution where state land was given away: 15 acres of cultivable soil to every soldier and larger grants to officers in accordance with rank. This policy was most probably instituted because the regime was becoming increasingly hard-pressed to meet its wage commitment to the army, and the soldiers were paid off with the only thing of value available, the land seized from the old planter class.

The end result was serious decline in large-scale agriculture and tremendous drop in production of money crops as small-scale producers shifted to subsistence farming. Pétion's efforts to encourage sugar production failed, as cultivators refused to invest in the costly imputs needed for sugar production.

Politically, Pétion's rule was characterized by moderation and reliance on persuasion. He maintained some pretense of representative government, allowing the Senate to reelect him in 1811 and 1815, but in 1816 he was declared President for Life, the first of many to hold that title.

Despite the profound negative consequences of his policies for the economy, Pétion's tolerant and understanding nature, his willingness to attempt to please every sector of society, his success in moderating tensions between mulattoes and blacks, and his genuine commitment to freedom all endeared him to the people. There was a genuine outpouring of sadness when he died.

BIBLIOGRAPHY

Beard, John R. *The Life of Toussaint L'Ouverture*. Westport, Conn.: Negro University Press, 1970.
Cole, Herbert. *Christophe: King of Haiti*. London: Eyre and Spottiswoode, 1967.
James, C.L.R. *The Black Jacobins*. London: Allison and Busby, 1980.
Moran, Charles. *Black Triumvirate*. New York: Exposition, 1957.
Syme, Ronald. *Toussaint: The Black Liberator*. New York: William Morrow, 1971.

PERCY C. HINTZEN

PIEROLA, NICOLÁS DE (1839–1913), twice president of Peru, was born in Arequipa and received his education in Catholic schools. After accepting some business representations in Lima, he became editor of *El Progreso Católico* (1860–1861) and founded the newspaper *El Tiempo* in 1864. He served as minister of the treasury in President José Balta's cabinet. Thereafter, he was in exile in Chile and France, until he became acting president of Peru from December 23, 1879, to November 28, 1881. While in Europe, Pierola and his followers founded the Democratic Party. After several attempts to overthrow the military governments, he finally succeeded in imposing a provisional civilian administration in 1895. Pierola served as constitutional president from 1895 to 1899, and was in business from 1899 to 1909. The schism within the Democratic Party, caused by his withdrawal of support from the presidential candidacy of Guillermo Billinghurst,* proved to be Pierola's last historical act.

BIBLIOGRAPHY

Alisky, Marvin. *Historical Dictionary of Peru*. Metuchen, N.J.: Scarecrow Press, 1979.
Dulanto Pinillos, Jorge. *Nicolás de Pierola*. Lima: Compañía de Impresiones y Publicidad, 1947.
Pike, Frederick B. *The Modern History of Peru*. New York: Praeger, 1967.
Ulloa, Alberto. *Don Nicolás de Pieirola: Una época de la historia del Peru*. Lima: Imprenta Santa María, 1950.

EUGENIO CHANG-RODRÍGUEZ

PINDLING, LYNDEN OSCAR (1930–   ), was the first prime minister of the Bahamas. The son of a local merchant, he attended local schools before enrolling at London University. He was called to the bar in 1953, and that same year joined the newly formed Progressive Liberal Party (PLP) in the Bahamas. Three years later, in the new party's first electoral effort, the PLP won six seats in the House of Assembly, and Pindling was soon chosen parliamentary leader of the PLP. He served as Leader of the Opposition in the House from 1964 to 1967.

The PLP carried out a stunning electoral ''revolution'' over the white ''establishment'' in January 1967. The islands' black voters turned out in record numbers, forcing a tie between the United Bahamian Party (UBP) and PLP, each winning 18 seats. The stalemate was broken when a black, Randol Fawkes, the sole elected candidate of the Labour Party, and independent Alvin Braynen, joined forces with the PLP, permitting Lynden Pindling to form a government and become premier.

In 1963 and 1968 Pindling participated in constitutional conferences in London, promoting self-government for the Bahamas. In 1968 he served as chairman of the Commonwealth Parliamentary Association. Following independence for the Bahamas in 1973, Pindling became prime minister.

Pindling and the PLP won an additional five years in office in general elections in June 1982, but with a reduced electoral margin. In spite of widespread drug and corruption charges, Pindling and his party won reelection early in 1987.

BIBLIOGRAPHY

Alexander, Robert J. ''The Bahamas,'' in Robert J. Alexander (ed.). *Political Parties of the Americas*. Vol. 1. Westport, Conn.: Greenwood Press, 1982.
Anonymous. ''The Prime Minister, The Past and the Future. *The (Nassau) Herald*, July 9, 1981.

Collingwood, Dean. "The Bahamas," in Jack W. Hopkins (ed.). *Latin America and Caribbean Contemporary Record*. Vols. 1–3. New York: Holmes and Meier, 1983, 1984, 1985.

Craton, Michael. *A History of the Bahamas*. London: Collins, 1962.

Fawkes, Sir Randol. *The Faith That Moved the Mountain*. Nassau: Nassau Guardian, 1979.

PERCY C. HINTZEN AND W. MARVIN WILL

PINOCHET UGARTE, AUGUSTO (1915–), led the military coup that overthrew the government of Salvador Allende Gossens,* and presided over the second dictatorship which Chile suffered in the twentieth century. He graduated from military school in 1938, and subsequently studied at the Infantry School, the War Academy, and the National Defense Academy. As a junior officer, he saw service in several different infantry regiments and taught in the War Academy. After several overseas assignments, he served successively after 1956 as a regimental commander, subdirector of the War Academy, and a division commander and commanding general of the garrison of Santiago. He also wrote six books on geography, geopolitics, and the War of the Pacific.

During most of the Allende administration, General Pinochet was second-in-command of the army, under General Carlos Prats, who led the group within the armed forces which insisted on the military maintaining its traditional apolitical constitutional role. When political pressures forced the resignation of General Prats in August 1973, General Pinochet succeeded him.

It is not clear when General Pinochet entered the conspiracy to overthrow Allende. However, he headed the military movement of September 11, 1973, and was named president of the military junta that took power after the overthrow and death of Allende. In June 1974 Pinochet was proclaimed president of Chile.

General Pinochet has presided over the most oppressive regime which Chile has experienced in the twentieth century. It did away with Congress and outlawed all political parties. Hundreds of people were murdered by the regime, thousands "disappeared," and tens of thousands were driven into exile. Military men were named to run all of the universities. During the first years, freedom of the press was nonexistent. For two years, an official "state of war" and a curfew were kept in effect, and thereafter a modified form of martial law continued.

Proving himself a capable military politician, Pinochet was able to convert the regime from one of the leadership of the armed forces into a personal dictatorship, which relied for its support principally on the armed forces. A semblance of legality was given to this arrangement in 1981 when a new constitution was approved by a plebiscite which, among other things, confirmed Pinochet's continuance in power at least until 1989.

The economic policies of the Pinochet government have been characterized by monetarist and extreme free trade policies. Faced with an inflation rate of over 1000 percent during its first year, the regime adopted a drastic "shock treatment" that provoked an economic depression almost as bad as that of the

1930s. This was accompanied by an almost complete dismantling of tariffs and other devices to protect Chilean industry, as a consequence of which a major segment of the country's manufacturing sector was destroyed. Although from 1978 to 1981 the economy showed evidences of modest recovery, thereafter the situation again reached crisis proportions. By 1984 an unemployment rate of about 30 percent was officially recognized to exist, and Chile had the fifth largest foreign debt among the Latin American countries.

BIBLIOGRAPHY

Alexander, Robert J. *The Tragedy of Chile*. Westport, Conn.: Greenwood Press, 1978.
Chile Under Military Rule. New York: IDOC/North America, 1974.

ROBERT J. ALEXANDER

PINTO DÍAZ, FRANCISCO ANTONIO (1775–1858), the last *pipiolo* (novice) or Liberal president of Chile before the 1829–1830 civil war, received his law credentials in 1808, joined the independence movement two years later, and was named diplomatic representative first to Buenos Aires and then to Great Britain. In 1817 Pinto participated in the independence struggle in Bolivia, and in 1820 he was sent by Supreme Director Bernardo O'Higgins* to serve under General José de San Martín* in Peru.

Pinto became minister of war, interior, and foreign relations in 1824. In 1827 he was elected vice president and, when President Ramón Freire Serrano* resigned, became president in May 1827. He dissolved Congress, called elections for a new constituent assembly, and was elected president under the new constitution. But a bitter controversy over selection by Congress of the *pipiolo* nominee for vice president over two Conservatives who had more votes than he precipitated the Civil War of 1829–1830. Pinto resigned the presidency.

In 1841 Pinto was named the Liberal Party presidential candidate. He did not campaign and lost. He was subsequently elected to the Senate and was named to the Council of State by President Manuel Bulnes Prieto.

BIBLIOGRAPHY

Cortes, Lia, and Jordi Fuentes. *Diccionario Político de Chile*. Santiago: Editorial Orbe, 1967.
Enciclopedia Universal Ilustrada Europeo-Americana. Barcelona: José Espasa e Hijos.
Galdames, Luis. *Historia de Chile*. Santiago: Editorial Zig Zag, 1945.

ROBERT J. ALEXANDER

PINTO GARMENDÍA, ANÍBAL (1825–1884), was president of Chile at the beginning of the War of the Pacific (1879–1883) against Bolivia and Peru. He began a professional diplomatic career as secretary of the Chilean Legation in Rome in 1848, where he remained for three years. After returning home, he was elected to the Chamber of Deputies in 1852 and continued there until elected to the Senate in 1870. During most of the administration of President Federico Errázuriz Zañartu* (1871–1876), he was minister of war and navy, and in the election of 1876, he was the government's candidate, backed by the National Party and most Liberals. He came to office in the midst of a serious economic recession. Pinto imposed a series of new taxes and decreed the inconvertibility of government-issued paper currency.

Even more serious was the Pacific War. For a number of years Chile and Bolivia had been in dispute over the coastal areas, where Chilean mining interests (often in conjunction with British investors) had been exploiting nitrate. When Bolivia imposed new taxes on the Anglo-Chilean enterprises in Antofagasta Province, in violation of accords with Chile, the Pinto administration declared war on Bolivia. Peru, which had a "secret" mutual assistance treaty with Bolivia, immediately entered the conflict. During the last two years of the Pinto government, the Chileans totally defeated their opponents and conquered not only the Bolivian/Pacific coastal province of Antofagasta, but also the Peruvian provinces of Tarapaca, Arica, and Tacna, and even occupied the Peruvian capital of Lima.

BIBLIOGRAPHY

Cortes, Lia, and Jordi Fuentes. *Diccionario Político de Chile*. Santiago: Editorial Orbe, 1967.
Enciclopedia Universal Ilustrada Europeo-Americana. Barcelona: José Espasa e Hijos.
Galdames, Luis. *Historia de Chile*. Santiago: Editorial Zig Zag, 1945.

ROBERT J. ALEXANDER

PLAZA GUTIÉRREZ, LEÓNIDAS (1865–1932), was the second in the series of Liberal Party presidents who governed Ecuador between 1895 and 1944. He first appeared on the political scene as an aide to (José) Eloy Alfaro* in an unsuccessful Liberal uprising in 1884. Subsequently, Plaza spent a number of years abroad, engaging in insurrectional activities in El Salvador and Costa Rica and being named a general. Back in Ecuador by 1895, he supported Eloy Alfaro's successful insurrection of that year.

Plaza was a member of the Alfaro government. Alfaro designated him as his successor as president in 1901, and he served until 1905, expanding the Liberal reforms Alfaro had started.

After Plaza left office, there was growing discontent with Eloy Alfaro's attempts to continue to dominate the Liberal regime. This culminated with the lynching of ex-President Alfaro in January 1912.

Soon after Alfaro's death, Leónidas Plaza was elected president again. His second administration (1912–1916) was marked not only by extensive railroad construction, but also by close alliance of the administration with cacao-growing interests, particularly the Banco Comercial y Agricola, which continued to dominate policies of the governments of Plaza's immediate successors. After again leaving office, Leónidas Plaza continued to control the military until the revolution of July 1925, which resulted in his arrest and exile.

BIBLIOGRAPHY

Enciclopedia Universal Ilustrada Europeo-Americana. Barcelona: José Espasa e Hijos.
                                                          ROBERT J. ALEXANDER

PLAZA LASSO, GALO (1906–   ), a president of Ecuador, was born in New
York while Leónidas Plaza,* his father, was Ecuadorian minister to the United
States. He got his early schooling in Ecuador but for his higher education went
to the universities of California, Maryland, and Georgetown. Thereafter, he
spent a few years in the Ecuadorian diplomatic service, starting with a post in
the Washington Embassy. He entered politics in 1936, when he was elected
mayor of Quito. Afterwards, he was minister of defense, ambassador to the
United States, and senator.

After the overthrow of the second dictatorship of José María Velasco Ibarra,*
Galo Plaza was the successful candidate of the Liberal Party in the election of
1948, although he did not formally belong to the party. His administration was
the first one in several decades both to go into office and to give up office through
democratic election.

Galo Plaza governed principally with Liberals and Socialists in his cabinet.
His government promoted political freedom, expansion of a new export industry,
benanas, and some industrialization, but made no efforts to launch social reforms.

After leaving the presidency, Galo Plaza returned for a time to management
of his substantial highland estates. He served on a number of United Nations
committees and peacekeeping missions. Between 1968 and 1975 he was secretary
general of the Organization of American States.

BIBLIOGRAPHY

Blank, David Eugene. "Ecuador," in Robert J. Alexander (ed.). *Political Parties of the
    Americas*. Westport, Conn.: Greenwood Press, 1982.
Blanksten, George I. *Ecuador: Constitutions and Caudillos*. Berkeley: University of
    California Press, 1951.
Linke, Lilo. *Ecuador: Country of Contrasts*. London: Royal Institute of International
    Affairs, 1955.
Plaza, Galo. *Problems of Democracy in Latin America*. Chapel Hill: University of North
    Carolina Press, 1955.
                                                          ROBERT J. ALEXANDER

PONCE ENRÍQUEZ, CAMILO (1912–   ), was president of Ecuador from
1956 to 1960 and founder of the Social Christian Party. Born into a family of
landowning elite in the sierra region, after studying both in Ecuador and overseas
he got his law degree from the Central University in Quito in 1938.

Ponce became a successful lawyer in Quito. At first active in the Conservative
Party, in 1951 he led in the formation of the Social Christian Movement, a right-
wing Christian Democratic party. During the third administration of José María
Velasco Ibarra* between 1952 and 1956, Ponce Enríquez served as minister of

government. In the election at the end of the Velasco Ibarra regime, he enjoyed the president's support and was elected by a narrow majority.

The Ponce government followed a rigid fiscal policy. It gave very modest impetus to the economic development of the country, particularly to the banana export industry.

During his administration, President Ponce Enríquez broke with his patron, Velasco Ibarra, siding instead with the Conservatives. By the end of his term, differences between the two men were so great that Ponce Enríquez resigned one day before the end of his term to avoid turning the presidency over to Velasco Ibarra, who was elected to succeed him in 1960.

After leaving the presidency, Ponce Enríquez remained active in politics. He ran for the presidency again in 1968 but was badly defeated, again by Velasco Ibarra.

BIBLIOGRAPHY

Blank, David Eugene. "Ecuador," in Robert J. Alexander (ed.). *Political Parties of the Americas*. Westport, Conn.: Greenwood Press, 1982.
Williams, Edward J. *Latin American Christian Democratic Parties*. Knoxville: University of Tennessee Press, 1967.

ROBERT J. ALEXANDER

PORRAS, BELISARIO (1856–1942), served as president of Panama in 1912–1916; 1918–1920; and 1920–1924, giving him the distinction of holding the office the longest of any president in Panama's history. As leader of the Liberal Party, Porras dominated Panamanian politics between 1910 and 1924.

The Porras administrations were concerned largely with building the new nation. Panama earned a relatively high income, and Porras was able to undertake numerous public works; he left virtually no place in Panama untouched by construction or improvement. Nonetheless, the oligarchy, which Porras represented, enjoyed a disproportionate share of the wealth.

During Porras' first administration, the Panama Canal was completed and opened in August 1914 with appropriate ceremonies. The following year, Panama hosted the International Exposition which honored the event. However, relations between Panama and the United States were strained over the status of the Canal Zone and Panamanian sovereignty. Numerous incidents, particularly U.S. intervention in Panamanian elections and expanded commercial activities in the Zone, caused Panamanians to regret the relationship and fomented passionate nationalistic sentiment. Porras' apparent tolerance of U.S. domination, particularly his yielding to American pressure in a boundary dispute with Costa Rica, led to an unsuccessful attempt to overthrow him in February 1921.

BIBLIOGRAPHY

Alba C., Manuel Maria. *Cronologia de los Gobernantes de Panama, 1510–1967*. Panama: 1967.
Alfaro, Ricardo J. *Biográficos esbozos*. Panama: Instituto Nacional de Cultura, 1974.

Castillero R., Ernesto J. *Historia de Panama*. Panama: Editora Panama America, 1959.
Ropp, Steve C. *Panamanian Politics: From Guarded Nation to National Guard*. New York: Praeger, 1982.

CHARLES D. AMERINGER

PORTALES PALAZUELOS, DIEGO (1793–1837), without ever being president of Chile, was the principal influence in establishng a stable system of government in that country in the 1830s. His ideas were particularly felt in the Constitution of 1833, which remained in force for nearly a century.

Before entering politics, Portales had a business career of varying success. After overthrow of the Liberal government in the Battle of Lircay in April 1830, he dedicated himself to politics. He established a political organization that became the Conservative Party, dedicated to bringing into existence, in Portales' words, a government "obeyed, strong, respected and respectable, impersonal, superior to the parties and to the prestige of individuals."

From April 1830 until his death, Portales held various cabinet positions in the governments of Presidents Tomás Ovalle and Manuel Bulnes Prieto,* sometimes handling more than one portfolio at a time. For a while he was also governor of Valparaíso and commanding officer of the navy.

Portales was largely responsible for establishing a centralized, presidential system of government in which the chief executive had great power, limited only by the right of Congress to pass the annual budgets and to have annual parliamentary authorization to maintain a standing army and navy. Witness to the success of Portales' endeavors was the longevity of the 1833 constitution and the fact that between 1830 and 1891 no successful effort was made to overthrow the government.

Portales was assassinated. Reviewing troops that were to confront the Confederation of Peru and Bolivia on which Chile had recently declared war, Portales was seized by the regiment Maipo and shot without trial.

BIBLIOGRAPHY

Cortes, Lia, and Jordi Fuentes. *Diccionario Político de Chile*. Santiago: Editorial Orbe, 1967.
Enciclopedia Universal Ilustrada Europeo-Americana. Barcelona: José Espasa e Hijos.
Galdames, Luis. *Historia de Chile*. Santiago: Editorial Zig Zag, 1945.

ROBERT J. ALEXANDER

PRADO, JORGE DEL (1910–   ), long-time secretary general of the pro-Moscow Peruvian Communist Party, was born in Arequipa. When his father, a senator, died, Jorge, then 17 years old, had to interrupt his high school education and go to work. He became associated with the journal *Amauta* and José Carlos Mariátegui's* Socialist Party. When the Socialist Party was transformed into the Peruvian Communist Party (PCP), del Prado joined it. He rose in the party's ranks and the administration of Commander Luís M. Sánchez Cerro* jailed him for six months in 1930. Subsequently, he suffered several other periods of incarceration, as well as exile in Bolivia, Brazil, and Chile. From 1933 on he continued his underground work until the Peruvian Communist Party began its support of the banker Manuel Prado,* the official presidential candidate of the dictator Oscar R. Benavides.* Under Prado (1939–1945), the PCP enjoyed government protection. The first Congress of the PCP met freely in 1942 and elected Prado its national secretary of organization, a position he held until President Manuel A. Odría* outlawed the Aprista, Communist, and Trotskyist parties in 1948. Then, after three years of underground activities, del Prado was exiled to Bolivia and Brazil.

Del Prado returned to Peru in 1956, when Manuel Prado was again elected president. He was elected secretary general of the PCP in 1961, and when the PCP split into the pro-Moscow and pro-Peking branches, Jorge del Prado continued as secretary general of the former organization. He attended all the congresses of the Communist Party of the USSR after 1959 as well as congresses of the Communist parties of Chile, Cuba, the German Democratic Republic, Bulgaria, and Czechoslovakia.

Del Prado was elected to the Constituent Assembly in 1978 and to the Senate in 1980 and 1985. In 1980 he ran for the first vice presidency of the republic on the ticket of the Unidad de Izquierda, a conglomerate of leftist groups.

BIBLIOGRAPHY

Alisky, Marvin. *Historical Dictionary of Peru.* Metuchen, N.J.: Scarecrow Press, 1979.
Chang-Rodríguez, Eugenio. *Opciones políticas peruanas.* Lima: Centro de Documentación Andina, 1985.
Del Prado, Jorge. *Mariátegui y el seudomariateguismo actual.* Lima: Ediciones Unidad, S.A., 1983.
Tauro, Alberto. *Diccionario enciclopédico del Peru ilustrado: Apendice.* Lima: Editorial Mejía Baca 1975.

EUGENIO CHANG-RODRÍGUEZ

PRADO UGARTECHE, MANUEL (1889–1967), twice president of Peru (1939–1945 and 1956–1962), was born in Lima into a family of political leaders and bankers. He earned degrees in science and engineering. Although he received limited reserve officer training, he was promoted to lieutenant for helping Colonel Óscar R. Benavides* overthrow the constitutional government of Guillermo Billinghurst* (1914). President Benavides helped him get elected president in 1939 for a six-year term, during which he continued persecution of the Aprista Party but received the collaboration of the Communist Party.

Prado lived in Europe from 1945 to 1956, when he returned to become presidential candidate of a newly formed Partido Democratico Pradista. He won with the aid of the Apristas, whose reward was abrogation of the law banning their party. Prado's second term ended with the military coup of June 1962, organized by conservative forces to prevent electoral victory of the Apristas. He lived in Europe and returned to Peru shortly before his death.

BIBLIOGRAPHY

Anonymous. *Puede ser un Prado presidente del Peru*. Lima: 1936.
Basadre, Jorge. *Historia de la República del Peru*. Lima: Editorial Universitaria, 1968.
Gilbert, Dennis L. *La oligarquía peruana: Historia de tres familias*. Lima: Editorial
    Horizonte, 1982.
Ramírez y Berrios, M. Guillermo. *Grandezas y miserias de un proceso electoral en el
    Peru*. Lima: Talleres Gráficos P.L. Villanueva, 1957.

                                                        EUGENIO CHANG-RODRÍGUEZ

PRESCOD, SAMUEL JACKMAN (1806–1871), was the first nonwhite to be
elected to the House of Assembly of Barbados. The unacknowledged illegitimate
son of a white planter, he had no opportunities for a formal education and was
largely self-educated.

Prescod began his campaign in support of the rights of the Barbadian coloured
population in 1838. He became the acknowledged leader of the free colored
population, and it was largely through his efforts that in 1831 the franchise was
extended to them and all civil restriction on their activities was removed.

With the abolition of slavery in 1834, Prescod fought for the rights of the ex-
slaves and against the system of apprenticeship required of the slaves prior to
full emancipation.

Prescod saw the struggle as one of the "poor and middle classes of all com-
plexions against the unjust assumptions of the wealthy few." His goal was to
unite the coloureds, the ex-slaves, and the whites into a "grand radical alliance"
against the privileged. He became the editor of the first coloured newspaper on
the island and for 25 years was editor of a radical journal, *The Liberal*, which
he saw as a means of bridging the racial divide among blacks, coloureds, and
whites. *The Liberal* became one of the most popular journals in Barbados and
throughout the West Indies.

Prescod's prosecution on libel charges intensified his popularity. He won a
seat in the Barbados Assembly from Bridgetown, the capital city, in 1843, the
first nonwhite to sit in the Assembly. As a legislator, he quickly developed ties
with persons of enlightened opinion in the British Parliament and came to be
the leader of the Liberal Party in the Barbados House. He fought unsuccessfully
for universal adult suffrage and for an Executive Committee system of government, which was not finally adopted in Barbados until 1881.

Prescod retired from the Assembly in 1860, to become judge of the assistant
court of appeals, a position he retained until he died.

BIBLIOGRAPHY

Hoyos, F. A. *Barbados: A History*. London: Macmillan Co., 1978.
————. *Builders of Barbados*. London: Macmillan Co., 1973.
————. *Our Common Heritage*. Bridgetown: Advocate Press, 1953.

Tree, Ronald. *A History of Barbados*. 2d ed. London: Franada, 1977.
Vaughn, H. A. "Samuel Jackman Prescod." *New World Quarterly* 3, Nos. 1 and 2.
                                                    PERCY C. HINTZEN AND W. MARVIN WILL

PRESTES, LUIS CARLOS (1898–   ), internationally known Communist leader, has played a role in Brazilian politics since 1924. Born in Porto Alegre, Rio Grande do Sul, the son of a federal army officer, he graduated from the Realengo Military Academy in 1919 with top honors and was commissioned a second lieutenant. In 1922 he was transferred to the First Engineering Company involved in railroad construction for the Central Brazilian Railroad, and was promoted to captain, although he had filed reports charging graft and collusion between railroad contractors and government officials. In 1924 he was transferred to another railroad construction battalion in Rio Grande do Sul.

In October 1924 Prestes led an insurrection in solidarity with the revolt of the *tenentes* in São Paulo. Driven from Rio Grande do Sul, Prestes and his troops joined forces with the São Paulo rebels near Iguazú Falls. There they began a two and a half year guerrilla campaign of what became known as the Prestes Column through the backlands of Brazil. After marching over 25,000 kilometers and engaging in hundreds of skirmishes with the Brazilian Army, they went into voluntary exile in Bolivia. By this time Luis Carlos Prestes had gained fame as the "Knight of Hope."

Prestes settled in Buenos Aires, where he refused to join the other *tenentes* who supported Getúlio Vargas* and the Liberal Alliance in the March 1930 elections, and subsequently in the October 1930 Revolution.

Prestes went to Moscow to work as a civil engineer in 1931. He was coopted into the Executive Committee of the Communist International, returned clandestinely to Brazil in 1934, and soon assumed leadership of the Brazilian Communist Party (PCB). During this period when Moscow favored a Popular Front policy, Prestes helped form and dominated the National Liberation Alliance which attempted an ill-fated military uprising in October 1935 against the Vargas government. After eluding the police, he was arrested in March 1936.

Prestes was released from prison in April 1945, took control of the Communist Party, but instead of condemning Getúlio Vargas urged him to remain in office. After Vargas' ouster by the military in October, general elections were held and Prestes was elected senator from the Federal District.

The Communist Party was declared illegal in May 1947, and in October Prestes was forced to give up his seat in the Senate. He lived underground for a decade, until the Juscelino Kubitschek de Oliveira* administration allowed him to be legally cleared of charges against him. Prestes and the Communist party supported General Henrique Lott who lost the 1960 presidential elections. However, when Vice President João Belchior Marques Goulart* succeeded to the presidency in August 1961, Prestes and his party strongly backed Goulart and gained extensive influence in organized labor.

When the March 1964 revolution overturned Goulart, Prestes left the country, spending most of his exile in Moscow and returning only in November 1979 when amnesty was granted to all political exiles. In 1980 the PCB was in disagreement with Luis Carlos Prestes and asked him to step down as secretary general. Subsequently, he was expelled from the party.

BIBLIOGRAPHY

Amado, Jorge. *Vida de Luis Carlos Prestes*. Saõ Paulo: Livraria Martins Editora, n.d. (1945).
Bastos, Abguar. *Prestes y a Revolucão Social*. Rio de Janeiro: Editorial Calvino Ltda., 1946.
Chilcote, Ronald D. *The Brazilian Communist Party: Conflict and Integration 1922–1972*. New York: Oxford University Press, 1974.
Dulles, John W.F. *Brazilian Communism 1935–1945*. Austin: University of Texas Press, 1983.
McCauley, Neill. *The Prestes Column*. New York: New Viewpoints, 1974.

JORDAN YOUNG

PRICE, GEORGE (1919–   ), led a 30-year battle to gain independence for Belize (formerly British Honduras), which was realized on September 21, 1981, when the colony became an independent nation under his prime ministership. Price was of part-Mayan ancestry, came from a prestigious family, and attended the country's most select secondary school. He attended St. Augustine Seminary in Mississippi. In 1942 he joined the firm of a businessman-politician as a secretary.

Under the tutelage of his boss, Price developed an interest in politics, first campaigning unsuccessfully for a seat on the Town Board in 1943. In 1947 he again campaigned for a seat on the Belize Town Council, and this time was successful.

In 1949 Price joined a member of the Legislative Council to form an ad hoc Peoples Committee to protest Great Britain's devaluation of the colony's currency. The committee established strong ties with the General Workers Union and began to hold joint public meetings with the union, calling for improved labor legislation, constitutional reform, and West Indian federation. In April 1950 Price became a member of the Executive Council of the union. In September the Peoples Committee became the Peoples United Party (PUP), and George Price became its general secretary. In 1950 the party won six seats in the Belize municipal elections.

In 1951 the PUP began to make demands for self-government under a new constitution. Price's position in the party was becoming preeminent, and finally in 1956, he was elected party leader.

Meanwhile, in April 1954 Belize had held its first election under universal adult suffrage. The PUP won eight out of nine elective seats in the Legislative Council and 65 percent of the votes. Price became a member of the colony's

Executive Council. The victory was particularly impressive in view of an official investigation of Price for allegedly receiving money from sources in neighboring Guatemala, which was claiming sovereignty over Belize.

Price's alleged pro-Guatemalan sentiments fueled a leadership struggle within the PUP. When Price went to London in November 1957 seeking financial aid for the colony, the Colonial Secretary released allegations that he had been engaged in secret negotiations with a Guatemalan minister. The talks were suspended, and Price returned home to a tremendous outpouring of support from the population. The governor thereupon called in a British frigate and removed Price from the Executive Council.

Under Price's leadership, the party took a position of strong opposition to Belizean involvement in the West Indies Federation and made this the central issue of the 1957 elections. Price proposed that Belize seek to become an independent nation within the Commonwealth.

With superior organization, a well-defined policy, and a clear appeal to the political sentiments of the people, the PUP swept all nine elective seats in the Legislative Council in 1957. They again won all elected council positions in 1961, when the number of seats doubled to 18. In 1965 and 1969 the PUP won 16 and 17 of the 18 sets, respectively.

Price went to London in July 1963 for constitutional talks, which resulted in full internal self-government for Belize. As a result, Price became premier in January 1965.

During the 1970s Belize was plagued by a decline in the sugar industry and by problems of international inflation and a rise in energy costs. With growing unemployment, particularly in the capital city, Price and his PUP began to lose support. In 1974 they lost control of the Belize City Council and won only 12 of 18 seats in the House of Representatives. The PUP was expected to lose the elections in 1979, but hard campaigning by Price produced a surprise victory. He then fulfilled a campaign promise to negotiate with Britain for full independence, which was achieved in September 1971. Price became the first prime minister.

Unable to manage the economic crisis, Price and his PUP were defeated in 1984 by the United Democratic Party, led by Manuel Esquivel.* With this defeat, George Price became Leader of the Opposition.

BIBLIOGRAPHY

Alexander, Robert J. "Belize," in Robert J. Alexander (ed.). *Political Parties of the Americas*. Vol. 1. Westport, Conn.: Greenwood Press, 1982.

Grant, C. H. *The Making of Modern Belize*. Cambridge: Cambridge University Press, 1976.

Peoples United Party. *25 Years of Struggle and Achievement 1950–1975*. Belize: 1976.

Shoman, Assad. "Birth of a Nationalist Movement in Belize." *Occasional Paper No. 7*. Belize: Bisra, 1979.

Young, Alma, and Jacqueline Braveboy-Wagner. "Territorial Disputes in the Caribbean
    Basin," in W. Marvin Hill and Richard Millett (eds.). *Crescents of Conflict*. New
    York: Praeger Publishers, 1985.

PERCY C. HINTZEN AND W. MARVIN WILL

PRIETO FIGUEROA, LUIS BELTRÁN (19?–   ), was one of the founders
of Acción Democrática (AD) and long-time political leader of the teachers of
Venezuela. Even before the death of Juan Vicente Gómez* in December 1935,
Prieto had organized the Teachers Federation of Venezuela. In 1936 he became
one of the founders of Organización Venezolana (ORVE), the core of what was
to become Acción Democrática, and mobilizied many teachers in its support.
He was one of the leaders of the National Democratic Party (PDN), into which
ORVE merged, and was deported by the Eleazar López Contreras* government
in early 1937. Upon his return, he became one of the principal figures of the
PDN.

With legalization of PDN as Acción Democrática, Luis Beltrán Prieto was
elected its second vice president. He was the principal liaison between the AD
leadership and the young military in the conspiracy that overthrew President
Isaías Medina Augarita.*

With the overthrow of Medina Angarita in October 1945, Prieto became a
member of the seven-man Revolutionary Government Junta presided over by
Rómulo Betancourt,* and also minister of education. He presided over a massive
expansion and modernization of the country's educational system.

When the AD regime was overthrown in November 1948, Prieto went into
exile and during most of the next nine years worked for various United Nations
agencies. After the Marcos Pérez Jiménez* dictatorship fell, he was elected
secretary general of AD, and in the 1958 election was elected to the Senate. He
also became President of Acción Democrática.

At the end of President Raúl Leoni's* administration, there were two candidates for the AD nomination, Luis Beltrán Prieto and Gonzalo Barrios.* Prieto
had the support of AD Secretary General Jesús Paz Galarraga but was strongly
opposed by Rómulo Betancourt and President Leoni. Prieto and his followers
withdrew from AD to form the Electoral Movement of the People (MEP), which
nominated Prieto. He came in third, behind Social Christian Copei Party nominee
Rafael Caldera Rodríguez* and Barrios.

Prieto harbored great bitterness toward his old party. He continued as president
of MEP, many of whose leaders and rank and file returned to Acción Democrática. Prieto continued to be a senator until 1983, but his presidential candidacies of 1978 and 1983 got such small support as to reduce MEP to a minor
party.

BIBLIOGRAPHY

Alexander, Robert J. *Rómulo Betancourt and the Transformation of Venezuela*. New
    Brunswick, N.J.: Transaction Books, 1981.

———. *The Venezuelan Democratic Revolution*. New Brunswick, N.J.: Rutgers University Press, 1964.

Betancourt, Rómulo. *Venezuela, Oil and Politics*. Boston: Houghton Mifflin, 1979.

Martz, John D. *Acción Democrática: Evolution of a Modern Political Party in Venezuela*. Princeton, N.J.: Princeton University Press, 1966.

ROBERT J. ALEXANDER

PRIETO VIAL, JOAQUÍN (1786–1854), was the first Chilean president during the so-called Conservative Republic. He became a cavalry lieutenant in 1805, and with the independence movement he took part in military campaigns in both Chile and Argentina. By 1817 he was commander-in-chief in Santiago and in 1822 was named field marshal.

Prieto was also active in politics. He was twice governor of Concepción Province. In 1823 he was elected deputy in the national Congress, serving there during most of the rest of the 1820s.

Liberal governments controlled Chile during the 1820s. In the 1828 election, all factions accepted Francisco Antonio Pinto Díaz* as president, but there was a contest for the vice presidency. One candidate was Joaquín Prieto, who was aligned with the conservative forces as was Francisco Ruiz Tagle. When no candidate received the required number of votes and the Liberal-controlled Congress chose the third nominee, Joaquín Vicuña, a Liberal, the result was a civil war. The military leader of the insurgents was Joaquín Prieto, who gained a decisive victory over Liberal forces in April 1830 in the Battle of Lircay. Elected president the following year, Prieto took office in September 1831.

During much of the Prieto administration, its predominant figure was Diego Portales Palazuelos,* who had exercised a virtual dictatorship between the Battle of Lircay and the inauguration of President Prieto. Prieto summoned a constitutional congress. It drew up the Constitution of 1833, which provided for a very strong presidency, and a highly centralized national government. The Prieto regime had a strongly authoritarian tendency.

President Prieto was overwhelmingly reelected in 1836. In the following year, Chile became involved in a war with the Peru-Bolivia Confederation, one result of which was the murder of Diego Portales as the consequence of a plot in which enemy agents were probably involved.

Considerable economic progress was made during the Prieto administration, owing in part to the political stability of the period. Copper mining received particular impetus, an effective tax system was established, and a coastal shipping company was started.

During the last years of the Prieto regime, its authoritarian tone relaxed somewhat. Prieto turned over power to an elected successor, General Manuel Bulnes Prieto.* Upon leaving the presidency, Joaquín Prieto became a member of the Council of State. He also was named commander of the national military forces in the port city of Valparaíso. In 1843 he was elected senator.

BIBLIOGRAPHY

Cortes, Lia, and Jordi Fuentes. *Diccionario Político de Chile*. Santiago: Editorial Orbe, 1967.
Enciclopedia Universal Ilustrada Europeo-Americana. Barcelona: José Espasa e Hijos.
Galdemes, Luis. *Historia de Chile*. Santiago: Editorial Zig Zag, 1945.

                                                                          ROBERT J. ALEXANDER

PRÍO SOCARRÁS, CARLOS (1903–1977), president of Cuba from 1948 until 1952, attended the University of Havana, gained national attention in the late 1920s as secretary general of the Havana Student Directorate and one of the chief student leaders fighting Gerardo Machado,* and spent nearly three years in prison. He was chief representative of the students who met with Sergeant Fulgencio Batista y Zaldívar* at Camp Columbia on the night of September 4, 1933, to found the Revolutionary Junta that led to the installation of Ramón Grau San Martín* as president.

When Batista, encouraged by the United States, deposed Grau in January 1934, Prío immediately worked to form the Partido Revolucionario Cubano (Auténtico), founded in February 1934, to fight for social and economic reforms and to seek the election of Ramón Grau. In 1939 he was an Auténtico member of the Constituent Assembly.

When Ramón Grau was elected president in 1944, Carlos Prío, a member of the Senate from 1940 until 1948, became prime minister in 1945 and minister of labor in 1947. He aided the successful Auténtico takeover of the Communist-dominated Confederación de Trabajadores de Cuba. Early in 1948 Prío resigned his cabinet post to become his party's successful presidential candidate.

Like his predecessor, President Prío maintained wide respect for civil liberties. Unlike Grau, he secured passage of vital pieces of legislation necessary to implement the social democratic system of government called for in the Constitution of 1940, including acts creating the National Bank of Cuba, the Constitutional Rights Tribunal, and the Organic Law of Budgets.

After breaking with Grau in 1949, Prío decided to prosecute his former political mentor on charges of corruption. Although a trial was never held because evidence against Grau was mysteriously stolen, Prío's moral stance on corruption turned out to be tragically ironic. By the time Prío was overthrown by Batista on March 10, 1952, he had also become corrupt. Under his presidency gangsterism and political terrorism were rampant. Because Carlos Prío possessed such a strong revolutionary record, his dishonesty did much to permanently discredit social democracy in Cuba.

Between 1952 and 1959 Carlos Prío was in exile, except for a few months in 1955. Returning after the overthrow of Batista, Prío again went into exile in 1960, as the regime of Fidel Castro* began to evolve in a Communist direction.

BIBLIOGRAPHY

Farber, Samuel. *Revolution and Reaction in Cuba, 1933–1960*. Middletown, Conn.: Wesleyan University Press, 1976.

Ruiz, Ramon Eduardo. Cuba: The Making of a Revolution. New York: W. W. Norton, 1968.

Thomas, Hugh. *Cuba: The Pursuit of Freedom*. New York: Harper and Row, 1971.

Wright, Stephen J. "Cuba, Sugar and the United States: Diplomatic and Economic Relations During the Administration of Ramón Grau San Martín, 1944–1948." Ph.D. diss., Pennsylvania State University, 1983.

                                                            STEPHEN J. WRIGHT

Q

QUADROS, JÂNIO (1917–   ), was one of the most disruptive politicians in twentieth-century Brazil. His spectacular 1960 presidential victory so raised the Brazilians' political expectations that his unexpected and apparently unnecessary resignation from the presidency on August 24, 1961, left them stunned and helped create the conditions that led directly to the army takeover in March 1964.

Quadros was born in Mato Grosso in 1917, but his family moved in 1930 to the city of São Paulo, where he was educated. He entered the small Christian Democratic Party (PDC) in 1945 and was elected to the São Paulo City Council in 1948. He became a state deputy in 1950. In March 1953 he was elected mayor of São Paulo, where he projected an image of a fresh and honest political leader with no ties to any one political or economic group.

In 1954 Quadros became governor of the state of São Paulo, defeating the powerful populist political boss, Ademar de Barros. Quadros' constant political theme was an appeal to hard work and honesty. As governor, he was able to channel funds into industrial projects, and the business and financial community was impressed with his administration.

Quadros switched political parties and states as he climbed the political ladder. After his term as São Paulo governor, he was elected to the national Congress from the neighboring state of Mato Grosso representing the National Labor Party.

In 1960, after a great deal of political maneuvering, the União Democrática Nacional (UDN) party and several smaller groups nominated him as their presidential candidate to run against General Henrique Lott, candidate of the parties from the Getúlio Vargas* tradition. Quadros won a substantial victory but resigned after nine months. He brought substantial changes in economic policy and proposed a number of major socioeconomic reforms. Quadros also initiated political moves which he hoped would free him from dependence on the legislative branch. He began to funnel federal funds to various state governors.

Quadros was an innovator in foreign policy and wanted to break Brazil's deep dependence on the United States. He embarked on a program of close cooperation with Third World nations, especially Africa. But his insistence on granting Brazil's highest award to Che Guevara,* Fidel Castro's* Argentine-born economic minister, was a deliberate slap in the face of the United States and provoked much internal resistance in Brazil.

When he resigned, Quadros apparently was sure that the Congress and military would recall him. When they did not, he went into self-imposed exile. After the 1964 military coup, he was deprived of his civil rights, which were not restored until 1979. He repeatedly attempted to regain office and in November 1985 was finally elected mayor of São Paulo once again.

BIBLIOGRAPHY

Castro, José Viriato de. *O Fenomeno Jânio Quadros*. 1959.
Ribeiro, Mauro. *Diario de Um Confinado*. 1968.

JORDAN YOUNG

R

RAVINES, EUDOCIO (1897–1969), one of the most controversial political figures of Peru, was born in Cajamarca. After finishing high school in his hometown, he moved to Lima to work for a commercial firm. There he joined the studuent-labor forces led by Víctor Raúl Haya de la Torre* opposed to the autocratic rule of President Augusto B. Leguía.* As a result, he was deported to Santiago de Chile in 1925, but soon the Chilean police sent him by train to Buenos Aires. There he joined the Aprista Committee, which in 1926 assigned him to collaborate with Haya de la Torre, then exiled in Europe. He became a leader of the Paris Aprista Committee and with Haya attended the International Anti-Imperialist Congress in Brussels in 1927.

The following year Ravines began working surreptitiously against the Apristas under orders of the Third International, as he had secretly joined the Communist Party. After receiving training in the Soviet Union, he returned to Lima in 1930 and became secretary general of the Peruvian Socialist Party, founded by José Carlos Mariátegui* two years earlier. Soon after Mariátegui's death, Ravines changed the name of the party to the Peruvian Communist Party. Following Comintern instructions, he launched a campaign against the nationalist and personal interpretation of Marxism that Mariátegui had passed on to his followers. Ravines was captured by the police in October 1933 but managed to escape from prison, and traveled to the Soviet Union.

The Comintern sent Ravines to Chile to organize the Popular Front, and when the Civil War broke out in Spain, he was dispatched there as a trusted aparatchik. The Stalin-Hitler Pact began to weaken his faith in communism, and by the end of the war, he was expelled from the Chilean Communist Party.

In 1945 he returned to Lima, where he first joined the Peruvian Socialist Party, and then organized his own Authentic Socialist Party. In his later years, he was closely associated with the conservative newspaper *La Prensa* and its owner, Pedro Beltrán. The Revolutionary Government of the Armed Forces deported him to Mexico, where a car ran over and killed him.

BIBLIOGRAPHY

Alisky, Marvin. *Historical Dictionary of Peru*. Metuchen, N.J.: Scarecrow Press, 1979.
Prieto Celi, Federico. *El deportado: Biografía de Eudocio Ravines*. Lima: Editorial Andina, 1979.
Ravines, Eudocio. *The Yenan Way*. New York: Charles Scribner and Sons, 1952.

EUGENIO CHANG-RODRÍGUEZ

RECABARREN SERRANO, LUIS EMILIO (1876–1924), founder of the Communist party of Chile, began his political career in the Democratic party in 1894 in Valparaíso. In 1903 he moved to the northern nitrate area, where he published several left-wing labor newspapers and helped organize trade unions in the nitrate fields and ports. In 1906 he was elected to the Chamber of Deputies, but the Chamber refused to seat him.

As major leader of the Democatic party left wing, Recabarren led a split in 1912, which established the Socialist Labor Party. The new party gained extensive influence in organized labor in the nitrate region and Santiago-Valparaíso area. In 1919 Recabarren presided over a congress of the Federación Obrera de Chile, and two years later he led its next Congress' decision to join the Red International of Labor Unions. A few weeks later, the Socialist Labor Party became the Communist party.

Meanwhile, in 1920 Recabarren was his party's unsuccessful candidate for president, and in 1922–1923 he visited the Soviet Union. Recabarren committed suicide in December 1924.

BIBLIOGRAPHY

Alexander, Robert J. *Communism in Latin America*. New Brunswick, N.J.: Rutgers University Press, 1957.
Boizard, Ricardo. *Cuatro Retratos en Profundidad: Ibáñez, Lafertte, Walker, Leighton*. Santiago: Imprensa el Imparcial, 1950.
Cortes, Lia, and Jordi Fuentes. *Diccionario Político de Chile*. Santiago: Editorial Orbe, 1967.
Jobet, Julio César. *Recabarren y los Origines del Movimiento Obrero y el Socialismo Chilenos*. Santiago: Editorial Prensa Latinoamericana, 1973.

ROBERT J. ALEXANDER

REMÓN CANTERA, JOSÉ ANTONIO (1908–1955), rose to power in Panama as an officer of the National Police, becoming colonel and commandant in February 1947. He modernized and upgraded the force and made it the arbiter of political affairs. Between 1948 and 1952 five different persons filled the office of president, largely at the will of "kingmaker" Remón.

Remón was a member of an old but impoverished Panamanian family. He attended the National Institute, Panama's prestigious secondary school. His connections then enabled him to secure a scholarship in Mexico at the National Military Academy. He graduated third in his class in 1931 and entered the Panamanian National Police with the rank of captain.

In that same year, when the United States refrained from intervening in the overthrow of President Florencio Harmodio Arosemena, the National Police became a factor in political affairs. Its power expanded after the coup ousting President Arnulfo Arias Madrid* in 1941, again with U.S. blessing.

After shuttling civilian politicians in and out of the presidency, Remón put together the National Patriotic Coalition and won his own election in 1952. He established the primacy of the military, even though he denied he was a dictator. He won the support of the masses by promising economic and social reform, even though he amassed a fortune under Panama's corrupt political system and capitalized on Panamanian nationalism. He negotiated the new Remón-Eisenhower Canal Treaty, which did not answer the demands of ultranationalists but provided Panama with increased revenues and eliminated discriminatory wage policies in the Zone. Remón completed the negotiations only days before he was assassinated in January 1955.

Remón kept the civilian politicians in line by limiting the number of political parties, but he made a fetish of constitutionality and civilian authority. He promoted economic development, extensive public works, improvement of education, housing, and health care, and inauguration of an ambitious agrarian reform program. On the other hand he outlawed labor's right to strike and maintained the system of private monopolies and concessions that sustained the ruling families. He converted the National Police into the National Guard in 1953, improving its professionalism and training but tolerating graft and corruption that enriched its leaders.

BIBLIOGRAPHY

Alba C., Manuel María. *Cronología de los Gobernantes de Panamá, 1510–1967*. Panamá: 1967.
Pippin, Larry LaRae. *The Remón Era: An Analysis of a Decade of Events in Panama, 1947–1957*. Stanford, Calif.: Stanford University Press, 1964.
Ropp, Steve C. *Panamanian Politics: From Guarded Nation to National Guard*. New York: Praeger, 1982.

CHARLES D. AMERINGER

REYES, RAFAEL (1850–1921), Colombian general and president, came to power in the wake of the devastating civil War of the Thousand Days (1899–1902). He was born in Santa Rosa, Boyacá, into a prominent local family. In his young manhood, he explored Colombia's Amazon region with his brothers and established several commercial enterprises along the frontier. In the civil war of 1885, Reyes won distinction on the Conservative side. The following year he took an active role in formulating Colombia's centralist constitution. When disgruntled Liberals rebelled in 1895, Reyes led government forces in a successful four-month campaign.

Reyes saw his presidential ambition frustrated by political intrigues within the Conservative Party and another Liberal uprising, the War of the Thousand Days.

When it was over, an exhausted party finally accepted him in 1904. He inherited a country in ruins; 100,000 had perished, much of the economy was destroyed, and the United States had successfully detached Panama.

Reyes attempted political reconciliation by bringing moderate Liberals into his government and dealing harshly with intransigents of both parties. He began an ambitious program of highway and railroad construction; carried out fiscal reforms and foreign debt renegotiation; and promoted technical education. He gave indigenous peoples representation in the government. He sought to professionalize the armed forces; the army was reorganized, and a military school was established by Chilean advisers.

Reyes responded to growing opposition with increasingly dictatorial methods, including creation of a subservient "National Assembly" that effectively overrode Congress. Dissatisfaction over his personalist rule, the terms granted foreign creditors, and what were regarded as unequal treaties over Panama that he negotiated with the United States brought Liberals and Conservatives to form the anti-Reyes Republican Union.

During debates over the Panama treaties, nationalist students led by Enrique Olaya Herrera* and encouraged by the Republican Union staged major demonstrations in Bogotá. With support for his regime crumbling, Reyes resigned and left the country in July 1909. He spent most of the following decade in exile.

BIBLIOGRAPHY

Camacho Carrizosa, Guillermo. *Criítica y política*. Bogotá: 1924.
Henao, Jesús María, and Gerardo Arrubla. *History of Colombia*. Chapel Hill: University of North Carolina Press, 1938.
Liévano Aguirre, Indalecio. *Los grandes conflictos sociales y económicos de nuestra historia*. Bogotá: 1963.
López de Mesa, Luis. *Escrutinio sociólogico de la historia colombiana*. Bogotá: 1956.
RICHARD E. SHARPLESS

RIESCO ERRÁZURIZ, GERMÁN (1854–1916), was president of Chile during the first few years of the twentieth century. He received his law degree in 1875. Thereafter, he served as attorney for several government ministries. In 1891 he was named to the Santiago Appeals Court and in 1897 to the Supreme Court. He retired from the judiciary in the following year.

In 1901 Germán Riesco was elected president with support of the Liberal Alliance. His principal accomplishments as president were in foreign affairs. Peace treaties with Peru and Bolivia put an official end to the War of the Pacific (1879–1883). An arbitration agreement in 1903 ended a boundary dispute with Argentina.

Domestically, the Riesco regime was marked by extensive unrest, including a violent strike in Valparaíso in May 1903 which brought intervention by the navy; widespread rioting in Santiago in 1905; and disturbances in the northern nitrate regions.

After his presidency, Germán Riesco played no further significant political role.

BIBLIOGRAPHY

Cortes, Lia, and Jordi Fuentes. *Diccionario Político de Chile*. Santiago: Editorial Orbe, 1967.

Enciclopedia Universal Ilustrada Europeo-Americana. Barcelona: José Espasa e Hijos.

Galdames, Luis. *Historia de Chile*. Santiago: Editorial Zig Zag, 1945.

ROBERT J. ALEXANDER

RÍOS MORALES, JUAN ANTONIO (1888–1946), was the second of three Radical Party leaders who served as presidents of Chile between 1938 and 1952. He received his law degree from the University of Chile in 1914. Although active in the Radical party, he did not enter the Chamber of Deputies until 1924. During the dictatorship of President Carlos Ibáñez del Campo (1927–1931), Ríos headed that Radical faction which collaborated with the regime. serving as president of the party after 1927. Following the overthrow of Ibáñez, he was expelled from the party. However, he was shortly readmitted, and in 1936–1937 he was leader of the faction that favored entering the Popular Front. After the Radicals joined the Front, the party's convention in May 1937 resolved to withdraw from the cabinet of President Arturo Alessandri Palma* and chose Juan Antonio Ríos as party president.

When the Popular Front named its candidate for the presidential election of 1938, however, it chose Pedro Aguirre Cerda*, who had led the faction opposed to entering the Front. It was not until Aguirre Cerda's death at the end of 1941 that Juan Antonio Ríos was elected president with the support of his own party, the Socialists, Communists, and the Falange Nacional, as well as of a Liberal faction headed by ex-President Arturo Alessandri, who wanted to defeat Carlos Ibáñez, Rios' opponent.

President Juan Antonio Ríos broke diplomatic relations with the Axis powers in World War II and finally declared war on them. His government energetically pushed economic development, most notably starting construction of the Huachipato steel mill. In the last months of 1945, President Ríos became gravely ill, turning over the government to Vice President (Acting President) Alfredo Duhalde at the end of September. Although resuming the presidency for about a month and a half in December 1945-January 1946, he once again turned over power to Duhalde on January 17, 1946, and died a few months later.

BIBLIOGRAPHY

Alexander, Robert J. "Chile," in Robert J. Alexander (ed.). *Political Parties of the Americas*. Vol. 1. Westport, Conn.: Greenwood Press, 1982.

Bowers, Claude G. *Chile Through Embassy Windows*. New York: Simon and Schuster, 1958.

Cortes, Lia, and Jordi Fuentes: *Diccionario Político de Chile*. Santiago: Editorial Orbe, 1967.

Stevenson, John Reese. *The Chilean Popular Front*. Philadelphia: University of Pennsylvania Press, 1962.

ROBERT J. ALEXANDER

RIVADAVIA, BERNARDINO (1780–1845), was one of the precursors of Argentine independence and was president in 1826–1827. He was educated in the Colegio de San Carlos in Buenos Aires, and while still a schoolboy took part in the successful defense of Buenos Aires under Governor Santiago Liniers against British attempts to capture the city. In 1809, when Liniers faced a successful revolt, Rivadavia continued to support the governor. On May 25, 1810, he took part in the *cabildo abierto* meeting in Buenos Aires which launched the Argentine independence movement.

Rivadavia became minister of war of the new Argentine government in 1811, and subsequently was also minister of finance and of government. However, he withdrew from the government in 1812, when the incumbent regime was overthrown. In 1814 he was named minister to various European countries and did not return home until 1820.

Upon his return, Rivadavia was named minister of government of Buenos Aires Province, in which capacity he contributed to the organization of a viable provincial administration. He laid the basis of the public education system of the province and sponsored the creation of a university.

Subsequently, Rivadavia was named Argentine minister to Great Britain. In 1826 he was elected president. In that post, he devoted a lot of his energies to the extension of public education, bringing a number of European teachers to Argentina. He also fomented expansion of agriculture and recognized the independence of Uruguay.

With the eruption of caudillo-led revolts in various parts of the country, Rivadavia resigned in June 1827. Two years later he went back to Europe, returning home only in 1834, when he presented himself to the courts to answer charges made by his political enemies. He was exiled first to Brazil and then to Spain, where he died.

BIBLIOGRAPHY

Enciclopedia Universal Ilustrada Europeo-Americana. Barcelona: José Espasa e Hijos.

Galvan Moreno, C. *Rivadavia, el Estadista Genial: Reseña documentaria de su vida y su obra*. Buenos Aires: Claridad, 1940.

Palcos, Alberto. *Rivadavia: Ejecutor del Pensamiento de Mayo*. La Plata: Universidad de la Plata, 1960.

Piccirilli, Ricardo. *Rivadavia y su Tiempo*. Buenos Aires: Ediciones Peuser, 1960.

JOHN T. DEINER

RIVERA, FRUCTUOSO (1784?–1854), was the first constitutional president of Uruguay and founder of the Colorado Party. He was born some time between 1784 and 1789. When the struggle for independence began, he joined the independence forces. He won quick promotion and was a captain by 1811. He resisted Portuguese attempts to control the country, as well as supporting José Gervasio Artigas'* early efforts to resist Argentine attempts to establish hegemony in Uruguay.

Rivera again led Uruguayan resistance to Portuguese efforts to control Uruguay between 1816 and 1820. After he was defeated, however, he signed an agreement making his native land part of Brazil. By 1824 he was a general and commander of Brazilian forces in Uruguay.

Nevertheless, when Juan Antonio Lavalleja* launched another effort to obtain Uruguayan independence in 1825, Rivera again switched sides and soon became the second-in-command of the Uruguayan forces. He objected to Buenos Aires' control of Lavalleja's forces, however, and in 1826 he withdrew from the struggle. He went to the Argentine province of Santa Fe, where he joined forces with the local caudillo Estansilao López and cooperated in a campaign to capture the Brazilian missions region. In the process, he developed an army that was loyal to him. His influence was significant in Brazil's decision to recognize the independence of Uruguay in 1828.

Rivera was the minister of war in the provisional government first set up by the Uruguayans, and in October 1830 was chosen as first constitutional president of the country. As president and subsequently, Rivera got involved in the politics of both Argentina and Brazil. He sided with opponents of Argentine dictator Juan Manuel de Rosas* and with Rio Grande do Sul rebels against the Brazilian government.

While out of office, Rivera established what became the Uruguayan Colorado Party. In March 1839 he returned to the presidency. Soon afterward, he declared war on the Rosas regime in Argentina. He defeated an Argentine force late in 1839, but in 1842 and 1845 was defeated by the Argentine-backed forces of his major rival, Manuel Oribe,* and took refuge in Brazil. He returned to Uruguay in 1846 to lead a Colorado army. After being forced out of command in the wake of military defeat in 1847, Rivera went to Rio de Janeiro, where he lived for four years.

Rivera attempted to return to Uruguay again in 1851. The Brazilian government put many impediments in his way, and although he was named member of a triumvirate junta in 1853, he died without having reached Montevideo.

BIBLIOGRAPHY

Antuna, José Gervásio. *Un caudillo, el General Fructuoso Rivera, Prócer del Uruguay.* Madrid: 1948.
Enciclopedia Universal Ilustrada Europeo-Americana. Barcelona: José Espasa e Hijos.
Lepro, Alfredo. *Fructuoso Rivera, hombre del pueblo. Sentido revolucionario de su vida y de su acción.* Montevido: 1945.

ROBERT J. ALEXANDER

RIVIÉREZ, HÉCTOR (1913–), was French Guiana deputy in the French National Assembly between 1967 and 1981. He studied in schools in Cayenne and the Faculty of Law in Paris. He worked for many years in Oubangi C! ari in French Equatorial Africa and was a member of the French Senate from that territory. Returning to French Guiana, he was elected to the National Assembly by the Gaullists in 1967 and served until the Socialist Party victory in 1981. Between 1973 and 1979 he was a French representative in the European Parliament.

BIBLIOGRAPHY

Who's Who in France 1984–1985. 17th ed. Paris: Editions Jacques Lafitte S.A., 1984.

ROBERT J. ALEXANDER

ROBLES, MARCO AURELIO (1905–   ), was president of Panama from 1964 to 1968. A banker and representative of the political elite, he tried to continue the Liberal Party's comeback in the wake of the assassination of strongman José Antonio Remón* by convincing his fellow oligarchs of the need for reform, a message backed by pressure from the United States. He sponsored relatively mild tax reform and a modest agrarian reform, which had the effect of splitting the Liberal Party.

Robles' task was complicated by nationalistic passions aroused by the Panama Canal issue. Violent rioting in January 1964, before he took office, had strained U.S.-Panamanian relations severely. Negotiations with the United States for a series of treaties on the status and operation of the existing canal, defense of it, and construction of a sea-level canal, explicitly recognizing Panama's sovereignty over the Isthmus, made progress until 1967, when unofficial texts of the treaties were leaked to the press. Public outcry against the proposed terms caused Robles to refuse to submit the treaties to the National Assembly.

BIBLIOGRAPHY

Alba C., Manuel María. *Cronología de los Gobernantes de Panama, 1510–1967*. Panama: 1967.
LaFeber, Walter. *The Panama Canal: The Crisis in Historical Perspective*. New York: Oxford University Press, 1978.
Ropp, Steve C. *Panamanian Politics: From Guarded Nation to National Guard*. New York: Praeger, 1982.

CHARLES D. AMERINGER

ROCA, BLAS (1898–1987), formerly Francisco Calderío, was a major leader of the Cuban Communist Party from the early 1930s until 1961, and thereafter a prominent figure in the regime of Fidel Castro.* He had only a grammar school education. He worked as a cobbler, entering radical politics when he served as an official of the Shoe Workers' Union in 1929. Roca joined the Communist party in the 1920s and fought in the struggle against Gerardo Machado,* resulting in his imprisonment in 1930. Subsequently, he became secretary general of the party, a post he continued to hold in the Unión Revolucionaria Comunista and the Partido Socialista Popular (PSP). In 1939 he was elected to the Constituent Assembly.

Blas Roca worked out arrangements in 1937 with Fulgencio Batista y Zaldívar,* by which the party was legalized as the Unión Revolucionaria Comunista and was assured control of the labor movement. Collaboration with Batista paid handsome dividends for the Communists, with both Juan Marinello* and Carlos Rafael Rodríguez Rodríguez* serving for short periods in Batista's cabinet. Communist Party membership rose to 150,000 in 1946, and the Communists polled 200,000 votes in the 1946 elections, 10 percent of the total.

During the second Batista era (1952–1958), Blas Roca led the party in a bland policy toward the dictatorship and in opposition to popular insurrection against it. Given his dominant role as the long-time leader of the old Communist Party, Blas Roca's future in the revolutionary government of Fidel Castro was anything but assured.

When the Organizaciones Revolucionarias Integradas was formed in mid–1961, bringing together the 26th of July Movement, the old PSP and the Revolutionary Directorate, Blas Roca was the only ex-PSP leader named to its Secretariat. At the same time, he took over editorship of the party newspaper, *Hoy*, a position he held until 1965.

When the new Partido Comunista de Cuba (PCC) was formed in 1965, its Secretariat contained only two stalwarts from the pre–1961 PSP, Carlos Rafael Rodríguez and Blas Roca. Also in 1965, Roca was given responsibility for writing a new socialist constitution for Cuba. In the mid–1970s he was appointed to the powerful Politburo of the PCC. Roca also served Fidel Castro as vice president of the Council of State and as president of the National Association of People's Power from 1976 to 1979.

BIBLIOGRAPHY

García Montes, Jorge, and Alonso Avila, Antonio. *Historia de Partido Comunista de Cuba*. Miami: Ediciones Universal, 1970.

Karol, K. S. *Guerrillas in Power: The Course of the Cuban Revolution*. New York: Hill and Wang, 1970.

Thomas, Hugh. *Cuba: The Pursuit of Freedom*. New York: Harper and Row, 1971.

                                                              STEPHEN J. WRIGHT

ROCA, JULIO ARGENTINO (1843–1914), an Argentine military hero who eradicated Indian opposition from the South, was twice elected president and was a dominant political leader in the last quarter of the nineteenth century. Son of a military officer who had fought for Argentine independence, he was born in the Province of Tucumán, and began his own military activities at age 15 in fighting between the interior and Buenos Aires armies. He later became an officer in the national army and took part in the Paraguayan War and in battles against regional caudillos.

By 1874, at age 31, Roca won promotion to general. He was given command of the frontier armies and embarked on the conquest of Patagonia from hostile

Araucanian Indians, opening up the southern third of the country for white settlement.

During Roca's first presidency (1880–1886), Patagonian lands were opened for settlement and Argentine agricultural and livestock production expanded. He undertook development of the ports, doubled railroad mileage, and improved public education. This was a period of heavy immigration from southern Europe, but Roca effectively denied immigrants political representation.

During Roca's second presidency (1898–1904) he continued many of the same policies pursued earlier, although the political and social situation had dramatically altered with the creation of the Unión Cívica Radical and greatly increased the militancy of labor and immigrant groups. Roca continued to deny representation to these groups, controlled elections by fraud, used violence to break up demonstrations, utilized the military to maintain control, and passed a law that allowed the government to expel any foreign "troublemakers." After the 1904 election, Roca retired from active political life.

BIBLIOGRAPHY

Arce, José. *Roca, 1843–1914 Su vida—su obra*. Buenos Aires: 1961.
Bucich Escobar, Ismael. *Historia de los Presidentes Argentinos*. Buenos Aires: Roldon, 1934.
Ferns, Henry S. *Argentina*. New York: Praeger, 1969.
Levene, Gustavo Gabriel. *Historia de los presidentes argentinos*. Buenos Aires: 1973.
Levene, Ricardo. *A History of Argentina*. Chapel Hill: University of North Carolina Press, 1937.

JOHN T. DEINER

ROCAFUERTE, VICENTE (1783–1847), was president of Ecuador and founder of the Liberal Party. He was educated in Madrid and Paris. In 1814 he was a republican member of the Spanish Cortes, representing Guayaquil. After the restoration of King Ferdinand VII, and the king's efforts to reestablish an authoritarian regime, Rocafuerte went to Mexico, where he joined those fighting for Spanish-American independence. Between 1824 and 1830 he was secretary of the Mexican Legation in London.

Rocafuerte returned to Ecuador in 1833 and soon became leader of the Liberals in the national legislature. In 1835 he participated in a rebellion in Guayaquil, was captured, but entered into an agreement with the Conservative leader Juan José Flores* by which Rocafuerte soon afterward became president.

During his four years in office, Rocafuerte established a solid fiscal system and carried out educational reforms that included forcing convents in the cities to provide schools. He also had a penal code written, and he established naval and military colleges.

When Flores returned to power in 1839, he appointed Rocafuerte as governor of Guayas Province. When Flores sought to perpetuate himself in office, however, Rocafuerte led a successful revolt against him. By 1846 he was back in

Quito as president of the Senate. He died in Lima, where he had gone on a diplomatic mission.

BIBLIOGRAPHY

Blanksten, George. *Ecuador: Constitutions and Caudillos*. Berkeley: University of California Press, 1951.
Enciclopedia Universal Ilustrada Europeo-Americana. Barcelona: José Espasa e Hijos.
Linke, Lillo. *Ecuador: Country of Contrasts*. London: Royal Institute of International Affairs. 1954.

ROBERT J. ALEXANDER

RODRÍGUEZ LARA, GUILLERMO (1923–   ), was president of Ecuador between 1972 and 1976. He graduated from the Quito Military Academy and subsequently enjoyed a normal army career, with a variety of assignments, including several overseas. By 1971 he was brigadier general and commander-in-chief of the army.

In 1972 General Rodríguez Lara led the army chiefs in overthrowing President José María Velasco Ibarra,* and assumed the presidency himself. He headed a reformist military regime, patterned frankly on that of President Juan Velasco Alvarado* in Peru. It decreed an agrarian reform and various other measures. It also presided over a very expansive oil boom, which allowed the government carry out a large public works program.

Charges of mismanagement of the oil bonanza, extensive corruption, social discontent, and growing civilian resentment at military rule undermined the Rodríguez Lara regime. The general was finally ousted by his military colleagues in 1976, although several more years were to pass before an elected civilian regime was restored.

BIBLIOGRAPHY

Americana Annual. New York: Grolier Inc., 1973–1976.
The International Who's Who 1985–86. 49th ed. London: Europa Publications Ltd., 1985.

ROBERT J. ALEXANDER

RODRÍGUEZ RODRÍGUEZ, CARLOS RAFAEL (1913–   ), was by the early 1980s vice president of the Council of State and Council of Ministers, member of the Politburo, and fourth secretary of the Cuban Communist Party. Rodríguez was ranked third in the Cuban hierarchy after Fidel* and Raúl Castro.* He was the most prominent of the trio of "old guard" Communists (along with Juan Marinello* and Blas Roca*) who played major roles in the revolutionary government after 1959.

Rodríguez received his doctorate in economics from the University of Havana in 1939. He held appointments as mayor of Cienfuegos during the Revolution of 1933 and as a member of the national Civil Service Commission from 1934 until 1944. He joined the old Communist Party in 1932 and became a member of the Central Committee of the reorganized Partido Socialista Popular (PSP) in 1939. In 1944 he was appointed to Fulgencio Batista y Zaldívar's* cabinet as Minister Without Portfolio. Rodríguez was the only person to serve in both Batista's and Castro's cabinets.

As one of the dominant leaders of the PSP, Rodríguez visited Fidel Castro in the Sierra Maestra in July 1957, where he signed a mutual aid pact with the 26th of July Movement. Opposed by many PSP members, this agreement led to Communist support of both the clandestine struggle and the guerrillas in the mountains.

Rodríguez made the transition to the Castro era with relative ease. From 1959 to 1962 he served as editor of the Communist daily paper, *Hoy*; from 1962 until 1965, he was president of the National Institute of Agrarian Reform; and when Castro created the Organizaciones Revolucionarias Integradas in 1961, as the regime's single party, he was given a major role over economic matters in the new organization. In 1965 he became a member of the Secretariat of the newly created Partido Comunista de Cuba (PCC).

During the late 1960s Rodríguez fell from favor with Fidel Castro but made a strong comeback in the early 1970s, when he directed a regulatory commission overseeing Cuban-Soviet economic, technical, and scientific exchanges. He was appointed to the Politburo in 1975 and to the Council of State in 1976. Thereafter, he played a vital role in the development of foreign policy and management of the economy.

BIBLIOGRAPHY

Domínguez, Jorge I. *Cuba: Order and Revolution*. Cambridge, Mass.: Harvard University Press, 1978.
Karol, K. S. *Guerrillas in Power*. New York: Hill and Wang, 1970.
Thomas, Hugh. *Cuba: The Pursuit of Freedom*. New York: Harper and Row, 1971.
Who Is Who—Government and Politics in Latin America. New York: Media Books Inc., 1984.

                                                            STEPHEN J. WRIGHT

ROJAS PINILLA, GUSTAVO (1900–1975), commander of Colombia's armed forces, seized power in 1953 in a military coup and remained as president until ousted by the military in 1957. He was born in Tunga, Boyacá, and educated at the Colombian military academy, where he received his commission in 1920. He also studied in the United States. Rojas served in various posts throughout the country. In 1950 he was named head of the armed forces during a period of intense rural violence. In 1953 leading Liberal and moderate Conservative politicians urged the military to act against the rightist Conservative president, Laureano Gómez.* In June, the military ousted Gómez and installed Rojas for a four-year term as president.

Rojas attempted limited social reforms to build a base of popular support. When his efforts began to threaten the traditional Conservative and Liberal parties, opposition increased. He responded by increasingly dictatorial methods, repressing the political parties. Economic problems and the inefficiency of his administration precipitated a nationwide strike and riots that finally led the military high command, supported by politicians of both parties, to force him from office in 1957.

Although temporarily stripped of his civil rights by the Senate, Rojas formed the Alianza Nacional Popular (ANAPO) in 1961 and unsuccessfully ran for president the following year. He organized ANAPO into a cohesive opposition to the ruling Liberal-Conservative National Front, and in elections from the municipal to the national level, ANAPO candidates frequently won office. By the end of the 1960s ANAPO was a mass party, with organizations down to the ward level, rallies, membership cards and dues, party training schools, and party media. ANAPO was dominated by the personalist style of Rojas, assisted by his daughter María Eugenia Rojas de Moreno and her husband Samuel Moreno Díaz. It appealed for support principally to the "popular class," which included the working classes, the poor, and those marginalized by the socioeconomic system. Support was solidified by distribution of food, clothing, and health services to the needy. ANAPO's ideological orientation was at best ambiguous; its programs were vaguely nationalist and developmentalist.

In 1970, Rojas came close to regaining power, when he lost to the Conservative Misael Pastrana Borrero by less than 60,000 votes. Rojas charged that he was defrauded in the official count, which was a possibility. Failing health forced him to take a less active role in ANAPO. That, combined with restoration of political competition following the end of the National Front, resulted in ANAPO's poor showing in the 1974 election.

BIBLIOGRAPHY

Berry, R. Albert, Ronald G. Hellman, and Mauricio Solaun. *Politics of Compromise*. New Brusnwick, N.J.: Transaction Books, 1980.
Dix, Robert H. *Colombia: The Political Dimensions of Change*. New Haven, Conn.: Yale University Press, 1967.
Fluharty, Vernon Lee. *Dance of the Millions*. Pittsburgh: University of Pittsburgh Press, 1957.
Premo, Daniel. "Alianza Nacional Popular: Populism and the Politics of Social Class in Colombia, 1961–1970." PhD. diss., University of Texas at Austin, 1972.

                                                              RICHARD E. SHARPLESS

ROMERO BARCELÓ, CARLOS (1932–   ), governor of Puerto Rico for the period 1976–1984, was one of the most dynamic of the young political leaders to emerge after the end of the Muñoz Marín* era in the 1960s. He was also one of the strongest advocates of Puerto Rico's admission to U.S. statehood.

Romero was born in San Juan into a prominent political family. His father was a judge of the insular Supreme Court and his mother a president of the now defunct Liberal Party, a position she inherited from her father, Antonio R. Barceló, the party's founder, and first president of the Puerto Rican Senate in 1917.

Romero was educated in private schools in San Juan, at Philips-Exeter Academy, and at Yale, where he graduated in 1953. He got a law degree from the University of Puerto Rico in 1956. Over the following decade he practiced law.

Romero entered politics in the mid–1960s. He joined those who called for statehood and soon became a prominent member of the Statehood Republican Party, then the principal opposition to the Popular Democrats. When the Statehood Republicans refused to participate in a referendum on the status question in 1967, Romero bolted from the party to join with Luis Antonio Ferré Aguayo* in organizing the United Statehooders, forerunner of the New Progressive Party.

As a vice president of the New Progressives, Romero supported Ferré's successful gubernatorial race in 1968, while simultaneously running for mayor of San Juan. He campaigned in the American "shirt-sleeve" style and was elected in a landslide. His two terms as mayor of San Juan were notable for administrative reorganization of municipal agencies and conservative fiscal policies. Political friends and foes alike praised him as an efficient and competent administrator.

Following Ferré's defeat by the Popular Democrats in 1972, Romero assumed leadership of the party and was its candidate for governor in 1976. He traveled widely throughout the island, emphasizing the need to restructure the island's economy, hard hit by unemployment, inflation, and dislocation caused by the flight of American-owned enterprises. He relegated the statehood question to the future when the economic situation had substantially improved.

Elected governor by a narrow margin, Romero drew on political contacts in the United States, made during the years when he served as a top official of the National League of Cities, to push for additional federal aid to help solve Puerto Rico's growing economic problems. He also instituted a public works program and established a Puerto Rico Development Fund to promote housing construction and infrastructure rebuilding. He also sought to stimulate the island's dormant agricultural sector. Primary emphasis was on private capital, which he sought to attract to the island. His initiatives to denationalize the telephone company and other government-owned enterprises, were intended to reassure the private sector, but also were in keeping with his political ideas.

Despite Romero's efforts and the New Progessives' influence with both U.S. parties, the Puerto Rican economy continued to suffer. In 1980 the electorate failed to give the party a majority in the legislature, although Romero Barceló narrowly won reelection. In 1984 in the wake of a police scandal, he was decisively defeated by the Popular Democratic former Governor Rafael Hernández Colón.*

BIBLIOGRAPHY

Sharpless, Richard. "Puerto Rico," in Robert J. Alexander (ed.). *Political Parties of the Americas*. Vol. 2. Westport, Conn.: Greenwood Press, 1982.
Who's Who in America 1984–1985. Chicago: Marquis Who's Who Inc., 1984.
                                                          RICHARD E. SHARPLESS

ROSAS, JUAN MANUEL DE (1793–1877), was Argentina's most important political leader in the first half of the nineteenth century. A famous fighter against the Indians, an *estanciero* (large ranch owner), and governor of Buenos Aires

Province from 1829 to 1832 and 1835 to 1852, Rosas forced the warring and divided provinces of Argentina to submit to federalist control. Many revere Rosas as a national hero because of his unification of the country; others vilify him for the undemocratic, and often cruel, practices he followed.

Rosas fought against British invasions of Buenos Aires as a young teenager, and became manager and owner of *estancias* in his late teens. His *estancia* was on the southern frontier, and the government gave him the job of organizing an army to protect the frontier against Indian attacks. He defeated the Indians. During the 1832–1835 period, following his first term as governor, Rosas again led expeditions against the Indians, exploring much of Argentina's south and southwest, and effectively ending Indian raids on Buenos Aires. He was given huge expanses of land as a reward and was acclaimed as governor of Buenos Aires in 1835, with virtually unlimited powers. He used a spy system to secure his control. He suppressed all opposition without mercy and demanded adulation. His supporters wore a red ribbon emblematic of support for Rosas and his Federalist cause. Rosas, although a Federalist, forced the unity of Argentina by coopting or eliminating rival provincial caudillos.

Rosas's economic policies aided the cattle and beef producers. He overcame attacks by regional caudillos, foreign interests, and those who opposed his political and economic policies, and kept the British and French out of Argentina. Finally, in 1852 one of Rosas' own generals, Justo José de Urquiza,* led a revolt. Rosas was defeated and forced into exile in England, where he lived for the next 25 years.

BIBLIOGRAPHY

Ferns, Henry S. *Argentina*. New York: Praeger, 1969.
Ibarguren, Carlos. *Juan Manuel de Rosas: su vida su tiempo su drama*. Buenos Aires: 1930.
Kroeber, Clifton. *Rosas y la revisión de la historia argentina*. Buenos Aires: 1965.
Levene, Ricardo. *A History of Argentina*. Chapel Hill: University of North Carolina Press, 1937.
Whitaker, Arthur P. *Argentina*. Englewood Cliffs, N.J.: Prentice-Hall, 1964.

JOHN T. DEINER

ROZENDAL, SYLVUS (1928–), was the third leader of the Curaçao Democratic Party and was twice Minister President (prime minister) of Netherlands Antilles. He was educated at Peter Stuyvesant College in Curaçao and received further schooling in Geneva. He joined the Democratic Party in 1958, was a member of the island legislature of Curaçao between 1959 and 1969, and leader of the Democratic Party delegation there between 1963 and 1967. He became a member of the Staten (Parliament) of Netherlands Antilles in 1966. In 1969 he was Minister President and minister of finance. He was again Minister President between 1977 and 1979 until the Curaçao Democratic Party suffered the worst defeat in its history. Thereafter, he continued merely to be the party's leader.

BIBLIOGRAPHY

Alexander, Robert J. "Netherlands Antilles," in Robert J. Alexander (ed.). *Political Parties of the Americas*. Vol. 2. Westport, Conn.: Greenwood Press, 1982.
Personalities Caribbean Seventh Edition, 1982–83. Binghamton, N.Y.: Vail Ballou Press, n.d.

ROBERT J. ALEXANDER

S

SAAVEDRA, BAUTISTA (1860–1939), was one of the last great caudillos of Bolivian politics. He was born in La Paz, completed his legal studies in 1896, and became reknowned as a professor of penal law.

Saavedra was originally a Liberal, but in 1914 he and several other prominent Liberals founded the Republican Party, of which he became second vice president. In the Republican Party, "revolution" of July 1920, the Liberal government fell and Saavedra organized an interim governing junta. A national convention in December 1920 split the Republican Party over the rival presidential candidacies of Saavedra, Daniel Salamanca Urey,* and two other members of the junta. Saavedra became chief of the Socialist Republican Party and Salamanca leader of the Genuine Republicans. The schism between these two parties and political chieftains dominated public life in the 1920s.

The national convention elected Bautista Saavedra president of the republic for 1921–1925. His term was punctuated by 48 insurrectionary plots and attempted coups, and five cabinet reorganizations. The achievements of his "plebeian government" included a new electoral law, legislation that established an 8-hour workday and legalized strikes, and a reform of mining taxes that doubled government revenues from tin exports. He vigorously pursued negotiations of the Tacna-Arica problem with Chile.

Through Saavedra, North American economic interests expanded in Bolivia. He negotiated a $33 million loan with New York banks, under terms of high interest rates and external control over Bolivia's tax system. This and the extremely favorable concessions to Standard Oil provoked rival political parties to call his government antinational. Although his mildly reformist labor legislation attracted the support of lower and middle classes, harsh repression of a strike in Uncía Mines and the Indian uprising in the highland town of Jesús de Machaca in 1923 aroused wide resentment.

Based on an agreement with his party, Saavedra transferred the presidency to his rival, Hernando Siles Reyes* and became minister to various European governments and to the League of Nations. Exiled in June 1936 by the military socialist government of David Toro, Saavedra died in Santiago de Chile.

BIBLIOGRAPHY

Baptista Gumucio, Mariano. *Historia Contemporanea de Bolivia, 1930–1978*. 2d ed. La Paz: Gisbert, 1978.
Céspedes, Augusto. *El Dictador Suicida, 40 Años de Historia de Bolivia*. 3d ed. La Paz: Juventud, 1979.
Díaz Machicao, Porfirio. *Historia de Bolivia, Saavedra, 1920–1925*. La Paz: Alfonso Tejerina, 1954.
Fellman Velarde, José. *Historia de Bolivia, La Bolivianidad Semicolonial*. Vol 3. Cochabamba: Lose Amigos del Libro, 1981.
Klein, Herbert S. *Parties and Political Change in Bolivia, 1880–1952*. Cambridge: Cambridge University Press, 1969.

WALTRAUD QUEISER MORALES

SABLE, VICTOR (1911–   ), a leading politcal figure of Martinique after World War II, was educated at the Lycée of Fort-de-France and at the Law Faculty of Paris, where he received a doctorate. For many years he conducted a law practice in Martinique. he was counselor of the French Republic from December 1946 to November 1948. He was elected as a Gaullist deputy from Martinique in 1958 and reelected in 1962, 1967, 1968, 1978, and 1981. He aligned with the Union de la Democratie Française in Parliment. In 1979 he was elected to the European Parliament in the first popular election for that body, on the list of the Union pour la France en Europe, headed by Simone Weil, and was the only non-European to be chosen.

BIBLIOGRAPHY

Personal contacts of the writer.
Who's Who in France. 17th ed. Paris: Editions Jacques Lafitte, 1984.

ROBERT J. ALEXANDER

SÁENZ PEÑA, ROQUE (1851–1914), Argentina's president from 1910 to 1913, is remembered primarily for his election reforms, which changed the nature of Argentine politics and allowed the Radicals to come to power. During his own era he was equally well known as a spokesman for Argentine opposition to U.S. dominance in the Western Hemisphere.

Sáenz Peña was the son of President Luis Sáenz Peña. Born in Buenos Aires, he graduated from law school in 1875 and briefly fought in Argentina's civil wars. he later was wounded while fighting on the Peruvian side in the War of the Pacific. Upon his return to Argentina, he was one of the founders in 1885 of the journal *Sud America* in which he urged that Argentina should resist U.S. hemispheric domination and that the nation should engage in world, not just hemispheric, politics. He was a consistent spokesman for this position at the many international meetings he attended as Argentine delegate.

In 1890 Sáenz Peña became Argentina's foreign minister, and the following year he was nominated by the "modernist" faction of the Autonomist Party as presidential candidate. More traditional elements in the party opposed this, however, and nominated his father. Sáenz Peña withdrew his candidacy and retired from public life during his father's 1892–1895 presidency. After 1895 he returned to politics and held a number of diplomatic posts before being elected president of Argentina in 1910.

Sáenz Peña's major contributions to Argentine politics was reform of the electoral laws in 1912. Under the previous unfair and corrupt election procedure, only about 10 percent of the population voted, and the Radicals abstained in protest of the system.

Sáenz Peña's reforms ensured more complete and honest voter registration, a secret ballot, compulsory voting, and minority representation. As a result, the Radical party ended its electoral boycott, and elected its candidate, Hipólito Yrigoyen* to the presidency in 1916.

A year after his electoral reforms were passed, Sáenz Peña retired from the presidency for health reasons. He died the following year.

BIBLIOGRAPHY

Barreda Laos, Felipe. *Roque Sáenz Peña*. Buenos Aires.
Canton, Darío. *Elecciones y partidos políticos en la Argentina: Historia, interpretación y balance*. 1910–1966. Buenos Aires: Siglo Veintiuno. Buenos Aires.
Gálvez, Manuel. *Vida de Hipólito Yrigoyen: el hombre de misterio*. 2d ed. Buenos Aires: Kraft, 1939.
Levene, Gustavo Garbriel. *Historia de los presidentes argentinos*. Buenos Aires: 1973.
Smith, Peter H. *Argentina and the Failure of Democracy, 1904–1955*. Madison: University of Wisconsin Press, 1974.

JOHN T. DEINER

ST. JOHN, HAROLD BERNARD (1931–   ), Barbadian prime minister and leader of the Barbados Labour Party, received his primary and secondary education on the island, then attended London University and earned his law degree at Inner Temple, by age 23. He then opened a successful legal practice in Bridgetown, Barbados, served as president of the Barbados Bar Association, and was named Queen's Counsel (QC) in 1969.

Active in the Barbados Labour Party (BLP), St. John was appointed to represent the BLP in the Senate. In 1966 and 1970 he was elected to the House of Assembly. Following resignation of Sir Grantley Herbert Adams* in 1970, St. John became leader of the BLP, until he was narrowly defeated in the 1971 general election. He was succeeded as leader by John Michael, G.M. (Tom) Adams,* son of Sir Grantley. From 1971 to 1976 St. John was again in the Senate and served in the BLP "Shadow Cabinet."

St. John was reelected to the House of Assembly in 1976 and 1981. With the BLP victory in 1976, St. John became deputy prime minister, as well as holding several portfolios in Prime Minister Adams' cabinet. He also served as president

of both the Council of Ministers of the African, Caribbean, and Pacific subgroup
of Commonwealth states, and of the Latin American Commonwealth subgroup.

With the unexpected death of Prime Minister Tom Adams in March 1985,
H. Bernard St. John became prime minister and BLP leader.

BIBLIOGRAPHY

International Who's Who, 1984–85. Vol. 48. London: Europa Publications, Ltd., 1984.
Manifesto, Barbados Labour Party. 1976 General Elections. Bridgetown, Barbados:
      1976.
Smith, Lloyd (ed.). *The Caribbean: Who, What, Why.* Port of Spain, Trinidad: 1969.
Will, W. Marvin. "Barbados," in Jack W. Hopkins (ed). *Latin America and Caribbean
      Contemporary Record,* Vols. 2–4. New York: Holmes and Meier, 1984, 1985,
      1986.

                                        PERCY C. HINTZEN AND W. MARVIN WILL

SALAMANCA UREY, DANIEL (1868–1935), was Bolivia's president during
the critical Chaco War years and leader of the Genuine Republican party. He
obtained his primary and secondary education in Cochabamba, where he passed
the bar exam in 1880. He was national deputy, senator, and minister of finance
in the government of General José Manuel Pando.* Salamanca was one of the
founders of the Republican Party in 1914, along with General Pando and Bautista
Saavedra, * and in May 1917 ran as Republican Party candiate for vice president.
At its December convention, following the Republican Revolution of July 1920,
the party split over rival presidential candidacies of Saavedra and Salamanca,
whose faction organized as the Genuine Republic Party.

Salamanca's bid for the presidency was only successful in 1931, after the
government of President Hernando Siles Reyes* was overthrown in a bloody
revolt. In March 1931 the Republican-Liberal coalition ticket of Daniel Salamanca and José Luis Tejada Sorzano was victorious.

Despite other achievements of his administration, Salamanca is largely remembered as a president who sought to solve domestic ills by a "good little
foreign war," the Chaco War with Paraguay. Although Bolivia's economy was
severely depressed, Salamanca approved extensive defense spending for ag-
gressive colonization of the Chaco region, and in July 1932 he escalated one of
many border clashes into full-scale war.

His critics indict Salamanca not only for involving Bolivia in one of its most
devastating wars, but also for mismanaging the war effort. The Bolivian High
Command had opposed the timing of the hostilities and chafed at Salamanca's
constant interference. In turn, Salamanca deeply mistrusted them and overruled
many military decisions. In November 1934, with the war going badly, Salamanca traveled to Chaco headquarters in Villamontes, where he was arrested
and deposed by the military.

A broken and bitter man, Salamanca retired to Cochabamba and died only a
month after the war's conclusion, in June 1935.

BIBLIOGRAPHY

Alvesteguí, David. *Salamanca: su gravitación sobre el destino de Bolivia.* Vols. 1 and 2. La Paz: Talleres Gráficos Bolivianos, 1947 and 1962.
Céspedes, Augusto. *Salamanca o el metafísico del fracaso.* La Paz: Editorial Juventud, 1973.
Díaz Arguedas, Julio. *Como fue derrocado el hombre símbolo: Salamanca. Un capítulo de la guerra con el Paraguay.* La Paz: Empresa Editora Universo, 1957.
Salamanca, Daniel. *Las dudas y las visiones del camino.* Barcelona: n.p., 1951.
———. *Mensajes y memorias póstumas.* Cochabamba: Editorial Canelas, 1976.

WALTRAUD QUEISER MORALES

SALOMON, LOUIS-FÉLICITÉ LYSIUS (1815–1888), elected president by the National Assembly of Haiti in August 1879 after 11 years of turmoil, was born to a wealthy black landowning family in the South. Well educated, he very early became committed to preventing political domination of Haiti by mulattoes. When Faustin Soulouque* reestablished black dominance, Salomon served as his minister of finance for 11 years. He was made duke of Saint Louis de Sud after Soulouque declared himself emperor in 1849.

After the overthrow of Soulouque in 1858, Salomon lived in exile. In 1867 He was named Haiti's diplomatic representative in Europe. He used his exile to broaden his knowledge , to travel, and to become acquainted with world affairs. He also married a French woman, Louise Magnus.

While abroad, Salomon acquired the reputation as the leading defender of black interests in Haiti. This reputation, which elevated him in the twentieth century to the status of a patron saint of Haitian black nationalism, prolonged his exile.

During Salomon's period abroad, the Haitian elite coalesced into factions of mulattoes, "Liberals," and blacks, "Nationalists." Salomon became the acknowledged leader of the Nationalists. When President Boisrond Canal stepped down after a turbulent period in office, Salomon returned an overwhelming number of Nationalists to the National Assembly, which in October, by a vote of 74–13, elected Salomon president.

Salomon's regime was characterized by a certain degree of subservience to French interests and ideas. He brought together a group of French bankers to capitalize and administer a national bank. He resumed payment on outstanding debts to France which were entirely liquidated. He recruited French teachers and established an expanded French-style system of education which still prevails. His military was reorganized with French assistance.

Salomon secured the admission of Haiti to the Universal Postal Union and granted a British company the concession to lay a cable between Haiti and Jamaica. An agrarian law of 1883 facilitated foreign ownership of land, previously proscribed. Despite the best intentions, these policies have been blamed for undermining Haitian independence and have been seen by many as beginning a pattern of foreign intervention which culminated in U.S. occupation of Haiti in 1915.

Salomon faced mulatto rebellions early in his regime. In 1883 a major rebellion resulted in the pillaging and burning of mulatto properties and murdering of mulattoes by black soldiers and mobs, which ended only when U.S. and European powers threatened intervention. The rebellion forced the expenditure of enormous amounts on the military, did irreparable damage to commerce and industry, further intensified racial animosities, and precipitated a spiral of inflation and state bankruptcy from which the regime never recovered.

Salomon had the constitution rewritten in 1886 to allow his reelection after a seven-year term. From the beginning of his second term, there was internal turmoil and discontent, stemming partly from fears that he might become president for life. By August 1888, the embittered Salomon, facing a rebellion from the predominantly black North, left for France, where he died a few months later.

BIBLIOGRAPHY

Davis, H. P. *Black Democracy: The Story of Haiti*. Toronto: Longmans, Green and Co., 1929.
Heinl, R. D. and N. G. Heinl. *Written in Blood*. Boston: Houghton Mifflin, 1978.
Leyburn, James G. *The Haitian People*. New Haven, Conn.: Yale University Press, 1941.
Logan, R. W. *Haiti and the Dominican Republic*. London: Oxford University Press, 1968.
Nicholls, David. *Haiti in Caribbean Context*. London: Macmillan Co. 1985.

PERCY C. HINTZEN

SANABRIA MARTÍNEZ, VICTOR (1898–1952), was the politically active archbishop of Costa Rica, 1940–1962. He emerged as a powerful political figure in the 1940s by giving attention to economic and social issues that had been ignored by the political liberals. Affected by the new social teachings of the church and having studied in Rome, where he received his doctorate in canon law in 1921, he sensed need for change in Costa Rica.

Sanabria became allied with President Rafael Angel Calderón Guardia* (1940–1944) who, at Sanabria's urging, established social security and a labor code. He also sanctioned Calderón's alliance with Communist leader Manuel Mora Valverde.* Sanabria gave vigorous public support to Calderón's choice for president in 1944, Teodoro Picado Michalski. However, he also sponsored the non-Communist labor federation "Rerum Novarum," under the young priest, Benjamín Núñez.

BIBLIOGRAPHY

Aguilar Bulgarelli, Oscar R. *Costa Rica y sus hechos políticos de 1948*. San José: Editorial Costa Rica, 1969.
Ameringer, Charles D. *Don Pepe: A Political Biography of José Figueres of Costa Rica*. Albuquerque: University of New Mexico Press, 1979.

Barahona Jiménez, Luis. *El pensamiento político en Costa* Rica. San José: Editorial Fernández-Arce, 1971.

Bell, John Patrick. *Crisis in Costa Rica: The Revolution of 1948.* Austin: University of Texas Press, 1971.

Segura, Ricardo Blanco. *Monseñor Sanabria: apuntes biográficos.* San José: Editorial Costa Rica, 1971.

CHARLES D. AMERINGER

SÁNCHEZ, LUIS ALBERTO (1900–   ), senator and president of the Political Commission of the Peruvian Aprista Party (PAP), was born in Lima, where he received all his formal education. He graduated with a bachelor of law and a doctorate in literature from the National University of San Marcos, of which he later was a professor and president on three occasions. Author of more than 30 books on literature, history, and political economy, he was a teacher of two generations of Peruvians who have excelled in politics, diplomacy, and literature. He was one of the founders of the PAP in 1931, the year he was elected to the Constituent Assembly. The following year he and the other Aprista representatives to the assembly were exiled. In Santiago de Chile he became president of Ercilla, a well-known publishing house. Sánchez was a member of the Chamber of Deputies (1945–1948), the Senate (1963–1968 and 1981–1985), and the 1978 Constituent Assembly, and was candidate for the second vice presidency (1962) and the first vice presidency of the Republic (1985). He was elected senator in 1985 with the highest number of preferential votes.

BIBLIOGRAPHY

Chang-Rodríguez, Eugenio. *Opciones políticas peruanas.* Lima: Centro de Documentación Andina, 1985.

Henderson, Donald C., and Grace R. Perez, trans. and compilers. *Literature and Politics in Latin America: An Annotated Calendar of the L.A. Sánchez Correspondence 1919–1980.* University Park, Pa.: Pennsylvania State University Libraries, 1982.

Tauro, Alberto. *Diccionario enciclopédico del Peru.* Lima: Editorial Mejía Baca, 1967.

EUGENIO CHANG-RODRÍGUEZ

SÁNCHEZ CERRO, LUÍS M. (1890–1933), president of Peru (1930–1931 and 1932–1933), was born in Piura. After graduating from the Chorrillos Military Academy in 1910, he was promoted for his assistance in overthrowing the constitutional government of Guillermo Billinghurst* (1914). Later, he alternated service and training abroad with efforts to overthrow President Augusto B. Leguía.* In 1929 President Leguía promoted Sánchez Cerro to lieutenant colonel, but he nonetheless overthrew Leguía in 1930 and ruled as head of a military junta until 1931. That year he founded the Unión Revolucionaria (UR), a party that used swastikas in its political propaganda and black shirts for its shock troops.

In the 1931 national elections, Sánchez Cerro ran as UR candidate against Víctor Raúl Haya de la Torre,* of the Peruvian Aprista Party (PAP). Sánchez

Cerro was proclaimed president-elect. Upon assuming power, he executed eight rebellious sailors, deported the 23 Aprista representatives in the Constituent Assembly, crushed rebellions in Trujillo, Huaraz, and Cajamarca, and ordered thousands of Apristas to be imprisoned. Sánchez Cerro was assasinated on April 30, 1933.

BIBLIOGRAPHY

Chang-Rodríguez, Eugenio. *Opciones políticas peruanas*. Lima: Centro de Documentación Andina, 1985.
Miró Quezada, Carlos. *Sánchez Cerro y su tiempo*. Buenos Aires: Libreria El Ateneo, 1947.
Muillo Garaycochea, Percy. *Historia del APRA, 1919–1945*. Lima: Enrique Delgado Valenzuela, (ed.). 1976.
Ugarteche, Pedro. *Sánchez Cerro: papeles y recuerdos de un presidente del Peru*. Lima: E. Universitaria, 1969–1970.

EUGENIO CHANG-RODRÍGUEZ

SANDINO, AUGUSTO CÉSAR (1895–1934), was a guerrilla leader whose resistance to U.S. Marines and Nicaraguan government forces made him a hero to all in Latin America who objected to U.S. military intervention. Half a century later, he was the symbol around whom anti-Somoza leftists molded the Sandinista National Liberation Front (FSLN).

Augusto Nicolás Sandino Calderón—his real name—was the son of a moderately prosperous farmer and an Indian servant. Little is known about his education. In 1921 he left Nicaragua and in the next five years held various jobs in Honduras, Guatemala, and Mexico.

In May 1926, hearing that a Liberal revolution had broken out in Nicaragua, he returned home. Starting with a band of 20 followers, within a year he headed a group of about a hundred. They participated in several successful combats with Conservative troops.

When Liberal Party leader José María Moncada negotiated a truce with the Conservatives in May 1927, Sandino refused to accept it, announcing that he was going back to the northern mountains to fight ''while even one gringo remains in Nicaragua.'' For nearly six years, the U.S. Marines and the Nicaraguan National Guard that they trained battled against Sandino without success. Finally, President Herbert Hoover ordered the Marines withdrawn shortly before leaving office in 1933.

For some months in 1929–1930, Sandino was in Mexico, seeking to gain support from the government there. His efforts were unavailing, but in Mexico he gathered around himself a number of Latin American supporters.

With the Marines gone in 1933, Sandino entered into negotiations with President Juan Bautista Sacasa. Coming into Managua, he dined with Sacasa and National Guard commander Anastasio Somoza García* on February 18, 1934. Three days later, members of the National Guard arrested and killed Sandino and his two principal aides.

Neil MacAulay has said of Sandino that he ''was one of the precursors of modern revolutionary guerrilla warfare—the process used to seize political control of an entire country by guerrilla action, without resort to conventional military operations, except perhaps in the final stages of the struggle, when the guerrilla army has acquired many of the characteristics of a regular army.''

BIBLIOGRAPHY

Beals, Carleton. *Banana Gold*. Philadelphia: J. B. Lippincott Co., 1932.
MacAulay, Neil. *The Sandino Affair*. Chicago: Quadrangle Books, 1967.
Millett, Richard. *Guardians of the Dynasty, a History of the U.S. Created Guardia Nacional de Nicaragua and the Somoza Family*. Maryknoll, N.Y. Orbis Books, 1977.
Selser, Gregorio. *Sandino* (translated by Cedric Belfrage). New York: Monthly Review Press, 1981.
Walker, Thomas W. *Nicaragua, The Land of Sandino*. Boulder, Colo.: Westview Press, 1980.

NEALE J. PEARSON

SANFUENTES, JUAN LUIS (1858–1930), was elected president of Chile after having served for many years as head of the Liberal Democratic Party, organized soon after the Civil War of 1891 by supporters of the defeated President José Manuel Balmaceda Fernández.* A graduate of the Law School of the University of Chile in 1879, he was elected to the Chamber of Deputies for the firt time in 1888. As a supporter of the martyred ex-president, he returned temporarily to private life. However, he took a prominent part in organizing the Liberal Democratic Party and became its president in 1900.

Sanfuentes was elected senator in 1900 and continued in that body until his election to the presidency. He was president of the Senate in 1906, and minister of finance and minister of justice and public instruction.

Sanfuentes was elected president in 1915 with support of the Coalition, the alliance of the National, Liberal Democratic, and Conservative parties. The most important events of his administration (1915–1920) were its maintenance of neutrality throughout World War I and its enactment of the first compulsory primary education law.

BIBLIOGRAPHY

Cortes, Lia, and Jordi Fuentes. *Diccionario Político de Chile*. Santiago: Editorial Orbe, 1987.
Enciclopedia Universal Ilustrada Europeo-Americana. Barcelona: José Espasa e Hijos.
Galdames, Luis. *Historia de Chile*. Santiago: Editorial Zig Zag, 1945.

ROBERT J. ALEXANDER

SANGSTER, DONALD BURNS (1911–1967), was Jamaica's second prime minister. Born into a middle-class farming family, he attended one of the country's premier secondary schools and completed studies to become a solicitor in

1937. His political career began in 1933, when he was elected to the local government council of the parish of St. Elizabeth.

When universal adult suffrage was introduced in 1944, Sangster failed to win a seat in the House of Representatives. In 1949 he joined the Jamaica Labour Party (JLP), won a seat in the House, and was immediately appointed minister for social welfare. He was appointed deputy leader of the JLP in 1950, and minister of finance and leader of the House in 1963. In 1955 Sangster lost his seat in a general election which the JLP lost to the People's National Party (PNP). He was reelected the following year.

Sangster was fiercely loyal to the leader of the JLP, Sir William Alexander Bustamante.* This loyalty was demonstrated over the issue of federation, which Sangster advocated and supported although most JLP leaders did not. He played an active role in the first two years of the federal government, which was formally inaugurated in 1958. However, in 1960 he supported the party leadership's position that the country should secede from the union, in spite of his own personal preference.

Sangster helped draw up a new constitution for independent Jamaica and was on the team that negotiated independence in London. Elections in April 1962 were won by the JLP, and Sangster was again made minister of finance, leader of the House, and deputy prime minister. In 1965 Bustamante became so incapacitated that Sangster assumed the post of acting prime minister until the prime minister retired two years later.

After Bustamante retired, Sangster called general elections in February, 1967. His party won an overwhelming victory. In March of the same year, however, Donald Sangster suffered a cerebral seizure from which he never recovered.

BIBLIOGRAPHY

Hurwitz, Samuel, and E. F. Hurwitz. *Jamaica: A Historical Portrait*. New York: Praeger, 1971.
Lindsay, Louis. *The Myth of Independence: Middle Class Politics and Non-mobilization in Jamaica*.
Kingston: Institute of Social and Economic Research, 1975.
McDonald, Frank. *Jamaica: A Political Overview*. New York: Institute of Current World Affairs, 1970.
Mettleford, Rex. *Manley and the Politics of Jamaica: Towards an Analysis of Political Change in Jamaica*, 1938–1966. Mona, Jamaica: Institute for Social and Economic Research, 1971.
Who's Who in Jamaica 1963. Kingston: Who's Who Ltd. 1964.
                                              PERCY C. HINTZEN AND W. MARVIN WILL

SANGUINETTI, JULIO MARÍA (1936–   ), was the first president of Uruguay elected after a dozen years of military dictatorship. He graduated from the law school of the University of Montevideo and was a practicing attorney. He became a member of the Chamber of Deputies in 1962, serving until Congress was dissolved by the military regime in 1973. He was minister of labor and industry (1969–1972) and minister of culture (1972–1973).

The military dictatorship deprived Sanguinetti of his political rights between 1976 and 1981. However, after the regime allowed legal reestablishment of political parties in 1982, Sanguinetti became secretary general of the Colorado Party. In 1985, when the military finally permitted more or less democratic elections, Sanguinetti was the victorious candidate of the Colorado Party for president of Uruguay. Once in office, he fully restored a democratic regime but was cautious about supporting the punishment of those guilty of atrocities during the military dictatorship.

BIBLIOGRAPHY

International Who's Who 1985–86. London: Europa Publications, 1985.
New York Times, November 27, 1984.
Who is Who in Government and Politics in Latin America. New York: Decade Media Books, 1984.

ROBERT J. ALEXANDER

SAN MARTÍN, JOSÉ DE (1778–1850), was the principal Liberator of the southern part of South America from Spanish control. Born in Yapeyu in northeastern Argentina, the son of a Spanish military officer, he returned with his father to Spain and served from 1808 to 1811 in the Spanish struggle against the Napoleonic invasion of Spain.

However, in 1812 San Martín returned to Argentina and joined the forces which had revolted against Spain two years before. He became a member of the Lautaro Lodge, which in October 1812 overthrew the regime headed by Bernardino Rivadavia.* In February 1813, San Martín won his first conflict with Spanish forces at San Lorenzo near Rosario. Subsequently, he became ill, but in 1814 was named governor of Cuyo in Western Argentina. Two years later, when the Argentine Congress met in Tucuman, he strongly supported the majority which decided to declare the formal independence of Argentina.

In January 1817, San Martín led the expedition of Argentines and Chileans across the Andes and defeated the Spanish forces at Chacabuco in February 1817 and Maipu in April 1818, finally freeing Chile from Spanish control. Then, in September 1820, he led Argentine-Chilean troops into Peru, with support of a fleet commanded by British Admiral Thomas Cochrane, and in July 1821 declared the independence of that country.

In July 1822, San Martín met with Simón Bolívar* in Guayaquil, Ecuador. It is still not clear what the two Liberators discussed or decided upon. However, it is clear that San Martín left completion of the liberation of western South America to Bolivar. San Martín resigned as Protector of Peru on September 20, 1822, and after staying for a while in Chile, he returned to Cuyo, Argentina.

Refusing to get involved in the internal quarrels of Argentina, San Martín left for Europe in February 1824. Except for a short return to South America in

1828—although not to Argentina—San Martín remained in Europe until his death in Boulogne, France.

BIBLIOGRAPHY

Genta, Jordan B. *Doctrina Politica de San Martin a Traves de su Correspondencia*. Buenos Aires: Nuevo Orden, 1965.
Metri, Bartolome. *Historia de San Martin y de la Emancipación Sudamericana*. Buenos Aires: F. Lajouame, 1889–1890.
Rojas, Ricardo. *San Martin, Knight of the Andes*. Garden City: Doubleday, Doran and Company, 1945.
Vicuña MacKenna, Benjamin. *El General Don Jose de San Martin*. Buenos Aires: Editorial Francisco de Aguirre, 1971.

JOHN DEINER

SANTA ANNA, ANTONIO LÓPEZ DE (1794–1876), dominated Mexican politics from 1825 to 1855 as an army general and as president. He is remembered as the leader who lost Texas in 1836 and what is today the southwestern United States in the Mexican War of 1846–1848.

Santa Anna was born in Jalapa in the state of Veracruz in 1794 and became a cadet at age 16. In 1823 he commanded troops that helped oust Agustín de Iturbide* as self-proclaimed emperor of Mexico. Elected president of Mexico in 1833, Santa Anna remained at his hacienda and allowed his vice president, Valentín Gómez Farias, to function as chief executive. When Gómez established a reform program in 1834, Santa Anna took over and canceled the program.

Santa Anna frequently shifted his loyalty between federalists and centralists, contributing to Mexico's political instability. In 1836 he proclaimed a centralized constitution to replace the federal one of 1824, thereby giving Texans an excuse to declare independence from Mexico in the name of states' rights.

At the Alamo in San Antonio, Santa Anna left no defender alive. Six weeks later, in April 1836, General Sam Houston defeated Santa Anna's army at the Battle of San Jacinto. Texas became a republic for nine years, until joining the United States in 1845. That action triggered the war in which Mexico also lost New Mexico, Arizona, California, and areas adjacent to the United States. Santa Anna had served as president again for brief periods during 1841–1844. As commander of all Mexican forces, he was defeated by American troops in 1848 and signed the Treaty of Guadalupe giving up the aforementioned territories.

Serving as an unelected dictator in 1854–1855, again he was ousted. In 1863 he went into exile in Nassau, returning to Mexico in 1872.

BIBLIOGRAPHY

Callcott, Wilfrid H. *Santa Anna, an Enigma*. Hamden, Conn.: Connecticut Universities Press, 1964.
Jone, Oakah. *Santa Anna*. New York: Twayne Publishers, 1968.
Pletcher, David M. *The Diplomacy of Annexation—the Mexican war*. Columbia: University of Missouri, 1973.

Santa Anna, Antonio López de. *The Eagle: The Autobiography of Santa Ana*. (Translated by Sam Guyler and Jaime Platon.) Austin, Texas: Pemberton Press, 1967.

MARVIN ALISKY

SANTA CRUZ, ANDRÉS DE (1792?–1865), president of Peru's Government Junta (1826–1827), president of Bolivia (1829–1836), and protector of the Peru-Bolivia Confederatica (1836–1839), ws born in La Paz, Bolivia. Many Bolivians consider him a pro-Peru Bolivian general, while most Peruvians recognize him as an ambitious Bolivian. Lima's white aristocracy pejoratively called him "El Cholo" Santa Cruz because he was descended from a Spanish family paternally and from Inca nobility maternally.

Santa Cruz first served in the Spanish Army fighting Argentine and Peruvian insurgents (1810–1821). In 1821 he joined José de San Martín's* Liberation Army and thereafter fought in the revolutionary forces. As Simón Bolívar's * chief of staff, he participated in the decisive battles of Junín and Ayacucho (1824).

In power, Santa Cruz proved himself an able and efficient administrator. Jealous and envious Peruvian generals collaborated with Chile and Aregntina in war against the confederation sponsored by Santa Cruz. After his defeat in 1839, he was exiled to Ecuador (1839–1843), suffered imprisonment in Chile (1843–1845), and, although exiled to Europe, served as Bolivian minister to France (1845–1855).

BIBLIOGRAPHY

Alisky, Marvin. *Historical Dictionary of Peru*. Metuchen, N. J.: Scarecrow Press, 1979.
Basadre, Jorge. *Historia de la República del Peru*.Lima: Editorial Universitaria, 1968.
Chang-Rodríguez Eugenio. *Opciones políticas peruanas*. Lima: Centro de Documentación Andina, 1985.

EUGENIO CHANG-RODRÍGUEZ

SANTA MARÍA GONZÁLEZ, DOMINGO (1825–1889), was president of Chile from 1881 to 1886. Upon receiving his law degree in 1847, he was named Intendente (governor) of the Province of Colchagua for three years. Strongly Liberal in his politics, he participated in the revolt in 1851 against the election of President Manuel Montt Torres.* As a result, he was exiled to Peru until 1853.

Returning home, Domingo Santa María practiced his profession, as well as being a journalist and publishing studies of Chilean history. In 1858 his political activities again brought exile for four years. He returned under an amnesty law in 1862.

During the next four years, Santa María was a member of the appeals court of Santiago and the Supreme Court. He also was minister of justice and public instruction for some months. During the 1865–1866 war with Spain, he had diplomatic assignments. After that war, he again served on the Supreme Court and was minister of foreign relations, interior, and war and navy.

Domingo Santa María was the government's candidate for president in 1881. General Manuel Baquedano, victor in the War of the Pacific against Peru and Bolivia, returned home amidst great acclaim and was put forward by the Conservatives as their candidate. However, all Liberal factions, as well as other groups, rallied behind Santa María, fearing that Baquedano's selection might bring militarism.

President Santa María had as his most pressing task the liquidation of the War of the Pacific, which had already been won militarily. By 1884 preliminary peace treaties were signed with Chile's defeated opponents.

At home, the state-church conflict reached a high point. The Vatican not only refused to accept the Chilean regime's nominee for archbishop of Santiago, but also publicly challenged the longstanding right of the government to make such a nomination. President Santa María expelled the Apostolic Delegate.

This controversy stimulated the Liberal-controlled Congress to pass laws ending Catholic control of existing cemeteries and forbidding the church to establish new ones; requiring a civil ceremony for a marriage to be legal; and turning over registration of births and deaths to civil authorities.

In the last months of the Santa María regime, controversy arose over the 1886 election. The president favored José Manuel Balmaceda Fernández,* but a congressional minority opposed him. In an effort to make Santa María withdraw support from Balmaceda, the congressional opposition unsuccessfully sought to prevent enactment of the 1886 budget by the deadline.

After leaving the presidency, Domingo Santa María was elected to the Senate in 1888. When he died, he was president of the Senate.

BIBLIOGRAPHY

Cortes, Lia, and Jordi Fuentes. *Diccionario Político de Chile*. Santiago: Editorial Orbe, 1967.
Enciclopedia Universal Ilustrada Europeo-Americana. Barcelona: José Espasa e Hijos.
Galdames, Luis. *Historia de Chile*. Santiago: Editorial Zig Zag, 1945.

ROBERT J. ALEXANDER

SANTANA, PEDRO (1801–1864), was one of the two most important political leaders of the Dominican Republic during its first two decades as an independent country. Soon after it achieved separation from Haiti in 1844, Santana overthrew Juan Pablo Duarte,* the major architect of independence. Santana remained in power that time until 1848 and fought off attempts of the Haitians to reassert control, dissolved Congress, and had the constitution changed to give the president almost unlimited power.

Ousted through the efforts of his major rival, Buenaventura Báez,* Santana returned to power again in 1853 remaining president for three years. Once again ousted by Báez in 1856, Santana became president for the third time in 1859.

Constantly plagued by Haitian attempts to regain control of the Dominican Republic, Santana decided in 1861 that the only solution was to allow Spain to reannex the country as a colony. He was named captain general of the colony by the Spanish government, but when revolts against Spanish control developed, he finally resigned his post. He died before the end of Spanish control.

BIBLIOGRAPHY

Enciclopedia Universal Ilustrada Europeo-Americana. Barcelona: José Espasa e Hijos.
ROBERT J. ALEXANDER

SANTANDER, FRANCISCO DE PAULA (1792–1840), Colombia's "Man of Laws," associate of Simón Bolívar,* general in the independence struggle, and first administrator of Gran Colombia, also inspired the Liberal party which, along with the Conservative Party, has dominated Colombian politics ever since. He was born into a prominent provincial landowning family in Cucutá. While still in his teens he was sent to study law at the College of San Bartolomé in Bogotá, where he was when the independence struggle broke out in 1810.

Santander abandoned his studies to join the patriot cause and fought both in the internal civil conflicts in New Granada and against the Spanish. When the fortunes of war turned against the patriots, Santander retreated northeastward with the French General Manuel Serviez, who had joined the colonials' cause. In the llanos, or plains, they joined forces with José Antonio Páez,* later chief executive of Venezuela. From Páez, Santander learned bold cavalry and guerrilla tactics.

In 1819, after several years of harassing Spanish columns and garrisons, Simón Bolívar promoted Santander to brigadier general and made him a top field commander. In the ensuing struggle, Santander displayed remarkable talents for organization and intrepid action. Bolívar named the 27-year old general administrator of the liberated territories.

With Bolívar absent on campaigns in southern Colombia, Ecuador, and Peru, Santander set about organizing a government. He viewed his task as one of reconciling conflicting regional and institutional interests, and of reconstruction without further upsetting the fragile social order. Much of his attention was given to countering separatist tendencies in Venezuela and Ecuador, which together with Colombia, comprised Gran Colombia.

Santander's government promoted secular, public education; education had been dominated by the Catholic Church and limited to members of the upper class. As government educational institutions grew and expanded, the opposition of the church increased, and Santander moved to restrict clerical influence. In the economic area, Santander retained protectionist policies of the past, but the influence of liberal, individualist ideas about private property began to prevail.

One of Santander's principal concerns was to develop a constitutional framework based upon a sound legal structure. These efforts earned him the informal title of "Man of Laws." He was elected vice president of Gran Colombia in 1821 (with Bolívar as titular president).

Opposition of the church, of conservatives, and, finally, of Bolívar himself led to Santander's ouster in 1827. Upon his return from Peru, Bolívar sought to impose his vision of a grand confederation of Andean states reaching from Bolivia to Venezuela, ruled by a president-for-life but with a republican constitution. When he could not convince the Colombians to pass the necessary constitutional reforms, he established a military dictatorship. After an attempt on the Liberator's life in Bogotá in 1828, Bolívar suspended many of the liberal reforms of the Santander administration, epecially in the religious and financial areas, and exiled Santander.

After the dissolution of Gran Colombia and the death of Bolívar, Santander was elected the first president of the Republic of New Granada in 1832. As a legacy of the turbulent final years of Bolívar's dictatorship, he encountered resistance, especially among disgruntled elements in the army, which had been reduced in size and which Santander was attempting to limit in influence. When a major conspiracy against the regime was discovered, Santander had a number of the plotters executed. He showed little inclination to bring about reconciliation with the former supporters of Bolívar.

Santander did not succeed in liquidating the national debt of the former Gran Colombian countries or in reaching agreement with Venezuela over boundaries. He was more successful in fostering education, however. By the time Santander left office, over 17,000 students were reported to be in primary schools throughout the country, and there were thriving colleges and universities in major cities.

When a political foe of Santander, José Ignacio de Márquez, was elected president in 1836, the "Man of Laws" peacefully turned over the presidency. After a short retirement, he was elected to the Chamber of Representatives, where he led the opposition to the Márquez administration. Santander died while serving in Congress.

BIBLIOGRAPHY

Bushnell, David. *El régimen de Santander en la gran colombia*. Bogotá: 1966.
Fals Borda, Orlando. *Subversion and Social Change in Colombia*. New York: Columbia University Press, 1967.
Gómez, Laureano. *El mito de Santander*. 2 vols. Bogotá: 1966.
Henao, Jesús María, and Gerardo Arrubla. *History of Colombia*. Chapel Hill: University of North Carolina Press, 1938.
Hoenigsberg, Julio. *Santander ante la historia*. 3 vols. Barranquilla: 1969–1970.

RICHARD E. SHARPLESS

SANTOS, EDUARDO (1888–1974), was president of Colombia from 1938 to 1942. Of aristocratic background, he was educated at the Colegio del Rosario and in Paris. Upon return home in 1913, he founded the Liberal Party daily *El Tiempo* of Bogotá, which he owned until his death.

With the return of the Liberals to power under President Enrique Olaya Herrera* in 1931, Eduardo Santos served as foreign minister, governor of the

Province of Santander, and head of the Colombian delegation to the League of Nations. He also was head of the Colombian delegation which negotiated the settlement of the Leticia dispute with Peru (1933–1934).

Representing more moderate elements of the Liberal Party, Santos was elected president in 1938, as successor to Alfonso López Pumirejo* and his "Revolution on the March." His administration was widely labeled "the pause," although it also established a number of new institutions to stimulate government support for the country's economic development.

After leaving the presidency in 1942, Santos served on the National Directorate of the Liberal Party. Between 1944 and 1948 he was an official of the United Nations relief agency UNRRA (United Nations Relief and Rehabilitation Administration).

During the Conservative Party administration of Laureano Gómez,* Santos unsuccessfully sought to rally Liberal forces against the regime. In the subsequent dictatorship of General Gustavo Rojas Pinilla,* Santos' newspaper *El Tiempo* was closed for almost two years in 1955–1957, which became an international *cause célebre*. With the overthrow of Rojas Pinilla, control of *E! Tiempo* was returned to Santos.

During the National Front alliance of Liberal and Conservative parties following the overthrow of Rojas Pinilla, Santos was a strong supporter of the Front. He was a particularly strong backer of the government of Carlos Lleras Restrepo,* who had been one of his ministers.

BIBLIOGRAPHY

New York Times, March 28, 1974.
Santos, Eduardo. *La Crisis de la Democracia en Columbia y "El Tiempo."* Mexico: Gráfica Panamericana, 1955.

RICHARD E. SHARPLESS

SARAVIA, APARICIO (1855–1904), was the most significant Uruguayan Nationalist (Blanco) Party leader at the end of the nineteenth century and the beginning of the twentieth. His father was Brazilian, and he spent much of his life in that country. He participated in the federalist revolution in the state of Rio Grande do Sul between 1893 and 1895.

In Uruguay, Saravia was affiliated with the Blanco Party, and upon returning there, he led a short uprising against President Juan Idiarte Borda's Colorado party regime in November 1896. Four months later, Saravia led a more serious revolt which at first was successful. After President Idiarte Borda was assassinated in August, his successor, President Juan Lindolfo Cuestas, agreed to a settlement that gave the Blancos control of six of the country's nineteen departments, provided for a guaranteed Blanco minority representation in Congress, pardoned all those participating in the uprising, and gave financial "compensation" to the rebels for their expenses in undertaking the revolt.

Saravia "retired" to his rural estate but threw his political support to the Cuestas regime. At the time of the 1903 presidential election, he indicated his opposition to Colorado candidate José Batlle y Ordóñez* but did not specifically support any opponent to Batlle. Saravia's antipathy to Batlle intensified when the new president named several Blancos who were not supporters of Saravia as "jefes políticos" of Blanco-controlled departments. Although a revolt led by Saravia was narrowly averted in March 1903, a fulls scale insurrection broke out in the following year under Saravia's leadership. His death in battle in September 1904 ended the last Uruguayan civil war of the twentieth century and paved the way for the democratic regime that prevailed in that country during most of the twentieth century.

BIBLIOGRAPHY

Enciclopedia Universal Ilustrada Europeo-Americana. Barcelona: José Espasa e Hijos.
                                                              ROBERT J. ALEXANDER

SARMIENTO, DOMINGO FAUSTINO (1811–1888), was president of Argentina from 1868 to 1874 and principal founder of its public school system. He came from a moderately well-to-do family, a fact that was helpful during his long period in exile.

Sarmiento's father was a member of José de San Martín's* army which liberated Chile during the Wars of Independence. Sarmiento was largely self-educated and went to Chile when Juan Manuel de Rosas* seized control of Argentina in the late 1820s. There, he was particularly engaged in teaching and journalism, working on *El Mercurio* and founding the newspaper *El Nacional* and other periodicals in Santiago. He also founded the first normal school in Chile in 1842.

Sarmiento became involved in Chilean politics as a supporter of President Manuel Montt Torres.* This finally made it necessary for him to leave Chile, and he traveled widely in Europe, North Africa, and the United States, where he met Horace Mann, the philosopher of U.S. public education.

During the long exile, Sarmiento wrote books on history and literary criticism. Undoubtedly his most important work was *Facundo: Civilization or Barbarism*, a study of Facundo Quirós, one of the caudillo contemporaries of Rosas. The volume's subtitle emphasized Sarmiento's belief in the need to "civilize" Argentina by Europeanizing it, a bias that persisted as a major strain in Argentine politics during the next century or more.

With the uprising of Justo José de Urquiza* against Rosas in 1852, Sarmiento returned to Argentina to participate in the struggle, and in the process became a colonel. After the overthrow of Rosas and the separation of Buenos Aires from the Argentine Confederation led by Urquiza, Sarmiento served as director of public instruction of Buenos Aires. After reunification of the country, he was named minister to Chile and Peru in 1865, and in 1866 became minister to the United States.

Domingo Faustino Sarmiento was elected president in 1868. He faced serious problems of compromising conflicts between followers of Urquiza and those of Bartolomé Mitre,* Sarmiento's predecessor and Buenos Aires leader. However, his most notable achievement was reorganization and expansion of the educational system. He also sponsored expansion of the public library system and establishment of the Academy of Exact Sciences and of the National Observatory, and administered the country's first national census. Immigration was encouraged, and expansion of agriculture was fomented.

Sarmineto was elected senator after leaving the presidency. In that capacity, he strongly opposed the election of President Juárez Celman in 1886. For a while, Sarmiento served as director general of schools in the government of Buenos Aires.

Sarmiento died in Paraguay, where he had gone frequently in his later years for health reasons.

BIBLIOGRAPHY

Bunkley, A. W. *The Life of Sarmiento*. Princeton, N. J.: Princeton University Press, 1952.
Enciclopedia Universal Ilustrada Europeo-Americana. Barcelona: José Espasa e Hijos.
                                                                    JOHN T. DEINER

SEAGA, EDWARD P. G. (1930–   ), became prime minister of Jamaica in 1980. Born in Boston, Massachusetts, of Jamaican parents, he attended secondary schools in Jamaica and Harvard University, graduating with a B. A. in social science in 1952. He returned to Jamaica to conduct research for the Institute for Social and Economic Research in rural villages and urban slums in Jamaica where he later developed a strong political following.

In 1959, the president of the Jamaican Labour Party (JLP), Sir William Alexander Bustamante*, invited Seaga to serve in the Upper House of the Jamaican Legislative Assembly, the youngest person ever to hold such a position. In 1962 he helped draft the Jamaican independence constitution. The same year he was elected a member of Parliament, on the JLP ticket, from one of the poorest constituencies in Kingston. Between 1962 and 1967 he served as minister of development and welfare and between 1967 and 1972 he was minister of finance and planning. He helped set up the Jamaica Stock Exchange and the Jamaica Development Bank, and initiated a program of Jamaicanization in banking, insurance, utilities, and agriculture, transferring foreign ownership to majority Jamaican ownership. He was concerned primarily with making Jamaica as self-reliant as possible. During his tenure as minister of finance and planning, the country experienced its greatest period of economic growth. Seaga was also an active promoter of national culture, promoting indigenous music, as well as local performing and graphic arts.

In 1960 Seaga was elected assistant secretary of the JLP, two years later he was elevated to the post of secretary, and in 1974 he was elected leader of the

JLP and leader of the Parliamentary Opposition. Seaga came to be popularly perceived as the person who could bring the country out of the severe economic plight it was facing in the latter half of the 1970s. He led the JLP to a massive electoral victory over the democratic socialist government of the People's National Party (PNP) headed by Michael Norman Manley* in 1980.

Seaga sought to attract foreign investment and to stimulate the private sector. He also undertook a pro-Western and particularly pro-U. S. foreign policy, reversing that of the previous government. He became the region's staunchest advocate of the Caribbean Basin Initiative, the Reagan administration's economic plan for the Caribbean. Seaga also played a pivotal role in the United States' decision to invade neighboring Grenada after the murder of Maurice Herbert Bishop* in 1983. Jamaica sent one of the largest contingents of troops from the Caribbean to participate in the invasion force.

In December 1983 the JLP was reelected unopposed after the PNP refused to contest national elections in protest of the Seaga government's failure to update electoral registration.

BIBLIOGRAPHY

Bajan. January 1981.
Profile: The Honorable Edward Seaga. Kingston, Jamaica: Government of Jamaica, 1981.
Will, W. Marvin. *"Jamaica." Colliers 1984 Yearbook*. New York: Macmillan Educational Co., 1983.

                                                          PERCY C. HINTZEN AND W. MARVIN WILL

SHARPE, SAMUEL (?–1832), was organizer of a slave rebellion in Jamaica which contributed to the abolition of slavery throughout the British colonial empire in 1838. Born into slavery, Sharpe was the property of a slaveowner who was sufficiently tolerant to provide him to opportunity to become literate. He was attracted to the Baptist Church because of its assertion that all people were born equal in the sight of God and because of its opposition to slavery.

The Baptist Church was becoming enormously popular among the slaves, particularly after the passage in Great Britain of a Humane Code in 1823–1824, which encouraged religious instruction of the slave population. The Baptist Church in the parish of St. James, where Sharpe lived, began to grow rapidly, and he became a church class leader.

Sharpe formulated a nonviolent course of passive resistance to end slavery in Jamaica, by which all slaves would simply cease working on an appointed day until they were paid for their labor. Sharpe's position as a class leader in the Baptist Church afforded him the opportunity to proselytize the plan and organize support for it. In the face of planters' threats to resist the movement toward emancipation, Sharpe, guaranteed massive support from the slave population, decided to implement his campaign of passive resistance on December 28, 1831. But the planters learned of the proposed action. Troops were sent to St. James parish, where Sharpe lived and did most of his organizing.

On the night of December 27, overzealous militants began to set fire to buildings and canefields, followed by similar action elsewhere. The government used this destruction of property as an excuse for massive retaliation against the slaves. More than 500 slaves and 14 whites were killed, with most of the slaves executed. Samuel Sharpe was hanged.

BIBLIOGRAPHY

Brathwaite, E. *Nancy, Sam Sharpe and the Struggle for People's Liberation.* Kingston, Jamaica: National Heritage Week Committee, 1977.
Hart, Richard. *Slaves Who Abolished Slavery.* Kingston, Jamaica: Institute for Social and Economic Research, 1980.
Wynter, Sylvia. *Jamaica's National Heroes.* Kingston, Jamaica: National Trust Commission, 1971.

                                                PERCY C. HINTZEN AND W. MARVIN WILL

SILES REYES, HERNANDO (1881–1942), was president of Bolivia from 1926 to 1930 and founder of the Nationalist Party. He received his law degree in Sucre in 1905 and was a professor of civil law at the National Institute of Commerce in La Paz (1911–1917) and the University of San Andrés. He was rector of the San Francisco Xavier University in Sucre (1917–1920). He entered politics in 1920 as deputy for Oruro and later was senator for Chuquisaca. In the administration of President Bautista Saavedra* he was minister of education, minister of war and colonization, and minister to Peru.

In 1925 President Saavedra unable to engineer his own reelection, hand-picked Hernando Siles, with Saavedra's brother, Abdón, as vice president. Siles assumed office in January 1926. Although having signed a pact with the Saavedra brothers to allow the Socialist Republican Party and Bautista Saavedra to dominate political affairs, Siles broke his pledge and founded the Nationalist Party in January 1927.

Siles' government initiated important constitutional and electoral reforms, and continued the economic development policies of the previous regimes. A labor law was passed and the Department of Labor was established and university reform in 1928 guaranteed university autonomy. That year, the North American Kemmerer Mission created the Central Bank. The government sponsored new roads and rail connections and opened up new telegraph lines. In 1927–1928 important loans were negotiated with U. S. banks, but critics charged that terms were too onerous for Bolivia. On the other hand, Siles faced a decline in tin prices, the onset of the Depression, and chronic budget deficits. A major Indian uprising in 1927 at Chayanta in Potosi was put down by the army.

The dispute with Paraguay over the Chaco escalated. On December 5, 1928, Paraguayans attacked Bolivian Fort Vanguardia. In reprisal, Siles ordered the seizure of two Paraguayan forts. A conciliation commission met in Washington in 1929, found Paraguay at fault, and ordered reconstruction of Fort Vanguardia.

Against the advice of members of his own party, Siles decided to alter the constitution to permit his own reelection. In early May 1930, he created a provisional government and stepped down in order to run. When a student was killed in an antigovernment demonstration, the crisis escalated into a general uprising of students, workers, opposition parties, and the army. Siles was toppled on June 25, 1930, in a bloody revolt.

Fleeing to Brazil, Siles later returned to Bolivia and served in various diplomatic posts. He died in an airplane crash en route from La Paz to Lima.

BIBLIOGRAPHY

Carrasco, Benigno. *Hernando Siles*. La Paz: Editorial del Estado, 1961.
Céspedes, Augusto. *El Dictador Suicida, 40 Años de Historia de Bolivia*. Santiago de Chile: Editorial Universitaria, 1956.
Díaz Machicao, Porfirio. *Historia de Bolivia, Guzmán, Siles, Blanco Galindo, 1925–1931*. La Paz: Gisbert, 1955.
Fellman Velarde, José. *Historia de Bolivia*. Vol 3.2d ed. La Paz: Los Amigos del Libro, 1981.
Finot, Enrique. *Nueva Historia de Bolivia (Ensayo de Interpretación Sociológica)*. 2d ed. La Paz: Gisbert, 1954.

WALTRAUD QUEISER MORALES

SILES ZUAZO, HERNÁN (1913–   ), was president of Bolivia twice (1956–1960, 1982–1985). He was born in La Paz, and his father was Hernando Siles Reyes,* president of Bolivia from 1926 to 1930. He graduated as a lawyer from the Universidad Mayor de San Andrés, was a founder of the Bolivian Institute of Statistics, and director of the Bolivian Library of Congress. He was a twice-decorated veteran of the Chaco War.

During the 1940s, Siles emerged as a major figure in the Nationalist Revolutionary Movement (MNR), second to party leader Víctor Paz Estenssoro,* and in 1952 was a key organizer of the successful MNR revolutionary uprising. He served as vice president from 1952 to 1956 and was elected president in 1956.

As president, Siles pursued a program of monetary stabilization which partly alienated the labor movement from the MNR and caused Vice President Ñuflo Chávez Ortíz to resign. The Bolivian Labor Central (COB), led by Juan Lechín Oquendo,* launched a series of strikes.

Siles greatly strengthened the army, which had been dissolved after the 1952 revolution, but revived a few years later, as a counterweight to peasant and miner militias. He used the army to establish order in restive mining districts. Despite these tensions, Siles consolidated the revolutionary reforms of former President Paz—nationalization of the mines, agrarian and educational reforms, and a new petroleum code.

The first schism in the MNR took place during Siles' first term. Walter Guevara Arze* split to form the Authentic Revolutionary Party (PRA), when the MNR leadership failed to support him for the presidency in 1960. Although Siles had supported Paz' second presidency, he became disaffected when Paz was named for a third time in 1964. Siles then began to conspire with Generals René Barrientos Ortuño* and Alfredo Ovando Candia,* who overthrew the newly reelected Paz in November. Later falling out with the military regime, Siles went into exile, returning to Bolivia only briefly in November 1970 to support the government of General Juan José Torres González Torres.*

In January 1971, Siles and Paz signed a Unity Pact, but when Paz Estenssoro supported Colonel Hugo Banzer Suarez'* military coup against Torres, the agreement collapsed. After Siles was ousted from an MNR congress in early 1972, he formed the Leftist National Revolutionary Movement (MNRI), which entered into a loose electoral coalition, the Democratic and Popular Unity (UDP), with several minor parties of the left.

The UDP selected Siles as its presidential candidate in 1978. He was credited with the second highest popular vote, but the election results were annulled by a coup. In July 1979 Siles was again the UDP nominee, and although he beat Paz and Banzer in popular votes, he did not receive the majority required by the constitution. Walter Guevara Arze was then chosen by Congress as interim president but was soon overthrown.

In June 1980 Siles again ran for the UDP, received 39 percent of the vote, and a congressional majority was ready to elect him. However, the brutal coup of General García Meza on July 17 forced Siles into exile in Lima until October 1982, when the 1980 Congress finally met and confirmed Siles as constitutional president and first legally elected civilian president after nearly 18 years of military rule.

Siles faced several major crises: a foreign debt of $4 billion; natural disasters in 1983 which left millions of Bolivians hungry and agriculture disrupted; deep political party splits which divided and stalemated the governing coalition; and crippling national strikes and skyrocketing inflation which left the Bolivian peso at 270,000 to a U.S. dollar in mid–1985. Siles refused to implement a stringent International Monetary Fund stabilization program, making Bolivia the first Latin American nation officially to default on its debt. The Siles government initiated a crackdown on the cocaine mafia but found itself hampered by powerful connections and insufficient resources. Internationally, Siles pursued an activist foreign policy; relations with the United States were proper but distant.

In early 1985 Siles bowed to interest group pressures and called elections for July, a year before schedule. Given the political, economic, and social disintegration of Bolivia under the last military rulers, the strong record of Siles on democratic liberties, his attempts to improve social welfare, and simply his ability to remain in office represented a positive legacy.

BIBLIOGRAPHY

Antezana, Luis E. *Hernán Siles Zuazo, el Estratega y la Contrarevolución.* La Paz: Editorial Luz, 1979.
Baptista Gumucio, Mariano. *Historia Contemporanea de Bolivia, 1930–1978.* 2d ed. La Paz: Gisbert, 1978.

412

SIMMONDS, KENNEDY ALPHONSE

Dunkerley, James. *Rebellion in the Veins, Political Struggle in Bolivia, 1952–1982.* London: Thet-Press, 1984.

Fellman Velarde, José. *Historia de Bolivia, La Bolivianidad Semicolonial.* Vol. 3. Cochabamba: Los Amigos del Libro, 1981.

Klein, Herbert S. *Parties and Political Change in Bolivia.* Cambridge: Cambridge University Press, 1969.

WALTRAUD QUEISER MORALES AND GUILLERMO DELGADO

SIMMONDS, KENNEDY ALPHONSE (1936–   ), became the first prime minister of St. Kitts-Nevis when it achieved its independence in September 1983. Born in the capital city of Basseterre, St. Kitts, Simmonds received his primary and secondary education in his home island. He entered the University of the West Indies Medical School in Jamaica in 1955, receiving his degree in 1962.

On his return home in 1964, Simmonds soon became involved in an Electricity Tarifffs Protest Committtee formed to oppose an electricity bill pending in the legislature. The Peoples Action Movement (PAM), officially constituted as a political party on January 15, 1965, under the leadership of Dr. William Herbert, emerged out of this committee and Simmonds was its secretary. He contested elections on the PAM ticket in 1966 and was defeated. However, PAM did capture two constituencies, one in Nevis and one in Anguilla, which, at the time, was part of the colony. Simmonds then left the colony for graduate study in the Bahamas and the United States.

Simmonds returned to St. Kitts in 1969. While overseas, he had remained first vice president of PAM, and in the 1971 and 1975 general elections he contested a seat but lost both times, when the ruling Labour Party, under the leadership of Robert Llewellyn Bradshaw,* swept all seven seats on the island. In 1976 he succeeded William Herbert as leader of PAM.

At this time, Nevisian resistance to participation as a political entity with St. Kitts was becoming hardened. Fears of St. Kittsian domination, on the part of the population of Nevis, were not assuaged by the attitude of Labour leadership. Threats of secession were becoming more real when the Nevis Reformation Party (NRP), formed in 1970 by Simeon Daniel, captured both Nevisian seats in the House of Assembly by 1975 on a secessionist platform. The issue forestalled attainment of independence for the colony under a Labour Party government.

Under Simmonds, the strength of PAM grew substantially. When the popular charismatic leader of the Labour Party, Robert Bradshaw, died, Simmonds contested his seat in a by-election in January 1979. He was declared winner by a mere 22 votes, the first non-Labour candidate elected in St. Kitts since 1952.

The ruling party then decided to dissolve the House of Assembly before Simmonds could take his seat. Elections were not held until February 1980, 12 months later. In the interim, Caleb Azariah Paul Southwell,* Bradshaw's successor, also died suddenly. The Labour party government came under the premiership of Lee Llewellyn Moore,* who lacked the prestige of his two predecessors. Under Simmonds, PAM won three of seven seats in St. Kitts, with NRP retaining the two Nevis seats. Simmonds and NRP then entered into a coalition, with a parliamentary majority.

The Simmonds government immediately embarked on a program of economic development that was based on growth of tourism and diversification of agriculture. Simmonds emphasized the social and economic development of Nevis, particularly in agriculture, education, and cottage industries. The Nevisian secession issue was defused and a federal arrangement in 1982 paved the way for independence for the twin-island colony in September 1983.

In the spring 1984 elections, PAM was able to capture six of seven seats in St. Kitts, while NRP won all of the Nevis seats, now increased to three.

BIBLIOGRAPHY

Alexander, Robert J. "Saint Kitts-Nevis," in Robert J. Alexander (ed). *Political Parties of the Americas*. Vol. 2. Westport, Conn.: Greenwood Press, 1982.
Caricom Perspectives 18 (March/April 1983).
Hopkins, Jack W. "British Colonies and Associated States," in Jack W. Hopkins (ed). In *Latin America and Caribbean Contemporary Record*. Vol 1. New York: Holmes and Meier, 1983.
Jones-Hendrickson, Simon B. "St. Kitts-Nevis," in Jack W. Hopkins (ed.). *Latin America and Caribbean Contemporary Record*. Vol. 2. New York: Holmes and Meier, 1984.
The Nation (Barbados), September 15, 1983, supplement.
PERCY C. HINTZEN AND W. MARVIN WILL

SOMOZA DEBAYLE, ANASTASIO (1925–1980), was the second of three sons of Anastasio Somoza García.* At age 11, young Anastasio, nicknamed "Tachito," was sent with his brother Luis* to the La Salle Military Academy in Oakdale, New York, and in 1942 entered West Point, already holding the rank of captain in the Nicaragua National Guard.

Tachito Somoza rose through the National Guard to become its commander in the 1960s. When brother Luis refused to run for a second term, Tachito ran as the Nationalist Liberal Party candidate for president in the February 1967 elections and won 70.8 percent of the votes, illustrating not only the party's strength as a vote mobilizer but also a considerable degree of popular support.

According to the 1950 constitution, the president was not eligible to succeed himself. Instead, with the connivance of Fernando Aguero Rocha,*, a leader of the Traditional Conservative Party, and U.S. Ambassador Turner Shelton, Congress dissolved itself on August 31, 1971, and provided for executive power to be shared by two Liberals and one Conservative, until a new constitution could be prepared. Under the new constitution, a new Congress chose Tachito for a six-year term beginning December 1, 1974.

Meanwhile, a December 23, 1972, earthquake destroyed about three quarters of the buildings in Managua. Somoza then took over effective control as head of the National Guard and of a new National Emergency Committee. Although he promised to rebuild downtown Managua, government buildings were relocated in other parts of the city on property owned by Somoza or his close friends. In this period of post-earthquake corruption and authoritarian politics, many former supporters of the regime or of an opposition still loyal to the system though not sharing in political power, came to favor violent overthrow of Somoza.

The most important group pursuing armed action was the Sandinista Front of National Liberation (FSLN), originally organized in 1962. A small FSLN force seized 35 hostages at a December 27, 1974, Christmas party in Managua honoring U. S. Ambassador Turner Shelton. Three days later, in return for a $1 million ransom, release of 14 political prisoners, and publication in *La Prensa* and over Managua radio stations of a lengthy FSLN communique, the hostages were released and the guerrillas given safe passage to Cuba. President Somoza then declared a state of siege, suspended constitutional guarantees, and ordered creation of a special counterinsurgency unit.

The assassination on January 10, 1978, of Pedro Joaquín Chamorro Cardenal,* editor of the antigovernment newspaper *La Prensa*, provoked two days of rioting and a 17-day general strike. Sixteen opposition groups, including three labor unions, the Conservative, Nicaraguan Socialist, and Independent Liberal parties, and "Los Doce," a group of businessmen, intellectuals, and priests, formed the Broad Opposition Front (FAO), which called for Somoza's resignation and developed a program for a future government.

Although the National Guard regained control of the cities after the first "offensive" of the FSLN in November 1978, the number of FSLN forces increased. When Tachito broke off negotiations designed to get him to leave peacefully, the United States, in February 1979, ended all military and economic assistance to his regime.

In June 1979, the FSLN launched a "final offensive" and established a government in exile, together with elements of the FAO, in Costa Rica. Somoza finally fled the country in July. Somoza family properties, worth an estimated $500 million, were then confiscated.

Being denied asylum in the United States, Somoza went to Paraguay. He was killed there, when the car in which he was riding was blown up by bazooka rockets and machine guns.

BIBLIOGRAPHY

Millett, Richard. *Guardians of the Dynasty, A History of the U. S.-Created Guardia Nacional and the Somoza Family*. Maryknoll, N. Y.: Orbis Books, 1977.
Pearson, Neale J. "Nicaragua," in Robert J. Alexander (ed). *Political Parties of the Americas*, Vol. 2. Westport, Conn.: Greenwood Press, 1982.
Walker, Thomas W. *Nicaragua, The Land of Sandino*. Boulder, Colo.: Westview Press, 1980.

NEALE J. PEARSON

SOMOZA DEBAYLE, LUIS (1922–1967), eldest son of Anastasio Somoza García,* succeeded his father as president of Nicaragua. He received his earliest education at the Christian Brothers School in Managua and at the age of 14 was sent to LaSalle Military Academy in Oakdale, New York, and received a commission as captain in the National Guard. He subsequently studied at the University of California, Louisiana State, and the University of Maryland. While at Maryland, he was Nicaraguan military attaché to the United States.

Upon his return to Nicaragua, Luis Somoza had a rapid rise to colonel in the National Guard by 1950. He then retired, ran for deputy of the Nationalist Liberal Party (PNL), was elected president of Congress in early 1956, and First Designate, to succeed to the presidency if his father should die.

Somoza filled the presidency on a temporary basis when his father was shot on September 21, 1956, and was named president by Congress on September 30, upon his father's death, until new elections in January 1957. Not wishing to run unopposed, Luis Somoza persuaded several Conservative leaders to participate as a ''loyal opposition,'' and to form the Nicaraguan Conservative Party (PCN), nicknamed *Zancudo* (pest or mosquito) because of its small size and inability to be anything more than a nuisance.

Luis Somoza announced that he would serve only one term, and in 1959 he restored constitutional articles prohibiting the immediate reelection or succession to the presidency by any relative of the incumbent. Somoza inaugurated some programs of economic modernization, low-cost housing, and land reform. He reduced the budget of the National Guard. Freedom of the press and new opposition publications appeared. However, for four of his five years suspension of constitutional guarantees was in effect, and the Guard announced on September 30, 1960, that it has repelled the twentieth armed invasion since Luis Somoza became president. The most serious threat occurred in 1959: a land attack from Costa Rica and the airlifting of two planeloads of men led by young Conservative Party editor of *La Prensa*, Pedro Joaquín Chamorro Cardenal,* and Independent Liberal Enrique Lacayo Farfán.

Luis Somoza contributed to improved Central American relations by accepting the World Court's decision on Nicargua's border dispute with Honduras and by seeking to avoid conflict with Costa Rica. Nicaragua joined the new Central American Common Market in 1961. On the other hand, Somoza was an early opponent of Fidel Castro* and allowed Nicaraguan territory to be used by Cuban exiles for the abortive April 1961 Bay of Pigs invasion.

Keeping his promise to step down, Luis Somoza imposed selection of Minister of Education René Schick. The principal opposition forces withdrew from the 1963 election when Somoza rejected their demand for Organization of American states supervision of the polling.

In August 1967 the PLN nominated Anastasio Somoza Debayle,* Luis's brother, despite reported opposition by Luis. The sudden death of Luis Somoza of a heart attack 17 days before his brother's inauguration removed a restraining influence on the more military-minded Anastasio.

BIBLIOGRAPHY

English, Burt H. *Nicaragua Election Factbook, February 5, 1967*. Washington, D. C. Institute for the Comparative Study of Political Systems, December 1966.

Millett, Richard. *Guardians of the Dynasty, A History of the U. S. Created Guardia Nacional and the Somoza Family.* Maryknoll, N. Y.: Orbis Books, 1977.
Pearson, Neale J. "Nicaragua," in Robert J. Alexander (ed). *Political Parties of the Americas.* Westport, Conn.: Greenwood Press, 1982.
———. "Nicaragua in Crisis." *Current History*, February 1979.

NEALE J. PEARSON

SOMOZA GARCÍA, ANASTASIO ("TACHO") (1896–1956), established a family dynasty that dominated Nicaragua from the early 1930s until 1979. Son of prosperous middle-class landowners, he attended the Intituto Nacional de Oriente at Granada, Nicaragua, and later graduated from the Pierce Commercial College in Philadelphia, where he studied bookkeeping, baseball and English. On his return to Nicaragua, this experience helped ingratiate him with influential Americans for whom he acted as interpreter during the Marine occupation of 1926–1932.

One of the first things Somoza did upon his return from Philadelphia was to marry Salvadora Debayle, whom he had met in Philadelphia. She was daughter of one of Nicaragua's leading families, and niece of Liberal politician Juan Bautista Sacasa.

In August 1926 "General" Somoza, only 30 years old, commanded a Liberal force that occupied San Marcos on behalf of Liberal "General" Benjamín Moncada, in revolt against the government of Conservative General Emiliano Chamorro Vargas.* Going into hiding after a defeat, Somoza accepted a pardon in return for a promise "not to join any other subversive activities." When Moncada later became president, Somoza was his subsecretary for foreign affairs and acting foreign minister.

After Liberal Juan Bautista Sacasa won the presidential election conducted under U. S. supervision in 1932, he appointed his nephew-in-law Anastasio Somoza to head the National Guard. However, relations between the two deteriorated after the U. S. Marines left in 1933, and Somoza ousted his uncle from the presidency in 1936—after having permitted the assassination of Augusto César Sandino,* the Liberal guerrilla leader, in Managua under a flag of truce.

Inaugurated president in January 1937, Somoza reorganized the Liberal Party into a personalist party to maintain his family's control. Making himself a general, he ruled directly (1937–1947 and 1950–1956) or through puppets until his death.

Somoza was clever enough to see that more than force was needed to stay in power. He juggled the constitution until he had a document that enabled him to do whatever he wanted. Roads, schools, hospitals, and hydroelectric plants were built; agriculture was diversified by stimulating the production of sugar and cotton. Somoza also benefited mightily from this economic development, amassing a fortune worth at least $150 million.

A labor code was adopted in 1944, an income tax in 1952, a National Development Institute in 1953, and a National Institute of Social Security in 1956. By tempting Conservative opponents and independents with jobs and influence on a minor scale, Somoza weakened the opposition. Twice, the Conservatives under Emiliano Chamorro negotiated formal agreements with him that provided them with a stated percentage of government posts in return for a relaxation of opposition.

Somoza was wise enough to cultivate good relations with the United States. In 1939, when he paid a state visit to the United States, he was elaborately received by Washington officials. However, his relations with other Central American countries, especially Costa Rica, after World War II were not so cordial. Somoza gave support to Costa Rican conservatives wishing to overthrow the democratic Junta governing that country in December 1948, and in January 1955, the government of Jose Figueres Ferrer.*

On September 21, 1956, Somoza was shot. He died on September 30 in a U. S. Army hospital in Panama, to which he had been transported under orders of President Dwight Eisenhower. He succeeded by his son, Luis Somoza Debayle.*

BIBLIOGRAPHY

English, Burt E. *Nicaraguan Election Factbook, February 5, 1967.* Washington D.C.: Institute for the Comparative Study of Political Systems, 1967.

Kantor, Harry. *Patterns of Politics and Political Systems in Latin America.* Chicago: Rand McNally, 1969.

Millett, Richard. *Guardians of the Dynasty, A History of the U.S. Created Guardia Nacional and the Somoza Family.* Maryknoll, N. Y.: Orbis Books, 1977.

Parker, Franklin D. *The Central American Republics.* London: Oxford University Press, 1964.

Pearson, Neale J. "Nicaragua," in Robert J. Alexander (ed). *Political Parties of the Americas.* Vol 2. Westport, Conn: Greenwood Press, 1982.

NEALE J. PEARSON

SOTO, MARCO AURELIO (1846–1908), planted the ideas of the Liberal Revolution of the late nineteenth century in the 1880 constitution of Honduras. Largely educated in Guatemala, he worked there in the govenment of the great Liberal caudillo Justo Rufino Barrios.* He became president of Honduras in 1876 largely becauuse of Barrios' influence.

Soto initiated an ambitious program of reforms. A Department of Finance and National Mint were established to reorganize public finances. Civil, commercial, mining, and customs codes were reformed. Marriage, divorce, and the operation of schools and cemeteries were taken away from the Catholic Church and transferred to secularized public institutions. A national library and archives were opened, and faculties of law, social sciences, and medicine were established at the University of Honduras. A postal and telegraph service was established.

Construction was begun on a road from Tegucigalpa to Amapala on the Pacific coast. More than 100 American and British companies were formed to rework old silver and gold mines with new technology and imported machinery. However, only the New York and Honduras-Rosario Mining Company survived, owing to declining silver prices and a resurgence of domestic turmoil between 1891 and 1894.

Under the 1880 constitution, Soto was reelected president. He resigned in March 1883, ostensibly because of illness but more likely because Guatemalan President Barrios was planning a revolution to oust him. Congress refused to accept his resignation and granted him a leave of absence. Soto sent another resignation from San Francisco, California, on August 27, 1893, rather than plunge Honduras into war with Guatemala.

Although Soto never joined the Liberal party, or any party, his minister of public instruction, Ramón Rosa, welded the disorganized factions of liberalism into a compact and disciplined party, the Liberal League, in 1884. Soto himself remained active in politics and as late as 1902 launched an abortive campaign to succeed President Terencio Sierra.

BIBLIOGRAPHY

Durón y Gamero, Rómulo E. *Bosquejo Histórico de Honduras, 1502 a 1921.* San Pedro Sula, Honduras: Tipografía del Comercio, 1927.

Stokes, William S. *Honduras, an Area Study in Government.* Madison: University of Wisconsin Press, 1959.

Vallejo, Antonio R. *Compendio de la Historia Social y Política de Honduras.* Tegucigalpa: Tipografía Nacional, 1926. Tomo I.

NEALE J. PEARSON

SOTO ALFARO, BERNARDO (1854–1931), was president of Costa Rica from 1885 to 1890. As vice president, he succeeded upon the death of Prospero Fernández* in 1885 and was elected to a full term in his own right in April 1886. Soto retained Education Minister Mauro Fernández, who issued the landmark General Law of Education in 1886. Costa Rica's commitment to free, compulsory, secular education was fixed during Soto's tenure. Soto also established the Liceo de Costa Rica in 1887. However, he and Minister Fernández closed the University of Santo Tomás as elitist and under control of the Jesuits, which left the Law School as the only institution of higher learning in Costa Rica until 1940.

The Liberals established absolute separation of church and state. They were also paternalistic. Soto tried to hand-pick his successor, but amid a popular outcry against his meddling in the election of 1890, he finally allowed José Joaquín Rodríguez, his political opponent, to win the election.

BIBLIOGRAPHY

Ameringer, Charles D. *Democracy in Costa Rica.* New York: Praeger, 1982.

Maris, Richard, and Karen Biesanz. *Los Costarricenses.* San José: Editorial Universidad Estatal a Distancia, 1979.

Monge, Carlos. *Historia de Costa Rica*. San José: Editorial Fondo de Cultura de Costa
   Rica, 1948.

CHARLES D. AMERINGER

SOUBLETTE, CARLOS (1789–1870), was twice president of Venezuela. He
emerged as a second-rank military figure during the independence struggle after
1810. When José Antonio Páez* led the movement to separate Venezuela from
Simón Bolívar's* Gran Colombia republic, Soublette supported him.

When Páez, first president of Venezuela, decided not to run again after his
first term, he chose Soublette to be vice presidential running mate of Páez' choice
for president, José María Vargas. When Vargas finally withdrew from the presidency in 1837, Soublette succeeded him.

After Soublette's first presidency, Páez returned to office in 1839. However,
four years later, Páez again decided to turn the post over to Carlos Soublette,
whose administration was the last securely Conservative regime to hold office.

During the Federal War of 1859–1863, Soublette held secondary positions in
the Conservative regime of that period. He also reappeared, for the last time,
playing a small role in the very short-lived Conservative regime of 1869.

BIBLIOGRAPHY

Diccionario Biográfico de Venezuela. Madrid: Cárdenas-Sáenz de la Calzada y Cia.,
   1953.
Enciclopedia Universal Ilustrada Europeo-Americana. Barcelona: José Espasa e Hijos.
Magallanes, Manuel Vicente. *Los Partidos Políticos en la Evolución Histórica de Venezuela*. Caracas: Monte Avila Editores, 1977.

ROBERT J. ALEXANDER

SOULOUQUE, FAUSTIN (1788–1873), ruled Haiti for 12 years after a period
of turmoil following a revolution that deposed President Jean-Pierre Boyer* in
1843, ending a period of mulatto domination that had begun with Alexandre
Pétion* in 1806. The choice of Faustin Soulouque as president was made by the
mulatto-dominated Senate almost on a whim, in the belief that he would be
completely subservient to the mulatto political elite.

Soulouque was illiterate, superstitious, and widely recognized to be almost
totally incompetent. He was born to slave parents who had newly arrived from
Africa just before his birth. He managed to move up in the predominantly black
army to become general of the Palace Guard of his predecessor, General Riche.

Soon, Soulouque made it clear that he was nobody's pawn. He named his
own council of advisers and staffed the army with his own loyal black generals.
He organized a secret police and a system of personal tyranny to ensure loyalty
among his advisers and to suppress organized opposition. The mulattoes, real-
izing their mistake, soon made an effort to get rid of him by revolution, which
was brutally quashed. Most prominent mulattoes were either executed or forced
to go into exile.

With potential and actual opposition neutralized, Soulouque turned his attention to reestablishing Haitian domination of the Dominican Republic, which had declared its independence from Haiti in 1844. He invaded on March 9, 1849, but his forces were defeated and had to retreat, leaving a path of pillage and destruction in their wake.

Despite the defeat, Soulouque declared the invasion a succcess and began a campaign to make himself emperor, declaring it the will of God. On September 20, a new constitution was approved, declaring him Emperor Faustin I. Black generals, eager for prestige, were provided with peerages, mostly in exchange for a fee: 4 princes, 59 dukes, 2 marquises, 90 counts, 215 barons and 30 chevaliers.

Voodoo, tolerated by his predecessors, was openly practiced and encouraged by Soulouque and his wife, Adelina. Voodoo priests were installed in his household, and voodoo beliefs and practices became one of the pillars of the emperor's power.

Soulouque, always intent on recapturing Santo Domingo, engaged in frequent unsuccessful but costly invasions. There was also enormous expenditure on court rituals and royal pomp. Corruption and graft were rampant. Soulouque's printing of money greatly devalued Haitian currency. Revenue was also raised through state monopolization of exports and imports, steep increases in import duties, and heavy taxes on capital.

With a world depression during 1857–1858 hitting prices of coffee and cotton particularly hard, with corruption running rampant, a bankrupt treasury, and escalating international debt, Soulouque found himself isolated from his former supporters. In December 1858 he was deserted by one of his most trusted ministers, Fabre Nicholas Géffrard,* who pronounced an end to the empire, made Soulouque a virtual prisoner, and was made president by acclamation. Soulouque and his family, after his signing an Act of Abdication, left for Jamaica. He returned to Haiti in 1867 and lived there until his death.

BIBLIOGRAPHY

Davis, H. P. *Black Democracy: The Story of Haiti*. Toronto: Longmans, Green and Co., 1929.
Heinl, R. D., and N. G. Heinl. *Written in Blood*. Boston: Houghton Mifflin, 1978.
Leyburn, James G. *The Haitian People*. New Haven, Conn.: Yale University Press, 1941.
Logan, R. W. *Haiti and the Dominican Republic*. London: Oxford University Press, 1968.

PERCY C. HINTZEN

SOUTHWELL, CALEB AZARIAH PAUL (1913–1979), became the second premier of St. Kitts-Nevis after the sudden death of Robert Llellwyn Bradshaw.* Born in Dominica, he completed elementary school and became a pupil teacher. He gained a teacher's certificate and continued to teach until January 1938 when he joined the Leeward Islands Police Force and was stationed in St. Kitts. He remained in the force until 1944, resigning to go to work in the only sugar factory in St. Kitts. There he met Robert Bradshaw, president of the St. Kitts-Nevis Trades and Labour Union, immediately became involved in the activities of the union, was elected its vice president and organizer in 1947, while retaining his job at the factory.

Southwell also became active in the St. Kitts-Nevis-Anguilla Labour Party, also headed by Bradshaw. In 1952 he won a seat in the Legislative Council. In 1956 the Labour Party won five of eight elective seats under a revised constitution that ushered in a quasi-ministerial system, under which St. Kitts, Nevis, and Anguilla were combined into a separate colony. Southwell again won election and was appointed minister of works and communications, a position he held for three years.

Bradshaw, meanwhile, involved in federal politics, gave up his post in the St. Kitts Legislature after being elected to the Federal House in March 1957, and became federal minister of finance the following year. Southwell assumed the party leadership and became a member of the St. Kitts-Nevis-Anguilla Executive Council. He was appointed chief minister at the inauguration of the ministerial system of government in February 1960 and led the party to another electoral victory in 1961.

Bradshaw, back in St. Kitts after the collapse of the West Indies Federation in 1962, resumed his position on the Legislative Council. However, Southwell remained chief minister until 1966, when Bradshaw, who was again party leader, became chief minister following another electoral victory.

When St. Kitts-Nevis-Anguilla was granted Associated Statehood in 1967, Southwell became deputy premier and minister of trade, industry, and tourism. Upon Bradshaw's death in May 1978, he became party leader and premier. He died suddenly in May 1979.

BIBLIOGRAPHY

Bajan, July 1978.
Bulletin of Eastern Caribbean Affairs 4 (May/June 1978).
Hopkins, Jack W. "British Colonies and Associated States," in Jack W. Hopkins (ed). *Latin America and Caribbean Contemporary Record*. Vol. 1. New York: Holmes and Meier, 1983.
Jones-Hendrickson, Simon B. "St. Kitts-Nevis," in Jack W. Hopkins (ed.). *Latin America and Caribbean Contemporary Record*. Vol. 2. New York: Holmes and Meier, 1984.
Rickards, Colin: *Caribbean Power*. London: Dobson, 1963.

PERCY C. HINTZEN AND W. MARVIN WILL

SPRINGER, SIR HUGH WORRELL (1913–   ), was the third black, native-born governor-general of Barbados. A graduate of Harrison College in Barbados in 1931, he received a B.A. and an M.A. from Oxford University, and became a barrister in 1938 following studies at Inner Temple. In 1939 he returned to

Barbados to practice law and teach the classics. He soon became active in politics and the trade union movement.

Springer was elected to the Barbadian House of Assembly in 1944. He also served as secretary general of the newly formed Barbados Labour Party (BLP) and, with Sir Grantley Herbert Adams,* was instrumental in organizing the Barbados Workers Union (BWU), becoming its secretary general in 1944. In addition, Springer became a member of the Barbadian Governmental Executive Committee, along with Adams.

Springer resigned all of these positions in 1947 to become registrar of the new University of the West Indies (UWI), near Kingston, Jamaica, where he remained until 1963. He was awarded a Guggenheim Fellowship and became a fellow in the Harvard Center for International Affairs (1961–1962), was a visiting fellow at Oxford (1962–1963), and served as director of the Institute of Education for the University of the West Indies (1963–1966). In 1964 he returned to Barbados to be acting governor.

Between 1966 and 1980 Springer held posts as assistant secretary general of the (British) Commonwealth, director of the Commonwealth's educational liaison unit, and secretary general of Commonwealth Universities. In February 1984 he again returned to Barbados, as governor-general.

BIBLIOGRAPHY

Alexander, Robert J. "Barbados," in Robert J. Alexander (ed.). *Political Parties of the Americas*. Vol 1. Westport, Conn.: Greenwood Press, 1982.
Hoyos, F. A. *Grantley Adams and the Social Revolution*. London: MacMillan Co., 1974.
International Who's Who. London: Europa Publications, 1984.
Who's Who in the World. 7th ed. Chicago: Marquis Who's Who, Inc., 1984.
Will, W. Marvin. "Barbados," in Jack W. Hopkins (ed.). *Latin America and Caribbean Contemporary Record*. Vols. 2–4. New York: Holmes and Meier, 1983, 1984, 1985.

PERCY C. HINTZEN AND W. MARVIN WILL

STOUTT, HAMILTON LAVITY (1929–   ), was leader of the Virgin Islands Party and first chief minister of the British Virgin Islands. He received his primary and secondary education in the British Virgin Islands, and was a contractor between 1946 and 1964. He was first elected to the Legislative Council in 1957, served as member for Works and Communications between 1960 and 1967, and in 1967 became the first chief minister of the territory, serving until 1971. Between 1971 and 1975 he was Leader of the Opposition, he was minister of natural resources and public health between 1975 and 1979, and again he served as chief minister after the election of 1979.

BIBLIOGRAPHY

Personalities Caribbean, Seventh Edition 1982–83, Binghamton, N. Y.: Vail Ballou
    Press, n.d.

                                                        ROBERT J. ALEXANDER

STROESSNER, ALFREDO (1912–   ), has served as president of Paraguay
for more than three decades since 1954. His father was an immigrant from
Germany who went to Paraguay in the 1890s and began a beer factory. Alfredo
Stroessner entered Paraguay's military school at age 16 and was sent to fight in
the Chaco War even before completing his studies. He was promoted to first
lieutenant during the war. By 1940 he was a major.

Stroessner was sent to Brazil for artillery training, and then to the Superior
War School, which was critical for any officer desiring to ascend to the rank of
colonel or general. In November 1945 Stroessner was promoted to lieutenant
colonel and placed in command of the principal artillery unit of Paraguay. In
1946 he was appointed to the army's general staff.

Stroessner was one of the minority of military officers who stayed loyal to
President Higinio Morínigo* during the 1947 Civil War. As Southern Front
commander, he was instrumental in preventing rebel armies from encircling
Asunción. He was hailed as a hero by the victorious Colorados.

Although a supporter of Morínigo in the Civil War, Stroessner turned against
him to support Felipe Molas López in the coup that ousted Morínigo. Molas
López promoted him to general, but this did not prevent Stroessner from turning
against Molas López and siding with Federico Cháves' "democratic" faction
of the Colorado Party which ousted Molas López from the presidency.

Cháves appointed Stroessner commander-in-chief of the Armed Forces, but
again this promotion failed to ensure Stroessner's loyalty. He and Epifanio
Méndez of the Colorado Party planned the coup that ousted Cháves on May 5,
1954, following which Stroessner was the Colorado Party presidential candidate,
and won the election, running unopposed. He assumed the presidency on August
15, 1954, at age 41.

Once Stroessner was president, he knew that he would have to eliminate the
rival factions of the Colorado Party if he intended to stay in office. Although
he had not been active in Colorado Party politics prior to 1954, he proved himself
an expert in factional struggles. By 1966 Stroessner had broken the power of
all Colorado factional leaders.

Stroessner's trusted associates, both military and political, were appointed to
top cabinet positions and to posts on the Colorado Executive Committee. Organized from the top down, the party stressed discipline and unquestioning
obedience to superiors, with Stroessner being the ultimate superior. In addition
to the patronage possibilities the Colorado Party gave Stroessner, it had a large
number of functioning organizations associated with it: labor, women's, peasant,
youth, veterans, and professional associations, which support the regime.

The second major source of support for General Stroessner has been the military. Two of his most outstanding characteristics helped him maintain control over the armed forces: his organizational abilities, and his thoroughness and hard work. He has remained commander-in-chief and kept a close watch over military promotions and appointments, met with officers on a regular basis, and has taken a direct part in supervising the allocation of military resources.

There has been a great deal of corruption in Stroessner's Paraguay. High-ranking military officers have often been its direct beneficiaries, and some became very wealthy because of their control over certain areas of illegal activities such as smuggling.

All of these factors have kept Stroessner in power more than 30 years. He has changed the constitution several times. Although he has usually permitted opposition parties to function, he has very closely circumscribed their activities and carefully controlled elections. Imprisonment, torture, exile, and even death have awaited any opposition that came to constitute, in the eyes of Stroessner and his close associates, a possible danger to the regime.

BIBLIOGRAPHY

Bourne, Richard. *Political Leaders of Latin America*. Baltimore: Penguin, 1969.
Kolinski, Charles J. *Historical Dictionary of Paraguay*. Metuchen, N. J.: Scarecrow Press, 1973.
Lewis, Paul H. *Paraguay Under Stroessner*. Chapel Hill: University of North Carolina Press, 1980.
Lott, Leo B. *Venezuela and Paraguay: Political Modernity and Tradition in Conflict*. New York: Holt, Rinehart and Winston, 1972.
Weil, Thomas, et al. *Area Handbook for Paraguay*. Washington, D. C.: Department of Defense, 1972.

JOHN T. DEINER

SUCRE ALCALÁ, ANTONIO JOSÉ DE (1795–1830), was Bolivia's first constitutionally elected president. Born in Venezuela, he joined the independence revolt against Spain in 1810, when only 15, and served in the armies of the first and second Venezuelan republics. Forced to flee in 1814, he returned to Venezuela in 1816 to renew the struggle, first under General Santiago Mariño* and then under Simón Bolívar.*

With Bolívar's victory over the Spanish forces, Sucre, his chief lieutenant, helped negotiate an armistice in November 1820. Sent in 1821 to support the independence struggle in Ecuador, Sucre won a decisive victory at Pichincha on May 24, 1822. He then led Gran Colombian troops to liberate Peru in 1824, and commanding an independence army of 7,000 men defeated a 10,000-man royalist force in the Battle of Ayacucho on December 9, 1824, which guaranteed the independence of Peru.

Surce was then ordered to La Paz. There, he issued the decree of February 9, 1825, proclaiming the independence of Upper Peru. An assembly of notables resolved to create the Republic of Bolivia, and on August 13, 1825, they appointed Bolívar its first president. When Bolívar returned to Peru in December 1825, Sucre was elected president under Bolívar's constitution to serve for life.

Despite a major economic decline, President Surce attempted to rebuilt wartorn Bolivia, introducing progressive reforms in taxation, mining, and education. However, his government was forced to heavily tax the Indians and church properties. Sucre's programs left the Bolivian church firmly under secular control. However, the Bolivians became restive with his liberal reforms and foreign rule. A revolt in April 1828, an assassination attempt, and the invasion of General Agustín Gamarra* from Peru ultimately forced Sucre's resignation in August 1828.

Sucre returned to Venezuela, but with the outbreak of war between Gran Colombia and Peru, he led the Colombians in defeating a Peruvian force invading Ecuador. In 1830 he served as president of a constitutional congress in Bogotá, which failed to solve Colombian divisivenes. While returning to Quito, he was assassinated.

BIBLIOGRAPHY

Arnade, Charles. *The Emergence of the Republic of Bolivia*. New York: Russell and Russell, 1970.

Lofstrom, William Lee. *The Promise and the Problem of Reform, Attempted Social and Economic Change in the First Years of Bolivian Independence*. Ithaca, N. Y.: Cornell University Press, 1972.

O'Connor d'Arlach, Tomás. *Los presidentes de Bolivia desde 1825 hasta 1912*. La Paz: González y Medina, 1912.

Rumazo González, Alfonso. *Sucre, gran mariscal de Ayacucho; biografía*. Madrid: Aguilar, 1984.

Sherwell, Guillermo Antonio. *Antonio José de Sucre (Gran Mariscal de Ayacucho), Hero and Martyr of American Independence: A Sketch of His Life*. Washington, D.C.: Press of B. S. Adams, 1924.

WALTRAUD QUEISER MORALES

T

TERRA, GABRIEL (1873–1942), established Uruguay's first dictatorship of the twentieth century. A teacher and lawyer, Terra became active in Colorado Party politics as a relatively young man. He served in the cabinets of Presidents Claudio Williman (1907–1911) and Baltasar Brum (1919–1923), and was minister to Italy. He also served for five years as a member of the National Council of Administration, which shared executive powers with the president of the republic during the 1920s.

In 1930 Gabriel Terra was the victorious Colorado Party candidate for president. Coming to power at the beginning of the Great Depression, he felt himself hampered by the split presidency established in the 1918 constitution. In 1933, with support of opposition Blanco Party leader Luis Alberto de Herrera,* he carried out a coup with the backing of the national police, dissolving the National Council of Administration and Parliament, and suspending the 1918 constitution.

A new constitution reestablished the full power of the president and guaranteed the Blancos strong representation in Parliament and the cabinet. The convention which adopted that constitution elected Terra as president for the 1934–1938 period. During his "constitutional" period, Terra maintained a severe dictatorship. In 1938 he gave up his office to General Alfredo Baldomir,* the Colorado Party candidate and his brother-in-law, who dismantled the Terra dictatorship.

BIBLIOGRAPHY

Fitzgibbon, Russell H. *Uruguay: Portrait of a Democracy*. New Brunswick, N. J.: Rutgers University Press, 1954.
New York Times, September 16, 1942.
Taylor, Philip B., Jr. "The Uruguayan Coup d'Etat of 1933." *Hispanic American Historical Review* 32 (August 1952).
Terra, Gabriel. *La Revolución de Marzo, Principales Discursos*. Buenos Aires: M. Gleizer, 1938.

ROBERT J. ALEXANDER

THIEL, BERNARDO AUGUSTO (1850–1907), was archbishop of Costa Rica during the intense struggle over church-state relations in the 1880s. Born in Eberfield, Germany, he came to Costa Rica in 1877 and was appointed bishop in 1880. Within two years, he faced the powerful attack against the church by Liberal reformers under President Prospero Fernández Oreamuno,* who demanded absolute separation of church and state, civil marriage and divorce, and secular education. Thiel's vigorous objection to the Liberal laws of 1884 caused him to be expelled for two years.

During the 1890s, Thiel rallied the anti-Liberal forces around the Catholic Union Party. Attacking the Liberals for both their anticlericalism and their lack of social conscience, he took up the cause of the Costa Rican workers, calling for "just wages" and better treatment. The Liberal program rejected the concept of intervention by the state in political and economic affairs. In this social posture, Thiel was ahead of his time.

BIBLIOGRAPHY

Creedman, Theodore S. *Historical Dictionary of Costa Rica*. Metuchen, N. J.: Scarecrow Press, 1977.
Mavis, Richard, and Karen Biesanz. *Los Costarricenses*. San José: Editorial Universidad Estatal a Distancia, 1979.
Monge, Carlos. *Historia de Costa Rica*. San José: Editorial Fondo de Cultura de Costa Rica, 1948.

                                                          CHARLES D. AMERINGER

TINOCO GRANADOS, FEDERICO (1870–1931), was president of Costa Rica from January 1917 to August 1919, ruling as a military dictator, an aberration in a nation that has had few dictators. He was able to seize power owing to the unpopularity of President Alfredo González Flores* and the uncertain economic conditions accompanying World War I.

Tinoco would not tolerate any criticism, established press censorship, exiled, jailed, or murdered his political opponents, and increased the size of the army and police. His family and cronies dominated the government, and police spies seemed to be everywhere.

Costa Ricans sought to recover their lost freedoms. In June 1919, when a group of schoolteachers marched on the government newspaper, *La Información*, and set the building ablaze, Tinoco's troops, in an unprecedented action, fired on the crowd. Soon afterward, at the urging of the diplomatic corps, Tinoco appeared before Congress, resigned, and received safe-conduct from the country.

The United States withheld recognition of Tinoco. Gonzalez Flores had fled to Washington, where he enlisted the aid of President Woodrow Wilson. Other American countries supported the U. S. position, a strong factor in resistance in Tinoco, and in his decison to resign.

BIBLIOGRAPHY

Ameringer, Charles D. *Democracy in Costa Rica*. New York: Praeger, 1982.
Gamboa G., Francisco. *Costa Rica: ensayo histórico*. San José: Ediciones Revolución, 1971.

Mavis, Richard, and Karen Biesanz. *Los Costarricenses*. San José: Editorial Universidad
Estatal a Distancia, 1979.

CHARLES D. AMERINGER

TORRES GONZÁLEZ, JUAN JOSE (1921–1976), was one of the most radical
Bolivian generals to serve as president. Although in his youth he had been a
militant of the conservative Bolivian Socialist Falange and had led a military
unit against the Ché Guevara* guerrilla insurgency in 1967, he emerged as an
idealistic politician of the left.

When General Alfredo Ovando Candia* seized power in September 1969,
Torres became commander-in-chief of the armed forces but was removed in July
1970, under conservative pressure. In the confusion after the fall of Ovando
during October 4–7, 1970, Torres assumed power, beginning a new, but brief,
experiment in populist politics.

Under Torres, organized labor created a Popular Assembly, two-thirds of the
delegates representing urban unions and the rest from leftist parties and peasant
organizations. It was intended to be a "dual power." Although the Assembly
adjourned without major policy changes, it permitted the radical parties a greater
influence on politics than at any time in the past.

In April 1971 Torres pardoned imprisoned guerrilla activists. The lease of the
Matilda zinc mine by U. S. Steel was cancelled and the Popular Assembly
directed the U. S. Peace Corps to leave Bolivia. Torres sought agreements with
the Eastern Bloc countries and received promises of Soviet and East European
economic assistance.

From the start, the Torres government was the object of sharp internal and
external opposition. Relations with the United States were strained and aid was
cut, although a decree on February 8, 1971, provided a $78 million compensation
to Gulf Oil. Hugo Banzer Suárez,* dismissed head of the army's military college,
organized a successful revolt during August 19–21. Despite bloody worker and
student resistance, the ultraconservative military won out, since General Torres
refused to arm civilians.

Torres went into exile and ultimately was assassinated in Buenos Aires in
1976.

BIBLIOGRAPHY

Gallardo Lozada, Jorge. *De Torres a Banzer: Diez Meses de Emergencia en Bolivia*.
Buenos Aires: Ediciones Periferia, 1972.
Sandoval Rodríguez, Isaac. *Culminación y Ruptura del Modelo Nacional-Revolucionario:
Torres en el Escenario Político Boliviano*. La Paz: n.p., 1979.
Torres Goitia, Hugo. *El Gobierno Revolucionario y la Asamblea del Pueblo*. La Paz:
Editorial del Estado, 1971.

Torres González, Juan José. *El General Torres Habla a Bolivia*. Buenos Aires: Editorial
   Crisis, 1973.

WALTRAUD QUEISER MORALES

TORRIJOS HERRERA, OMAR (1929–1981), was one of the strongest political figures ever to exercise power in Panama. His parents were schoolteachers,
and he attended the military academy of El Salvador between 1947 and 1952.
He had the rank of lieutenant colonel in the National Guard at the time of the
1968 coup which overthrew the ten-day government of Arnulfo Arias Madrid.*
Relatively unknown outside of Panamá, within the country he enjoyed a swashbuckler's image as a counterinsurgency officer. He vaulted past several senior
officers and consolidated his control within six months, becoming a general.

Torrijos was determined to bring change and proclaimed himself Maximum
Leader of the Revolution, placing figureheads in the presidency. He banned
political parties, creating a corporative system to provide some opportunity for
particular sectors of society to influence decisions, denied traditional urban elites
access to power, and strengthened the influence of provincial leaders and representatives. He enlarged the public sector and instituted social programs for the
masses.

Torrijos also undertook a new vitality in foreign relations. He revived the
Canal talks, which had been virtually suspended in 1967. He played on U. S.
fears. Although not a Marxist, he permitted the Communist Party to function
when other parties were banned, and he exchanged *abrazos* with Fidel Castro.*
The more liberal foreign policy of the Carter administration provided the final
ingredient for Torrijos' greatest triumph, the Panama Canal treaties of 1977. He
attained the Panamanian dream of isthmian sovereignty and eventual ownership
and control of the Canal.

A downturn in the economy brought Torrijos to announce a "return to the
barracks" in 1978 and to appoint Aristídes Royo as president, with some independence of action. Torrijos estabished the Democratic Revolutionary Party,
apparently hoping to create a Mexican-style, single-party political system and a
return to an elected president in 1984. However, Torrijos remained final arbiter
of Panamanian affairs until his death in an airplane crash in 1981.

BIBLIOGRAPHY

American University Foreign Area Studies. *Panama: A Country Study*. Washington, D.C:
   March 1980.
Greene, Graham. *Getting to Know the General: The Story of an Involvement*. New York:
   Simon and Schuster, 1984.
Ropp, Steve C. *Panamanian Politics: From Guarded Nation to National Guard*. New
   York: Praeger, 1982.

CHARLES D. AMERINGER

TOWNSEND EZCURRA, ANDRÉS (1915–   ), twice Peruvian vice presidential candidate, was born in Chiclayo. Soon after he finished high school at
the Colegio Nacional de Guadalupe, he joined the Federación Aprista Juvenil

(FAJ) in 1934. The following year he was deported to Argentina. There he received a doctorate in law at the University of La Plata. From 1945 to 1948 he was editor of *La Tribuna*, the Aprista daily. In 1948 he was again exiled. He lectured in Panama, taught history at the National University of San Carlos in Guatemala and worked at the United Nations until his return to Peru in 1956. During the second Manuel Prado* administration (1956–1962), Townsend was on three occasions on the Peruvian Delegation to the United Nations General Assembly. He was elected as an Aprista to the Chamber of Deputies in 1963 and was its president when the constitutional regime was deposed by the armed forces in October 1968. While a deputy, he was elected secretary general of the Latin American Parliament. He was elected to the Constituent Assembly in 1978 and to a five-year term in the Senate in 1980. He was a candidate for the first vice presidency on the Aprista ticket in 1980, and in 1985 on the ticket of Convergencia Democrática, an electoral alliance of Luis Bedoya Reyes'* Partido Popular Christiano and the Movimiento de Bases Hayistas, a party established by Andrés Townsend after he left the Aprista Party in 1982. He was reelected senator for a five-year term in 1985.

BIBLIOGRAPHY

Arriola Grande, Marilio. *Diccionario literario del Peru*. Lima: Editorial Universo, 1980.
Goldenberg, Sonia, (ed.). *Dedicamos nuestro futuro*. Lima: Universidad del Pacífico-Fundación Friedrich Ebert, 1985.
Townsend Ezcurra, Andrés. *Pan y Libertad*. Lima: Ediciones Pueblo, 1968.

EUGENIO CHANG-RODRÍGUEZ

TRUJILLO MOLINA, RAFAEL LEÓNIDAS (1891–1961), was the dictator of the Dominican Republic from 1930 to 1961. Of lower middle-class origins, he had a minimal education and worked for some years as a telegraph operator on a sugar estate. When the United States Marines, who occupied the Dominican Republic between 1916 and 1924, organized a National Guard as a new, supposedly ''non-political'' army, Trujillo received a commission and soon after the Marines left emerged as commander of the force, becoming a brigadier general in 1927.

When a revolt broke out in 1930 against President Horacio Vázquez,* General Trujillo proclaimed his ''neutrality.'' The upshot was that he ran for president shortly afterward with his opponent virtually unable to campaign because of intimidation by Trujillo goon squads.

After 1930 Trujillo completely dominated the Dominican regime. He served as president during 1930–1938 and 1943–1952; in other periods he had puppets in the office, the last of them being Joaquín Balaguer.* When he was not president, Trujillo was commander of the armed forces.

The Trujillo dictatorship was the most absolutist regime in Latin America during the years it was in power. During most of the period, there was only one legal party, the Partido Dominicano, and its chief, who was always Trujillo, constitutionally filled any vacancies in Congress and all other legislative bodies. There were several secret police forces that kept control over all political activities and reported directly to Trujillo. The dictator constantly rotated people in office. Press censorship was complete. A "cult of personality" was established according to which the dictator had to be credited as the ultimate authority in all fields of human knowledge, and numerous things and places, including the capital city, were renamed in his honor.

Trujillo also became dominant in the Dominican economy. He and the government under his control allotted virtually all sectors of the economy directly to the dictator, to members of his family, or to the dictator's favorites. In his own interest, Trujillo brought about substantial development of the Dominican economy, including the sugar industry, grazing, and manufacturing, as well as the infrastructure. One consequence of this development was that when the post-Trujillo regime confiscated the Trujillo family holdings, it took over a large part of the Dominican economy.

During most of his regime, Trujillo sought to maintain good relations with the United States. However, during his last half dozen years, he ran into serious international difficulties, when a prominent critic of the regime, the Basque leader Jesús de Galíndez was kidnapped from the streets of New York and a U. S. pilot of Dominican Airlines "disappeared" in the Dominican Republic, provoking a very critical investigation by the United States State Department.

Trujillo was finally assassinated in May 1961, presumably by people who had personal rather than political grievances against him.

BIBLIOGRAPHY

Bosch, Juan. *Trujillo*. Caracas: 1959.
Crassweiler, Robert D. *Trujillo: The Life and Times of a Caribbean Dictator*. New York: Macmillan Co., 1966.
Galíndez, Jesús. *La Era de Trujillo*. Santiago de Chile: Editorial del Pacífico, 1956.
Ornes, Germán. *Trujillo: Little Caesar of the Caribbean*. New York: Thomas Nelson and Sons, 1958.
Wiarda, Howard J. *Dictatorship and Development: The Methods of Control in Trujillo's Dominican Republic*. Gainesville: University of Florida Press, 1970.

ROBERT J. ALEXANDER

U

UBICO Y CASTAÑEDA, JORGE (1878–1946), was president of Guatemala between 1931 and 1944. The only son of a wealthy lawyer, he attended the national military college and rose to the rank of lieutenant colonel by the time he was 25.

After losing presidential campaigns in 1922 and 1926, General Ubico won the 1931 election on a platform that included rejection of reelection. By 1934, however, he had succeeded in assuming all governmental responsibilities, destroying the Communist Party, disbanding all unions, and changing the constitution to allow for his reelection.

Ubico stabilized the Guatemalan economy and utilized highly favorable concessions to attract U.S. business interests. The national treasury and Guatemala's international credit were built up. Working conditions deteriorated, however. A strictly enforced vagrancy law provided forced labor to coffee planters who supported the dictator. A decree in 1933 required all Indian men to work two weeks a year without pay unless they had paid a tax. All Indians had to work 150 days a year at minimal pay.

Ubico had a highly efficient secret police. Cultural life in the country suffered greatly because the dictator refused to permit the expression or exchange of any ideas that might even faintly resemble criticism.

Active opposition to the dictatorship began in 1941, mostly in the universities where with all the publicity on fighting for freedom and democracy against the Axis, students and young professionals considered the Ubico dictatorship unacceptable. When the president reacted to student protests in 1944 by declaring a state of siege, a general strike paralyzed the capital. On July 1, 1944, the dictator finally resigned in favor of General Federico Ponce, fled to Mexico, and then to New Orleans, where he died.

BIBLIOGRAPHY

Grieb, K. J. *Guatamelan Caudillo: The Regime of Jorge Ubico 1931–1944.* Athens, Ohio: 1979.

Immerman, R. H. *The CIA in Guatemala*. Austin: University of Texas Press, 1982.
Monteforte Toledo, Mario. *La Revolución de Guatemala, 1944–1954*. Guatemala City: 1975.
Samayoa Chinchilla, Carlos. *El Dictador y Yo: Verdadero Relato Sobre la Vida del General Ubico*. Guatemala City: 1975.
Whetten, Nathan L. *Guatemala: The Land and the People*. New Haven, Conn.: Yale University Press, 1961.

JOSÉ M. SÁNCHEZ

ULATE BLANCO, OTILIO (1892–1973), was elected president of Costa Rica in 1948, but it required a civil war to enable him to take office. As editor and publisher of *Diario de Costa Rica*, he had opposed the rule of Rafael Angel Calderón Guardia,* who, in addition to authoritarian tendencies, was enlarging the role of the state through the enactment of social reforms that Ulate opposed. When Calderón sought to return to office in 1948, a broad spectrum of political forces supported Ulate against him. When Calderón attempted to annul Ulate's victory, the same forces successfully rose up in arms.

The victorious rebels, led by José Figueres Ferrer,* representing the Social Democrats, did not install Ulate in the presidency immediately. Figueres led the Founding Junta of the Second Republic for 18 months (May 1948-November 1949), preserving Calderón's social reforms, inaugurating new economic programs, and drafting the constitution of 1949. When Ulate finally assumed the presidency, Costa Rica had been changed vastly.

As president (1949–1953), Ulate became a bitter enemy of Figueres. However, Figueres respected the traditions of Costa Rican democracy, and Ulate abided by the constitution that had been imposed on him. Figueres formed the National Liberation party (PLN) in 1951 and became president in 1953.

Ulate spent the remainder of his political career in opposition to Figueres and the PLN. He ran for president again in 1962 and was soundly defeated. He joined with his former enemy Calderón in the National Unification coalition in 1966, which backed the successful candidacy of José Joaquín Trejos. Four years later, however, when Figueres was reelected, he appointed Ulate ambassador to Spain. Ulate held that position at the time of his death.

BIBLIOGRAPHY

Aguilar Bulgarelli, Oscar R. *Costa Rica y sus hechos políticos de 1943*. San José: Editorial Costa Rica, 1969.
Ameringer, Charles D. *Dom Pepe: A Political Biography of José Figueres of Costa Rica*. Albuquerque: University of New Mexico Press, 1979.
Bell, John Patrick. *Crisis in Costa Rica: The Revolution of 1948*. Austin: University of Texas Press, 1971.
Gamboa G., Francisco. *Costa Rica: ensayo histórico*. San José: Ediciones Revolución, 1971.

CHARLES D. AMERINGER

UNZAGA DE LA VEGA, OSCAR (1916–1959), founded and led the Bolivian Socialist Falange (FSB). Born in Cochabamba, he was educated there and in the School of Agriculture at the University of Chile. Later, he taught at the Colegio Nacional Sucre.

While exiled in Chile, Unzaga founded the FSB in 1937 and served as its general secretary from 1937 to 1944. Inspired by the fascist Spanish Falange of José Antonio Primo de Rivera, the FSB was the first of the new post-Chaco War political parties. It came to represent right-wing interests in the 1950s but gained the support of the urban middle class disaffected with the 1952 revolution. The FSB favored hierarchical discipline and nationalistic mysticism. Under Unzaga's leadership, it supported the reactionary regime of General Hugo Ballivian in 1951 and refused to support the 1952 revolution.

On November 9, 1953, Unzaga led an FSB coup attempt against President Víctor Paz Estenssoro,* who responded by forming a state security apparatus that subjected the FSB and other opposition parties to violent reprisals and internal exile. Subsequently, Unzaga led four other major coup attempts.

In May 1956 Unzaga returned from exile in Chile to participate in the presidential election against MNR candidate Hernán Siles Zuazo.*. The FSB gained 130,000 votes and became the second largest party and major opposition to the MNR

Bitter feuding between the MNR and FSB climaxed in the revolutionary uprising of April 19, 1959—the birthday of Unzaga. FSB activists were slaughtered as they attempted to seize a military barracks in La Paz. Unzaga's body was found, and his death was officially termed an "assassination-suicide." An Organization of American States investigating commission concurred with the official finding that the FSB chief shot himself and that a second shot, fired by his loyal secretary and ex-cadet, René Gallardo, ultimately killed him. Gallardo then also committed suicide. However, within the FSB the tradition persisted that Unzaga was murdered by the MNR government.

BIBLIOGRAPHY

Acha Alvarez, Enrique, and Mario Ramos y Ramos. *Unzaga: Martir de America*. Buenos Aires: n.p., 1960.
Baptista Gumucio, Mariano. *Historia Contemporánea de Bolivia, 1930–1978*. 2d. ed. La Paz: 2d Gisbert, 1978.
Landivar Flores, Hernán. *Infierno en Bolivia*. La Paz: n.p. 1965.

WALTRAUD QUEISER MORALES

URDANETA, RAFAEL (1789–1845), one of the major lieutenants of Simón Bolívar,* was an active participant in the political life of both Colombia and Venezuela. Educated in Venezuela, in 1804 he went to Bogotá, where he held posts in the bureaucracy of the viceroyalty.

When the independence struggle began in 1810, Urdaneta joined it and by age 26 was a general. In 1819, he was a deputy in the Congress of Guayana and commander of the Colombia Guard. In 1821 he was a senator and member of the Cucutá Constituent Assembly. In 1823 he was president of the Senate of Gran Colombia. He was commander of the army in Zulia and then in Cundinamarca in 1824–1828. Between 1828 and 1830 he was secretary of war and navy of Gran Colombia. A member of the 1830 Constituent Assembly of Gran Colombia, he was made provisional chief of government by a coup on September 5. He offered the supreme command to Bolívar, who refused it. In May 1831 he resigned the presidency and went to Venezuela.

In Venezuela, Urdaneta served as deputy, senator, and twice as secretary of war and marine. He died in Paris, on the way to seek Spanish recognition of Venezuela's independence.

BIBLIOGRAPHY

Enciclopedia Universal Ilustrada Europeo-Americana. Barcelona: Espasa Calpe.
Madariagas, Salvador de. *Bolívar.* New York: Pellegrini and Cudahy, 1952.
Memorias del General Rafael Urdaneta. Madrid: Biblioteca Ayacucho, n.d.

                                                              ROBERT J. ALEXANDER

URQUIZA, JUSTO JOSÉ DE (1801–1870), led the uprising that overthrew Argentine dictator Juan Manuel de Rosas.* Born in the Province of Entre Rios, he attended the Colegio de San Carlos in Buenos Aires. He then became a businessman and landowner in Entre Rios and governor of the province in 1841. Ten years later, he organized the struggle against Rosas and defeated him in the Battle of Caseros in February 1852. He was then president of the Argentine Confederation (1854–1860) but failed to bring Buenos Aires into the Confederation. His forces were definitively defeated by those of Buenos Aires in the Battle of Pavón in 1861, although he continued to be governor of Entre Rios. His influence was essential in the election of Domingo Faustino Sarmiento;* as Argentine president in 1868. Urquiza was assassinated by supporters of a political rival.

BIBLIOGRAPHY

Santillán, Diego Abad de. *Gran Enciclopedia Argentina.* Vol. 8. Buenos Aires: Ediar Soc. Anon. Editores, 1963.
Udaondo, Enrique. *Diccionario Biográfico Argentino.* Buenos Aires: Institución Mitre, 1938.

                                                              JOHN T. DEINER

V

VALENTINO, PAUL (1902-?), the major political leader of Guadeloupe during and for a decade after World War II, was already leader of the Socialist party there at the beginning of the war. He led the resistance to the Vichy regime in the island and as a result was jailed for a considerable period.

Valentino was Guadelupean delegate to the French Provisional Consultative Assembly organized under General Charles De Gaulle in the latter part of the war. He was deputy to the two constitutional assemblies of 1945 and 1946. Thereafter, he served as Socialist deputy in the National Assembly for the next 15 years. He was also mayor of Pointe-à-Pitre from 1946 until 1959, when the Socialists were defeated by a coalition organized by the Communists. In the mid–1960s he led a split of the Guadeloupean Socialists with the French party.

BIBLIOGRAPHY

Alexander, Robert J. "Guadeloupe," in Robert J. Alexander (ed.). *Political Parties of the Americas*. Vol. 2. Westport, Conn.: Greenwood Press, 1982.
Who's Who in France, 1955–1956. Paris: Editions Jacques Lafitte, 1955.

ROBERT J. ALEXANDER

VALLE, JOSÉ CECILIO DEL (17?–1834), was born in Honduras. By 1820 he was writing articles that brought him prominence and amity among conservative elements. When Mexican leader Agustín Iturbide* invited Central America to join Mexico after Mexican independence, Valle wrote a circular asking each region to decide on the issue. Union with Mexico was finally accepted, and Valle became a representative in the Mexican Congress. However, he was soon jailed by Iturbide. He was freed on the overthrow of Iturbide and elected to the provisional government of the Central American Federation. A member of its second Federal Congress, after failing to be elected president, he ran for a second time but was narrowly defeated by Francisco Morazán.* In 1834 del Valle was finally elected president of the Central American Federation but died before he could take office.

BIBLIOGRAPHY

Diccionario Enciclopédico Hispano Americano. Vol. 22. Barcelona: Montaner y Simon
     Editores, 1897.
Enciclopedia Universal Ilustrada Europeo-Americana. Barcelona: José Espasa e Hijos.
                                                              NEALE J. PEARSON

VARAS DE LA BARRA, ANTONIO (1817–1886), was one of Chile's leading political figures in the mid nineteenth century. He largely organized the National Party, which for a long time was popularly known as the Montt-Varista Party because of the role of President Manuel Montt Torres* and Antonio Varas.

Varas received his law degree at the University of Chile in 1842. First elected to the Chamber of Deputies in 1843, he remained there (except for the period 1849–1852) until elected to the Senate in 1876. He died a senator. He served as presiding officer of both the Chamber and the Senate. He was in the cabinets of Presidents Manuel Bulnes Prieto,* Manuel Montt and Aníbal Pinto,* holding the portfolios of Justice, Interior, Foreign Relations, and War and Navy.

Varas was the closest political aide and adviser of President Montt, playing a particular role in Montt's quarrel with the church, which led to the formation of the National Party in 1857. Although Varas was nominated by that party for president in 1861, he refused to run. He was leader of the National Party at the time of his death, President Montt having predeceased him six years before.

BIBLIOGRAPHY

Cortes, Lia, and Jordi Fuentes. *Diccionario Político de Chile.* Santiago: Editorial Orbe,
     1967.
Enciclopedia Universal Ilustrada Europeo-Americana. Barcelona: José Espasa e Hijos.
Galdames, Luis. *Historia de Chile.* Santiago: Editorial Zig Zag, 1945.
                                                          ROBERT J. ALEXANDER

VARGAS, GETÚLIO DORNELLES (1883–1954), dominates the political history of twentieth century Brazil. His social, economic, and political reforms profoundly affected and altered the life of the nation.

Born in São Borja, a small town in the state of Rio Grande do Sul, Vargas was the son of General Manuel do Nascimento Vargas, a rancher of Azorian descent and a local political boss.

Vargas went to two military schools before entering the Porto Alegre Law School, where he graduated in 1909. He was soon elected to the State Assembly where he worked for the state political caudillo, Borges de Medeiros, but resigned as a result of a disagreement with him and entered private law practice. In 1917 he returned to the Rio Grande do Sul State Assembly. He became majority leader and secretary of the Budget Committee in 1921.

In 1922, Vargas was elected a federal congressman, and in 1927 President Washingon Luis,* after consultation with Borges de Medeiros, appointed Vargas federal finance minister. Borges de Medeiros then selected him as governor of the state in the November 1927 gubernatorial elections. Vargas took office in January 1928. He eased the previous political tension between the state's two political parties and assisted in the economic development of private industry.

In 1930 President Washington Luis of São Paulo refused to honor a previous political agreement to alternate the presidency of Brazil with the state of Minas Gerais. Angry political leaders from Minas Gerais established contacts with Borges de Medeiros, and a reluctant Getúlio Vargas was offered as the candidate of the opposition Liberal Alliance.

Vargas accepted his defeat, but his supporters in Rio Grande Do Sul charged that the election had been stolen and began to plot revolution. They were joined by the *tenentes* revolutionaries of 1922 and 1924, and on October 4, 1930, an armed rebellion broke out. Less than a month later, the triumphant Vargas entered Rio de Janeiro. He dominated Brazil from 1930 to 1945.

The revolutionary government suspended the 1891 constitution, disbanded all existing political parties and governed by decree. When Vargas failed to grant a constitution, São Paulo dissidents in July 1932 rose in a three-month-long armed rebellion.

In May 1933, Vargas called for a constituent assembly which, after presenting Vargas with the new consititution also voted him president for the years 1934–1938. On November 7, 1937, amidst maneuvers of various candidates for the presidential election of 1938, Vargas, with the backing of the military led by General Goes Monteiro, established a dictatorship, the Estado Novo.

Vargas embarked on a program of economic nationalism that reserved the mineral wealth of the country for Brazilians, enacted extensive labor legislation, exercised strict censorship, and suppressed all political opposition. When war broke in Europe in 1939, a strong faction inside the Brazilian government favored closer relations with the Axis powers. However, Vargas decided in favor of the United States when President Roosevelt promised the construction of a steel mill in return for use of air and naval bases in Brazil by U.S. military forces. Shortly after Pearl Harbor, Brazilian shipping became the target of German submarines. On August 21, 1942, Brazil declared war on Germany. A Brazilian army of 25,000 men was sent to fight in Italy.

Vargas, sensing that Allied victory was close, promised early in 1945 a return to democracy and presidential elections for late 1945. Vargas then sought to create a new political power based on the labor unions and the working class. The armed forces removed Vargas from office on October 28, 1945, and he returned to Rio Grande do Sul.

In the election of December 1945, Vargas was elected senator; and as a senator, he maintained a low profile. Five years later, in 1950, he returned to the presidency in the free election.

Vargas discovered that governing Brazil with a free press, an independent Congress, and a watchful military was much more difficult than being a dictator. However, he secured two major pieces of legislation: the law establishing Petrobras and blocking major foreign oil companies from developng Brazil's petroleum resources, and the law establishing the National Bank of Economic Development.

Growing charges of fraud and corruption resulted in demands from civil and military opponents that Vargas resign. He refused, and on August 24, 1954, he committed suicide.

BIBLIOGRAPHY

Dulles, John W. F. *Vargas of Brazil: A Political Biography*. Austin: University of Texas Press, 1967.
Frischauer, Paul. *Presidente Vargas*. São Paulo: 1944.
Levine, Robert J. *The Vargas Regime: The Critical Years, 1934–1938*. New York: Columbia University Press, 1970.
Lowenstein, Karl. *Brazil Under Vargas*. New York: Macmillan Co., 1942.

JORDAN YOUNG

VASCONCELOS, JOSÉ (1882–1959), was Mexico's leading philosopher in the twentieth century, an educator and politician whose publications made him known throughout the Spanish-speaking world. Born in Oaxaca, he attended primary school in Northern Mexico and secondary school in Campeche City. He graduated from the Escuela Nacional Preparatoria in Mexico City in 1900 and received his law degree from the Escuela Nacional de Jurisprudencia in 1905. He became president of the Ateneo de la Juventud, a graduate research entity, in 1909.

Vasconcelos supported Francisco I. Madero* after the Mexican Revolution began in 1910. He went into exile during 1915–1920 and upon his return to Mexico served as president of the National Autonomous University of Mexico from June 1920 to October 1921. He was minister of education under President Alvaro Obregón from October 1921 through July 1924. He was the driving force behind the adult literacy campaigns and expansion of rural education by the federal government during 1920–1928. In fine arts, he was a patron of muralists Diego Rivera and José Orozco.

In 1929 Vasconcelos failed to get the Revolutionary coalition's nomination. Former President Plutarco Elías Calles* instead persuaded the Revolutionary Party to choose Pascual Ortíz Rubio, who defeated independent candidate Vasconcelos in a special election.

A prolific writer, Vasconcelos' most famous work is *La Raza Cósmica (The Cosmic Race)*, in which he envisions a dynamic ethnic group growing out of the intermarriage of Indians and Europeans. It is still read throughout Latin America and Europe. As a political philosopher and leader in the Mexican Revolution, Vasconcelos was given academic and civic awards. He died in Mexico City.

BIBLIOGRAPHY

Alba, Victor. *The Mexicans—The Making of a Nation*. New York: Praeger, 1967.
Briggs, Donald C., and Marvin Alisky. *Historical Dictionary of Mexico*. Metuchen, N. J.: Scarecrow Press, 1981.

Haddox, John H. *Vasconcelos of Mexico*. Austin: University of Texas Press, 1976.
Romanell, Patrick. *Making of the Mexican Mind*. Lincoln: University of Nebraska Press, 1952.
Vasconcelos, José. *A Mexican Ulysses*. Bloomington: Indiana University Press, 1963.

MARVIN ALISKY

VÁSQUEZ, HORACIO (1860–1936), was the most important political leader of the Dominican Republic during the first three decades of the twentieth century. Three times president, he presided over the most democratic government in that period, but paved the way for the advent of the totalitarian regime of Rafael Leónidas Trujillo Molina.*

Vásquez participated in the overthrow of the dictatorship of Ulíses Heureaux,* who was assassinated in 1899. Vasquez served as president in 1899 and again in 1902–1903. Thereafter, his followers, the *horacistas*, constituted one of the country's principal political factions.

The United States Marines occupied the Dominican Republic in 1916 and stayed until 1924. In elections preceding the Marines' withdrawal, Horacio Vásquez was the victor. He had been one of the Dominican negotiators arranging the elections.

The government of Horacio Vásquez was one of the few administrations of the first half of the twentieth century which was more or less democratic. However, when Vásquez attempted to extend his term, his opponents revolted and Trujillo emerged as the victor.

Vásquez died in exile.

BIBLIOGRAPHY

Crassweiler, Robert D. *Trujillo: The Life and Times of a Caribbean Dictator*. New York: Macmillan Co., 1966.
Galíndez, Jesús de. *La Era de Trujillo*. Santiago de Chile: Editorial del Pacífico, 1956.

ROBERT J. ALEXANDER

VELASCO ALVARADO, JUAN (1910–1977), president of the Revolutionary Government of the Armed Forces of Peru, was born in Piura. He attended the Liceo San Miguel, the Non-Commissioned Officers School at Chorrillos and the Escuela Militar, Peru's West Point, where he graduated in 1934. He also attended the Escuela Superior de Guerra (1945–1946) and the United States Army Caribbean Institute in the Canal Zone. Velasco was promoted to brigadier general in 1959 and in 1962 was sent to France as military attaché. In 1964 he returned home and President Fernando Belaúnde Terry* (1963–1968) appointed him inspector general and chief of staff of the army. On October 3, 1968, he led the military coup against President Belaúnde and became president of the Revolutionary Govenment of the Armed Forces. He was forced to resign the presidency by the military leaders on August 29, 1975. The most important measures adopted by his administration were the agrarian reform, nationalization of the petroleum and mining industries, and reduction of economic and political dependency on the great powers.

BIBLIOGRAPHY

Alisky, Marvin. *Historical Dictionary of Peru*. Metuchen, N.J.: Scarecrow Press, 1979.
Chang-Rodríguez, Eugenio. *Opciones políticas peruanas*. Lima: Centro de Documentación Andina, 1985.
Guerra, Garciá. *Velasco: Del Estado oligárquico al capitalismo de Estado*. Lima: CEDEP 1983.
Lowenthal, Abraham (ed.). *The Peruvian Experiment: Continuity and Change Under Military Rule*. Princeton, N. J.: Princeton University Press, 1975.
Quijano, Aníbal. *Nationalism and Capitalism in Peru: A Study in Neo-Imperialism*. New York: Monthly Review, 1971.

EUGENIO CHANG-RODRÍGUEZ

VELASCO IBARRA, JOSÉ MARÍA (1893–1979), was five times president of Ecuador and the country's most durable political leader of the twentieth century. He was educated in the country and received a law degree. This served him well during his various periods of exile, in which he served as a law professor in various Latin American countries.

Velasco Ibarra became chief executive for the first time as provisional president after a military coup in 1934. He remained in office for only a year; another military movement deposed him and drove him into exile in Colombia.

In 1944 Velasco Ibarra returned to Ecuador in the wake of a border conflict with Peru which had resulted in the loss of most of the Ecuadorian Amazonian region to its neighbor. Liberal President Carlos Alberto Arroyo del Rio,* who had presided over that disaster, was highly unpopular, and Velasco Ibarra soon became the head of a coalition of Conservatives, Socialists, Communists, and dissident Liberals which organized a successful coup in May 1944. Velasco Ibarra became provisional president once again.

A new constituent assembly elected Velasco Ibarra constitutional president. Although he had first governed with a cabinet with representatives of all the parties that had helped bring him to power, he soon dispensed with all parties except the Conservatives, and his regime became a dictatorship. He was overthrown again in August 1947 and once more went into exile, this time in Argentina.

At the end of the term of Galo Plaza Lasso* as elected constitutional president in 1948, Velasco Ibarra was elected president for the first time. This time, too, he served out his full constitutional term, and in 1956 he turned over his post to an elected successor.

In 1960, Velasco Ibarra returned from self-exile in Argentina to run for the presidency once more and was victorious. However, in November 1961 he was overthrown by a military coup and returned to exile in Argentina.

When a popular insurrection put an end to a military regime in March 1966, Velasco Ibarra returned home, and although virtually all existing parties opposed him, he triumphed in the elections of 1968. Once again, President Velasco Ibarra declared a dictatorship in mid–1970, and although he subsequently modified his strong-arm policies, he was once more overthrown by the armed forces in February 1972. For the last time, he went into exile in Argentina.

Throughout his long career, José Mariá Velasco Ibarra had no clearly defined ideology. At one time or another, he allied himself with virtually every party and group in Ecuadorian politics. His various administrations were marked by bureaucratic incompetence and corruption. However, his oratorical ability, personal charisma, and ability to portray himself as the champion of the humble Ecuadorian citizen allowed him to return from apparent defeat on four separate occasions.

BIBLIOGRAPHY

Blank, David Eugene. "Ecuador," in Robert J. Alexander (ed.). *Political Parties of the Americas*. Vol. 1. Westport, Conn.: Greenwood Press, 1982.
Blanksten, George I. *Ecuador: Constitutions and Caudillos*. Berkeley: University of California Press, 1951.

ROBERT J. ALEXANDER

VICTORIA, GUADELUPE (1785–1843), was the first elected president of Mexico. Born Miguel Fernández in Durango, he studied law in Mexico City, quitting school to become a military leader in the fight for independence from Spain. He changed his name to Guadalupe Victoria. Refusing to surrender when the Spaniards defeated his troops, he hid in the mountains of Veracruz until 1821.

Disenchanted with the govenment of Emperor Agustín de Iturbide during 1822–1823, Victoria helped overthrow him. He was elected president under the federal constitution of 1824. Under Victoria, the federalists organized in the York Rite Masons and the centralists in the Scottish Rite, making freemasonry central to the poltical system.

Victoria backed war Minister Manuel Gómez Pedraza as his successor in 1829, and Gómez won the election. But a rebellion placed Vicente Guerrero in office instead. Victoria retired to his hacienda where he died.

BIBLIOGRAPHY

Callcot, Wilfrid H. *Church and State in Mexico, 1822–1857*. Durham, N. C.: Duke University Press, 1926.
Jones, Oakah L. *Santa Anna*. New York: Twayne Publishers, 1968.
Randall, Robert W. *Real del Monte*. Austin: University of Texas Press, 1972.
Robertson, William S. *Iturbide of Mexico*. Durham, N. C.: Duke University Press, 1982.

MARVIN ALISKY

VICUÑA MACKENNA, BENJAMÍN (1831–1886), a leading Chilean political figure in the third quarter of the nineteenth century, as a very young man was secretary of the Sociedad de la Igualdad organized by Francisco Bilbao Barquin* in 1850. He participated in an attempted military coup in April 1851 and was sentenced to death. However, he escaped from jail, and went abroad, first to California and then to Europe. Returning home in 1856, he edited a newspaper that opposed the government of President Manuel Montt Torres.* He was again exiled to Europe in 1858, returning home in 1863.

A Liberal, Benjamín Vicuña Mackenna was elected to the Chamber of Deputies in 1864, serving until his election to the Senate in 1876. He also served as mayor of Santiago from 1872 to 1876, during which period he contributed extensively to modernizing and beautifying the capital city.

In the election of 1876, Vicuña Mackenna organized the Liberal Deomcratic party to support his presidential aspirations. He garnered wide popular support but a few days before the election he withdrew his candidacy.

Benjamín Vicuña Mackenna was an exceedingly prolific writer. He had more than 80 books published, as well as many articles in reviews and newspapers.

BIBLIOGRAPHY

Cortes, Lia, and Jordi Fuentes. *Diccionario Político de Chile*. Santiago: Editorial Orbe, 1967.
Enciclopedia Universal Ilustrada Europeo-Americana. Barcelona: José Espasa e Hijos.
Galdames, Luis. *Historia de Chile*. Santiago: Editorial Zig Zag, 1945.

                                                    ROBERT J. ALEXANDER

VIDELA, JORGE RAFAEL (1924–   ), was leader of the military coup that ousted Argentine President María Estela (Isabelita) Perón.* He was born in Buenos Aires Province, graduated from the Colegio Militar in 1944, and thereafter received regular promotions. He became commander-in-chief of the army in 1975.

By early 1976 inflation was running at 400 percent a year, and the country was undergoing a tremendous surge of violence by leftist guerillas, including the Peronist Montoneros and the Trotskyite Popular Revolutionary Army (ERP). The Peronists were rocked by internecine violence between contending trade union sectors. In addition, there was a growing rightist vigilantism, spearheaded by the Argentine Anti-Communist Alliance (AAA), which was kidnapping and killing suspected leftists. The government was riddled by corruption and scandal. Furthermore, many in the military disliked having a female president.

The coup of March 1976 came as no surprise, but the harshness of the Videla government was unexpected. It banned all civilian political activity and set out to destroy the guerrillas. Clandestine nightime arrests, imprisonment without charge, torture, and executions were used to eradicate the guerrillas and their sympathizers.

The government and its AAA allies ran secret prisons and torture centers. Wholesale violation of human rights claimed as many as 30,000 lives in three years. Governmental critics and the press were censored. Lawyers who attempted to protect or gain information about those arrested put their own lives in danger.

By 1979 the "dirty war" campaign was successful, and guerrilla activities had virtually ceased, but at great cost to the Argentine population and political system.

Although the Videla government was successful in eliminating guerillas, it was unable to straighten out the economic situation. Inflation averaged over 200 percent per year, the government was unable to lure private and foreign investment and there were numerous bank failures and bankruptcies. The government also ran up a very large foreign debt.

When Videla stepped down, he was succeeded in office by General Roberto Viola. Civilian government was not restored until December 1983, with the election and inauguration of President Raúl Ricardo Alfonsín Foulkes,* following Argentina's defeat by Great Britain in the war over the Malvinas Islands.

The Alfonsín government set up an investigation of the many disappearances and human rights violations that occurred under the military governments. As a result of that investigation, Videla and all members of the military juntas that governed from 1976 to 1983 were put on trial. Videla was convicted and sentenced to a long prison term.

BIBLIOGRAPHY

Page, Joseph AA. *Perón: A Biography*. New York: Random House, 1983.

Snow, Peter G. *Political Forces in Argentina*. New York: Praeger, 1979.

Wynia, Gary W. *Argentina in the Postwar Era: Politics and Economic Policy Making in a Divided Society*. Albuquerque: University of New Mexico Press, 1978.

Wright, Ione S., and Lisa Nekhorn. *Historical Dictionary of Argentina*. Metuchen, N.J.: Scarecrow Press, 1978.

JOHN T. DEINER

VILLA, PANCHO (1877–1923), was the most colorful of the Mexican Revolution generals during 1910–1920. He was born Doroteo Arango in the state of Durango. In 1894 while working as a peon, he wounded the owner of the ranch in defense of his sister's honor and had to flee, adopting the name Pancho Villa. In 1898 he entered the United States and enlisted as an army private in the Spanish-American War. When he returned to Mexico, he had acquired the basic training of a soldier.

In November 1910 Villa joined the Revolution. The regular army's 20th Battalion turned the *Villistas* back, wounding Villa himself in the leg. On December 10, 1910, Villa met with General Pascual Orozco, who had authority from Francisco I. Madero* to name commanding officers in key regions as colonels. With his new title, Villa was now in charge of the Revolution in Chihuahua.

Lacking sufficient horses for each of his soldiers, Villa and his men began raiding ranches. Villa earned a press image as "bandit," as his soldiers stole almost 500 horses in one week. They also attacked a detachment of federal police south of Chihuahua City, taking their horses and arms.

446   VILLA, PANCHO

In March 1911 Madero had returned to Mexico from Texas and met Villa at a Chihuahua stronghold of the revolutionaries. Thereafter, Villa captured federal posts in the northern part of Chihuahua near the Texas border and took Ciudad Juárez, after Madero concluded cease-fire negotiations with envoys from Porfirio Díaz.* Villa captured most of the other provincial cities of the state of Chihuahua. President Porfirio Díaz resigned on May 25 and went into exile.

Villa returned to Chihuahua from Mexico City early in 1912 and publicly questioned army commander Victoriano Huerta's* loyalty to the Revolution. Huerta's officers arrested Villa, but a telegram from President Madero's brother, Colonel Raúl Madero, countermanded the execution order and directed that Villa be sent by train to Mexico City. There Villa served six months in a military prison for insubordination to General Huerta.

After Huerta murdered Madero in February 1913 in Mexico City, Villa fled across the border to El Paso. On March 9, 1913, however, he returned to Mexico and during the 15 months before Huerta's fall, Villa recruited a new large Army of the North, which won battle after battle.

In 1915 Villa's Division of the North began to lose volunteers. To discredit President Venustiano Carranza,* Villa raided Columbus, New Mexico, provoking President Woodrow Wilson to send General John Pershing and a punitive expedition into Mexico after Villa. Wounded, Villa was never captured by the American troops.

Villa's defeat of Huerta was perhaps the most brilliant military operation of the Revolution and insured the continuance of Carranza's presidency. Yet Carranza criticized Villa for launching the attack without his permission.

From 1916 to 1919 Villa concerned himself with dominating Chihuahua, as Carranza and Alvaro Obregón* militarily controlled much of the remainder of Mexico. Carranza's ingratitude and Obregón's rivalry had reduced Villa's status from the third most powerful leader of the Revolution to a regional boss.

In May 1920 Congress elected Adolfo de la Huerta of Sonora as provisional president, and de la Huerta persuaded Villa to sign a peace agreement on July 28, 1920, pledging to lay down his arms and retire to the Canutillo hacienda in Durango. Villa was given title to the large ranch and $120,000 in U. S. currency to buy equipment and run the estate, plus 5,000 peso pensions for each widow of his officers from the Division of the North.

Villa's retirement was a short one. A cattle dealer, Melitón Lozoya, who hated Villa whom he accused of appropriating some of his livestock, hired eight assassins for an ambush at Parral. On July 23, 1923, the eight gunmen killed Villa and five of his six campanions.

BIBLIOGRAPHY

Braddy, Haldeen. *Pershing's Mission in Mexico*. El Paso: Texas Western Press of the University of Texas at El Paso, 1966.
Clendenen, Clarence C. *The United States and Pancho Villa—Unconventional Diplomacy*. Ithaca, N. Y.: Cornell University Press, 1961.

Grieb, Kenneth J. *The United States and Huerta*. Lincoln: University of Nebraska Press, 1968.
Guzmán, Martín Luis. *Memoirs of Pancho Villa*. Austin: University of Texas Press, 1965.
Tannenbaum, Frank. *Mexico—The Struggle for Peace and Bread*. New York: Alfred A. Knopf, 1956.

MARVIN ALISKY

VILLALBA, JÓVITO (1908–   ), was head of what for several decades was one of Venezuela's principal political parties. One of the three principal leaders in February 1928 of the Student Week protest against the dictatorship of Juan Vicente Gómez,* Villalba spent most of the rest of the Gómez regime in jail, being exiled to Trinidad only about a year befoe Gómez' death. After Gómez died in December 1935, Villalba returned as leader of the Venezuelan Students Federation (FEV) and then head of its Political Organization.

The FEV-Political Organization joined in establishing the National Democratic party (PDN), and Villalba was named PDN secretary general. However, in February 1937 the government of General Eleazar López Contreras* exiled him once again.

When he returned home, Jóvito Villalba did not rejoin the PDN, nor did he become a member of its legal successor, Acción Democrática (AD). During the administration of López Contreras' successor, General Isaías Medina Angarita,* Villalba was elected an independent senator. In 1945 he supported Medina's hand-picked successor in the election campaign cut short by the coup of October 18, 1945, which brought AD to power for the first time, with Rómulo Betancourt* as provisional president.

Early in 1946 Jóvito Villalba joined the Republican Democratic Union (URD), a new party established by some of these asociated with the Medina government. He soon became the virtually undisputed leader of that party. The URD was bitterly critical of the Acción Democrática (AD) governments of Rómulo Betancourt and Rómulo Gallegos.*

When the government of President Gallegos was overthrown in November 1948, Jóvito Villalba and the URD strongly supported the new military regime, although urging it to return to constitutional democracy as soon as possible. Several leaders of URD held key positions in the regime for some time, although Villalba was not among those.

By the time of the election called by the military regime late in 1952, however, Villalba and the URD were in strong opposition to the dictatorship. They received the support of the underground AD as a result of which the URD won the election. However, Colonel Marcos Pérez Jiménez* stopped the counting of ballots and proclaimed himself president. Jóvito Villalba was deported and spent the rest of the Pérez Jiménez regime in exile in the United States.

Returning home after the fall of Pérez Jiménez in January 1958, Villalba dedicated himself to rebuilding the URD. In the election of December 1958, the

URD supported the candidacy of Admiral Wolfgang Larrazábal and became the second largest party, outdistanced only by AD.

For a year and a half, the URD was represented in the cabinet of President Betancourt. But by the time of the 1963 election, it was strongly in opposition, and Jóvito Villalba was the first person to announce his candidacy for president. He came in third, and the strength of the URD in the congressional election was much reduced. The URD again served in the cabinet of President Raúl Leoni,* but then went into the opposition. In 1968 Villalaba and the URD, together with three other parties, supported an "independent" candidate.

Five years later, the URD again began to participate in an electoral coalition, the New Force. When that coalition failed to choose Villalba as its presidential nominee, the URD withdrew and ran him on its own. Again he was badly defeated, coming in fifth, with only 3.07 percent of the total vote. The URD was no longer a major party.

In 1978 Jóvito Villalba supported the Social Christian Copei nominee, Luis Herrera Campins.* Copei supported some URD congressional candidates, and Jóvito Villalba returned to the Senate. Finally, in 1983, with his nemesis Rómulo Betancourt dead, Villalba at last endorsed the successful Acción Democrática candidate, Jaime Lusinchi.*

BIBLIOGRAPHY

Alexander, Robert J. "Chile," in Robert J. Alexander (ed.) *Political Parties of the Americas*, Vol 1. Westport, Conn.: Greenwood Press, 1982.
———. *Rómulo Betancourt and the Transformation of Venezuela*. New Brunswick, N. J.: Transactions Press, 1982.
Betancourt, Rómulo. *Venezuela: Oil and Politics*. Boston: Houghton Mifflin, 1979.
Blank, David Eugene. *Venezuela: Politics in a Petroleum Republic*. New York: Praeger, 1984.
Magallanes, Manuel Vicente. *Los Partidus Políticos en la Evolución Histórica de Venezuela*. Caracas: Monte Avila Editores, 1977.

ROBERT J. ALEXANDER

VILLANUEVA, ARMANDO (1915–   ), presidential candidate of the Peruvian Aprista Party (PAP) in 1980 and member of its Political Commission, received his basic education in religious schools and studied journalism at the National University of San Marcos. At the age of 15 he joined the PAP, and shortly before his eighteenth birthday co-founded the Aprista Youth Federation and became its first secretary general. Because of his ideas and underground work against the military-oligarchical administrations, Villanueva suffered imprisonment (1934, 1938–1940, 1941, and 1948–1952) and banishment from his country (1941–1945, 1952–1956, and 1975). While abroad, he practiced journalism and served as secretary general of the Coordinating Committee of Aprista Exiles.

In 1945, Villanueva was elected to the National Executive Committee of the PAP, and in 1963 he became its secretary general, a position to which he was reelected several times. From 1963 to 1968 Villanueva was a member of the

Chamber of Deputies, over which he presided from 1967 to 1968. In 1985 he was elected senator for a five-year term.

BIBLIOGRAPHY

Alisky, Marvin. *Historical Dictionary of Peru*. Metuchen, N. J.: Scarecrow Press, 1979.
Chang-Rodríguez, Eugenio. *Opciones políticas peruanas*. Lima: Centro Documentación Andina, 1985.
Rójas Samanéz, Alvaro. *Partidos políticos en el Peru*. Lima: Centro de Documentación e Información Andina, 1984.

EUGENIO CHANG-RODRÍGUEZ

VILLARROEL LÓPEZ, GUALBERTO (1908–1946), was the third in a line of reformist military presidents which preceded the 1952 Bolivian National Revolution. Born in the department of of Cochabamba, Villarroel attended grade school and high school in the city of Cochabamba. He entered the military college in 1925 and graduated in 1928. He served in the Chaco War and in 1935 was promoted to captain. He entered the Superior War College and became a major in 1940. By 1943 he was in a junior position in the General High Command of the army.

Although Villarroel was a relatively unknown military figure, he became president of the first government in which the Nationalist Revolutionary Movement (MNR) participated. His influence derived from his commanding position in the military lodge called "Reason of the Fatherland," which joined with the MNR in the revolt of December 20, 1943. Serving as provisional president until August 6, 1944, Villarroel was elected constitutional president for 1944–1948 by a national convention. The new government was branded by the tin interests, the political parties of the left, and the U. S. State Department as "Nazi-Fascist," and was denied recognition by most governments in the hemisphere until the removal of the MNR from the cabinet in June 1944. However, by January 1945 MNR leaders had returned to the cabinet. The national Congress and nascent labor movement were rent by rivalry between the MNR and the Revolutionary Left Party (PIR) of José Antonio Arze.* Coup attempts in November 1944 and June 1945 were occasions for the murder and imprisonment of many opposition party leaders. This brought about the alliance of the Stalinist PIR and the conservative parties in the Democratic Antifascist Front against Villarroel's government.

The Villarroel rule benefited labor and the urban middle classes. Its reforms threatened the entrenched power elite. A new 1945 constitution reaffirmed the principles of economic nationalism and social welfare, and interests of the state over individualism. The government forced companies to sell 60 percent of foreign exchange earnings to the state and increased tax revenues. Pro-labor laws protected job security and the right to unionization. The MNR gained leadership of the Federation of Mine Workers in 1944: the PIR controlled most nonmining workers.

A major move of the Villarroel government was convocation of the First National Indian Congress in May 1945. A National Federation of Campesinos was formed and two decrees abolished the free labor service obligations of the Indian peasantry on haciendas and in mines. Although land reform was not considered and the rural landlords ignored the new reforms, for the first time the Indian was mobilized as a potential political power base.

The popularity of some Villarroel reforms did not protect the regime from the chaotic political environment. On July 21, 1946, street demonstrations by students, striking teachers, and railworkers overran the presidential palace. Villarroel and several close associates were seized and strung up from lampposts in the main plaza. Villarroel thus became a martyr of the forthcoming 1952 Revolution.

BIBLIOGRAPHY

Baptista Gumucio, Mariano. *Historia Contemporánea de Bolivia, 1930–1978.* 2d ed. La Paz: Gisbert, 1978.

Céspedes, Augusto. *El President Colgado: Historia Boliviana.* 2d ed. La Paz: Juventud, 1971.

Fellman Velarde, José. *Historia de Bolivia, La Bolivianidad Semicolonial.* Vol. 3. Cochabamba: Los Amigos del Libro, 1981.

Ríos Reinaga, David. *Civiles y Militares en la Revolución Boliviana, 1943–1966.* La Paz: Difusión, 1967.

WALTRAUD QUEISER MORALES

VILLEDA MORALES, RAMÓN (1908–1971), led a revived Liberal party back to power in Honduras after a long period of National Party rule. He was born in Ocotepeque, studied medicine at the National University of Honduras, where he was president of the Federation of University Students, and began practicing medicine. In 1936 he married Alejandra Bermúdez Milla, a schoolteacher from a politically active Liberal family. The two pursued graduate studies in Berlin. In 1940 he established a private clinic in Tegucigalpa.

After Tiburcio Carías Andino* turned over power in December 1948 to Juan Manuel Gálvez Durón,* who began to relax the Carías dictatorship, Villeda Morales helped reorganize the Liberal Party and emerged as party chairman in 1949. He founded a daily newspaper, *El Pueblo*, and managed a vigorous campaign in the 1953 municipal elections.

Named Liberal presidential candidate in the October 1954 election, Villeda won a plurality over Carías Andino, the nominee of one faction of the National Party, and over General Abraham Williams, the candidate of a dissident faction of that party. Nationalist deputies refused to attend the session of Congress to choose between the two top nominees, and after President Gálvez went to Panama for medical treatment, Vice President Julio Lozano Díaz proclaimed himself constitutional dictator on December 5, 1954. Lozano exiled Villeda Morales, who went to Costa Rica.

After fraudulent elections on October 7, 1956, which Lozano claimed to have won, a military *golpe* expelled him and set up a three-man military junta. It appointed Villeda Morales ambassador to the United States. The September 22, 1957 elections gave the Liberal party a smashing victory. On November 16, Congress elected Villeda Morales president, and he was inaugurated on December 11.

During Villeda's term, more schools, health centers, roads, and bridges were built than existed when he took office. A modern labor code was adopted. The United States and various international organizations granted loans and technical assistance to build roads and a hydroelectric plant, and to diversify agriculture and grazing. Two new peasant movements pressed for an agrarian reform law, approved September 29, 1962, which established a progressive land tax on unused land and created an Agrarian Institute to settle landless peasants on publicly owned land.

On October 3, 1963, ten days before scheduled presidential elections, the armed forces under Colonel Oswaldo López Arrellano* ousted Villeda Morales to prevent the election of Modesto Rodas Alvarado, the Liberal candidate, who strongly supported presidential control over the armed forces. Villeda Morales went into exile. He died of a heart attack in New York shortly after López Arrellano appointed him ambassador to the United States.

BIBLIOGRAPHY

Baciu, Stefan. *Ramón Villeda Morales, Ciudadano de America*. San José, Costa Rica: Litografía Lehmann, 1970.

Kantor, Harry. *Patterns of Politics and Political Systems in Latin America*. Chicago: Rand McNally, 1969.

Morris, James A. *Honduras, Caudillo Politics and Military Rulers*. Boulder, Colo.: Westview Press, 1984.

Pearson, Neale J. "Peasant Pressure Groups and Agrarian Reform in Honduras, 1962–1977," in William P. Avery, Richard E. Lonsdale, and Ivan Volgyes (eds.). *Rural Change and Public Policy, Eastern Europe, Latin America and Australia*. New York: Pergamon Press, 1980.

NEALE J. PEARSON

VINCENT, STÉNIO (1874–1959), was president of Haiti at the time the U. S. military occupation came to an end. A member of the mulatto elite, he had an extensive career as a lawyer and diplomat, serving in Paris, Berlin, and the Hague. During the U. S. occupation, he headed the anti-interventionist Nationalist Party and the Patriotic Union, which demanded withdrawal of U. S. troops.

In November 1930 Vincent was elected president by the National Assembly, and in 1934 he visited the United States and convinced President Franklin D. Roosevelt to withdraw the U. S. Marines occupation force. In 1935 his tenure in office was extended for five years by a referendum.

As president, Vincent was widely regarded as antiblack. He was particularly suspicious of the army which the U. S. Marines had left behind, which was predominantly officered by blacks. He built up his own special presidential guard, and his policy was to deposit the army's weapons in the presidential palace.

When, in 1941, Vincent again sought to have his period in office extended, Washington suggested that another extension would be unwise. He then finally retired, pleading "ill health," giving way to President Élie Lescot,* another member of the mulatto elite. He remained in Haiti and died in Port-au-Prince.

BIBLIOGRAPHY

Logan, R. W. *Haiti and the Dominican Republic*. London: Oxford University Press, 1986.
Rothberg, Robert I. *Haiti: The Politics of Squalor*. Boston: Houghton Mifflin, 1971.
Weinstein, Brian, and Aaron Segal. *Haiti: Political Failures, Cultural Successes*. New York: Praeger, 1984.

PERCY C. HINTZEN

VOLIO JIMÉNEZ, JORGE (1882–1955), was one of Costa Rica's more colorful and influential politicians of the 1920s. He studied at the University of Louvain in Belgium, where progressive Cardinal Mercier strongly influenced him. A Catholic priest, he gave up his calling in 1915, but he took seriously the social Christian philosophy and was deeply moved by the poverty and social injustice he perceived around him. As a political activist, he fought the tyranny of Federico Tinoco Granados.* After Tinoco resigned, Volio returned from exile in Nicaragua and founded the Reformist Party in 1923.

The Reformist Party was the first true political party in Costa Rica, organized around a body of ideas, not a personality. It challenged the benign rule of the liberal patriarchs and the economic domination of the coffee barons. Volio addressed the problems of low wages, poor working conditions, inadequate housing, and unemployment, and demanded that the government act to narrow the gap between the poor and the rich. In 1924 he ran for president in a three-way contest, in which no candidate received a majority. Volio, despite insistence that there could be no compromise with the status quo, gave his support to Ricardo Jiménez Oreamuno* and accepted the post of vice president.

In 1926, Volio tried to overthrow Jiménez, who sent him abroad to seek psychiatric care. After this episode, Volio never recovered his influence, although he was actually a deputy in the national congress at the time of his death.

BIBLIOGRAPHY

Ameringer, Charles D. *Democracy in Costa Rica*. New York: Praeger, 1982.
Barohona Jiménez, Luis. *El pensamiento político en Costa Rica*. San José: Editorial Fernández-Arce, 1971.
Creedman, Theodore S. *Historical Dictionary of Costa Rica*. Metuchen, N. J.: Scarecrow Press, 1977.

CHARLES D. AMERINGER

W

WALCOTT, FRANK LESLIE (1916–), was the principal organizer of the labor movement of Barbados and a major figure in stimulating mass participation in politics. He received his formal education at Wesley Hall Boys School. He became an early associate of Sir Grantley Herbert Adams* and Hugh Springer* in the Barbados Labour Party (BLP) and Barbados Workers Union (BWU), formed in 1938. He was first elected in 1945 as a BLP member of the House of Assembly, a seat he would hold for most of the next three decades. In the 1970s he would serve in the appointed upper house, the Senate.

In 1948 Walcott served as a member of the government's Executive Committee, representing the BLP. Shortly afterward, following a major BLP electoral victory, a serious split developed between Walcott and Grantley Adams. The governor asked Adams to assume leadership of the new semiministerial government. Agreeing to do so, he resigned his position as secretary general of the BWU, sensing a possible conflict-of-interest arising from holding both posts. Walcott succeeded Adams in his BWU post, and Adams expected that he would thereupon resign from the cabinet. When Walcott refused, Adams finally forced him out.

Subsequently, when a revolt within the BLP in 1955 produced the Democratic Labour Party (DLP), Walcott led the BWU into alignment with the DLP. The support of the Barbados Workers Union was a major element in the victory of the DLP at the end of 1961 and its maintenance in power for 15 years. Walcott served in the cabinet of Prime Minister Errol Walton Barrow* for some years.

Walcott remained BWU secretary general for nearly 40 years. He led in the establishment of collective bargaining as the normal pattern of labor relations in the island and in the achievement of one of the highest levels of living of any workers in the Caribbean area. He also remained one of the most powerful figures in national politics.

BIBLIOGRAPHY

Knowles, William. *Trade Union Development and Industrial Relations in the British West Indies.* Berkeley: University of California Press, 1959.

Mark, Francis. *The History of the Barbados Workers Union*. Bridgetown, Barbados: Advocate Press, 1965.

Will, W. Marvin. "Barbados." in Jack W. Hopkins (ed.). *Latin America and Caribbean Contemporary Record*. Vols. 2 and 3. New York: Holmes and Meier, 1984 and 1985.

————. "Political Development in the Mini-State Caribbean." Ph.D. diss., University of Missouri-Columbia, 1972.

PERCY C. HINTZEN AND W. MARVIN WILL

WALKER, WILLIAM (1824–1860), a North American adventurer who took over the government of Nicaragua in 1856–1857 and united the rest of Central America against him, was born in Nashville, Tennessee. He graduated from the University of Nashville at age 14 and from the University of Pennsylvania Medical School at 19.

Walker had a career as a journalist in New Orleans and San Francisco. In 1853–1854 he was involved in an ill-fated expedition to occupy Mexico's Baja California. In 1854 the Nicaraguan Liberals, seeking to unseat the Conservative government of the time, sought help from Byron Cole, who owned the San Francisco paper for which Walker then worked. Cole turned to Walker, who soon mustered a comic opera force of 58 men, which arrived in Nicaragua on June 1, 1855.

Walker's first battle was an attack on the town of Rivas, where Ponciano Corral, perhaps the ablest Conservative commander, had barricaded the streets. Although Walker's force was not able to win control of Rivas, they reduced Corral's forces from 500 men to 200, while losing only six dead and five wounded. Walker was soon joined by Cole and 20 new volunteers, and went to Chinandega, where he augmented his forces by another 100 men. Ignoring orders from Liberal leader Francisco Castellón to go to Léon, Walker's force went to Virgin Bay, principal harbor on Lake Nicaragua, operated by Cornelius Vanderbilt's trans-isthmus company. After a three-hour battle, the Conservatives fled.

Walker and his 230 men then captured Granada, the Conservative capital, at which point the Conservatives agreed to negotiate. The resulting agreement provided for a single army, with Walker as commander-in-chief, the sharing of government posts by Conservatives and Liberals, and a minor Conservative figure, Patricio Rivas, as president. Rivas was inaugurated on December 1, 1855.

In the following months, a Costa Rican force, subsidized by Cornelius Vanderbilt, with whom Walker had quarreled, invaded Nicaragua and was defeated more by cholera than by Walker's troops. After a quarrel between Walker and President Rivas, fraudulent elections were held on June 29, 1856, in which Walker was declared victor.

Soon after Walker's election, Honduras, El Salvador, and Guatemala formed an alliance against him. It finally triumphed on May 1, 1857, when Walker surrendered to the captain of a U. S. warship off the Pacific Coast. Two later attempts by Walker to return proved unsuccessful. On September 13, 1860, he was executed by a Honduran firing squad at Trujillo, on the north coast.

BIBLIOGRAPHY

Gerson, Noel B. *Sad Swashbuckler, The Life of William Walker.* Nashville and New York: Thomas Nelson Inc., 1976.
Rosengarten, Frederic, Jr. *Freebooters Must Die!* Wayne, Pa.: Haverford House Publishers, 1976.
Scroggs, William O. *Filibusters and Financiers.* New York: Macmillan Co., 1916.
Soto V., Marco Antonio. *Guerra Nacional de Centro América.* Guatemala: Editorial del Ministerio de Educación Publica, 1957.
Walker, William. *The War in Nicaragua.* Detroit: Ethridge Books, 1971.

NEALE J. PEARSON

WALTER, GEORGE HERBERT (1928–   ), was premier of Antigua and Barbuda between 1971 and 1976. He completed primary school and received some secondary education in Antigua. He joined the Antigua Trade and Labour Union (ATLU) during the 1950s and became the union's general secretary and primary negotiator. He acquired the reputation as an effective representative of the workers.

During the 1960s Walter became concerned about the conflict of interest in the highest reaches of government: many government officials also were executives of the ATLU. He led a group of the union's middle-level leaders in asking that the premier, Vere Cornwall Bird*, and other government ministers resign from either their government or union positions. When Bird refused, Walter and his followers left the ATLU and formed a rival Antigua Workers Union (AWU), which immediately attracted a large number of workers.

Walter also formed the country's first real political party, the Progressive Labour Movement (PLM), in April 1968. Formerly, politics was organized through the political committee of the ATLU, which used the name Antigua Labour Party (ALP), although not formally organized as a political party. With formation of the PLM, Walter resigned his position in the AWU.

Both parties contested the general elections in 1971, and Walter led his PLM to a stunning victory, winning 13 of the 17 seats. Walter became premier and immediately set about the task of agricultural development while closing down the last of the sugar factories on the island, which had been a financial disaster. His government expanded livestock production for both internal consumption and export, revived the production of sea island cotton, and developed fruit and vegetable output. It also established a social security system and comprehensive labor legislation.

In the elections of 1976 the PLM, despite capturing a majority of the popular vote, was defeated by Bird's ALP. Walter became Leader of the Opposition. In 1980 his party won only 3 seats in the Legislative council. Walter continued as Leader of the Opposition after independence was achieved in 1981.

BIBLIOGRAPHY

Alexander, Robert J. "Antigua," in Robert J. Alexander (ed.) *Political Parties of the Americas*. Vol. 1. Westport, Conn.: Greenwood Press, 1982.

Carmody, C. M. "First Among Equals: Antiguan Patterns of Local Level Leadership." Ph.D. diss., New York University, 1978.

Richards, Novell H. *The Struggle and the Conquest: Twenty-five Years of Social Democracy in Antigua*. St. Johns: Workers Voice, 1964.

PERCY C. HINTZEN AND W. MARVIN WILL

WEEKS, GEORGE (1921–), was one of the most influential figures in the politics and trade union movement of Trinidad from the 1960s. After leaving school at age 14 to work on his father's small farm, at the beginning of World War II he joined the West Indian Regiment and was trained in the United States. While in Newport News, Virginia, Weeks became sensitized to racism, especially the U. S. variant. Later, his sense of racial injustice was deepened by de facto segregation between the British Regiment and troops from Britain's colonial possessions.

After the war, Weeks joined the party of Tubal Uriah Butler,* became active in the Oilfield Workers Trade Union (OWTU), and was elected Executive Council member and then vice president and president of the union's most important branch. He soon gained full control of the branch. He attacked the national leadership of the union for conservative pro-company sentiments and undemocratic practices.

Weeks was instrumental in forcing the union to call a strike in 1960, out of which came large wage concessions and greatly increased benefits. He was elected president general of the OWTU in 1962.

Weeks used the union as a base for forging a political alliance between the black and East Indian workers. In 1965, as president of the National Trade Union Congress, he was instrumental in mobilizing support for a strike by sugar workers. The government immediately declard a state of emergency and implemented an Industrial Stabilization Act which Weeks strongly opposed.

In 1970 the Black Power Movement emerged primarily as a result of Weeks' union action. At its height, the movement involved massive demonstrations, strikes, civil unrest, and an army mutiny. Weeks and two officers of the OWTU were among the first to be detained after the government declared a state of emergency on April 21, 1970. He remained imprisoned for seven months.

Weeks led in the formation in 1975 of the United Labour Front (ULF), an alliance among unions and parties representing the predominantly East Indian sugar workers, the OWTU, and the Transport and Industrial Workers Trade Union, a radical union with close ties to Weeks. A month after its formation, the ULF leadership staged a march for "Peace, Bread and Justice" which was broken up by the police. Weeks was again arrested.

The ULF contested national elections in 1976, capturing 10 of 36 elective seats in Parliament and becoming the official oposition. George Weeks, however, was unable to win a seat because he failed to galvanize black unionists against the predominantly black PNM. However, Weeks was appointed a senator and argued for a revolutionary transformation of the country's political economy, particularly nationalization of foreign investments.

Unable to overcome ideological and racial divisions within the ULF leadership, the radicals, led by Weeks, resigned their positions in 1977. Weeks, however, continued working through his union.

BIBLIOGRAPHY

Hintzen, Percy C. "The Cost of Regime Survival: Racial Mobilization, Elite Domination and Control of the State in Guyana and Trinidad," unpublished manuscript, University of California, Berkeley, 1985.
Oilfield Workers Trade Union: July 1937–1977. San Fernando, Trinidad: OWTU, 1977.
Oxaal, Ivar. *Race and Revolutionary Consciousness.* Cambridge, Mass.: Schenkman 1971.
Ryan, Selwyn. *Race and Nationalism in Trinidad and Tobago.* Toronto: University of Toronto Press, 1972.
Weeks, George. *Why I Resigned.* Pamphlet of the Oilfield Workers Trade Union, San Fernando, Trinidad, 1965.

PERCY C. HINTZEN AND W. MARVIN WILL

WHEATLEY, WILLARD (1915–   ), was chief minister of the British Virgin Islands during most of the 1970s. He got his primary schooling in the British Virgin Islands, and then went to the government Teaching College in Trinidad and the University of Nottingham. He was a teacher for 35 years and permanent secretary of the Ministry of Natural Resources and Public Health for four years. He was first elected to the Legislative Council in 1971 as an independent, but he joined with two members of the Democratic Party to form the government, of which he became chief minister. In 1978 he was again elected to the Council, that time by the United Party, but he abandoned that party to continue as chief minister, with the support of the Virgin Islands party. He ceased being chief minister after the election of 1979.

BIBLIOGRAPHY

Alexander, Robert J. "British Virgin Islands," in Robert J. Alexander (ed.). *Political Parties of the Americas.* Vol. 1. Westport, Conn.: Greenwood Press, 1982.
Personalities Caribbean, Seventh Edition 1982–83. Binghamton, N. Y.: Vail Ballou Press, n.d.

ROBERT J. ALEXANDER

WICKHAM, CLENNEL WILSDEN (1895–1938), was one of the major precursors of the mass political movement that emerged in Barbados during the 1930s. After serving with the British West Indies Regiment during World War I, he returned to Barbados and joined the staff of the *Herald*, a left-of-center weekly, through which he aroused the political consciousness of the Barbadian masses.

Wickham joined with Charles Duncan O'Neale* in launching the Democratic League in 1924, of which the *Herald* became the semiofficial spokesman. The successes of the league—electing members of the assembly from 1924 to 1936, in spite of the severe limitation of the franchise—were largely due to Wickham's campaigns in the *Herald*.

In 1930 Wickham wrote an attack in the *Herald* on those he alleged were putting financial pressure on the paper. The result was a libel suit which Wickham and the paper lost, forcing the *Herald* into bankruptcy. Shortly thereafter, Wickham moved to Grenada, where he lived until his death. He has come to be known as the "greatest interpreter of the aspirations of the common people that Barbados has ever known."

BIBLIOGRAPHY

Hoyos, F. A. *Barbados: A History*. London: Macmillan Co., 1973.
———. *Builders of Barbados*. London: Macmillan Co., 1973.
———. *Our Common Heritage*. Bridgetown, Barbados: Advocate Press, 1953.
Wickham, John. "Clennel Wickham: A Man for All Time." in *New World Quarterly* 3, Nos. 1 and 2.

PERCY C. HINTZEN AND W. MARVIN WILL

WILLIAMS, ERIC (1911–1981), was prime minister of Trinidad and Tobago from the time it gained independence from Great Britain in 1962 until his death. The son of a civil servant, he studied at Queen's Royal College in Trinidad and in 1931 won the Island Scholarship to Oxford University where he received a Ph.D. in modern history in 1938.

In 1939 Williams became an assistant professor at Howard University and betwen 1940 and 1942 was able to travel to Cuba, Puerto Rico, Haiti, and the Dominican Republic as a recipient of a Julian Rosenwald Fellowship to conduct research that led to the publication of three volumes.

In 1944 Williams joined the staff of the Anglo-American Caribbean Commission, formed jointly by Britain and the United States to further social and economic cooperation within the Caribbean and to coordinate research efforts. He resigned this post in 1946 but was named duputy chairman of the Caribbean Research Council of a restructured commission in 1948.

Williams remained with the commission until 1955. During his last year in this office he became increasingly hostile toward what he considered the colonial character of the commission. When it refused to renew his contract, he called a public meeting in Port of Spain, which marked his entry into the nationalist politics of Trinidad and Tobago.

Over the next six months Williams gave a series of public lectures while making preparations to start a new political party, the Peoples National Movement

(PNM), launched on January 24, 1956. He conducted 109 political meetings throughout the twin-island colony between January and September 1956 and turned the new party into the most powerful political organization in the country.

The PNM won the September 1956 elections, and Williams was made chief minister: he remained head of government, in one capacity or another, for the remainder of his life. He began a program of industrialization based on the country's oil resources.

Williams launched a campaign in 1957 to remove an American military base from the colony, seeing it as a blatant symbol of foreign domination. He also began a campaign for full self-government as a prelude to independence. Britain was induced to concede on both issues by 1960. Williams then led the PNM to a massive electoral victory in 1961. The new government immediately prepared and circulated a Draft Constitution for an independent Trinidad and Tobago, which was granted on August 31, 1962. Williams became the first prime minister.

One noted failure of the Williams pre-independence government was over the issue of federation. An ardent integrationist, Williams fought hard for a centralized federal government. Unable to sufficiently influence the eventual federal structure, which was inaugurated as the West Indies Federation in 1958, Williams saw the experiment fail in 1962, when Jamaica seceded. Upon hearing the news, Williams also withdrew his country from the federation.

Williams' efforts at integration were revived after independence. In 1966, upon his initiative, a Caribbean Free Trade Area was organized with Antigua, Barbados, and Guyana. It was soon expanded to embrace all the Anglophone Caribbean except the Bahamas, which did not join until 1983. In 1973, the Free Trade Area became the Caribbean Community and Common Market (Caricom).

Domestically, Williams oversaw fundamental reform of the public service sector as well as educational reform. He embarked on a second Five-Year Development Plan, presented in 1963, with primary emphasis on import substitution industrialization.

In 1968 Williams formulated a highly comprehensive third Five-Year Development Plan aimed at creation of a "peoples sector," including small-scale industry, handicrafts, and service activities. The new plan focused on development of the locally owned capitalist sector as "the pivot of efforts at economic transformation," with emphasis on private rather than public enterprises. However, an oil-related economic crisis which sparked serious political disturbances in 1970, as well as serious opposition to the Williams government between 1970 and 1973, hampered fulfillment of the Third Development Plan.

After 1973 Williams used revenue generated by the phenomenal increase in the price of oil to embark on an industrialization and massive state spending program. The result was tremendous growth in the economy and an explosion in the income level of the entire Trinidadian population. The state became the major investor in the economy, with most foreign enterprises being relegated to partnership status.

BIBLIOGRAPHY

Bryan, Anthony. Chapter in Richard Millett and M. Marvin Will (eds.). *The Restless Caribbean*. New York: Praeger, 1979.

Deosaran, R. *Eric Williams: The Man, His Ideas, His Politics*. Port of Spain: Signum, 1981.

Oxaal, Ivar. *Black Intellectuals Come to Power*. Cambridge, Mass.: Schenkman, 1968.

Ryan, Selwyn. *Race and Nationalism in Trinidad and Tobago*. Toronto: University of Toronto Press, 1974.

Williams, Eric E. *Inward Hunger: The Education of a Prime Minister*. London: Andre Deutsch, 1969.

PERCY C. HINTZEN AND W. MARVIN WILL

Y

YRIGOYEN, HIPÓLITO (1852–1933), was twice president of Argentina and was the longtime leader of the Radical Civic Union (UCR), founded by his uncle, Leandro Nicebro Alem.* Until passage of the Rogue Sáenz Peña* laws in 1912, the UCR abstained from elections to protest electoral fraud.

Hipólito Yrigoyen was born in Buenos Aires. He became interested in politics at an early age and held a number of minor governmental positions before becoming a police official and member of the Buenos Aires provincial legislature. He worked with his uncle in the 1890 Radical revolution and was named police chief of Buenos Aires. In 1893 Yrigoyen became president of the Radical Party. He solidified his control over the party after his uncle's suicide in 1896.

When Yrigoyen was elected president in 1916, he faced serious economic difficulties because World War I had interrupted Argentina's traditional trade patterns with Europe, and because new groups in society were making economic demands. He kept Argentina neutral during the war and responded to increased labor militancy with a show of force.

In 1918 there were many strikes, which culminated in a mass demonstration of 150,000 workers in January 1919. Yrigoyen sent military forces to attack the demonstrators, and the clash resulted in many injuries and deaths during the week of rioting and fighting that followed (the "Semana Tragica"). Although opposed to the old oligarchy, the Radicals under Yrigoyen were not sympathetic to the demands for change coming from the working class.

Two major changes did occur under Yrigoyen. First, in the University Reform of 1918, the professors were now to be chosen on the basis of merit rather than political or personal connections within the oligarchy. Students obtained a role in university administration, the curriculum was reorganized to fit more closely with national needs, and new teaching methods were introduced. These University Reforms spread throughout Latin America.

Second, in June 1922, Yrigoyen signed the decree creating a government oil firm, Yacimientos Petrolíferos Fiscales (YPF), with control over the development of Argentina's petroleum resources. YPF was responsible for the exploration and production of Argentina's oil, and controlled and regulated the activities of any private or foreign company engaged in the oil business.

Yrigoyen's first term was also notable for his use of the presidential power of "intervention." He removed provincial governments over 20 times. Most of these officials were Conservatives, representing the old oligarchical interests, and critics charged that many of Yrigoyen's acts were motivated by narrow political advantage. The man who had fought so long for electoral reform used presidential power to impose his choices on the nation.

In 1922 Yrigoyen was succeeded in the presidency by Marcelo T. de Alvear. The Radical Party was fragmented at the time into the Personalists, who supported Yrigoyen, and the anti-Personalists, led by de Alvear.

In 1928 Yrigoyen was reelected president but he was unable to exert any leadership to meet the economic and social problems provoked by the Great Depression. Extensive corruption in high governmental circles further undermined national confidence. On September 6, 1930, Yrigoyen was overthrown in a coup led by General José F. Uriburu.

BIBLIOGRAPHY

Gálvez, Manuel. *Vida de Hipólito Yrigoyen: El hombre del misterio*. Buenos Aires: 1939.
Luna, Féliz. *Yrigoyen, el templario de la libertad*. Buenos Aires: 1954.
Rock, David. *Politics in Argentina, 1890–1930: The Rise and Fall of Radicalism*. New York: Cambridge Latin American Studies, 1975.
Smith, Peter H. *Argentina and the Failure of Democracy, 1904–1955*. Madison: University of Wisconsin Press, 1974.
Snow, Peter G. *Argentine Radicalism: The History and Doctrine of the Radical Civic Union*. Iowa City: University of Iowa Press, 1965.

JOHN T. DEINER

Z

ZAPATA, EMILIANO

ZAPATA, EMILIANO (1879–1919), principal agrarian leader in the Mexican Revolution after 1910, was born in the state of Morelos to a family of peasant farmers. He worked as a stableboy and a sharecropper. In 1910–1911 he quickly established himself as a general by winning battles via ambushes of the regular army. Impatient with President Francisco I. Madero's* slowness in getting land for peasants, Zapata disavowed his allegiance to Madero in November 1911. With a lawyer, Antonio Díaz Soto y Gama, phrasing his proclamations for him, marginally literate Zapata recruited a large army with the promise of "Land, Bread and Justice." In 1915 he ignored the orders of President Venustiano Carranza* and began his own land reform program.

After his military operations had been reduced to guarding the ramparts of the state of Morelos, he got word that an army colonel wanted to turn over large numbers of arms to *zapatistas* to insure that their lands would not be confiscated. When Zapata rode to take possession of the arsenal on April 10, 1919, he was shot in the back.

BIBLIOGRAPHY

Dunn, Harry H. *Zapata*. New York: Crimson Press, 1934.
Gruening, Ernest. *Mexico and its Heritage*. New York: Century Publishers, 1928.
Millon, Robert P. *Ideology of a Peasant Revolution, Zapata*. New York: International Publishers, 1969.
Womack, John, Jr. *Zapata and the Mexican Revolution*. New York: Vintage Books, 1968.

MARVIN ALISKY

ZAYAS Y ALFONSO, ALFREDO

ZAYAS Y ALFONSO, ALFREDO (1861–1934), served as president of Cuba from 1921 to 1925. He earned a law degree and in 1896 was serving as a member of the Autonomist Party Junta Central, when he was imprisoned by Spanish General Valeriano Weyler. Upon release a year later, Zayas joined the revolutionary forces. Following the defeat of the Spanish, he served in the Department of Justice under the administration of General Leonard Wood.

Alfredo Zayas, a long-time member of the Liberal Party, served as vice president during the José Miguel Gómez* administration (1909–1913) but was defeated for the presidency in 1912, when a feud with Gómez gave the election to the Conservatives. When the Liberals refused him the nomination in 1920, Zayas formed the Partido Popular which, with backing of the Conservatives, gave him victory over his old Liberal Party mentor, Gómez. His administration was the most corrupt up to that time in Cuban history. Bribery, tax frauds, grafting in customs, and manipulation of lottery collectorships were all used for personal enrichment by Zayas, his family and friends.

Another hallmark of the Zayas administration was the "special relationships" between the Cuban president and the U. S. presidential envoy, General Enoch Crowder. Originally appointed by President Wilson to set Cuba's financial house in order, Crowder soon became adviser to President Zayas. Throughout 1922, Crowder virtually ran the nation, telling the Cuban president what to spend and hand-picking a new "honest cabinet" in an effort to deal with the rampant corruption. Only when Zayas received a $50 million loan from the Morgan bank in 1923 did he dismiss the "honest cabinet" chosen by his U.S. mentor.

The later years of Zayas' administration witnessed a resurgence of the economy as sugar prices began to rebound. In response to Zayas' rule, there emerged a generation of militant young people dedicated to revitalizing their nation; this radical backlash was Zayas' only lasting legacy.

BIBLIOGRAPHY

Aguilar, Luis. *Cuba 1933: Prologue to Revolution*. Ithaca, N. Y.: Cornell University Press, 1972.
Strode, Hudson. *The Pageant of Cuba*. New York: Harrison Smith and Robert Haas, 1934.
Suchlicki, Jaime. *University Students and Revolution in Cuba 1920–1968*. Coral Gables, Fla.: University of Miami Press, 1969.
Thomas, Hugh. *Cuba: The Pursuit of Freedom*. New York: Harper and Row, 1971.

STEPHEN J. WRIGHT

ZELAYA, JOSÉ SANTOS (1853–1919), was president of Nicaragua between 1893 and 1909. In 1859 Nicaragua had entered a period in which Conservatives from Granada succeeded one another in office every four years. The circle was broken when, after the death of Evaristo Caraza (1887–1889), Vice President Roberto Sacasa was unable to finish his term of office. A Conservative, General Francisco Gutiérrez, began the revolt, and Liberal forces led by General Santos Zelaya, supported Gutiérrez and drove Sacasa out of office. He was succeeded by Salvador Machado, another Conservative, but in July 1893, the Liberals staged their own revolt, and Zelaya became president.

With a Positivist outlook acquired through years of study in France, Zelaya worked to separate church and state, especially in education. He built libraries,

and museums, and attempted to modernize agriculture, industry, and the army—
and thus help himself stay in office.

Relations between Nicaragua and the United States were initially cordial, as
the United States joined Nicaragua in pressuring Great Britain to withdraw its
military forces from disputed territory along the Mosquito Coast. But relations
deteriorated after 1902, when the United States decided to construct its trans-
Isthmian Canal through Panama instead of Nicaragua. Then, alarmed at the
prospect of Nicaraguan dominance of the region after Nicaraguan forces in 1906
defeated both the Honduran Army and a force sent from El Salvador, the United
States and Mexico invited the Central American nations to meet in Washington.

Zelaya rejected the ''right'' of the United States, which also signed the Conference Treaty, to intervene in Central American affairs. Moreover, he discussed
a canal across Nicaragua with various foreign powers and gave a British firm
the right to construct and operate a railroad across Nicaragua. The United States,
however, considered it essential that Nicaragua's potential canal route be kept
out of European hands. Consequently, when Zeyala's presidency was threatened
by a revolt in 1909, his opponents were assured of success by open financial
and military support form the United States.

Conservatives played a major role in organizing an uprising against Zelaya,
but its nominal leader was the local governor, a Liberal and Zelaya appointee,
General Juan José Estrada. Zelaya resigned on December 17, 1909. His departure
began a period of Conservative dominance and U.S. armed intervention in
Nicaragua.

BIBLIOGRAPHY

English, Burt H. *Nicaragua Election Factbook, February 5, 1967*. Washington, D.C.:
    Institute for Comparative Study of Political Systems, 1967.
Millett, Richard. *Guardians of the Dynasty, A History of the Guardia Nacional and the
    Somoza Family*. Maryknoll, N.Y.: Orbis Books, 1977.
Parker, Franklin D. *The Central American Republics*. London and New York: Oxford
    University Press, 1964.
Pearson, Neale J. ''Nicaragua,'' in Robert J. Alexander (ed.). *Political Parties of the
    Americas*. Vol. 2. Westport, Conn.: Greenwood Press, 1982.

NEALE J. PEARSON

APPENDIX A: CHRONOLOGY

1804	Final success of slave revolt under Jean-Jacques Dessalines, assuring independence of Haiti
1808	Napoleonic invasion of Iberian Peninsula, capturing Spanish monarchs, setting in motion movement for Spanish-American independence. Transfer of Portuguese court to Brazil
1811	Establishment of Paraguayan independence under Dr. José Gaspar Rodríguez de Francia
1821	Establishment of Central American Federation
1822	Independence of Brazil, under Emperor Pedro I
1824	Battle of Ayacucho, conclusive battle for Spanish-American independence
1828	Establishment of Uruguay as buffer state between Argentina and Brazil
1830	Breakup of Republic of Gran Colombia into Colombia, Venezuela, and Ecuador
1831	Abdication of Brazilian Emperor Pedro I in favor of his son Pedro II
1835	Independence of Texas from Mexico
1837–1838	Dissolution of Central American Federation
1844	Independence of Dominican Republic from Haiti
1846–1848	War between Mexico and the United States
1852	Overthrow of Juan Manuel de Rosas in Argentina
1853	Adoption of Argentine constitution still in effect today
1857	Adoption of Mexican Liberal constitution
1861	Short civil war consolidating Argentine unity. Establishment of Empire of Maximilian in Mexico due to French armed intervention
1861–1865	Dominican Republic under General Santana cedes sovereignty and becomes Spanish colony

1865–1870	War of the Triple Alliance of Argentina, Brazil, and Uruguay against Paraguay, ending in total defeat and decimation of Paraguay
1866	War of Chile, Bolivia, and Peru with Spain
1867	Overthrow of Emperor Maximilian of Mexico, triumph of Liberals under Benito Juárez
1868–1878	First Cuban War of Independence
1876	Beginning of 35-year rule of Porfirio Díaz in Mexico
1879–1884	War of the Pacific, of Chile against Bolivia and Peru
1886	Longstanding Conservative Colombian constitution adopted
1889	Overthrow of Brazilian empire, proclamation of the republic
1891	Civil war in Chile leading to ouster and suicide of President José Manuel Balmaceda; beginning of "parliamentary republic"
1895–1898	Second Cuban War of Independence; intervention by United States in 1898 (Spanish-American War); U. S. annexation of Puerto Rico
1899–1902	War of Thousand Days establishing definitive Conservative regime in Colombia
1902	Formal independence of Cuba after passage of Platt Amendment
1903	Separation of Panama from Colombia, with help of U. S. intervention
1906–1908	Second U. S. military occupation of Cuba
1908	Coming of Juan Vicente Gómez to power in Venezuela
1909	End of long period of Liberal rule in Nicaragua with overthrow of President José Santos Zelaya; beginning of 23-year period of U. S. military intervention
1910	Outbreak of Mexican Revolution
1911–1915	Second presidency of José Batlle in Uruguay; enactment of extensive social and economic nationalist legislation
1914	Opening of Panama Canal
1915	U. S. military occupation of Haiti
1916	U. S. military occupation of Dominican Republic
1917	Mexican revolutionary constitution adopted
1917–1919	Short-lived dictatorship of Federico Tinoco Granados in Costa Rica
1920	Last successful move to overthrow a Mexican government with ouster of President Venustiano Carranza
1924	Withdrawal of U. S. troops from Dominican Republic; presidency of Horacio Vásquez begins. Presidency of Gerardo Machado in Cuba begins. Establishment of Alianza Popular Revolucionaria Americana (APRA) by Peruvian exiles, led by Víctor Raúl Haya de la Torre, in Mexico

1924–1925	Ouster and subsequent return of President Arturo Alessandri Palma of Chile; end of parliamentary republic with 1925 constitution; beginning of Chilean social legislation
1924–1927	Uprising of Brazilian *tenentes* and guerrilla war of Prestes Column in interior
1927–1931	Chilean dictatorship of General Carlos Ibáñez del Campo
1928	"Student week" insurrection against Gómez regime in Venezuela; beginning of "Generation of '28"
1929	Establishment of National Revolutionary Party as governing party of Mexico; party still in power almost 60 years later under name of Institutional Revolutionary Party (PRI)
1930	End of Old Republic of Brazil; coming to power of Getúlio Vargas. Seizure of power by General Rafael Leónidas Trujillo Molina in Dominican Republic
1932–1935	Chaco War between Paraguay and Bolivia; followed by short-lived reformist regimes in both countries
1932–1938	Return of Arturo Alessandri to power in Chile through election; stabilization of democratic regime
1933	Overthrow of dictator Gerardo Machado in Cuba; short-lived reformist regime of Ramón Grau San Martín. End of U.S. military occupation of Nicaragua
1933–1938	Dictatorship of President Gabriel Terra in Uruguay
1934	End of U. S. military occupation of Haiti
1934–1940	Administration of President Lázaro Cárdenas in Mexico; extensive agrarian reform; nationalization of railroads and petroleum; completion of "institutionalization" of Mexican Revolution
1934–1944	Control of Cuban regime by Fulgencio Batista y Zaldívar, as dictator and then constitutional president
1935	Death of Juan Vicente Gómez, last of Venezuelan caudillos
1935–1938	Series of political strikes and demonstrations in British West Indies
1936	Seizure of power in Nicaragua by General Anastasio Somoza García, establishing dynastic regime that lasts until 1979
1937	Establishment of Estado Novo dictatorship by Getúlio Vargas in Brazil
1938	Reorganization of Mexican government party as "collegial" organization under name of Party of the Mexican Revolution (PRM)
1943	Overthrow of Argentine government by the military, paving way for rise to power of General Juan Domingo Perón on basis of labor/military support; large-scale labor reforms and economic development effort
1944–1954	Democratic interregnum in Guatemala

1945	Overthrow of President Getúlio Vargas of Brazil; beginning of 19-year democratic interregnum
1945–1948	"Trienio" of rule of Democratic Action Party in Venezuela; extensive social and economic development legislation; ended by military coup inspired by Colonel Marcos Pérez Jiménez
1946–1955	Regime of Juan Perón in Argentina, most of time as thinly disguised dictatorship
1948	"Bogotazo" uprising in Colombia following murder of Jorge Eliécer Gaitán Short but bloody civil war in Costa Rica bringing José Figueres Ferrer to power for first time
1952	Overthrow of Cuban democratic regime and return of Fulgencio Batista to power as dictator. Bolivian National Revolution, followed by redistribution of land to the Indian peasants, nationalization of Big Tin mines, and other broad changes under leadership of Movimiento Nacionalista Revolucionario (MNR)
1953	Overthrow of President Laureano Gómez of Colombia by General Gustavo Rojas Pinilla, establishing four-year military dictatorship. Beginning of first constitutional presidency of José Figueres, inaugurating domination of National Liberation Party in Costa Rican politics
1954	Advent of General Alfredo Stroessner to power in Paraguay, starting dictatorship of more than three decades
1955	Overthrow of regime of Juan Perón in Argentina
1956–1961	Administration of President Juscelino Kubitschek de Oliveira in Brazil; period of intense economic development, democratic government, and cultural expansion
1958	Overthrow of Venezuelan dictator Marcos Pérez Jiménez; beginning of stable democratic regime
1958–1962	Elected government of President Arturo Frondizi encourages democracy and economic development in Argentina
1959	Overthrow of dictatorship of Fulgencio Batista in Cuba by revolutionary forces led by Fidel Castro
1959–1964	Administration of President Rómulo Betancourt establishes democratic regime in Venezuela, with program of social reform and economic development
1961	Assassination of Dominican Republic dictator Rafael Leónidas Trujillo. Proclamation of Cuba as "socialist state" by Castro; Bay of Pigs invasion of exiles with U. S. support; beginning of establishment of one-party state
1962	Independence of Jamaica, first British West Indian colony to achieve that status; followed in next 24 years by independence of virtually all of the other colonies. Cuban missile crisis
1963	First Dominican democratic regime in three decades takes office; President Juan Bosch overthrown seven months later

1964	Democratically elected president turns over office to democratically elected successor for the first time in Venezuelan history. Overthrow of MNR regime in Bolivia, followed by 18 years of military dictatorship. Overthrow of Brazilian President João Belchior Marques Goulart; beginning of 21-year military dictatorship
1964–1970	Administration of Christian Democratic President Eduardo Frei in Chile, carrying out agrarian reform, "Chileanization" of mining, unionization of rural workers, and other changes
1965	Formal establishment of Castroite Communist Party of Cuba. Civil war in Dominican Republic and U.S. armed intervention (1965–1966)
1969	"Cordobazo" uprising in Argentina; beginning of guerilla warfare by far left. Coming to power of opposition party through elections for the first time in Venezuelan history
1970	Failure of "10 million tons campaign" of Castro regime in Cuba to greatly expand sugar production; followed in next decade by "institutionalization" of Cuban Revolution
1970–1973	Administration of Socialist/Communist coalition in Chile led by Salvador Allende Gossens; period of extensive social and political conflict; ended by bloody military coup led by General Augusto Pinochet Ugarte
1973	Return of Juan Perón to power in Argentina. Establishment of 12-year long military-controlled dictatorship in Uruguay
1974	Death of President Juan Perón, succeeded by wife Isabel, who is overthrown after a year and a half, launching nearly eight-year period of military dictatorship
1975	Independence of Surinam from The Netherlands
1976	Signing of U.S.–Panama treaties gradually passing control of Canal to Panama
1979	Outbreak of civil war in El Salvador. Overthrow of domination of Somoza family in Nicaragua and establishment of revolutionary Sandinista regime
1982	Unsuccessful invasion of Malvinas (Falkland) Islands by Argentine dictatorship of President Leopoldo Fortunato Galtieri. Return of civilian government to Bolivia under President Hernán Siles Zuazo
1983	Democratic election of President Raúl Ricardo Alfonsín Foulkes in Argentina
1985	Return to civilian government in Brazil. Return to civilian government in Uruguay under President Julio María Sanguinetti. Return of Víctor Paz Estenssoro to presidency of Bolivia in election. Election and installation of first government of Aprista Party in Peru, under President Alan García Pérez

APPENDIX B: BIOGRAPHIES BY COUNTRY

ANTIGUA

Vere Cornwall Bird
George Herbert Walter

ARGENTINA

Leandro Nicebro Alem
Raúl Ricardo Alfonsín Foulkes
Pedro Eugenio Aramburu
Ricardo Balbín
Héctor José Cámpora
Arturo Frondizi
Leopoldo Fortunato Galtieri
Américo Ghioldi
Arturo Umberto Illia
Agustín Pedro Justo
Juan Bautista Justo
Alejandro Agustín Lanusse
Bartolomé Mitre
Juan Carlos Onganía
Alfredo Lorenzo Palacios
Eva María Duarte de Perón
Juan Domingo Perón
María Estela Martínez de Perón
Bernardino Rivadavia
Julio Argentino Roca
Juan Manuel de Rosas
Roque Sáenz Peña
José de San Martín
Domingo Faustino Sarmiento
Justo José de Urquiza
Jorge Rafael Videla
Hipólito Yrigoyen

BAHAMAS

Kendall George Lamon Isaacs
Lynden Oscar Pindling

BARBADOS

Sir Grantley Herbert Adams
John Michael G. M. Adams
Errol Walton Barrow
Charles Duncan O'Neale
Samuel Jackman Prescod
Harold Bernard St. John
Sir Hugh Worrell Springer
Frank Leslie Walcott
Clennel Wilsden Wickham

BELIZE

Manuel Esquivel

George Price

BOLIVIA

José Antonio Arze

Hugo Banzer Suárez

Mariano Baptista Caserta

René Barrientos Ortuño

Manuel Isidoro Belzú

Germán Busch

Eliodoro Camacho

Walter Guevara Arze

Juan Lechín Oquendo

Guillermo Lora Escobar

Mariano Melgarejo

Ismael Montes

Alfredo Ovando Candia

José Manuel Pando

Víctor Paz Estenssoro

Bautista Saavedro

Daniel Salamanca Urey

Andrés de Santa Cruz

Hernando Siles Reyes

Hernán Siles Zuazo

Antonio José de Sucre Alcalá

Juan José Torres González

Oscar Unzaga de la Vega

Gualberto Villarroel López

BRAZIL

Luis Alves de Lima (Duque de Caxias)

Oswaldo Aranha

Ruy Barbosa

Artur Bernardes

José Bonifácio de Andrada e Silva

Leonel Brizola

Humberto Castelo Branco

Benjamin Constant Botelho de Magalhães

Manuel Deodoro da Fonseca

Padre Diogo Antônio Feijó

João Belchior Marques Goulart

Juscelino Kubitschek de Oliveira

Carlos Lacerda

Washington Luis

Emílio Garrastazú Médici

Joaquim Barreto Nabuco de Araujo

Tancredo Neves

Dom Pedro I (Alcântara de Bragança Bourbon)

Dom Pedro II (de Alcântara)

Floriano Peixoto

Luis Carlos Prestes

Jânio Quadros

Getúlio Dornelles Vargas

BRITISH VIRGIN ISLANDS

Hamilton Lavity Stoutt

Willard Wheatley

CHILE

Pedro Aguirre Cerda

Arturo Alessandri Palma

Jorge Alessandri Rodríguez

Salvador Allende Gossens

José Manuel Balmaceda Fernández

Ramón Barros Luco

Francisco Bilbao Barquín

Manuel Bulnes Prieto

José Miguel Carrera Verdugo

Luis Malaquías Concha Ortíz

Federico Errázuriz Echaúren
Federico Errázuriz Zañartu
Emiliano Figueroa Larraín
Eduardo Frei Montalva
Ramón Freire Serrano
Gabriel González Videla
Marmaduque Grove Vallejo
Carlos Ibáñez del Campo
Elías Lafertte Gaviño
Enrique MacIver Rodríguez
Juan Esteban Montero Rodríguez
Jorge Montt Alvarez
Pedro Montt Montt
Manuel Montt Torres
Bernardo O'Higgins
José Joaquín Pérez Mascayano
Augusto Pinochet Ugarte
Francisco Antonio Pinto Díaz
Aníbal Pinto Garmendía
Diego Portales Palazuelos
Joaquín Prieto Vial
Luis Emilio Recabarren Serrano
Germán Riesco Errázuriz
Juan Antonio Ríos Morales
Juan Luis Sanfuentes
Domingo Santa María González
Antonio Varas de la Barra
Benjamín Vicuña MacKenna

COLOMBIA

Belisario Betancur Cuartas
Miguel Antonio Caro
Jorge Eliécer Gaitán
Laureano Gómez
Alberto Lleras Camargo
Carlos Lleras Restrepo
Alfonso López Michelson

Alfonso López Pumarejo
Tomás Cipriano de Mosquera
Rafael Núñez Moledo
José María Obando
Enrique Olaya Herrera
Mariano Ospina Pérez
Rafael Reyes
Gustavo Rojas Pinilla
Francisco de Paula Santander
Eduardo Santos

COSTA RICA

Rafael Angel Calderón Guardia
Rodrigo Carazo Odio
Braulio Carrillo Colina
León Cortés Castro
Mario Echandi Jiménez
Próspero Fernández Oreamuno
José Figueres Ferrer
Alfredo González Flores
Cleto González Víquez
Tomás Guardia Gutiérrez
Rafael Iglesias Castro
Ricardo Jiménez Oreamuno
Luis Alberto Monge Alvarez
Juan Rafael Mora Porrás
Manuel Mora Valverde
Daniel Oduber Quirós
Francisco José Orlich Bolmarcich
Víctor Sanabria Martínez
Bernardo Soto Alfaro
Bernardo Augusto Thiel
Federico Tinoco Granados
Otilio Ulate Blanco
Jorge Volio Jiménez

CUBA

Fulgencio Batista y Zaldívar
Fidel Castro Ruz
Raúl Castro Ruz
Carlos Manuel de Céspedes
Eduardo René Chibás
Tomás Estrada Palma
Calixto García Iñiguéz
José Miguel Gómez
Máximo Gómez
Miguel Mariano Gómez
Ramón Grau San Martín
Ernesto (Che) Guevara de la Serna
Federico Laredo Brú
Antonio Maceo y Grajales
Gerardo Machado y Morales
Juan Marinello
José Martí
Carlos Mendieta y Montefur
Mario García Menocal
Carlos Prío Socarrás
Blas Roca
Carlos Rafael Rodríguez Rodríguez
Alfredo Zayas y Alfonso

DOMINICA

Mary Eugenia Charles
Patrick Roland John
Edward Oliver LeBlanc

DOMINICAN REPUBLIC

Buenaventura Báez
Joaquín Balaguer
Juan Bosch
Juan Pablo Duarte

Ulíses Heureaux
José Francisco Peña Gómez
Pedro Santana
Rafael Leónidas Trujillo Molina
Horacio Vásquez

ECUADOR

Eloy Alfaro
Carlos Alberto Arroyo del Río
Juan José Flores
Gabriel García Moreno
Leónidas Plaza Gutiérrez
Galo Plaza Lasso
Camilo Ponce Enríquez
Vincente Rocafuerte
Guillermo Rodríguez Lara
José María Velasco Ibarra

EL SALVADOR

Manuel José Arce
José Napoleón Duarte
Francisco Dueñas
Maximiliano Hernández Martínez
Francisco Malespín
Oscar Osorio

FRENCH GUIANA

Justin Catayée
Léopold Héder
Hector Riviérez

GRENADA

Maurice Rupert Bishop
Herbert Augustus Blaize

Eric Matthew Gairy
Theophilus Albert Marryshow

GUADELOUPE

Henri Bangou
Fréderic Jalton
Hégépappe Légitimus
Paul Valentino

GUATEMALA

Jacobo Arbenz Guzmán
Juan José Arévalo Bermejo
Justo Rufino Barrios
Rafael Carrera
Carlos Castillo Armas
Vinicio Cerezo
Manuel Estrada Cabrera
Mariano Gálvez
Jorge Ubico y Castañeda

GUYANA

Linden Forbes Sampson Burnham
Hubert Nathaniel Critchlow
Cheddi Jagan
Janet Jagan

HAITI

Jean Pierre Boyer
Henri Christophe
Jean-Jacques Dessalines
François Duvalier
Jean-Claude Duvalier
Dumarsais Estimé
Fabre Nicholas Géffrard

Élie Lescot
Toussaint L'Ouverture
Paul Eugène Magloire
Alexandre Pétion
Louis-Félicité Lysius Salomon
Faustin Soulouque
Sténio Vincent

HONDURAS

Manuel Bonilla
Policarpo Bonilla
Tiburcio Carías Andino
Juan Manuel Gálvez Durón
Oswaldo López Arellano
Francisco Morazán
Marco Aurelio Soto
José Cecilio del Valle
Ramón Villeda Morales

JAMAICA

Paul Bogle
William Alexander Bustamante
Marcus Mosiah Garvey
George William Gordon
Edward Jordan
Michael Norman Manley
Norman Washington Manley
Donald Burns Sangster
Edward P. G. Seaga
Samuel Sharpe

MARTINIQUE

Aimé Césaire
Victor Sable

MEXICO

Miguel Alemán Valdés
Manuel Ávila Camacho
Plutarco Elías Calles
Lázaro Cárdenas
Venustiano Carranza
Miguel de la Madrid
Porfirio Díaz
Gustavo Díaz Ordaz
Miguel Hidalgo y Costilla
Victoriano Huerta
Agustín de Iturbide
Benito Juárez
Sebastián Lerdo de Tejada
Vicente Lombardo Toledano
Adolfo López Mateos
José López Portillo
Francisco I. Madero
Alvaro Obregón
Antonio López de Santa Anna
José Vasconcelos
Guadelupe Victoria
Pancho Villa
Emiliano Zapata

MONTSERRAT

Percival Austin Bramble
William Henry Bramble
John Alfred Osborne

NETHERLANDS ANTILLES

Gilbert François Croes
Efraín Jonckheer
Ciro de Kroon
Maria Liberia-Peters
Sylvus Rozendal

NICARAGUA

Fernando Agüero Rocha
Frutos Chamorro
Pedro Joaquín Chamorro Cardenal
Emiliano Chamorro Vargas
Carlos Fonseca Amador
José Daniel Ortega Saavedra
Augusto César Sandino
Anastasio Somoza Debayle
Luis Somoza Debayle
Anastasio Somoza García
William Walker
José Santos Zelaya

PANAMA

Ricardo Joaquín Alfaro
Manuel Amador Guerrero
Arnulfo Arias Madrid
Harmodio Arias Madrid
Rodolfo E. Chiari
Roberto Francisco Chiari Remón
Ernesto de la Guardia
Ricardo Adolfo de la Guardia
Enrique Adolfo Jiménez
Belisario Porras
José Antonio Remón Cantera
Marco Aurelio Robles
Omar Torrijos Herrera

PARAGUAY

Cecilio Báez
Bernardino Caballero
Federico Cháves
José Félix Estigarribia
Dr. José Gaspar Rodríguez de Francia

Rafael Franco
Juan Natalicio González
Carlos Antonio López
Francisco Solano López
Higinio Morínigo
Alfredo Stroessner

PERU

Alfonso Barrantes Lingan
Luis Bedoya Reyes
Fernando Belaúnde Terry
Óscar R. Benavides
Guillermo Billinghurst
Hugo Blanco Galdós
José Luís Bustamante y Rivero
Andrés A. Cáceres
Ramón Castilla
Luciano Castillo
Agustín Gamarra
Alan García Pérez
Manuel González Prada
Abimael Guzmán Reynoso
Víctor Raúl Haya de la Torre
Augusto B. Leguía
Fernando León de Vivero
José Carlos Mariátegui
Francisco Morales Bermúdez
Manuel A. Odría
José Pardo y Barreda
Manuel Pardo y Lavalle
Nicolás de Pierola
Manuel Prado Ugarteche
Jorge del Prado
Eudocio Ravines
Luis Alberto Sánchez
Luís M. Sánchez Cerro
Andrés Townsend Ezcurra

Juan Velasco Alvarado
Armando Villanueva

PUERTO RICO

Pedro Albizu Campos
Ramón Baldorioty de Castro
José Celso Barbosa
Luis Antonio Ferré Aguayo
Rafael Hernández Colón
Eugenio María de Hostos y Bonilla
Santiago Iglesias Pantín
Luis Muñoz Marín
Luis Muñoz Rivera
Carlos Romero Barceló

ST. KITTS AND NEVIS

Robert Llewellyn Bradshaw
Lee Llewellyn Moore
Kennedy Alphonse Simmonds
Caleb Azariah Paul Southwell

ST. LUCIA

George Frederic Charles
John George Melvin Compton
Allan Louisy

ST. VINCENT

R(obert) Milton Cato
James Fitz Allen Mitchell

SURINAM

Henck A. E. Arron
Desi Bouterse

Jaggernath Lachmon
Johan Adolf Pengel

TRINIDAD

Tubal Uriah Butler
Rudranath Capildeo
George Michael Chambers
Arthur Andrew Cipriani
Albert Gomes
Cyril Lionel Robinson James
Bhadase Sagan Maraj
George Weeks
Eric Williams

URUGUAY

Gregorio Alvarez
José Gervasio Artigas
Alfredo Baldomir
Luis Batlle Berres
José Batlle y Ordóñez
Juan María Bordaberry
Venancio Flores
Luis Alberto de Herrera
Juan Antonio Lavelleja
Aparicio Méndez Manfredini
Manuel Oribe
Fructuoso Rivera
Julio María Sanguinetti
Aparicio Saravia
Gabriel Terra

VENEZUELA

Gonzalo Barrios
Rómulo Betancourt
Simón Bolívar

Rafael Caldera Rodríguez
Cipriano Castro
Joaquín Crespo
Carlos Delgado Chalbaud
Juan Cristósomo Falcón
Rómulo Gallegos
Juan Vicente Gómez
Antonio Leocadio Guzmán
Antonio Guzmán Blanco
José Manuel Hernández
Luis Herrera Campins
Raúl Leoni
Eleazar López Contreras
Jaime Lusinchi
Gustavo Machado
Santiago Mariño
Isaías Medina Angarita
Francisco de Miranda
José Gregorio Monagas
José Tadeo Monagas
José Antonio Páez
Carlos Andrés Pérez
Marcos Pérez Jiménez
Luis Beltrán Prieto Figueroa
Carlos Soublette
Rafael Urdaneta
Jóvito Villalba

VIRGIN ISLANDS OF THE UNITED STATES

Ron De Lugo
Melvin Evans
Cyril Emmanuel King
Juan Luis
John David Merwin
Ralph Paiewonsky

INDEX

Italic page numbers indicate the location of biographical entries in the dictionary.

AAA, 444
ABC Party, 276
Acción Comunal, 23–24, 119
Acción Democrática. *See* Democratic Action (*various entries*)
Acción Popular, 50–51, 304
Acción Socialista, 183
Achá, José Maria, 290
AD. *See* Democratic Action (*various entries*)
Adams, Grantley Herbert, *1–2*, 45, 72, 116, 391, 422, 453
Adams, John, 269
Adams, John Michael G. M. (Tom), *2–4*, 45, 392
Agrupación Cívica Bolivariana, 262
Agrupación Revolucionaria de Izquierda, 41, 53, 252
Agüero Rocha, Fernando, *4–5*, 8–9, 114, 413
Aguirre Cerda, Pedro, 5, 10, 14, 165, 193, 199, 220, 377
Aguirre Gainsborg, José, 202
Agustín I, 224–25, 400, 437, 443
Albizu Campos, Pedro, *5–6*
Alcántara Herran, Pedro, 307
Alem, Leandro Nicebro, *6–7*, 461
Alemán Valdés, Miguel, *7–8*
Alfrey, Phyllis, 248
Alessandri Palma, Arturo, *8–10*; and Aguirre Cerda, his first interior minister, 5; attempted uprising against, by

Chilean Nazi Party, 220, as candidate of Liberal Alliance, 276; decisive political role of, in later years, 193; opposes President Montt in Congress, 301; and problems with young military officers, 199, 219; returns to office (1925), 199; second administration of (1932–1938), 245; second resignation and exile of, 159, 219; second return to presidency of (1932), 199; supported by González Videla (1932); 193; supports Ríos Morales, 377
Alessandri Rodríguez, Fernando, 10
Alessandri Rodríguez, Jorge, *10–11*, 15, 166
Alfaro, (José) Eloy, *11–12*, 357
Alfaro, Ricardo Joaquín, *12–13*, 232
Alfonsín Foulkes, Rául Ricardo, *13–14*, 33, 176, 445
Alfonso, Pedro Enrique, 165
Alliance for Progress, 11, 119, 256
Alianza Nacional Popular, 385
Allende, Ignacio, 215
Allende Gossens, Salvador, 11, *14–16*, 54, 166, 194, 355
ALP, 58, 455
Altamirano, Carlos, 16
Alvarez, Gregorio, *16–17*
Alvarez, Juan, 235
Alvear, Marcelo T. de, 462
Alves de Lima, Luis (Duque de Caxias), *17–18*, 133

Amador Guerrero, Manuel, *18*
Amauta, 284, 350
American Federation of Labor, 222
American People's Revolutionary Alliance, 40, 192, 209, 251, 319, 361
American Sanitary Mission, 140
ANAPO, 385
Anaya, Ricardo, 28
Andean Bloc, 166
Andrade, Ignacio, 128
Andueza Palacio, Raimundo, 128
ANEC, 165
Antigua Labour Party, 58, 455
Antigua Trade and Labour Union, 57–58, 455
Antigua Workers Union, 58, 455
Antigua Workingman's Association, 57
Anti-Imperialist League of the Americas, 274
Anti-Personalista Radical Party, 462
AP, 50–51, 304
APRA. *See* American People's Revolutionary Alliance
Aprista Committee, 373
Aprista Party. *See* American People's Revolutionary Alliance
Aprista Youth Federation, 430, 448
Aramburu, Pedro Eugenio, *18–19*, 91
Arana, Francisco Javier, 21, 104
Arango, Doroteo. *See* Pancho Villa
Aranha, Oswaldo, *19–21*
Arbenz Gúzman, Jacobo, *21–22*, 23, 104, 203
Arce, Manuel José, *22*
ARDI, 41, 53, 252
Arévalo Bermejo, Juan José, *22–23*, 104
Argentine Anti-Communist Alliance, 444
Arias, Juan Angel, 66–67
Arias Madrid, Arnulfo, 12, *23–24*, 25, 119, 120, 200, 375
Arias Madrid, Harmodio, *24–25*, 119, 430
Arosemena, Florencio Harmodio, 12, 119, 375
Arron, Henck A. E., *25–26*, 70, 244, 344

Arroyo del Río, Carlos Alberto, *26–27*, 442
Artigas, José Gervasio, *27*, 247, 324, 379
Arze, José Antonio, *27–29*, 449
ATLU, 57–58, 455
Austin, Gen. Hudson, 3
Auténtico Party, 121, 198, 368
Authentic Nationalist Revolutionary Movement, 202
Authentic Revolutionary Party, 202, 338, 410
Authentic Revolutionary Party of Democratic Unification, 329
Authentic Socialist Party, 199
Autonomist Party (Argentina), 391
Autonomist Party (Cuba), 463
Automonist Party (Puerto Rico), 34, 41, 311
Avellaneda, Nicolás, 296
Ávila Camacho, Manuel, *29*
Ayala, Eusebio, 149, 164
Azules, the, 323

Báez, Buenaventura, *31*, 402
Báez, Cecilio, *31–32*
Bahamian Democratic Party, 224
Bajo el oprobio, 52
Balaguer, Joaquín, *32*, 431
Balbín, Ricardo, 13, *32–33*, 168, 223
Baldomir, Alfredo, *33–34*, 212, 427
Baldorioty de Castro, Ramón, *34–35*
Ballivián, Adolfo, 37
Ballivian, Hugo, 435
Balmaceda Fernández, José Manuel, *35–36*; and formation of Liberal Democratic Party, 397; opposition to, during congressional revolt and 1891 Civil War, 8, 44, 146, 276, 300, 301; supported by Concha in 1891 Civil War, 126; supported by Santa María in 1886 election, 402
Balta, José, 353
Bangou, Henri, *36*
Banzer Suárez, Hugo, *36–37*, 338, 411, 429
Baptista Caserta, Mariano, *37–38*
Baquedano, Manuel, 402

Barbados Labour Party, 1–3, 45, 392, 422, 453
Barbados Progressive League, 1
Barbados Transport and General Workers' Union, 45
Barbados Workers Union, 1–2, 422, 453
Barbosa, José Celso, *38–39*
Barbosa, Ruy, *39–40*
Barceló, Antonio R., 309, 385
Barrantes Lingan, Alfonso, *40*, 50
Barrientos Ortuño, René, 36, *40–41*, 202, 249, 330, 338, 411
Barrios, Gonzalo, *41–42*, 366
Barrios, Justo Rufino, *42–44*, 151, 417
Barros, Ademar de, 371
Barros Luco, Ramón, *44*
Barrow, Errol Walton, 2, *44–46*, 453
Batista y Zaldívar, Fulgencio, *46–47*; Castro's guerilla struggle against, 106–7, 203; elected president against Grau (1940), 47, 198; electoral defeat of Saladrigos, 198; impeachment of Mariano Gómez, 46; leads military coup against Prío, 198, 368; overthrow of, 368; overthrows Grau, 292; and presidency of Laredo Bru, 47, 247; relations with communist leaders, 285, 381, 384; role of, in making Grau president, 368
Batlle, Lorenzo, 48
Batlle Berres, Luis, *47–48*
Batlle y Ordóñez, José, 47, *48–49*
Bayou, Monsieur, 268
BDP, 224
Beacon, 184
Bedoya Reyes, Luis, *49–50*, 431
Belaúnde Terry, Fernando, 49, *50–51*, 210, 304, 441
Bell, Alexander Graham, 340
Belzú, Manuel Isidoro, 37, *51–52*
Beltrán, Pedro, 373
Benavides, Óscar R., *52*, 57, 82, 209, 361
Bernardes, Antonio da Silva, 52
Bernardes, Artur, *52–53*, 270
Berreta, Tomás, 47
Bertrand, Francisco, 67
Betancourt, Rómulo, *53–56*; and choice of a successor, 253; as constitutional
president (1959–1964), 88, 253, 344; endorses Pérez in 1973, 344; and establishment of ARDI, 41; exile in Chile, 252; offers Caldera post in junta government, 87; opposes candidacy of Prieto, 336; opposition to his government by URD, 447–48; pledges with Caldera and Villalba to restore Venezuelan democracy, 87; as president of Revolutionary Junta, 344, 364; proposes Gallegos as PDN candidate, 175; and revolution of October 18, 1945, 346, 447; as secretary general of Democratic Action (1941–1945), 252, 290; sends Pérez Jiménez on mission abroad, 346; underground activity of, during rule of López Contreras, 175
Betancur Cuartas, Belisario, *56*, 573
BGLU, 128–29
Biaggini, Angel, 290
Biassou, 268
Bilbao Barquín, Francisco, *56–57*, 443
BITU, 80, 279, 281
Billinghurst, Guillermo, 52, *57*, 192, 354, 361, 395
Bird, Vere Cornwall, *57–59*, 455
Bishop, Maurice Rupert, 3, *59–61*, 62, 118, 268, 408
Black Man, 181
Black Power movement, 456
Blaize, Herbert Augustus, 60, *61–62*, 172
Blanco, Salvador Jorge, 343
Blanco Galdós, Hugo, *62–63*
Blanco Party, 17, 33–34, 48–49, 69, 161, 213, 247, 291, 324–25, 405–6, 427
BLP. *See* Barbados Labour Party
"Blue Revolution" movement, 297
Bogle, Paul, *63–64*, 195
Boisrond Canal, President, 393
Bolívar, Simón, *64–66*, 178, 307; and Battle of Carabobo, 160, 333, 404; establishes military dictatorship in Gran Colombia, 404; is joined by Páez after return (1816), 333; meets with San Martín at Guayaquil, 333, 404; objects to federal form of government for Ven-

ezuela, 294; persuades Obando to join army of Gran Colombia, 317; prevents departure of Miranda, 294; relations with Santander, 403–4; resigns presidency and dies enroute to exile, 404; and separatist movement by Páez in Venezuela, 333, 419; Urdaneta as a major lieutenant of, 435–36

Bolivarian Civic Group, 262

Bolivian Labor Central, 249, 267, 410

Bolivian Leftist Front, 28

Bolivian Revolutionary Front, 41

Bolivian Socialist Falange, 36, 338, 429, 434–35

Bonaparte, Napoleon, 70, 100, 134, 269, 339, 352

Bonifácio de Andrada e Silva, José, *66*, 339, 340

Bonilla, Manuel, *66–67*, 68, 95

Bonilla, Policarpo, *67–68*

Bordaberry, Juan María, *68–69*, 291

Borno, Louis, 149

Bosch, Juan, *69–70*, 342–43

Boukman, 134

Bourricaud, François, 180

Bouterse, Desi, 25, *70*

Boyd, Augusto Samuel, 12

Boyer, Jean-Pierre, *70–71*, 139

Bradshaw, Robert Llewellyn, *71–73*, 303, 412, 420–21

Bramble, Percival Austin, *73–74*, 75, 328

Bramble, William Henry, *74–75*, 328

Braynen, Alvin, 354

Brazilian Anti-Slavery Society, 313

Brazilian Democratic Movement, 314

Brazilian Labor Party, 75–76, 196

Brezhnev, Leonid, 108

British Broadcasting Company, 3

British Empire Workers and Citizens Home Rule Party, 83

British Empire Workers, Peasants and Ratepayers Union, 84

British Guiana and West Indies Labour Congress. *See* Caribbean Labour Congress

British Guiana Labor Union, 128–29

British Labour Party, 3, 124

Brizola, Leonel, *75–76*, 106

Broad Opposition Front, 326, 414

Brooke, John, 222

Brum, Baltasar, 427

Bryan-Chamorro Treaty, 113

Bulnes Prieto, Manuel, 56, *76–77*, 302, 346, 356, 360, 438

Bunau-Varilla, Philippe, 18

Burnham, Linden Forbes Sampson, *77–79*, 227

Busch, Germán, 40, *79–80*, 201, 338

Bustamante, William Alexander, *80–82*, 281–83, 398, 407

Bustamante Industrial Trade Union, 80, 279, 281

Bustamante y Rivero, José Luís, 49, 52, *82–83*, 209, 319

Butler, Tubal Uriah, *83–84*, 124, 456

Butler Party, 84

BWU, 1–2, 422, 453

Caballero, Bernardino, 85

Cáceres, Andrés A., 57, *85–86*

Caldera Rodríguez, Rafael, 42, *86–88*, 214, 271, 366

Calderón Guardia, Rafael Angel, *88–89*, 127, 145, 157, 305, 394, 434

Calles, Plutarco Elías, *89–90*, 94–95, 262, 318, 440

Camacho, Eliodor, *90–91*

Campaign Against Racial Discrimination, 59

Campero, Narciso, 90

Cámpora, Héctor José, 13, 32–33, *91–92*, 246, 351

Campos, Roberto, 102

Capildeo, Rudranath, *92–93*, 283

Carazo Odio, Rodrigo, *93*

Cárdenas, Lázaro, 8, 29, *93–95*, 258

Carías Andino, Tiburcio, *95–97*, 177, 450

Caribbean Basin Initiative, 118, 408

Caribbean Bauxite, Mineworkers, and Metal Workers Federation, 280

Caribbean Common Market, 58, 459

Caribbean Community, 113, 459

Caribbean Free Trade Area, 45, 248, 459

Caribbean Labour Congress, 2, 72, 129, 287
Caricom, 113, 459
CARIFTA, 45, 248, 459
Carlota Joaquina, Queen, 339
Caro, José Eusebio, 97
Caro, Miguel Antonio, *97–98*, 316
Carranza, Venustiano, *98–99*, 318, 446, 463
Carrera, Rafael, *99–100*, 176, 306
Carrera Verdugo, José Miguel, *100–101*, 320
Carrillo Colina, Braulio, *101*
Carter, Jimmy, 32, 142, 327, 430
Castañeda Cástro, Salvador, 328
Castellón, Francisco, 454
Castelo Branco, Humberto, *101–3*, 244
Castilla, Ramón, 85, *103*
Castillo, Luciano, *103–4*
Castillo, Ramón, 236
Castillo Armas, Carlos, 21, *104–5*
Castro, Cipriano, *105–6*, 186, 211, 261, 346
Castro, Julián, 155, 204, 297, 334
Castro Ruz, Fidel, *106–8*, 198, 244, 327, 372; continued support of, by Mexico under López Mateos, 263; disaffection of Prío with, 368; guerilla struggle of, 47; his impact on the region, 145, 158, 161, 164, 228, 430; lands in Oriente Province, 47, 203; meets Guevara in Mexico, 203; opposition to, by Luis Somoza, 415; relations with Rodríguez, 383–84; role of brother Raúl in guerilla war and regime, 108–9; role of Juan Marinello in his regime, 286; signs mutual aid pact with PSP in July 1957, 384; student of Máximo Gómez's ideas on guerilla warfare, 189
Castro Ruz, Raúl, 107, *108–9*, 383
Castro y Argiz, Angel, 106
Catayée, Justin, *109*, 210
Catholic Action, 86
Catholic Union Party, 428
Cato, R(obert) Milton, *109–10*, 295
CBI, 118, 408
Celman, Juárez, 6, 407

Center for the Study of National Problems, 319, 325
Central American Common Market, 415
Central American Federation, 99, 101, 176, 305, 437
Central Intelligence Agency, 21, 104
Central Obrero Bolatino, 249, 267, 410
Cerezo, Vinicio, *110–11*
Césaire, Aimé, *111*
Céspedes, Carlos Manuel de, 46, *111–12*, 189, 197, 247
CGOCM, 258
CGTP, 284
Chambers, George Michael, *112–13*
Chamorro, Diego Manuel, 115
Chamorro, Frutos, *113–14*
Chamorro, Pedro Joaquín, 326
Chamorro, Violeta Barrios de, 326
Chamorro Cardenal, Pedro Joaquín, 45, *114*, 414, 415
Chamorro Vargas, Emiliano, *114–16*, 416, 417
Chamorro Zelaya, Pedro Joaquín, 114
Charles, George Frederic, *116–17*
Charles, James Luc, 116, 125
Charles, Mary Eugenia, *117–18*
Cháves, Federico, *118–19*, 190–91, 423
Chávez Ortíz, Ñuflo, 410
Chiape, Anna, 284
Chiari, Rodolfo E., *119–20*
Chiari Remón, Roberto Francisco, *120*
Chibás, Eduardo René (Eddy), 106, *120–21*
Chilean Development Corporation, 5
Chilean Nazi Party, 220
Christian Democratic Organizations, Latin American Congress of, 214
Christian Democratic Party (Brazil), 371
Christian Democratic Party (Chile), 15, 165–66
Christian Democratic Party (El Salvador), 138
Christian Democratic Party (Guatemala), 110
Christian Democratic Party (Peru), 49
Christian Popular Party, 49
Christophe, Henri, 70–71, *121–23*, 134–35, 352

Churchill, Winston, 78
Cienfuegos, Camillo, 107
Cipriani, Arthur Andrew, 83, *123–24*, 184, 231
Círculo Literario, 192
Civic Union, 296
Civil Party, 52
Claridad, 284
Clarke, William Alexander. *See* Bustamante, William Alexander
CNC, 93–94
CNS, 117–18, 233
Coard, Bernard, 3, 60
COB, 249, 267, 410
Cochrane, Thomas, 321
Cole, Byron, 454
Colorado Party (Paraguay), 31, 85, 119, 164, 190–91, 307, 423
Colorado Party (Uruguay), 17, 33–34, 48–49, 69, 213, 379, 399, 405, 427
Colorados (Argentina), 323
Combato, 298
Comintern, 363, 373
Committee for National Salvation, 117–18, 233
Committee of Concerned Citizens, 59
Committee of Independent Electoral Political Organization. *See* Social Christian Copei Party
Communist International, 363, 373
Communist Parties, Latin American, meeting of, 285
Communist Party (Brazil), 243, 363
Communist Party (Bulgaria), 361
Communist Party (Chile), 14–15, 193–94, 199, 219–20, 245, 361, 373–74, 377
Communist Party (Costa Rica), 53, 89, 127, 205, 394
Communist Party (Cuba), 47, 107–9, 198, 274, 285, 361, 383–84
Communist Party (Czechoslovakia), 361
Communist Party (Ecuador), 26, 442
Communist Party (El Salvador), 211
Communist Party (France), 230
Communist Party (German Democratic Republic), 361
Communist Party (Guadeloupe), 36, 437

Communist Party (Guatemala), 21, 23, 433
Communist Party (Mexico), 258, 263
Communist Party (Nicaragua), 161
Communist Party (Panama), 430
Communist Party (Peru), 40, 103, 360–61, 373
Communist Party (USSR), 361
Communist Party (Venezuela), 88, 253, 290
Communist Party–Shining Path (Peru), 207
Communist Revolutionary Union, 285, 380
Communist Trade Union Conference, 245
Communist Youth, 108
Communist Youth Federation, 243
Compton, John George Melvin, *124–26*, 267
Comrade Gonzalo, 207
Comte, Auguste, 126
Concentración Revolucionaria Febrerista, 164
Concha Ortiz, Luis Malaquías, *126*
Concordancia, 236
Confederación de Trabajadores de Cuba, 47, 198, 368
Confederación de Trabajadores de Mexico, 198, 258
Confederación General de Obreros y Campesinos Mexicanos, 258
Confederación Regional Obrera Mexicana, 258
Confederation of Workers of Cuba, 47, 198, 368
Confederation of Workers of Mexico, 198, 258
Conservative Nationalists, 96
Conservative Party (Bolivia), 38, 336
Conservative Party (Brazil), 17, 313, 341
Conservative Party (Central American Federation), 305–6
Conservative Party (Chile), 146–47, 165–67, 220, 299, 300–302, 347, 356, 360, 397, 402
Conservative Party (Colombia), 56, 97, 173–74, 187–88, 256–57, 264–66,

308, 315, 318, 321–22, 329–30, 375–76, 384–85, 403–5

Conservative Party (Cuba), 185, 292–93, 464

Conservative Party (Ecuador), 11–12, 26, 358–59, 382, 442

Conservative Party (Guatemala), 42–43, 99

Conservative Party (Honduras), 67, 95

Conservative Party (Mexico), 235

Conservative Party (Nicaragua), 4, 114–15, 326, 396, 413–17, 454, 464–65

Conservative Party (Venezuela), 155, 204–5, 296, 333–34, 419

Conservative Republic, 367

Constant Botelho de Magalhães, Benjamin, *126–27*, 134

Constitutionalist Party, 86

Constitutionalists, 98

Constitutional Progressive Party, 277

Convergencia Democrática, 50, 431

Coolidge, Calvin, 275

Cooperative Republic of Guyana, 79

Coordinating Committee of Aprista Exiles, 448

COPEI. *See* Social Christian Copei Party

Córdova, Jorgé, 51

Córdova Rivas, Rafael, 326–27

Corral, Ponciano, 454

Cortés Castro, León, 80, 89, *127*, 305

Costa e Silva, Artur da, 102, 289

Council of Venezuelan Catholic Youth, 86

"Country" Party, 195

Creelman, James, 136

Crespo, Joaquín, *127–28*, 206, 211

Crippled Hernández. *See* Hernández, José Manuel

Cristeros, 94

Critchlow, Hubert Nathaniel, *128–29*

Croes, Gilbert François (Batico), *129–30*

CROM, 258

Crowder, Enoch, 464

Cruz, Ramón Ernesto, 261

Cruz Porras, Arturo, 327

CSTB, 28

CTM, 198, 258

Cuban Confederation of Labor, 47, 198, 368

Cuban Confederation of Women, 108

Cuban People's Party, 121

Cuban Revolutionary Committee, 288

Cuban Revolutionary Party, 288

Cuban Revolutionary Party (Authentic), 121, 198, 368

Cuestas, Juan Lindolfo, 405

Curaçao Democratic Party, 234, 239, 387

Cuyamel Fruit Company, 67

Daniel, Simeon, 303, 412

Das Kapital, 237

Daza, Hilarión, 90

Debayle, Salvadora, 416

Declaration of Rights of the Negro Peoples of the World, 181

De Gaulle, Charles, 437

Dejoie, Louis, 141

de la Guardia, Ricardo Adolfo, 24

de la Madrid, Miguel, *131–32*, 264

de la Mar, José, 178

Delgado Chalbaud, Carlos, 87, *132–33*, 346

Delgado Chalbaud, Román, 132

del Río, Arturo, 9

De Lugo, Ron, *133*

del Valle, Aristóbulo, 6

Democratic Action (Costa Rica), 325

Democratic Action (Peru), 50

Democratic Action (Venezuela), 41–42, 54–55, 87–88, 93, 132, 174–75, 213–14, 252–53, 262, 271, 290, 344–45, 366, 447–48

Democratic Alliance, 26

Democratic and Popular Unity, 411

Democratic Antifascist Front, 28, 449

Democratic Conservative Party, 4

Democratic Coordination Council, 327

Democratic Front of the National Union, 297

Democratic Labor Party (Brazil), 76

Democratic Labour Party (Barbados), 2–3, 45, 453

Democratic Labour Party (Trinidad), 92, 283

Democratic League, 323, 457

Democratic Liberation Party, 283–84
Democratic National Committee, 334
Democratic Party (Bolivia), 37
Democratic Party (British Virgin Islands), 457
Democratic Party (Chile), 9, 57, 74, 126
Democratic Party (Peru), 57, 354
Democratic Party (U.S. Virgin Islands), 133, 239
Democratic Revolutionary Party, 430
Democratic Societies, 315, 318
Deodoro da Fonseca, Marshal Manuel, 127, *133–34*, 342
Dessalines, Jean-Jacques, 70–71, 122, *134–35*, 352–53
d'Estaing, Admiral, 122
d'Eu, Comte, 341
DFP, 117
Diario de Costa Rica, 434
Díaz, Adolfo, 115
Díaz, Porfirio, 43, 98, *135–37*, 254, 277, 446
Díaz Ordaz, Gustavo, 95, *137–38*
Díaz Serrano, Jorge, 264
Díaz Soto y Gama, Antonio, 463
DLP. *See* Democratic Labour Party; Dominica Labour Party
Dominica Freedom Party, 117
Dominica Labour Party, 118, 233, 248
Dominica Liberation Alliance, 233
Dominican Liberation Party, 69–70
Dominican Party, 431
Dominican Revolutionary Party, 32, 69, 42–43
Doña Bárbara, 174
Donavan, William, 287
Duarte, José Napoleón, *138–39*
Duarte, Juan Pablo, *139–40*, 402
DuBois, W. E. B., 181
Dueñas, Francisco, *140*
Duhalde, Alfredo, 377
Dulles, John Foster, 21
Duque de Caxias, 17–18, 133
Dutra, Eurico, 20, 102
Duvalier, François, *140–42*, 143, 149–50
Duvalier, Jean-Claude, 140, *142–43*
Duvalier, Michele Bennett, 143

Duvalier, Simone Ovide, 142
Duvalier Ovide, Marie-Denise, 142

Eastern Caribbean Regional Defense Force, 118
Eastern Caribbean Regional Security and Defense Pact, 110, 295
Echandi Jiménez, Mario, *145–46*
Echeverría, Luis, 131, 264
Edun, Ayube, 129
Eguiguren, Luís Antonio, 52
Eisenhower, Dwight David, 107, 200, 241, 375, 417
Ejercito Revolucionario del Pueblo, 444
El Arqitecto Peruana, 50
El Derecho, 34
El Día, 47–48
Electoral Action, 86–87
Electoral Movement of the People, 42, 344, 366
Electricity Tariffs Protest Committee, 412
El Liberal, 256
El Mercurio, 406
El Mocho Hernández. *See* Hernández, José Manuel
El Nacional, 406
El Porvenir, 37
El Progreso Católico, 353
El Pueblo, 450
El Siglo, 56, 187
El Tarapacá, 165
El Tiburón, 185
El Tiempo (Colombia), 256, 405
El Tiempo (Peru), 284, 353
El Tradicionalista, 97
El Venezolano, 204
Emanuels, D. H., 344
Ensayo Obrero, 222
ERP, 444
Errázuriz Echaúren, Federico, *146*, 356
Errázuriz Zañartu, Federico, *146–47*, 356
Erro, Enrique, 69
Escalante, Diogenes, 252, 290
Espín, Vilma, 108
Esquivel, Ascensión, 221
Esquivel, Manuel, *147–48*, 365
Estado Novo, 20, 240, 314, 439
Estigarribia, José Félix, *148–49*, 306

Estimé, Dumarsais, 141, *149–50*, 278
Estrada, Emilio, 12
Estrada, Juan José de, 115, 465
Estrada Cabrera, Manuel, *150–51*
Estrada Palma, Tomás, *151–52*, 185
European Economic Community, 113
Eva Duarte de Perón Welfare Foundation, 349
Evans, Melvin, *152–53*
Eyre, Governor, 195

Fabian Society, 124
Facundo: Civilization or Barbarism, 406
FAJ, 430, 448
Falange Naciónal, 165, 193, 377
Falange Socialista Boliviana, 36, 338, 429, 434–35
Falangism, 188
Falcón, Juan Cristósomo, 127, *155–56*, 205, 297, 334
FAO, 326, 414
Farrell, Edelmiro, 349
Fawkes, Randol, 354
FDN, 50, 52, 82, 209
Febrerista Party, 163–64, 307
Federación Aprista Juvenil, 430, 448
Federación Nacional de Cafeteros de Colombia, 257, 329
Federación Obrera de Chile, 245, 374
Federalist and Grenada, The, 287
Federalists (Argentina), 387
Federalists (Venezuela), 155
Federal Labor Party (West Indies Federation), 231
Federal League for Rural Action, 27, 69
Federal Party (Puerto Rico), 311
Federal Party (Venezuela), 204
"Federal Revolution," 299
Federated Workers Trade Union, 184
Federation of Mine Workers, 449
Federation of Peasants, 62
Federation of Sugar Workers and Cane Farmers, 283
Federation of University Students (Honduras), 450
Federation of University Students (Peru), 209
Feijó, Padre Diogo Antonio, *156*

Feminine Peronist Party, 348
Ferdinand VII, King of Spain, 215, 382
Fernández, Miguel. *See* Victoria, Guadelupe
Fernández, Mauro, 418
Fernández Albano, Elías, 159
Fernández Oreamuno, Próspero, *156–57*, 418, 428
Ferré Aguayo, Luis Antonio, *157*, 386
FEV, 86, 447
Fignolé, Daniel, 140
Figueres Ferrer, José, 93, 145, *157–59*, 298, 319–20, 325, 417
Figueroa Larraín, Emiliano, *159*, 219, 298
First National Indian Conference, 450
First World Conference of Christian Democratic Parties, 214
Flores, Juan José, *159–60*, 382
Flores, Venancio, *160–61*
FNM, 223–24
FOCh, 245, 374
Fonseca Amador, Carlos, *161–62*
FORUM, 59
Founding Junta of the Second Republic, 158
Fourth International, 267
Fourth Miners' Congress, 266
FPN, 36
Francia, Dr. José Caspar Rodríguez de, *162–63*, 259
Franco, Rafael, 149, *163–65*, 190
FRAP, 15
Free Federation of Puerto Rican Workers, 222
Free National Movement, 223–24
Frei Montalva, Eduardo, 15, *165–67*
Freire Serrano, Ramón, *167*, 356
Frejuli, 91
Frente Ampla, 241, 244
Frías, Tomás, 37
Frondizi, Arturo, 19, 33, *167–69*, 335, 350
Front of Democratic Youth, 50
Front of Popular Action, 15
Front of the Revolutionary Left, 62
FSB, 36, 338, 429, 434–35

FSLN, 4, 161–62, 326–27, 396, 414
FSTMB, 249, 267

Gairy, Eric Matthew, 59–61, *171–73*
Gaitán, Jorge Eliécer, *173–74*, 257, 333
Galíndez, Jesús de, 432
Gallegos, Rómulo, *174–75*; in exile under Gómez, 41; government of, 42, 132, 447; named PDN candidate (1941), 54; overthrow of, 42, 55, 87, 132
Galtieri, Leopoldo Fortunato, *175–76*
Gálvez, Mariano, *176–77*
Gálvez Barnes, Robert, 260
Gálvez Durón, Juan Manuel, 96, 150, *177–78*
Gamarra, Agustín, 51, *178*, 425
Gamarra, Francisco, 178
García Granados, Miguel, 43
García Iñiguéz, Calixto, *178–79*, 189, 273, 288, 292
García Meza, Luís, 202, 339, 411
García Moreno, Gabriel, 12, 160, *179–80*
García Pérez, Alan, 50, *180*
Garvey, Marcus Mosiah, *180–82*
Gaullists (French Guiana), 210, 379
Gaullists (Martinique), 390
Géffrard, Fabre Nicholas, *182–83*, 420
General Association of Students, 274
General Confederation of Mexican Workers and Peasants, 258
General Confederation of Peruvian Workers, 284
General Union of Mexican Workers and Peasants, 258
General Workers Union, 364
Genuine Republican Party, 389, 392
Gestido, Oscar, 69
Ghioldi, Américo, *183–84*
Gill, Juan Bautista, 85
Giró, Juan Francisco, 161, 247
GIWU, 229
GNP, 60–62, 172
Goes Monteiro, Pedro Aurelio, 439
Gomes, Albert, *184–85*
Gómez, José Miguel, *185–86*, 190, 275, 292–93, 464
Gómez, Juan Vicente, *186–87*; attempted

overthrow of, by Román Delgado Chalbaud (1919), 132; death of, 86, 174, 261, 366, 447; dictatorship of, 41, 289; during Castro regime, 105; joins forces with Castro in the "Restoring Liberal Revolution," 105; opposes Machado, 274; and role of López Contreras in Gómez' regime and afterwards, 261–62; seizes power during absence of Castro, 106, 211; Student Week protest against, 53, 252, 261, 447; and voluntary exile of Gallegos, 174
Gómez, Laureano, *187–88*, 256–57, 265–66, 329, 387, 405
Gómez, Máximo, 112, *188–90*, 273, 288
Gómez Miguel Mariano, 46, *190*, 247
Gómez Farias, Valetín, 400
Gómez Pedraza, Manuel, 443
Gompers, Samuel, 222
González, Juan Natalicio, 119, 164, *190–91*
González Flores, Alfredo, *191–92*, 428
González Prada, Manuel, 52, 284, *192–93*
González Prada People's University, 284
González Videla, Gabriel, 10–11, 15, *193–94*, 220
González Víquez, Cleto, 157, *194–95*, 232
Gordon, George William, 63, *195*
Goulart, João Belchior Marques, *195–97*; assumes presidency after resignation of Quadros, 314; backed by Prestes, 363; becomes Brizola's brother-in-law, 75; elected vice president (1955), 243; as Kubitschek's running mate, 240; overthrown by revolution of March 31, 1964, 76, 241; political warfare with Lacerda, 244; stripped of political rights, 102; support of, by Brizola, 76
Goulart, Neusa, 75
Granadine Confederation, 308
Grant, Ulysses S., 235
Grau San Martín, Ramón, 46–47, 106, 121, *197–98*, 292, 368
Grenada Manual and Menial Workers Union, 171

Grenada National Party, 60–62, 172
Grenada United Labour Party, 61, 171–72
Grenada Workers' Association, 287
Griffith, Robert, 74
Griots, the, 140–41
"Groups of 11," 76
Grove Vallejo, Marmaduque, 15, *199–200*, 219
Guadeloupe Federation of the French Socialist Party, 250
Guardia, Ernesto de la, *200*
Guardia, Ricardo Adolfo de la, *200–201*
Guardia Gutiérrez, Tomás, 156, *201*
Guerrero, Vicente, 443
Guerrilla Warfare, 203
Guevara Arze, Walter, *201–3*, 338, 410–11
Guevara de la Serna, Ernesto (Che), 41, 107, 168, 189, *203–4*, 244, 372, 429
Guiana Industrial Workers Union, 229
Guianese Federation of Trade Unions, 129
Guianese Labour Party, 129
Guión Rojo, 190, 307
GULP, 61, 171–72
Gutiérrez, Francisco, 464
Gutiérrez, Rafael Antonio, 68
Gutiérrez Guerra, José, 300
Guyana Industrial Workers Union, 227
Guyanese Socialist Party, 109
Guzmán, Antonio Leocadio, *204–5*
Guzmán Blanco, Antonio, 32, 127–28, 155, *205–7*, 211
Guzmán Reynoso, Abimael, *207*

Hague Court, 105
Hassan Morales, Moíses, 326
Havana Student Directorate, 360
Havana Summit Meeting of the Non-aligned Nations, 327
Hawley, R. B., 292
Haya de la Torre, Víctor Raúl, 50, *209–10*, 284, 373, 395
Héder, Léopold, *210–11*
Hédouville, 269
Herald (Barbados), 457
Herbert, William, 412

Hernández, José Manuel, 105, 128, *211–12*
Hernández Colón, Rafael, *212*, 352
Hernández Martínez, Maximiliano, *212–13*
Herrera, Luis Alberto de, 34, *213*, 427
Herrera Campins, Luis, 88, *213–14*, 448
Heureaux, Ulíses, *214–15*, 441
Hidalgo y Costilla, Miguel, *215–16*, 224
Historia de Belgrano y de la Independencia Argentina, 296
Holguín, Carlos, 316
Hoover, Herbert, 396
Horacistas, 441
Hostos y Bonilla, Eugenio María de, *216–17*
Houston, Sam, 400
Hoy, 381, 384
Huerta, Adolfo de la, 92, 318, 446
Huerta, Victoriano, 97, *217*, 277, 446
Hull, Cordell, 20
Humphrey, Hubert, 239

Ibáñez del Campo, Carlos, *219–21*; dictatorship of, 5, 165, 377; forces Jorgé Alessandri into exile, 11; handpicks "Thermal Congress," 293; insists on running for president (1926), 9; opposed only by Lafertte in 1927, 245; overthrow of, 245, 298; Radical Party and others support Figueroa (1925), 298; relations with Grove, 199; supported by PSP in 1952 election, 15; undermines government of Figueroa, 159
ICM, 239, 270
Iglesias, Miguel, 86
Iglesias Castro, Rafael, *221*
Iglesias Pantín, Santiago, *222*
Illia, Arturo Umberto, 13, 33, 91, 168, *223*, 246, 323
ILP, 231, 322
Independence Conference, 92
Independent Citizens Movement, 239, 270
Independent Labor Party, 231, 322
Independent Liberal Party, 4, 114, 327, 414, 416

Independents, 315
Indianist movement, 192
Innis, Clement, 323
Institutional Revolutionary Party, 8, 94–95, 131, 138, 258, 262
Integrated Revolutionary Organizations, 381, 384
Inter-American Institute of Political Education, 298
Inter-American Regional Organization of Workers, 298
Inter-American System, 158
International African Opinion, 231
International African Service Bureau, 231
International Anti-Imperialist Congress, 373
International Confederation of Free Trade Unions, 72
International Congress of Anti-Imperialists, 209
International Congress of Catholic University Students, 165
International Federation of Trade Unions, 128
International Labor Organization, 253
International Monetary Fund, 3, 241, 280
Intransigent Radical Civic Union, 19, 33, 168
Irish, James, 328
Isaacs, Kendall George Lamon, *223–24*
Isabel, Princess, 341
Iturbide, Agustin de, *224–25*, 400, 437, 443
Izquierda Unida–IU, 40, 50, 63

Jagan, Cheddi, 77–78, *227–28*
Jagan, Janet (Rosenberg), 78, 227, *228–30*
Jalton, Fréderic, *230*
Jamaica Labour Party, 81, 279–82, 398, 407–8
Jamaica Workers' and Tradesmen's Union, 80
James, Cyril Lionel Robinson, *230–31*
Jean-François, 268
Jewel, 59, 62
Jiménez, Enrique Adolfo, 12, *231–32*

Jiménez Oreamuno, Ricardo, 157, 194, *232*, 452
JLP, 81, 279–82, 398, 407–8
João VI, King of Portugal, 339
John, Patrick Roland, 117–18, *232–34*
Johnson, Lyndon Baines, 120, 334
Joint Endeavour for the Welfare, Education and Liberation of the People, 59, 62
Jonckheer, Efraín, *234*, 239
Jordon, Edward, *234*
Jornado, 49
José Martí People's University, 209
Joshua, Ebenezer, 295
Journal of Commerce (Brazil), 313
Juárez, Benito, 136, *234–36*, 254
Justicialismo, 349
Justo, Agustín Pedro, *236–37*
Justo, Juan Bautista, *237*
JWTU, 80

Kennedy, John Fitzgerald, 32, 142, 334
Kenyatta, Jomo, 231
Khrushchev, Nikita, 147
King, Cyril Emmanuel, *239*
Kingston Proclamation, 178
Kroon, Ciro de, *239–40*
Kubitschek de Oliveira, Juscelino, *240–41*, 243–44, 314, 363

La Alborada, 174
La Aurora de Chile, 110
Labor (Peru), 284
Labor Federation of Chile, 245, 374
Labour Party (Bahamas), 354
Labour Party (Montserrat), 73–75
Lacayo Farfán, Enrique, 415
Lacerda, Carlos, 240–41, *243–44*
Lachmon, Jaggernath, *244–45*
La Crítica, 25
La Crónica, 34
La Democracia (Colombia), 315
La Democracia (Puerto Rico), 309, 311
La Época, 96
Lafertte Gaviño, Elías, 219, *245–46*
La Gaceta del Comercio, 56
La Hora, 25
La Justicia, 8

La Nación, 296
Lantern Club, 243
Lanusse, Alejandro Agustín, *246*, 324, 350
La Prensa (Argentina), 19
La Prensa (Peru), 284, 373
La Prensa (Nicaragua), 114, 326–37, 414–15
La Raza Cosmica, 440
La Razón, 284
Laredo Brú, Federico, 46, *246–47*
La República, 344
Larrazábal, Wolfgang, 448
La Ruche, 255
Laski, Harold, 45
Latin American Congress (1847), 103
Latin American Free Trade Area, 11
Latin American Parliament, 431
La Tribuna, 431
La Trinitaria, 139
La Unidad, 187
Lavalleja, Juan Antonio, 161, *247–48*, 324, 379
La Vanguardia, 183, 237
Laveau (French governor of St. Domingue), 268
League of Colored Peoples, 77
League of National Defense, 86
League of Nations, 220, 322, 390, 405
LeBlanc, Edward Oliver, 233, *248–49*
LeBlanc Labour Party, 248
Lechín Oquendo, Juan, 202, *249–50*, 338
Leclerc, Charles, 122, 134, 269, 352
Leftist National Revolutionary Movement, 411
Left Union, 361
"Legalist Revolution," 211
Légitimus, Hégépape, *250*
Leguía, Augusto B., 82, 209, *250–51*, 284, 337, 373, 395
Leíva, Ponciano, 68
Lémus, José María, 328
Lenin, Vladimir Ilyich, 203
León de Vivero, Fernando, *251–52*
Leoni, Raúl, 51, 87–88, *252–53*, 346, 366, 448
Lerdo de Tejada, Sebastián, 136, *253–54*
Lescot, Élie, 141, 149, *254–55*, 278, 452

Liberal, 362
Liberal Alliance (Brazil), 314, 363, 439
Liberal Alliance (Chile), 9, 276, 301, 376
Liberal Democratic Party, 397, 444
Liberal League, 418
Liberal Nationalist Party, 105, 211
Liberal Party (Barbados), 362
Liberal Party (Bolivia), 90, 299, 335–36, 389, 392
Liberal Party (Brazil), 39, 341
Liberal Party (Central American Federation), 70, 306
Liberal Party (Chile), 8–10, 35, 146–47, 167, 220, 299–300, 347, 356–57, 360, 367, 377, 402, 444
Liberal Party (Colombia), 56, 97, 173–74, 188, 256–57, 264–66, 308–9, 315–16, 318, 321–22, 329–30, 375–76, 384–85, 404–5
Liberal Party (Costa Rica), 101–2, 194, 221, 418, 428
Liberal Party (Cuba), 152, 185, 190, 275, 293
Liberal Party (Ecuador), 11–12, 26, 160, 179, 357–58, 382, 442
Liberal Party (Guatemala), 42–43, 99
Liberal Party (Haiti), 393
Liberal Party (Honduras), 66–67, 95–96, 177, 417–18, 450–51
Liberal Party (Mexico), 35, 235
Liberal Party (Nicaragua), 4, 114–15, 327, 396, 414–15, 454, 464–65
Liberal Party (Panama), 119–20, 231, 359, 380
Liberal Party (Paraguay), 31, 85, 119, 149, 164
Liberal Party (Peru), 192
Liberal Party (Puerto Rico), 38, 309, 385
Liberal Party (Spain), 311
Liberal Party (Venezuela), 155, 204–6, 296–97, 334
Liberal Republic, 35, 44, 346
"Liberal Restoring Revolution," 211
Liberal Revolution, 417
Liberal Revolutionary Movement, 264
Liberal Society of Caracas, 204
"Liberating Revolution," 105

Liberia-Peters, Maria, *255*
Lincoln, Abraham, 235
Lindo, Juan, 279
Linieres, Santiago, 378
Livingston, Roberto, 246
Lleras Camargo, Alberto, *255–56*, 266
Lleras Restrepo, Carlos, *256–57*, 405
Llovera Páez, Luis Felipe, 345
Lobo, Aristides. *See* Luis Carlos Prestes
Lombardo Toledano, Vicente, *257–58*
Lonardi, Eduardo, 18
López, Carlos Antonio, *258–59*, 260
López, Estansilao, 379
López, Francisco Solano, 161, *259–60*
López, José Hilario, 308, 317, 318
López Arellano, Oswaldo, *260–61*, 451
López Contreras, Eleazar, *261–62*; aspirations to return to presidency (1945) opposed by Caldera, 87; deports Machado, Villalba, and 41 others in 1937, 274, 447; Gallegos briefly in his government before joining opposition, 174; handpicked Congress chooses president (1941), 54; and Medina, his minister of war and navy and chosen successor, 289, 447; outlaws PDN and its leaders (1937), 42, 54, 252; and "symbolic" candidacy of Gallegos, 54, 175
López Gutierrez, Rafael, 96
López Mateos, Adolfo, 137–38, *262–63*
López Michelson, Alfonso, 257, *263–64*, 322
López Portillo, José, 131, 138, *264–65*
López Pumarejo, Alfonso, 173, 188, 257, 263, *265–66*, 405
Lora Escobar, Guillermo, 249, *266–67*
Los Aventureros, 174
"Los Doce," 414
Lott, Henrique, 243, 371
Louisy, Allan, *267–68*
L'Ouverture, Toussaint, 70–71, 122–23, *268–70*, 352–53
Lozano Días, Julio, 177, 260, 450–51
Lozoya, Melitón, 446
Luis, Juan, *270*
Luis, Washington, 53, *270–71*, 439
Lusinchi, Jamie, 88, 214, *271*, 448

Luz, Carlos, 243
Lynch, Elisa Alicia, 260

MacAulay, Neil, 397
Maceo y Grajales, Antonio, 178–79, 189, *273–74*, 288, 291
Machado, Gustavo, *274–75*, 292
Machado, Salvador, 464
Machado Lopes, José, 76, 196
Machado y Morales, Gerardo, 121, 190, 197, *275–76*, 285, 368, 380
MacIver Rodríguez, Enrique, *276–77*
Madero, Francisco I., 98, 137, 219, *277*, 318, 440, 445–46, 463
Madero, Raúl, 446
Magloire, Paul Eugène, 141, 149–50, 255, *277–79*
Magnus, Louise, 393
Malespín, Francisco, *279*
Man and Socialism in Cuba, 203
Manley, Michael Norman, *279–81*, 408
Manley, Norman Washington, 80–81, 279–80, *281–82*
Mann, Horace, 406
Man Power Citizen's Association, 227
MAP, 59
Maraj, Bhadase Sagan, 92, *282–84*
Maria I, Queen of Portugal, 340
Mariátegui, José Carlos, 40, 103, *284–85*, 360, 373
Marighela, Carlos, 289
Marinello, Juan, 47, 121, *285–86*, 381, 383
Mariño, Santiago, *286–87*, 333, 424
Maritain, Jacques, 165
Marof, Tristán. *See* Gustavo Navarro
Marquesa de Santos, 66
Márquez, José Ignacio de, 307, 317, 404
Marryshow, Theophilus Albert, 171, *287–88*
Martí, José, 152, 189, 273, 285, *288–89*, 292, 311
Martínez, Bartolomé, 115
Martinican Progressive Party, 111
Marx, Karl, 203, 237, 285
Masas, 267
Matos, Manuel Antonio, 105

Maximilian, Emperor of Mexico, 135, 235

MDB, 314

Medeiros, Borges de, 438

Médici, Emílio Garrastazú, *289*

Medina Angarita, Isaías, *289–90*; AD seeks agreement with him on joint candidate (1945), 252; his election imposed by López Contreras, 175, 262; his handpicked successor supported by Villalba, 447; legalizes PDN as AD, 54, 252; overthrow of, planned by AD and Military Patriotic Union, 42, 54, 87, 132, 175, 252, 262, 345, 366, 447

Mejía Colindres, Vicente, 96

Melgarejo, Mariano, 51, *290–91*

Melo, José María, 308, 318

Mena, Luis, 115

Méndex, Abadía, 173

Méndez Manfredini, Aparicio, 17, 69, *291*

Mendieta y Montefur, Carlos, 46, 247, 275–76, *291–92*

Mendive, Rafael María, 288

Menocal, Mario García, 185, 190, 276, *292–93*

MEP, 42, 344, 366

Mercier, Cardinal, 88, 452

Merwin, John David, *293*

Mexican Federation of Labor, 93–94, 131

Mexican Labor Party, 258

Mexican Regional Confederation of Labor, 258

MID, 169

Mikoyan, Anastas, 107

Military Club of Rio de Janeiro, 126

Military Patriotic Union, 132, 346

Military Peasant Pact, 36, 41

Miners' Bloc, 249

Miners Federation of Bolivia, 249, 267

Miners Parliamentary Bloc, 266

MIR. *See* Movement of the Revolutionary Left

Miranda, Francisco de, 64, 286, *293–94*

Mitchell, James Fitz Allen, 110, *294–95*

Mitre, Bartolomé, 161, 407, *295–96*

Mitterand, François, 230

MNR. *See* Nationalist Revolutionary Movement

MNRA, 202

MNRI, 411

Moderate Party. *See* Conservative Party (Cuba)

Molas López, Felipe, 119, 190–91, 423

Monagas, José Gregorio, 155, 204, *296–97*

Monagas, José Tadeo, 155, 204, 286, *297–98*, 333

Moncada, Benjamín, 416

Moncada, José María, 115, 396

Monge Alvarez, Luis Alberto, 93, *298*

"Mongoose Gang," 172

Montealegre, José Maria, 305

Montero, Juan Estebán, 9

Montero Rodríguez, Juan Esteban, *298–99*

Montes, Ismael, *299–300*

Montoneros, 444

Montserrat Trades and Labour Union, 74–75

Montt Alverez, Jorge, 35, 146, *300–301*

Montt Montt, Pedro, 159, *301–2*

Montt Torres, Manuel, 35, 77, 147, 301, *302–3*, 346–47, 401, 406, 438, 444

Montt–Varista Party, 438

Moore, Lee Llewellyn, *303–4*, 412

MOP, 140

Morales, Agustín, 290

Morales, Franklin, 96

Morales Bermúdez, Francisco, *304*

Mora Porrás, Juan Rafael, *304–5*

Mora Valverde, Manuel, 89, 127, *305*, 394

Morazán, Francisco, 22, 99, 101, 279, *305–6*, 437

Moreno Díaz, Samuel, 385

Morínigo, Higinio, 164, 191, *306–7*, 423

Mosquera, Joaquín, 307

Mosquera, Manuel, 307–8

Mosquera, Tomás Cipriano de, *307–9*

Movement for Assemblies of the People, 59

Movement for Renovation and Change, 13

Movement for the Advancement of Community Effort, 59
Movement of Integration and Development, 169
Movement of the Revolutionary Left (Chile), 15–16
Movement of the Revolutionary Left (Venezuela), 88
Movimiento de Bases Hayistas, 50, 431
Movimiento de Integración y Desarrollo, 169
Movimiento Electoral del Pueblo (Aruba), 129
Movimiento Electoral del Pueblo (Venezuela), 42, 344, 366
Movimiento Nacionalista Revolucionario. See Nationalist Revolutionary Movement
Movimiento Nacionalista Revolucionario Auténtico, 202
Movimiento Revolucionario Liberal, 264
Monyne, Lord, 83
MRL, 264
MTLU, 74–75
Muñoz Marín, Luis, 6, 222, *309–11*, 385
Muñoz Rivera, Luis, 302, *311–12*
Mussolini, Benito, 24, 173, 349

Nabuco de Araujo, Joaquim Barreto, *313*
Nardone, Benito, 69
Nation, 231
National Action, 87
National Antireelectionist Party, 277
National Association of Catholic Students, 165
National Association of People's Power, 381
National Campesino Federation, 93–94
National Coffee Federation of Colombia, 257, 329
National Concentration, 321
National Council of Administration, 49
National Democratic Front, 50, 52, 82, 209
National Democratic Party, 41, 54, 252, 366, 447
National Democratic Union, 196, 243–44
Nationale Militaire Rand, 70

National Federation of Campesinos, 450
National Federation of Students, 103
National Front, 56, 188, 256, 264, 266, 330, 385, 405
Nationalist Liberal Party, 413
Nationalist Party (Bolivia), 409
Nationalist Party (Haiti), 451–52
Nationalist Party (Uruguay). See Blanco Party
Nationalist Revolutionary Movement, 36, 40, 201–2, 249, 266–67, 330, 337–38, 410, 435, 449
National Labor Party, 371
National Labour Movement, 116, 125
National Liberation Alliance, 363
National Liberation Party, 93, 158, 298, 325, 434
National Party (Chile), 35, 146–47, 301–2, 346–47, 357
National Party (Colombia), 308
National Party (Haiti), 393
National Party (Honduras), 66, 68, 95–96, 177, 261, 450
National Patriotic Coalition, 200, 377
National People's Party, 255
National Phalanx, 165, 193, 377
National Popular Alliance, 385
National Republican Association. See Colorado Party (Paraguay)
National Republican Party, 305
National Revolution, 249
National Revolutionary Movement, 138
National Revolutionary Party. See Institutional Revolutionary Party
National Security Volunteers, 141
National Sergeants Command, 76
National Student Strike Committee, 137
National Trade Union Congress, 456
National Unification, 434
National Union, 192
National Union of Opposition, 4, 114
National Union of Students, 86–87, 213
National Workers Union, 279
Natusch Busch, Alberto, 339
Navarro, Gustavo, 79
NDP, 110, 295
"Negritude" movement, 111
Negro World, 181

Neves, Tancredo, 196, *313–15*
Nevis Reformation Party, 303, 412–13
New Democratic Party, 110, 295
"New Force," 446
New Jamaican, 182
New Jewel Movement, 59, 62
New National Party, 62
New Progessive Party, 156, 386
New York Sun, 288
Nicaraguan Patriotic Youth, 326
Nicaraguan Socialist Party, 414
Niemeyer, Oscar, 240
Nixon, Richard, 16, 40, 62
NJM, 59, 62
NLM, 116, 125
NMR, 70
NPP, 156, 386
NPS, 25, 244, 344
NRP, 303, 412–13
Nuestra Epoca, 284
Núñez Moledo, Rafael, 97, *315–16*
Núñez Portuondo, Ricardo, 121
NWU, 279

OAS. *See* Organization of American States
Obaldia, José Domingo de, 231
Obando, Jośe María, 308, 315, *317–18*
Obregón, Alvaro, 89, 98, *318–19*, 440, 446
O'Connor, Quintin, 184
Odlum, George, 267–68
O'Donojú, Juan, 224
Odría, Manuel A., 82, 209, 251, *319*, 361
Odriísta National Union, 319
Oduber Quirós, Daniel, 93, 158, *319–20*
OECS, 110, 118, 125
O'Higgins, Bernardo, 100–101, 167, *320–21*, 356
Oilfield Workers Trade Union, 83, 456
Olaya Herrera, Enrique, 256, 265–66, *321–22*, 376, 404
O'Neale, Charles Duncan, 1, *322–23*, 457
Onganía, Juan Carlos, 246, *323–24*
Operation Pan America, 241

Organizaciones Revolucionarias Integradas, 381, 384
Organización Venezolana. *See* Democratic Action (Venezuela)
Organization of American States, 4, 45, 120, 256, 358, 415, 435
Organization of Eastern Caribbean States, 110, 118, 125
Oribe, Manuel, 161, 247, *324–25*, 379
ORIT, 298
Orlich Bolmarcich, Francisco José, 158, 298, 320, *325–26*
Orozco, José, 440
Orozco, Pascual, 445
Ortega Saavedra, (José) Daniel, *326–27*
Ortíz, Roberto, 236
Ortíz Rubio, Pascual, 440
Ortodoxo Party. *See* Cuban People's Party
ORVE. *See* Democratic Action (Venezuela)
Osborn, Robert, 234
Osborne, John Alfred, 73, *327–28*
Osorio, Oscar, *328–29*
Ospina, Pedro Nel, 322, 329
Ospina Pérez, Mariano, 174, 188, 256–57, 308, *329–30*
Ospina Rodríguez, Mariano, 329
Our View, 282
Ovalle, Tomás, 360
Ovando Candia, Alfredo, 36, 41, 228, *330–31*, 411, 429
OWTU, 83, 456

PAC, 77, 227, 229
Pacheco, Gregorio, 37
Pacheco Areco, Jorge, 69
Páez, José Antonio, 65, 204, 286, *333–34*, 296–97, 403, 419
Paiewonsky, Ralph, *334*
Palacios, Alfredo Lorenzo, 237, *334–35*
PAM, 303, 412–13
Pan Africanists, 181
Pan American Federation of Labor, 222
Pan American Sanitary Bureau, 96
Pando, José Manuel, 90, 299, *335–36*, 392
PAP. *See* Peruvian Aprista Party

Pardo y Aliago, Felipe, 337
Pardo y Barreda, José, 52, 250, *336–37*
Pardo y Lavalle, Manuel, *337*
Paris Aprista Committee, 373
Parliamentary Republic, 35, 44
Partido Civil, 52, 250, 336
Partido Comunista de Cuba. *See* Communist Party (Cuba)
Partido Comunista Peruano—Bandera Roja, 207
Partido del Pueblo Cubano, 121
Partido Democrático Pradista, 361
Partido Dominicano, 431
Partido Liberación Dominicana, 69–70
Partido Obrero Revolucionario, 202, 266–67
Partido Popular, 464
Partido Popular Cristiano, 49
Partido Reformista. *See* Reformist Party
Partido Revolucionario Auténtico (Bolivia), 202, 338, 410
Partido Revolucionario Cubana (Auténtico), 121, 198, 368
Partido Revolucionario Dominicana, 32, 69, 342–43
Partido Social Cristiano Copei. *See* Social Christian Copei Party
Partido Socialista Popular. *See* Popular Socialist Party (*various entries*)
Parti Progressiste Martiniquais, 111
Party of Political Progress Group, 184
Party of the Mexican Revolution. *See* Institutional Revolutionary Party
Party of the Revolutionary Left, 28, 449
Pastrana Borrero, Misael, 385
Patria, 190
Patriotic Junta of Venezuela, 204
Patriotic Union, 451
Paulista Republican Party, 270
Paz Barahona, Miguel, 96, 177
Paz Estenssoro, Víctor, *337–39*; attempted coup against, by Falange Socialista Boliviana in 1953, 435; candidacy of, in 1978 presidential election, 202; opposition to, by Jugo Banzer, 36; overthrown by Generals Ovando and Barrientos, 36, 41, 202, 249; participant in Germán Busch gov-

ernment, 79; pressured into naming General Barrientos as vice presidential candidate, 41; put in power by 1952 Revolution, 80, 249, 410; reelected president in 1960, 202, 249; reelected president in 1985, 250
Paz Galarraga, Jesús, 366
PCC. *See* Communist Party (Cuba)
PCN. *See* Conservative Party (Nicaragua)
PCP, 40, 103, 360–61, 373
PCT. *See* Conservative Party (Nicaragua)
PDC. *See* Christian Democratic Party (*various entries*)
PDN, 41, 54, 252, 366, 447
PDP. *See* Peoples Democratic Party; Progressive Labour Party
PDT, 76
PDV, 290
Pearson's Magazine, 136
Peasant Congress, 40
Peasant Development Scheme, 58
Pedro I, Dom (Alcântara de Bragança e Bourbon), 17, 66, 156, *339–40*
Pedro II, Dom (de Alcântara), 18, 39, 53, 66, 126, 133, 270, 313, *340–42*
Peixoto, Floriano, 127, 134, *342*
Pelucones, 76, 167, 302
Peña Gómez, José Francisco, 69, *342–43*
Peñaranda, Enrique, 28, 338
Pengel, Johan Adolf, 25, 244, *343–44*
Peoples Action Movement, 303, 412–13
Peoples Alliance, 60, 62
People's Army, 60
Peoples Assembly, 249, 267
Peoples Committee, 364
Peoples Democratic Party, 283
Peoples Liberation Movement, 328
Peoples National Congress, 78
Peoples National Movement, 84, 92, 113, 184, 231, 283, 457, 458–59
Peoples National Party, 80–81, 92, 279–82, 398, 408
People's Political Party (Jamaica), 181
Peoples Political Party (St. Vincent), 295
Peoples Progressive Party (Guyana), 77–78, 227, 229
Peoples Progressive Party (St. Lucia), 125

Peoples' Radical Civic Union, 13, 33, 91, 168, 223

People's Revolutionary Government, 60, 62, 172

People's United Movement, 326

Peoples United Party, 364–65

People's Universities, 209

Perdue, Michael Eugene, 233

Pereda Asbún, Juan, 37

Pereira, Gabriel Antonio, 161

Pérez, Carlos Andrés, 55, *344–45*

Pérez, Jiménez, Marcos, *345–46*; allowed to return home by Delgado Chalbaud (1948), 132; and close watch kept on Caldera during his regime, 87; open plotting against, by Gallegos, 175; overthrow of, 42, 55, 175, 214, 253, 271, 274, 344, 366, 447; deportation of Villalba, 447; seizes power (1952), 87, 447

Pérez Mascayano, José Joaquín, 147, 302, *346–47*

Permanent Assembly for Human Rights, 13

Perón, Eva María Duarte de (Evita), *347–49*, 350

Perón, Juan Domingo, *349–51*; elected to presidency with Isabelita as vice president (1973), 33, 91; endorses candidacy of Frondizi, 168; marries Eva Duarte, 347; marries María Estela Martínez, 351; 1943 coup, 237; opposition to, by Balbin, 32; opposition to, by Ghioldi, 183; opposition to, by Palacios, 335; ouster of, in 1955 coup, 33, 91; relations with Aramburu, 18–19; relations with Cámpora, 13, 91; supports Paraguayan President Morínigo, 307; use of his name barred in 1958 elections, 19

Perón, María Estela Martínez de (Isabelita), 91, *351–52*, 444

Peronist Party, 91, 168, 349–50

Peronists, 13–14, 168–69

Pershing, John, 446

Personalist Radical Party, 462

Peru-Bolivian Confederation, 103, 178

Peruvian Aprista Party, 50, 52, 82, 180, 209–10, 395–96, 431, 448

Peruvian Socialist Party, 103, 284–85, 360, 373

Pétion, Alexandre, 64, 70–71, 123, 135, *352–53*, 419

Petroleos Mexicanos, 131, 264–65

Picado Michalski, Teodoro, 89, 127, 158, 305, 394

Pierola, Nicolás de, 57, 86, *353–54*

Pindling, Lynden Oscar, 224, *354–55*

Pinochet Ugarte, Augusto, 11, 16, 37, 166, 194, *355–56*

Piño Suárez, José, 277

Pinto Bernardes, Maria Aniceta, 53

Pinto Garmendía, Aníbal, 35, *356–57*, 438

Pipiolos (Novices), 167, 356

Plan of San Luis, 277

Platt Amendment, 152

Plaza Gutiérrez, Leónidas, 12, *357–58*

Plaza Lasso, Galo, *358*, 442

PLD, 69–70

PLM. *See* Mexican Labor Party; Peoples Liberation Movement; Progressive Labour Movement

PLN, 93, 158, 298, 325, 434

PLP, 224, 354

PNC, 78

PNM. *See* Peoples National Movement

PNP. *See* Peoples National Party

Political Affairs Committee, 77, 227, 229

Political Organization of the Venezuelan Students Federation, 447

Ponce, Federico, 433

Ponce Enríquez, Camilo, *358–59*

Popular Action, 50–51, 304

Popular Assembly, 249, 267

Popular Christian Movement, 41

Popular Democratic Party, 212, 222, 309–10, 386

Popular Democratic Unity, 40

Popular Front, 5, 14, 193, 363, 373, 377

Popular Liberating Alliance Coalition, 220

Popular Nationalist Front, 36

Popular Party (Cuba), 464

Popular Party (Mexico), 257–58

Popular Socialist Party (Chile), 15
Popular Socialist Party (Cuba), 108, 286, 380, 384
Popular Socialist Party (Mexico), 257–58
Popular Unity, 15, 166
Popular Vanguard Party, 305
POR, 202, 266–67
PORRA, 276
Porras, Belisario, 119, *359–60*
Portales Palazuelos, Diego, *360*, 367
Portinari, Candido, 240
Positivists, 315
PPP. *See* People's Political Party (Jamaica); Peoples Political Party (St. Vincent); Peoples Progressive Party (Guyana); Peoples Progressive Party (St. Lucia)
PRA, 202, 338, 410
Prado, Jorge del, *360–61*
Prado, Mariano Ignacio, 103, 337
Prado Democratic Party, 361
Prado Ugarteche, Manuel, 50, 52, 82, *361–62*, 431
Prats, Carlos, 16, 355
PRD, 32, 69, 342–43
Prescod, Samuel Jackman, *362–63*
Presidential Succession in 1910, The, 277
Prestes, Julio, 271
Prestes, Luis Carlos, *363–64*
Prestes Column, 363
PRG, 60, 62, 172
Price, George, 148, *364–66*
Prieto Figueroa, Luis Beltrán, 42, *366–67*
Prieto Vial, Joaquín, 302, *367–68*
Primo de Rivera, José Antonio, 435
Prío Socarrás, Carlos, 47, 106, 121, 198, *368–69*
Progressive Democratic Party, 73–74, 328
Progressive Labour Movement, 58, 455
Progressive Liberal Party, 224, 354
Progressive Party, 18, 314
Progressive Reformed Party, 244
Progressive Republican Party, 153, 293
Proletarian Tendency, 326
Prolonged Popular War Tendency, 326
PRP, 270

PRUD, 328–29
PRUD (Auténtico), 329
PSD. *See* Social Democratic Party
PSG, 109
PSO, 245, 374
PSP. *See* Popular Socialist Party (*various entries*); Socialist Party (Peru)
PTB, 75–76, 196
PU, 15, 166
Public Opinion, 279
Puerto Rican Nationalist Party, 5
PUP, 364–65
"Puros," 38
PVP, 305

Quadros, Jânio, 76, 102, 196, 241, 244, 314, *371–72*
Quiros, Facundo, 406

RADEPA, 338, 449
Radical Civic Union. *See* Radical Party (Argentina)
Radical Civic Union of the People, 13, 33, 91, 168, 223
Radical Party (Argentina), 6–7, 13–14, 32–33, 168, 223, 236–37, 382, 390–91, 461–62
Radical Party (Chile), 5, 9–10, 15, 35, 57, 126, 147, 165, 193–94, 199, 276, 298–99, 300, 347, 377
Radical Party (Peru), 193–94
Railroad Workers Union, 263
Ramírez Mercado, Sergio, 326–27
Rastafarian movement, 233, 248
Ravines, Eudocio, *373–74*
Reagan, Ronald W., 3, 60, 118, 143, 153, 176, 295, 327
"Reason of the Fatherland," 338, 449
Recabarren Serrano, Luis Emilio, 243, *374*
Red International of Labor Unions, 374
Reformist Party (Costa Rica), 452
Reformist Party (Dominican Republic), 32
Reinaldo Solar, 174
Reis Velloso, João Paulo, 289
Remón Cantera, José Antonio, 24, 120, 200, *374–75*, 380

Representative Government Association, 287
Republica Mayor de Centro America, 68
Republican Democratic Union, 87, 447–48
Republican Party (Argentina), 6
Republican Party (Bolivia), 300, 336, 389, 392
Republican Party (Brazil), 39, 53, 133, 341
Republican Party (Puerto Rico), 38, 222, 311
Republican Party (Spain), 382
"Republic in Arms," 111, 151
Republic of Central America, 114
Republic Union, 376
"Rerum Novarum," 298, 394
"Restoring Liberal Revolution," 105
Revista de Lima, 337
Revolutionary Governing Junta, 42, 132
Revolutionary Government of the Armed Forces, 50, 441
Revolutionary Group of the Left, 41, 53, 252
Revolutionary Insurrectional Movement, 106
Revolutionary Movement, 285
Revolutionary National Leftist Union, 173
Revolutionary Party, 29, 440
Revolutionary Party of Democratic Unification, 328
Revolutionary Party of the National Left, 249
Revolutionary Union (Cuba), 285
Revolutionary Union (Peru), 395
Revolutionary Workers Party, 202, 266–67
"Revolution on the March," 256, 265–66, 405
Reyes, Rafael, 322, 375–76
Riche, Jean Baptiste, 182, 419
Rienzi, Andrian, 124
Riesco Errázuriz, Germán, 376–77
Riguad, André, 70, 134, 269, 352
Riggs, E. Francis, 6
Ríos Morales, Juan Antonio, 10, 14, 165, 193, 199, 220, 377–78

Rivadavia, Barnardino, 378
Rivas, Patricio, 454
Rivera, Diego, 440
Rivera, Fructuoso, 161, 247, 324, 378–79
Riviérez, Héctor, 379–80
Robello Calleja, Alfonso, 326–27
Robles, Marco Aurelio, 380
Roca, Blas, 380–81, 383
Roca, Julio Argentino, 146, 381–82
Rocafuerte, Vicente, 160, 179, 382–83
Rodas Alvarado, Modesto, 451
Rodríguez, José Joaquín, 221, 418
Rodríguez, Simón, 64
Rodríguez Lara, Guillermo, 383
Rodríguez Rodríguez, Carlos Rafael, 47, 381, 383–84
Rojas, Isaac, 18
Rojas de Moreno, María Eugenia, 385
Rojas Paúl, Juan Pablo, 128, 206
Rojas Pinilla, Gustavo, 188, 256, 384–85, 404–5
Romero, Carlos Humberto, 139
Romero Barceló, Carlos, 285–86
Roosevelt, Franklin Delano, 20, 276, 309, 439, 451
Roosevelt, Theodore, 152, 222
Rosas, Juan Manuel de, 161, 259, 295, 324, 379, 386–87, 406, 436
Rosenberg, Janet. See Jagan, Janet
Rosenwald, Julian, 458
Royo, Aristides, 430
Rozendal, Sylvus, 387–88
Ruíz Cortines, Adolfo, 7, 258
Ruiz Tagle, Francisco, 367
Ruz González, Lina, 106

Saavedra, Abdón, 409
Saavedra, Bautista, 389–90, 392, 409
Sable, Victor, 390
Sacasa, Juan Bautista, 396, 416
Sacasa, Roberto, 464
Sáenz Peña, Luis, 390
Sáenz Peña, Roque, 390–91, 461
Sagasta, Praxedes Mateo, 311
Sailors Enlisted Men's Organization, 76
St. George's Chronicle and Grenada Gazette, 287

St. John, Harold Bernard, 3, *391–92*

St. Kitts–Nevis–Anguilla Labour Party, 72–73, 303, 412, 421

St. Kitts Workers League, 72

St. Lucia Labour Party, 116–17, 125, 267–68

St. Lucia Workers Union, 116

St. Vincent Labour Party, 109–10, 295

Saladrigas, Carlos, 47, 198

Salamanca Urey, Daniel, 389, *392–93*

Salnave, Sylvain, 183

Salomon, Louis-Félicité Lysius, *393–94*

Sanabria Martínez, Victor, 89, *394–95*

Sánchez, José Aurelio, 291

Sánchez, Luis Alberto, *395*

Sánchez Cerro, Luís M., 52, 82, 209, 360, *395–96*

Sánchez Vilella, Roberto, 310

Sandinista Front of National Liberation, 4, 161–62, 326–27, 396, 414

Sandino, Augusto César, 162, *396–97*, 416

Sanfuentes, Juan Luis, *397*

Sangster, Donald Burns, *397–98*

Sanguinetti, Julio María, *398–99*

San Martín, José de, *399–400*; and Army of the Andes, 167, 320, 406; campaigns in Peru, 178, 356, 401; capture of Ramón Castilla, 103; meeting with Bolívar, 65; relations with Carrera, 100–101; support of O'Higgins, 321

Santa Anna, Antonio López de, 235, *400–401*

Santa Cruz, Andrés de, 178, 290, *401*

Santa María González, Domingo, 35, 44, 146, *401–2*

Santana, Pedro, 31, 139, *402–3*

Santander, Francisco de Paula, 65, 317, *403–4*

Santos, Eduardo, 366, *404–5*

Saravia, Aparicio, 48, *405–6*

Sarmiento, Domingo Faustino, *406–7*, 436

Sarney, José, 314

Schick Gutiérrez, René, 162, 415

Scottish Rite Masons, 443

Seaga, Edward P. G., 280, *407–8*

Seamen and Waterfront Workers Union, 232

Semana, 56

"Semana Trágica," 461

Serviez, Manuel, 403

Shearer, Hugh, 453

7 ensayos de interpretación de la realidad peruana, 284

SFIO, 210, 230, 437

"Shark, The," 185

Sharpe, Samuel, *408–9*

Sheldon, Turner, 162, 413

Shoe Workers Union, 380

Sierra, Terencio, 66–68, 95, 418

Siles Reyes, Hernando, 389, 392, *409–10*

Siles Salinas, Luis Adolfo, 330

Siles Zuazo, Hernán, 202, 249–50, 338, *410–12*, 435

Simmonds, Kennedy Alphonse, 305, *412–13*

Sixth International Conference of American States, 275

SLP. *See* St. Lucia Labour Party; St. Vincent Labour Party

Sociabilidad Chilena, 56

Social Christian Copei Party, 42, 86–88, 213–14, 250, 253, 271, 366, 448

Social Christian Movement (Ecuador), 358

Social Christian Movement (Guatemala), 110

Social Christian Party (Ecuador), 358

Social Christian Party (Nicaragua), 4, 114

Social Democratic Party (Brazil), 240, 314

Social Democratic Party (Costa Rica), 319, 325

Socialist Alliance. *See* Socialist Party (Chile)

Socialist International, 128, 320, 345–44

Socialist Labor Party, 245, 374,

Socialist Party (Argentina), 183, 236–37, 335

Socialist Party (Chile), 14–16, 54, 126, 166, 199, 377

Socialist Party (Ecuador), 26, 358

Socialist Party (France), 210, 230, 437

Socialist Party (French Guiana), 379
Socialist Party (Guadeloupe), 230, 250, 437
Socialist Party (Nicaragua), 161
Socialist Party (Peru), 103, 284–85, 360, 373
Socialist Party (Puerto Rico), 221–22, 309
Socialist Republican Party, 389, 409
Socialist Republic of Chile, 199
Socialist Workers Party, 231
Sociedad de la Igualdad, 56, 443
Soldiers and Sailors Union, 124
Solorzano, Carlos, 115
Somoza Debayle, Anastasio, 4, 114, *413–14*, 415
Somoza Debayle, Luis, 114, 326, 413, *414–16*, 417
Somoza family, 326, 396, 414
Somoza García, Anastasio (''Tacho''), 89, 115–16, 145, 396, 413, 414, *416–17*
Sonthonax, 269
Soto, Marco Aurelio, 194, *417–18*
Soto Alfaro, Bernardo, *418–19*
Soublette, Carlos, 333, *419*
Soulouque, Adelina, 420
Soulouque, Faustin, 182, 393, *419–20*
Southwell, Caleb Azariah Paul, 72, 303, 412, *420–21*
Spanish Falange, 435
Springer, Sir Hugh Worrell, *421–22*
Statehood Republican Party, 157, 386
Stimson, Henry L., 115
Stoutt, Hamilton Lavity, *422–23*
Stroessner, Alfredo, 164, 191, 199, *423–24*
Student Directorate, 275
Students Federation, 252
Suazo Córdova, Roberto, 95
Sucre Alcalá, Antonio José de, 65, *424–25*
Sud America, 390
Surinam National Party, 25, 244, 344
SWU, 116

Teachers Federation of Venezuela, 366
Tejada Sorzano, José Luis, 392

Tenentes, 53, 439
Terra, Gabriel, 33, 47, 213, *427*
''Thesis of Pulacayo,'' 249, 266
Thiel, Bernardo Augusto, *427–28*
Third International, 373
Thirty-Three, The, 324
Thunder, 229
Tinoco Granados, Federico, 191, *428–29*, 452
TLP, 126
Tomic, Radomiro, 166
Tonton macoutes, 141
Toriello, Jorge, 21
Toro, David, 28, 79, 390
Torres González, Juan José, 36, 249, 267, 333, 338, 411, *429–30*
Torrijos Herrera Omar, 24, *430*
Tosta, Vicente, 96
''Town'' Party, 195
Townsend Ezcurra, Andrés, 50, *430–31*
Trades Union Council (Guyana), 129
Trade Union Congress (Jamaica), 81, 281
Traditional Conservative Party. *See* Conservative Party (Nicaragua)
Transport and Industrial Workers Trade Union, 456
Trejos, José Joaquín, 434
Tribuna da Imprensa, 243
Tribuna Popular, 274
Trinidad Labour Party, 126
Trinidad Workingmen's Association 83, 124
Trotskyists, 231, 249, 266, 361, 444
Trujillo, Hector, 32
Trujillo family, 423
Trujillo Molina, Rafael Leónidas, 32, 69, 254, 342, *431–32*, 441
Truman, Harry S., 6
Tugwell, Rexford, 310
Tupamaros, 69
Turbay, Gabriel, 56, 174
TWA, 83, 124
26th of July Movement, 108, 381, 384

Ubico y Castañeda, Jorge, 21, 23, *433–34*
UBP, 354
UCR. *See* Radical Party (Argentina)

UCRI, 19, 33, 168
UCRP, 13, 33, 91, 168, 223
UDN, 196, 243–44
UDP. *See* Democratic and Popular Unity; United Democratic Party
UGOCM, 258
Ulate Blanco, Otilio, 89, 145, 158, *434*
ULF, 457
UNE, 86–87, 213
Ungo, Guillermo, 138
Unidad de Izquierda, 361
Unidad Democrática Popular, 40
Unión Cívica, 296
Unión Cívica Radical. *See* Radical Party (Argentina)
Unión Cívica Radical del Pueblo, 13, 33, 91, 168, 223
Unión Cívica Radical Intransigente, 19, 33, 168
Union Confederation of Bolivian Workers, 28
Union de la Democratie Française, 390
Union for France in Europe, 390
Union for French Democracy, 390
Unión General de Obreros y Campesinos Mexicanos, 258
Unión Insurreccional Revolucionaria, 106
Unionist Party, 311
Unión Nacional, 192
Unión Nacional Izquierdista Revolucionaria, 173
Unión Nacional Odriísta, 319
Union of Students of France, 36
Unión para Avanzar, 88, 253, 290
Unión Patriótica Militar, 132, 346
Union pour la France en Europe, 390
Unión Revolucionaria. *See* Revolutionary Union
Unión Revolucionario Communista, 285, 380
UNIR, 173
United Bahamian Party, 354
United Brands. *See* United Fruit Company
United Democratic Party, 148, 365
United Force, 78
United Fruit Company, 21, 23, 67, 96, 151, 177, 261

United Labour Front, 457
United Left, 40, 50, 63
United Nations, 82, 253, 266, 405, 431
United Negro Improvement Association, 181
United Party, 457
United Peoples Party, 60, 62
United Statehooders, 386
United States of Indo-America, 210
United Workers Party, 125, 267
Unity Coalition, 93
University Federation of Bolivia, 28
Unzaga de la Vega, Oscar, *434–35*
UPM, 132, 346
UR. *See* Revolutionary Union
URD, 87, 447–48
Urdaneta, Rafael, 317, *435–36*
Urdaneta Arbeláez, Roberto, 188
Uriburu, José F., 236, 462
Urquiza, Justo José de, 161, 295, 387, 406, *436*
Urriolagoitia, Mamerto, 338
Urrutia, Manuel, 107
Utopian Socialists, 56
UWP, 125, 267

Valencia, Guillermo Leon, 56
Valentino, Paul, *437*
Valle, José Cecilio del, 306, *437–38*
Vallejo, Demetrio, 263
Vanderbilt, Cornelius, 454
Vanguard Party, 224
Varas de la Barra, Antonio, 302, 347, *438*
Vargas, Getúlio Dornelles, *438–40*; commits suicide, 102, 196, 240, 243; elected constitutional president in 1950, 20, 196, 243; and fall of Estado Novo, 363; first period in office (1930–1945), 53; followers of, after his death, 240, 244, 371; as governor of Rio Grande do Sul, 19; 1930 election campaign of, 314, 363; relations with Oswaldo Aranha, 20; revolutionary regime after October 1930, 19–20, 271; sets up Estado Novo dictatorship, 20, 240
Vargas, José María, 286, 297, 333, 419

Vargas, Manuel do Nascimento, 438
Vasconcelos, José, 209, 262, *440–41*
Vásquez, Horacio, 431, *441*
Velasco Alvarado, Juan, 50, 63, 304, 383, *441–42*
Velasco Ibarra, José María, 26, 358, 359, 383, *442–43*
Venezuelan Democratic Party, 290
Venezuelan Popular Union, 88, 253, 290
Venezuelan Revolutionary Party, 274
Venezuelan Students Federation, 86, 447
Vesco, Robert, 158, 320
VHP, 244
Victoria, Guadelupe, *443*
Victory Bloc, 305
Vicuña Mackenna, Benjamín, 147, 167, *443–44*
Videla, Jorge Rafael, 183, *444–45*
Vilatte, General, 269
Villa, Pancho, 94, 98, *445–47*
Villalba, Jóvito, 87, *447–48*
Villanueva, Armando, 50, *448–49*
Villarroel López, Gualberto, 28, 40, 201, 249, *449–50*
Villazón, Eliodoro, 300
Villeda, Alejandra Bermúdez de, 450
Villeda Morales, Ramón, 95, 177, 260, *450–51*
Villistas, 445
Vincent, Sténio, 254, 278, *451–52*
Viola, Roberto, 176, 445
Virgin Islands Party, 422, 457
Vision, 250
Vittorio Emanuel III, 313
Volio Jiménez, Jorge, *452*

Walcott, Frank Leslie, 2, *453–54*
Wallace, Cecil, 224
Walker, William, 52, 140, 201, 305, *454–55*
Walter, George Herbert, 58, *455–56*
War of the Thousand Days, 97
Washington, Booker T., 46
Watchman, 181, 234
Weekly Herald, 323
Weeks, George, *456–57*
Weil, Simone, 390

Welles, Sumner, 276
West Indian, 287
West Indian Federal Labour Party, 72, 81
West Indian Federation, 2, 58, 61, 81, 116, 125, 231, 282–83, 287, 364–65, 421, 459
West Indian Federation of Trade Unions, 129, 248
West Indian Labour Party, 129
West Indies Students' Union, 77
We The People, 231,
Weyler, Valeriano, 463
Wheatley, Willard, 457
Wickham, Clennel Wilsden, 1, 323, *457–58*
"Wigged Ones," 76, 167, 302
Williams, Eric, 84, 92, 113, 184, 231, 283, *458–60*
Williams Calderón, Abraham, 177, 450
Williman, Claudio, 427
Wilson, Woodrow, 192, 428, 446, 464
Wood, Leonard, 152, 463
Worker–Peasant Movement, 140
Workers and Peasants Party, 231
Worker's Circle, 221
Workers Party, 231
Workers University of Mexico, 257
Workingmen's Association 323
World Bank, 3

York Rite Masons, 443
Yrigoyen, Hipólito, 7, 236–37, 391, *461–62*

Zañartu, Anibal, 146
Zañartu, Enrique, 301
"Zancudo." *See* Conservative Party (Nicaragua)
Zapata, Emiliano, 94, 98, 217, 277, *463*
Zapatistas, 463
Zayas y Alfonso, Alfredo, 185, 285, 292, *463–64*
Zelaya, José Santos, 67–68, 115, *464–65*
Zemurray, Samuel, 67, 96
Zúñiga Augustinius, Ricardo, 261
Zúñiga Hueste, Angel, 96

CONTRIBUTORS

ROBERT J. ALEXANDER received his B.A., M.A., and Ph.D. degrees from Columbia University, and has been teaching economics, political science, and history at Rutgers University since 1947. He is author of several books on Latin America and edited *Political Parties of the Americas* (Greenwood Press, 1982).

MARVIN ALISKY, Professor of Political Science at Arizona State University (ASU), founded the ASU Center for Latin American Studies and directed it for seven years. He is author of more than a dozen books and monographs and two hundred magazine articles. He has had two Fulbright professorships, was U.S. delegate to UNESCO in Ecuador, has taught at Indiana University and the University of California at Irvine, and was a research scholar at Princeton and Stanford. He has lectured for the International Communications Agency, been an NBC network news correspondent throughout Latin America, and a consultant on hemispheric relations at the Institute of Defense and Strategic Studies in London. He was named to the Board of Foreign Scholarships for the 1984–1987 term.

CHARLES D. AMERINGER received his Ph.D. degree from the Fletcher School of Law and Diplomacy. He is author of *The Democratic Left in Exile: The Antidictatorial Struggle in the Caribbean, 1945–1959*; *Don Pepe: A Political Biography of José Figueres of Costa Rica*; and *Democracy in Costa Rica*; and has contributed to numerous professional journals. He was founder and first president of the Middle Atlantic Council on Latin American Studies. Dr. Ameringer is Professor of Latin American History at the Pennsylvania State University.

EUGENIO CHANG-RODRÍGUEZ is Professor of Romance Languages at Queens College of the City University of New York and Professor *honoris causa* at the National University of San Marcos of his native Peru. He formerly taught at the University of Pennsylvania. He is editor of the *Boletin* of the North

American Academy of the Spanish Language, and editorial board member of *Bilingual Review*, *Caribe*, and *Revista Hispanica Moderna*. He is a director of the International League for Human Rights and member of the New York Academy of Science, and has held numerous other posts in professional organizations. He has a Ph.D. from the University of Washington and an honorary doctorate from the National University Federico Villareal of Lima, Peru. He has authored, co-authored, and edited more than a dozen books.

JOHN T. DEINER is Associate Professor of Political Science at the University of Delaware. He has traveled widely in Latin America and has published various articles on Argentine politics, Eva Perón, the political role of the Catholic Church in Latin America, and guerrillas, and is author of a manual, *Politics in Developing Nations*. He has been a member of the Executive Committee of the Middle Atlantic Council on Latin American Studies.

GUILLERMO DELGADO is a Bolivian anthropologist, specializing in political anthropology and peasant studies. He is a Research Associate at the Institute of Latin American Studies at the University of Texas at Austin.

PERCY C. HINTZEN is an Associate Professor of Afro-American Studies and Associate at the Institute for International Studies at the University of California, Berkeley. He received his Ph.D. in Comparative Political Sociology from Yale. His research and publications focus on race, politics, and elite domination in small, formerly colonial, less-developed countries. He has completed a book entitled *The Costs of Regime Survival: Racial Mobilization, Elite Domination, and Control of the State in Guyana and Trinidad*, which is soon to be published.

WALTRAUD QUEISER MORALES is Associate Professor of International and Comparative Studies at the University of Central Florida. She received her Ph.D. from the University of Denver. She is author of *Bolivia: Land of Struggle; Social Revolution: Theory and Historical Application*; and country studies in *Violence and Repression in Latin America,* by Ernest A. Duff and John F. McCamant with Waltraud Q. Morales. She has published articles in *Current History, International Philosophical Quarterly, Journalism Quarterly*, and *Revista/Review Interamericana*.

NEALE J. PEARSON, Professor of Political Science at Texas Tech University, received his doctorate at the University of Florida. He has had chapters or articles in six books, is a regular contributor to the *Annual Yearbook of the Encyclopedia Americana* and the *Yearbook on International Communist Affairs*, and has had numerous articles in professional journals.

JOSÉ M. SÁNCHEZ received his Ph.D. from Colombia University and his J.D. from Hofstra University's School of Law. He is currently Associate Professor of Political Studies at Adelphi University. He is a Cuban-American scholar whose principal fields of publication and research are U.S. foreign policy in the Caribbean and comparative legal systems. His current projects include an article on the impact of Marxism on the Cuban legal system, and *Hollywood Politics*, a book on the American political system as depicted in commercial films.

RICHARD E. SHARPLESS is an Associate Professor at Lafayette College in Easton, Pennsylvania, where he teaches Latin American history and American economic and labor history. He is author of *Gaitán of Colombia*, a biography of the Colombian populist leader, and various articles on Latin American and U.S. politics, immigration, and labor.

W. MARVIN WILL is Associate Professor of Political Science at the University of Tulsa. He has edited (with R. Millett) a book entitled *The Restless Caribbean*, as well as two other studies, *Crescents of Conflict* and *Revolution or Order?* He is Vice President of the Midwest Association of Latin American Studies and a past board member and newsletter editor of the Caribbean Studies Association.

STEPHEN J. WRIGHT is Assistant Professor and Director of the Department of Independent Learning of the Pennsylvania State University, and Affiliate Assistant Professor of History at Penn State. Dr. Wright received his Ph.D. from Penn State in 1983, where his doctoral dissertation was entitled, ''Cuba, Sugar and the United States: Diplomatic and Economic Relations During the Administration of Ramón Grau San Martín, 1944–1948.''

JORDAN YOUNG is Professor of History at Pace University, having been there since 1957. He has also been Visiting Professor at Columbia University, New York University, and the College of the City of New York. He was in Brazil during World War II, from 1941 to 1944, originally as a student and later working for the Office of Inter American Affairs. For two years in the 1950s, he worked for the Chase Manhattan Bank in Brazil; subsequently, he has visited the country virtually every year. He has lectured at various Brazilian universities as well as in the Rio Branco Institute of the Brazilian Foreign Office. His many publications include *The Brazilian Revolution of 1930* and *The Aftermath*.